G000123898

CLYMER ®

Publisher Shawn Etheridge

EDITORIAL

Managing Editor
James Grooms

Associate Editor
Steven Thomas

Technical Writers
Jay Bogart
Jon Engleman
Michael Morlan
George Parise
Mark Rolling
Ed Scott
Ron Wright

Editorial Production Manager
Dylan Goodwin

Senior Production Editor
Greg Araujo

Production Editors
Holly Messinger
Darin Watson

Associate Production Editors
Susan Hartington
Julie Jantzer-Ward
Justin Marciniak

Technical Illustrators
Steve Amos
Errol McCarthy
Mitzi McCarthy
Bob Meyer

MARKETING/SALES AND ADMINISTRATION

Sales Channel & Brand Marketing Coordinator
Melissa Abbott Mudd

New Business Marketing Manager
Gabriele Udell

Art Director
Chris Paxton

Sales Managers
Justin Henton
Dutch Sadler
Matt Tusken

Business Manager
Ron Rogers

Customer Service Manager
Terri Cannon

Customer Service Representatives
Felicia Dickerson
Courtney Hollars
Jennifer Lassiter
April LeBlond

Warehouse & Inventory Manager
Leah Hicks

PRiSM
BUSINESS MEDIA™
P.O. Box 12901, Overland Park, KS 66282-2901 • 800-262-1954 • 913-967-1719

The following books and guides are published by Prism Business Media

More information available at *clymer.com*

CLYMER®

HONDA

GL1500C VALKYRIE • 1997-2003

CLYMER®

P.O. Box 12901, Overland Park, Kansas 66282-2901

Copyright ©2003 Prism Business Media Inc.

FIRST EDITION
First Printing November, 2000

SECOND EDITION
Updated by James Grooms to include 2001-2003 models.
First Printing October, 2003
Second Printing April, 2006

Printed in U.S.A.

CLYMER and colophon are registered trademarks of Prism Business Media Inc.

ISBN: 0-89287-885-1

Library of Congress: 2003111937

AUTHOR: Ed Scott.

TECHNICAL PHOTOGRAPHY: Ron Wright.

TECHNICAL ILLUSTRATIONS: Mitzi McCarthy.

WIRING DIAGRAMS: Bob Meyer.

TOOLS AND EQUIPMENT: K & L Supply Co. at www.klsupply.com.

EDITOR: James Grooms.

PRODUCTION: Dennis Conrow.

COVER: Photographed by Mark Clifford Photography at www.markclifford.com. GL1500CT provided by Rice Motorsports, LaPuerrte, CA.

Contents

QUICK REFERENCE DATA

MOTORCYCLE DATA

MODEL:_____ YEAR:_____

VIN NUMBER:_____

ENGINE SERIAL NUMBER:_____

CARBURETOR SERIAL NUMBER OR I.D. MARK:_____

TUNE-UP SPECIFICATIONS

Valve clearance (cold)	
Intake	0.15 mm (0.006 in.)
Exhaust	0.22 mm (0.009 in.)
Cylinder compression-standard	171 psi (1177 kPa)
Spark plug type	
Standard heat range	NGK DPR7EA-9 or ND X22EPR-U9
Cold weather*	NGK DPR6EA-9 or ND X20EPR-U9
Extended high-speed riding	NGK DPR8EA-9 or ND X24EPR-U9
Spark plug gap	0.8-0.9 mm (0.031-0.035 in.)
Ignition timing	
"F" mark	3.5° BTDC @ 800-1000 rpm
Vacuum advance	
Starts	See text
Stops	See text
Idle speed	800-1000 rpm
Firing order	1-4-5-2-3-6

* Temperature below 5° C (41° F).

TIRE INFLATION PRESSURE (COLD)*

Load	Air pressure
Up to 200 lbs. (90 kg)	
Front	33 psi (225 kPa)
Rear	33 psi (225 kPa)
Maximum load limit**	
Front	33 psi (225 kPa)
Rear	36 psi (250 kPa)
Maximum weight capacity	
GL1500C, GL1500CT	396 lbs (180 kg)
GL1500CF	414 lbs (188 kg)

* Tire inflation pressure for original equipment tires. Aftermarket tire inflation pressure may vary; refer to manufacturer's instructions.

** Maximum load limit includes total weight of motor accessories, rider(s) and luggage.

ENGINE OIL CAPACITY

	Liters	U.S. quarts	Imp. quarts
At oil and filter change	3.7	3.9	3.3
At engine disassembly	4.3	4.5	3.8

COOLING SYSTEM CAPACITY

	Liters	U.S. qt.	Imp. qt.
Radiator and engine	3.75	3.9	3.3
Reserve tank	1.0	1.1	0.9

FINAL DRIVE GEAR OIL CAPACITY

	mL	U.S. oz.	Imp. oz.
Oil change	150	5.1	5.3
After disassembly	170	5.7	6.0

FUEL CAPACITY

	L	U.S. Gal.	Imp. Gal.
Fuel tank			
GL1500C, GL1500CT	20	5.3	4.4
GL1500CF	26	6.9	5.7
Reserve			
GL1500C, GL1500CT	4.3	1.14	0.95
GL1500CF	4.0	1.06	0.88

RECOMMENDED OIL AND FLUIDS

Item	Lubricant
Engine oil	See text
Final drive gear	Hypoid gear oil, SAE 80
Front fork	Honda Suspension Fluid SS-7
Brake and clutch fluid	DOT 4
Speedometer cable	Light weight oil
Throttle and choke cables	Light weight oil
Grease	NGLI No. 2

TIGHTENING TORQUES

	N•m	in.-lb.	ft.lb
Oil filter	10	88	-
Engine drain plug	34	-	25
Oil pressure switch	12	106	-
Valve adjuster locknut	23	-	17
Spark plugs	12	106	-
Final drive unit			
Filler cap	12	106	-
Drain plug	20	-	15

CHAPTER ONE

GENERAL INFORMATION

This manual covers all models of the 1997-on Honda Valkyrie GL1500.

Troubleshooting, tune-up, maintenance and repair are not difficult, if the proper tools and instructions are available. Step-by-step instructions guide anyone through jobs ranging from simple maintenance to complete engine and suspension overhaul.

Table 1 lists model coverage with starting engine and frame serial numbers.

Table 2 lists general vehicle dimensions.

Table 3 lists vehicle weight specifications.

Table 4 lists fuel capacity.

Table 5 lists decimal and metric equivalents.

Table 6 lists conversion tables.

Table 7 lists general torque specifications.

Table 8 lists metric tap and drill sizes.

Table 9 lists technical abbreviations.

Tables 1-9 are at the end of the chapter.

MANUAL ORGANIZATION

All dimensions and capacities are expressed in U.S standard units and metric units.

This chapter provides general information and discusses equipment and tools useful both for preventive maintenance and troubleshooting.

Chapter Two provides methods and suggestions for quick and accurate diagnosis and repair of problems. Troubleshooting procedures discuss typical symptoms and logical methods to pinpoint the trouble.

Chapter Three explains all periodic lubrication and routine maintenance necessary to keep the motorcycle operating well. Chapter Three also includes recommended tune-up procedures, thereby eliminating the need to constantly consult other chapters on the various assemblies.

Subsequent chapters describe specific systems such as the engine and transmission, clutch, fuel, exhaust, electrical, cooling system, suspension, drive train, steering, brakes and body panels Each chapter provides disassembly, repair, and assembly procedures in simple step-by-step form. If a repair is impractical for a home mechanic, it is so indicated. It is usually faster and less expensive to take such repairs to a Honda dealership or a competent repair shop. Specifications concerning a particular system are included at the end of the appropriate chapter.

NOTES, CAUTIONS AND WARNINGS

The terms NOTE, CAUTION and WARNING have specific meanings in this manual. A NOTE provides additional information to make a step or procedure easier or clearer. Disregarding a NOTE could cause inconvenience, but it would not cause damage or personal injury.

A CAUTION emphasizes an area where equipment damage could occur. Disregarding a CAUTION could cause permanent mechanical damage; however, personal injury is unlikely.

A WARNING emphasizes an area where personal injury or even death could result from negligence. Mechanical damage may also occur. WARNINGS *are to be taken seriously*. In some cases, serious injury and death have resulted from disregarding similar warnings.

SAFETY FIRST

Professional mechanics can work for years and never sustain a serious injury. If simple rules of common sense and safety are observed, most accidents can be avoided. Ignoring these rules can cause personal injury or damage the motorcycle.

1. *Never* use gasoline or any type of low flash point solvent to clean parts. See *Cleaning Parts* and *Handling Gasoline Safely* in this chapter for additional information on parts cleaning, gasoline use, and safety.

NOTE
The flash point is the lowest temperature at which the vapors from a combustible liquid ignite when contacting an open flame. A low flash point solvent ignites at a lower temperature than a high flash point solvent.

2. *Never* smoke or use a torch in the vicinity of flammable liquids, such as gasoline or cleaning solvent, in open containers.

3. If welding or brazing is required on the machine, remove the fuel tank, carburetors and rear shocks to a safe distance, at least 50 feet (15 m) away.

4. Use the correct size wrenches to avoid damaging fasteners and injuring yourself.

5. When loosening a tight or stuck nut, be guided by what would happen if the wrench should slip.

6. When replacing a fastener, make sure to use one with the same measurements and strength as the old one. Incorrect or mismatched fasteners may result in damage to the vehicle and possibly personal injury. Beware of fastener kits that are filled with poorly made nuts, bolts, washers and cotter pins. Refer to *Fasteners* in this chapter for additional information.

7. Keep all hand and power tools in good condition. Wipe greasy and oily tools after using them; they are difficult to hold and can cause injury. Replace or repair worn or damaged tools.

8. Keep the work area clean and uncluttered.

9. Use a motorcycle lift when any procedure requires raising the motorcycle off the ground. The motorcycle is not equipped with a centerstand and a lift is required to safely work on the motorcycle while it is raised.

10. Wear protective eyewear during all operations involving drilling, grinding, the use of a cold chisel, using chemicals, cleaning parts, when using compressed air or *anytime* eye safety is in question.

11. Be sure to wear the correct type of clothes for the job. Long hair should be tied back or covered by a cap so that it cannot accidentally fall out where it could be quickly grabbed by a piece of moving equipment or tool.

12. Keep an approved fire extinguisher nearby. Be sure it is rated for gasoline (Class B) and electrical (Class C) fires.

13. When drying bearings or other rotating parts with compressed air, never allow the air jet to rotate the bearing or part. The air jet is capable of rotating

the part at speeds far in excess of those for which it was designed. The bearing or rotating part is very likely to disintegrate and cause serious injury and damage. To prevent bearing damage when using compressed air, hold the inner bearing race by hand.

WARNING
*The improper use of compressed air is very dangerous. Using compressed air to dust off clothes, the motorcycle or the workbench can cause flying particles to be blown onto the eyes or skin. **Never** direct or blow compressed air into skin or through any body opening (including cuts) as this can cause severe injury or death. Compressed air should be used carefully; never allow children to use or play with compressed air.*

14. Never work on the motorcycle while someone is working underneath it.

15. When placing the motorcycle on a stand, make sure the motorcycle is secure before walking away from it.

16. Never carry sharp tools in your pockets.

17. There is always a right and wrong way to use tools—learn to use them the right way.

18. Do not start and run the motorcycle in a closed area. The exhaust gasses contain carbon monoxide, an odorless, colorless, tasteless poisonous gas. Carbon monoxide levels build quickly in a small enclosed area and can cause unconsciousness and death in a short time. When it is necessary to start and run the motorcycle during a service procedure, always do so outside or in a service area equipped with a ventilating system.

CLEANING PARTS

Cleaning parts is one of the more tedious and difficult service jobs performed in the home garage. While there are a number of chemical cleaners and solvents available for home and shop use, most are poisonous and extremely flammable. To prevent chemical overexposure, vapor buildup, fire and serious injury, observe all manufacturer's directions and warnings while noting the following.

1. Read the entire product label before using the chemical. Observe the precautions and warnings on the label.

2. If the chemical product must be mixed, measure the proper amount according to the directions.

3. When a warning label specifies that the product should only be used with adequate ventilation, care must be taken to prevent chemical vapors from collecting in the shop. Always work in a well-ventilated area. Use a fan or ventilation system to remove vapor. If working in a small area, simply opening a door or window may not provide adequate ventilation. Remember, when the chemical can be smelled, there is some vapor in the air. The stronger the smell, the stronger the vapor concentration.

4. When a product is listed as combustible, flammable or an extremely flammable liquid, the danger of fire increases as the vapor collects and builds up in the shop.

5. When a product is listed as a poison, the vapor is poisonous as well as the liquid.

6. To prevent skin exposure, wear protective gloves when cleaning parts. Select a pair of chemical-resistant gloves suitable for the type of chemicals being used. Replace the gloves when they become thin, damaged, discolored, or swollen.

7. Wear protective eyewear when using chemicals and cleaning parts.

8. Do not use more than one type of cleaning solvent at a time.

9. If a part must be heated to remove a bearing, clean it thoroughly to remove all oil, grease and cleaner residue. Then wash with soapy water and rinse with clear water.

10. Wear a respirator, if instructed.

11. Keep chemical products out of reach of children and pets.

12. To prevent sparks, use a nylon bristle brush when cleaning parts.

13. When using a commercial parts washer, read and follow the manufacturer's instructions for selecting the type of solvent to use. Parts washers must be equipped with a fusible link designed to melt and drop the cover in the event of fire.

14. Wash both hands and arms thoroughly after cleaning parts.

HANDLING GASOLINE SAFELY

Gasoline, a volatile flammable liquid, is one of the most dangerous items in the shop. However, because gasoline is used so often, many people forget that it is a dangerous product. Gasoline should be used only as fuel for internal-combustion engines. Never use gasoline to clean parts, tools or to wash hands with. When working on a motorcycle or any other type of gasoline engine, gasoline will always be present in the fuel tank, fuel lines and carburetors. To avoid a disastrous accident when working around gasoline or on the fuel system, carefully observe the following cautions:

1. *Never* use gasoline to clean parts. See *Cleaning Parts* in this chapter for additional information on parts cleaning and safety.

2. When working on the fuel system, work outside or in a well-ventilated area.

3. Do not add fuel to the fuel tank or service the fuel system while the motorcycle is in the vicinity of open flames, sparks, appliance pilot lights or where someone is smoking. Gasoline vapors are actually more dangerous than liquid gasoline. Because these vapors are heavier than air, they collect in low areas and are easily ignited.

4. Allow the engine to cool completely before working on any fuel system component.

5. When draining the carburetors, catch the gasoline in a plastic container and then pour it into an appropriate gasoline storage container.

6. Do not store gasoline in any type of glass container. If the glass should break, a serious explosion or fire could occur.

7. Wipe up spilled gasoline immediately with dry rags. Store the rags in a metal container with a lid until they can be properly disposed of, or place them outside in a safe place to dry.

8. Do not pour water onto a gasoline fire. Water spreads the fire and makes it more difficult to extinguish. Use a class B, BC, or ABC fire extinguisher to smother the flames and put the fire out.

9. Always turn the engine off before refueling. Use a wide-mouth funnel to prevent spilling gasoline onto the engine, exhaust pipe or muffler. Do not overfill the fuel tank. Leave an air space at the top of the fuel tank to prevent fuel from spilling when installing the cap.

10. Always refuel the motorcycle with it parked outside and away from all open flames and sparks.

11. When transporting the motorcycle in another vehicle, keep it upright and with the fuel valve turned off.

12. Do not perform a spark test, as described in Chapter Two, if there is any gasoline leaking from the fuel tank, fuel line or carburetors.

SERVICE HINTS

Most of the service procedures covered are straightforward and can be performed by anyone reasonably competent with tools. It is suggested, however, that personal capabilities be considered carefully before attempting any operation involving major disassembly of the engine assembly.

Take time to do the job correctly. Do not forget that a newly rebuilt engine must be broken in the same way as a new one. Refer to the *Engine Break-In* procedure listed in Chapter Five.

1. Front as used in this manual, refers to the front of the vehicle; the front of any component is the end closest to the front of the vehicle. The left and right sides refer to the position of the parts as viewed by a rider sitting on the seat facing forward. For example, the throttle control is on the right side. These rules are simple, but confusion can cause a major inconvenience during service. See **Figure 1**.

2. Whenever servicing an engine or suspension component, safely secure the vehicle on a motorcycle lift with tie downs.

3. Tag all similar parts for location and mark all mating parts for position. Record the number and thickness of any shims as they are removed. Placing them in plastic sandwich bags helps identify small parts, such as bolts. Seal and label them with masking tape.

4. Tag disconnected wires and connectors with masking tape and a marking pen. Do not rely on memory alone.

5. Protect finished surfaces from physical damage or corrosion. Keep gasoline and other chemicals off painted surfaces.

6. Use penetrating oil on corroded or tight bolts, then strike the bolt head a few times with a hammer and punch (use a screwdriver on screws). Avoid the use of heat where possible, as it can warp, melt or affect the hardness temper of parts. Heat also damages finishes, especially paint and plastics.

7. When a part is a press fit or requires a special tool to remove it, the necessary information or type of tool will be called out in the text. Otherwise, if a part is difficult to remove or install, find out why before proceeding.

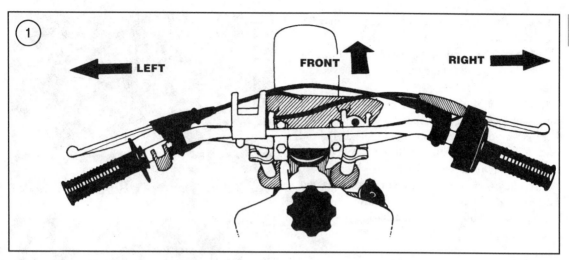

8. To prevent small objects and abrasive dust from falling into the engine, cover all openings after exposing them.

9. Read each procedure completely while looking at the actual parts before starting a job. Make sure the procedural steps are thoroughly understood then follow the procedure, step by step.

10. Recommendations are occasionally made to refer service or maintenance to a Honda dealership or a specialist in a particular field. In these cases, the work may be performed more quickly and economically by a professional.

11. In procedural steps, the term *replace* means to discard a defective part and replace it with a new or exchange unit. *Overhaul* means to remove, disassemble, inspect, measure, repair and or replace parts as required.

12. Some operations require using a hydraulic press. If a press is not available, have these operations performed by a shop equipped for such work, rather than to try to do the job with makeshift equipment that may damage the machine.

13. Repairs go much faster and easier if the motorcycle is clean before beginning work. There are many special cleaners on the market, like Bel-Ray Degreaser, for washing the engine and related parts. Follow the manufacturer's directions on the container for the best results. Clean all oily or greasy parts with cleaning solvent as they are removed.

WARNING
Never use gasoline to clean parts or tools. It presents an extreme fire hazard. Be sure to work in a well-ventilated area when using cleaning solvent. Keep a fire extinguisher, rated for gasoline fires, on hand.

CAUTION
If using a car wash to clean the motorcycle, do not direct the high pressure water hose at steering bearings, carburetors hoses, suspension components, wheel bearings, electrical components or the final drive unit. The water will flush grease out of the bearings or damage the seals.

14. Much of the labor charges for repairs made by dealerships are for the time involved during the removal, disassembly, assembly, and reinstallation of other parts in order to reach the defective part. When possible, perform the preliminary operations at home, then take the defective unit to the dealership for repair at considerable savings.

15. When special tools are required, make arrangements to get them before starting. It is frustrating and time-consuming to begin a job and then be unable to complete it. When special tools are required, they will be described (including part number) at the beginning of a procedure.

16. Make diagrams wherever similar-appearing parts are found. For instance, crankcase bolts are often not the same lengths. Failure to remember where everything was installed may result in costly mistakes. There is also the possibility of being sidetracked and not returning to work for days or even

weeks, at which time the carefully laid parts may become disturbed.

17. When assembling parts, make sure all shims and washers are reinstalled exactly as they came out.

18. Whenever a rotating part contacts a stationary part, look for a shim or washer. Use new gaskets if there is any doubt about the condition of the old ones. A thin coating of oil on non-pressure type gaskets may help them seal more effectively.

19. Use heavy grease to hold small parts in place if they tend to fall out during assembly. However, keep grease and oil away from electrical and brake components.

SERIAL NUMBERS

Honda motorcycles can be identified by serial numbers stamped into the frame and engine. Always record these numbers and use them when ordering parts from a Honda dealership. If a question should arise about a part number or production change with the motorcycle, these numbers will be required before the part in question can be ordered. These numbers are also useful when trying to identify a motorcycle that may have been repainted or modified in some way.

1. The Vehicle Identification Number (VIN) is attached to the left side of the frame next to the steering head (**Figure 2**). Use these numbers to identify and register the Honda.

2. The frame serial number is stamped to the right side of the steering head (**Figure 3**). Use these numbers to identify and register the Honda.

3. The engine number is stamped on a raised pad on the right side crankcase next to the engine oil fill cap (**Figure 4**).

4. The carburetor's serial number is stamped on the intake side of the carburetor body (**Figure 5**).

5. The color label is attached to the frame down tube, under the left side cover (**Figure 6**).

WARNING LABELS

A number of warning labels are located on the Honda motorcycles covered in this manual. These labels contain information that is important to the rider's safety. Refer to the Owner's Service Manual for a description and location of each label. If a label

is missing, order a replacement label from a Honda dealership.

TORQUE SPECIFICATIONS

The materials used in the manufacture of the Honda may be subjected to uneven torque stresses if the fasteners used to hold the sub-assemblies are not installed and tightened correctly. Loose or missing fasteners can cause cylinder head warpage, crankcase leaks, premature bearing and seal failure, and

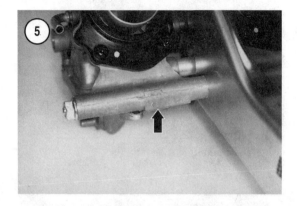

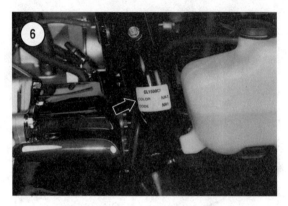

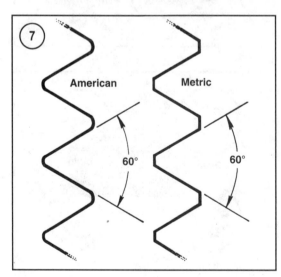

Torque wrenches calibrated in meter kilograms can be used by performing the following conversion: mkg × 9.8 = N•m. For example, 3.5 mkg × 9.8 = 34.3 N•m.

To mathematically convert foot-pounds to Newton meters, multiply the foot pounds specification by 1.3558 to achieve a N•m equivalent. For example 150 ft.-lb. × 1.3558 = 203 N•m.

Refer to **Table 7** for general torque specifications for various size screws, bolts and nuts that may not be listed in other chapters.

FASTENERS

Fasteners such as screws, bolts, nuts, studs, pins and clips join various pieces of the engine, frame and suspension together. Proper selection and installation of fasteners are important to ensure that the motorcycle operates satisfactorily and can be serviced efficiently. Stripped, broken and missing fasteners cause excessive vibration, leaks and other performance and service related problems. For example, a loose or missing engine mount fastener can increase engine vibration that will eventually lead to a cracked frame tube or damaged crankcase.

Threaded Fasteners

Most of the components on the Honda are held together by threaded fasteners—screws, bolts, nuts, and studs. Most fasteners are tightened by turning clockwise (right-hand threads), although some fasteners may have left-hand threads (turned counterclockwise) if the rotating parts can cause loosening. If a left-hand thread is used on a specific fastener it is noted in the procedure.

Two dimensions are needed to match threaded fasteners: the number of threads in a given distance and the nominal outside diameter of the threads. Two standards are currently used in the United States to specify the dimensions of threaded fasteners, the U.S. common system and the metric system (**Figure 7**). Pay particular attention when working with unidentified fasteners; mismatching thread types can damage threads.

suspension failure. Therefore, use an accurate torque wrench (described in this chapter) together with the torque specifications listed at the end of most chapters.

Torque specifications throughout this manual are given in Newton-meters (N•m), foot-pounds (ft.-lb.) and inch-pounds (in.-lb.).

NOTE
During reassembly, start all fasteners by hand. This will help ensure that the fastener threads are not mismatched

or cross-threaded. If a fastener is hard to start or turn, stop and determine the cause before tightening with a wrench.

Metric screws and bolts are classified by length (L, **Figure 8**), nominal diameter (D) and distance between thread crests (T). A typical bolt can be identified by the numbers 8—1.25 × 130, which would indicate that the bolt has a nominal diameter of 8 mm, the distance between thread crests is 1.25 mm and bolt length is 130 mm.

The strength of metric screws and bolts is indicated by numbers located on top of the screw or bolt as shown in **Figure 8**. The higher the number the stronger the screw or bolt. Unnumbered screws and bolts are the weakest.

> *WARNING*
> ***Do not*** *install screws or bolts with a lower strength grade classification than installed originally by the manufacturer. Doing so may cause vehicle failure and possible bodily injury.*

Tightening a screw or bolt increases the clamping force it exerts, the stronger the screw or bolt, the greater the clamping force. Critical torque specifications are listed in a table at the end of appropriate chapter. If not, use the torque specifications in **Table 7**. The Honda torque specifications in the manual are for clean, dry threads (unless specified differently in text). Screws and bolts are manufactured with a variety of head shapes to fit specific design requirements. The Honda Valkyrie is equipped with the common hex, Phillips and Allen head types.

The most common nut used is the hex nut (**Figure 9**). The hex nut is often used with a lockwasher. Self-locking nuts have a nylon insert that prevents loosening; no lockwasher is required. Wing nuts, designed for fast removal by hand, are used for convenience in non-critical locations. Nuts are sized using the same system as screws and bolts. On hex-type nuts, the distance between two opposing flats indicates the proper wrench size to use.

Self-locking screws, bolts and nuts may use a locking mechanism that uses an interference fit between mating threads. Manufacturers achieve interference in various ways: by distorting threads, coating treads with dry adhesive or nylon, distorting the top of an all-metal nut, using a nylon insert in the

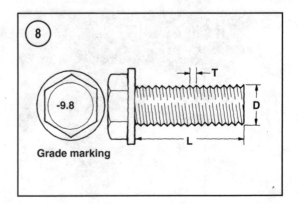
Grade marking

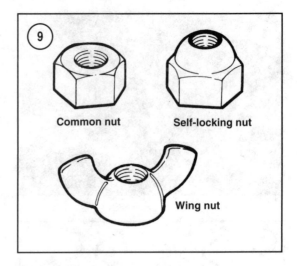
Common nut   Self-locking nut

Wing nut

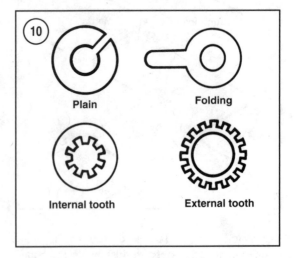
Plain   Folding

Internal tooth   External tooth

center or at the top of a nut, etc. Self-locking fasteners offer greater holding strength and better vibration resistance than standard fasteners. For greatest safety, install new self-locking fasteners during reassembly.

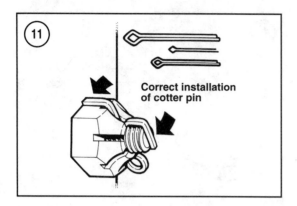

Correct installation of cotter pin

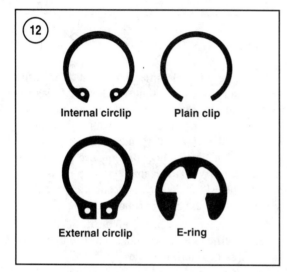

Internal circlip   Plain clip

External circlip   E-ring

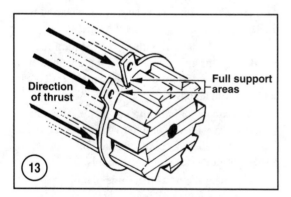

Direction of thrust   Full support areas

Washers

There are two basic types of washers used on the Honda: flat washers and lockwashers. Flat washers are simple discs with a hole to fit a screw or bolt. Lockwashers are designed to prevent a fastener from working loose. **Figure 10** shows several types

of washers. Washers can be used in the following functions:

1. As spacers.
2. To prevent the fastener from galling or damaging the equipment.
3. To help distribute fastener load when tightening the fastener.
4. As fluid seals.

Note that flat washers are often used between a lockwasher and a fastener to provide a smooth bearing surface. This allows the fastener to be turned easily with a tool.

Cotter Pins

In certain applications, a fastener must be secured so it cannot possibly loosen. The front and rear axles are two such applications. For this purpose, a cotter pin and slotted or castellated nut is often used. To use a cotter pin, first make sure the pin fits snugly, but not too tight. Then align the slot in the fastener with the hole in the bolt or axle. Insert the cotter pin through the nut and bolt or axle and bend the ends over to secure the cotter pin tightly (**Figure 11**). If the holes do not align, tighten the nut just enough to obtain the proper alignment. Unless specifically instructed to do so, never loosen the fastener to align the slot and the hole. Because the cotter pin is weakened after installation and removal, never reuse a cotter pin. Cotter pins are available in several styles, lengths and diameters. Measure the cotter pin length from the bottom of its head to the tip of the shortest prong.

Circlips

Circlips can be internal or external design (**Figure 12**). Circlips retain items on shafts (external type) or within tubes (internal type). In some applications, circlips of varying thickness are used to control the end play of assembled parts. These are often called selective circlips. Replace circlips during re-assembly and installation, as removal weakens and deforms them. Two other types of clips used on the Honda are the plain snap ring and E-clip (**Figure 12**).

Two basic styles of circlips are available: machined and stamped circlips. Machined circlips (**Figure 13**) can be installed in either direction (shaft or housing) because both faces are machined, thus creating two sharp edges. Stamped circlips (**Figure 14**) are manufactured with one sharp edge and one rounded edge. When installing stamped circlips in a thrust situation, the sharp edge must face away from the part producing the thrust. When installing circlips, observe the following:

1. Compress or expand circlips only enough to install them. If overly expanded, they will lose their locking ability

2. After installing a circlip, make sure it seats in its groove completely.

Transmission circlips become worn with use and increase side play. For this reason, always use new circlips whenever a transmission is reassembled.

E-Clips

E-clips (**Figure 12**) are used when it is impractical or impossible to use a circlip. There are many different sizes of E-clips available.

Remove E-clips by prying between the shaft and E-clip. To install an E-clip, center it into its shaft groove, then tap or push it into place.

Plain Clip

The plain clip (**Figure 12**) is used to secure the piston pin in the piston. See *Piston* in Chapter Four. Plain clips are sometimes used to secure bearings in suspension components.

LUBRICANTS

Periodic lubrication helps ensure long life for any type of equipment. The type of lubricant used is just as important as the lubrication service itself, although in an emergency the wrong type of lubricant is better than none at all. The following paragraphs describe the types of lubricants used most often when servicing motorcycles. Be sure to follow the manufacturer's recommendations for lubricant types.

Generally, all liquid lubricants are called oil. They may be mineral-based (including petroleum bases), natural-based (vegetable and animal bases), synthetic-based or emulsions (mixtures). Grease is an oil to which a thickening base has been added so that the end product is semi-solid. Grease is often classified by the type of thickener added; lithium soap is commonly used.

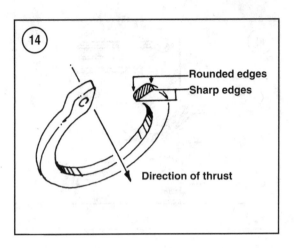

Engine Oil

Engine oil is classified by two standards: the American Petroleum Institute (API) service classification and the Society of Automotive Engineers (SAE) viscosity rating. This information is on the oil container label. Two letters indicate the API service classification. The number or sequence of numbers and letters (10W-40 for example) is the oil's viscosity rating. The API service classification and the SAE viscosity index are not indications of oil quality.

The service classification indicates that the oil meets specific lubrication standards. The first letter in the classification S indicates that the oil is for gasoline engines. The second letter indicates the standard the oil satisfies. The classification started with the letter A and is currently at the letter J.

Always use an oil with a classification recommended by the manufacturer. Using an oil with a classification different than that recommended can cause engine damage.

Viscosity is an indication of the oil's thickness. Thin oils have a lower number while thick oils have a higher number. Engine oils fall into the 5- to 50-weight range for single-grade oils.

Most manufacturers recommend multigrade oil. These oils perform efficiently across a wide range of operating conditions. Multigrade oils are identified by a W after the first number, which indicates the low-temperature viscosity.

Engine oils are most commonly mineral (petroleum) based; however synthetic and semi-synthetic types are used more frequently. When selecting engine oil, follow the manufacturer's recommendation for type, classification and viscosity.

Grease

Greases are graded by the National Lubricating Grease Institute (NLGI). Greases are graded by number according to the consistency of the grease; these range from No. 000 to No. 6, with No. 6 being the most solid. A typical multipurpose grease is NLGI No. 2. For specific applications, equipment manufacturers may require grease with an additive such as molybdenum disulfide.

Antiseize Lubricant

An antiseize lubricant may be specified in some assembly applications. The antiseize lubricant prevents the formation of corrosion that may lock parts together.

SEALANT, CEMENTS AND CLEANERS

Sealants

Many mating surfaces of an engine require a gasket or seal between them to prevent fluids and gasses from passing through the joint. Note that a sealing compound may be added to the gasket or seal during manufacture and adding a sealant may cause premature failure of the gasket or seal. Recommended sealants are referred to in the service procedures.

> *NOTE*
> *If a new gasket leaks, check the two mating surfaces for warpage, old gasket residue or cracks. Also check to see if the new gasket was properly installed and if the assembly was tightened correctly.*

RTV Sealants

One of the most common sealants is RTV (room temperature vulcanizing) sealant. This sealant hardens (cures) at room temperature over a period of several hours, which allows sufficient time to reposition parts, if necessary, without damaging the gaskets.

RTV sealant is available in different strengths. For example, while many RTV compounds offer excellent chemical resistance in bonding and sealing applications where oil and water is prevalent, most RTV compounds offers poor chemical resistance to gasoline. Always follow the manufacturer's recommendations when purchasing and using a particular compound.

Cements and Adhesives

A variety of cements and adhesives are available, their use is dependent on the type of materials to be sealed, and to some extent, the personal preference of the mechanic. Automotive parts stores offer cements and adhesives in a wide selection. Some points to consider when selecting cements or adhesives: the type of material being sealed (metal, rubber, plastic, etc.), the type of fluid contacting the seal (gasoline, oil, coolant, etc.) and whether the seal is permanent or must be broken periodically, in which case a pliable sealant might be desirable. Experience is required in the selection of cements and adhesives. Follow the recommendation if the text specifies a particular sealant.

Cleaners and Solvents

Cleaners and solvents are helpful in removing oil, grease and other residue when maintaining and overhauling the motorcycle. Before purchasing cleaners and solvents, consider how they will be used and disposed of, particularly if they are not water-soluble. Local ordinances may require special procedures for the disposal of certain cleaners and solvents.

> *WARNING*
> *Some cleaners and solvents are harmful and may be flammable. Follow any safety precautions noted on the container or in the manufacturer's literature. Use petroleum-resistant gloves to protect hands and arms from the harmful effect of cleaners and solvents; wear safety glasses to protect eyes.*

Figure 15 shows a variety of cleaners and solvents. Cleaners designed for ignition contact cleaning are excellent for removing light oil from a part without leaving a residue. Cleaners designed to remove heavy oil and grease residues, called degreasers, contain a solvent that usually must work awhile. Some degreasers wash off with water.

One of the more powerful cleaning solutions is carburetor cleaner. It is designed to dissolve the deposits that may build up in the carburetor's jets and orifices. A good carburetor cleaner is usually expensive and requires special disposal. Carefully read directions before purchase; do not immerse nonmetallic parts in a carburetor cleaner.

When using a degreaser, follow the manufacturer's instructions for proper cleanup and disposal.

Refer to *Cleaning Parts* in this chapter for more information.

Gasket Remover

Stubborn gaskets can present a problem during engine service, as they can be difficult to remove. Consequently, there is the added problem of damage occurring to the gasket mating surfaces from the incorrect use of gasket scraping tools. To remove stubborn gaskets, use a spray gasket remover. Spray gasket remover can be purchased through automotive parts houses. Follow the manufacturer's directions for use.

THREADLOCKING COMPOUND

A threadlocking compound is a fluid applied to fastener threads. After tightening the fastener, the fluid dries to a solid filler between the mating threads, thereby locking the threads in position and preventing loosening due to vibration. Threadlocking compounds are also used on threaded parts to form a seal.

Before applying a threadlocking compound, clean the contacting threads with an aerosol electrical contact cleaner. Use only as much threadlocking compound as is necessary, depending on the size of the fastener. Excess fluid can work its way into adjoining parts.

Threadlocking compound is available in different strengths, so make sure to follow the manufacturer's recommendations when using their particular compound. Two manufacturers of threadlocking compound are ThreeBond of America and the Loctite Corporation. The following threadlocking

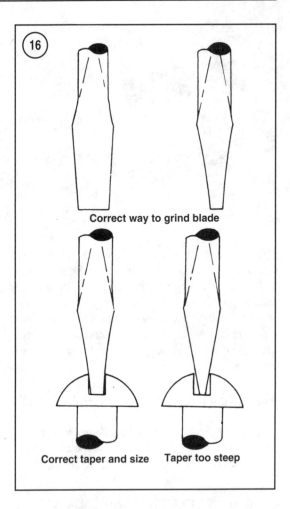

Correct way to grind blade

Correct taper and size   Taper too steep

compounds are recommended for many threadlock requirements described in this manual:

1. ThreeBond 1342: low strength, frequent repair for small screws and bolts.

2. ThreeBond 1360: medium strength, high temperature.

3. ThreeBond 1333B: medium strength, bearing and stud lock.

4. ThreeBond 1303: high strength, frequent repair.

5. Loctite 242 (blue): low strength, frequent repair.

6. Loctite 271 (red): high strength, frequent repair.

BASIC HAND TOOLS

Many of the procedures in this manual may be carried out with simple hand tools and test equipment familiar to the average home mechanic. Keep the tools clean and in a toolbox. Keep them organized with related tools together. After using a tool,

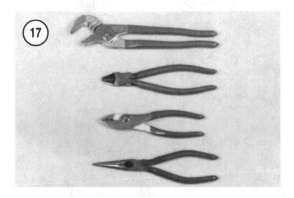

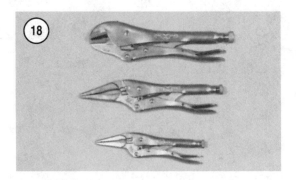

wipe off dirt and grease with a clean cloth and return the tool to its correct place.

High quality tools are essential; they are also more economical in the long run. If starting to build a tool collection, stay away from the advertised specials featured at some parts houses, discount stores and chain drug stores. These are usually a poor grade tool that can be sold inexpensively. They are usually made of inferior material, and are thick, heavy and clumsy. Their rough finish makes them difficult to clean and they usually do not last very long.

Quality tools are made of alloy steel and are heat treated for greater strength. They are lighter and better balanced than poorly crafted ones. Their surface is smooth, making them a pleasure to work with and easy to clean. The initial cost of good quality tools may be more, but they are less expensive in the long run. Do not try to buy everything in all sizes in the beginning; buy a few at a time until all the necessary tools are acquired.

Screwdrivers

The screwdriver is a very basic tool, but if used improperly it will do more damage than good. The slot on a screw has a specific dimension and shape.

A screwdriver must be selected to conform to that shape. Use a screwdriver that matches the screw, or the screw head will be damaged.

Two basic types of screwdrivers are required: common (flat-blade) screwdrivers and Phillips screwdrivers.

Screwdrivers are available in sets that often include an assortment of common and Phillips blades. If purchased individually, obtain the following:
1. Common screwdriver—5/16 × 6 in. blade.
2. Common screwdriver—3/8 × 12 in. blade.
3. Phillips screwdriver—size 2 tip, 6 in. blade.
4. Phillips screwdriver—size 3 tip, 6 and 10 in. blade.

Use screwdrivers only for driving screws. Never use a screwdriver for prying or chiseling metal. Do not try to remove a Phillips or Allen-head screw with a common screwdriver (unless the screw has a combination head that accepts either type); the head will be damaged so that the proper tool cannot remove it.

Keep screwdrivers in the proper condition and they will last longer and perform better. Always keep the tip of a common screwdriver in good condition. **Figure 16** shows how to grind the tip to the proper shape if it becomes damaged. Note the symmetrical sides of the tip.

Pliers

Pliers come in a wide range of types and sizes. Pliers are useful for cutting, bending and crimping. Do not use them to cut hardened objects or to turn bolts or nuts. **Figure 17** shows several pliers useful in motorcycle repair. Each type of pliers has a specialized function. Slip-joint pliers are general-purpose pliers and are used mainly for holding things and for bending.

Needlenose pliers are used to hold or bend small objects. Adjustable pliers can be adjusted to hold various sizes of objects; the jaws remain parallel to grip around objects such as pipe or tubing. There are many more types of pliers. The ones described here are most suitable for vehicle repairs.

Locking Pliers

Locking pliers (**Figure 18**) are used to hold objects very tightly like a vise. Because their sharp jaws can permanently scar the objects they hold, select and use them carefully. Locking pliers are available in many types for more specific tasks.

Circlip Pliers

Circlip pliers (**Figure 19**) are designed to remove and install circlips. When purchasing circlip pliers, there are two kinds to distinguish from. External pliers (spreading) are used to remove circlips that fit on the outside of a shaft. Internal pliers (squeezing) are used to remove circlips that fit inside a gear or housing.

> *WARNING*
> *Circlips can slip and fly off during re-moval and installation. Always wear safety glasses when using circlip pli-ers.*

Box-end, Open-end and Combination Wrenches

Box-end, open-end and combination wrenches are available in sets or separately in a variety of sizes. On open- and box-end wrenches, the number stamped near the end refers to the distance between two parallel flats on the hex head bolt or nut. On combination wrenches, the number is stamped near the center.

Open-end wrenches (A, **Figure 20**) work well in areas with limited overhead access. Their wide flat jaws make them unstable for situations where the bolt or nut is sunken or close to the edge of a cast-ing. These wrenches grip only two flats of a fastener so if either the fastener head or the wrench jaws are worn, the wrench may slip off. While there are many instances where an open-end wrench can be used, use a box-end wrench or socket whenever possible, especially when loosening or tightening the fastener.

Box-end wrenches (B, **Figure 20**) require clear overhead access to the fastener but can work well in situations where the fastener head is close to an-other part. They grip all six edges of a fastener for a very secure grip. They are available in either 6-point or 12-point. The 6-point provides superior holding power and durability but requires a greater swinging radius. The 12-point works better in situa-tions with a limited swinging radius.

Combination wrenches (C, **Figure 20**) have an open-end on one side and a box-end on the other with both ends being the same size. Professional mechanics favor these wrenches because of their versatility.

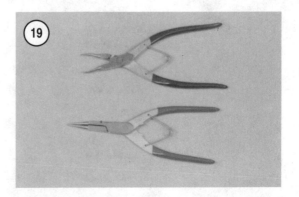

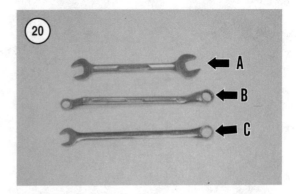

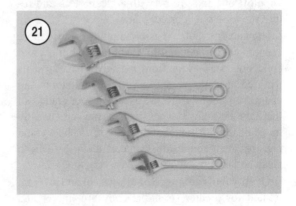

Adjustable Wrenches

An adjustable wrench (sometimes called a cres-cent wrench) can be adjusted to fit nearly any nut or bolt head that has clear access around its entire per-imeter. Adjustable wrenches (**Figure 21**) are best used as a backup wrench to keep a large nut or bolt from turning while the other end is being loosened or tightened with a box-end or socket wrench.

Adjustable wrenches have only two gripping sur-faces that make them more likely to slip from the fastener, causing damage to the part and possibly

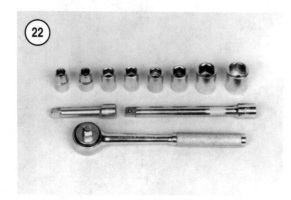

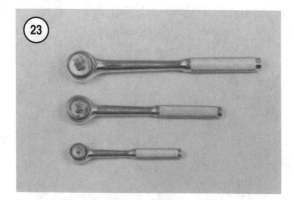

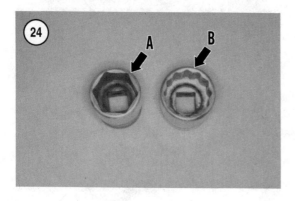

ratchet handle (**Figure 22**) are available with 6-point or 12-point openings and 1/4, 3/8, ½, and 3/4 inch drives. The drive size indicates the size of the square hole that mates with the ratchet handle (**Figure 23**).

When purchasing and using sockets, note the following:

1. When working on the motorcycle, use metric sockets. Individual sockets can be identified by the fastener sizes stamped on the side of the socket.

2. While using metric sockets, the drive hole in the bottom of all sockets is always measured in inches: 1/4, 3/8 and ½ inch drive (larger drive sizes are available for industrial use). Socket adapters are available in order to use a 3/8 in. drive socket on a ½ in. drive ratchet (and vise versa).

3. Sockets are available with either 6- or 12- points. Point size refers to the number of points between the grooves cut inside the socket walls.

4. The 6-point socket (A, **Figure 24**) provides greater holding power and durability but requires a longer swinging radius than the 12-point socket.

5. The 12-point socket (B, **Figure 24**) needs to be moved only half as far as a 6-point socket before it is repositioned on the fastener. However, because of the larger number of points (and a smaller holding area between the points), the 12-point socket provides less holding power than a 6-point socket.

6. Sockets are available in hand sockets and impact sockets. Hand sockets can be chrome-plated or have a black finish. Impact sockets generally have a black finish. Use hand sockets with ratchets and torque wrenches (hand use only). Use impact sockets when loosening or tightening fasteners with air tools and hand impact drivers. Impact sockets are made of thicker material for more durability. Compare the size and wall thickness of the regular 19 mm hand socket (A, **Figure 25**) with the corresponding 19 mm impact socket (B, **Figure 25**).

> *WARNING*
> *Do not use hand sockets with air tools and hand impact drivers, as they may shatter and cause injury. Use only impact-approved sockets and always wear eye protection when using any type of impact or air tool.*

personal injury. The fact that one jaw is adjustable only aggravates this shortcoming.

These wrenches are directional; the solid jaw must be the one transmitting the force. If using the adjustable jaw to transmit the force, it can loosen and possibly slip off.

Socket Wrenches

This type is undoubtedly the fastest, safest and most convenient to use. Sockets that attach to a

Impact Driver

The hand impact driver makes removing fasteners easy and eliminates damage to bolts and screw slots. Impact drivers and interchangeable bits (**Figure 26**) are available at most large hardware, motorcycle or auto parts stores. Sockets can also be used with a hand impact driver, however make sure that the socked is designed to be used with an impact driver or air tool. Do not use regular hand sockets, as they may shatter during use.

Allen Wrenches

Allen wrenches are available in sets or separately in a variety of sizes. Honda motorcycles require a metric set (**Figure 27**). Allen bolts are sometimes called socket bolts.

Hammers.

The correct hammer (**Figure 28**) is necessary for certain repairs. A hammer with a face (or head) of rubber or plastic or the soft-faced type that is filled with lead or steel shot is sometimes necessary during engine disassembly. Never use a metal-faced hammer on engine or suspension parts, as severe damage will result in most cases. The same amount of force can be produced with a soft-faced hammer. The shock of a metal-faced hammer, however, is required for using a hand impact driver or cold chisel.

Torque Wrench

A torque wrench is used with a socket, torque adapter or similar extension to measure how tightly a nut, bolt or other fastener is installed. They come in a wide price range and with either 1/4, 3/8 or ½ in. square drive. The drive size indicates the size of the square drive that mates with the socket, torque adapter or extension. Popular types are the deflecting beam (A, **Figure 29**), the dial indicator and the audible click (B, **Figure 29**) torque wrenches. As with any series of tools, there are advantages and disadvantages with each type of torque wrench. When choosing a torque wrench, consider its torque range, accuracy rating and price. The torque specifications listed at the end of most chapters in this manual will give an idea on the range of torque wrench needed to service the motorcycle.

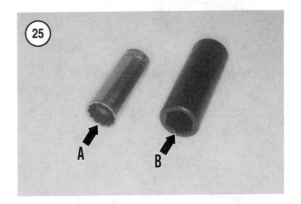

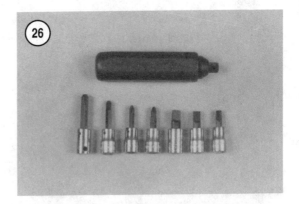

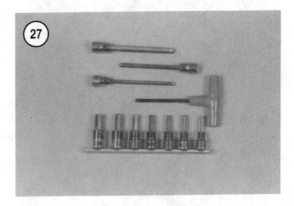

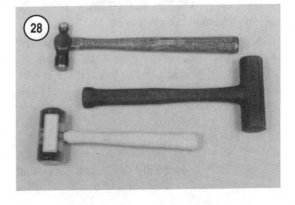

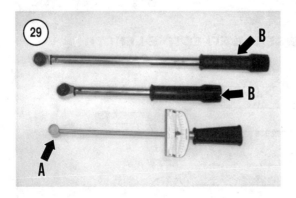

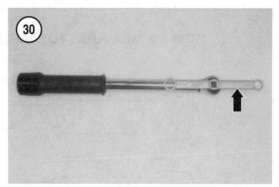

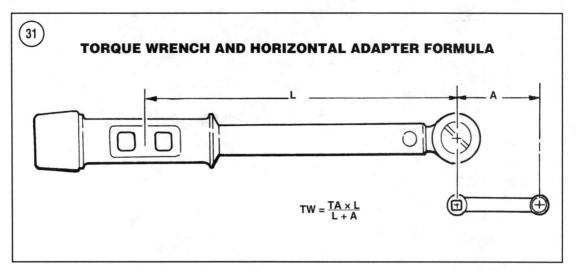

TORQUE WRENCH AND HORIZONTAL ADAPTER FORMULA

$$TW = \frac{TA \times L}{L + A}$$

Because the torque wrench is a precision tool, it must be cared for properly to maintain its accuracy. Always store a torque wrench in its carrying case or in a padded tool box drawer. All torque wrenches require periodic recalibration. To find out more about this, read the information provided with the torque wrench or contact the manufacturer.

Torque Wrench Adapters

Torque adapters and extensions offer greater flexibility of the torque wrench. For example, the torque adapter wrench shown in **Figure 30** can be used to extend the length of the torque wrench to tighten fasteners that cannot be reached with a torque wrench and socket. When a torque adapter lengthens or shortens the torque wrench, the torque reading on the torque wrench will not be the same amount of torque that is applied to the fastener. It is then necessary to recalibrate the torque specification to compensate for the effect of the added or re-

duced torque adapter length. When a torque adapter is set at a right angle to the torque wrench, relcalibration is not required (see information and following figure).

To recalculate a torque reading when using a torque adapter, it is first necessary to know the lever length of the torque wrench, the length of the adapter from the center of the square drive to the center of the nut or bolt and the actual amount of torque desired at the nut or bolt (**Figure 31**). The formula can be expressed as:

$$TW = \frac{TA \times L}{L + A}$$

TW = This is the torque setting or dial reading to set on the torque wrench when tightening the fastener.

TA = Actual torque specification. This is the torque specification listed in this service manual and will be the actual amount of torque applied to the fastener.

A = This is the lever length of the adapter from the centerline of the square drive (at the torque

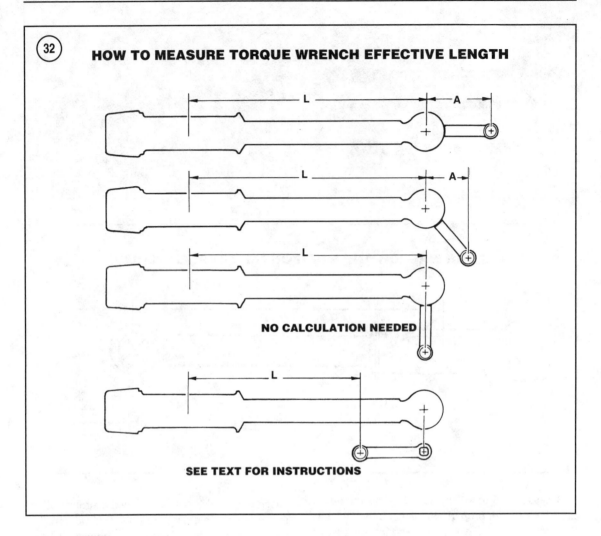

HOW TO MEASURE TORQUE WRENCH EFFECTIVE LENGTH

NO CALCULATION NEEDED

SEE TEXT FOR INSTRUCTIONS

wrench) to the centerline of the nut or bolt. If the torque adapter extends straight from the end of the torque wrench (**Figure 32**), the centerline of the torque adapter and torque wrench are the same.

However, when the centerlines of the torque adapter and torque wrench do not align, the distance must be measured as shown in **Figure 32**. Also note in **Figure 32** that when the torque adapter is set at a right angle to the torque wrench, no calculation is needed; the lever length of the torque wrench did not change.

L = This is the lever length of the torque wrench. This specification is usually listed in the instruction manual provided with the torque wrench, or the length can be determined by measuring the distance from the center of the square drive on the torque wrench to the center of the torque wrench handle (**Figure 32**).

Example:
Calculate the torque wrench preset reading or dial reading when:

TA = 20 ft.-lb.

A = 3 in.

L = 14 in.

$$TW = \frac{20 \times 14}{14 + 3} = \frac{280}{17} = 16.5 \text{ ft.-lb.}$$

In this example, the recalculated torque value of 16.5 ft.-lb. would be the amount of torque to set on the torque wrench. When using a dial or beam-type torque wrench, torque would be applied until the pointer aligns with the 16.5 ft.-lb. dial reading. When using a click-type torque wrench, the micrometer dial would be preset to 16.5 ft.-lb. In all cases, even though the torque wrench dial or preset reading was 16.5 ft.-lb., the fastener will actually be tightened to 20 ft.-lb.

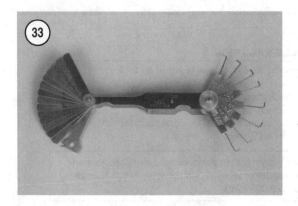

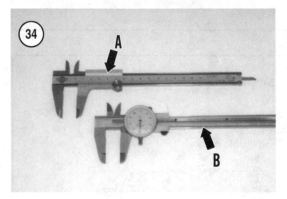

PRECISION MEASURING TOOLS

Measurement is an important part of engine and suspension service. When performing many of the service procedures in this manual, a number of measurements are required. These include basic checks such as engine compression and spark plug gap. As shop experience progresses into engine disassembly and service, many measurements are required to determine the size and condition of the piston and cylinder bore, crankshaft runout, and other components. When making these measurements, the degree of accuracy will dictate which tool is required.

Precision measuring tools are expensive. If this is the first experience at engine or suspension service, it may be more worthwhile to have the checks and measurements made at a Honda dealership, a competent independent vehicle repair shop or a machine shop. However, as skills and enthusiasm for service work increase, it may be desirable to purchase some of these specialized tools. The following is a description of the measuring tools required to perform the service procedures described in the various chapters in this manual.

Feeler Gauge

Feeler gauges come in assorted sets and types. The feeler gauge is made of either a piece of flat or round hardened steel of a specified thickness (**Figure 33**). Wire gauges are used to measure spark plug gap. Flat gauges are used for most other measurements. Feeler gauges are also designed for special uses. For example, the end of a gauge can be small and angled to facilitate checking valve clearances on models requiring adjustment.

Vernier Caliper

This tool is invaluable when reading inside, outside and depth measurements to close precision. Although this tool is not as precise as a micrometer, it allows reasonable, non-close tolerance measurements, typically to within 0.025 mm (0.001 in.). Common uses of a vernier caliper are measuring the length of clutch springs, the thickness of clutch plates, shims and thrust washers, brake pad thickness or the depth of a bearing bore. The jaws of the caliper must be clean and free of burrs at all times in order to obtain an accurate measurement. There are several types of vernier calipers available. The standard vernier caliper (A, **Figure 34**) has a highly accurate graduated scale on the handle in which the measurements must be calculated. The dial indicator caliper (B, **Figure 34**) is equipped with a small dial and needle that indicates the measurement reading. The digital electronic type with an LCD display that shows the measurement on a small display screen. Some vernier calipers must be calibrated prior to making a measurement to ensure an accurate measurement. Refer to the manufacturer's instructions for this procedure.

Outside Micrometers

An outside micrometer is a precision tool used to accurately measure parts using the decimal divisions of the inch or meter (**Figure 35**). While there are many types and styles of micrometers, this section will describe steps on how to use the outside micrometer. The outside micrometer is the most common type of micrometer used when servicing motorcycles. It is useful in accurately measuring the outside diameter, length and thickness of parts. These parts include the piston, piston pin, crank-

DECIMAL PLACE VALUES*

0.1	Indicates 1/10 (one tenth of an inch or millimeter)
0.010	Indicates 1/100 (one one-hundredth of an inch or millimeter)
0.001	Indicates 1/1,000 (one one-thousandth of an inch or millimeter)

*This chart represents the values of figures placed to the right of the decimal point. Use it when reading decimals from one-tenth to one one-thousandth of an inch or millimeter. It is not a conversion chart (for example: 0.001 in. is not equal to 0.001 mm).

STANDARD INCH MICROMETER

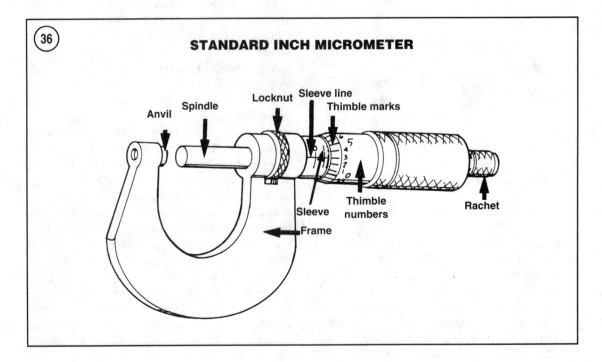

shaft, piston rings and shims. The outside micrometer is also used to measure the dimension taken by a small hole gauge or a telescoping gauge described later in this section. After the small hole gauge or telescoping gauge has been carefully expanded to a limit within the bore of the component being measured, carefully remove the gauge and measure the distance across its arms with the outside micrometer.

Other types of micrometers include the depth micrometer and screw thread micrometer. **Figure 36** illustrates the various parts of an outside micrometer with its part names and markings identified.

Micrometer Range

A micrometer's size indicates the minimum and maximum size of a part that it can measure. The usual sizes include: 0-1 in., 1-2 in., 2-3 in. and 3-4 in./0-25 mm, 25-50 mm, 50-75 mm and 75-100 mm. These micrometers use fixed anvils.

Some micrometers use the same frame with interchangeable anvils of different lengths. This allows the installation of the correct length anvil for a particular job. For example, a 0-4 in. interchangeable micrometer is equipped with four different length anvils. While purchasing one or two micrometers to

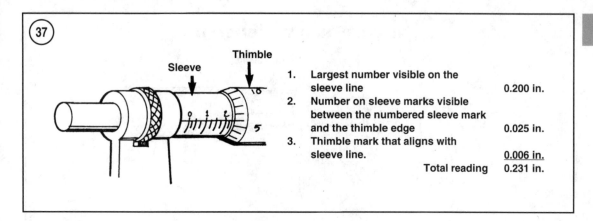

1.	Largest number visible on the sleeve line	0.200 in.
2.	Number on sleeve marks visible between the numbered sleeve mark and the thimble edge	0.025 in.
3.	Thimble mark that aligns with sleeve line.	0.006 in.
	Total reading	0.231 in.

cover a range from 0-4 or 0-6 inches is less expensive, its overall frame size makes it less convenient to use.

How to Read a Micrometer

When reading a micrometer, numbers are taken from different scales and then added together. The following sections describe how to read the standard inch micrometer, the vernier inch micrometer, the standard metric micrometer and the metric vernier micrometer.

Standard inch micrometer

The standard inch micrometer is accurate up to one-thousandth of an inch (0.001 in.). The heart of the micrometer is its spindle screw with 40 threads per inch. Every turn of the thimble will move the spindle 1/40 of an inch or 0.025 in.

Before learning how to read a micrometer, study the markings and part names in **Figure 36**. Then take the micrometer and turn the thimble until its zero mark aligns with the zero mark on the sleeve line. Now turn the thimble counterclockwise and align the next thimble mark with the sleeve line. The micrometer now reads 0.001 in. (one one-thousandth) of an inch. Thus each thimble mark is equal to 0.001 in. Every fifth thimble mark is numbered to help with reading: 0, 5, 10, 15 and 20.

Reset the micrometer so that the thimble and sleeve line zero marks line up. Then turn the thimble counterclockwise one complete revolution and align the thimble zero mark with the first line in the sleeve line. The micrometer now reads 0.025 in.

(twenty-five thousandths) of an inch. Thus each sleeve line represents 0.025 in.

Now turn the thimble counterclockwise while counting the sleeve line marks. Every fourth mark on the sleeve line is marked with a number ranging from 1 through 9. The last digit on the sleeve line is usually a zero (0) mark. The zero mark indicates that the end of the micrometer's measuring range has been reached. Each sleeve number represents 0.100 in. For example, the number 1 represents 0.100 in. and the number 9 represents 0.900 in.

When reading a standard inch micrometer, take the three measurements described and add them together. The first two readings are taken from the sleeve. The last reading is taken from the thimble. The sum of the three readings gives the measurement in thousandths of an inch (0.001 in.).

To read a standard inch micrometer, perform the following steps while referring to the example in **Figure 37**.

1. Read the sleeve line to find the largest number visible—each sleeve number mark equals 0.100 in.

2. Count the number of sleeve marks visible between the numbered sleeve mark and the thimble edge—each sleeve mark equals 0.025 in. If there is no visible sleeve marks, continue with Step 3.

3. Read the thimble mark that lines up with the sleeve line—each thimble mark equals 0.001 in.

NOTE
If a thimble mark does not align exactly with the sleeve line but falls between two lines, estimate the decimal amount between the lines. For a more accurate reading, a vernier inch micrometer must be used.

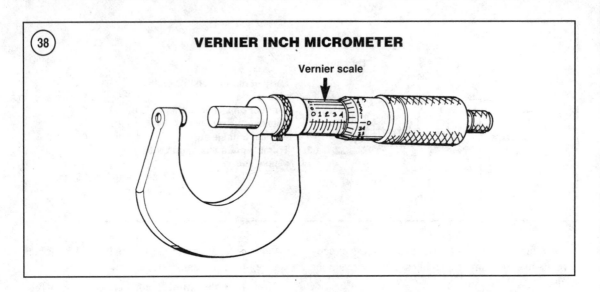

(38)

VERNIER INCH MICROMETER

Vernier scale

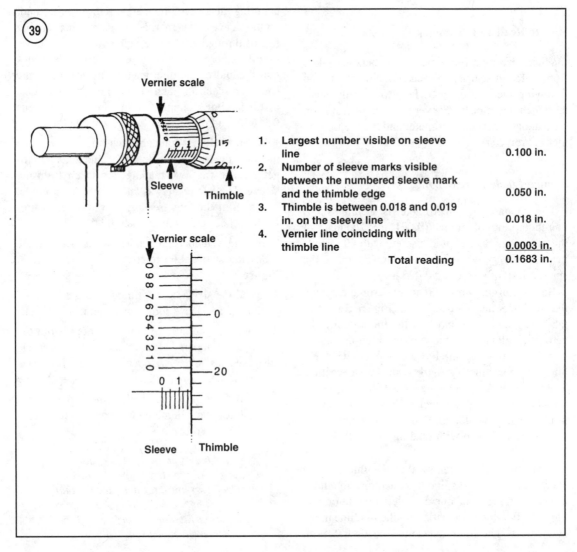

(39)

Vernier scale

Sleeve

Thimble

Vernier scale

Sleeve   Thimble

1. Largest number visible on sleeve
   line   0.100 in.
2. Number of sleeve marks visible
   between the numbered sleeve mark
   and the thimble edge   0.050 in.
3. Thimble is between 0.018 and 0.019
   in. on the sleeve line   0.018 in.
4. Vernier line coinciding with
   thimble line   0.0003 in.
                          Total reading   0.1683 in.

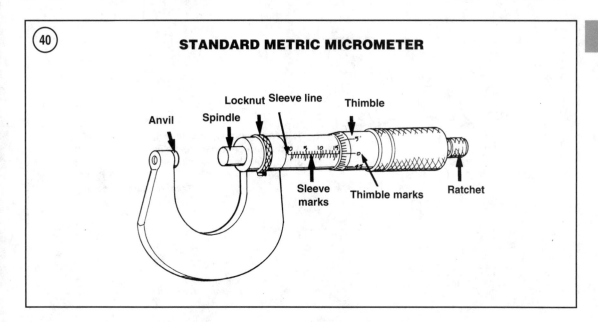

STANDARD METRIC MICROMETER

Anvil · Spindle · Locknut · Sleeve line · Thimble · Sleeve marks · Thimble marks · Ratchet

4. Adding the micrometer readings in Steps 1, 2 and 3 gives the actual measurement.

Vernier inch micrometers

A vernier inch micrometer can accurately measure in ten-thousandths of an inch (0.0001 in.). While it has the same markings as a standard micrometer, a vernier scale scribed on the sleeve (**Figure 38**) makes it unique. The vernier scale consists of eleven equally spaced lines marked 1-9 with a 0 on each end. These lines run parallel on the top of the sleeve where each line is equal to 0.0001 in. Thus the vernier scale divides a thousandth of an inch (0.001 in.) into ten-thousandths of an inch (0.0001 in.).

To read a vernier inch micrometer, perform the following steps while referring to the example in **Figure 39**.

1. Read the micrometer in the same way as on the standard inch micrometer. This is the initial reading.

2. If a thimble mark aligns exactly with the sleeve line, reading the vernier scale is not necessary. If a thimble mark does not line up exactly with the sleeve line, read the vernier scale in Step 3.

3. Read the vernier scale to find which vernier mark lines up with one thimble mark. The number of that vernier mark is the number of ten-thousandths of an inch to add to the initial reading taken in Step 1.

Metric micrometers

The metric micrometer is very similar to the standard inch type. The differences are the graduations on the thimble and sleeve, as shown in **Figure 40**.

The standard metric micrometer accurately measures to one one-hundredth of a millimeter (0.01 mm). On the metric micrometer, the spindle screw is ground with a thread pitch of one-half millimeter (0.5 mm). Thus every turn of the thimble moves the spindle 0.5 mm.

The sleeve line is graduated in millimeters and half millimeters. The marks on the upper side of the sleeve line are equal to 1.00 mm. Every fifth mark above the sleeve line is marked with a number. The actual numbers depend on the size of the micrometer. For example, on a 0-25 mm micrometer, the sleeve marks are numbered 0, 5, 10, 15, 20 and 25. On a 25-50 mm micrometer, the sleeve marks are numbered 25, 30, 35, 40, 45 and 50. This numbering sequence continues with larger micrometers (50-75 and 75-100). Each mark on the lower side of the sleeve line is equal to 0.50 mm.

The thimble scale is divided into fifty graduations where one graduation is equal to 0.01 mm. Every fifth thimble graduation is numbered 0-45 to help with reading. The thimble edge is used to indicate which sleeve markings to read.

To read a metric micrometer, add the number of millimeters and half-millimeters on the sleeve line to the number of one one-hundredth millimeters on

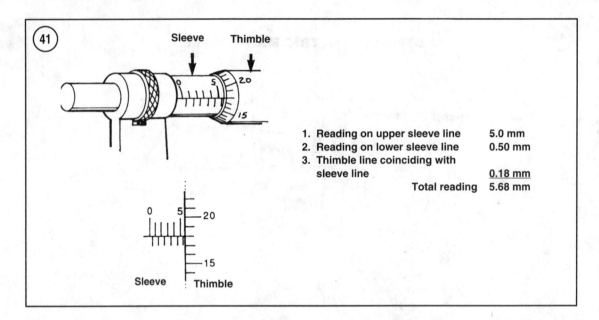

1. Reading on upper sleeve line   5.0 mm
2. Reading on lower sleeve line   0.50 mm
3. Thimble line coinciding with
   sleeve line   <u>0.18 mm</u>
                 Total reading   5.68 mm

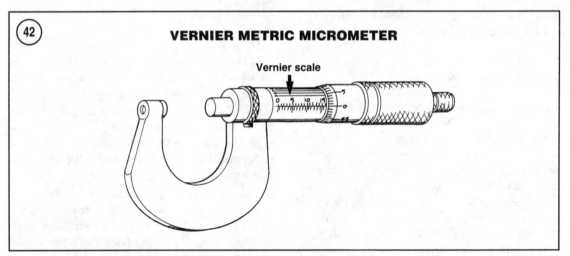

VERNIER METRIC MICROMETER

the thimble. To do so, perform the following steps while referring to the example in **Figure 41**.

1. Take the first reading by counting the number of marks visible on the upper sleeve line. Record the reading.

2. Look below the sleeve line to see if a lower mark is visible directly past the upper line mark. If so, add 0.50 to the first reading.

3. Now read the thimble mark that aligns with the sleeve line. Record this reading.

NOTE
If a thimble mark does not align exactly with the sleeve line but falls between two lines, estimate the decimal amount between the lines. For a more accurate reading, a metric vernier micrometer must be used.

4. Adding the micrometer readings in Steps 1, 2 and 3 gives the actual measurement.

Metric vernier micrometers

A metric vernier micrometer is accurate to two thousandths of a millimeter (0.002 mm). While it has the same markings as a standard metric micrometer, a vernier scale scribed on the sleeve (**Figure 42**) makes it unique. The vernier scale consists of five equally spaced lines marked 0, 2, 4, 6 and 8.

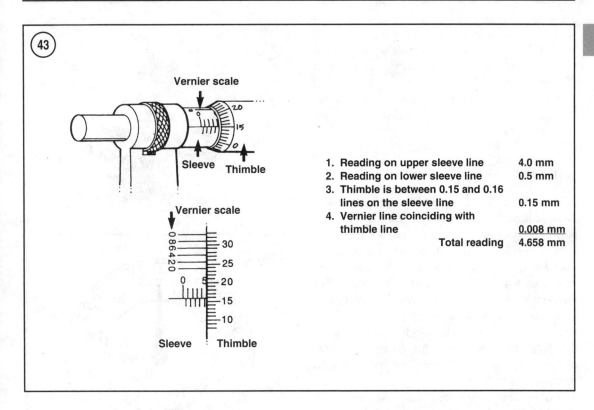

43

1. Reading on upper sleeve line	4.0 mm
2. Reading on lower sleeve line	0.5 mm
3. Thimble is between 0.15 and 0.16 lines on the sleeve line	0.15 mm
4. Vernier line coinciding with thimble line	0.008 mm
Total reading	4.658 mm

These lines run parallel on the top of the sleeve where each line is equal to 0.002 mm.

To read a metric vernier micrometer, perform the following steps while referring to the example in **Figure 43**:

1. Read the micrometer in the same way as the metric standard micrometer. This is the initial reading.

2. If a thimble mark lines up exactly with the sleeve line, reading the vernier scale is not necessary. If a thimble mark does not line up exactly with the sleeve line, read the vernier scale in Step 3.

3. Read the vernier scale to find which vernier mark lines up with one thimble mark. The number of that vernier mark is the number of thousandths of a millimeter to add to the initial reading taken in Step 1.

Micrometer Accuracy Check

Before using a micrometer, check its accuracy as follows:

1. Make sure the anvil and spindle faces (**Figure 36**) are clean and dry.

2. To check a 0-1 in. or 0-25 mm micrometer, perform the following:

a. Turn the thimble until the spindle contacts the anvil. If the micrometer has a ratchet stop, use it to ensure that the proper amount of pressure is applied against the contact surfaces.

b. Read the micrometer. If the adjustment is correct, the zero mark on the thimble will align exactly with the zero mark on the sleeve line. If the zero marks do not align, the micrometer is out of adjustment

c. To adjust the micrometer, follow the manufacturer's instructions supplied with the micrometer.

3. To check the accuracy of micrometers above the 1 in. or 25 mm size, perform the following:

a. Manufacturers usually supply a standard gauge with these micrometers. A standard is a steel block, disc or rod that is ground to an exact size to check the accuracy of the micrometer. For example, a 1-2 in. micrometer is equipped with a 1-inch standard gauge. A 25-50 mm micrometer is equipped with a 25 mm standard gauge.

b. Place the standard gauge between the micrometer's spindle and anvil and measure its outside diameter or length. Read the micrometer. If the adjustment is correct, the zero mark on the thimble will align exactly with the zero mark on the sleeve line. If the zero marks do not align, the micrometer is out of adjustment.

c. To adjust the micrometer, follow the manufacturer's instructions provided with the micrometer.

Proper Care of the Micrometer

The micrometer is a precision instrument and must be used correctly and with great care. When handling a micrometer, note the following:

1. Store a micrometer in its box or in a protected place where dust, oil, and other debris cannot come in contact with it. Do not store micrometers in a drawer with other tools or hang them on a tool board.

2. When storing a 0-1 in. (0-25 mm) micrometer, turn the thimble so that the spindle and anvil faces do not contact each other. If they do, rust may form on the contact ends or the spindle can be damaged from temperature changes.

3. Do not clean a micrometer with compressed air. Dirt forced into the tool can cause premature wear.

4. Occasionally lubricate the micrometer with lightweight oil to prevent rust and corrosion.

5. Before using a micrometer, check its accuracy. Refer to *Micrometer Accuracy Check* in this section.

Dial Indicator

Dial indicators (A, **Figure 44**) are precision tools used to check dimension variations on machined parts such as transmission shafts and axles and to check crankshaft and axle shaft end play. Dial indicators are available with various dial types; for motorcycle repair, select an indicator with a continuous dial face (**Figure 45**).

When using a dial indicator, it must be mounted rigidly to a magnetic stand (B, **Figure 44**) or other support so that only the dial indicator plunger can move. An error in the reading will occur if the dial body or its mounting stand moves in relation to the plunger.

> *NOTE*
> *A dial indicator and spark plug adapter set are not required to check the ignition timing on the Honda models covered in this manual. See **Ignition Timing** in Chapter Three.*

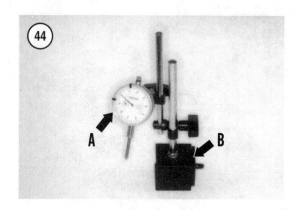

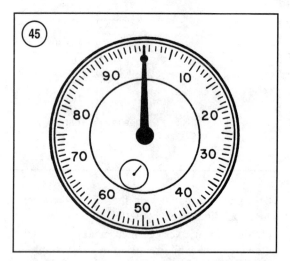

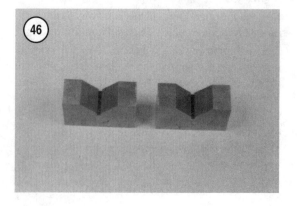

V-Blocks

V-blocks (**Figure 46**) are precision ground blocks used to hold a round object when checking its runout or condition. V-blocks can be used when checking the runout of such items as the transmission shafts and axles.

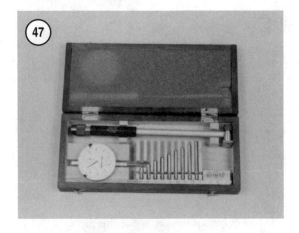

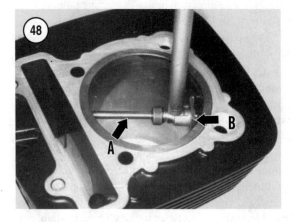

Cylinder Bore Gauge

The cylinder bore gauge is a very specialized precision tool. The gauge set shown in **Figure 47** is comprised of a dial indicator, handle, and a number of length adapters to adapt the gauge to different bore sizes. The bore gauge can be used to make cylinder bore measurements such as bore size, taper and out-of-round. In some cases, an outside micrometer must be used to calibrate the bore gauge to a specific bore size.

Select the correct length adapter (A, **Figure 48**) for the size of the bore to be measured. Zero the bore gauge according to its manufacturer's instructions, insert the bore gauge into the cylinder, carefully move it around in the bore to make sure it is centered and that the gauge foot (B, **Figure 48**) is sitting correctly on the bore surface. This is necessary to obtain a correct reading. Refer to the manufacturer's instructions for reading the actual measurement obtained.

Small Hole Gauges

A set of small hole gauges measure a hole, groove or slot. The small hole gauge is used for the smallest measurements and the telescoping gauges are used for slightly larger measurements. A small hole gauge is required to measure rocker arm bore and brake master cylinder bore diameters. The telescoping gauge does not have a scale for direct readings. An outside micrometer must be used together with the telescoping gauge to determine the bore dimension.

Carefully insert the small hole gauge into the bore of the component to be measured. Tighten the knurled end of the gauge to carefully expanded the gauge fingers to the limit within the bore—*do not overtighten* the gauge as there is no built-in release feature. If overtightened, the gauge fingers can damage the bore surface. Carefully remove the gauge and measure the outside dimension of the gauge with a micrometer. See *Outside Micrometer* in this chapter.

Telescoping Gauges

A telescoping gauge is used to measure hole diameters from approximately 8 mm (5/16 in.) to 150 mm (6 in.). For example, it could be used to measure brake caliper bore and cylinder bore diameters. Like the small hole gauge, the telescoping gauge does not have a scale for direct readings. An outside micrometer must be used together with the telescoping gauge to determine the bore dimension.

Select the correct size telescoping gauge for the bore to be measured. Compress the moveable side of the gauge post and carefully install the gauge into the bore of the component to be measured, then release the movable post against the bore. Carefully move the gauge around in the bore to make sure it is centered. Tighten the knurled end of the gauge to hold the movable gauge post in this position. Carefully remove the gauge and measure the outside dimension of the gauge posts with a micrometer. See *Outside Micrometer* in this chapter.

TEST EQUIPMENT

Spark Tester

A quick way to check the ignition system is to connect a spark tester to the end of the spark plug wire and operate the engine's starter. A visible spark should jump the gap on the tester. A variety of spark testers are available from engine and after-market manufacturers. This tool and its use are de-scribed in Chapter Two.

Compression Gauge

An engine with low compression cannot be prop-erly tuned and will not develop full power. A com-pression gauge (**Figure 49**) measures engine compression. The one shown has a flexible stem with an extension that can allow holding it while turning the engine over. Open the throttle all the way when checking engine compression. See Chap-ter Three.

Multimeter or VOM

A multimeter or VOM (Volt and Ohm Meter) is a valuable tool for all electrical system troubleshoot-ing (**Figure 50**). The voltage application is used to indicate the voltage applied or available to various electrical components. The ohmmeter portion of the meter is used to check for continuity, or lack of con-tinuity, and to measure the resistance of a compo-nent. Some tests are easily accomplished using an analog meter, but other components must be tested with a digital multimeter, as indicated in the text.

In some test procedures, the vehicle's manufac-turer will suggest using their specific test meter due to the internal design of their meter. They will spec-ify that the resistance reading may differ if another type of test meter is used in the test procedure. If this requirement occurs relating to any of the test proce-dures in this book it will be noted.

See *Electrical Troubleshooting* in Chapter Two for its use.

Voltage

Voltage is the pressure in an electrical circuit. The more pressure (voltage) in the circuit, the more work can be accomplished. Always measure volt-age in a simple parallel connection. The connection of a voltmeter directly to the negative and positive terminals of a battery is an example of a parallel connection. Nothing must be disconnected to make a parallel connection.

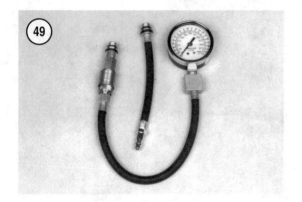

Direct current (DC) voltage means that electricity flows in one direction only. All circuits powered by a battery are DC circuits.

Alternating current (AC) means that the electric-ity flows in one direction momentarily then switches to the opposite direction. The frequency at which AC voltage changes direction is referred to a hertz. In motorcycle applications, the charging sys-tem output is AC voltage until the AC is converted to DC for storage in the battery.

Since resistance causes voltage to drop, resis-tance can be measured on an active circuit using a voltmeter. This is called a voltage drop test. Ba-sically, a voltage drop test compares the voltage at the beginning of a circuit to the voltage available at the end of the circuit while the circuit is being oper-ated. If the circuit has no resistance, there will be no voltage drop and the meter will read zero volts. The more resistance the circuit has, the higher the volt-age meter reading will be. Generally, a voltage drop of one or more volts is considered excessive. The advantage to the voltage drop test over a resistance test is that the circuit is tested during operation. It is important to remember that a zero reading on a volt-age drop test is desired while a reading of battery voltage indicates an open circuit.

When measuring voltage, select the meter volt-age range one scale higher than the expected volt-age of the circuit to prevent damage to the meter.

Resistance

> *NOTE*
> *In most cases, to obtain an accurate resistance measurement, the compo-nent must be at approximately 20° C (68° F).*

Resistance is the opposition to the flow of electricity in a circuit and is measured in ohms. Resistance causes a reduction in current flow and a reduction or drop in available voltage. Resistance is measured with an ohmmeter. To measure resistance, the ohmmeter sends a small amount of electricity through the circuit and measures how difficult it is push the electricity back to the ohmmeter.

CAUTION
An ohmmeter must only be used on a circuit or component that is isolated from any other circuits or components and has no voltage present. The meter will be damaged if it is connected to a circuit with voltage present.

An ohmmeter, although useful, is not always a good indicator of a component's condition. This is primarily because resistance tests do not simulate actual operating conditions. For example, the power source in most ohmmeters is only 6-9 volts. The voltage in the secondary windings of an ignition coil, however, can be several thousand volts during normal operation. Such high voltage can cause coil insulation leakage that cannot be detected using an ohmmeter.

Because resistance generally increases with temperature, perform resistance tests with the component or circuit at room temperature. Resistance tests on a hot component will indicate increased resistance and may result in unnecessary replacement of a good component.

To calibrate an analog ohmmeter

Every time an analog ohmmeter is used or if the scale is changed, the ohmmeter must be calibrated

to zero the needle. Most digital ohmmeters are auto ranging—when switched on they are automatically set to zero.

1. Make sure the meter's battery is at full power. If the battery condition is questionable, replace the battery.
2. Make sure the test probes are clean and free of corrosion.
3. Touch the two test probes together and observe the meter needle location on the ohms scale. The needle must be aligned with the zero mark on the scale.
4. If necessary, rotate the *ohms adjust* knob on the meter in either direction until the needle is directly aligned with the zero mark.

Continuity Test

A continuity test determines the integrity of a circuit or component. A broken wire or open circuit has no continuity, a complete circuit has continuity. Continuity can be checked using an ohmmeter or a self-powered test lamp. Using an ohmmeter, a low-resistance reading, usually 0 ohms, indicates continuity. An infinity reading indicates no continuity. Using a self-powered test lamp, continuity is indicated if the test lamp glows. If the lamp does not glow, no continuity is present.

The circuit or component must be isolated or disconnected from any other circuit to check continuity.

Amperage

Amperes (amps) are the units used to measure current flow in a circuit or through a component. Current is the actual flow of electricity. The more current that flows, the more work that can be accomplished. However, if excessive current flows through a wire, the wire will overheat and probably melt. Melted wires are caused by excessive current, not excessive voltage.

Amperes are measured using an ammeter attached in a simple series connection. Amperage measurement requires that the ammeter be spliced into the circuit in a series connection. Always use an ammeter that can read higher that the anticipated current flow to prevent damaging the meter. Connect the red lead of the ammeter to the electrical source and the black lead to the electrical load.

SPECIAL TOOLS

A few special tools are required for engine and suspension service. These are described in the appropriate chapters and are available either from a Honda dealership or other manufacturers as indicated in the text.

MOTORCYCLE LIFT

The Honda 1500 Valkyrie is not equipped with a centerstand. Therefore, purchase a motorcycle lift (**Figure 51**); it is an essential piece of equipment if the motorcycle is going to be serviced. The motorcycle is heavy and must be supported securely when performing many of the service procedures in this book, even wheel removal. Do not try to balance the motorcycle on makeshift jacks or wooden blocks, as this will certainly lead to the motorcycle falling over, causing damage not only to the motorcycle but to anyone working around it.

There are many motorcycle lifts available. The middle to upper price range lift is suitable for working on the Valkyrie and is shown in some of the procedures in this manual. Most lifts have receptacles for attaching tie downs that add to the security of the motorcycle on the lift (**Figure 52**).

Research the types of lifts that are available; all lifts do not fit all motorcycles and some lifts have adapters to fit a variety of motorcycles. Remember the Valkyrie is large and heavy, so do not purchase a small lift that may not be strong enough to raise the motorcycle or large enough to *securely support* the motorcycle.

When using a motorcycle lift, make sure it is placed on a flat, stable surface. Concrete flooring is ideal—do *not* place the lift on a dirt or soft surface that may shift after the motorcycle has been raised on the lift.

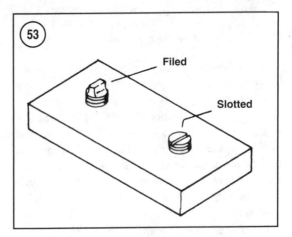

Filed

Slotted

MECHANICS' TIPS

Removing Frozen Nuts and Screws

If a fastener rusts and cannot be removed, several methods may be used to loosen it. First, apply penetrating oil such as Liquid Wrench or WD-40 (available at hardware or auto supply stores). Apply it liberally and let it penetrate for 10-15 minutes. Tap the fastener several times with a small hammer; do not hit it hard enough to cause damage. Reapply the penetrating oil, if necessary.

For frozen screws, apply penetrating oil as described, then insert a screwdriver in the slot and tap the top of the screwdriver with a hammer. This loosens the rust so the screw may be removed normally. If the screw head is too damaged to use this method, try gripping the fastener head with locking pliers and twisting the screw out.

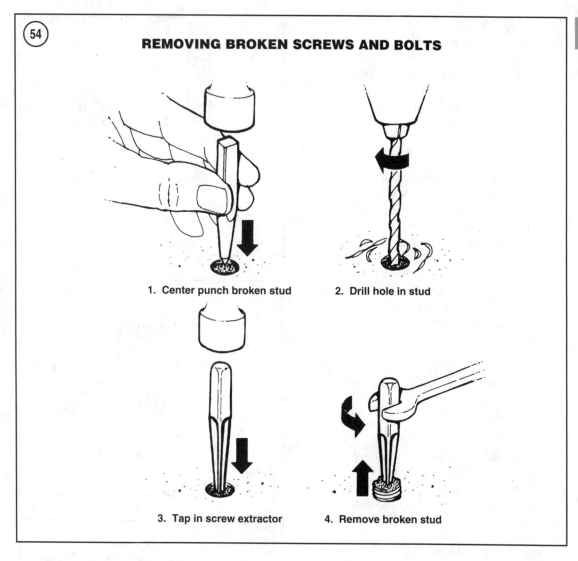

(54)

REMOVING BROKEN SCREWS AND BOLTS

1. Center punch broken stud

2. Drill hole in stud

3. Tap in screw extractor

4. Remove broken stud

Avoid applying heat unless specifically in-structed, as it may melt, warp or remove the temper from parts.

Removing Broken Screws or Bolts

If the head breaks off a screw or bolt, several methods are available for removing the remaining portion.

If a large portion of the remainder projects out, try gripping it with locking pliers. If the projecting por-tion is too small, file it to fit a wrench or cut a slot in it to fit a screwdriver tip (**Figure 53**). Then loosen the fastener with a hand impact driver. See *Impact Driver* in this chapter.

If the head breaks off flush, use a screw extractor. To do this, centerpunch the exact center of the re-maining portion of the screw or bolt. Drill a small hole in the screw and tap the extractor into the hole. Back the screw out with a wrench on the extractor. See **Figure 54**.

Remedying Stripped Threads

Occasionally, threads are stripped through care-lessness or impact damage. Often the threads can be repaired by running a tap (for internal threads on nuts) or die (for external threads on bolts) through the threads. See **Figure 55**. To clean or repair spark plug threads, use a spark plug tap.

If an internal thread is damaged, it may be necessary to install a thread insert. These are available for individual thread sizes and in large sets. Follow the manufacturer's instructions when installing an insert.

If it is necessary to drill and tap a hole, refer to **Table 8** for metric tap and drill sizes.

Replacing Studs

1. Measure the height of the installed stud so that the new stud can be installed correctly.

2A. If some threads of a stud are damaged, but others remain, possible removal of the stud can be accomplished as follows. If there are no usable threads, remove the stud as described in Step 2B.

   a. Thread two nuts onto the damaged stud (**Figure 56**), then tighten the nuts against each other so that they are locked together.

   b. Turn the bottom nut (**Figure 57**) to unscrew and remove the stud.

> *NOTE*
> *To prevent damaging the cylinder surface when replacing the cylinder studs, install the old head gasket over the cylinder.*

2B. If the threads on the stud are damaged, remove the stud with a stud remover or, if possible, with a pair of locking pliers.

3. When reusing the stud, clean the threads with solvent or contact cleaner and allow them to dry thoroughly.

4. Clean the threaded hole with contact cleaner or solvent and a wire brush (a rifle cleaning brush works well). Try to remove as much of the threadlocking compound residue from the hole as possible.

> *NOTE*
> *After removing a stud, do not chase the mating hole threads with a tap (to clean it), as the hole may have been threaded with a close class thread fit. The close class thread fit is often used in stud holes where no looseness is permitted between the stud and threaded hole. It is usually possible to tell what type of thread tolerance is being used when threading the stud into the hole by hand. If the stud can be screwed into the hole by hand, a me-*

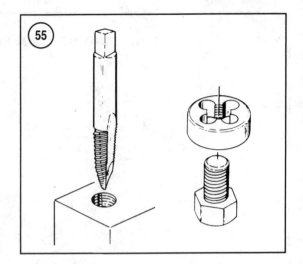

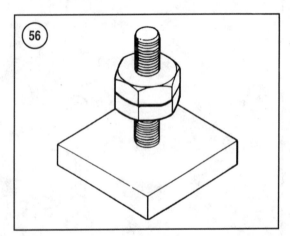

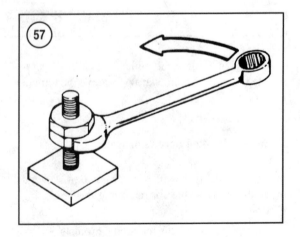

dium fit thread is used. If a wrench or some other tool must be used to install the stud, the hole uses close-fit threads. Chasing a close fit hole with a standard (medium fit) tap will enlarge the

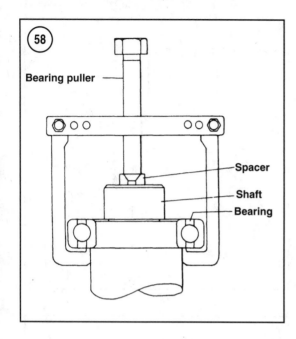

Bearing puller — Spacer — Shaft — Bearing

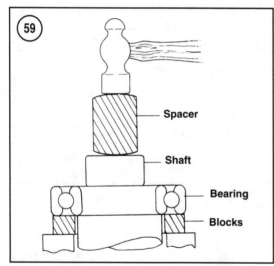

Spacer — Shaft — Bearing — Blocks

6. Apply a high-strength threadlocking compound to the bottom threads on the new stud.

7. Turn the top nut and thread the new stud in. Install the stud to its correct height position (Step 1) or tighten it to its correct torque specification if one is listed (see appropriate chapter).

8. Remove the nuts and repeat for each stud as required.

BEARING REPLACEMENT

Bearings are used throughout the engine and chassis to reduce power loss, heat and noise resulting from friction. Because bearings are precision-made parts, they must be maintained with proper lubrication and maintenance. If a bearing is damaged, replace it immediately. However, when installing a new bearing, use caution to prevent damaging the new bearing. While bearing replacement is covered in the individual chapters, the following should be used as a guideline.

NOTE
Unless otherwise specified, install bearings with their manufacturer's mark or number facing outward.

Bearing Removal

While bearings are normally removed only if damaged, there may be times when it is necessary to remove a bearing that is in good condition. However, improper bearing removal may damage the bearing, the mounting bore or shaft. Note the following when removing bearings.

1. When using a puller to remove a bearing from a shaft, take care that the shaft is not damaged. Always place a metal spacer (**Figure 58**) between the end of the shaft and the puller screw. In addition, place the puller arms next to the bearing's inner bearing.

2. When using a hammer to drive a shaft from a bearing, do not strike the shaft with the hammer. Doing so can crack or spread the end of the shaft, permanently damaging it. Instead, use a brass or aluminum driver between the hammer and shaft, making sure to support both bearing races with wooden blocks, as shown in **Figure 59**.

3. The ideal method of bearing removal is with a hydraulic press. However, certain procedures must be followed to prevent damaging the bearing,

hole and increase the looseness between the threads in the hole and stud. It will then be difficult to install the stud properly, and it will probably loosen later on. This can cause blown head and base gaskets and other damage. If the threaded hole is damaged and requires re-tapping, take the part to a motorcycle dealership or machine shop where the correct tap (thread fit) can be used.

5. Install two nuts on the top half of the new stud, as in Step 2A. Make sure they are locked securely.

mounting bore or shaft. Note the following when using a press:

    a. Always support the inner and outer bearing races with a suitably sized wood or aluminum spacer (**Figure 60**). If only the outer race is supported, the balls and/or the inner race will be damaged.

    b. Make sure the press ram (**Figure 60**) aligns with the center of the shaft. If the ram is not centered, it may damage the bearing and shaft.

    c. The moment the shaft is free of the bearing, it will drop to the floor. Secure or hold the shaft to prevent it from falling.

Bearing Installation

1. When installing a bearing in a housing, apply pressure to the *outer* bearing race (**Figure 61**). When installing a bearing on a shaft, apply pressure to the *inner* bearing race (**Figure 62**).

2. When installing a bearing as described in Step 1, some type of driver is required. Never strike the bearing directly with a hammer, or the bearing will be damaged. When installing a bearing, a bearing driver or a socket with an outside diameter slightly smaller than the bearing race is required. **Figure 63** shows the correct way to use a bearing driver and hammer when installing a bearing over a shaft.

3. Step 1 describes how to install a bearing into a housing or over a shaft. However, when installing a bearing over a shaft and into a housing at the same time, a snug fit is required for both outer and inner bearing races. In this situation, a spacer must be installed underneath the driver tool to apply pressure evenly across *both* races (**Figure 64**). If the outer race is not supported as shown in **Figure 64**, the balls push against the outer bearing race and damage it.

Shrink Fit

1. *Installing a bearing over a shaft*: If a tight fit is required, the bearing inside diameter will be smaller than the shaft. In this case, driving the bearing on the shaft using normal methods may cause bearing damage. Instead, heat the bearing before installation. Note the following:

    a. Secure the shaft so that it is ready for bearing installation.

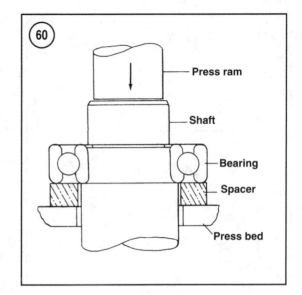

60 Press ram, Shaft, Bearing, Spacer, Press bed

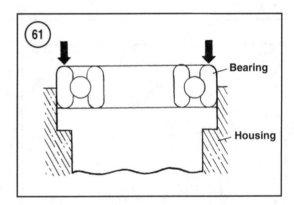

61 Bearing, Housing

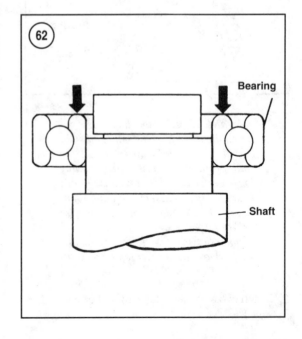

62 Bearing, Shaft

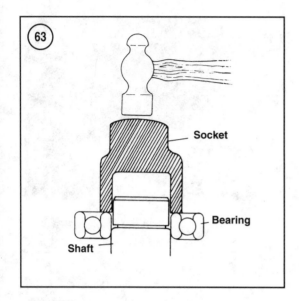

63

Socket

Bearing

Shaft

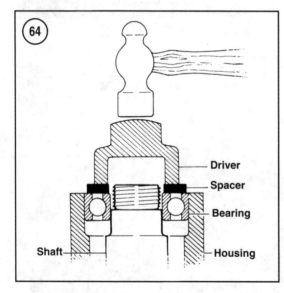

64

Driver

Spacer

Bearing

Shaft

Housing

e. Turn the heat on and monitor the thermometer. When the oil temperature rises to approximately 120° C (248° F), remove the bearing from the pot and quickly install it. If necessary, place a socket on the inner bearing race (**Figure 62**) and tap the bearing into place. As the bearing chills, it will begin to tighten on the shaft. To prevent the bearing from locking onto the shaft at the wrong spot, work quickly while installing it. Make sure the bearing is installed completely.

2. *Installing a bearing in a housing*: Bearings are generally installed in a housing with a slight interference fit. Driving the bearing into the housing using normal methods may damage the housing or cause bearing damage. Instead, the housing should be heated before the bearing is installed. Note the following.

CAUTION
Before heating the housing in this procedure to remove the bearings, wash the housing thoroughly with detergent and water. Rinse and rewash the housing as required to remove all traces of oil and other chemical deposits.

a. Heat the housing to a temperature to about 100° C (212° F) in a shop oven or on a hot plate. To monitor the temperature, drop tiny drops of water on the housing as it starts to heat up; when they start to sizzle and evaporate, the temperature is correct. Heat only one housing at a time.

CAUTION
Do not heat the housing with a torch—never bring open flames into contact with the bearing or housing. The direct heat will destroy the case hardening of the bearing and will likely warp the housing.

b. Remove the housing from the oven or hot plate. Hold onto the housing with a kitchen pot holder, heavy gloves, or heavy shop cloths—*it is hot.*

NOTE
An appropriate size socket and extension are suitable for removing and installing bearings.

b. Clean the bearing surface on the shaft of all residue. Remove burrs with a file or sandpaper.

c. Fill a suitable pot or beaker with clean mineral oil. Place a thermometer (rated higher than 120° C [248° F]) in the oil. Support the thermometer so that it does not rest on the bottom or side of the pot.

d. Secure the bearing with a piece of heavy wire bent to hold it in the pot. Hang the bearing in the pot so that it does not touch the bottom or sides of the pot.

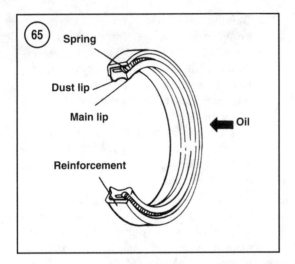

c. Hold the housing with the bearing side down and tap the bearing out. Repeat for all bearings in the housing.

d. Before heating the housing, place the new bearings in a freezer, if possible. Chilling them slightly reduces their overall diameter while the hot housing assembly is larger due to heat expansion. This makes installation much easier.

NOTE
Always install bearings with their manufacturer's mark or number facing outward unless the text directs otherwise.

e. While the housing is still hot, install the new bearing(s) into the housing. Install the bearings by hand, if possible. If necessary, lightly tap the bearing(s) into the housing with a socket placed on the outer bearing race. *Do not* install new bearings by driving against the inner bearing race. Install the bearing(s) until it seats completely.

SEALS

Seals are used to prevent leakage of oil, grease or combustion gasses from forming between a housing and a shaft. The seal has a rubber or neoprene lip (**Figure 65**) that rests against the shaft to form a seal. Depending on the application, the seal may have one or more lips, as well as a garter spring behind the lip to increase pressure on the seal lips. Improper procedures to remove a seal can damage the housing or shaft. Improper installation can damage the seal. Note the following:

a. Before removing a seal, note its installed position in its mounting bore. Is the seal flush with the top of the bore or is it installed down in the bore?

b. It is sometimes possible to remove a seal without damaging it. Prying is generally the easiest and most effective method of removing a seal from its mounting bore. Seals can usually be removed by prying with a wide-blade screwdriver as shown in **Figure 66**. A rag placed underneath the screwdriver prevents the screwdriver from damaging the housing bore. Seals will generally pop out, but when trying to remove a really tight seal or remove a seal without damaging it, do not apply excessive pressure in one spot along the seal, as this may damage the housing bore and seal. Instead, apply pressure in one spot, then stop and move the screwdriver around the seal and apply pressure in a different spot. Continue to walk the screwdriver around the seal, applying small amounts of pressure, until the seal starts to move out of its mounting bore. If this technique does not work, use a hooked seal driver like the one shown in **Figure 67**. These tools work well but will damage the seal.

c. Pack the seal lips before installing the seal. If the procedure does not specify a certain type of grease, use a waterproof grease.

d. Install seals with their manufacturer's marks facing out, unless the text directs otherwise.

e. A socket of the correct size can often be used as a seal driver. Select a socket that fits the seal's outer diameter properly and clears any protruding shafts. See **Figure 68**.

f. Some seals can be installed by pressing them into place by hand. When doing so, make sure the seal is positioned squarely in its bore.

g. Make sure the seal is driven squarely into the housing. Never install a seal by hitting directly against the top of the seal with a hammer.

Table 1 ENGINE AND FRAME SERIAL NUMBERS

Year	Engine	Frame
1997		
49-state		
GL1500C	SC34E-2000101-on	SC340-VA000001-on
GL1500CT	SC34E-2000101-on	SC343-VA000001-on
California		
GL1500CL	SC34E-2000101-on	SC341-VA000001-on
GL1500CTL	SC34E-2000101-on	SC344-VA000001-on
1998		
49-state		
GL1500C	SC34E-2100101-on	SC340-WA100001-on
GL1500CT	SC34E-2100101-on	SC343-WA100001-on
California		
GL1500CL	SC34E-2100101-on	SC340-WA000001-on
GL1500CTL	SC34E-2100101-on	SC343-WA100001-on
1999		
49-state		
GL1500C	SC34E-2200101-on	SC340-XA200001-on
GL1500CT	SC34E-2200101-on	SC343-XA200001-on
GL1500CF	SC41E-2000001-on	SC410-XA000000-on
California		
GL1500CL	SC34E-2200101-on	SC341-XA200001-on
GL1500CTL	SC34E-2200101-on	SC344-XA200001-on
GL1500CFL	SC41E-2000000-on	SC411-XA200000-on
2000		
49-state		
GL1500C	SC34E-2300101-on	SC341-YA300001-on
GL1500CT	SC34E-2300101-on	SC343-YA300001-on
GL1500CF	SC41E-2100001-on	SC410-YA100001-on
California		
GL1500CL	SC34E-2300101-on	SC341-YA300001-on
GL1500CTL	SC34E-2300101-on	SC344-YA300001-on
GL1500CFL	SC41E-2100000-on	SC411-YA100001-on
2001-2003	NA	NA

C = Standard model
CF = Interstate model
NA = Not available, contact your Honda dealership
CT = Touring model
L = California

Table 2 GENERAL SPECIFICATIONS

	mm	in.
Overall length		
GL1500C, GL1500CT	2525	99.4
GL1500CF	2660	104.7
Wheelbase	1690	66.5
Overall height		
GL1500C	1185	46.7
GL1500CT	1485	58.5
GL1500CF	1490	58.7
Overall width		
GL1500C, GL1500CT	980	38.6
GL1500CF	970	38.2
Seat height		
GL1500C, GL1500CT	740	29.1
GL1500CF	730	28.7
Ground clearance		
GL1500C, GL1500CT	155	6.1
GL1500CF	150	5.9

Table 3 WEIGHT SPECIFICATIONS

	kg	lb.
Dry weight		
49-state and Canada		
GL1500C	309	681
GL1500CT	324	714
GL1500CF	351	774
California		
GL1500C	310	683
GL1500CT	325	716
GL1500CF	352	776
Curb weight		
49-state and Canada		
GL1500C	334	736
GL1500CT	349	769
GL1500CF	380	838
California		
GL1500C	335	739
GL1500CT	350	772
GL1500CF	381	840
Maximum weight capacity		
GL1500C, GL1500CT	180 kg	396 lb.
GL1500CF	188 kg	414 lb.

Table 4 FUEL CAPACITY

	Liters	U.S. gallons	Imp. gallons
Fuel tank capacity			
GL1500C, GL1500CT	20	5.3	4.4
GL1500CF	26	6.9	5.7
Reserve capacity			
GL1500C, GL1500CT	4.3	1.14	0.95
GL1500CF	4.0	1.06	0.88

Table 5 DECIMAL AND METRIC EQUIVALENTS

Fractions	Decimal in.	Metric mm	Fractions	Decimal in.	Metric mm
1/64	0.015625	0.39688	33/64	0.515625	13.09687
1/32	0.03125	0.79375	17/32	0.53125	13.49375
3/64	0.046875	1.19062	35/64	0.546875	13.89062
1/16	0.0625	1.58750	9/16	0.5625	14.28750
5/64	0.078125	1.98437	37/64	0.578125	14.68437
3/32	0.09375	2.38125	19/32	0.59375	15.08125
7/64	0.109375	2.77812	39/64	0.609375	15.47812
1/8	0.125	3.1750	5/8	0.625	15.87500
9/64	0.140625	3.57187	41/64	0.640625	16.27187
5/32	0.15625	3.96875	21/32	0.65625	16.66875
11/64	0.171875	4.36562	43/64	0.671875	17.06562
3/16	0.1875	4.76250	11/16	0.6875	17.46250
13/64	0.203125	5.15937	45/64	0.703125	17.85937
7/32	0.21875	5.55625	23/32	0.71875	18.25625
15/64	0.234375	5.95312	47/64	0.734375	18.65312
1/4	0.250	6.35000	3/4	0.750	19.05000
17/64	0.265625	6.74687	49/64	0.765625	19.44687
9/32	0.28125	7.14375	25/32	0.78125	19.84375
19/64	0.296875	7.54062	51/64	0.796875	20.24062
5/16	0.3125	7.93750	13/16	0.8125	20.63750
21/64	0.328125	8.33437	53/64	0.828125	21.03437
11/32	0.34375	8.73125	27/32	0.84375	21.43125
23/64	0.359375	9.12812	55/64	0.859375	22.82812
3/8	0.375	9.52500	7/8	0.875	22.22500
25/64	0.390625	9.92187	57/64	0.890625	22.62187
13/32	0.40625	10.31875	29/32	0.90625	23.01875
27/64	0.421875	10.71562	59/64	0.921875	23.41562
7/16	0.4375	11.11250	15/16	0.9375	23.81250
29/64	0.453125	11.50937	61/64	0.953125	24.20937
15/32	0.46875	11.90625	31/32	0.96875	24.60625
31/64	0.484375	12.30312	63/64	0.984375	25.00312
1/2	0.500	12.70000	1	1.00	25.40000

Table 6 CONVERSION TABLES

	Multiply by:	To get the equivalent:
Length		
Inches	25.4	Millimeter
Inches	2.54	Centimeter
Miles	1.609	Kilometer
Feet	0.3048	Meter
Length		
Millimeter	0.03937	Inches
Centimeter	0.3937	Inches
Kilometer	0.6214	Mile
Meter	0.0006214	Mile
Fluid volume		
U.S. quarts	0.9463	Liters
U.S. gallons	3.785	Liters
U.S. ounces	29.573529	Milliliters
Imperial gallons	4.54609	Liters
Imperial quarts	1.1365	Liters
Liters	0.2641721	U.S. gallons

(continued)

Table 6 CONVERSION TABLES (continued)

	Multiply by:	To get the equivalent of:
Fluid volume (continued)		
Liters	1.0566882	U.S. quarts
Liters	33.814023	U.S. ounces
Liters	0.22	Imperial gallons
Liters	0.8799	Imperial quarts
Milliliters	0.033814	U.S. ounces
Milliliters	1.0	Cubic centimeters
Milliliters	0.001	Liters
Torque		
Foot-pounds	1.3558	Newton-meters
Foot-pounds	0.138255	Meters-kilograms
Inch-pounds	0.11299	Newton-meters
Newton-meters	0.7375622	Foot-pounds
Newton-meters	8.8507	Inch-pounds
Meters-kilograms	7.2330139	Foot-pounds
Volume		
Cubic inches	16.387064	Cubic centimeters
Cubic centimeters	0.0610237	Cubic inches
Temperature		
Fahrenheit	$(°F - 32) \times 0.556$	Centigrade
Centigrade	$(°C \times 1.8) + 32$	Fahrenheit
Weight		
Ounces	28.3495	Grams
Pounds	0.4535924	Kilograms
Grams	0.035274	Ounces
Kilograms	2.2046224	Pounds
Pressure		
Pounds per square inch	0.070307	Kilograms per square centimeter
Kilograms per square centimeter	14.223343	Pounds per square inch
Speed		
Miles per hour	1.609344	Kilometers per hour
Kilometers per hour	0.6213712	Miles per hour

Table 7 GENERAL TORQUE SPECIFICATIONS

	N•m	in.-lb.	ft.-lb.
5 mm bolt and nut	5	44	–
6 mm bolt and nut	10	88	–
8 mm bolt and nut	22	–	16
10 mm bolt and nut	35	–	26
12 mm bolt and nut	55	–	41
5 mm screw	4	35	–
6 mm screw	9	80	–
6 mm flange bolt (8 mm head)	9	80	–
6 mm flange bolt (10 mm head) and nut	12	106	–
8 mm flange bolt and nut	27	–	20
10 mm flange bolt and nut	40	–	29

Table 8 METRIC TAP AND DRILL SIZES

Metric	Drill size	Decimal equivalent	Nearest (mm) fraction
3 × 0.50	No. 39	0.0995	3/32
3 × 0.60	3/32	0.0937	3/32
4 × 0.70	No. 30	0.1285	1/8
4 × 0.75	1/8	0.125	1/8
5 × 0.80	No. 19	0.166	11/64
5 × 0.90	No. 20	0.161	5/32
6 × 1.00	No. 9	0.196	13/64
7 × 1.00	16/64	0.234	15/64
8 × 1.00	J	0.277	9/32
8 × 1.25	17/64	0.265	17/64
9 × 1.00	5/16	0.3125	5/16
9 × 1.25	5/16	0.3125	5/16
10 × 1.25	11/32	0.3437	11/32
10 × 1.50	R	0.339	11/32
11 × 1.50	3/8	0.375	3/8
12 × 1.50	13/32	0.406	13/32
12 × 1.75	13/32	0.406	13/321-7

Table 9 TECHNICAL ABBREVIATIONS

ABDC	After bottom dead center
API	American Petroleum Institute
ATDC	After top dead center
BBDC	Before bottom dead center
BDC	Bottom dead center
BTDC	Before top dead center
C	Celsius (Centigrade)
CAV	Carburetor air vent
cc	Cubic centimeters
CDI	Capacitor discharge ignition
cu. in.	Cubic inches
ECT	Engine coolant temperature sensor
EVAP	Evaporative emission purge control valve
F	Fahrenheit
ft.-lb.	Foot-pounds
gal.	Gallons
hp	Horsepower
ICU	Ignition control unit
in.	Inches
kg	Kilograms
kg/cm^2	Kilograms per square centimeter
kgm	Kilogram meters
km	Kilometer
l	Liter
LCD	Liquid crystal display
m	Meter
mm	Millimeter
N•m	Newton-meters
oz.	Ounce
PAIR	Pulse secondary air injection
PCU	Purge control valve
psi	Pounds per square inch
pts.	Pints
qt.	Quarts
rpm	Revolutions per minute
SAE	Society of American Engineers
SE	Starting enrichment
W	Watts

CHAPTER TWO

TROUBLESHOOTING

Diagnosing mechanical problems is relatively simple if you use orderly procedures and keep a few basic principles in mind. The first step in any troubleshooting procedure is to define the symptoms and then localize the problem. Subsequent steps involve testing and analyzing those areas that could cause the symptoms. A haphazard approach may eventually solve the problem, but it can be very costly with wasted time and unnecessary parts replacement.

Proper lubrication, maintenance and periodic tune-ups, as described in Chapter Three, will reduce the necessity for troubleshooting. Even with the best of care, however, all vehicles may require troubleshooting.

Never assume anything; do not overlook the obvious. If the engine will not start, the engine stop switch or start button may be shorted out or damaged. While trying to start the engine, you may have flooded it.

If the engine suddenly quit, what sound did it make? Consider this and check the easiest, most accessible problem first. If the engine sounded as if it ran out of fuel, check to see if there is fuel in the tank. If there is fuel in the tank, is it reaching the carburetors? Is the fuel shutoff valve turned to the ON position?

If nothing obvious turns up in a quick check, look a little further. Learning to recognize and describe symptoms will make repairs easier. Describe problems accurately and fully.

Gather as many symptoms as possible to aid in diagnosis. Note whether the engine lost power gradually or all at once, what color smoke came from the

right time. If one basic requirement is missing, the engine will not run. Four-stroke engine operating principles are described in Chapter Four under *Engine Principles*.

If the motorcycle has been sitting for some time and refuses to start, check and clean the spark plugs. If the plugs are not fouled, inspect the fuel delivery system. This includes the fuel tank, fuel shutoff valve, fuel filter and fuel lines. If the motorcycle sat for awhile with fuel in the carburetor, fuel deposits may have gummed up carburetor jets and air passages. Gasoline tends to lose its potency after standing for long periods. Condensation may contaminate it with water. Drain the old gas and try starting with a fresh tankful.

EMERGENCY TROUBLESHOOTING

If the engine turns but is difficult to start, do not discharge the battery with the electric starter. Check for obvious problems first. Go down the following list step by step while remembering the three engine operating requirements described under *Operating Requirements* earlier in this chapter.

If it still does not start, refer to the appropriate troubleshooting procedure in this chapter.

1. Check fuel flow from the tank to the carburetors. Is there fuel in the tank? On GL1500C and GL1500CT models, remove the fuel filler cap and rock the motorcycle from side to side. Listen for fuel sloshing around in the tank. On GL1500CF models, turn the ignition switch ON and read the fuel gauge on the instrument panel. The fuel gauge readout shows the approximate fuel supply in the fuel tank. If necessary, refill the tank.

2. An auto fuel valve (**Figure 1**) is used on all models. Fuel flows to the carburetor assembly only when the engine is being started or when the engine is running.

3. The engine stop switch mounted next to the throttle grip is a two-position switch (**Figure 2**). The switch has one RUN position and one OFF position. The engine should start and operate when the switch is in the RUN position. This switch is used primarily as an emergency or safety switch and should be left in the RUN position. Check that the switch is in the RUN position when starting the engine.

4. Are all six spark plug wires and caps (**Figure 3**) on tight? Check the spark plugs as described under *Tune-Up* in Chapter Three.

exhaust and so on. Remember that the more complicated a machine is, the easier it is to troubleshoot because symptoms point to specific problems.

After defining the vehicle's symptoms, test and analyze areas that could cause the problem. Guessing at the cause of a problem may provide the solution, but it can easily lead to frustration, wasted time and a series of expensive, unnecessary parts replacements.

Expensive equipment or complicated test gear is not required to determine whether repairs can be attempted at home. A few simple checks could save a large repair bill and lost time while the motorcycle sits in a dealership's service department. On the other hand, be realistic and do not attempt repairs beyond personal capabilities. Dealership service departments tend to charge heavily for working on a disassembled engine that may have been abused. Some will not even accept such work. Use common sense to avoid getting involved in a procedure that cannot be completed satisfactorily.

OPERATING REQUIREMENTS

An engine needs three basics to run properly: correct air/fuel mixture, compression and a spark at the

5. Is the enrichment (choke) lever (**Figure 4**) in the correct position? Pull the lever all the way down (ON) for a cold engine and pushed all the way forward (OFF) for a warm engine.

ENGINE STARTING PROCEDURES

If experiencing engine starting trouble, it is easy to work out of sequence and forget basic engine starting procedures. The following sections list the recommended starting procedures for the GL1500 Valkyrie engine at the following ambient temperatures and engine conditions:
1. Cold engine with normal air temperature.
2. Cold engine with low air temperature.
3. Warm engine and/or high air temperature.
4. Flooded engine.

Starting Preparation

1. All models are equipped with a side stand ignition cutoff system. The position of the side stand will affect engine starting. Note the following:
   a. The engine cannot start when the side stand is down and the transmission in any gear except NEUTRAL.
   b. The engine can start when the side stand is down and the transmission in NEUTRAL. The engine will stop if the transmission is put in gear with the side stand down.
   c. The engine can be started when the side stand is up and the transmission in NEUTRAL or in any gear with the clutch lever pulled in.
2. Before starting the engine, shift the transmission into NEUTRAL and confirm that the engine stop switch (**Figure 2**) is in its RUN position.
3. Turn the ignition switch to ON and confirm the following:
   a. The neutral indicator light is on (when transmission is in NEUTRAL).
   b. The engine oil pressure warning light is on.
4. The engine is now ready to start. After reading Steps 5 and 6, refer to the starting procedure in this section that best meets the air temperature and engine conditions.
5. If the engine idles at a fast speed for more than five minutes and/or the throttle is snapped on and off repeatedly at normal air temperatures, the exhaust pipes may discolor.

6. Excessive enrichment (choke) use can cause an excessively rich fuel mixture. This condition can wash oil off of the piston and cylinder walls, causing piston and cylinder scuffing.

CAUTION
*Once the engine starts, the red oil pressure warning light should go off in a few seconds. If the light stays on longer than a few seconds, stop the engine immediately. Check the engine oil level as described in Chapter Three. If the oil level is acceptable, the oil pressure may be too low or the oil pressure switch may be shorted. Check the lubrication system and correct the problem before starting the engine. If the oil pressure switch is good, the system is warning that some type of blockage has occurred in the lubrication system and that oil is not being delivered to vital engine components. Severe engine damage will occur if the engine is run with low oil pressure. Refer to **Engine Lubrication** in this chapter.*

NOTE
Do not operate the starter motor for more than five seconds at a time. Wait approximately 10 seconds between starting attempts.

Starting Procedures

Cold engine with normal air temperature

Normal air temperature is between 10-35° C (50-95° F).
1. Perform the procedures under *Starting Preparation* in this section.

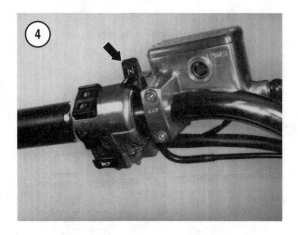

2. Turn the ignition switch to ON.

3. Pull the enrichment (choke) lever all the way down (ON).

4. Push the starter button and start the engine. Do not open the throttle.

> *NOTE*
> *When attempting to start a cold engine with the throttle open and the enrichment (choke) ON, a lean fuel mixture will result, causing hard starting.*

5. After the engine starts, operate the choke lever to maintain engine idle at 1500-2500 rpm.

6. After approximately 30 seconds, push the enrichment (choke) lever all the way forward to the fully closed position (OFF). If the idle is rough, open the throttle slightly until the engine warms up.

Cold engine with low air temperature

Low air temperature is 10° C (50° F) or lower.

1. Perform the procedures under *Starting Preparation* in this section.

2. Turn the ignition switch to ON.

3. Pull the enrichment (choke) lever all the way down (ON).

4. Push the starter button and start the engine. Do not open the throttle.

> *NOTE*
> *When attempting to start a cold engine with the throttle open and the choke ON, a lean fuel mixture will result, causing hard starting.*

5. After the engine starts, operate the choke lever to maintain engine idle at 2200-2800 rpm.

6. After approximately five minutes, push the enrichment (choke) lever all the way forward to the fully closed position (OFF). If the idling is rough, open the throttle slightly until the engine warms up.

Warm engine and/or high air temperature

High air temperature is 35° C (95° F) or higher.

1. Perform the procedures under *Starting Preparation* in this section.

2. Turn the ignition switch to ON.

3. Open the throttle slightly and push the starter button. Do not use the enrichment (choke).

Flooded engine

If the engine will not start after a few attempts, it may be flooded. If a gasoline odor is noticed after attempting to start the engine and the engine will not start, the engine is probably flooded. To start a flooded engine:

1. Turn the engine stop switch to OFF.

2. Push the enrichment (choke) lever all the way forward to the fully closed position (OFF).

3. Open the throttle completely and push the starter button for five seconds. Then release the starter button and close the throttle.

4. Wait 10 seconds, then continue with Step 5.

5. Turn the engine stop switch to ON.

6. Turn the ignition switch to ON.

7. Open the throttle slightly and push the starter button to start the engine. Do not use the choke.

Spark Test

Perform the following spark test to determine if the ignition system is operating properly.

> *NOTE*
> *There are three separate ignition coils. Test each coil. The first coil provides spark for plugs one and two, the second for plugs three and four, and the third*

*for plugs five and six. The cylinders and plugs are identified in **Figure 5**.*

CAUTION
*Before removing the spark plugs in Step 1, clean all dirt and debris away from the plug receptacle in the cylinder head (**Figure 6**). If any dirt falls into the cylinder, it will cause rapid piston, ring and cylinder wear.*

1. Disconnect the plug wires and remove all six spark plugs as described in Chapter Three.
2. Securely ground five of the spark plugs as shown in **Figure 7**. The remaining spark plug is to be used in this test.

NOTE
*A spark tester is a useful tool to check the ignition system. **Figure 8** shows the Motion Pro Ignition System Tester (part No. 08-122). This tool is inserted in the spark plug cap and its base is placed against the cylinder head to provide a ground. The tool's air gap is visible and adjustable, this makes it possible to observe the intensity of the spark. This tool is available through most motorcycle dealerships or from Motion Pro.*

NOTE
If using a spark tester, set its air gap to 6 mm (1/4 in.).

3. Insert the spark plug (or spark tester) into the plug cap and ground the spark plug base against the cylinder head and away from the plug hole. Position the spark plug so the electrodes are visible.

NOTE
If the spark plug is fouled, use a new spark plug.

CAUTION
Place the spark plug or spark tester away from the plug hole in the cylinder head so the spark from the plug or tester cannot ignite the gasoline vapors in the cylinder.

WARNING
Do not hold the spark plug, wire or connector or a serious electrical shock may result.

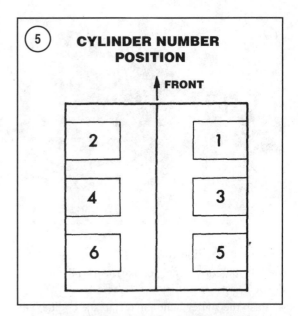

CYLINDER NUMBER POSITION

4. Turn the engine over with the starter. A fat blue spark should be evident across the spark plug electrodes or spark tester terminals. Note the following:
   a. If the spark is intermittent, weak (white or yellow in color) or if there is no spark, continue with Step 5.
   b. If the spark is good, proceed to Step 6.
5. Make sure the engine stop switch (**Figure 2**) is not stuck or working improperly or that a wire is broken and shorting out. Disconnect the engine stop switch leads and recheck the spark. Note the following:
   a. If there is now spark, the engine stop switch is damaged. Replace the switch and retest.
   b. If there is still no spark, test the engine stop switch with an ohmmeter (Chapter Nine) before reconnecting it into the wiring harness to make sure it is not a secondary problem. If the

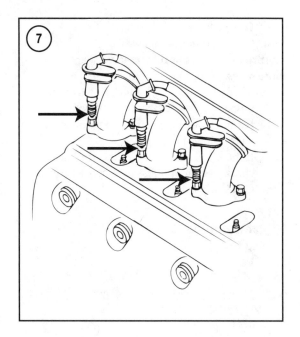

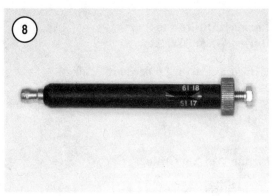

looseness, the terminal inside the cap may have pulled away from the coil wire.

b. Insert the spark plug into the plug cap. The terminal ring inside the plug cap should snap tightly onto the spark plug when connecting them together.

c. If there is a problem, remove the plug wire from the coil wire.

d. Check the metal terminal for corrosion or other damage. Remove any corrosion with a file or sandpaper. Check the terminal where it connects onto the plug wire.

e. Check the wire strands in the plug wire end for corrosion or other damage.

f. Check the coil wire at the end of its outer rubber cover for excessive looseness or play that may indicate a weak or broken plug wire. The plug wire can be damaged from vibration or mishandling.

g. Pack the plug cap or the coil wire end with dielectric grease to prevent moisture from entering the plug cap and corroding the connection.

h. Install the plug cap securely; ensure good contact between the plug wire core and the plug cap terminal. Repeat the spark test. If there is still no spark, continue with Step 7.

7. If the spark plug cap was not the problem, test the ignition system as described in Chapter Nine.

8. Repeat this test for the remaining two ignition coils.

9. If the spark is good, review the *Engine Starting Troubleshooting* section in this chapter.

ENGINE STARTING TROUBLESHOOTING

An engine that refuses to start or is difficult to start is very frustrating. More often than not, the problem is very minor and its source can be found with a simple and logical troubleshooting approach.

First, review the steps under *Engine Starting Procedures* in this chapter. If the engine will not start by following the engine starting procedure steps, continue with this section.

The following are beginning points from which to isolate engine starting problems.

> *NOTE*
> *Do not operate the starter motor for more than five seconds at a time. Wait*

switch tests good, reconnect it and continue with Step 6.

> *NOTE*
> *If the engine stop switch is faulty, install a new one as soon as possible. It is not safe to operate the motorcycle with a missing or disconnected engine stop switch.*

6. A loose, corroded or damaged spark plug cap terminal is a common source of ignition system problems, especially when the problem is intermittent. Perform the following:

a. Disconnect the spark plug cap from the spark plug. Then hold the plug wire and try to turn the cap. The cap must fit tightly. If there is any

approximately 10 seconds between starting attempts.

Engine Fails to Start

Perform the following spark test to determine if the ignition system is operating properly.

1. Remove all of the spark plugs as described under *Tune-Up* in Chapter Three.

2. Connect a spark plug wire to each spark plug and secure the base of each spark plug to a good ground (away from the spark plug holes). Position the spark plugs so the electrodes are visible (**Figure 7**).

> *WARNING*
> *Turning the engine over with the spark plugs removed will force fuel out through the spark plug holes. When making a spark test, do not place the spark plugs next to the open spark plug holes because the air/fuel mixture may ignite and cause a fire or explosion.*

3. Crank the engine over with the starter. A fat blue spark should be evident across each of the electrodes. If the spark is good, continue with Step 4. If the spark is weak or if there is no spark across one or more plugs, perform Step 6.

> *WARNING*
> *If it is necessary to hold a spark plug wire, do so with insulated pliers. The high voltage generated by the ignition control unit could produce serious or fatal shocks.*

4. Check engine compression as described in Chapter Three. If the compression is good, perform Step 5. If the compression is low, check for one or more of the following:
   a. Incorrectly adjusted valve clearance.
   b. Leaking cylinder head gasket(s).
   c. Cracked or warped cylinder head.
   d. Worn piston rings, pistons and cylinders.
   e. Valve(s) stuck open.
   f. Worn or damaged valve seat(s).
   g. Incorrect valve timing.

5. Check for proper fuel flow. Check for one of the following:
   a. Empty fuel tank.
   b. Plugged fuel tank cap vent hole.
   c. Clogged fuel line.
   d. Stuck carburetor fuel valve.

6. If spark is weak or if there is no spark at one or more plugs, perform the following:
   a. Check that the spark plug caps or wires are properly connected to the ignition coils.
   b. If a spark plug(s) is fouled, repeat the test with a new plug(s).
   c. If these steps do not solve the spark problem, check the ignition system as described in Chapter Nine.

Engine is Difficult to Start During Cold Weather

1. Incorrect engine oil weight.
2. Incorrect enrichment (choke) cable adjustment.
3. Low battery charge.
4. Water in the fuel.

Engine is Difficult to Start During Warm Weather

1. Incorrect starting procedures (choke).
2. Vapor lock in fuel lines or carburetors.
3. Defective purge control valve on California models.

Engine Will Not Crank

1. Discharged battery.
2. Defective starter motor, starter solenoid or start switch.
3. Seized piston(s).
4. Seized crankshaft bearings.
5. Broken connecting rod(s).
6. Locked-up transmission or clutch assembly.

ENGINE PERFORMANCE

In the following checklists, it is assumed that the engine is not operating at peak performance. This will serve as a starting point from which to isolate a performance malfunction.

The possible causes for each malfunction are listed in a logical sequence and in order of probability. Where ignition timing is mentioned as a problem, remember that there is no method of adjusting the ignition timing. If ignition timing is incorrect, there is a defective part(s) within the ignition system and that part must be tested and replaced if necessary, as described in Chapter Nine.

Engine Will Not Start or is Hard To Start

1. Fuel tank empty.
2. Engine flooded with fuel.
3. Fouled or improperly gapped spark plug(s).
4. Obstructed fuel line or fuel shutoff valve.
5. Improper enrichment valve (choke) operation.
6. Improper throttle operation.
7. Carburetor(s) incorrectly adjusted.
8. Carburetor(s) float valve stuck.
9. Contaminated fuel.
10. Incorrect ignition timing.
11. Improper valve timing.
12. Clogged air filter element.

Engine Will Not Idle or Idles Erratically

1. Enrichment valve (choke) stuck in the ON position.
2. Obstructed fuel line or fuel shutoff valve.
3. Fouled or improperly gapped spark plug(s).
4. Weak or faulty ignition control unit or pulse generator(s).
5. Slow air cutoff valve faulty.
6. Carburetors incorrectly adjusted (too lean or too rich).
7. Clogged slow jet(s) in the carburetor(s).
8. Clogged air filter element.
9. Leaking head gasket(s) or vacuum leak.
10. Low engine compression.
11. Incorrect ignition timing.
12. Improper valve timing.

Engine Misfires at Idle

1. Damaged spark plug caps.
2. Deteriorated spark plug cables.
3. Incorrect spark plug gap.
4. Poor fuel system operation.
5. Clogged air filter element.

Engine Misses at High Speed

1. Defective ignition system.
2. Fouled or improperly gapped spark plugs.

3. Obstructed fuel line or fuel shutoff valve.
4. Clogged carburetor jet(s).
5. Intake pipe(s) vacuum leak.
6. Low battery charge.
7. Low alternator voltage.
8. Ignition timing incorrect.
9. Incorrect valve timing.
10. Leaking cylinder head gasket(s).
11. Weak or damaged valve spring(s).

Engine Continues to Run after Turning Ignition Off

1. Intake pipes vacuum leak.
2. Contaminated or incorrect fuel octane rating.
3. Incorrect ignition timing.
4. Excessive carbon buildup in engine.

Engine Backfires

1. Fouled or improperly gapped spark plugs.
2. Spark plug caps faulty.
3. Ignition cable insulation deteriorated (shorting out).
4. Incorrect carburetor adjustment (too lean).
5. Contaminated fuel.
6. Ignition timing retarded.
7. Improper valve timing.
8. Burned or damaged intake and/or exhaust valves.
9. Weak or broken intake and/or exhaust valve springs.

Pre-ignition (Fuel Mixture Ignites Before Spark Plug Fires)

1. Hot spot in combustion chamber(s) (piece of carbon).
2. Valve(s) stuck.
3. Engine overheating.

Engine Overheating

1. Low coolant level.
2. Thermostat stuck in the closed position.
3. Defective fan motor.
4. Fan blades cracked or missing.
5. Passages blocked in the radiator, hoses or water jackets in the engine.
6. Defective radiator cap.

7. Defective temperature gauge or gauge sensor (GL1500CF).

8. Incorrect ignition timing.

9. Improper spark plug heat range.

Engine Runs Roughly and Excessive Exhaust Smoke

1. Enrichment valve (choke) not operating correctly.

2. Carburetor mixture too rich.

3. Water or other contaminants in fuel.

4. Clogged fuel line.

5. Dirty air filter element.

Engine Loses Power at Normal Riding Speed

1. Dragging brake(s).

2. Incorrectly gapped spark plugs.

3. Defective ignition system.

4. Incorrect ignition timing.

5. Carburetors incorrectly adjusted.

6. Engine overheating.

7. Obstructed mufflers.

Engine Lacks Acceleration

1. Dragging brake(s).

2. Carburetor mixture too lean.

3. Clogged fuel line.

4. Incorrect ignition timing.

ENGINE NOISES

1. Knocking or pinging during acceleration—Caused by using a lower octane fuel than recommended. May also be caused by poor fuel. Pinging can also be caused by spark plugs of the wrong heat range. Refer to *Spark Plug Selection* in Chapter Three.

2. Slapping or rattling noises at low speed or during acceleration—May be caused by piston slap (excessive piston-to-cylinder wall clearance).

3. Knocking or rapping while decelerating—Usually caused by excessive rod bearing clearance.

4. Persistent knocking and vibration—Usually caused by excessive main bearing clearance.

5. Rapid on-off squeal—Compression leak around cylinder head gasket(s) or spark plugs.

LOW CYLINDER COMPRESSION

1. Drain the engine oil and check it for contamination.

2. Check the engine oil pressure as described in Chapter Three.

3. If the oil pressure is within specification, check for the following conditions:

    a. Worn or damaged rocker arm or rocker arm shaft.

    b. Incorrect valve adjustment.

    c. Improper camshaft holder/camshaft installation.

4. If the camshaft holder assembly is in good condition, remove the cylinder heads and check for worn or damaged valves and valve seats.

ENGINE LUBRICATION

An improperly operating engine lubrication system will quickly lead to engine damage. The engine oil level should be checked weekly and topped off if necessary, as described in Chapter Three. Oil pump service is described in Chapter Five.

Incorrect Oil Pressure

The oil pressure can be checked as described under *Oil Pressure Test* in this chapter. If the oil pressure reading is incorrect, check for the following conditions:

1. Incorrect oil level (too low).

2. Clogged oil filter.

3. Clogged oil control orifice.

4. Clogged oil passage.

5. Clogged oil pipe.

6. Damaged oil pump.

7. Oil pump relief valve stuck open.

8. Worn or damaged crankshaft bearings.

Oil Consumption High or Engine Smokes Excessively

1. Worn valve guides.

2. Worn or damaged piston rings.

Engine Leaks Oil

1. Clogged crankcase breather hose.
2. Loose or warped engine mating surfaces.
3. Damaged gasket sealing surfaces.

High Oil Level

1. Pressure relief valve stuck closed.
2. Clogged oil filter.
3. Clogged oil gallery or metering orifice.

Low Oil Level

1. Oil not maintained at correct level.
2. External oil leakage.
3. Worn piston rings.
4. Worn cylinders.
5. Worn valve guides.
6. Worn valve guide stem seals.
7. Piston rings incorrectly installed during engine rebuild.

Oil Contamination

1. Oil and filter not changed at specified intervals or when abnormal operating conditions demand more frequent changes.
2. Blown head gasket(s) allowing coolant to leak into the engine.

No Oil Pressure

1. Excessively low oil level or no oil.
2. Internal oil leakage.
3. Damaged oil pump.
4. Faulty oil pump drive shaft.

OIL PRESSURE TEST

The low oil pressure indicator will come on when the oil pressure is below its normal operating range. Under normal operating conditions, the indicator should come on when the ignition switch is turned ON while the engine is not running. When the engine is started, the indicator should go off. It is normal to see an occasional flicker from the indicator when the engine is operating at or near idle speed and the engine temperature is warm.

If the oil pressure warning light comes on while riding, or if the engine starts to knock, stop the engine as soon as it is safe to do so. Then check the oil pressure using an external oil pressure gauge. The remote gauge consists of a direct reading gauge connected to a pressure hose. The hose is equipped with a threaded fitting so that it can be installed into the oil pressure switch port in the engine. To install the gauge on the engine, remove the oil pressure switch (located on the front cover to the left side of the oil filter) and install the remote gauge into its port. Start the engine and observe the oil pressure on the gauge. Check oil pressure at various engine speeds and temperatures.

NOTE
During the first part of the following test, the engine oil temperature must be below 35° C (95° F).

1. Pull back the rubber boot and remove the screw securing the electrical connector (A, **Figure 9**) to the oil pressure switch.
2. Unscrew the oil pressure warning switch (B, **Figure 9**) from the cylinder block.
3. Screw an oil pressure gauge into the switch port in the cylinder block.
4. Turn the engine stop switch to the RUN position and start the engine.
5. Run the engine at the speeds indicated in **Table 1** and compare the cold oil pressure readings with those listed in **Table 1**.
6. After the engine has warmed to normal operating temperature (5-10 minutes at idle) run the engine at the speeds indicated in **Table 1**. Compare the hot oil pressure readings with those listed in **Table 1**. Note the following:
   a. If the oil pressure readings are low, refer to *Low Oil Pressure* and *No Oil Pressure* under *Engine Lubrication* in this chapter. Both sec-

tions list possible causes. If oil pump or engine service is required, refer to Chapter Five.

   b. If the oil pressure readings are correct but the low oil pressure indicator light comes on, the oil pressure switch may be damaged. Test the oil pressure switch as described under *Switches* in Chapter Nine. If the oil pressure switch is good, the oil pump relief valve may be stuck; refer to *Oil Strainer and Main Oil Pump* in Chapter Five.

   c. If the oil pressure readings are correct and the low oil pressure indicator light operates correctly, remove the oil pressure gauge. Apply sealant to the oil pressure threads. Install the switch and tighten it to 12 N•m (106 in.-lb.).

7. Attach the electrical wire. Make sure the connection is tight and free from oil.

8. Slide the rubber boot back into position.

FUEL SYSTEM

This section isolates problems that are fuel-related.

Engine Cranks
But Will Not Start

If the engine is cold and cranks but will not start and there is no electrical problem, check the following:

NOTE
If the fuel reserve indicator light came on, add fuel to the fuel tank. Check that the fuel gauge is working properly. The fuel gauge should show the approximate supply in the fuel tank.

1. No fuel.
2. Blocked fuel tank vent.
3. Engine flooded.
4. Incorrect enrichment (choke) use.
5. Incorrect throttle use.
6. No fuel delivery to carburetors.
7. Clogged air cleaner.
8. Intake air leak.
9. Incorrect enrichment (choke) cable free play.

Engine Starts but
Idles Rough or Stalls

1. Clogged air cleaner.
2. Contaminated fuel.
3. Incorrect pilot screw adjustment.
4. Incorrect carburetor synchronization.
5. Incorrect idle speed.
6. Enrichment (choke) valve(s) stuck open.
7. Loose, disconnected or damaged fuel and emission control vacuum hoses.
8. Intake air leak.
9. Lean fuel mixture.
10. Rich fuel mixture.
11. Defective purge control valve on California models.
12. Defective air vent control valve on California models.

Incorrect Fast Idle Speed

1. Starting enrichment (SE) valve stuck.
2. Clogged SE air line.
3. Incorrect enrichment (choke) cable free play.
4. Incorrect carburetor synchronization.

Poor Fuel Mileage and
Engine Performance

Poor fuel mileage and engine performance may be caused by infrequent engine tune-ups. Check the service records to see when the Valkyrie was last tuned up and compare against the recommended tune-up service intervals in Chapter Three. If the last tune-up was within the specified service intervals, check for one or more of the following problems:
1. Dirty air filter.
2. Clogged fuel system.
3. Defective secondary air system.
4. Loose, disconnected or damaged fuel and emission control vacuum hoses.
5. Defective air vent control valve on California models.
6. Defective evaporative emission control system hoses on California models.

Rich Fuel Mixture

1. Dirty air filter.

2. Worn or damaged float valve and seat.
3. Clogged air jets.
4. Incorrect float level (too high).
5. SE valve damaged or stuck open.
6. Faulty primary air jet control system.

Lean Fuel Mixture

1. Clogged fuel tank cap vent.
2. Clogged fuel strainer screen in carburetor.
3. Restricted fuel line.
4. Intake air leak.
5. Incorrect float level(s) (too low).
6. Worn or damaged fuel valve(s).
7. Clogged air jets.

Engine Backfires

1. Lean fuel mixture.
2. Incorrect carburetor adjustment.

Engine Misfires
During Acceleration

When there is a pause before the engine responds to the throttle and acceleration is sluggish, the engine is misfiring. An engine miss can occur when starting from a dead stop or at any speed. Engine miss may be caused by one of the following conditions:
1. Lean fuel mixture.
2. Defective ignition coil secondary wires; check for cracking, hardening or bad connections.
3. Leaking vacuum hoses; check for kinks, splits or bad connections.
4. Vacuum leaks at the carburetor and/or intake manifold(s).
5. Fouled spark plug(s).
6. Damaged spark plug(s).
7. Low engine compression, especially at one cylinder only. Check engine compression as described in Chapter Three. Low compression may be caused by worn engine components.

CLUTCH

All clutch troubles, except for bleeding the system, require partial clutch disassembly to identify and solve the problem. Refer to Chapter Six for clutch service procedures.

Clutch Slips

1. Weak clutch spring.
2. Contaminated clutch hydraulic system.
3. Plugged master cylinder reservoir compensating port.
4. Worn or damaged plates.
5. Sticking clutch lifter system.
6. Sticking clutch hydraulic system.

Clutch Drags
with Clutch Disengaged

1. Warped clutch plates.
2. Low clutch fluid level.
3. Air in clutch hydraulic system.
4. Sticking clutch hydraulic system.
5. Leaking clutch hydraulic system.
6. Engine oil level too high.
7. Incorrect engine oil viscosity (too thick).

Rough Clutch Operation

1. Sticking clutch master cylinder piston.
2. Sticking clutch slave cylinder piston.

Excessive Clutch Lever Pressure

1. Damaged clutch lifter mechanism.
2. Sticking clutch hydraulic system.

Clutch Will Not Disengage

1. Warped clutch plates.
2. Low clutch fluid level.
3. Air in clutch hydraulic system.
4. Sticking clutch hydraulic system.
5. Leaking clutch hydraulic system.

Difficult or Rough
Transmission Shifting

1. Faulty gearshift linkage.
2. Faulty transmission.
3. Clutch not disengaged.

TRANSMISSION

Transmission symptoms are sometimes hard to distinguish from clutch symptoms. Refer to Chapter Seven for transmission service procedures. Be sure that the clutch is not causing the trouble before working on the transmission.

Excessive Output Shaft Noise

1. Faulty final drive or driven gears.
2. Faulty output shaft bearing.
3. Excessive final drive-to-driven gear backlash.

Difficult Shifting

1. Air in clutch hydraulic system.
2. Bent shift forks.
3. Bent shift claw.
4. Bent shift shaft.
5. Bent drum stopper.
6. Damaged shift drum cam grooves.
7. Loose shift spindle bolt.

Transmission Will Not Stay in Gear

1. Bent shift forks.
2. Bent shift shaft.
3. Worn or damaged gear dogs.
4. Broken shift drum stopper.

FINAL DRIVE

Excessive Final Drive Noise

1. Low oil level.
2. Worn or damaged pinion and ring gears.
3. Excessive pinion-to-ring gear backlash.
4. Worn or damaged drive pinion and splines.
5. Scored driven flange and wheel hub.
6. Scored or worn ring gear shaft and driven flange.

Oil Leakage

1. Loose or missing cover bolts.
2. Damaged final drive seals.
3. Clogged breather.
4. Oil level too high.

Rear Wheel Does Not Rotate Freely

1. Bent drive shaft.
2. Damaged ring gear and pinion bearing.
3. Stuck pinion and ring gear.

EXCESSIVE VIBRATION

If the mounting hardware is secure, vibration may be difficult to find without disassembling the engine.

Loose engine, frame, fairing or suspension mounting hardware usually causes vibration. A rough running engine can also cause abnormal vibration.

FRONT SUSPENSION AND STEERING

Improper tire pressure, a damaged or bent frame or worn front steering components, a worn front fork assembly, worn wheel bearings or dragging brakes, may cause poor handling.

Suspension Noise

1. Loose mounting fasteners.
2. Damaged shock(s).
3. Incorrect fork oil viscosity.

Wobble/Vibration

1. Loose front or rear axle fasteners.
2. Loose or damaged wheel bearing(s).
3. Damaged wheel rim(s).
4. Damaged tire(s).
5. Loose swing arm pivot bolt.

Hard Suspension (Front Fork)

1. Bent fork tubes.
2. Binding slider.
3. Incorrect fork oil.
4. Plugged fork hydraulic passage.

Hard Suspension (Rear Shock Absorbers)

1. Incorrect shock absorber spring pre-load adjustment.
2. Incorrect shock absorber oil viscosity.

Soft Suspension (Front Fork)

1. Incorrect fork oil viscosity.
2. Contaminated fork oil.
3. Weak or damaged fork springs.

Soft Suspension (Rear Shock Absorbers)

1. Weak or damaged shock absorber spring.
2. Damaged shock absorber.

BRAKE PROBLEMS

Sticking disc brakes may be caused by a stuck piston(s) in a caliper assembly or warped pad shim(s).

Brake Drag

1. Clogged brake hydraulic system.
2. Clogged master cylinder reservoir compensating port.
3. Sticking caliper pistons.
4. Sticking master cylinder piston.
5. Incorrectly installed brake caliper.
6. Warped brake disc.
7. Sticking caliper side slide pin.
8. Wheel alignment incorrect.

Brakes Grab

1. Contaminated brake pads.
2. Wheel alignment incorrect.
3. Warped brake disc.

Brake Squeal or Chatter

1. Contaminated brake pads.
2. Incorrectly installed brake caliper.
3. Warped brake disc.
4. Wheel alignment incorrect.

Soft or Spongy Brake Lever or Pedal

1. Low brake fluid level.
2. Air in brake hydraulic system.
3. Leaking brake hydraulic system.

Hard Brake Lever or Pedal Operation

1. Clogged brake hydraulic system.
2. Sticking caliper pistons.
3. Sticking master cylinder piston.
4. Glazed or worn brake pads.

ELECTRICAL TROUBLESHOOTING

The GL1500 Valkyrie has a number of complex electrical systems. This can make troubleshooting basic circuits and components frustrating, especially for those not completely familiar with motorcycle electrical systems.

The first part of this section contains basic information about electrical troubleshooting procedures and electrical test equipment. The second part details specific troubleshooting procedures for the following GL1500 Valkyrie electrical systems:

1. Charging system.
2. Ignition system.
3. Starting system.
4. Lighting system.
5. Cooling system.
6. Fuses.

TROUBLESHOOTING HINTS

What To Look For

Before attempting to troubleshoot any electrical problem, identify all of the symptoms involved. If a particular circuit exhibits more than one symptom, devote the attention to the components (also called load devices) and wiring within the circuit that could be the cause of all the symptoms. If more than one circuit is involved, check common components such as fuses and relays. Such components should be suspected first as the cause of problems in the circuits.

Be familiar with the appropriate test equipment and how to use it most efficiently. These tools and the appropriate electrical wiring diagrams help to devise a logical approach for troubleshooting the problem.

The correct wiring diagram is important since it helps to identify the interrelationship between the circuit components and select the correct wiring by its color code.

It can also be useful in determining those components in the circuit which are probably not involved in the problem—an important step in isolating the cause.

Troubleshooting Preliminary Checks

Many problems can be located without a great deal of effort. It is much easier to start with the simplest and shortest tests first. Before beginning any involved troubleshooting procedure, try the following prechecks:

1. Make sure all connectors are securely plugged together (**Figure 10**). It is much easier to service a connector than troubleshoot the entire circuit to find that an improperly connected or damaged connector is the cause of the problem.

2. If a connector or terminal is corroded, find out what caused the corrosion and correct the source of the problem in addition to cleaning or replacing the connector/terminal. This will prevent the problem from happening again.

3. Check the circuit protection devices. If a fuse is burned out, there is a short-to-ground in the circuit. Several other possibilities have been eliminated.

The Five-Step Method of Troubleshooting

To be effective, electrical circuit troubleshooting must be logical and sequential as described in the following five steps:

1. Make sure the extent of the problem is understood.

2. Once it has been determined exactly what is wrong, start to narrow the possible causes of the problem and location of the components and wiring involved using the wiring diagrams. There are only four places in a circuit where a problem can occur:
   a. At the power source.
   b. Between the power source and load.
   c. At the load.
   d. Between the load and ground.

3. Use electrical test equipment to check the suspected components and wiring for defects. There are only four possible things that can go wrong and cause a problem in the circuit:
   a. An open circuit.
   b. A short circuit or very low resistance.
   c. High resistance.
   d. A worn or damaged component.

4. Replace or repair the defective component or wiring. Make sure that this does not cause further

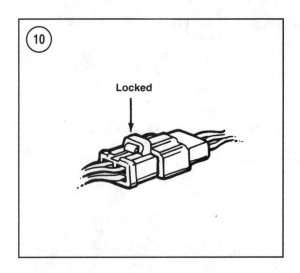

problems in the process of solving this one, such as burning the wiring insulation with a soldering iron.

5. Recheck the work. Test the repair to make sure the system functions correctly and that all connectors are properly secured. Be sure to correct all malfunctions without causing other potential problems.

CIRCUIT DESIGN

This section describes the motorcycle electrical circuit and the types of possible circuit malfunctions.

Electrical Circuit and Components

An electrical circuit is a complete path through which current flows. In a motorcycle circuit, current flow occurs between the positive (+) battery terminal through the components and back to the negative (−) battery terminal. In a motorcycle circuit, the frame provides the ground or negative side of the circuit. This greatly reduces the amount of wiring required for the circuit.

The motorcycle electrical circuit is composed of the battery, some form of circuit protection (fuse, relays or fusible link), a switch to control current flow, load devices or components (light bulbs, horns, electric motor, etc.) and conductors (wiring). See **Figure 11**.

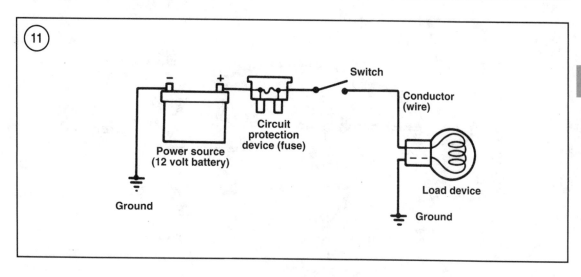

Malfunctioning Circuits

Opens or breaks

An electrical circuit requires a continuous path for current to flow. If there is a break in the circuit, current flow is stopped. This is called an open circuit or a break in the circuit.

An open circuit can be located by using a jumper wire to bypass parts of the circuit to make it operational. When this happens, the open circuit is located within that part of the circuit bypassed. It can also be found with an ohmmeter or self-powered test lamp (circuit disconnected) or with a voltmeter or 12-volt test lamp (circuit connected).

One of the most difficult problems to locate in a circuit is the intermittent open. An intermittent open circuit can be caused by a wire broken inside its insulation, poor wire crimps, molding flash, a pushed-out terminal, loose connection or a partially spread connection. The wire will make contact at rest, hindering efforts to find the intermittent open. However, movement and vibration of vehicle operation will cause the wire to flex, making and breaking contact. Wiggling the wiring or connector by hand is the only practical way to locate this type of open condition.

Short circuit

A short circuit is one that interrupts the normal current path through the circuit by providing a second continuous path for the current to follow. This is usually a short-to-ground, which allows the current to bypass the load device or component, although a short caused by wire-to-wire contact may lead directly into another circuit.

When a short occurs, circuit resistance drops considerably and a larger-than-normal amount of current flows. The excessive current causes the circuit protection device to open (blown fuse) and the circuit shuts down.

The effect of a short to ground will differ according to where it happens. If it occurs between a load device or component and the power source, the component will be bypassed and not operate. If it occurs after the component but ahead of the grounding type switch, the component will remain on. If it takes place on the ground side of the component's switch, the effect is to create an alternate path to ground.

An intermittent short to ground, like the intermittent open circuit, can be extremely difficult to locate. If no obvious fraying or bare wires are found, wiggling the wires is the best technique to locate the source of the problem.

Extremely high resistance

High resistance in a circuit often appears exactly like an open circuit, especially if it is very high. Such resistance effectively creates an excessive voltage drop, causing the rest of the circuit to function at reduced power. For example, an excessively corroded or loose ground terminal (whose resistance should be zero) may develop such high resis-

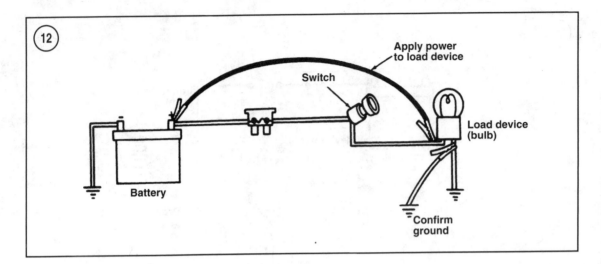

⑫

Apply power
to load device

Switch

Load device
(bulb)

Battery

Confirm
ground

tance that none of the loads in the circuit will function.

High resistance can be caused by contamination at terminals, connectors and grounds. Under some conditions, the heat caused by a loose connection will result in the formation of an oxide coating on the terminals. Load devices or components may develop high resistance due to internal damage, wear, vibration or overloads. Most causes of high resistance are difficult to spot visually. Connectors, terminals and grounds should be weatherproof and kept clean. Coating them with dielectric grease or petroleum jelly helps prevent corrosion.

WIRING DIAGRAMS

Wiring diagrams are the road maps used for troubleshooting an electrical circuit. A typical wiring diagram shows the various circuit components and their connecting wires. Refer to wiring diagrams at the end of this manual.

ELECTRICAL TEST EQUIPMENT

All but the most complicated electronic circuits can generally be checked with simple equipment. Testing can be accomplished efficiently with the following test equipment, providing there is an understanding of how to select the proper tester and use it correctly:

1. Jumper wires.
2. Test lights.
3. Ohmmeter.
4. Voltmeter.
5. Ammeter.

Jumper Wires

The jumper wire is a simple but valuable form of continuity tester, although it does not provide a reading. Temporarily connected across a circuit that might have an open or break in it (**Figure 12**), the jumper wire is simply a device to bypass a potential problem, and in doing so, tells if the problem is in the area being tested. A circuit that works properly with the jumper wire installed, but does not work without the jumper wire, indicates that there is an open or break in the circuit. Jumper wires can also be used to confirm or supply a good ground for a circuit or component.

In the example shown in **Figure 12**, the first step is to connect the jumper wire between the lamp and a good ground. If the lamp comes on at this point, it is established that the ground circuit is defective. If the lamp does not come on, a good ground has been provided and so the problem is between the lamp and its power source.

To isolate the problem, connect the jumper wire between the battery and lamp. If the lamp comes on, the problem is between these two points. Move the jumper wire from the battery to the switch side of the fuse. If the lamp continues to light, the fuse is good. A switch can be tested in the same way. By successively moving the jumper wire from one point to another, it will eventually isolate the part of the circuit where the break is located.

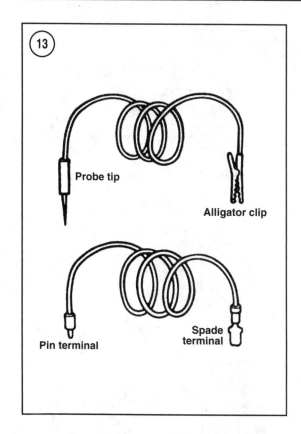

13

Probe tip

Alligator clip

Pin terminal

Spade terminal

14

Make different jumper wires in varying lengths, using alligator clips, terminals or probe tips as required (**Figure 13**). Old, discarded Honda wiring harnesses can be used to acquire different terminal ends. It is a good idea to have a wide variety of different jumper wires with various combinations of tips available in a tool box. Insulated boots should be installed over alligator clips. This will prevent accidental grounding, sparks or a possible shock when used in cramped quarters or areas that are difficult to reach.

There are a few precautions that should be heeded when using a jumper wire:

1. Make sure that the jumper wire is the same gauge (thickness) wire as that used in the circuit being tested. A jumper wire that is too small a gauge (too thin a wire) will overheat rapidly and if connected long enough, its insulation will melt.

2. Jumper wires are designed for temporary use in locating a problem. Do not leave the jumper wire installed with the idea that it is a permanent solution to the problem. It seems an easy way out of fixing the cause of the problem, but can be dangerous and may cause a fire resulting in the complete loss of the motorcycle.

Test Light

> *CAUTION*
> *Many of the circuits contain solid-state devices. Voltages in these circuits should be tested only with a 10-megohm or higher impedance digital multimeter (**Figure 14**).*

A test light can be constructed of a 12-volt light bulb with a pair of test leads carefully soldered to the bulb. To check the voltage in a circuit, attach one lead to ground and the other lead to various points along the circuit. Where voltage is present the light bulb will light.

> *CAUTION*
> ***Never** use a self-powered test light on circuits that contain solid-state devices, as these devices may be damaged.*

A self-powered test light can be constructed of a 12-volt light bulb, a pair of test leads and a 12-volt battery. When the test leads are touched together the light bulb will illuminate.

Use a self-powered test light as follows:

1. Touch the test leads together to make sure the light bulb comes on. If not, correct the problem prior to using it in a test procedure.

2. Disconnect the motorcycle's battery leads, refer to Chapter Three, or remove the fuse(s) that protects the circuit to be tested.

3. Select two points within the circuit where there should be continuity.

4. Attach one lead of the self-powered test light to each point.

5. If there is continuity, the self-powered test light bulb will come on.

6. If there is no continuity, the self-powered test light bulb will not come on, indicating an open circuit.

Voltmeter

A voltmeter is used in the same manner as the test light to find out if battery voltage is present in any given circuit. The voltmeter, unlike the test light, will also indicate how much voltage is present at each test point.

A voltmeter must be connected in parallel to a circuit (**Figure 15**) with the negative or black test lead connected to the ground side of the circuit and the positive or red test lead connected to the hot side. Its high internal resistance permits very little current to pass, allowing the meter scale to display the circuit voltage.

In addition to reading circuit voltage, the voltmeter can be used to locate points of high resistance by measuring the voltage drop across a component or in wiring and connectors (**Figure 16**). Voltage drop is the amount of voltage lost by resistance in the circuit. Generally speaking, a voltage drop should be less than one volt.

Ohmmeter

The ohmmeter is a continuity tester that reads actual circuit resistance in ohms (**Figure 17**). Like the self-powered test light, an ohmmeter contains its own power source and should not be connected to a live circuit.

Ohmmeters may be an analog type (needle scale) or a digital type (LCD or LED readout). Both types of ohmmeters have a switch that allows a different range of resistance for accurate readings. The analog ohmmeter also has a set-adjust control which is used to zero or calibrate the meter needle for accurate adjustments (digital ohmmeters do not require calibration).

Connect the ohmmeter test leads to the terminals or leads of the circuit or component being tested (**Figure 17**). If an analog meter is used, first calibrate it by touching the test leads together and adjusting the meter needle until it reads zero. When the leads are disconnected, the needle should move to the other end of the scale, indicating infinite resistance.

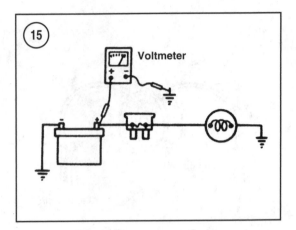

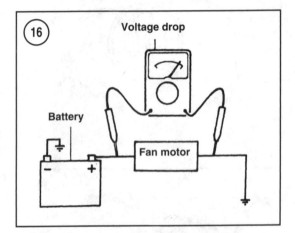

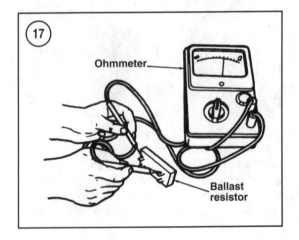

CAUTION
Many of the circuits contain solid-state devices. Do not use a low impedance analog ohmmeter to check any electronic circuit or component that operates in milliamperes. The low impedance of the ohmmeter will

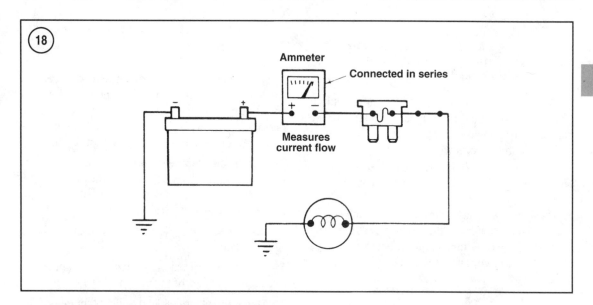

Ammeter

Connected in series

Measures
current flow

series in the circuit, the ammeter will determine whether current is flowing through the circuit, and whether the current flow is excessive because of a short in the circuit. This current flow is usually referred to as current draw. Comparing actual current draw in the circuit or component to the manufacturer's specified current draw rating will provide useful diagnostic information.

BASIC TEST PROCEDURES

Voltage Testing

Unless otherwise specified, all voltage tests are made with the electrical connector still connected. Insert the test lead(s) into the backside of the connector (**Figure 19**) and make sure the test lead touches the electrical wire or metal connector within the connector. If the test lead only touches the wire insulation, a false reading will result.

NOTE
If the connector is sealed against moisture, seal any holes made by the test leads with silicone sealer.

Always check both sides of the connector as one side may be loose or corroded and prevent electrical flow through the connector. This type of test can be performed with a test light or a voltmeter. A voltmeter will give the best results.

destroy the circuit or component. High impedance (10 megaohm) digital ohmmeters should be used when testing these circuits.

The infinite reading indicates that there is an open in the circuit or component. A reading of zero indicates continuity, which means there is no measurable resistance in the circuit or component being tested. If the meter needle falls between these two points on the scale, it indicates the actual resistance to current flow that is present. To determine the resistance, multiply the meter reading by the ohmmeter scale. For example, a meter reading of five multiplied by the R × 1,000 scale is 5000 ohms of resistance.

Ammeter

An ammeter measures the flow of current (amperes) in a circuit (**Figure 18**). When connected in

1. Attach the negative test lead (if using a voltme-ter) to a good ground (bare metal). Make sure the part used for ground is not insulated with a rubber gasket or rubber grommet.
2. Attach the positive test lead (if using a voltme-ter) to the point (electrical connector, etc.) to be checked.
3. If using a test light, the test light will come on. If using a voltmeter, note the voltage reading. The reading should be within one volt of battery voltage (12 volts). If the voltage is less, there is a problem in the circuit.

Voltage Drop Test

A voltage drop of one volt means there is a prob-lem in the circuit. All components within the circuit are designed for low resistance in order to conduct electricity with a minimum loss of voltage.
1. Connect the voltmeter positive test lead to the end of the wire or switch closest to the battery.
2. Connect the voltmeter negative test lead to the other end of the wire or switch.
3. Turn the components on in the circuit.
4. The voltmeter should indicate low voltage. If there is a reading of one volt or more, there is a problem within the circuit.
5. Check the circuit for loose or dirty connections within an electrical connector(s).

Continuity Test

A continuity test is made to determine if the cir-cuit is complete with no breaks in either the electri-cal wires or components within that circuit.

Unless otherwise specified, all continuity tests are made with the electrical connector still con-nected. Insert the test leads into the back side of the connector and make sure the test lead touches the electrical wire or metal connector within the con-nector. If the test lead only touches the wire insula-tion, a false reading will result.

Always check both sides of the connectors, as one side may be loose or corroded and prevent electrical flow through the connector. This type of test can be performed with a self-powered test light or an ohm-meter. An ohmmeter will give the best results.

If using an ohmmeter, touch the test leads to-gether and adjust the ohmmeter so the meter needle is on zero ohms. This is necessary in order to get ac-curate test results.

1. Disconnect the battery negative lead. Refer to Chapter Three.

2. Attach one test lead (test light or ohmmeter) to one end of the part of the circuit to be tested.

3. Attach the other test lead to the other end of the part of the circuit to be tested.

4. The self-powered test light will come on if there is continuity. The ohmmeter will indicate either a low or no resistance (a complete circuit) or infinite resistance (an open circuit).

Testing for a Short with a Self-Powered Test Light or Ohmmeter

1. Disconnect the battery negative lead. Refer to Chapter Three.

2. Remove the blown fuse from the fuse panel. Re-fer to Chapter Nine.

3. Connect one test lead of the test light or ohmme-ter to the load side (not battery side) of the fuse ter-minal in the fuse panel.

4. Connect the other test lead to a good ground (bare metal). Make sure the part used for a ground is not insulated with a rubber gasket or rubber grom-met.

5. With the self-powered test light or ohmmeter at-tached to the fuse terminal and ground, wiggle the wiring harness relating to the suspect circuit at six-inch intervals. Start next to the fuse panel and work away from the fuse panel. Observe the self-powered test light or ohmmeter while traveling along the harness.

6. If the test light blinks or the needle on the ohm-meter shows continuity, there is a short-to-ground at that point in the harness.

Testing for a Short with a
Test Light or Voltmeter

1. Remove the blown fuse from the fuse panel. Refer to Chapter Nine.

2. Connect the test light or voltmeter across the fuse terminals in the fuse panel. Check for battery voltage (12 volts). In some circuits the ignition switch must be turned to ON. Refer to the wiring diagrams at the end of the book.

3. With the test light or voltmeter attached to the fuse terminals, wiggle the wiring harness relating to the suspected circuit at six-inch intervals. Start next to the fuse panel and work away from the fuse panel. Watch the test light or voltmeter while traveling along the harness.

4. If the test light blinks or the needle on the voltmeter moves, there is a short-to-ground at that point in the harness.

CHARGING SYSTEM
TROUBLESHOOTING

With the engine running, alternating current is generated by the alternator and is rectified to direct current. The voltage regulator maintains a constant voltage to the battery and all additional electrical loads (lights, ignition, accessories and radio) regardless of variations in engine speed and load.

The electrical testing of individual charging system components is described under *Charging System* and *Alternator* in Chapter Nine. Individual switch testing is described under *Switches* in Chapter Nine. When making electrical tests to the charging system, refer to the wiring diagrams at the end of this book and in Chapter Nine.

The basic charging system complaints are:

1. Noisy alternator.
2. Battery discharging or overcharging.

Noisy Alternator

A noisy alternator could be due to loose alternator mounting, a loose coupler nut, damaged coupler rubber dampers, internal defects in the alternator or a worn or damaged alternator drive gear or driven gear. Alternator overhaul is described in Chapter Nine. Alternator drive gear and driven gear service is described in Chapter Five.

Battery Discharging or Overcharging

1. Make sure the battery is fully charged and in good condition. Refer to Chapter Three.

2. Check all connections. Make sure all are tight and free of corrosion.

3. Perform the charging system *Leakage Test*, as described in Chapter Nine. Interpret results as follows:

   a. Current leakage under 5 mA, perform Step 4.

   b. Current leakage above 5 mA, check for a faulty battery, a short circuit in the wire harness or for loose or damaged electrical connectors.

4. Perform the charging system *Output Test*, as described in Chapter Nine. Interpret results as follows:

   a. If the output voltage is normal (13.5-15.5 volts at 900 rpm), the battery is faulty. Replace the battery and retest.

   b. If the output voltage is excessive, the regulator/rectifier is damaged. Replace the regulator/rectifier as described in Chapter Nine.

   c. If the output voltage is the same as battery voltage (12-volts), perform Step 5.

5. Disconnect the black/green wire connector (**Figure 20**) from the alternator. Connect a voltmeter to the black/green connector (+) and ground (–). With the ignition switch ON, read the voltage indicated on the voltmeter. It should be 12 volts (battery voltage). Note the following:

   a. If the battery voltage is below the prescribed range, perform Step 6.

   b. If the battery voltage reading is 12 volts, perform Step 7.

6. Disconnect the subwire harness connector at the main wire harness black/green connector. Connect

a voltmeter to the black/green wire (+) on the main wire harness side and ground (–). With the ignition switch on, read the voltage indicated on the voltmeter. Note the following:

    a. A reading of 12 volts indicates an open circuit in the black/green subwire harness or a loose or dirty connector contact in the connector.

    b. A reading of 0 volts indicates an open circuit in the black/green main wire harness.

7. Remove the alternator from the motorcycle as described in Chapter Nine. Turn the rotor shaft coupler (**Figure 21**) by hand. The shaft should turn smoothly with no sign of roughness or excessive noise. Note the following:

    a. If the rotor shaft did not turn or if it turned roughly, disassemble the alternator (Chapter Nine) and check the following for damage: rotor coil, rotor shaft bearings and stator coil. If these components are not damaged, perform Step 9.

    b. If the rotor shaft turned smoothly, perform Step 8.

8. Disassemble the alternator and test or check the following components as described in Chapter Nine:

    a. Condenser.

    b. Brush wear length.

    c. Stator coil.

    d. Rotor coil.

Replace the damaged part and retest the alternator.

9. Assemble the alternator, if disassembled, as described in Chapter Nine.

IGNITION SYSTEM TROUBLESHOOTING

The ignition system is a solid-state capacitor discharge ignition (CDI) system. Direct current charges the capacitor. As the piston reaches the firing position, a pulse from the pulse generator triggers the silicon-controlled rectifier. The rectifier in turn allows the capacitor to discharge quickly into the primary circuit of the ignition coils. There, the voltage is stepped up in the secondary circuit to a value sufficient to fire the six spark plugs. The distribution of the pulses from the pulse generator is controlled by the rotation of the timing belt drive pulley on the front of the crankshaft. The electrical testing of individual ignition system components is described under *Ignition System Electrical Compo-*

nents in Chapter Nine. Individual switch testing is described under *Ignition System Electrical Components* and *Switches* in Chapter Nine. When making electrical tests on the ignition system, refer to the wiring diagrams in Chapter Nine.

The basic ignition system complaints are:

1. Engine cranks but does not start.
2. Engine starts but runs rough at speeds below 2000 rpm.
3. Engine starts but sidestand switch does not operate.
4. Poor engine performance and fuel economy.

Engine Cranks but Will Not Start

This section is divided into three sections (*Test 1*, *Test 2* and *Test 3*). Perform *Test 1* first, then proceed as instructed in the test procedures.

Test 1

1. Make sure the battery is fully charged and in good condition. Refer to Chapter Three. If necessary, install a replacement battery when making the following checks.
2. Remove all six spark plugs from the engine. Refer to Chapter Three.
3. Connect the spark plug wire to each spark plug and ground each plug base to the engine cylinder head (**Figure 7**). Position the spark plugs so the electrodes are visible.

WARNING
Turning the engine over with the spark plugs removed will force fuel out through the spark plug holes. When making a spark test, do not place the spark plugs next to the open

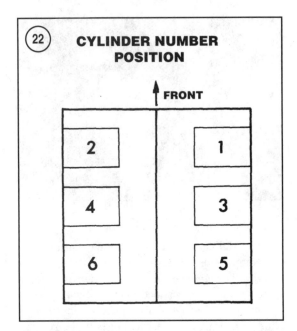

CYLINDER NUMBER POSITION

↑ FRONT

2	1
4	3
6	5

spark plug holes because the air/fuel mixture in the cylinders may ignite and cause a fire or explosion to occur.

4. Crank the engine over with the starter. A fat blue spark should be evident across the electrode on each spark plug.

WARNING
If it is necessary to hold a spark plug wire, do so with insulated pliers. The high voltage generated by the ignition system can produce a serious or fatal shock.

5. If there is a good spark at all of the spark plugs, check the fuel system as described in this chapter and Chapter Eight.

6. If there is no spark at one spark plug only, check for a fouled spark plug or a damaged spark plug secondary wire.

7. If there is no spark at all spark plugs, perform *Test 2* in this section.

8. If there is no spark at a pair of plugs that use the same coil, perform *Test 3* in this section.

NOTE
*There are three separate ignition coils. The first coil provides spark for plugs one and two, the second for plugs three and four, and the third for plugs five and six. The cylinders and plugs are identified in **Figure 22**.*

9. Reinstall the spark plugs. Refer to Chapter Three.

Test 2

1. Check the ignition control module (**Figure 23**) electrical connector. Make sure all of the connector pins and sockets are tight and free of corrosion.

NOTE
Clean contaminated electrical connectors with electrical contact cleaner if necessary.

NOTE
The manufacturer does not provide a test procedure for the ignition control module.

2. Check the pulse generator rotor bolt and rotor as follows:

  a. Remove the fairing lower covers and the fairing front cover as described in Chapter Fifteen. Then remove the timing cover (**Figure 24**).

  b. Check the pulse generator rotor bolt (**Figure 25**); the bolt must be secure. If the bolt is loose, reassemble the rotor assembly as described in Chapter Four.

NOTE
If the rotor bolt was loose, the pulse generator rotor can move out of time. Reassemble the rotor assembly as described in Chapter Four.

c. If the rotor bolt is tight, remove the timing belt covers and inspect the rotor for damage. Refer to Chapter Four.

d. If the rotor bolt is tight and the rotor is not damaged, the ignition control module is defective and must be replaced. Refer to Chapter Nine.

e. If necessary, reinstall the rotor and rotor bolt assembly as described in Chapter Four.

Test 3

1. Perform the *Ignition Coil Primary Voltage Inspection* as described in Chapter Nine.

2. Substitute the suspect ignition coil with a known working coil (from the motorcycle being tested) and repeat the spark test as described under Test 1 in this chapter. Note the following:

a. If there is a spark with the substitute coil, the suspect coil is damaged; replace the ignition coil and retest.

b. If there is still no spark, the ignition control module is faulty. Replace the unit and retest.

Engine Starts but Sidestand Switch Does Not Operate

1. Check the sidestand switch continuity as described in Chapter Nine. Note the following:

a. If there is no continuity, the sidestand switch is damaged; replace the switch and retest.

b. If there is continuity, check for an open or short circuit in the sidestand switch wiring harness or for damaged or contaminated electrical connectors.

Poor Engine Performance and Fuel Economy

1. Check the ignition timing as described in Chapter Three.

2. Check the fuel system as described in this chapter.

STARTING SYSTEM TROUBLESHOOTING

The basic starting system complaints are:
1. Starter is inoperative.
2. Engine cranks slowly.
3. Starter operates but does not crank engine .

4. Engine turns over, but does not start.

The electrical testing of individual starting system components is described under *Starting System Electrical Components* in Chapter Nine. Individual switch testing is described under *Starting System Electrical Components* and *Switches* in Chapter Nine. When making electrical tests to the starting system, refer to the wiring diagram in Chapter Nine.

Prior to troubleshooting the starting system, perform the following:

1. Ensure that the battery is fully charged and functioning. Refer to Chapter Three.

2. Make sure the bank angle sensor is properly installed and in good working order. Refer to *Bank Angle Sensor Testing/Replacement* in Chapter Nine.

3. Check main fuse A (30A). Refer to Chapter Nine.

4. If none of the above checks locates the starting problem, proceed to the following starting complaints that best describes the starting problem.

Starter is Inoperative

Test 1

1. Check the starter relay switch electrical connectors for contamination and looseness. Check the starter relay switch four-pin electrical connector for damaged or loose terminal pins.

2. Check the starter terminal connections at the starter motor.

3. Check the starter ground cable for a loose connection. Check the starter cables for an open or short circuit.

4. Remove the starter motor (Chapter Nine) and apply battery voltage to its positive cable terminal. The starter motor should run. Note the following:

a. If the starter motor runs, reinstall the starter and perform Step 5.

b. If the starter motor did not run, disassemble and inspect the starter motor as described in Chapter Nine.

5. Perform the *Starter Relay Switch Tests* in Chapter Nine. Note the following:

a. If the relay did not click, continue with Step 6.

b. If the relay clicked, check the starter relay switch continuity as described under the same procedure in Chapter Nine. If there is no continuity, replace the starter relay switch and retest.

6. Disconnect the four-pin electrical connector at the starter relay switch. Connect the voltmeter test lead to the yellow/red wire on the wire harness side and the voltmeter test lead to ground. With the ignition switch on, press the starter button. The voltmeter should show battery voltage. Note the following:

a. If there is no voltage at the connector, see *Test 2*.

b. If there is voltage at the connector, perform Step 7.

7. Connect the positive ohmmeter test lead to the green wire and the negative ohmmeter test lead to ground. There should be continuity with the clutch lever squeezed and the sidestand up or when the transmission is in NEUTRAL. If there is no continuity, perform *Test 2*.

Test 2

1. Test the following components as described under *Starter System Electrical Components* in Chapter Nine:

a. Diode(s).

b. Clutch lever switch.

2. Test the following components as described under *Ignition System Electrical Components* in Chapter Nine:

a. Coolant temperature sensor.

b. Sidestand switch.

3. If the problem has not been found after testing the components in Steps 1 and 2, recheck the starter system wiring harness for an open or short circuit. Check the electrical connectors for dirty or loose-fitting terminals.

Engine Cranks Slowly

1. Check for a low battery charge as described in Chapter Three.

2. Check for excessive resistance in the starting circuit.

3. Disassemble and bench test the starter motor as described in Chapter Nine.

Starter Operates but Does Not Crank Engine

Check the following components as described in Chapter Five:

1. Damaged starter idle gear.

2. Damaged starter clutch.

3. Damaged starter drive and/or driven gear.

Engine Turns Over but Does Not Start

1. Troubleshoot the ignition system as described in this chapter.

2. Check for a mechanical problem in the engine. See Chapter Two.

LIGHTING SYSTEM TROUBLESHOOTING

The basic lighting system complaints are:

a. Lights are dim; engine runs but lights or components do not work.

b. Lights do not work with ignition switch on (except for instrument illumination).

c. Headlight does not come on when the ignition switch is turned ON (U.S. models).

d. Parking lights do not come on with ignition switch in P position.

e. Neutral indicator does not come on.

f. Brake lights do not come on with ignition switch ON and brake applied.

g. Turn signals do not come on.

h. One turn signal light does not come on.

The electrical testing of individual lighting system components is described under *Lighting System Electrical Components* in Chapter Nine. Individual switch testing is described under *Switches* in Chapter Nine. When performing electrical tests to the lighting system, refer to the wiring diagrams for the specific model at the end of this book.

Prior to troubleshooting the lighting system, perform the following:

1. Make sure the battery is fully charged and in good condition. Refer to Chapter Three.

2. On U.S. models, the headlight should go off when the starter button is pressed.

3. Check for blown or damaged fuses. Refer to Chapter Nine.

4. If none of the above checks locates the starting problem, proceed to the following lighting system complaints that best describe the lighting problem.

Lights are Dim; Engine Runs but Lights or Components Do Not Work

1. Check for a defective bulb.

2. Check for dirty or loose-fitting terminals of related connectors.

3. Check for an open or short circuit in the related wiring harness.

Headlight is Inoperative When the Ignition Switch is Turned ON (U.S. Models)

1. Check for a defective headlight bulb.

2. Check for a damaged dimmer switch. Test the dimmer switch as described under *Switches* in Chapter Nine.

3. Check for dirty or loose-fitting terminals of related connectors.

4. Check for an open or short circuit in the related wiring harness.

Neutral Indicator is Inoperative

1. Check for a defective bulb.

2. Check for a damaged neutral position switch. Refer to *Ignition System Electrical Components* in Chapter Nine.

3. Check for dirty or loose-fitting terminals of related connectors.

4. Check for an open or short circuit in the related wiring harness.

Brake Lights are Inoperative with Ignition Switch On and Brake Applied

1. Check for a defective bulb(s).

2. Check for a damaged front and/or rear brake switch. Test as described under *Switches* in Chapter Nine.

3. Check for dirty or loose-fitting terminals of related connectors.

4. Check for an open or short circuit in the related wiring harness.

Turn Signals are Inoperative

NOTE
If one bulb is defective, the turn signals will blink faster than normal.

1. Check for defective bulbs. If the bulbs are good, perform Step 2.

2. Check the following connectors for dirty or loose-fitting terminals; clean and/or repair them as required. If the connectors are clean, or if they have been repaired and the problem still exists, perform Step 3.

3. Check the turn signal switch continuity as described under *Switches* in Chapter Nine. If the turn signal switch tested incorrectly, the switch is defective and should be replaced.

One Turn Signal Light is Inoperative

1. Check for a loose or defective bulb. Check the bulb for dirty or loose-fitting contacts; clean and repair as required.

2. Check for a defective turn signal switch. Refer to *Switches* in Chapter Nine.

COOLING SYSTEM TROUBLESHOOTING

The electrical testing of individual components is described under *Cooling System Electrical Components* in Chapter Nine. Individual switch testing is described under *Switches* in Chapter Nine. When performing electrical tests to the cooling system, refer to the wiring diagrams for the specific model at the end of this manual.

The most common electrical-related cooling system complaint is that the fan is inoperative.

Coolant Temperature Indicator Does Not Work Properly

1. Check main fuse A as described under *Fuses* in Chapter Nine:

2. Test the temperature gauge indicator unit as described under *Cooling System Electrical Components* in Chapter Nine.

3. Test the coolant temperature sensor as described in Chapter Nine. Note the following:

   a. If the test results are correct, check for a dirty or loose-fitting coolant temperature sensor wire connector.

   b. If the test results are not as specified, the coolant temperature sensor is defective and should be replaced.

4. Install by reversing these steps. Make sure all electrical connections are tight.

Fan Motor is Inoperative

1. Check main fuse A (30A) and the fan motor fuse (10A). Refer to *Fuses* in Chapter Nine.

2. Ground and test the thermostatic fan motor switch as described in Chapter Nine. Note the following:

   a. If the test results are not as specified, perform Step 3.

   b. If the switch tests correctly, perform Step 4.

3. Test the fan motor as described in Chapter Ten. Note the following:

   a. If the fan motor runs correctly, check for a dirty or loose-fitting fan motor wire or connector. Check for an open or short circuit in the wire harness.

   b. If the fan motor does not operate correctly, the fan motor is defective and should be replaced.

4. Remove the thermostatic fan motor switch and test it as described in Chapter Nine. Note the following:

   a. If the switch tests correctly, check the switch wire and connectors for dirty or loose-fitting terminals.

   b. If the switch did not test as specified, the switch is defective and should be replaced.

5. Install by reversing these steps. Make sure all electrical connections are tight.

Table 1 OIL PRESSURE SPECIFICATION

Cold 35° C (95° F)	127 kPa (18 psi) @ idle
	490 kPa (71 psi) @ 5000 rpm
Hot 80° C (176° F)	78 kPa (11 psi) @ idle
	78 kPa (11 psi) @ 5000 rpm

CHAPTER THREE

LUBRICATION, MAINTENANCE AND TUNE-UP

The service life and operation of the GL1500 Valkyrie depends on the maintenance it receives. A motorcycle, even in normal use, is subjected to tremendous heat, stress and vibration. When neglected, any motorcycle may become unreliable and actually dangerous to ride.

All motorcycles require attention before and after riding them. This is especially true on a high-mileage vehicle. The time spent on basic maintenance and lubrication provides the utmost in safety and performance. Minor problems found during these inspections are generally simple and inexpensive to correct. If they are not found and

corrected in time, they could lead to major and more expensive problems later on.

Regular cleaning of the motorcycle is also very important to the motorcycle's upkeep. It makes routine maintenance much easier by not having to work through a build-up of road dirt and grime to get to a component for adjustment or replacement. Routine cleaning also helps to find worn, damaged or leaking parts that can be repaired or replaced before they break or cause secondary damage.

When performing the maintenance tasks in this chapter, experience will be gained on how the Valkyrie works, identifying components and their

location and how to service them. This experience will more than pay for itself if troubleshooting or servicing the motorcycle while on the road.

Start by doing simple tune-up, lubrication and maintenance. Tackle more involved jobs after becoming better acquainted with the vehicle.

Certain maintenance tasks and checks should be performed weekly. Others should be performed at specific time or mileage intervals. Some maintenance procedures are included under *Tune-up* at the end of this chapter. Detailed instructions will be found there. Other steps are described in the following chapters. Chapter references are included with these steps.

Table 1 is a suggested maintenance schedule. **Tables 1-11** are at the end of this chapter.

ROUTINE CHECKS

Perform the following checks at each fuel stop.

Engine Oil Level

Refer to *Oil Level Check* under *Periodic Lubrication* in this chapter.

Coolant Level

Check the coolant level after the engine has reached normal operating temperature.

1. Start the engine, let it idle and place the motorcycle on the sidestand.

2. Hold the motorcycle vertically and check the coolant level in the reservoir tank. The level should be between the UPPER and LOWER marks on the side of the tank.

3. If the reservoir tank is low, perform the following:
   a. Remove the left frame cover as described in Chapter Fifteen.
   b. Remove the reservoir tank cap (A, **Figure 1**).
   c. Add a 50:50 mixture of coolant and distilled water to the reserve tank filler neck so the level is at the UPPER mark (B, **Figure 1**). If the reservoir tank is empty, perform Step 4.
   d. Install the left cover, as described in Chapter Fifteen.

4. If the reservoir tank is empty, perform the following:
   a. On models so equipped, remove the screw securing the radiator cap in place on the filler neck.

WARNING
Do not remove the radiator cap (Figure 2) when the engine is hot. The coolant is very hot and under pressure. Severe scalding will result if the coolant contacts skin.

   b. Loosen and remove the radiator cap (**Figure 2**). Check the coolant level in the radiator.

NOTE
If the coolant level is low in the radiator, there may be a leak in the cooling system. Test the cooling system as described in this chapter.

   c. Start and run the engine for 2-3 minutes to allow air in the system to escape. Turn the engine off.
   d. Top off the radiator with a 50:50 mixture of coolant and distilled water. Then, install and tighten the radiator cap. Install the screw and tighten it securely on models so equipped.

e. If necessary, fill the reservoir tank with coolant as described in Step 3. Reinstall the cap.

General Inspection

1. Quickly inspect the engine for signs of oil, fuel or coolant leakage.
2. Check the tires for embedded stones. Pry them out with the ignition key.
3. Make sure all lights work.

> *NOTE*
> *Test the brake light. It can burn out at any time. Automobiles cannot stop as quickly as motorcycles and drivers need as much warning as possible.*

Tire Pressure

Tire pressure must be checked with the tires cold. Correct tire pressure varies with the motorcycle's load. See **Table 3**. Refer to *Tires and Wheels* in this chapter.

Lights and Horn

With the engine running, check the following:
1. Pull the front brake lever on and check that the brake light comes on.
2. Push the rear brake pedal down and check that the brake light comes on soon after the pedal has been pressed.
3. Press the headlight dimmer switch to both the HI and LO positions and check to see that both headlight elements are working.
4. Turn the turn signal switch to the left and right positions and check that all four turn signals function.
5. Push the horn button and make sure the horn sounds loudly.
6. If the horn or any of the lights fail to operate properly, refer to Chapter Nine.

PRE-RIDE INSPECTION

Perform the following checks prior to the first ride of the day.
1. Walk around the vehicle and check for any fuel, brake fluid, clutch fluid, oil or coolant leaks.

2. Visually inspect both tires. If the tires appear low, check tire pressure with a gauge. Check the tread for severe wear or damage.
3. Visually check the cables for any looseness or damage.
4. Check that the rearview mirrors, footpegs and other items are mounted securely.

> *NOTE*
> *Perform Steps 5-7 while sitting on the motorcycle.*

5. Rock the vehicle and apply the front brake lever, then the rear brake pedal separately. Make sure that the lever and pedal return normally and that the brakes operate correctly.
6. Rotate the throttle, making sure it moves smoothly with no binding or roughness and that it closes in all steering positions.
7. Turn the ignition on. Check that all gauges and indicators work properly. Start the engine and listen to the engine for any abnormal sounds. Shut off the engine.
8. Check that all lights work properly.
9. Make sure the horn sounds loudly.
10. Make sure that the engine stop switch works properly. Use it to turn the engine off.
11. Make sure the side stand ignition cutoff system works properly. Check as follows:
    a. Have an assistant sit on the motorcycle.
    b. Check the spring on the side stand. Make sure the spring is in good condition and has not lost tension.
    c. Swing the side stand down and up a few times. The side stand should swing smoothly and the spring should provide proper tension.
    d. Swing the side stand up and while the assistant is straddling the motorcycle.
    e. Shift the transmission into NEUTRAL.
    f. Start the engine and allow it to idle. Then pull the clutch lever in and shift the transmission into first gear.
    g. Lower the side stand. The engine should stop as the side stand is lowered.
    h. If the side stand does not operate as described, inspect it as described in Chapter Nine.

SERVICE INTERVALS

The recommended maintenance schedule is shown in **Table 1**. Strict adherence to these recom-

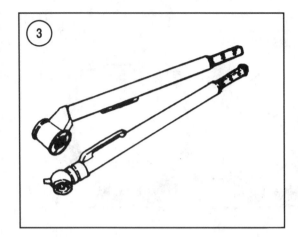

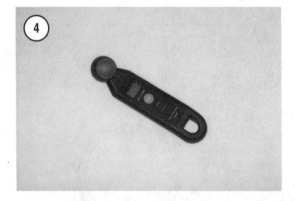

TIRES AND WHEELS

Check tires and wheels prior to each ride and daily when traveling.

Tire Pressure

Check the tire pressure and adjust it to maintain the tire profile, good traction and handling and to get maximum life out of the tire. A simple plunger-type gauge (**Figure 3**) can be purchased for a few dollars and, for a little more money, the more accurate digital type (**Figure 4**) is available. This gauge should be carried in the motorcycle tool kit. Check tire pressure when the tires are cold. The appropriate tire pressures are shown in **Table 3**.

> *NOTE*
> *After checking and adjusting the air pressure, make sure to reinstall the air valve cap (**Figure 5**) on both wheels. This cap prevents small pebbles and dirt from collecting in the valve stem; this could allow air leakage or result in incorrect tire pressure readings. Install and tighten finger-tight.*

> *NOTE*
> *A loss of air pressure may be due to a loose or damaged valve core. Place a few drops of water on the top of the valve core. If the water bubbles, tighten the valve core and recheck. If air is still leaking from the valve after tightening it, replace the valve as described in Chapter Twelve.*

Tire Inspection

The tires take a lot of punishment, so inspect them periodically for excessive wear. Inspect the tires for the following:
1. Deep cuts and imbedded objects like stones, nails and road debris. If an object is found in the tire, mark its location with a light crayon prior to removing it. This will help to locate the hole for repair. Refer to Chapter Eleven for tire changing and repair information.
2. Flat spots.
3. Cracks.
4. Separating plies.
5. Side wall damage.

mendations will ensure long service from the Valkyrie. If the vehicle is run in an area of high humidity, the lubrication services must be done more frequently to prevent rust damage.

For convenience when maintaining the motorcycle, most of the services shown in **Table 1** are described in this chapter. However, those procedures that require more than minor disassembly or adjustment are covered elsewhere in the appropriate chapter.

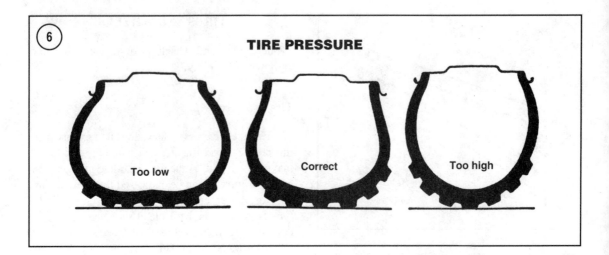

TIRE PRESSURE

Too low   Correct   Too high

Tire Wear Analysis

Analyze abnormal tire wear to determine its cause. The most common causes are the following:

1. Incorrect tire pressure—Check tire pressure as described in this chapter.
2. Overloading.
3. Incorrect wheel alignment.
4. Incorrect wheel balance—balance the tire/wheel assembly when installing a new tire, and then rebalance each time the tire is removed.
5. Worn or damaged wheel bearings.

Incorrect tire pressure is a significant cause of abnormal tire wear (**Figure 6**). Underinflated tires will result in higher tire temperatures, hard or imprecise steering and abnormal tire wear. Overinflated tires will result in a hard ride and abnormal tire wear. Examine the tire tread, comparing wear in the center of the contact patch with tire wear at the edge of the contact patch. Note the following:

1. If a tire shows excessive wear at the edge of the contact patch, but the wear at the center of the contact patch is normal, the tire has been underinflated.
2. If a tire shows excessive wear in the center of the contact patch, but the wear at the edge of the contact patch is normal, the tire has been overinflated.

Tread Depth

Check local traffic regulations concerning minimum tread depth. Measure the tread depth at the center of the tire (**Figure 7**) using a tread depth gauge or a small ruler. Honda recommends that original equipment tires be replaced when the front

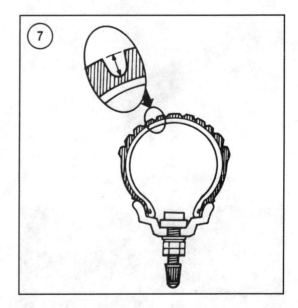

tire center tread depth has reached a minimum depth of 1.5 mm (1/16 in.) and when the rear tire center tread depth has reached a minimum depth of 2.0 mm (3/32 in.). Or when tread wear indicators appear across the tire indicating the minimum tread depth. If tires other than those originally equipped on the motorcycle have been installed, refer to the manufacturer's marking on the tire for minimum tread depth.

Rim Inspection

Frequently inspect the wheel rims. If a rim has been damaged, it might have been knocked out of alignment. Improper wheel alignment can cause se-

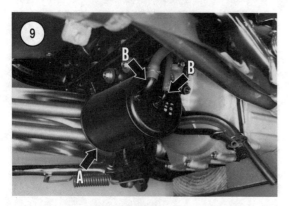

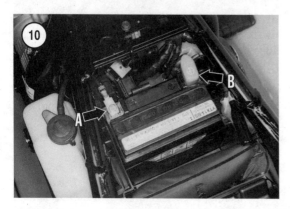

vere vibration and result in an unsafe riding condition. If the rim is damaged, the wheel must be replaced because it cannot be repaired.

CRANKCASE BREATHER HOSE (U.S. MODELS ONLY)

Service the breather hose and air box drain fitting (**Figure 8**) at the intervals indicated in **Table 1**. Service the system more often when riding at sustained full-throttle speed or in the rain. To service the

breather hose and fitting, refer to *Crankcase Breather System—U.S. Only* in Chapter Eight.

EVAPORATION EMISSION CONTROL (CALIFORNIA MODELS ONLY)

Inspect the canister (A, **Figure 9**) and hoses for cracks, kinks and deterioration. Make sure that all hoses (B, **Figure 9**) attach tightly to the various components. For correct hose routing, refer to the emission control decal on the motorcycle.

BATTERY

The battery is an important component in the electrical system. Yet, many electrical problems can be traced to battery neglect. Therefore, clean and inspect the battery as indicated in **Table 1**.

For maximum battery life, inspect the battery periodically for the state of charge and corrosion. All models are equipped with a maintenance-free sealed battery and the electrolyte level cannot be checked.

On all models covered in this manual, the negative side is grounded. When removing the battery, disconnect the negative cable (A, **Figure 10**) first, then the positive cable (B, **Figure 10**). This eliminates the chance of a tool shorting to ground when disconnecting the positive cable.

Disconnecting the Negative Battery Cable

Some of the tests in this manual require that the negative (–) battery cable be disconnected prior to performing a specific procedure.
1. Turn the ignition switch to the OFF position.
2. Park the motorcycle on its sidestand.
3. Remove the seat as described in Chapter Fifteen.
4. On GL1500CF models, remove the radio as described in Chapter Nine.
5. Remove the retaining strap (A, **Figure 11**) and the battery cover (B, **Figure 11**).
6. Disconnect the negative battery lead (A, **Figure 10**) and move it out of the way to avoid accidental contact with the battery negative post.
7. Reconnect the negative cable to the battery.
8. Install the battery cover and secure it with the retaining strap.
9. On GL1500CF models, install the radio as described in Chapter Nine.

10. Install the seat as described in Chapter Fifteen.

Safety Precautions

While a battery is being charged, highly explosive hydrogen gas forms in each cell. Some of this gas may escape through the sealing bar cap and may form an explosive atmosphere in and around the battery. This condition can persist for several hours. Sparks, an open flame or a lighted cigarette can ignite the gas, causing an internal battery explosion and possible serious personal injury. Take the following precautions to prevent an explosion:

1. Do not smoke or permit any open flame near any battery being charged or which has been recently charged.

2. Do not disconnect live circuits at battery terminals since a spark usually occurs when a live circuit is broken.

3. Do not connect or disconnect any battery charger when its power switch is on. Make sure the charger connections are secure. Poor connections are a common cause of electrical arcs that can cause an explosion.

4. Keep children and pets away from charging equipment and batteries.

Battery Removal/Installation

1. Turn the ignition switch to the OFF position.

2. Park the motorcycle on its sidestand.

3. Remove the seat as described in Chapter Fifteen.

4. On GL1500CF models, remove the radio as described in Chapter Nine.

5. Remove the retaining strap (A, **Figure 11**) and the battery cover (B, **Figure 11**).

6. Remove the protective cap (A, **Figure 12**) from the positive terminal.

7. Disconnect the battery negative lead (B, **Figure 12**) and then the positive lead (A, **Figure 12**) from the battery.

> *NOTE*
> *The battery is not secured with hold down straps or bolts.*

8. Carefully lift the battery (C, **Figure 12**) up and out of the frame and remove it.

9. Place the battery on several newspapers on the workbench.

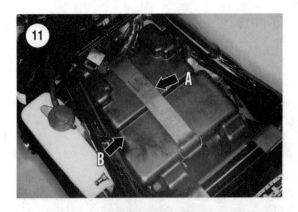

10. If necessary, wipe off any of the highly corrosive residue that may have escaped from the battery filler strip.

  a. Position the battery with the battery negative terminal on the left side of the frame.

  b. Install the battery (C, **Figure 12**) into the frame.

> *CAUTION*
> *Be sure the battery cables are connected to their proper terminals. Connecting the battery terminals backwards will reverse the polarity and damage the rectifier and ignition system.*

11. Install and tighten the positive battery cable (A, **Figure 12**) and tighten the screw securely.

12. Install and tighten the negative battery cable (B, **Figure 12**) and tighten the screw securely.

13. Coat the battery connections with dielectric grease or petroleum jelly to prevent corrosion.

14. Move the protective cap (A, **Figure 12**) back over the positive terminal.

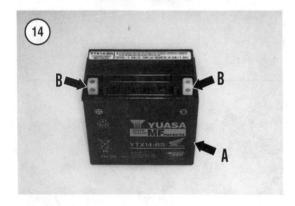

15. Install the battery cover and secure it with the retaining strap (A, **Figure 11**).

16. On GL1500CF models, install the radio as described in Chapter Nine.

17. Install the seat as described in Chapter Fifteen.

Inspection and Testing

The battery electrolyte level cannot be checked. *Never* attempt to remove the sealing bar cap from the battery (A, **Figure 13**). This bar cap was removed for the initial filling of electrolyte prior to delivery of the vehicle or the purchase of a new battery. This bar cap is not to be removed thereafter. The battery does not require periodic electrolyte inspection or water refilling.

> *WARNING*
> *Even though the battery is a sealed type, protect eyes, skin and clothing; electrolyte is corrosive and can cause severe chemical skin burns and permanent injury. The battery case may be cracked and leaking electrolyte. If any electrolyte is spilled or splashed on clothing or skin, immediately neu-*

tralize it with a solution of baking soda and clean water. Electrolyte splashed into the eyes is extremely harmful. Always wear safety glasses while working with a battery. If electrolyte enters the eyes, call a physician immediately. Then, force the eyes open and flood them with cool clean water for approximately 15 minutes.

1. Remove the battery as described in this chapter. Do not clean the battery while it is mounted in the frame.

2. Set the battery on a stack of newspapers or old shop cloths to protect the surface of the workbench.

3. Check the entire battery case (A, **Figure 14**) for cracks or other damage. If the battery case is warped, discolored or has a raised top surface, the battery has been overcharged or overheated.

4. Check the battery terminal bolts, spacers and nuts (B, **Figure 14**) for corrosion or damage. Clean parts thoroughly with a solution of baking soda and water. Replace severely corroded or damaged parts.

> *NOTE*
> *Do not allow the cleaning solution to enter the battery or the electrolyte will be seriously weakened.*

5. If necessary, clean the top of the battery with a stiff bristle brush using a baking soda and water solution. Rinse the battery case with clean water and wipe dry with a clean cloth or paper towel.

6. Check the battery cable clamps for corrosion and damage. If corrosion is minor, clean the battery cable clamps with a stiff wire brush. Replace severely worn or damaged cables.

7. Inspect the battery box for contamination or damage. Clean with a solution of baking soda and water and wipe dry.

8. Check the battery box and cover for cracks or other damage. Replace damaged or missing parts as required.

9. Connect a voltmeter between the negative and positive terminals (**Figure 15**). Note the following:

    a. If the battery voltage is 13.0-13.2 volts (at 20° C [68° F]), the battery is fully charged.

    b. If the battery voltage is below 12.3 volts (at 20° C [68° F]), the battery is undercharged and requires charging.

10. If the battery is undercharged, recharge it as described in this chapter. Then test the charging system as described in Chapter Two,

Charging

If recharging is required on a maintenance-free battery, the rate of charge (amperage) must be controlled. If a charger with a built-in ammeter is not available, have a Honda dealership perform the charging procedure. Overcharging a maintenance-free battery will permanently damage it.

If a battery not in use loses its charge within a week after charging, the battery is defective. A good battery should not self-discharge more than 1% (approximately 0.13 volts) each day. As outside temperature rises, so does the rate of discharge. A battery stored at 35° C (95° F) will discharge twice as fast as a battery stored at 24° C (75° F).

> *WARNING*
> *During the charging cycle, explosive hydrogen gas is released from the battery. Charge the battery only in a well-ventilated area, and always away from open flames (including pilot lights on some gas home appliances) that may be present in the work area. Do not allow any smoking in the area. Never check the charge of the battery by arcing across the terminals; the resulting spark can ignite the hydrogen gas.*

> *CAUTION*
> *Always remove the battery from the motorcycle before connecting the charging equipment. During the charging procedure, the charging amperage may damage the diodes within the voltage regulator/rectifier if the battery cables remain connected.*

1. Remove the battery from the motorcycle as described in this chapter.

2. Set the battery on a stack of newspapers or old shop cloths to protect the surface of the workbench.

3. Connect the positive charger lead to the positive battery terminal (A, **Figure 16**) and the negative charger lead to the negative battery terminal (B, **Figure 16**). Set the charger at 12 volts. If the output of the charger is variable, select the low setting.

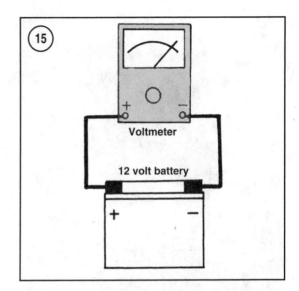

4. The charging time depends on the discharged condition of the battery. Use the suggested charging amperage and length of charge time on the battery label (B, **Figure 13**). The battery should be charged at a rate of one-tenth its amp-hour (AH) rating.

5. Turn the battery charger on. After the battery has been charged for the pre-determined time, turn the charger off, disconnect the charger leads and measure the battery voltage. Refer to the following:

   a. If the battery voltage is 13.0-13.2 volts (at 20° C [68° F]), or greater, the battery is fully charged.

   b. If the battery voltage is below 12.3 volts (at 20° C [68° F]), or less, the battery requires additional charging time.

6. If the battery voltage remains stable for one hour, the battery is charged.

7. Install the battery as described in this chapter.

New Battery Installation

A new battery must be *fully* charged (specific gravity of 1.260-1.280) before installing it in the vehicle. When electrolyte is added to a new battery, its charge or capacity at that time is approximately 80%. To bring the battery to a full charge, it must receive an initial or boost charge. Using a new battery without an initial charge will cause permanent battery damage. That is, the battery will never be able to hold more than an 80% charge. Charging a new battery after it has been in use will not bring its charge to 100%. When purchasing a new battery, verify its charge status. If possible, have the supplier add the electrolyte and perform the initial charge to bring the battery up to 100%.

NOTE
Recycle the old battery. *When the new battery is purchased, turn in the old one for recycling. The lead plates and the plastic case can be recycled. Most vehicle dealerships will accept the old battery in trade when the new one is purchased. Never place an old battery in the household trash since it is ille-*

gal, in most states, to place any acid or lead (heavy metal) contents in landfills.

PERIODIC LUBRICATION

Perform the services listed in this section at the maintenance intervals listed in **Table 1**. If the vehicle is exposed to harder than normal use with constant exposure to water and high humidity, perform the services more frequently.

Oil

Oil is graded according to its viscosity, which is an indication of how thick it is. The Society of Automotive Engineers (SAE) system distinguishes oil viscosity by numbers, called weights. Thick (heavy) oil has a higher viscosity number than thin (light) oil. For example, a 5 weight (SAE 5) oil is a light oil while a 90 weight (SAE 90) oil is relatively heavy. The viscosity of the oil has nothing to do with its lubricating properties.

Grease

Use waterproof grease when grease is called for. Water does not wash grease off parts as easily as it washes oil. In addition, grease maintains its lubricating qualities better than oil on long and strenuous rides.

Engine Oil Level Check

Check the engine oil level with the dipstick located on the right side of the engine (**Figure 17**).
1. Park the motorcycle on level ground and support it with its sidestand.
2. Start the engine and let it idle for 2-3 minutes.
3. Shut off the engine and allow the oil to drain into the crankcase for a few minutes.
4. Unscrew the dipstick and wipe it clean with a lint-free cloth.
5. Hold the motorcycle upright and reinsert the dipstick in the hole; do *not* screw it in.
6. Remove the dipstick and check the oil level.
7. The level should be between the two lines and not above the upper one on the dipstick (**Figure 18**).

8. If the level is below the lower line, remove the oil filler cap (**Figure 19**) and add the recommended type of engine oil to correct the level. See **Figure 20** for the recommended oil viscosity to use at different ambient temperatures.

9. Reinstall the oil filler cap and the dipstick and tighten securely.

Engine Oil and Filter Change

Regular oil and filter changes contribute more to engine longevity than any other maintenance performed. The recommended oil and filter change interval is listed in **Table 1**. This assumes that the motorcycle is operated in moderate conditions. If it is operated under dusty conditions, the oil gets contaminated faster and must be changed more frequently.

The manufacturer recommends using only high-quality detergent motor oil with an API (American Petroleum Institute) service classification of SF or SG. The classification is printed on the container. Use the same brand of oil at each change. Refer to **Figure 20** for the correct oil viscosity to use under anticipated ambient temperatures (not engine oil temperature).

To change the engine oil and filter the following items are required:

a. Drain pan.
b. Funnel.
c. Wrench (drain plug).
d. Oil filter wrench.
e. Engine oil. Refer to **Figure 20** and **Table 5**.
f. New oil filter.

NOTE
Never dispose of motor oil in the trash, on the ground, or down a storm drain. Many service stations accept used motor oil and waste haulers provide curbside used motor oil collection. Do not combine other fluids with motor oil to be recycled. To locate a recycler, contact the American Petroleum Institute (API) at www.recycleoil.org.

NOTE
Running the engine allows the oil to heat up; thus it flows freely and carries contamination and sludge with it.

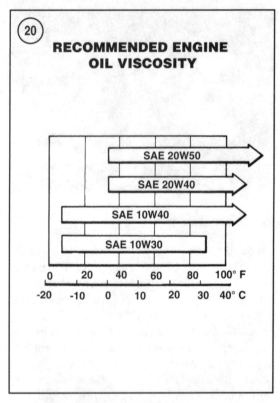

RECOMMENDED ENGINE OIL VISCOSITY

SAE 20W50
SAE 20W40
SAE 10W40
SAE 10W30

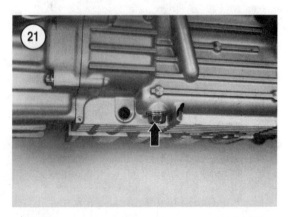

1. Start the engine and let it reach normal operating temperature; 15-20 minutes of riding is usually sufficient.

2. Turn the engine off and place the motorcycle on the sidestand (on a level surface). Make sure the ignition switch is turned OFF.

3. Place a drain pan under the oil drain plug.

4. Remove the oil drain plug and gasket (**Figure 21**). Be careful, the oil and plug will be hot.

5. Remove the oil filler cap (**Figure 19**); this will speed up the flow of oil.

CAUTION
Do not let the engine start and run without oil in the crankcase.

6. Let the oil drain for at least 15-20 minutes.

NOTE
Before removing the oil filter in Step 7, thoroughly clean off all debris around it.

7. The oil filter (**Figure 22**) is mounted at the front of the engine, next to the water pump.

8. Move the drain pan under the oil filter, as residual oil will drain out when the filter is loosened and removed.

9. Install the Honda oil filter wrench (part No. 07HAA-PJ70100) or equivalent onto the filter (**Figure 23**). Turn the wrench and filter *counterclockwise* until the oil begins to drain out. Wait until the oil stops.

10. Remove the oil filter and hold it over the drain pan and pour out all remaining oil. Place the filter in a reclosable plastic bag and close the bag. Discard the oil filter properly.

11. Wipe the engine filter flange surface (**Figure 24**) with a clean rag.

12. Coat the O-ring (**Figure 25**) on the new filter with clean engine oil.

13. Install the new filter onto the engine. If using the Honda filter wrench or equivalent, tighten the oil filter to the torque specification in **Table 6**. Otherwise, tighten the filter by hand until the O-ring contacts the flange surface, and then tighten it an additional ½ to 3/4 of a turn.

CAUTION
Overtightening the oil filter will cause it to leak.

14. Check the drain plug sealing washer for damage and replace it if necessary.

15. Install the sealing washer onto the drain plug and install the drain plug (**Figure 21**). Tighten the drain plug to the torque specification in **Table 6**.

16. Insert a funnel into the oil fill hole and fill the engine with the recommended viscosity and quantity of oil. Refer to **Figure 20** and **Table 5**.

17. Reinstall the oil filler cap and dipstick and tighten securely.

18. Start the engine, making sure not to over-rev the engine. The oil pressure warning light should go out within 1-2 seconds. If it stays on, shut off the engine immediately and locate the problem. Do not run the engine with the oil warning light on.

19. Allow the engine to idle for a few minutes, then turn it off.

20. Check visually for leaks around the oil filter and the drain plug.

21. Recheck the oil level as described in this chapter.

22. If the engine was rebuilt, check the oil pressure as described under *Oil Pressure Test* in Chapter Two.

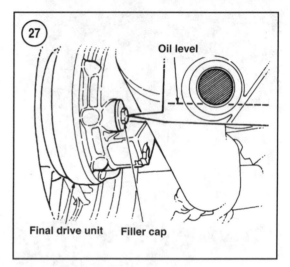

Final Drive Oil Level Check

When checking or changing the final drive oil, do not allow any debris to enter the case opening.

1. Park the motorcycle on a level surface. Support it on its sidestand.

NOTE
Figure 26 shows the right side muffler removed for clarity. It is not necessary to remove the muffler to check the final drive oil level.

2. Wipe the area around the oil filler cap clean and loosen the oil filler cap (A, **Figure 26**).

3. Have an assistant hold the motorcycle vertically.

4. Remove the oil filler cap (A, **Figure 26**).

5. The oil level is correct if the oil is even with the bottom of the filler hole (**Figure 27**). If the oil level is low, add the gear oil specified in **Table 8** to correct the oil level.

6. Inspect the O-ring seal on the oil filler cap. Replace the O-ring if it has deteriorated or is starting to harden.

7. Install the oil filler cap and tighten it to the torque specification in **Table 6**.

Final Drive Oil Change

The recommended oil change interval is listed in **Table 1**.

To drain the oil the following is required:

   a. Drain pan.

   b. Funnel.

   c. Hypoid gear oil (see **Table 7** and **Table 8**).

Discard old final drive oil as outlined under *Engine Oil and Filter Change* in this chapter.

1. Ride the motorcycle until normal operating temperature is obtained. Usually 15-20 minutes of riding is sufficient.

2. Park the motorcycle on a level surface. Support it on its sidestand.

3. Place a drain pan under the drain plug.

NOTE
Figure 26 shows the right side muffler removed for clarity. It is not necessary

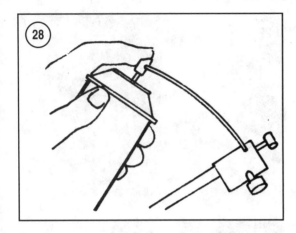

to remove the muffler to change the final drive oil level.

4. Remove the oil filler cap (A, **Figure 26**) and the drain plug (B, **Figure 26**).

5. Let the oil drain for at least 15-20 minutes.

6. Inspect the sealing washer on the drain plug; replace a damaged or missing washer.

7. Install the drain plug and washer. Tighten the drain plug to the torque specification in **Table 6**.

8. Insert a funnel into the oil filler cap hole.

9. Add the correct amount of hypoid gear oil; see **Table 7** and **Table 8**. Note that there are two different capacities—oil change and overhaul. Remove the funnel and make sure the oil level is even with the bottom of the filler cap hole (**Figure 27**).

10. Install the oil filler cap and tighten it to the torque specification in **Table 6**.

11. Test ride the motorcycle and check for oil leaks. After the test ride, recheck the oil level as described in this chapter and readjust it if necessary.

Front Fork Oil Change

Due to the inverted fork design, it is not possible to change the fork oil with the fork assembly mounted on the motorcycle. The fork leg assemblies must be partially disassembled to completely drain and refill the fork oil. Refer to Chapter Twelve.

Control Cable Lubrication

Periodically lubricate all control cables to ensure proper cable operation. Inspect the cables at this time for fraying and check the cable sheath for chaf-ing. The cables are relatively inexpensive and should be replaced if they are worn or damaged.

Control cables can be lubricated with a cable lubricant and a cable lubricator.

1. Remove the screws that clamp the throttle control/switch housing together to access the cable ends. Disconnect the cables from the throttle grip assembly.

2. Remove or disassemble those parts required to access the top end of the control cable(s).

3. Examine the exposed end of the inner cable. If it is dirty or if the cable feels gritty when moved up and down in its housing, first spray it with a lubricant/solvent such as WD-40.

4. Attach a lubricator to the cable sheath.

5. Insert the nozzle of the lubricant can in the lubricator (**Figure 28**), press the button on the can and hold it down until the lubricant begins to flow out of the other end of the cable.

> *NOTE*
> *Place a shop cloth at the ends of the cables to catch all excess lubricant that will flow out.*

6. Remove the lubricator.

7. Reconnect the throttle cable(s) and adjust the cable(s) as described in this chapter.

8. Repeat these steps for the enrichment (choke) cable.

General Lubrication Points

Table 9 lists general lubrication points.

PERIODIC MAINTENANCE

Disc Brake Fluid Level Check and Fill

Maintain the hydraulic brake fluid in the reservoirs at its maximum level. If necessary, correct the level by adding fresh DOT 4 brake fluid.

> *WARNING*
> *Use brake fluid from a sealed container marked DOT 4 (specified for disc brakes). Others may vaporize and cause brake failure. Do not intermix different brands or types of brake fluid as they may not be compatible. Do not use a silicone-based (DOT 5) brake fluid as it can cause brake com-*

ponent damage and lead to brake system failure.

CAUTION
Be careful when handling brake fluid. Do not spill it on painted or plated surfaces, as it will destroy the surface. Wash the area immediately with soapy water and thoroughly rinse it off.

The fluid level in the front brake reservoir should be above the lower level mark on the outside of the reservoir. The upper level mark is visible only when the master cylinder top cover is removed. If the brake fluid level is even with the lower level mark (**Figure 29**), add brake fluid.

On the rear master cylinder, the fluid level should be between the upper and lower reservoir level marks (A, **Figure 30**). If the fluid level is even with or lower than the lower level mark, add brake fluid.

WARNING
Use brake fluid clearly marked DOT4 from a sealed container. Other types may vaporize and cause brake failure. Always use the same brand name; do not intermix them because many brands are not compatible. Do not use silicone-based (DOT5) brake fluid, as it can cause brake component damage and lead to brake system failure.

NOTE
To control the flow of hydraulic fluid, punch a small hole into the seal of the new container of hydraulic brake fluid, next to the edge of the pour spout. This will help eliminate fluid spillage, especially while adding fluid to the small reservoirs.

1. To add brake fluid to the front master cylinder, perform the following:
  a. Park the motorcycle on level ground on the sidestand. Then position the handlebars so the brake master cylinder reservoir is level.
  b. Clean any dirt from the area around the top cover before removing the cover.
  c. Remove the screws, top cover, set plate, diaphragm and float (**Figure 31**). Add brake fluid until the level is at the upper level line (**Figure 32**) within the master cylinder body. Use new brake fluid from a sealed brake fluid container.

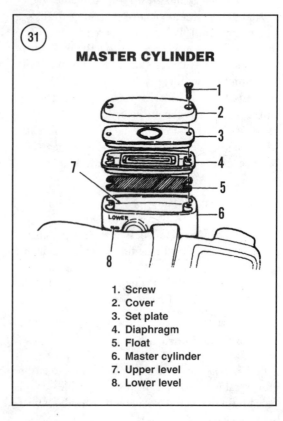

MASTER CYLINDER

1. Screw
2. Cover
3. Set plate
4. Diaphragm
5. Float
6. Master cylinder
7. Upper level
8. Lower level

d. Reinstall the cover assembly (substep c) and tighten the cover screws securely.

2. To add brake fluid to the rear master cylinder, perform the following:

a. Place the motorcycle on level ground on the side stand.

b. Remove the bolt (B, **Figure 30**) securing the master cylinder cover (C, **Figure 30**) and remove the cover.

c. Clean any dirt from the area around the master cylinder top cover before removing the cover.

d. Remove the screws, the top cover (**Figure 33**), set plate and the diaphragm. Add new brake fluid from a sealed brake fluid container. Fill it to the upper level line.

e. Reinstall the diaphragm and the top cover. Screw on the top cover securely.

Disc Brake Lines

Check the brake lines between the master cylinder and the brake calipers. If there is any leakage, tighten the connections and bleed the brakes as described under *Bleeding the System* in Chapter Fourteen. If tightening the connection does not stop the leak or if a brake line(s) is obviously damaged, cracked or chafed, replace the brake line and bleed the system as described in Chapter Fourteen.

Disc Brake Pad Wear

1. Inspect the brake pads for excessive or uneven wear, scoring and oil or grease on the friction surface.

2. Inspect the pads from the back of the caliper assembly for wear. See **Figure 34** for the front and **Figure 35** for the rear. Replace the pads if the wear line on the pads reaches the brake disc; see **Figure 36**.

3. If necessary, replace the brake pads as described in Chapter Fourteen.

CAUTION
When replacing the front brake pads, replace the brake pads in both caliper assemblies at the same time. When replacing the rear brake pads, replace both pads as a set. If not, uneven disc pressure may result.

Disc Brake Fluid Change

Every time the reservoir cap is removed, a small amount of dirt and moisture enters the brake fluid. This also occurs if a leak develops or any part of the hydraulic system is loosened or disconnected. Dirt can clog the system and cause unnecessary wear. Water in the brake fluid vaporizes at a high temperature, impairing the hydraulic action and reducing the brake's stopping ability.

To maintain peak performance, change the brake fluid at the interval listed in **Table 1**. To change brake fluid, follow the *Bleeding the Brake System* procedure in Chapter Fourteen. Continue adding new fluid to the master cylinder and bleeding old fluid out at the calipers until the fluid leaving the calipers is clean and free of contaminants.

> *WARNING*
> *Use brake fluid from a sealed container marked DOT 4 (specified for disc brakes). Others may vaporize and cause brake failure. Do not intermix different brands or types of brake fluid, as they may not be compatible. Do not use a silicone-based (DOT 5) brake fluid; it can cause brake component damage and lead to brake system failure.*

Clutch Fluid Level Check

The clutch is hydraulically operated and requires no routine adjustment.

Check the hydraulic fluid in the clutch master cylinder at the intervals in **Table 1** or whenever the level drops. Clutch bleeding and service are covered in Chapter Six.

> *CAUTION*
> *If the clutch operates correctly when the engine is cold or in cool weather, but operates erratically (or not at all) after the engine warms up or in hot weather, there is air in the hydraulic line and the clutch must be bled. Refer to Chapter Six.*

Maintain the hydraulic fluid level in the reservoir at its maximum level mark on the outside of the reservoir. The upper level mark is visible only when the master cylinder top cover is removed. If the fluid level is even with the lower level mark (A,

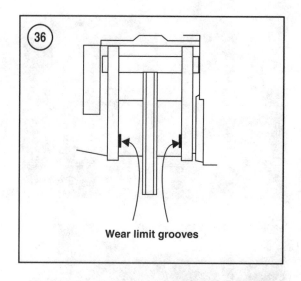

Wear limit grooves

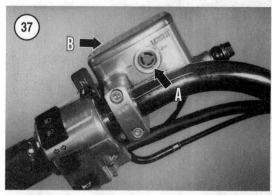

Figure 37), add brake fluid. Use DOT 4 brake fluid from a sealed container.

1. Park the motorcycle on level ground and position the handlebars so the clutch master cylinder reservoir is level.

2. Clean any dirt from the area around the top cover before removing the cover.

3. Remove the top cover (B, **Figure 37**), set plate, diaphragm and float (**Figure 31**). Add brake fluid until the level is to the upper level line within the master cylinder body.

> *WARNING*
> *Use brake fluid from a sealed container marked DOT 4. Others may vaporize and cause brake failure. Do not intermix different brands or types of brake fluid as they may not be compatible. Do not use a silicone-based (DOT 5) brake fluid as it can cause*

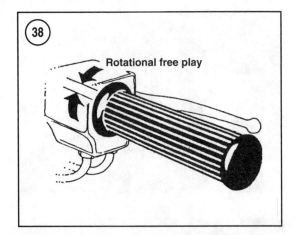

Rotational free play

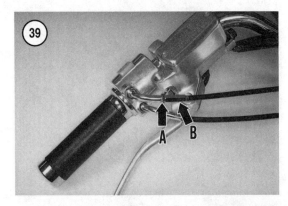

A   B

B

A

brake component damage leading to brake system failure.

CAUTION
Be careful when handling brake fluid. Do not spill it on painted or plated surfaces as it will destroy the surface. Wash the area immediately with soapy water and thoroughly rinse with clean water.

4. Reinstall the float, diaphragm, set plate and cover. Tighten the screws securely.

Clutch Hydraulic Lines

To check the clutch hydraulic lines, remove the following components:

    a. Fuel tank, see Chapter Eight.

    b. Left side cover, see Chapter Fifteen.

Check clutch lines between the master cylinder and the clutch slave cylinder. If there is any leakage, tighten the connections and bleed the clutch as described in Chapter Six. If this does not stop the leak or if a clutch line is obviously damaged, cracked or chafed, replace the clutch line and bleed the system as described in Chapter Six.

Throttle Adjustment and Operation

The throttle grip should have 2-6 mm (1/12-1/4 in.) rotational free play (**Figure 38**).

1. If minor adjustment is necessary, loosen the upper adjuster locknut (A, **Figure 39**) and turn the adjuster (B, **Figure 39**) at the throttle grip in or out to achieve proper free play rotation. Tighten the locknut.

2. If major adjustment is necessary, remove the fuel tank as described in Chapter Eight.

3. On the right side, loosen the lower adjuster locknut (A, **Figure 40**) and turn the adjuster (B, **Figure 40**) at the carburetor in or out to achieve proper free play rotation. Tighten the locknut.

4. Make sure the throttle grip rotates freely from a fully closed to fully open position. Check with the handlebar at center, at full right and at full left.

5. If removed, install the fuel tank as described in Chapter Eight.

If the correct throttle adjustment cannot be achieved, the throttle cable(s) has stretched and must be replaced.

Air Filter Element Replacement

Replace the air filter element at the interval indicated in **Table 1**.

The air filter removes dust and abrasive particles from the air before the air enters the carburetors and engine. Without the air filter, very fine particles could enter the engine and cause the rapid wear of the piston rings, cylinders and bearings and might clog small passages in the carburetors. Never operate the motorcycle without the air filter element installed.

Proper air filter servicing helps to ensure long service from the engine.

> *NOTE*
> *The viscous paper element type air filter element cannot be cleaned because the element contains a dust adhesive. Do not try to clean the element as it will be damaged and will no longer filter properly.*

1. Remove the fuel tank as described in Chapter Six.
2. Using compressed air or a soft brush, remove any debris that may have collected between the fuel tank and the air filter case cover. Do not allow any debris to fall into the air filter case after the cover has been removed.
3. Remove the screws securing the air filter case cover (**Figure 41**) and remove the cover.

> *CAUTION*
> *After the air filter element is removed in Step 4, plug the carburetor openings with clean, lint-free shop cloths.*

4. Remove the air filter element (**Figure 42**) and discard it.
5. Wipe out the interior of the air box (A, **Figure 43**) with a clean shop rag dampened with cleaning solvent. Remove any foreign matter that may have passed through the element.
6. Install by reversing these steps while noting the following:
   a. Before installing the case cover, make sure the rubber seal is in place in the groove on both the case cover (**Figure 44**) and the air box (B, **Figure 43**).
   b. Position the new air filter element with the screen side (**Figure 45**) facing down.
   c. If necessary, move the clutch hydraulic line (C, **Figure 43**) away from the air filter air box on the left side to allow the case cover to seat completely onto the air box.

Fuel Line Inspection

Inspect the fuel lines from the fuel tank to the carburetor assembly. If any are cracked or starting to

deteriorate they must be replaced. Make sure the small hose clamps are in place and secure.

> *WARNING*
> *A damaged or deteriorated fuel line presents a dangerous fire hazard if fuel should spill onto a hot engine or exhaust pipe.*

Cooling System Inspection

At the interval indicated in **Table 1**, check the following items. If the test equipment is not available, the tests can be performed by a Honda dealership, automobile dealer or radiator shop.

1. Have the radiator cap pressure tested. The specified radiator cap relief pressure is 16-20 psi (108-137 kPa). The cap must be able to hold this pressure for six seconds. Replace the radiator cap if it does not hold pressure or if the relief pressure is too high or too low.

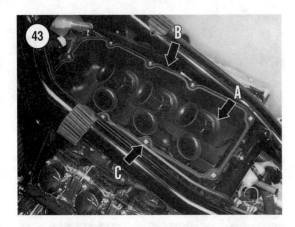

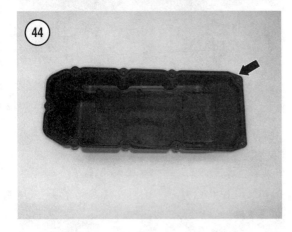

cooling system for leaks if it is unable to hold pressure.

3. Test the specific gravity of the coolant with a coolant tester to ensure adequate temperature and corrosion protection. The system must have at least a 50:50 mixture of distilled water and coolant. Never allow the mixture to become less than 40% coolant or corrosion protection will be impaired.

4. Check all cooling system hoses for damage or deterioration. Replace any hose that is questionable. Make sure all hose clamps are tight.

5. Carefully clean any debris from the radiator core. Use a whisk broom, compressed air or low-pressure water. If a small rock or other item has hit the radiator, carefully straighten out the fins with a thin flat-blade screwdriver.

> *NOTE*
> *If the radiator has been damaged across approximately 20% or more of the frontal area, repair or replace the radiator.*

Coolant Change

Drain and refill the cooling system at the interval indicated in **Table 1**.

It is sometimes necessary to drain the coolant from the system to perform a service procedure on some part of the engine. If the coolant is still in good condition, the coolant may be reused if it is kept clean. Drain the coolant into a *clean* drain pan and then pour it into a *clean* sealable container, such as a clean plastic milk or soft drink bottle and screw on the cap.

Use only a high-quality ethylene glycol coolant specifically labeled for use with aluminum engines. Do not use an alcohol-based coolant or a coolant with silicate inhibitors, as it will cause premature wear of the coolant pump seal and/or block radiator passages. Make sure the percentage of coolant to water is 50:50.

> *CAUTION*
> *If the applied test pressure exceeds the specifications in Step 2, the radiator may be damaged.*

2. Have the entire cooling system pressure tested. The entire cooling system should be pressurized up to, but not exceeding, 20 psi (137 kPa). Inspect the

> *WARNING*
> *Coolant is classified as an environmental toxic waste by the EPA and cannot be legally disposed of by flushing down a drain or pouring it onto the ground. Place coolant in a suitable container and dispose of it according to local EPA regulations. Do*

not store coolant where it is accessible to children or animals.

> **CAUTION**
> *Be careful not to spill coolant on painted surfaces; it will destroy the surface. Wash immediately with soapy water and rinse it thoroughly with clean water.*

1. Park the motorcycle on level ground. Then support it with its sidestand.

2. On models so equipped, remove the small screw securing the radiator cap.

3. Remove the radiator cap (**Figure 46**). This will speed up the draining process.

4. Place a drain pan under the engine on the left side of the motorcycle, under the water pump. Remove the drain bolt (**Figure 47**) and sealing washer on the water pump cover and let the coolant drain. Do not install the drain bolt at this time.

> **CAUTION**
> *Step 5 must be performed with the assistance of another person. Do not try this with only one person; the motorcycle may fall over due to the weight of the vehicle.*

5. Take the motorcycle off the sidestand and with an assistant's help. Tip the motorcycle from side to side to drain any residual coolant from the cooling system. Then support the motorcycle once again on its sidestand.

6. Install the drain bolt and sealing washer (**Figure 47**) on the water pump cover and tighten it securely.

7. Remove the left side cover as described in Chapter Fifteen.

8. Remove the bolt securing the reservoir tank (A, **Figure 48**). Disconnect the siphon tube and breather hose, then remove the reservoir tank (B, **Figure 48**).

9. Rinse out the reservoir tank and reinstall it onto the frame and install the mounting bolt. Reconnect the siphon and breather hoses to the correct fittings.

> **CAUTION**
> *Use only low-mineral, distilled or purified water in the cooling system. Using tap water will lead to internal radiator and engine damage.*

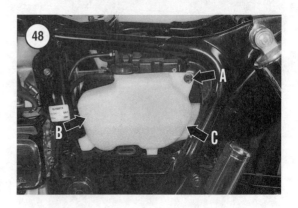

10. Refill the cooling system. Add the coolant through the radiator filler neck, then fill the reservoir tank to the upper line. Use a 50:50 mixture of coolant and distilled water.

11. Do not install the radiator cap at this time.

12. Bleed air from the cooling system as follows:

   a. Start the engine and let it run at idle speed for 2-3 minutes.

   b. Snap the throttle 3-4 times to rapidly circulate the coolant through the system thus bleeding the air from the system. Repeat this several

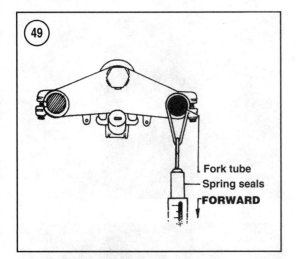

Fork tube
Spring seals
FORWARD

troubleshooting a steering or handling problem. The correct service procedures are covered in Chapter Eleven.

Steering Head Adjustment Check

Check the steering head for looseness at the intervals listed in **Table 1**, or whenever one or more of the following symptoms or conditions exist:

a. The handlebars vibrate more than normal.
b. A clicking or clunking noise is made when the front brake is applied.
c. The steering feels tight or slow.
d. The motorcycle does not steer straight on level road surfaces.

The motorcycle must be supported on a lift (see Chapter One) with the front wheel off the ground. Have an assistant sit on the seat to steady the motorcycle. Hold onto the front fork tubes and gently rock the fork assembly back and forth. If there is looseness, the steering stem bearings must be adjusted; refer to Chapter Twelve. To accurately check the steering head adjustment, perform the following.

1. Support the motorcycle on a motorcycle lift (see Chapter One) with the front tire off the ground.
2. Remove the handlebar as described in Chapter Twelve.
3. Attach a spring scale to one of the fork tubes as shown in **Figure 49**.

NOTE
The steering stem must be able to turn freely in Step 4 with no electrical harness or cable interference.

4. Center the wheel. Pull the spring scale and note the reading on the scale when the steering stem begins to turn. The correct preload adjustment reading is listed in **Table 10**. If any other reading is obtained, refer to *Steering Stem* in Chapter Twelve.
5. Install by reversing these steps.

Front Suspension Check

1. Apply the front brake and pump the fork up and down as vigorously as possible. Check for smooth operation and check for any oil leaks.
2. Make sure the upper and lower fork bridge bolts are tight (**Figure 50**).
3. Make sure the handlebar upper holder (**Figure 51**) bolts are tight.

times if necessary until there are no air bubbles in the coolant. Turn off the engine.

c. Add coolant to both the radiator and reservoir tank to bring the coolant to the correct level (C, **Figure 48**).
d. Install the radiator cap (**Figure 46**). On models so equipped, install the small screw securing the radiator cap in place.

13. Install the left side cover as described in Chapter Fifteen.
14. Test ride the motorcycle and readjust the coolant level in the reservoir tank if necessary.

Wheel Bearings

There is no recommended mileage interval for replacing the wheel bearings. Inspect the wheel bearings whenever the wheels are removed or whenever

4. Make sure the front axle bolt (A, **Figure 52**) is tight. Check the tightness of the axle pinch bolts (B, **Figure 52**) on each side.

> *CAUTION*
> *If any of the previously mentioned bolts and nuts are loose, refer to Chapter Twelve for correct procedures and torque specifications.*

Rear Suspension Check

1. Park the motorcycle on a level surface and support it on the sidestand.
2. Push hard on the rear wheel (sideways) to check for side play in the rear swing arm bushings.
3. Check the tightness of the upper and lower shock absorber mounting bolts or nuts (**Figure 53**) on each shock absorber.
4. Make sure the rear axle nut is tight (**Figure 54**).

> *CAUTION*
> *If any of the previously mentioned bolts and nuts are loose, refer to Chapter Eleven and Chapter Thirteen for correct procedures and torque specifications.*

Fasteners

Constant vibration can loosen many of the fasteners on the motorcycle. Check the tightness of all fasteners, especially those on:
1. Engine mounting hardware.
2. Handlebar and front fork assembly.
3. Gearshift lever.
4. Brake pedal and lever.
5. Exhaust system.

Sidestand Switch
System Inspection

Make sure the side stand ignition cut-off system works properly. Check as follows:
1. Park the motorcycle on its sidestand.
2. Check the spring (**Figure 55**) on the side stand. Make sure the spring is in good condition and has not lost tension. If the spring is weak or damaged, replace it before continuing with Step 3.
3. While sitting on the motorcycle, swing the sidestand down and up a few times. The side stand

should swing smoothly and the spring should provide proper tension.

4. While sitting on the motorcycle, raise the sidestand.

5. Shift the transmission into NEUTRAL.

6. Start the engine and allow it to idle. Then pull the clutch lever in and shift the transmission into first gear.

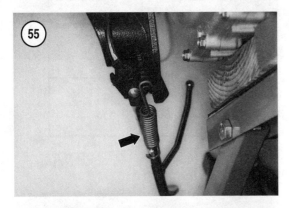

7. Lower the side stand. The engine should stop as the side stand is lowered.

8. Turn the engine off.

9. If the sidestand switch does not operate as described, inspect it as described in Chapter Nine.

REAR SUSPENSION SHOCK ADJUSTMENT

The spring pre-load can be adjusted to best suit the motorcycle's load and the ride preference. The spring pre-load can be adjusted to five different settings as follows:

    a. Position 1: for light load and smooth road conditions.

    b. Position 2: standard position.

    c. Positions 3-5: for varying heavy loads and rough road conditions.

WARNING
The spring preload adjustment must be set at the same number on both shock absorbers. If the shocks are set on different settings, it will affect the motorcycle's handling and may lead to an accident. Make sure both settings are identical on both shock absorbers.

CAUTION
To avoid internal damage to the shock absorber, rotate the adjuster slowly through all five positions in numerical sequence (1-2-3-4-5 and 5-4-3-2-1). Do not adjust directly from one to five or from five to one.

1. Support the motorcycle on its sidestand.

2. Use the pin spanner and extension bar in the motorcycle's tool kit.

3. Refer to the previous CAUTION and rotate the shock absorber adjuster (**Figure 56**) in either direction to the desired setting.

4. Repeat for the other shock absorber. Ensure both shocks are adjusted to the same setting.

TUNE-UP

Perform a complete tune-up at the interval indicated in **Table 1** for normal riding. More frequent tune-ups may be required if the motorcycle is ridden primarily in stop-and-go traffic. Refer to **Figure 57** for cylinder number location for the following procedures.

The following paragraphs discuss each phase of a proper tune-up, which should be performed in the given order. Unless otherwise specified, the engine should be thoroughly cool before starting any tune-up procedure.

Table 11 summarizes tune-up specifications.

1. Replace the air filter element.

2. Check and adjust the valve clearances.

3. Perform a compression test.

4. Check or replace the spark plugs.

5. Check the ignition timing.

6. Synchronize the carburetors.

7. Adjust the idle speed.

To perform a tune-up, the following tools are required:

1. Spark plug wrench.

2. Socket wrench and assorted sockets.

3. Compression gauge.

4. Spark plug wire feeler gauge and gapping tool.

5. Ignition timing light.

6. Tune-up tachometer.

7. Carburetor synchronization tool.

Valve Clearance Adjustment

The valve clearance is listed in **Table 11**. The exhaust valves are located at the bottom of the cylinder heads, next to the exhaust manifolds. The intake valves are located at the top of the cylinder head next to the intake manifolds.

Refer to **Figure 57** for cylinder number location.

1. Place the motorcycle on level ground on the side stand.

2. Shift the transmission into neutral.

3. Remove the cylinder head cover from each bank of cylinders as described in Chapter Four.

4. Remove the spark plug from each cylinder as described in this chapter. This will make it easier to turn the engine by hand.

5. Remove the Allen bolts securing the timing cover (**Figure 58**) and remove the cover. The O-ring seal (A, **Figure 59**) will usually stay with the timing belt cover. If it is loose, remove it at this time and keep it with the timing cover.

6. Rotate the engine *counterclockwise* as viewed from the front of the engine with the drive pulley bolt (B, **Figure 59**). Rotate the engine until the T1.2 mark on the timing plate is aligned with the index mark on the timing belt cover (**Figure 60**).

> *NOTE*
> *Check the valve clearance on the cylinders in the order listed in this procedure. Start with the No. 1 cylinder, then follow with the No. 4, No. 5, No. 2, No. 3 and the No. 6.*

7. The *No. 1 cylinder* must be at top dead center (TDC) on the compression stroke. The No. 1 cylin-

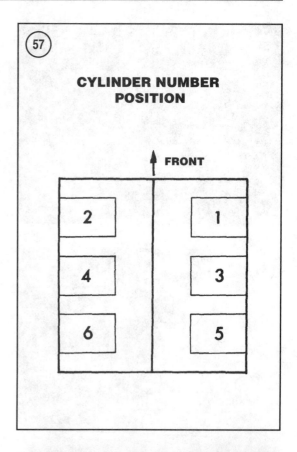

57

CYLINDER NUMBER POSITION

↑ FRONT

2		1
4		3
6		5

58

59

A

B

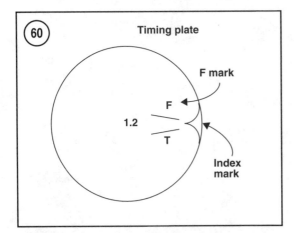

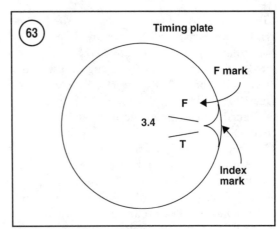

correct valve clearance is listed in **Table 11**. If the valve clearance is correct, there will be a slight resistance on the feeler gauge as it is inserted and withdrawn. If the feeler gauge passes through without any noticeable resistance or if it is difficult or impossible to insert, adjust the valve clearance.

9. To correct the clearance, perform the following:

  a. Use a wrench (A, **Figure 62**) and loosen the adjuster locknut .

  b. Use a narrow flat-blade screwdriver to turn the adjusting screw (B, **Figure 62**) in or out to achieve the correct clearance. Turn the adjuster until there is a slight resistance on the feeler gauge (C, **Figure 62**).

  c. Hold the adjuster to prevent it from turning and tighten the locknut to the torque specification in **Table 6**.

  d. Recheck the clearance to make sure the adjuster did not slip when tightening the locknut. Readjust the valve clearance if necessary.

10. Rotate the engine *counterclockwise* as viewed from the front of the engine using the drive pulley bolt (B, **Figure 59**). Rotate the engine 120° until the T3.4 mark on the timing plate is aligned with the index mark on the timing belt cover (**Figure 63**).

11. Check the valve clearance on the *No. 4 cylinder*. Perform Step 8 and, if necessary, Step 9.

12. Rotate the engine *counterclockwise* as viewed from the front of the engine using the drive pulley bolt (B, **Figure 59**). Rotate the engine 120° until the T5.6 mark on the timing plate is aligned with the index mark on the timing belt cover (**Figure 64**).

der is at TDC when both rocker arms have some valve clearance, indicating that both the intake and exhaust valves are closed. Move each rocker arm by hand. There should be some side movement. If the cylinder is not at TDC, rotate the engine *counterclockwise* 360° (one full rotation) and again align the T1.2 mark with the index mark (**Figure 60**).

8. Insert a flat feeler gauge between the rocker arm valve adjuster and the valve stem (**Figure 61**). The

13. Check the valve clearance on the *No. 5 cylinder*. Perform Step 8 and, if necessary, Step 9.

14. Rotate the engine *counterclockwise* as viewed from the front of the engine using the drive pulley bolt (B, **Figure 59**). Rotate the engine 120° until the T1.2 mark on the timing plate is aligned with the index mark on the timing belt cover (**Figure 60**).

15. Check the valve clearance on the *No. 2 cylinder*. Perform Step 8 and if necessary, Step 9.

16. Rotate the engine *counterclockwise* as viewed from the front of the engine using the drive pulley bolt (B, **Figure 59**). Rotate the engine 120° until the T3.4 mark on the timing plate is aligned with the index mark on the timing belt cover (**Figure 63**).

17. Check the valve clearance on the *No. 3 cylinder*. Perform Step 8 and if necessary, Step 9.

18. Rotate the engine *counterclockwise* as viewed from the front of the engine using the drive pulley bolt (B, **Figure 59**). Rotate the engine 120° until the T5.6 mark on the timing plate is aligned with the index mark on the timing belt cover (**Figure 64**).

19. Check the valve clearance on the *No. 6 cylinder*. Perform Step 8 and if necessary, Step 9.

NOTE
If a new O-ring seal is installed, apply a light coat of clean engine oil to it to ensure it will seal properly.

20. Make sure the O-ring seal (A, **Figure 59**) is still in place. Install the timing cover (**Figure 58**) and secure it with the Allen bolts. Tighten the bolts securely.

21. Install the spark plugs as described in this chapter.

22. Install the cylinder head cover onto each bank of cylinders as described in Chapter Four.

Compression Test

Check cylinder compression at each tune-up. Record the results and compare them at the next tune-up. A running record will show trends in deterioration so that corrective action can be taken before possible complete failure.

The results, when properly interpreted, can indicate general cylinder, piston ring and valve condition.

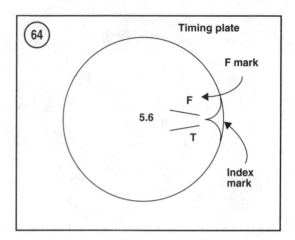

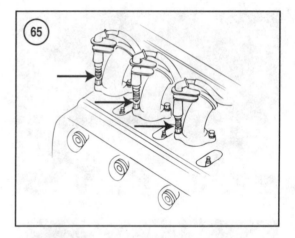

When interpreting the results, actual readings are not as important as the difference between the readings. Optimum readings should be 171 psi (1177 kPa). A maximum difference of 14 psi (1.0 kPa) between the cylinders is acceptable. Greater differences indicate worn or broken rings, leaking or sticking valves, a blown head gasket(s) or a combination of all.

If a low reading (10 percent or more) is obtained on one of the cylinders, it indicates valve or ring trouble. To determine which, insert a small funnel into the spark plug hole and pour about a teaspoon of engine oil into the cylinder. Turn the engine over once to distribute the oil, then take another compression test and record the reading. If the compression increases significantly, the valves are good but the rings are defective on that cylinder. If compression does not increase, the valves require servicing. A valve could be hanging open or a piece of carbon could be on a valve seat.

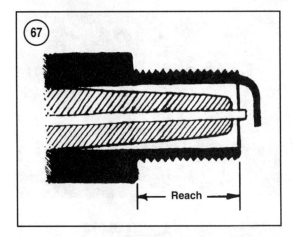

Reach

est voltage possible and the coils may overheat and be damaged.

7. Remove the tester and record the reading and the cylinder number
8. Repeat Steps 5-7 for the other five cylinders.

9. Install by reversing these removal steps.

Spark Plug Heat Range Selection

Spark plugs are available in various heat ranges, hotter or colder than plugs originally installed.

Select plugs of a heat range designed for the loads and temperature conditions under which the motorcycle will be operated.

In general, use a hot plug for low speeds, low engine loads and low temperatures. Use a cold plug for high speeds, high engine loads and high temperatures. The plug should operate hot enough to burn off deposits, but not so hot that it is damaged or causes preignition. A spark plug of the correct heat range will show a light tan color on the portion of the insulator within the cylinder after the plug has been in service.

The reach (length) of a plug is also important. A longer than normal plug could interfere with the valves and pistons, causing permanent and severe damage. Refer to **Figure 67**. Refer to **Table 11** for the recommended spark plug heat ranges.

Spark Plug Removal

The cylinders are numbered as shown in **Figure 60**. As each spark plug is removed, label it with its cylinder number.
1. On GL1500CF models, remove the radiator cover as described in Chapter Ten.
2. Disconnect the spark plug caps at the spark plugs (**Figure 68**). If the cap is stuck, twist it slightly to break it loose.

CAUTION
Whenever a spark plug is removed, dirt around it can fall into the spark plug hole. This can cause serious engine damage.

3. Use compressed air to blow away all loose debris that has accumulated in the spark plug receptacles (**Figure 69**).

1. Warm the engine to normal operating temperature. Shut off the engine. Make sure the enrichment (choke) valve is completely open and that the engine stop switch is in the OFF position.
2. Place the motorcycle on the sidestand.
3. Remove all six spark plugs as described in this chapter.
4. Reconnect the plug caps to the spark plugs and securely ground the plugs against the cylinder head as shown in **Figure 65**.
5. Connect the compression tester (**Figure 66**) to one cylinder following the manufacturer's instructions.
6. Open the throttle completely and using the starter, crank the engine over until there is no further rise in pressure. Maximum pressure is usually reached within 4-7 seconds of engine cranking.

CAUTION
Do not turn the engine over more than absolutely necessary. When spark plug leads are disconnected, the electronic ignition will produce the high-

> *NOTE*
> *Use a special spark plug socket equipped with a rubber insert that holds the side of the spark plug. This is necessary for removal and installation since the spark plugs are located within the cylinder head receptacles* **(Figure 69)**.

4. Use an 18 mm spark plug special tool and remove all spark plugs (**Figure 70**). Mark each spark plug's cylinder location.

> *NOTE*
> *If a plug is difficult to remove, apply penetrating oil around the plug base and let it soak in for 10-20 minutes.*

5. Inspect each spark plug carefully. Look for a plug with broken center porcelain, excessively eroded electrodes and excessive carbon or oil fouling. Replace such plugs. If the plugs are in good condition and they are going to be reused, regap the plugs as explained in this chapter.

> *NOTE*
> *Spark plug cleaning with a sand-blast type of device is not recommended. While this type of cleaning is thorough, the plug must be completely free of all abrasive material when finished. If not, it is possible for the cleaning material to fall into the cylinder during operation and cause damage.*

6. Also inspect the spark plug caps and secondary wires for damage. If either is damaged, the cap and secondary wire must be replaced as an assembly. The cap and secondary wire assemblies are available for each specific cylinder and are so marked next to the spark plug cap (**Figure 71**).

Gapping and Installing the Spark Plugs

Carefully adjust the electrode gap of new spark plugs to ensure a reliable, consistent spark. Use a special spark plug-gapping tool and a wire feeler gauge.

Replace all six spark plugs at the same time; all six plugs must be of the same heat range.

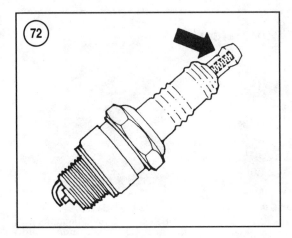

1. If installed, unscrew the small terminal end from the end of the plug (**Figure 72**). This terminal is not used.

2. Insert a wire feeler gauge between the center and the side electrode of each plug (**Figure 73**). The correct gap is listed in **Table 11**. If the gap is correct, there will be a slight resistance as the wire is pulled through. If there is no resistance, the gauge will not pass through; bend the side electrode with the gapping tool (**Figure 74**) to set the proper gap listed in **Table 11**.

3. Apply a *small* amount of antiseize compound on the threads of each spark plug prior to installing them Do not use engine oil on the threads.

> *CAUTION*
> *The cylinder head is aluminum and spark plug threads can be easily damaged by cross-threading the spark plug.*

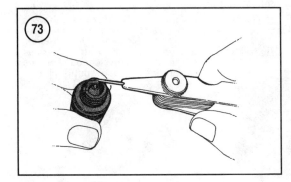

4. Install the spark plug into a spark plug wrench and extension.

5. Screw each spark plug in by hand until it seats. Very little effort is required. If force is necessary, the plug is cross-threaded; unscrew it and try again.

6. Tighten the spark plugs an additional ½ turn after the gasket has made contact with the head. If reinstalling old, regapped plugs with the old gasket, tighten only an additional 1/4 turn.

> *CAUTION*
> *Do not overtighten. This will damage the gasket and destroy its sealing ability.*

7. Install each spark plug lead. Check that each lead engages its respective spark plug.

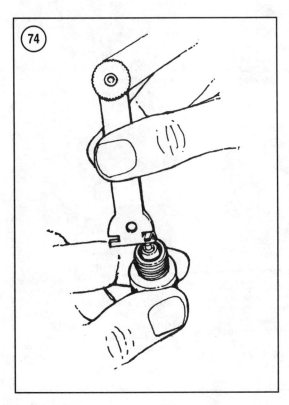

Reading Spark Plugs

A significant amount of information about engine and spark plug performance can be determined by careful examination of the spark plugs.

1. Remove the spark plugs and examine them. Compare them to **Figure 75**. If the electrodes are white or burned, the plug is too hot and should be replaced with a colder one.

A too-cold plug will have sooty or oily deposits ranging in color from dark brown to black. Replace with a hotter plug and check for excessively-rich

(75) **SPARK PLUG CONDITION**

NORMAL
- Identified by light tan or gray deposits on the firing tip.
- Can be cleaned.

GAP BRIDGED
- Identified by deposit buildup closing gap between electrodes.
- Caused by oil or carbon fouling. If deposits are not excessive, the plug can be cleaned.

OIL FOULED
- Identified by wet black deposits on the insulator shell bore and electrodes.
- Caused by excessive oil entering combustion chamber through worn rings and pistons, excessive clearance between valve guides and stems or worn or loose bearings. Can be cleaned. If engine is not repaired, use a hotter plug.

CARBON FOULED
- Identified by black, dry fluffy carbon deposits on insulator tips, exposed shell surfaces and electrodes.
- Caused by too cold a plug, weak ignition, dirty air cleaner, too rich fuel mixture or excessive idling. Can be cleaned.

LEAD FOULED
- Identified by dark gray, black, yellow or tan deposits or a fused glazed coating on the insulator tip.
- Caused by highly leaded gasoline. Can be cleaned.

WORN
- Identified by severely eroded or worn electrodes.
- Caused by normal ear. Should be replaced.

FUSED SPOT DEPOSIT
- Identified by melted or spotty deposits resembling bubbles or blisters.
- Caused by sudden acceleration. Can be cleaned.

OVERHEATING
- Identified by a white or light gray insulator with small black or gray brown spots with bluish-burnt appearance of electrodes.
- Caused by engine overheating, wrong type of fuel, loose spark plugs, too hot a plug or incorrect ignition timing. Replace the plug.

PREIGNITION
- Identified by melted electrodes and possibly blistered insulator. Metallic deposits on insulator indicate engine damage.
- Caused by wrong type of fuel, incorrect ignition timing or advance, too hot a plug, burned valves or engine overheating. Replace the plug.

76

carburetion or evidence of oil blowby at the piston rings.

If the plug has a light tan or gray colored deposit and no abnormal gap wear or electrode erosion is evident, the plug is correct for the engine operating conditions.

If the plug exhibits a black electrode tip, a damp and oily film over the firing end and a carbon layer over the entire nose, it is oil-fouled. An oil-fouled plug can be cleaned, but it is recommended to replace it.

If any one plug is found unsatisfactory, discard and replace all plugs.

Ignition Timing

The Honda Valkyrie is equipped with a capacitor discharge ignition (CDI) system consisting of an ignition control module, ignition pulse generator, three dual ignition coils and six spark plugs. This system uses no breaker points and is non-adjustable. The timing should be checked to make sure all ignition components are operating correctly.

The ignition control module (ICM) electronically varies the ignition timing in relation to engine speed and the engine coolant temperature.

Incorrect ignition timing can cause a drastic loss of engine performance and efficiency. It may also cause overheating.

Before starting this procedure, check all electrical connections related to the ignition system. Make sure all connections are tight and free from corrosion. Pay particular attention to ground connections.

Checking the ignition timing is a three-part procedure. When checking the ignition timing, perform the following procedures in order, recording each test result for a final determination.

1. Idle ignition timing inspection.
2. Coolant temperature timing shift inspection.
3. Ignition timing test results.

Idle ignition timing inspection

Refer to **Figure 57** for cylinder number locations when performing the following procedures.

A portable tachometer must be used when performing the following procedures. Install the tachometer following the manufacturer's instructions.

1. Support the motorcycle on its sidestand. Shift the transmission into NEUTRAL.
2. Remove the Allen bolts securing the timing cover (**Figure 58**) and remove the cover. The O-ring seal (A, **Figure 59**) will usually stay with the timing belt cover. If it is loose, remove it and keep it with the timing cover.
3. Start the engine and let it reach normal operating temperature. Shut the engine off.
4. Connect a timing light to the spark plugs on either the No. 1 or No. 2 cylinder (**Figure 57**) following the manufacturer's instructions.
5. Start the engine, and if necessary, adjust the idle speed to 800-1,000 rpm with the throttle stop screw (**Figure 76**).
6. Aim the timing light at the timing hole in the front cover.
7. Note the following:
   a. The F-1.2 mark should align with the index mark as shown in **Figure 60**.
   b. Turn the engine off and connect the timing light to the No. 3 or No. 4 spark plug wire (**Figure 57**). Start the engine and recheck the ignition timing. The F-3.4 mark should align with the index mark (**Figure 63**).
   c. Turn the engine off and connect the timing light to the No. 5 or No. 6 spark plug wire (**Figure 57**). Start the engine and recheck the ignition timing. The F-5.6 mark should align with the index mark (**Figure 64**).
8. Disconnect the timing light.
9. Turn off the engine.
10. Reverse to install all of the parts removed during the previous test procedures.
11. Install the timing cover and its O-ring. Tighten the Allen bolts securely.

3

Coolant temperature timing shift inspection

1. Remove the radiator as described in Chapter Ten.

2. Remove the ECT sensor from the right side of the thermostat housing.

3. Remove the right side steering head cover as described in Chapter Fifteen.

4. Disconnect the ECT two-pin blue electrical connector.

5. Reconnect the two-pin electrical connector to the ECT sensor.

6. Place the ECT sensor in ice water for approximately ten minutes.

7. Plug the ECT sensor hole in the thermostat housing and install the radiator. Refill the cooling system.

8. Start the engine and warm it to normal operating temperature.

NOTE
Allow the engine to run at idle speed when performing Step 9.

9. Connect the two pin blue connector to the ECT sensor. The engine speed should increase by 200 rpm.

10. Install the ECT sensor onto the thermostat housing.

Ignition timing test results

1. If the ignition system fails any one of these tests, test all of the ignition system components, except the ignition control unit (ICU), as described in Chapter Nine. If all of the individual components test correctly, replace the ignition control module. There is no method for adjusting ignition timing.

2. Reverse to install all of the parts removed during the previous test procedures.

Carburetor Synchronization

When the carburetors are properly synchronized the engine will warm up faster and there will be an improvement in throttle response, performance and mileage.

This procedure requires a carb-sync tool. This is a tool that measures the manifold vacuum for all cylinders simultaneously. A carb-sync tool is available from a Honda dealership (part No. 07LMJ-001000A

or M937B-021-XXXXX), motorcycle supply store or mail order firm. Make sure the tool is applicable to the Valkyrie GL1500.

1. Start the engine and let it warm up to normal operating temperature. Ten minutes of riding is usually sufficient. Shut off the engine.

2. Place the motorcycle on the sidestand.

3. Remove the screws securing the carburetor linkage cover (**Figure 77**). Remove the cover on each side.

4. Pinch the No. 6 cylinder vacuum tube (A, **Figure 78**) with a hemostat or similar clamping tool.

5. Disconnect the No. 4 cylinder vacuum tube (B, **Figure 78**) from the No. 4 cylinder intake manifold joint.

6. Remove the caps from the No.1 and No.5 cylinder intake manifold joints.

7. Disconnect the vacuum tube (**Figure 79**) from the No. 3 cylinder intake manifold joint.

8. Connect the carb-synch tubes to the No. 1, No. 3, No. 5 and No. 4 cylinders intake manifold vacuum joints

9. Start the engine, and if necessary, adjust the idle speed to 800-1000 rpm with the throttle stop screw (**Figure 76**).

NOTE
The No. 3 carburetor has no synchro-nization screw; it is the base carbure-tor that the remaining five carburetors are to be synchronized to.

10. If the difference in the two gauge readings is 40 mm Hg (1.6 in. Hg) or less, the carburetors are con-sidered synchronized. If not, proceed as follows.

11. Turn the carburetor synchronization adjusting screw (**Figure 80**, typical) on each carburetor re-quiring adjustment until the vacuum gauge readings are within specifications.

12. Open and close the throttle a few times; recheck carburetor synchronization. Readjust if necessary.

13. Disconnect the carb-synch tool and install the caps onto the No. 1 and No. 5 intake manifold joints.

14. Disconnect the vacuum tube from the No. 6 cylinder intake manifold joint.

15. Remove the cap from the No.2 cylinder intake manifold joint.

16. Connect the carb-synch tubes to the No. 2, No. 4, No. 6 and No. 3 cylinders intake manifold vac-uum joints.

17. Start the engine, and if necessary, adjust the idle speed to 800-1000 rpm with the throttle stop screw.

18. If the difference in the two gauge readings is 40 mm Hg (1.6 in. Hg) or less, the carburetors are con-sidered synchronized. If not, proceed as follows.

19. Turn the carburetor synchronization adjusting screw (**Figure 80**) on each carburetor requiring ad-justment until the vacuum gauge readings are within specifications.

20. Open and close the throttle a few times; re-check carburetor synchronization. Readjust if nec-essary.

21. Disconnect the carb-synch tool and install the cap onto the No. 2 intake manifold joint.

22. Connect the vacuum tubes to the No. 3, No. 4 and No. 6 intake manifold joints.

23. Install the carburetor linkage cover (**Figure 77**) on each side and tighten the screws securely.

24. Remove the hemostat or similar clamping tool from the No. 6 cylinder vacuum tube.

25. Restart the engine and readjust the idle speed, if necessary, as described in this chapter.

Idle Speed Adjustment

Before making this adjustment, the air filter ele-ment must be clean, the carburetors must be syn-chronized and the engine must have adequate compression. Otherwise, this procedure cannot be performed properly.

1. Start the engine. If the engine is cold, allow it to warm up to normal operating temperature.

2. Support the motorcycle on its sidestand.

3. On the right side, turn the idle speed stop screw (**Figure 76**) in to increase or out to decrease idle speed. The correct idle speed is listed in **Table 11**.

4. Open and close the throttle a few times; check for variations in idle speed. Readjust if necessary.

WARNING
With the engine idling and the trans-mission in NEUTRAL, move the han-dlebar from side to side. If idle speed increases during this movement, the throttle cables may need adjusting or they may be incorrectly routed through the frame. Correct this prob-lem immediately. Do not ride the mo-torcycle in this unsafe condition.

Table 1 SERVICE INTERVALS[1]

Initial 600 miles (1,000 km)	Change engine oil and filter Check and adjust idle speed Inspect entire brake system for leaks or damage Check and adjust rear brake pedal height Check chassis nuts and bolts for tightness Check that all cotter pins, hose clamps, safety clips and cable stays are in place and properly secured Inspect steering for looseness
Every 4,000 miles (6,400 km)	Inspect crankcase breather hose for cracks or loose hose clamps; drain out all residue[2] Check and adjust idle speed Check battery charge and condition Check fluid level in brake master cylinders Inspect brake pads for wear Check fluid level in clutch master cylinder
Every 8,000 miles (12,800 km)	Inspect fuel and vacuum lines for damage, leakage or age deterioration Replace worn or damaged hose clamps Check and adjust throttle operation and free play Check and adjust the choke Replace spark plugs Change the engine oil and filter Check and synchronize the carburetors Check and adjust idle speed Check coolant level in coolant reservoir tank Inspect entire cooling system for leaks or damage Inspect the radiator for damage and clean off debris Inspect the fuel system secondary air supply system—refer to Chapter Eight Check oil level in final drive unit Inspect entire brake system for leaks or damage Inspect the clutch hydraulic system for leaks or damage Check and adjust the rear brake light switch Check and adjust headlight aim Check the sidestand switch for loose or missing mounting bolts and a damaged switch push pin Check the sidestand switch for proper operation Check the front and rear suspension Inspect steering for looseness Check wheel bearings for smooth operation Check wheel runout Check minimum tire tread depth Check that all cotter pins, hose clamps, safety clips and cable stays are in place and properly secured
Every 12,000 miles (19,200 km)	Replace air filter element Inspect the evaporative emission control system—refer to Chapter Eight Change fluid in brake master cylinders Change fluid in clutch master cylinder Check valve clearance
Every 16,000 miles (25,600 km)	Perform a compression test
Every 24,000 miles (38,400 km)	Change coolant Change oil in final drive unit

1. This maintenance schedule should be considered as a guide to general maintenance and lubrication intervals. Harder than normal use and exposure to mud, water, sand, high humidity, etc., will naturally dictate more frequent attention to most maintenance items.
2. Increase service intervals when operating in rainy or wet conditions or when riding at full throttle for long periods.

Table 2 COOLING SYSTEM CAPACITY

	Liters	U.S. qt.	Imp. qt.
Radiator and engine	3.75	3.9	3.3
Reserve tank	1.0	1.1	0.9

Table 3 TIRE INFLATION PRESSURE (COLD)[1]

Load	Air pressure
Up to 200 lb. (90 kg)	
Front	33 psi (225 kPa)
Rear	33 psi (225 kPa)
Maximum load limit[2]	
Front	33 psi (225 kPa)
Rear	36 psi (250 kPa)
Maximum weight capacity	
GL1500C, GL1500CT	396 lbs (180 kg)
GL1500CF	414 lbs (188 kg)

1. Tire inflation pressure for original equipment tires. Aftermarket tire inflation pressure may vary; refer to manufacturer's instructions.
2. Maximum load limit includes total weight of motor accessories, rider(s) and luggage.

Table 4 STATE OF CHARGE

Specific gravity	State of charge
1.110-1.130	Discharged
1.140-1.160	Almost discharged
1.170-1.190	1/4 discharged
1.200-1.220	½ charged
1.230-1.250	3/4 charged
1.260-1.280	Fully charged

Table 5 ENGINE OIL CAPACITY

	Liters	U.S. quarts	Imp. quarts
At oil and filter change	3.7	3.9	3.3
At engine disassembly	4.3	4.5	3.8

Table 6 TIGHTENING TORQUES

	N•m	in.-lb.	ft.lb
Oil filter	10	88	–
Engine drain plug	34	–	25
Oil pressure switch	12	106	–
Valve adjuster locknut	23	–	17
Spark plugs	12	106	–
Final drive unit			
Filler cap	12	106	–
Drain plug	20	–	14

3

Table 7 FINAL DRIVE GEAR OIL CAPACITY

	mL	U.S. oz.	Imp. oz
Oil change	150	5.1	5.3
After overhaul	170	5.7	6.0

Table 8 RECOMMENDED OIL AND FLUIDS

Item	Lubricant
Engine oil	See text
Final drive gear	Hypoid gear oil, SAE 80
Front fork	Honda Suspension Fluid SS-7
Brake and clutch fluid	DOT 4
Speedometer cable	Light weight oil
Throttle and choke cables	Light weight oil
Grease	NGLI No. 2

Table 9 GENERAL LUBRICATION POINTS

Brake lever pivot
Brake pedal pivot
Center stand pivot
Clutch lever pivot
Drive shaft pinion joint splines and seal
Drive shaft, universal joint
Final driven flange splines
Front and rear wheel bearings
Front and rear wheel bearing dust seal lips
Side stand pivot
Speedometer drive
Steering head bearings
Steering head bearing dust seal
Swing arm pivot bearings
Swing arm pivot bearing dust seals
Throttle grip sliding surface
Windshield adjuster tension plate pivot

Table 10 STEERING STEM PRELOAD

GL1500C and GL1500CT	0.8-0.12 kgf (1.8-2.6 lbf)
GL1500CF	0.5-1.0 kgf (1.1-2.2 lbf)

Table 11 TUNE-UP SPECIFICATIONS

Valve clearance (cold)	
Intake	0.15 mm (0.006 in.)
Exhaust	0.22 mm (0.009 in.)
Cylinder compression—standard	171 psi (1177 kPa)
Spark plug type	
Standard heat range	NGK DPR7EA-9 or ND X22EPR-U9
Cold weather*	NGK DPR6EA-9 or ND X20EPR-U9
Extended high-speed riding	NGK DPR8EA-9 or ND X24EPR-U9
Spark plug gap	0.8-0.9 mm (0.031-0.035 in.)
Ignition timing	
F mark	3.5° BTDC @ 800-1000 rpm
Vacuum advance	
Starts	See text
Stops	See text
Idle speed	800-1000 rpm
Firing order	1-4-5-2-3-6
*Temperature below 41° F (5° C).	

3

CHAPTER FOUR

ENGINE TOP END

The Honda Valkyrie 1500 cc engine is a horizontally opposed six-cylinder, liquid-cooled, four-stroke design with a single overhead camshaft per cylinder head.

The three cylinder pairs are positioned 180° apart. The cylinder pairs are No. 1 and No. 2; No. 3 and No. 4; No. 5 and No. 6.

The engine fires every 120° of crankshaft rotation.

This chapter provides service and overhaul procedures for the engine top end that can be performed with the engine installed in the frame. Chapter Five covers engine removal and installation and service procedures to the engine lower end.

Service procedures for all models are virtually the same. Where differences occur, they are identified.

Tables 1-3 are located at the end of this chapter.

ENGINE PRINCIPLES

Figure 1 explains basic four-stroke operating principles. This will be helpful when troubleshooting or repairing the engine.

ENGINE ROTATION

Engine rotation is *counterclockwise* when viewed from the front of the engine.

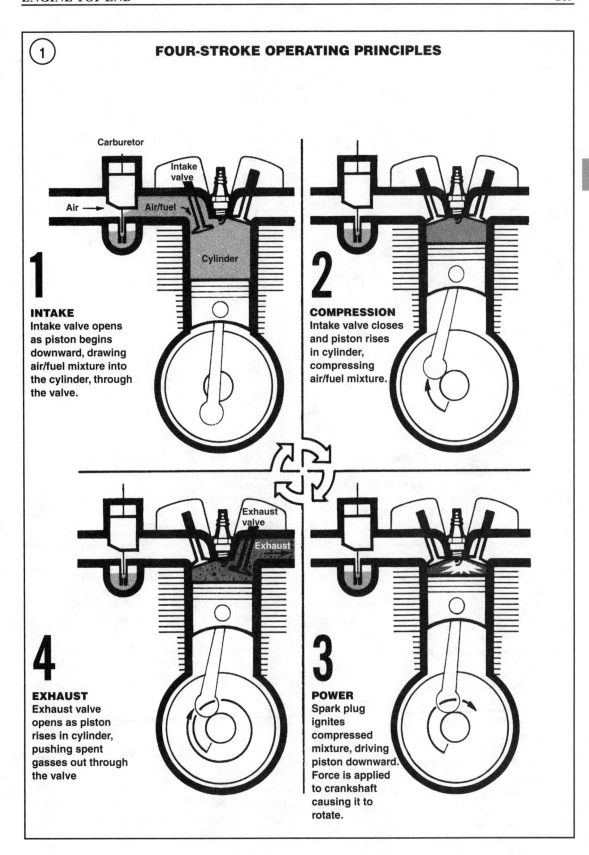

FOUR-STROKE OPERATING PRINCIPLES

1 INTAKE
Intake valve opens as piston begins downward, drawing air/fuel mixture into the cylinder, through the valve.

2 COMPRESSION
Intake valve closes and piston rises in cylinder, compressing air/fuel mixture.

4 EXHAUST
Exhaust valve opens as piston rises in cylinder, pushing spent gasses out through the valve

3 POWER
Spark plug ignites compressed mixture, driving piston downward. Force is applied to crankshaft causing it to rotate.

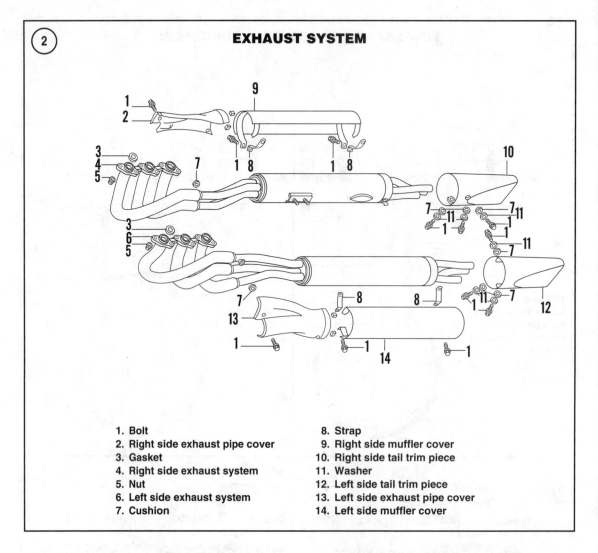

EXHAUST SYSTEM

1. Bolt
2. Right side exhaust pipe cover
3. Gasket
4. Right side exhaust system
5. Nut
6. Left side exhaust system
7. Cushion
8. Strap
9. Right side muffler cover
10. Right side tail trim piece
11. Washer
12. Left side tail trim piece
13. Left side exhaust pipe cover
14. Left side muffler cover

SERVICING ENGINE IN FRAME

The following components can be serviced while the engine is installed in the frame (the vehicle's frame is an excellent holding fixture for breaking loose stubborn bolts and nuts):

1. Exhaust system.
2. Timing belts.
3. Cylinder heads, camshafts and rocker arms.
4. Front cover.
5. Carburetor assembly (covered in Chapter Eight).

> **WARNING**
> *The Honda 1500 Valkyrie is not equipped with a centerstand. A motorcycle lift (see Chapter One) is an essential piece of equipment if the motorcycle is going to be serviced.*

> *The motorcycle is heavy and must be supported securely when performing many of the service procedures in this book, even wheel removal. Do not try to balance the motorcycle on makeshift jacks or wooden blocks. This unsafe condition may result in vehicle damage and/or personal injury.*

EXHAUST SYSTEM

The exhaust system should be free of corrosion, leaks, binding, grounding or excessive vibration. Loose, broken or misaligned clamps, brackets or pipes must be serviced as necessary to keep the exhaust system in a safe operating condition.

Refer to **Figure 2** for this procedure.

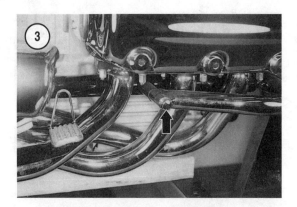

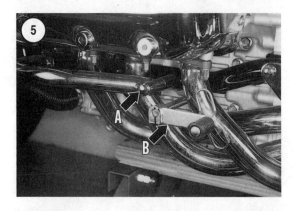

WARNING
The exhaust system is extremely hot under normal operating conditions. Do not work on the exhaust system until it has cooled down to room temperature.

1. Place the motorcycle on its sidestand.

2. On the right side, remove the bolt (**Figure 3**) and collar (**Figure 4**) securing the engine guard to the engine.

3. On the left side, perform the following:

   a. Remove the bolt (A, **Figure 5**) and collar (**Figure 6**) securing the engine guard to the engine

   b. Remove the clamping bolt on the gearshift pedal (B, **Figure 5**) and remove the pedal. Screw the bolt back onto the pedal to avoid misplacing it.

   c. Remove the bolts securing the driver's left footpeg (**Figure 7**) and remove the footpeg.

4. Loosen the two nuts (**Figure 8**) securing each section of the exhaust pipes to the cylinder head.

5. Loosen and remove the nuts (**Figure 9**) securing the muffler to the frame bracket.

6. Support the exhaust system (**Figure 10**) and re-move the six nuts securing the exhaust pipes to the cylinder head. Lower the exhaust system straight down off the cylinder head studs. Remove the ex-haust system from the engine and frame.

7. Remove the gaskets (**Figure 11**).

8. Repeat Steps 4-7 for the right exhaust system if necessary.

9. Inspect the exhaust system as described in this chapter.

10. If necessary, remove the bolts, washers and lockwashers securing the covers or tail trim pieces to the exhaust system and remove them. Tighten the bolts and nuts securely.

11. Installation of the exhaust pipe is the reverse of these steps. Note the following:

    a. Install a new gasket (**Figure 11**) at each ex-haust port.

    b. Tighten the mounting nuts to the torque speci-fication in **Table 3**.

    c. Align the split mark on the gearshift pedal with the index mark on the gearshift shaft (**Figure 12**) and install the pedal. Tighten the bolt securely.

    d. Start the engine and check for leaks. Tighten any nuts if necessary.

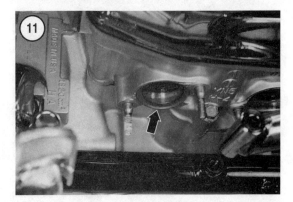

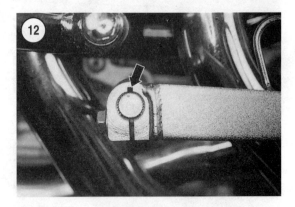

Inspection

1. Check the exhaust pipes for cracks or areas that are starting to rust through. A damaged or leaking pipe must be replaced.

2. Check the mufflers for dents or other damage.

3. Check the clamps securing the covers for dam-age, corrosion or weakness. Replace the clamps as required.

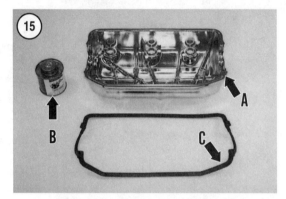

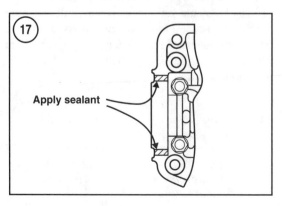

4. Replace fasteners that are bent, damaged or severely corroded.

CYLINDER HEAD COVER

Removal/Installation

1. Place the vehicle on level ground on the sidestand.
2. Shift the transmission into neutral.
3. Remove the bolts securing the cylinder head rear cover and remove the rear cover (**Figure 13**) and gasket.
4. Place a drain pan under the cylinder head cover, as some oil will drain out after the cover is removed.
5. Remove the rubber plug from each cylinder head cover mounting bolt.
6. Using a crisscross pattern, loosen and remove the cylinder head cover mounting bolts (**Figure 14**).
7. Remove the cylinder head cover and gasket.
8. Inspect the cylinder head cover gasket. Replace as follows if it is torn or starting to harden.
   a. Remove the old gasket from the cover.
   b. Clean off all old gasket sealer residue from the cover groove (A, **Figure 15**).
   c. Apply a light coat of No. 1521 sealant or Gasgacinch (B, **Figure 15**) to the cylinder head cover groove following the manufacturer's instructions.
   d. Install the new gasket (C, **Figure 15**) into the groove and press it in until it is completely seated around the entire perimeter (**Figure 16**).
9. Installation is the reverse of removal. Note the following:
   a. Apply a light coat of sealant to the mating surface at each end of the cylinder head as shown in **Figure 17**. Refer to **Figure 18** and **Figure 19**.

b. Make sure the rubber gaskets (**Figure 20**) are in place under each bolt head flange.

c. Install the cover bolts and tighten in a criss-cross pattern to the torque specification in **Table 3**. Install the rubber plugs.

d. If necessary, install a new gasket (**Figure 21**) on the rear cover.

e On the right side cover make sure the two wires are not pinched under the cover.

f. Check the engine oil level and top it off if necessary.

CAMSHAFT TIMING BELTS AND DRIVEN PULLEYS

The camshaft timing belts and driven pulleys can be removed with the engine installed in the frame.

Refer to **Figure 22** when servicing the camshaft timing belts.

Removal

> *CAUTION*
> *Do not allow the timing belts to become contaminated with oil, as it will cause the belts to swell. If contaminated, the belt will not maintain correct camshaft timing.*

> *NOTE*
> *This procedure is shown with the fork assembly removed for clarity. It is not necessary to remove the fork assembly for this procedure.*

1. Place the motorcycle on a motorcycle lift. Refer to *Motorcycle Lift* in Chapter One.

2. Shift the transmission into neutral.

3. Disconnect the negative battery cable as described in Chapter Three.

4. On GL1500CF models, remove the radiator cover from each side as described in Chapter Fifteen.

5. Using a crisscross pattern, loosen and remove the timing belt cover bolts. Remove the cover (**Figure 23**) and gasket.

6. Remove the spark plugs as described in this chapter. This will make it easier to rotate the engine by hand.

7. Rotate the engine *counterclockwise* as viewed from the front of the engine using the drive pulley bolt (**Figure 24**). Rotate the engine until the T1.2

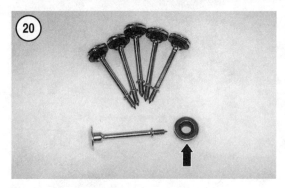

mark on the timing plate is aligned with the index mark on the timing belt cover (**Figure 25**).

8. The UP marks on both camshaft pulleys should be facing up; see **Figure 22** and **Figure 26**. If not, rotate the crankshaft an additional 360° and recheck the T1.2 timing mark alignment and the UP marks on the camshaft pulleys.

> *CAUTION*
> *In the following steps, left side and right side references refer to the engine as it sits in the motorcycle's frame. Clockwise and counterclockwise are references as viewed from the front of the motorcycle.*

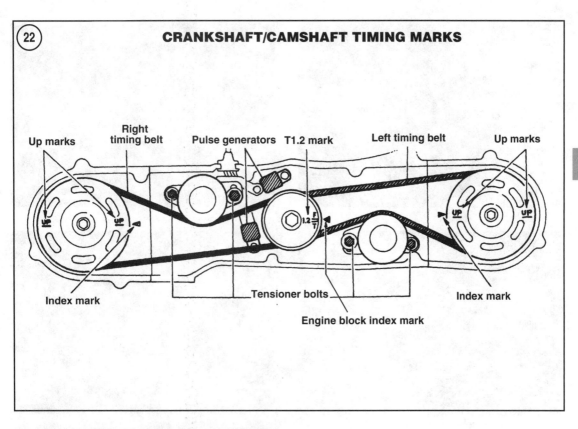

CRANKSHAFT/CAMSHAFT TIMING MARKS

Up marks · Right timing belt · Pulse generators · T1.2 mark · Left timing belt · Up marks · Index mark · Tensioner bolts · Index mark · Engine block index mark

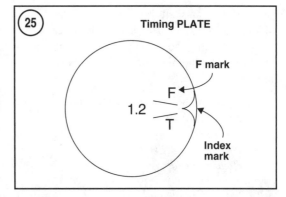

Timing PLATE

F mark

1.2

F

T

Index mark

9. Mark the camshaft timing belts with an R (right side) (**Figure 27**) or L (left side) (**Figure 28**) and an arrow indicating the direction of rotation. The top surfaces of both timing belts move toward the right side of the engine.

10. Loosen the bolts securing each belt tensioner assembly (**Figure 29**).

CAUTION
To prevent damage to the timing belts, do not use any sharp object to pry the belts off of the pulleys.

CAUTION
Do not rotate the crankshaft or camshaft driven pulleys after the timing belts have been removed. If the pulleys are rotated, the valve faces will contact the tops of the pistons and damage both parts.

11. Remove the right side belt tensioner assembly (**Figure 30**) and spring.

12. Remove the right side timing belt (**Figure 31**).

13. Remove the bolts securing both pulse generators (**Figure 32**). Remove both pulse generators and move them out of the way.

14. Remove the left side belt tensioner assembly (**Figure 33**) and spring.

15. Remove the left side timing belt (**Figure 34**).

> *CAUTION*
> *After the timing belts have been removed, handle them carefully. To prevent damage to the inner fiberglass material in the belts, do not twist or bend the belts.*

16. If removing the cylinder head(s), loosen the bolt (**Figure 35**) securing each camshaft driven pulley to the camshaft(s). Hold the pulley with a holder to prevent it from turning (**Figure 36**). Remove the Woodruff key from each camshaft and keep it with the driven pulley.

17. If removing the camshaft, rocker arms and/or cylinder head, remove the pulley cover as follows:

    a. Remove the bolts (A, **Figure 37**) securing the cover and remove the cover and side gasket (B, **Figure 37**).

    b. On the right side cover, release the wire harness from the clamp (A, **Figure 38**).

    c. Repeat for the left side cover.

Inspection

> *CAUTION*
> *Do not lubricate the tensioners. Do not allow any oil or solvents within the timing belt cover area, as it will damage the timing belts.*

1. Inspect the timing belts (**Figure 39**) for wear or damage.

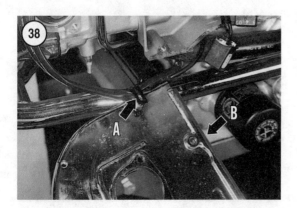

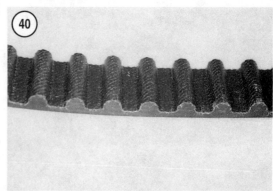

2. Check for cracks, worn teeth (**Figure 40**) or oil contamination. If the teeth are worn, check the cogs on the crankshaft drive pulley assembly (**Figure 41**) and the camshaft driven pulleys (**Figure 42**) for wear or damage. Replace the pulley(s) as necessary.

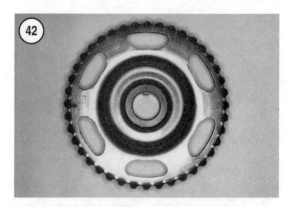

3. Check the Woodruff keyway (**Figure 43**) in the camshaft driven pulleys for wear or damage. Replace the pulley if necessary.

4. Check the camshaft driven pulley teeth (**Figure 44**) for wear or damage. Replace the pulley if necessary.

5. Inspect the belt tensioners (**Figure 45**). They must rotate smoothly with no binding. Replace if necessary.

6. Make sure the belt tensioner springs (**Figure 46**) are not stretched or damaged. Replace if necessary.

7. Check the pulley cover seal (**Figure 47**) in the cylinder head; replace the seal if it is worn or damaged.

Installation

1. If the pulley covers were removed, install them as follows:

a. Apply gasket sealer onto the rubber cover gasket and fit the gasket onto the side of the pulley cover (B, **Figure 38**).

b. The left and right pulley covers are different. The left side pulley is marked M20-L. The right side pulley is marked M20-R (C, **Figure 37**). Install the pulley covers onto the correct sides.

c. Apply ThreeBond TB1342, or Loctite 242 (blue), onto the pulley cover mounting bolts. Install the bolts (A, **Figure 37**) and tighten securely.

d. On the right cover, attach the wire harness onto the clamp (A, **Figure 38**).

2. If the crankshaft drive pulley assembly was not removed, make sure the pulley mounting bolt (**Figure 48**) is tight and that the pulleys and belt guides are tight. If any one part is loose, remove and then install the pulley assembly as described in this chapter.

3. If the camshaft driven pulleys were removed, perform the following:

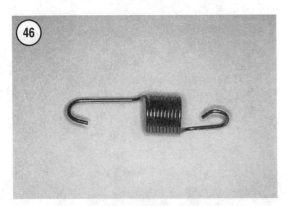

CAUTION
If the pulleys or guide plates loose, do not tighten the bolt. The guide plates may be out of alignment.

a. Install the Woodruff key on each camshaft. The Woodruff key should be facing straight up at the 12 o'clock position.

b. Align the pulley keyway with the Woodruff key and install the pulley (**Figure 49**).

c. Slide the pulley mounting bolt washer onto the bolt so the washer's chamfered side faces out (away from the bolt) (**Figure 50**). Thread the bolt into the camshaft.

CAUTION
Do not rotate the camshaft driven pulleys while tightening the bolts. If

the pulleys are rotated, the valve faces will contact the tops of the pistons and damage both parts.

d. Hold the pulley with a universal holding tool (**Figure 36**) and tighten the pulley mounting bolts to the torque specification in **Table 3**.

4. Check that the T-1.2 timing mark on the timing plate aligns with the fixed index mark on the cylinder block. See **Figure 51**.

> *CAUTION*
> *The belt tensioner bearings are sealed. Do not try to oil the bearings; the oil will contaminate the belts, causing belt damage.*

5. If removed, install both tensioners and position the springs with their open hook ends facing away from the engine case; see A, **Figure 52** (left side) and A, **Figure 53** (right side). Install the tensioner washer away from the pivot bolt side; see B, **Figure 52** (left side) and B, **Figure 53** (right side). Tighten the bolts only enough to allow the tensioner assembly to pivot freely at this time. The bolts will be tightened later in this procedure.

> *NOTE*
> *Refer to **Figure 54** when setting the camshaft timing in the following steps.*

6. The UP mark on each camshaft pulley must be facing up. Align the camshaft pulley timing mark with the alignment mark on the belt cover.

> *CAUTION*
> *To avoid damaging the timing belts, do not use any sharp object to install the belts onto the pulleys.*

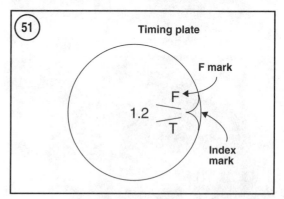

Timing plate

F mark

1.2

F

T

Index mark

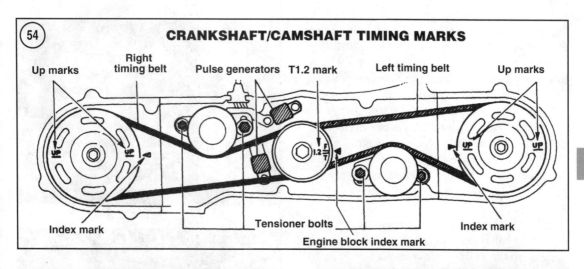

CRANKSHAFT/CAMSHAFT TIMING MARKS

54

Up marks · Right timing belt · Pulse generators · T1.2 mark · Left timing belt · Up marks · Index mark · Tensioner bolts · Engine block index mark · Index mark

55

57

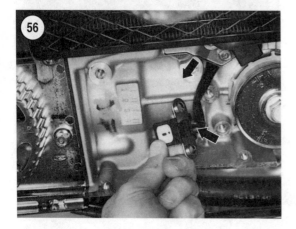

56

7. Refer to the marks made on the belts in *Removal* and install the left side camshaft timing belt (**Figure 55**).

8. Apply clockwise tension on the left side driven pulley to obtain some play in the tensioner. Then install the pulse generators (A, **Figure 57**). Tighten

the pulse generator bolts securely. Seat the pulse generator rubber plug (B, **Figure 57**) into the engine block securely.

NOTE
Make sure the locating collars on the mounting bracket (Figure 56) are indexed properly into the receptacle in the engine. This is necessary for proper ignition operation.

9. Refer to the marks made on the belts in *Removal* and install the right camshaft timing belt (**Figure 58**).

NOTE
Make sure the direction arrow made on the used belts points in the direction of engine rotation. The top surfaces of both timing belts move toward the right side of the engine.

10. Place a wrench on the crankshaft bolt (**Figure 59**) and turn the crankshaft *clockwise* 90°. Stop, then turn the crankshaft *counterclockwise* 90°. At this point, all timing marks must align as follows:

   a. The T1.2 timing mark on the drive pulley timing plate should align with the index mark on the cylinder block. See **Figure 51**.

   b. The UP mark on both camshaft pulleys must be facing up and aligned with the two index marks as shown in **Figure 54** and **Figure 60**.

11A. If the timing marks align, continue with Step 12.

11B. If the timing marks do not align, the belt position on the pulleys may be off by one or more teeth. Reposition the timing belt(s) and repeat Step 10. Repeat this step until all timing marks align.

CAUTION
Serious engine damage may result from improper camshaft, timing belt and crankshaft alignment. Recheck these steps several times to make sure alignment is correct.

12. The right side tensioner bolts are labeled A and B in **Figure 61**. Tighten bolt A and then bolt B to the torque specification in **Table 3**.

NOTE
The timing belt tensioners must be adjusted with the engine cold (at room temperature).

13. Push up on the *lower run* of the right side timing belt mid-way between the two pulleys with 2 kg (4.4 lb.) of force (**Figure 61**). There should be 5-7 mm (3/16-17/64 in.) of play.

14. If adjustment is necessary, perform the following:

   a. Loosen the right-hand tensioner bolts.

   b. Pivot the tensioner up or down to achieve the correct amount of play in the timing belt.

   c. Tighten the tensioner bolts as described in Step 12. Recheck tension on the belt and readjust if necessary.

15. Make sure the UP mark on the right side camshaft pulley is facing up (**Figure 60**).

16. The left side tensioner bolts are labeled A and B in **Figure 61**. Tighten bolt A and then bolt B to the torque specification in **Table 3**.

17. Push down on the *upper run* of the left side timing belt mid-way between the two pulleys with

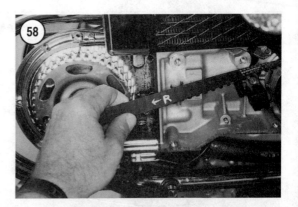

2 kg (4.4 lb.) of force (**Figure 61**). There should be 5-7 mm (3/16-17/64 in.) of play (**Figure 62**).

18. If adjustment is necessary, perform the following:

   a. Loosen the left side tensioner bolts.

   b. Pivot the tensioner up or down to achieve the correct amount of play in the timing belt.

   c. Tighten the left side tensioner bolts as described in Step 16. Recheck belt tension and readjust if necessary.

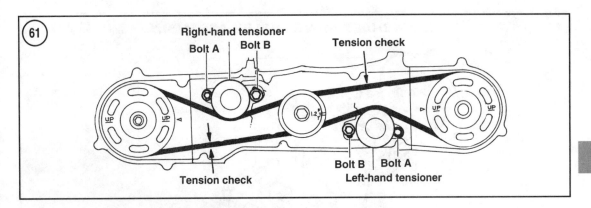

Right-hand tensioner
Bolt A   Bolt B   Tension check

Tension check

Bolt B   Bolt A
Left-hand tensioner

4

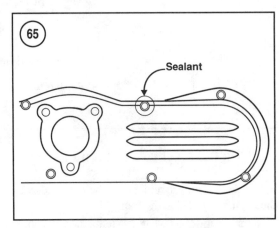

Sealant

19. Make sure the UP mark on the left side camshaft pulley is facing up (**Figure 61** and **Figure 63**).

20. Install the six spark plugs.

21. Inspect the gasket (**Figure 64**) on the timing belt cover. Replace if necessary.

22. Apply a light coat of sealant to the single bolt threads on the left side (**Figure 65**) prior to installation.

23. Install the timing belt cover and install the bolts (**Figure 66**). Tighten the bolts securely.

24. On GL1500CF models, install the radiator covers as described in Chapter Ten.

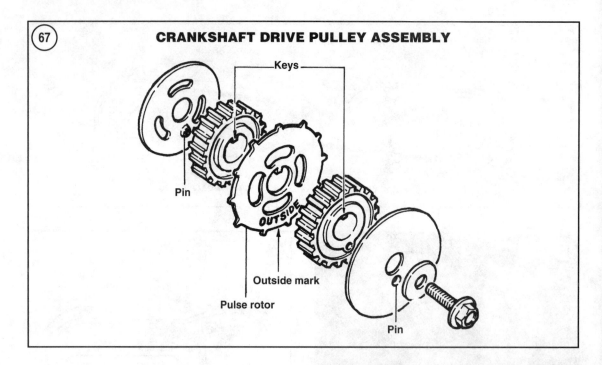

67

CRANKSHAFT DRIVE PULLEY ASSEMBLY

Keys

Pin

OUTSIDE

Outside mark

Pulse rotor

Pin

CRANKSHAFT DRIVE PULLEY

The drive pulley assembly can be removed with the engine installed in the frame.

Refer to **Figure 67** when servicing the crankshaft drive pulley.

Removal

1. Place the motorcycle on a motorcycle lift. Refer to *Motorcycle Lift* in Chapter One.
2. Remove the drive pulley mounting bolt (A, **Figure 68**) and washer.
3. Remove the right and left side timing belts as described in this chapter.
4. Remove the drive pulley assembly (B, **Figure 68**) in the order shown in **Figure 67**.

Installation

Refer to **Figure 67** for this procedure.
1. Lay out the parts in the order shown in **Figure 67**.
2. Slide on the notched timing belt guide so that the pin on the guide faces out (away from engine).
3. Slide the first drive gear onto the crankshaft, align the gear's key with the crankshaft keyway and slide it onto the crankshaft. Mate the hole in the

68

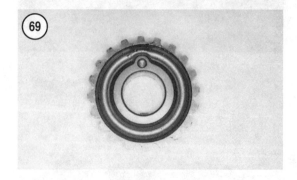

69

back of the gear (**Figure 69**) with the pin on the timing belt guide.

4. Position the pulse rotor (**Figure 70**) with its OUTSIDE mark facing out. Align the notch on the

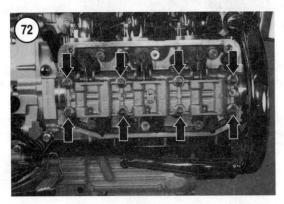

7. Push all of the components onto the crankshaft, then install the bolt (A, **Figure 68**) and washer. Tighten the bolt to the torque specification in **Table 3**.

CAMSHAFT AND ROCKER ARM ASSEMBLIES

The rocker arm assemblies are identical and will fit on either cylinder head. Either disassemble only one cylinder head's rocker arm assembly at a time or store the parts in separate boxes marked with an R (right side cylinder head) or L (left side cylinder head). All parts should be reinstalled on the same cylinder head from which they were removed during assembly. This is especially true on a high-mileage engine.

The camshafts are *not identical* due to the end for the driven pulley attachment. The camshafts must be installed on the correct side, otherwise the driven pulley cannot be attached.

Removal

1. Place the motorcycle on a motorcycle lift. Refer to *Motorcycle Lift* in Chapter One.
2. Remove the cylinder head rear cover and the cylinder head cover as described in this chapter.
4. Remove the timing belts and camshaft driven pulleys as described in this chapter.
5. Remove the driven pulley cover (**Figure 71**) as described under *Camshaft Timing Belts and Driven Pulleys* in this chapter

> *CAUTION*
> *Step 6 describes procedures for removing the camshaft holder to prevent if from binding when its mounting bolts are loosened. If the bolts are not loosened and removed as described in Step 6, damage to the camshaft holder and/or camshaft may occur.*

6. Using a crisscross pattern, loosen the camshaft holder bolts (**Figure 72**) in two to three stages. Hold onto the camshaft holder and remove the bolts.

> *CAUTION*
> *Do not let the camshaft fall out in the next step. The camshaft will be free when the camshaft holder is removed from the cylinder head.*

rotor with the crankshaft keyway and slide the pulse rotor onto the crankshaft.

5. Position the second drive gear with the pin hole in the gear (**Figure 69**) facing out. Slide the second drive gear onto the crankshaft, align the gear's key with the crankshaft keyway and slide it onto the crankshaft.

6. Position the belt guide/timing plate with the timing marks facing out and slide it onto the crankshaft; see B, **Figure 68**. Align the pin on the back of the timing plate with the hole in the drive gear.

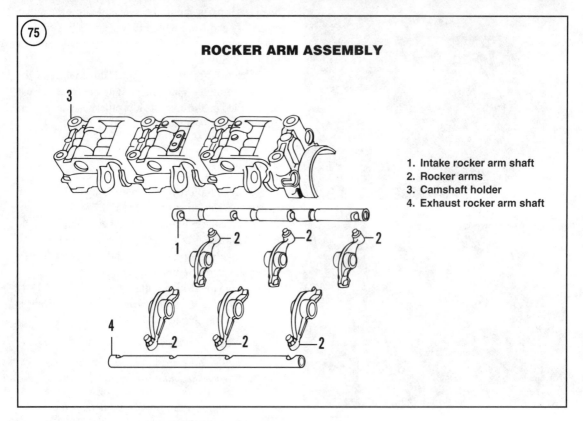

ROCKER ARM ASSEMBLY

1. Intake rocker arm shaft
2. Rocker arms
3. Camshaft holder
4. Exhaust rocker arm shaft

7. Hold onto the driven pulley end of the camshaft and remove the camshaft holder (**Figure 73**) and the camshaft (A, **Figure 74**) from the cylinder head. Account for the seal and end cap (B, **Figure 74**) at the ends of the camshaft.

8. Account for the locating dowels in the cylinder head (C, **Figure 74**).

9. Mark the camshaft holder with R (right side cylinder head) or L (left side cylinder head). The camshaft holder must be reinstalled onto the same cylinder head during assembly.

Disassembly

Refer to **Figure 75** for this procedure.

CAUTION
In Step 1 and Step 2, mark all parts removed as sets (cylinder number and intake or exhaust) so they will be reinstalled in their original positions. All rocker arms are identical (same Honda part No.). Place the rocker arms and rocker arm shafts into sepa-

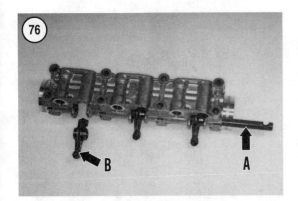

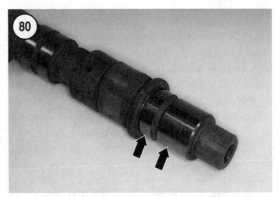

rate containers marked with the cylinder numbers, intake and exhaust.

> *NOTE*
> *The intake valve rocker arms are located at the top of the camshaft holder and the exhaust valve rocker arms are located at the bottom.*

1. Slowly withdraw the exhaust rocker arm shaft (A, **Figure 76**) and remove each rocker arm (B, **Figure 76**) from the camshaft holder.

2. Slowly withdraw the intake rocker arm shaft and remove each rocker arm from the camshaft holder.

3. Keep all parts in two separate sets (**Figure 77**).

Camshaft Inspection

> *NOTE*
> *Do not intermix the parts when cleaning and inspecting them in the following steps.*

1. Clean the camshaft in solvent and dry them with compressed air.

2. Apply compressed air into all oil control holes (**Figure 78**) in the camshaft. If necessary, clean the camshaft again in solvent and dry with compressed air.

3. Check the camshaft bearing journals (A, **Figure 79**) for wear and scoring.

4. Even if the camshaft bearing journal surfaces (**Figure 80**) appear to be satisfactory, with no visible signs of wear, the camshaft bearing journals must be measured with a micrometer (**Figure 81**). Record each camshaft journal measurement on a piece of paper. Replace the camshaft(s) if they are worn beyond the service limits in **Table 2**.

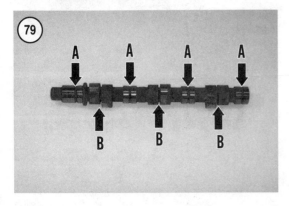

5. Check the camshaft lobes for wear (B, **Figure 79**). The lobes should not be scored and the edges should be square. Slight damage may be removed with a silicon carbide oilstone. Use No. 100-200 grit initially, then polish with No. 280-320 grit.

6. Measure the camshaft lobes with a micrometer (**Figure 82**). Replace the camshaft(s) if they are worn beyond the service limits in **Table 2**.

7. Measure camshaft runout with a dial indicator and V-blocks. Use one-half of the total runout and compare to the service limits in **Table 2**.

8. Check the camshaft bearing journals in the cylinder head (**Figure 83**) and camshaft holder (**Figure 84**) for wear and scoring. They should not be scored or excessively worn. If necessary, replace the cylinder head and cam holder as a matched set. If the journals do not show any visual damage, check the camshaft bearing clearance as described in this chapter.

Camshaft Bearing Clearance Measurement (Bore Gauge Measurement)

This procedure determines camshaft bearing journal clearance with a bore gauge. This procedure takes into account that the camshaft bearing journal outer diameter is within specification.

1. If removed, install all locating dowel pins into the cylinder head.

2. Install the camshaft holder onto the cylinder head. If the camshaft holder has been disassembled, it is not necessary to reassemble it.

3. Install all camshaft holder bolts and tighten them in 2-3 stages in a crisscross pattern to the torque specification in **Table 3**.

4. Using a bore gauge, measure the inside diameter of the bearing surfaces at each journal. Record each journal measurement.

5. If worn to the service limits in **Table 2**, replace the camshaft holder and cylinder head as a set. They cannot be replaced separately.

6. If the measurements are within specification for each journal, subtract the camshaft journal outside diameter from the camshaft bearing journal inside diameter and compare to the service limit in **Table 2**. If the camshaft journal outside diameter and the camshaft bearing journal inside diameter measurements were within specification as measured previously, the bearing clearance should also be within specification. If not, carefully measure each journal

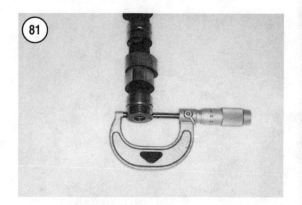

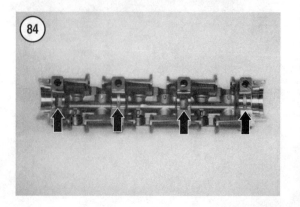

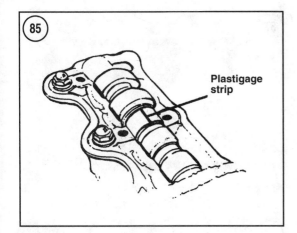

Plastigage strip

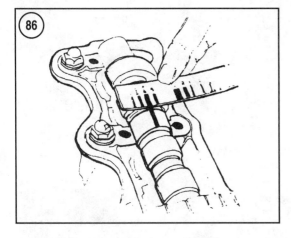

and bearing again. If the camshaft journals are within specifications, the bearing holder and cylinder head must be replaced as a set.

7. Loosen the camshaft holder bolts in a crisscross pattern in 2-3 steps. Remove the bolts and the camshaft holder.

Camshaft Bearing Clearance Measurement (Plastigage Measurement)

This procedure requires using a Plastigage set. The camshaft must be installed into the head. Prior to installation, wipe all oil residue from each camshaft journal and bearing.

NOTE
This procedure is easier to perform if the cylinder head is removed from the engine. If the cylinder head(s) is installed on the engine, make sure the

Plastigage does not slide off the camshaft journal.

1. Install all locating dowels into the cylinder head.

2. Wipe all oil from the cam bearing journals prior to using the Plastigage. Install the camshaft and hold it in place.

3. Place a strip of Plastigage on top of each camshaft bearing journal (**Figure 85**), parallel to the cam journal.

4. Hold the camshaft in place and install the camshaft holder onto the cylinder head. If the camshaft holder has been disassembled, it is not necessary to reassemble it.

5. Install all camshaft holder bolts and tighten in 2-3 stages in a crisscross pattern to the torque specification in **Table 3**.

CAUTION
Do not rotate the camshaft with the Plastigage in place.

6. Loosen the camshaft holder bolts in a crisscross pattern in 2-3 steps. Hold onto the camshaft and remove the camshaft holder.

7. Measure the width of the flattened Plastigage according to the manufacturer's instructions (**Figure 86**). Compare the Plastigage measurement with **Table 2**.

8. If the clearance is equal to or greater than the wear limit in **Table 2**, measure the camshaft journals with a micrometer as described in this chapter. If the camshaft bearing journals are less than specified, the camshaft will have to be replaced. If the camshaft bearing journals are within specification, the bearing holder and cylinder head must be replaced as a set.

CAUTION
Remove all Plastigage material from the camshaft bearing journals and camshaft holder surfaces. This material must not be left in the engine, as it can plug an oil orifice and cause severe engine damage.

Rocker Arm Inspection

Perform this procedure to inspect the rocker arms and rocker arm shafts for wear.

NOTE
*Do not intermix the parts (**Figure 87**)
when cleaning and inspecting them in
the following steps.*

1. Clean the parts in solvent and dry them with
compressed air.
2. Inspect the rocker arm pad where it contacts the
cam lobe (A, **Figure 88**) and where it contacts the
valve stem (B, **Figure 88**). If the pad is scratched or
unevenly worn, inspect the cam lobe for scoring,
chipping or flat spots. Replace the rocker arm if it is
defective.
3. Inspect the bore (C, **Figure 88**) in the rocker arm
for scoring or damage.
4. Measure the rocker arm inside diameter (C, **Figure 88**) with a snap gauge.
   Replace the rocker arm if the bore diameter exceeds the wear limit in **Table 2**.
5. Inspect the rocker arm shaft for severe wear or
damage. Replace the rocker arm shaft, if damaged.
6. Measure the rocker arm shaft outer diameter
(**Figure 89**) with a micrometer.
   Replace the rocker arm shaft if it is less than the
wear limit in **Table 2**.

Camshaft Holder Inspection

1. Clean the part in solvent and dry it with compressed air.
2. Make sure all oil control holes are clear. Clear
them with compressed air if necessary.
3. Inspect the camshaft holder for cracks or wear
(**Figure 90**).
4. If the camshaft holder is worn or damaged, it
must be replaced along with the cylinder head, as
both parts are sold as a set.

Assembly

   Refer to **Figure 75** for this procedure.

CAUTION
*During assembly, make sure to install
all parts into their correct locations in
the camshaft holder.*

NOTE
*Refer to **Figure 91** for cylinder number locations. The intake valve rocker
arms are located at the top of the cam-*

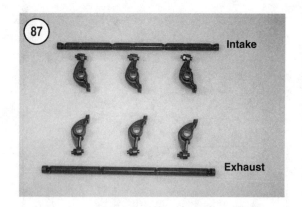

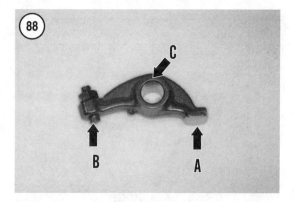

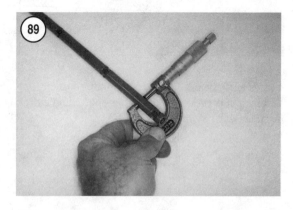

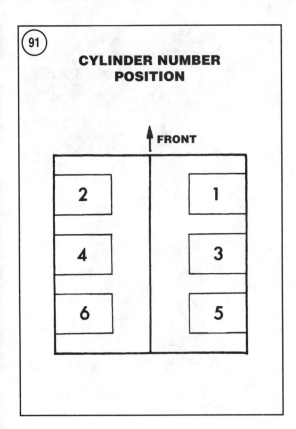

CYLINDER NUMBER POSITION

↑ FRONT

2	1
4	3
6	5

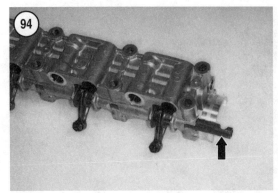

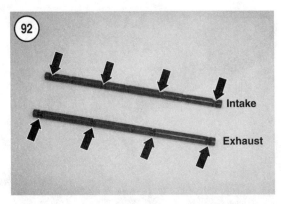

Intake

Exhaust

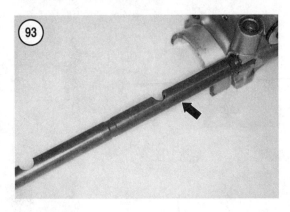

shaft holder and the exhaust valve rocker arms are located at the bottom.

1. Clean all camshaft holder passages and holes with compressed air.

2. Coat all rocker arm bores, needle bearings, and rocker arm shafts with molybdenum disulfide oil or assembly oil.

NOTE
*The intake rocker arm shaft has four notches (**Figure 92**), these must align with the camshaft holder bolts.*

NOTE
Either set of rocker arms can be installed first; there is no set order.

3. Slide the rocker arm into the camshaft holder as shown in **Figure 93** and stop before it enters the first rocker arm notch.

4. Slide a correct rocker arm into position in the camshaft holder.

5. Slide the rocker arm shaft into the camshaft holder until it engages with the first rocker arm, then stop.

6. Repeat Steps 4 and 5 for each rocker arm and rocker arm shaft. Do not push the rocker arm shaft all the way in at this time (**Figure 94**).

7. Align the notch in the end of the rocker arm shaft (A, **Figure 95**) with the camshaft holder bolt hole (B, **Figure 95**). This alignment is required so that each rocker arm notch is aligned with each bolt hole in the camshaft holder (**Figure 96**).

8. Repeat for the other set of rocker arms.

Installation

NOTE
*The camshaft holder appears to be symmetrical and could be installed upside down. To identify the top (intake) from the bottom (exhaust) sides, refer to the dowel pin receptacles (**Figure 97**) in the camshaft holder. The dowel pins fit into the bottom side of the camshaft holder.*

NOTE
When installing the camshaft holder, do not push it hard against the camshaft; this will cause the camshaft to rotate (the keyway will not be facing up), thus changing the camshaft timing.

1. Coat all camshaft lobes and bearing journals with molybdenum disulfide grease or assembly oil. Also coat the bearing surfaces in the cylinder head and camshaft bearing holders.

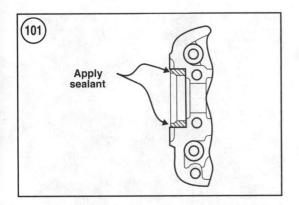

Apply sealant

4

NOTE
The left and right side camshafts are different. Install the camshaft with the R mark on the right side; install the camshaft with the L mark on the left side, as shown in **Figure 98**.

2. Pack the inner seal lip cavity with grease.

3. Install a *new* seal (**Figure 99**) onto the end of the camshaft. Apply a light coat of ThreeBond 1104 sealant to the outer edges of the seal.

4. Apply a light coat of ThreeBond 1104 sealant to the camshaft holder mating surfaces (**Figure 100**) and onto the cylinder head at each end as shown in **Figure 101**.

5. If removed, install the locating dowels into the cylinder head. Refer to **Figure 102** and **Figure 103**.

6. Apply a light coat of ThreeBond 1104 sealant to the camshaft end cap. Position the end cap with the sealed side facing out and install it into the cylinder head (**Figure 104**).

7. Position the cam so the keyway is toward the front (**Figure 105**) and install the camshaft into the cylinder head.

8. Position the keyway on the front of the camshaft in line with the mating surface of the cylinder (pointing UP at the 12 o'clock position toward the intake ports). See **Figure 105**.

9. Have an assistant hold the camshaft in place and check that the seal (A, **Figure 106**) and end cap (B, **Figure 106**) are installed properly. Reposition if necessary.

10. Refer to marks ® or L) made during removal and install the correct camshaft holder (**Figure 107**) onto the cylinder head.

11. Hold the camshaft holder in place and install the camshaft holder mounting bolts finger-tight (**Figure 72**).

NOTE
*The end cap (**Figure 108**) must be installed into the camshaft holder and cylinder head so it will not contact the cylinder head rear cover when it is installed.*

12. Check that the front seal and the end cap are seated squarely between the cylinder head and camshaft holder. Continue to check that these two parts remain correctly in place during the bolt tightening procedure.

13. Using a crisscross pattern (from the center outward), tighten the bolts 1/8 to 1/4 turn at a time (**Figure 109**). While tightening the bolts, check that the camshaft keyway is still facing UP (**Figure 110**)—it must remain in the UP position during the bolt tightening procedure, reposition it if necessary. Tighten the eight camshaft holder bolts to the torque specification in **Table 3**.

14. Install the cylinder head cover and rear cover as described in this chapter. Tighten the bolts securely.

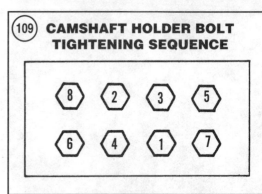

CYLINDER HEADS

Removal

1. Remove the camshafts and camshaft holders as described in this chapter.

2. Remove the exhaust system as described in this chapter.

3. Drain the cooling system as described in Chapter Three.

4. Place the motorcycle on a motorcycle lift. Refer to *Motorcycle Lift* in Chapter One.

5. Remove the bolts securing the engine guard and remove the guard.

6. Pull up and disconnect the spark plug caps (**Figure 111**). Move the caps and wires out of the way.

4

7. If the carburetor assembly is installed on the engine, support the assembly with a bungee cord—insert the cord underneath the intake manifolds, connecting both ends of the cord to the frame.

8. Remove the nuts securing the intake manifolds (A, **Figure 112**).

9. Disconnect and remove the secondary air pipes (B, **Figure 112**) from the cylinder head as described in Chapter Eight.

10. Remove the Allen bolts (A, **Figure 113**) and the bolt securing the air pipe to the cylinder head.

11. Loosen and remove the single 6 mm cylinder head bolt (B, **Figure 113**)

12. Loosen the cylinder head bolts (9 mm) in 2-3 stages in a crisscross pattern (**Figure 114**). Remove the bolts and washers (**Figure 115**).

NOTE
The cylinder heads are identical and can be installed on either side of the engine. The cylinder heads must be installed on the side from which they were removed. Mark them with an R (right side) or L (left side) so they can be identified during reassembly.

13. Loosen the head by tapping around the perimeter with a soft-faced mallet. Then remove the cylinder head from the cylinder block and coolant pipe.

14. Remove the head gasket and dowel pins from the crankcase and coolant pipe.

NOTE
After the cylinder head is removed, check both mating surfaces and the head gasket for signs of coolant leakage. A warped cylinder head or cylinder block can cause a blown gasket.

15. Remove the oil control orifice (**Figure 116**) from the cylinder block.

> *NOTE*
> *Store the oil control orifice in a plastic bag to avoid misplacing it.*

16. Repeat Steps 5-15 for the other cylinder head, if necessary.

Cylinder Head Inspection

1. Remove all traces of gasket material from the cylinder head and the cylinder block mating surfaces.
2. *Without* removing the valves, use a wire brush to remove all carbon deposits from the combustion chambers.
3. Examine the spark plug threads in the cylinder head for damage. If thread damage is minor or if the threads are dirty or clogged with carbon, use a spark plug thread tap to clean the threads following the manufacturer's instructions. If thread damage is severe, install a steel thread insert. Thread insert kits can be purchased at automotive supply stores, or have the inserts installed by a Honda dealership or machine shop.

> *NOTE*
> *When using a tap to clean the spark plug threads, apply an aluminum tap cutting fluid or kerosene to the tap's threads during use.*

> *NOTE*
> *Aluminum spark plug threads are commonly damaged due to galling, cross-threading and over tightening. To prevent galling, apply an anti-seize compound to the plug threads before installation and do not overtighten.*

4. After all carbon is removed from the combustion chambers and valve ports, clean the entire head in solvent.

> *CAUTION*
> *If the cylinder head was bead-blasted, make sure to clean the head thoroughly with solvent and then with hot water and soap. Residual grit seats in small crevices and other areas and can be difficult to remove. Also clean*

each exposed thread with a tap to remove grit between the threads. Any grit left in the engine will contaminate the oil and cause premature piston, ring and bearing wear.

5. Examine the piston crowns. The crowns should show no signs of wear or damage. If a piston crown appears pecked or spongy-looking, check the spark plug, valves and combustion chamber for aluminum deposits. If these deposits are noted, the cylinder is suffering from excessive heat caused by a lean fuel mixture or preignition.

> *CAUTION*
> *Do not clean the piston crowns with the pistons still installed. Carbon scraped from the tops of the pistons can fall between the cylinder wall and piston rings and into the crankcase. Because carbon grit is very abrasive, premature engine wear will result. If the piston crowns have heavy carbon deposits, remove the pistons as described in this chapter, then clean them. Excessive carbon build-up re-*

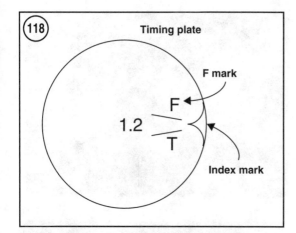

Timing plate

F mark

1.2

F

T

Index mark

duces the piston's ability to transfer heat away from the piston, resulting in increased compression and possible detonation and overheating.

6. Do not remove the carbon ridge at the top of the cylinder bore (**Figure 117**).

7. Check the cylinder head for rough or damaged gasket surfaces and cracks. Check for cracks in the combustion chamber and exhaust ports. A cracked head must be replaced.

8. After the head has been thoroughly cleaned, place a straightedge across the gasket surface at several points (crosswise and lengthwise). Measure for warp by inserting a flat feeler gauge between the straightedge and the cylinder head at each location. Compare with the warp limit in **Table 2**. If service is required, refer the work to a Honda dealership.

9. Measure cylinder block warpage as described in Chapter Five. If service is required, refer the work to a Honda dealership.

Installation

1. Prior to installing the cylinder head, perform the following steps to ensure maximum cylinder head bolt thread engagement and accurate cylinder head torque readings:

   a. Make sure the cylinder head and cylinder block mating surfaces are clean. Thoroughly remove all traces of old gasket residue from both surfaces.

   b. Clean the cylinder head bolts in solvent and dry thoroughly.

   c. Check the bolts and bolt threads for damage. Replace bent or damaged bolts. If the threads on a bolt are damaged, do not try to repair them with a die, as a portion of the thread will probably break off. Replace the bolt with an exact replacement.

   d. Check all of the cylinder head bolt washers (**Figure 115**) for cracks or cupping. Each washer must be flat.

   e. Cover the cylinder openings and blow out the cylinder block bolt holes with compressed air. Clean the threads with the correct size tap. Then use compressed air to remove all residue from the bolt holes.

   f. Check the dowel pins for rust or other debris. If the cylinder head was difficult to remove, there may have been rusted or damaged dowel pins. Replace the dowel pins if necessary.

2. To keep the valves from contacting the pistons, perform the following:

   a. Make sure the T1.2 drive pulley timing mark is aligned with the fixed index mark on the cylinder block (**Figure 118**).

   b. If the marks are not aligned, use the bolt on the crankshaft drive pulley (**Figure 119**) to rotate the crankshaft until the T1.2 timing mark (**Figure 118**) on the timing plate aligns with the fixed index mark on the cylinder block. Also make sure that the UP marks on both camshaft pulleys are facing up; see **Figure 54** and **Figure 120**. If not, rotate the crankshaft an additional 360° and recheck the T1.2 timing mark alignment and the UP marks on the camshaft pulleys.

   c. When the marks are properly aligned, use the bolt on the end of the crankshaft to rotate the crankshaft 40° clockwise to lower the No. 1

4

and No. 2 pistons 10-15 mm (0.4-0.6 in.) from the top cylinder surface. See **Figure 117**.

3. Install a new O-ring seal on the coolant pipe, then apply a light coat of clean engine oil to it.

4. Insert the oil control orifice into the cylinder block (**Figure 116**).

5. If removed, insert the two dowel pins into the cylinder block (**Figure 121**).

6. Install a new head gasket (**Figure 122**) onto the cylinder block. Align the gasket with the two dowel pins. Do *not* use any type of sealant on the head gasket.

7. Apply molybdenum disulfide grease to the 9 mm cylinder head bolt threads and to the underside of the bolt heads.

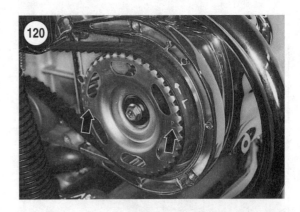

NOTE
Install the cylinder head onto its original side of the engine.

8. Place the cylinder head onto the cylinder block, engaging the cylinder head with the two dowel pins and the coolant pipe. Install a washer onto each 9 mm cylinder head bolt (**Figure 115**) and install the bolts finger tight. Then install the single 6 mm cylinder head bolt (B, **Figure 113**) finger tight.

CAUTION
Use an accurate torque wrench when tightening the cylinder head bolts in Step 9.

9. Tighten the 9 mm cylinder head bolts in 2-3 stages in the torque sequence shown in **Figure 123**. Tighten to the torque specification in **Table 3**.

10. Tighten the 6 mm bolt (B, **Figure 113**) to the torque specification in **Table 3**.

11. Use the bolt (**Figure 119**) on the crankshaft drive pulley to rotate the crankshaft *counterclockwise* until the piston is at the top of its stroke and the T1.2 timing mark (**Figure 118**) on the timing plate aligns with the fixed index mark on the cylinder block. Also make sure the timing mark on the crankshaft pulley is at the 12 o'clock position.

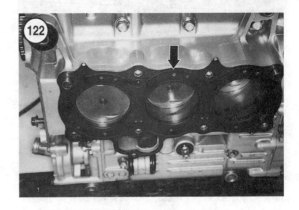

12. Install the secondary air pipes using new O-ring seals, as described in Chapter Eight.

13. Remove the b cord from around the intake manifolds.

14. Lower the carburetor assembly and intake manifolds onto the cylinder head.

15. Install the intake manifold bolts, making sure that the bolts align correctly with the cylinder head

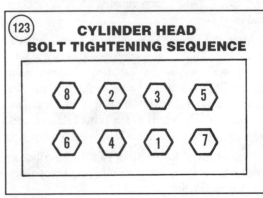

CYLINDER HEAD
BOLT TIGHTENING SEQUENCE

8   2   3   5

6   4   1   7

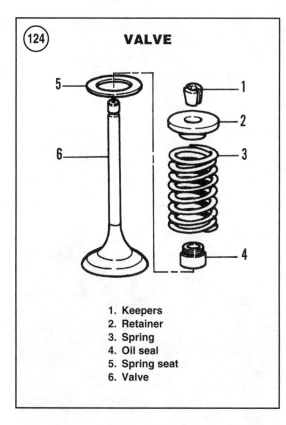

VALVE

5
6

1
2
3
4

1. Keepers
2. Retainer
3. Spring
4. Oil seal
5. Spring seat
6. Valve

bolt holes. Tighten the manifold bolts to the toque specification in **Table 3**.

16. Install the camshaft and camshaft holder as described in this chapter.

17. Install the exhaust system as described in this chapter.

18. Connect the spark plug caps (**Figure 111**) to each spark plug.

19. Repeat this procedure for the other cylinder head if necessary.

20. Install the engine guard and tighten the bolts securely.

21. Refill and bleed the cooling system as described in Chapter Three.

22. Remove the motorcycle from the lift.

VALVES AND VALVE COMPONENTS

Precision valve service requires special tools. The following procedures describe how to check for valve component wear and to determine what type of service is required. In most cases, valve troubles are caused by poor valve seating, worn valve guides and burned valves. A valve spring compressor is required to remove and install the valves.

Refer to **Figure 124** for this procedure.

1. Remove the cylinder head as described in this chapter.

2. Install a valve spring compressor squarely over the valve retainer with other end of tool centered against the valve head.

3. Tighten the valve spring compressor until the valve keepers separate (**Figure 125**). Lift the valve keepers out through the valve spring compressor with needle nose pliers or a magnet.

4. Gradually loosen the valve spring compressor and remove it from the head. Remove the retainer (**Figure 126**).

5. Remove the valve spring (**Figure 127**).

> *CAUTION*
> *Remove any burrs from the valve stem grooves before removing the valve (**Figure 128**); otherwise, the valve guides can be damaged.*

6. Push the valve (**Figure 129**) out and remove it.

7. Pull the oil seal (**Figure 130**) off of the valve guide and discard it.

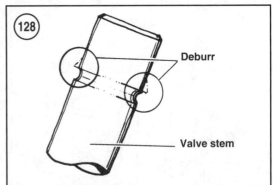

Deburr

Valve stem

8. Remove the lower spring seat (**Figure 131**).

> *CAUTION*
> *All component parts of each valve as-*
> *sembly remain together. Do not inter-*
> *mix components from other valves or*
> *excessive wear may result.*

9. Repeat Steps 2-8 to remove remaining valves.

Inspection

1. Clean the valves in solvent. Do not gouge or damage the valve seating surface.

2. Inspect the contact surface of each valve for burning (**Figure 132**). Remove minor roughness and pitting by lapping the valve as described in this chapter. Excessive unevenness to the contact surface is an indication that the valve is not serviceable.

3. Inspect the valve stems for wear and roughness. Then measure the valve stem outer diameter with a micrometer (**Figure 133**) and record the measurement. Compare the stem diameter to the specifications in **Table 2** and discard the valve if the stem diameter is less than the service limit.

4. Working from the combustion side of the cylinder head, remove all carbon and varnish from the valve guides with a stiff spiral wire brush before checking wear. Honda recommends removing carbon with a 5.5 mm valve guide reamer (Honda part No. 07984-2000001 or 07984-200000C).

> *NOTE*
> *If the required measuring devices are*
> *not available, proceed to Step 7.*

5. Measure the inner diameter of the valve guide using a small hole gauge. Measure at top, center and

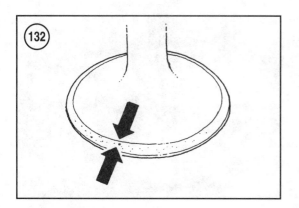

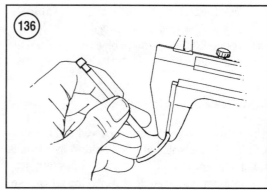

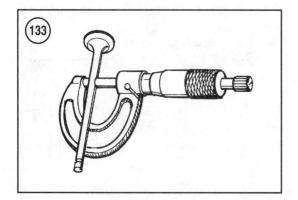

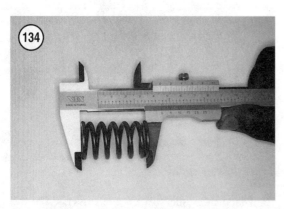

bottom. Then measure the hole gauge using a micrometer and compare the diameter to the specifications in **Table 2**. Replace the valve guide if the diameter exceeds the wear limit.

6. Subtract the measurement made in Step 3 from the measurement made in Step 5 above. The difference is the valve guide-to-valve stem clearance. See **Table 2** for the correct clearance. Replace any guide or valve that is not within tolerance. Valve guide replacement is described later in this chapter.

7. Measure the valve spring free length with a vernier caliper (**Figure 134**) and check against the specification in **Table 2**. Replace the spring if its free length is less than the service limit. Replace defective springs as a set.

8. Check the valve spring retainer and valve keepers. If they are in good condition, they may be reused.

9. Inspect the valve seats (**Figure 135**). If worn or burned, they may be reconditioned as described in this chapter. Seats and valves in near-perfect condition can be reconditioned by lapping with fine carborundum paste. Check as follows:

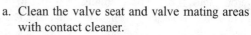

a. Clean the valve seat and valve mating areas with contact cleaner.

b. Coat the valve seat with machinist's blue (gear marking compound) or Dykem.

c. Install the valve into its guide and rotate it against its seat with a valve lapping tool. See *Valve Lapping* in this chapter.

d. Lift the valve out of the guide and measure the seat width with a vernier caliper (**Figure 136**).

e. The seat width for intake and exhaust valves should measure within the specifications in **Table 2** all the way around the seat. If the seat width exceeds the service limit (**Table 2**), regrind the seats as described in this chapter.

f. Remove all machinist's blue residue from the seats and valves.

Valve Guide Replacement

The valve guides must be removed and installed with special tools that are available from a Honda dealership. The required tools are listed as follows:

a. 5.5 mm valve guide driver (Honda part No. 07742-0010100).

b. 5.5 mm valve guide reamer (Honda part No. 07984-200000B or 07984-200000C).

1. Place the new valve guides in a freezer for 30 minutes.

NOTE
The freezing temperature will slightly reduce the guide's overall diameter while the hot cylinder head is slightly large due to expansion. This will make valve guide installation easier.

2. Measure the height of the valve guide from the cylinder head surface with a vernier caliper (**Figure 137**) and record the distance. Repeat for each valve guide.

CAUTION
Do not heat the cylinder head with a torch—never bring a flame into contact with the cylinder head. The direct heat may warp the cylinder head.

3. The valve guides are installed with a slight interference fit. The cylinder head must be heated to a temperature of approximately 130-140° C (275-290° F) in a shop oven or on a hot plate. Do not heat the cylinder head beyond 150° C (300° F). Heat sticks, available at most welding supply stores, can be used to accurately monitor cylinder head temperatures.

WARNING
Wear heavy gloves when performing this procedure—the cylinder head will be very hot.

4. Remove the cylinder head from the oven or hot plate and place onto wooden blocks with the combustion chamber facing *up*.

5. Drive the old valve guide straight out from the combustion chamber side of the cylinder head with the valve guide driver.

6. Reheat the cylinder head to the specified temperature.

7. Remove the cylinder head from the oven or hot plate and place it on wooden blocks with the combustion chamber facing *down*.

8. Remove the new valve guide from the freezer.

CAUTION
Failure to apply fresh engine oil to both the new valve guide and the guide bore in the cylinder head will result in damage to the cylinder head as well as the valve guide.

9. Apply fresh engine oil to the new valve guide and the guide bore in the cylinder head.

NOTE
The same Honda special tool is used for both removal and installation of the valve guide.

10. Using the same valve guide driver, drive the new valve guide from the rocker arm side of the cylinder head that distance from the cylinder head to the top of the valve guide is 18.5 mm (0.73 in.). See **Figure 137**.

11. Repeat for each valve guide.

12. After the cylinder head has cooled to room temperature, ream the new valve guides as follows:

a. Coat the valve guide and valve guide reamer with cutting oil.

b. Ream the valve guide by rotating the reamer in its cutting direction only. Do not turn the reamer in its non-cutting direction.

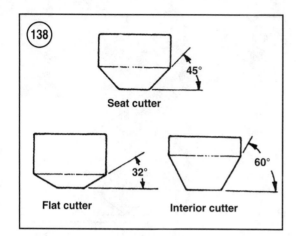

(138)

45°

Seat cutter

32°

Flat cutter

60°

Interior cutter

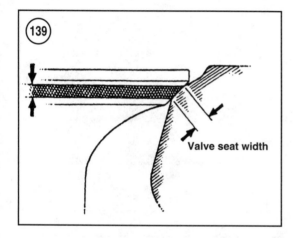

(139)

Valve seat width

c. Measure the valve guide inside diameter as previously described. The valve guide should be within the service specifications in **Table 2**.

d. Clean the valve guides with compressed air to remove all debris.

13. The valve seats must be refaced with a 45° cutter after replacing the valve guides. Reface the valve seats as described under *Valve Seat Reconditioning* in this chapter.

14. Clean the cylinder head thoroughly in solvent and blow dry. Lightly oil the valve guides to prevent rust.

Valve Seat Reconditioning

Valve facing equipment and considerable experience are required to properly recondition the valve seats in the cylinder head. If this is not available, save the expense and have a Honda dealership or machine shop recondition the valve seats.

The following tools will be required:
a. Valve facing equipment (see Honda dealership for part numbers).

NOTE
The valve facing equipment shown in Figure 138 is required for this procedure.

b. Vernier caliper.
c. Machinist's blue (gear marking compound) or Dykem.
d. Valve lapping tool.

NOTE
Follow the manufacturer's instructions with using valve facing equipment.

1. Inspect valve seats (**Figure 135**). If worn or burned, they may be reconditioned. Seats and valves in near-perfect condition can be reconditioned by lapping with fine carborundum paste. Check as follows:
a. Clean the valve seat and valve mating areas with electrical contact cleaner.
b. Coat the valve seat with machinist's blue or Dykem.
c. Install the valve into its guide and rotate it against its seat with a valve lapping tool. See *Valve Lapping* in this chapter.
d. Lift the valve out of the guide and measure the seat width with vernier calipers. See **Figure 139**.
e. The seat width for intake and exhaust valves should measure within the specifications in **Table 2** all the way around the seat. If the seat width exceeds the service limit in **Table 2**, regrind the seats as follows.

CAUTION
When grinding valve seats, work slowly to avoid over-grinding the valve seats. Over-grinding the valve seats will sink the valves into the cylinder head. Sinking the valves too far may reduce valve clearance and make it impossible to adjust valve clearance. If this condition exists, the cylinder head must be replaced.

2. Install a 45° cutter onto the valve tool and lightly cut the seat to remove roughness (**Figure 140**).

4

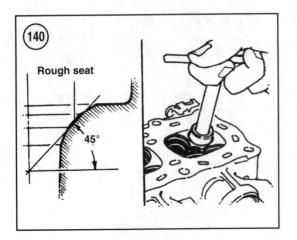

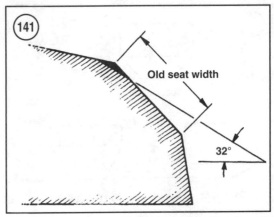

3. Measure the valve seat with a vernier caliper (**Figure 139**). Record the measurement to use as a reference point when performing the following.

> *CAUTION*
> *The 30° cutter removes material quickly. Work carefully and check the progress often.*

4. Install a 32° cutter onto the valve tool and lightly cut the seat to remove 1/4 of the existing valve seat (**Figure 141**).

5. Install a 60° cutter onto the valve tool and lightly cut the seat to remove the lower 1/4 of the existing valve seat (**Figure 142**).

6. Measure the valve seat with a vernier caliper (**Figure 139**). Then install a 45° cutter onto the valve tool and cut the valve seat to the specified seat width in **Table 2**. See **Figure 143**.

7. When the valve seat width is correct, check valve seating as follows.

8. Clean the valve seat and valve mating areas with contact cleaner.

9. Coat the valve seat with machinist's blue or Dykem.

10. Insert the valve into the guide and seat it against the valve seat.

11. Remove the valve and check the contact area on the valve (**Figure 144**). Note the following:

   a. The valve contact area should be approximately in the center of the valve seat area.

   b. If the contact area is too high on the valve, lower the seat with a 32° flat cutter.

   c. If the contact area is too low on the valve, raise the seat with a 60° interior cutter.

   d. Refinish the seat using a 45° cutter.

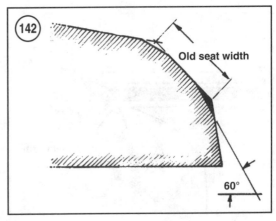

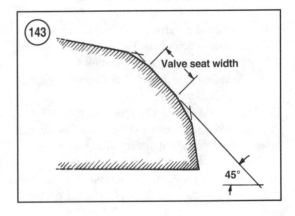

12. When the contact area is correct, lap the valve as described in this chapter.

Valve Lapping

Valve lapping is a simple operation that can restore the valve seal without machining if the amount of wear or distortion is not too great.

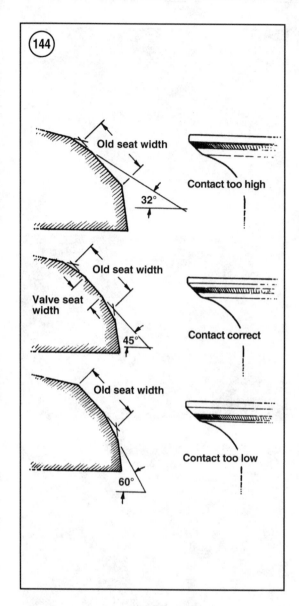

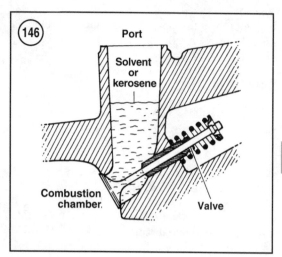

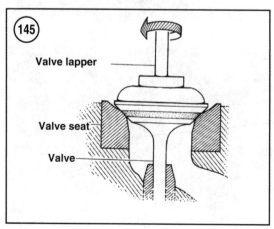

Perform this procedure after determining that valve seat width and outside diameter are within specifications.

1. Smear a light coating of fine-grade valve lapping compound on the seating surface of valve.

> *CAUTION*
> *Do not allow the valve lapping compound to fall into the valve guide.*

2. Insert the valve into the head.

3. Wet the suction cup of the lapping stick and stick it onto the head of the valve (**Figure 145**). Lap the valve to the seat by spinning the lapping stick in both directions. Every 5 to 10 seconds, rotate the valve 180° in the valve seat. Continue this action until the mating surfaces on the valve and seat are smooth and equal in size.

4. Closely examine the valve seat in the cylinder head (**Figure 135**). It should be smooth and even with a smooth, polished seating ring.

5. Thoroughly clean the valves and cylinder head in solvent to remove all grinding compound. Any compound left on the valves or the cylinder head will end up in the engine and cause excessive wear and damage.

6. After the lapping has been completed and the valve assemblies have been reinstalled into the head the valve seal should be tested. Check the seal of each valve by pouring solvent into each of the intake and exhaust ports (**Figure 146**). There should be no leakage past the seat. If leakage occurs, the combustion chamber will appear wet. If fluid leaks past any of the seats, disassemble that valve assem-

bly and repeat the lapping procedure until there is no leakage.

Installation

1. Carefully slide a new oil seal over the valve and seat it onto the end of the valve guide (**Figure 130**).

> *NOTE*
> *Replace the oil seals whenever a valve is removed.*

2. Coat a valve stem with molybdenum disulfide paste and install into its correct guide.

3. Install the lower valve seat so that the shoulder side faces up (see **Figure 131**).

> *NOTE*
> *To prevent the valve from damaging the valve guide oil seal when installing the valve in Step 4, turn the valve slowly as it enters and passes through the oil seal.*

4. Insert the valve through the valve guide (**Figure 129**) and hold in position.

5. Install the valve spring (**Figure 127**).

6. Center the upper valve spring retainer over the valve and spring (**Figure 126**).

7. Push down on the upper valve seat with the valve spring compressor and install the valve keepers (**Figure 125**). Slowly release tension from the compressor, making sure the valve keepers are seated correctly (**Figure 147**).

8. Tap the top of the valve with a plastic hammer to seat the valve keepers.

9. Repeat Steps 1-8 for remaining valve(s).

ENGINE FRONT COVER

The engine front cover can be removed with the engine installed in the frame.

Removal

1. Place the motorcycle on a motorcycle lift. Refer to *Motorcycle Lift* in Chapter One.

2. Shift the transmission into NEUTRAL.

3. Drain the engine oil and remove the oil filter as described in Chapter Three.

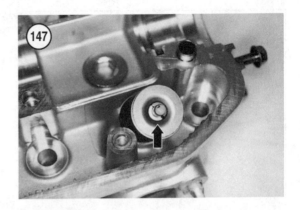

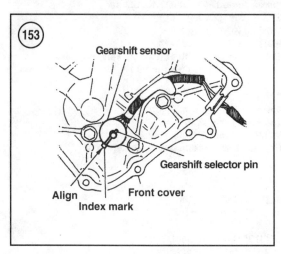

Gearshift sensor

Gearshift selector pin

Align   Front cover

Index mark

8. Remove the bolts (**Figure 148**) securing the front cover to the engine and remove the front cover.

9. Remove the two small cover dowel pins. See A, **Figure 149** and A, **Figure 150**.

10. Remove the large upper dowel pin and O-ring (B, **Figure 149**).

11. Remove the oil pipe (B, **Figure 150**).

12. Remove the O-ring (**Figure 151**) from the front cover oil orifice and O-ring from the front cover.

13. If necessary, remove the bearing holder (**Figure 152**).

Inspection

1. Remove all gasket residue from the front cover and engine block mating surfaces.

2. Check the O-rings for flat spots, deterioration or other damage. Replace all worn or damaged O-rings.

3. If necessary, remove the gearshift sensor from the front cover as described in Chapter Nine.

Installation

1. If necessary, shift the transmission into NEUTRAL.

2. Make sure that the neutral stopper arm is properly engaged in the neutral detent of the stopper plate.

3. If removed, install the bearing holder (**Figure 152**). Tighten its mounting bolts securely.

4. Install the O-ring onto the oil orifice in the front cover (**Figure 151**).

5. Install the oil pipe and two O-rings (B, **Figure 150**).

6. Install the large upper dowel pin and O-ring (B, **Figure 149**).

7. Install the two dowel pins. See A, **Figure 149** and A, **Figure 150**.

NOTE
Correct alignment is necessary for the
gearshift indicator to operate properly.

8. On the inside surface of the engine front cover, make sure that the gearshift sensor pin (long side) aligns with the switch body index mark as shown in **Figure 153**.

9. Apply gasket sealer to the two areas on the engine gasket surface as shown in **Figure 154**.

4. Drain the cooling system as described in Chapter Three.

5. Remove the water pump as described in Chapter Ten.

6. Disconnect the wire at the oil pressure switch on the front cover.

7. Disconnect the neutral switch 4-pin (red) electrical connector.

10. Install a new gasket, fitting it over the dowel pins.

11. Install the front cover and its mounting bolts, making sure to align the oil passages while bringing the cover into contact with the engine gasket surface. Tighten the bolts in a crisscross pattern.

12. Reconnect the neutral switch four-pin (red) electrical connector.

13. Reconnect the wire at the oil pressure switch on the front cover.

14. Install the water pump as described in Chapter Ten.

15. Install the oil filter as described in Chapter Three.

16. Refill the engine with the recommended type and quantity of engine oil and coolant. Refer to Chapter Three.

17. Install the under cover and the fairing front cover as described in Chapter Fifteen.

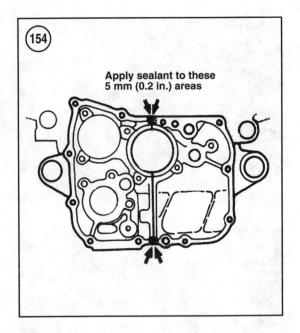

Table 1 GENERAL ENGINE SPECIFICATIONS

Engine type	Water-cooled, 4-stroke OHC, flat six
Bore and stroke	71 × 64 mm (2.8 × 2.5 in.)
Displacement	1520 cc (92.7 cu. in.)
Compression ratio	9.8:1
Valve train	Belt driven OHC with adjustable valves
Lubrication system	Wet sump with two oil pumps
Oil pressure	
Cold 35° C (95° F)	127 kPa (18 psi) @ idle
	490 kPa (71 psi) @ 5000 rpm
Hot 80° C (176° F)	78 kPa (11 psi) @ idle
	78 kPa (11 psi) @ 5000 rpm
Air filtration	Replaceable viscous paper element type
Valve timing	
49-state and Canada	
Intake valve	
Opens	5° BTDC (at 1 mm lift)
Closes	45° ABDC (at 1 mm lift)
Exhaust valve	
Opens	35° BBDC (at 1 mm lift)
Closes	5° ATDC (at 1 mm lift)
California	
Intake valve	
Opens	5° ATDC (at 1 mm lift)
Closes	40° ABDC (at 1 mm lift)
Exhaust valve	
Opens	40° BBDC (at 1 mm lift)
Closes	5° BTDC (at 1 mm lift)
Engine weight (dry)	
49-state and Canada	118.7 kg (261.6 lbs.)
California	119.0 kg (263.3 lbs.)
Firing order	1-4-5-2-3-6

Table 2 ENGINE TOP END SERVICE SPECIFICATIONS

	Specifications mm (in.)	Service limit mm (in.)
Camshaft		
Journal outside diameter		
Both inner journals	26.944-26.965	26.91
	(1.0608-1.0616)	(1.059)
Both outer journals	26.959-26.980	26.91
	(1.0614-1.0622)	(1.059)
Cam lobe height		
Intake	35.1350 35.2950	35.00
	(1.3833-1.3896)	(1.378)
Exhaust	35.1787 35.3387	35.03
	(1.3850-1.3913)	(1.379)
Runout	–	0.10
	–	(0.004)
Holder		
Journal inner diameter	27.000-27.021	27.05
	(1.0630-1.0638)	(1.065)
Bearing clearance		
Both outer journals	0.020-0.062	0.14
	(0.0008-0.0024)	(0.006)
Both inner journals	0.035-0.070	0.14
	(0.0012-0.0030)	(0.006)
Cylinder head warp	–	0.05
		(0.002)
Valve stem outer diameter		
Intake	5.475-5.490	5.45
	(0.2156-0.2161)	(0.215)
Exhaust	5.455-5.470	5.44
	(0.2148-0.2154)	(0.214)
Valve guide inside diameter		
Intake and exhaust	5.500-5.512	5.55
	(0.2165-0.2170)	(0.210)
Valve stem-to-guide clearance		
Intake	0.010-0.037	0.08
	(0.0004-0.0015)	(0.003)
Exhaust	0.030-0.057	0.10
	(0.0012-0.0022)	(0.004)
Valve seat width		
Intake and exhaust	1.2	–
	(0.05)	–
Valve spring free length		
Intake and exhaust	47.8	46.5
	(1.88)	(1.83)
Rocker arm inside diameter	12.000-12.018	12.03
	(0.4724-0.4731)	(0.474)
Rocker arm shaft outside diameter	11.966-11.984	11.95
	(0.4711-0.4718)	(0.470)
Rocker arm-to-shaft clearance	0.016-0.052	0.08
	(0.0006-0.0020)	(0.003)

Table 3 ENGINE TOP END TIGHTENING TORQUES

	N•m	in.-lb.	ft.-lb.
Camshaft holder bolts	20	-	15
Cylinder head cover bolts	12	106	–

(continued)

Table 3 ENGINE TOP END TIGHTENING TORQUES (continued)

	N•m	in.-lb.	ft.-lb.
Crankshaft drive/pulley bolt	74	–	54
Cylinder head bolt (6 mm)[1]	12	106	–
Cylinder head bolts (9 mm)[1]	45	–	33
Exhaust system			
Exhaust pipe to cylinder head nuts	10	88	–
Muffler mounting nuts	34	–	25
Intake manifold bolts	9	80	–
Spark plug	16	–	12
Timing belt tensioner bolt[2]	25	–	18
Timing belt driven pulley bolt	26	–	19

1. Apply molybdenum disulfide grease to the threads and bolt flange surfaces prior to installation.
2. Apply ThreeBond TB1343 or Loctite 242 (blue) to the threads prior to installation.

CHAPTER FIVE

ENGINE LOWER END

The crankshaft is supported by four main bearings and the camshafts are belt-driven from the drive pulley sprockets on the front end of the crankshaft. The cylinders are part of the crankcase, which also serves as the oil sump, as there is no oil pan. The crankcase is split vertically.

Engine lubrication is by wet sump, with the oil supply contained in the lower portion of the crankcase. There are two oil pumps with the main pump drawing oil from the crankcase and delivering oil under pressure throughout the engine. There is an additional scavenge pump that draws oil from the engine rear cover and supplies oil to the primary drive chain.

This chapter provides complete service and overhaul procedures for the lower end components in the Honda GL1500 engine. The rocker arms, camshafts, valves and cylinder heads are covered in Chapter Four.

Clutch and transmission procedures are covered in Chapter Six and Chapter Seven.

Tables 1-7 are at the end of the chapter.

SPECIAL TOOLS

When special tools are required or recommended for an engine overhaul procedure, the tool part numbers are provided. Purchase the special tools from a Honda dealership. Accessory tools can be purchased through most motorcycle dealerships and some mail-order houses.

PARTS REQUIRING ENGINE REMOVAL

The following parts or components require engine removal and partial or complete disassembly:

1. Rear engine cover.
2. Starter clutch.
3. Alternator clutch assembly.
4. Primary drive and driven gears.
5. Final drive gear.
6. Scavenging oil pump.
7. Oil strainer and main oil pump.
8. Crankcase.
9. Pistons and connecting rods.
10. Crankshaft.
11. Output shaft (covered in Chapter Seven).
12. Gearshift arm (covered in Chapter Seven).
13. Transmission (covered in Chapter Seven).

NOTE
The components that can be serviced while the engine is installed in the frame are covered in Chapter Four.

SERVICE PRECAUTIONS

Removing and installing the engine are important steps in engine overhaul. Removing the engine in a casual or disorganized manner prolongs installation and creates frustration while trying to locate a part or series of parts. Before removing the engine, note the following:

1. Review Chapter One of this manual. Having this information fresh in mind will result in doing a better job.
2. In the text, there is frequent mention of the left and right side of the engine. This refers to the engine as it is installed in the frame, not as it sits on the workbench.
3. Always replace a worn or damaged fastener with one of the same size, type and torque requirements. Make sure to identify each bolt before replacing it. Bolt threads should be lubricated with engine oil before torque is applied, unless otherwise specified. If a tightening torque is not in **Table 3** at the end of this chapter, refer to the general torque specifications and fastener information in Chapter One.
4. Use special tools where noted. In some cases, it may be possible to perform the procedure with makeshift tools, but this is usually not recommended. The use of makeshift tools can damage the components and may cause serious personal injury.

Where special tools are required, some of these may be purchased through a Honda dealership or aftermarket companies.

5. Have a number of boxes, plastic bags and containers on hand to store the parts in as they are removed (**Figure 1**).
6. There will be lot of disconnecting of wiring and hoses when removing the engine. Do not rely on memory alone when reconnecting these parts. Instead, tag each hose and wire as it is disconnected. Tag each disconnected hose and its connection or wire in numerical order. Reassembly is then a simple matter of matching the numbers. If it appears that there may be a routing problem with a hose or wire, photograph or draw the routing before proceeding with the next step.
7. Make identification tags from strips of masking tape and a fine-point permanent-marking pen. Use a permanent-marking pen because most ink or pencil marks fade on tape.
8. Use a vise with protective jaws to hold parts. If protective jaws are not available, insert wooden blocks on either side of the part(s) before clamping it in the vise.
9. Remove and install pressed-on parts with an appropriate mandrel, support and hydraulic press. Do not try to pry, hammer or otherwise force them on or off.
10. Refer to **Table 3** at the end of the chapter for torque specifications. Proper torque is essential to assure long life and satisfactory service from components.
11. Discard all O-rings and seals during disassembly. Apply a small amount of grease to the inner lips of each seal to prevent damage when the engine is first started.

12. Record the location and position of all shims. As soon as a shim is removed, inspect it for damage and record its thickness and location.

13. Work in an area where there is sufficient lighting and room for component storage.

14. A floor jack and a piece of plywood are required to remove the engine from the frame. The plywood should be 3/4 in. or thicker and cut to match the approximate size of the base of the engine. When placed between the engine and jack, the plywood allows the engine and jack to mate properly, thus providing additional control when rolling the jack and engine from underneath the frame. This is critical to prevent damage to the engine and frame.

ENGINE REMOVAL

Refer to the following illustrations for this procedure:

a. **Figure 2**: right side components and fasteners.

b. **Figure 3**: left side components and fasteners.

WARNING
*The GL1500 engine is heavy (see **Table 1** for engine weight). When removing the engine from the frame, it is essential that a minimum of two, preferably three, people assist in rolling the engine from underneath the frame.*

1. Park the motorcycle on the sidestand.

2. Disconnect the negative battery cable, then the positive cable as described in Chapter Three. Position the cables away from the battery to avoid any accidental contact with the battery terminals.

3. Drain the engine oil as described in Chapter Three.

4. Drain the engine coolant as described in Chapter Three.

5. Remove the engine guard from each side as described in Chapter Fifteen.

6. Remove the fuel tank as described in Chapter Eight.

7. Remove the exhaust system as described in Chapter Four.

8. Remove the air filter housing as described in Chapter Eight.

9. Remove the radiator as described in Chapter Ten.

10. Remove the starter motor as described in Chapter Nine.

11. Disconnect the spark plug wires at the spark plugs. Secure the wires so that they cannot interfere with engine removal.

12. Remove the right side steering head cover as described in Chapter Fifteen.

13. Disconnect the following sub-harness electrical connectors (**Figure 4**):

a. Four-pin white connector.

b. Two-pin blue connector.

c. Four-pin red connector.

14. Remove the bolts securing the right side radiator mounting bracket. Move the sub-harness from the bracket and move it out of the way.

15. On the left side, just in front of the coolant reservoir tank, disconnect the 2-pin white alternator electrical connector.

16. Remove the rubber cap and disconnect the white electrical cable from the alternator (**Figure 5**).

NOTE
*Cover the intake manifold openings in each cylinder head with duct tape (**Figure 6**) to prevent debris from entering the engine.*

17. Remove the carburetor assembly as described in Chapter Eight.

18. Remove the clutch slave cylinder as described in Chapter Six.

19. On the right side, perform the following and partially remove as an assembly:

a. Remove the rear brake master cylinder reservoir cover (A, **Figure 7**) and the rear brake master cylinder cover (B, **Figure 7**).

b. Remove the reservoir mounting bolt and reservoir hose clamp.

c. Remove the bolts securing the driver's right side front footpeg (C, **Figure 7**).

CAUTION
Do not suspend the assembly from the rear brake hose. Use a bungee cord or length of wire.

d. Move the assembly away from the frame and away from the engine mounting bolt areas. Keep the reservoir upright to prevent air from entering the rear brake system.

5

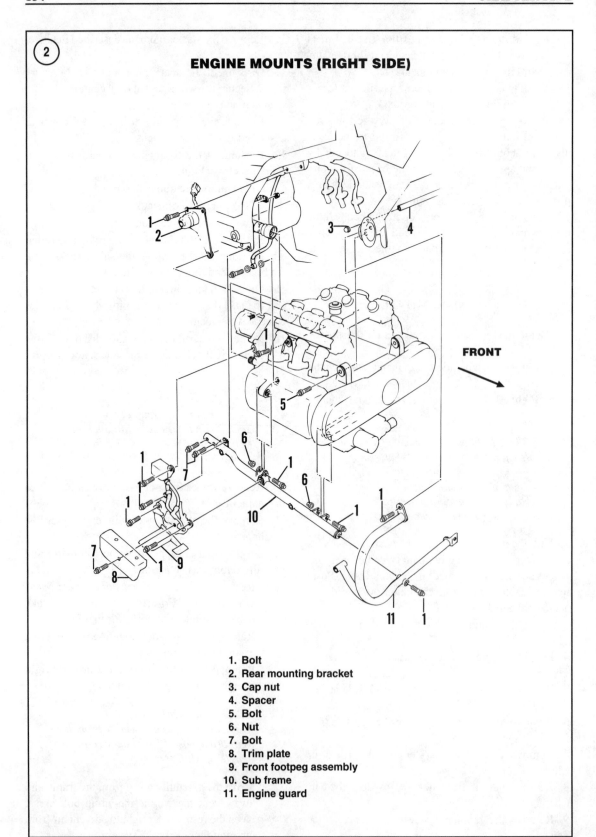

ENGINE MOUNTS (RIGHT SIDE)

FRONT

1. Bolt
2. Rear mounting bracket
3. Cap nut
4. Spacer
5. Bolt
6. Nut
7. Bolt
8. Trim plate
9. Front footpeg assembly
10. Sub frame
11. Engine guard

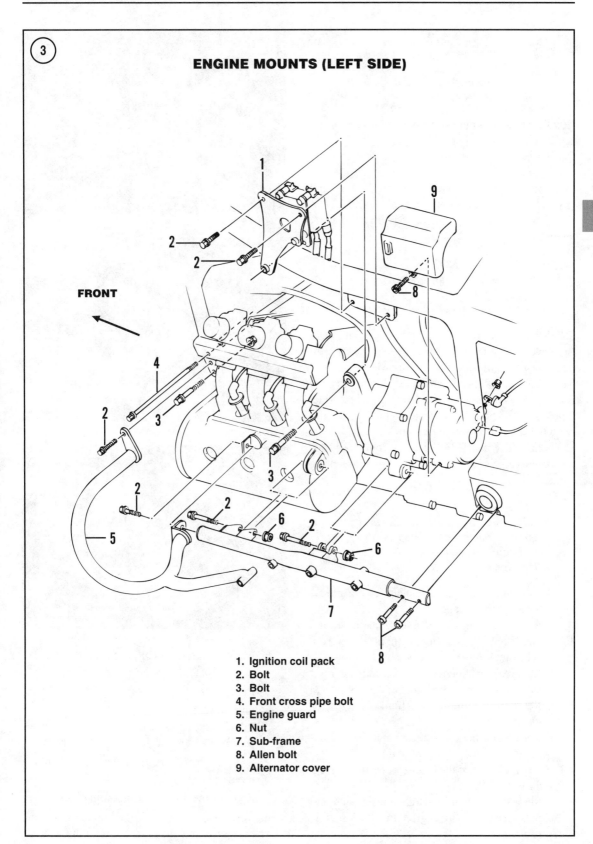

3

ENGINE MOUNTS (LEFT SIDE)

FRONT

1. Ignition coil pack
2. Bolt
3. Bolt
4. Front cross pipe bolt
5. Engine guard
6. Nut
7. Sub-frame
8. Allen bolt
9. Alternator cover

NOTE
The engine can be removed with the timing belt cover installed on the engine; removing the cover does provide additional clearance.

20. Remove the timing belt cover (**Figure 8**) as described in Chapter Four.
21. Disconnect the crankcase breather tube from the engine.
22. Disconnect the temperature sensor wire and ground wire from the thermostat case.
23. Remove the lower coolant hose from the water pump.

NOTE
If the cylinder heads are going to be serviced, remove them at this time; it makes engine removal much easier.

24. Make a final inspection of the engine to make sure everything has been disconnected.
25. Center the plywood on the floor jack (see *Service Precautions* in this chapter) and position the jack underneath the engine from the right side. Make sure the plywood is centered on the jack and with the engine. Raise the jack until it just contacts the engine. The jack height must be continually adjusted to relieve stress on the engine mounting bolts.

NOTE
When loosening and removing the engine mounting bolts in Steps 26-27, maintain constant pressure against the engine with the jack.

26. On the right side of the engine, refer to **Figure 2** to perform the following:
  a. Remove the front and rear lower bolts and nuts securing the engine to the right side sub-frame.
  b. Remove the Allen bolts securing the right side sub-frame to the frame at the rear.
  c. Remove the right side sub-frame from the engine and frame.
  d. Remove the nut from the upper cross pipe and the front upper engine mounting bolt.
27. On the left side of the engine, refer to **Figure 3** to perform the following:
  a. Remove the front and rear lower bolts and nuts securing the engine to the left side sub-frame.

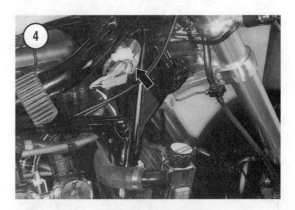

  b. Remove the Allen bolts securing the left side sub-frame to the frame at the rear.
  c. Remove the left side sub-frame from the engine and frame.
  d. Remove the upper cross pipe and the front upper engine mounting bolt.
  e. Disconnect the electrical connector from the ignition switch.
  f. Remove the upper rear mounting bolt.
  g. Remove the bolts securing the rear mounting bracket. Move the bracket out of the way.

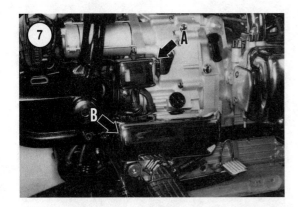

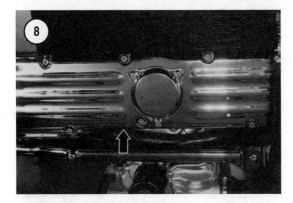

NOTE
Make a note of any loose or damaged engine mounting fasteners, dampers, spacers or collars. Damaged fasteners can cause vibration and handling problems when riding.

28. Make a second inspection to ensure that everything has been disconnected from the engine. Check that the engine and plywood will not catch on any-

thing as the engine is removed from the frame. Make sure not to damage the clutch and brake lines when removing the engine.

WARNING
Due to the weight of the engine, the following steps must be performed slowly and carefully to avoid dropping the engine, causing damage to the engine or injury to anyone involved in the removal. Never place hands or feet where the engine may tip over and crush them.

29. Move the engine slightly forward to disengage the output shaft from the universal joint on the drive shaft (**Figure 9**).

WARNING
The engine assembly is very heavy. This final step requires assistants to safely remove the engine from the frame.

30. Carefully and slowly lower the jack, then slide the jack out of the frame. During this time, assistants should be steadying the engine on the jack to prevent it from tipping over.
31. Place the engine in an engine stand or place it on a workbench for further disassembly.

ENGINE MOUNTS

Inspection

Whenever the engine is removed from the frame, inspect the engine mounts. Replace all worn or damaged parts before reinstalling the engine.
1. Check the engine mounting bolts for stripping, cross-threading or deposit buildup. Replace damaged bolts.
2. Inspect the engine brackets (**Figure 10**) for cracks, bending or other damage. Replace damaged brackets.
3. Check the sub-frame for cracks, bending or other damage.
4. Inspect the rubber mounts and bushings (**Figure 11**) for wear, cracks or other damage.
5. If paint was removed from the frame during engine removal, mask the surrounding areas and touchup the frame as required before installing the engine.

ENGINE INSTALLATION

Refer to the following illustrations for this procedure:

   a. **Figure 2**: right side components and fasteners.

   b. **Figure 3**: left side components and fasteners.

1. Identify and then lay out the engine mounting nuts and bolts.

2. Install all of the engine bushings and rubber mounts (**Figure 11**).

3. Make sure that all hoses, cables and tubes are out of the way.

4. Apply molybdenum disulfide grease onto the engine output shaft splines (**Figure 12**).

5. Center the plywood onto the jack pad as before and set the engine onto the plywood, centering it with the jack. The assistants should steady the engine while it is being rolled into the frame.

NOTE
Make sure the output shaft rubber boot is installed over the universal joint before performing Step 6.

6. Carefully roll the engine through the frame, aligning and engaging the output shaft with the universal joint.

7. Using the jack, align the engine mounting bosses with the main frame mounting areas.

8. Install the engine mounting bolts hand tight, in the following order:

   a. Front upper mounting bolts, brackets and nuts.

   b. The right and left side sub-frames and bolts and nuts.

   c. Front and rear lower mounting bolts and nuts.

   d. Front cross over pipe bolt and nut.

9. Release the jack pressure and remove the jack and plywood from underneath the engine.

10. Tighten the engine mounting bolts and nuts to the torque specifications in **Table 3**.

11. If the cylinder heads were previously removed, install them as described in Chapter Four.

12. Reverse Steps 1-23 under *Engine Removal* to complete engine installation. Note the following:

   a. Fill the crankcase with the recommended type and quantity of engine oil and coolant. Refer to Chapter Three.

   b. Start the engine and check for leaks.

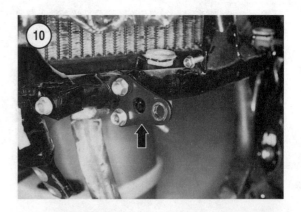

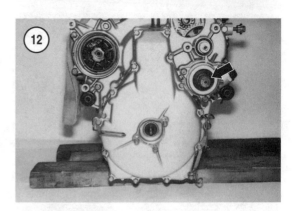

REAR ENGINE CASE

Refer to **Figure 13** for this procedure.

The following tools are required to remove and install the output shaft locknut:

   a. Mainshaft holder (Honda part No. 07JMB-MN50200), or equivalent.

   b. Locknut wrench, 30 × 64 mm (Honda part No. 07916-MB00001), or equivalent.

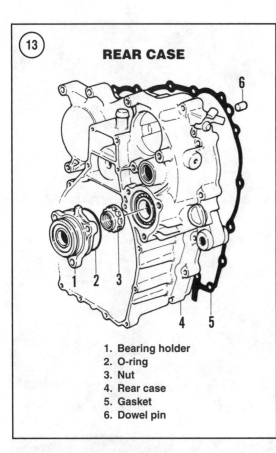

REAR CASE

1. Bearing holder
2. O-ring
3. Nut
4. Rear case
5. Gasket
6. Dowel pin

Rear Case Removal

1. Remove the engine from the frame as described in this chapter.

2. Remove the clutch as described in Chapter Six.

3. Remove the scavenge oil pump strainer.

4. If still attached, remove the alternator and coupler A as described in Chapter Nine.

5. Remove the bolts securing the bearing holder (**Figure 14**) to the rear cover. Remove the bearing holder.

6. The output shaft locknut (**Figure 15**) is staked to the output shaft in two places. Unstake the nut as follows:

   a. Mask off the bearing to prevent metal chips from entering the bearing.

   b. Wrap some cardboard or shim stock around the output shaft and secure in place with tape or plastic ties. This will help prevent damaging the output shaft when unstaking the nut.

   c. Remove the two staked areas with a grinder or drill.

   d. Clean off all metal residue from the grinding or drilling operation. Remove the cardboard or shim stock.

7. Shift the transmission into gear.

8. Install the mainshaft holder (A, **Figure 16**) onto the mainshaft and the locknut wrench (B, **Figure 16**) onto the output shaft locknut.

9. Hold the mainshaft securely, then loosen and remove the output shaft locknut. Discard the locknut.

10. Loosen and remove the bolts securing the rear case to the engine. Remove the rear case (**Figure 17**) from the engine.

11. Remove the dowel pins and gasket. Refer to **Figure 18** and A, **Figure 19**. Discard the gasket.

**Bearing Holder Seal and
O-ring Inspection and Replacement**

1. Check bearing holder seal (**Figure 20**) for excessive wear or damage. To replace the seal perform the following:

   a. Support the bearing holder and press or drive the seal out with a suitable bearing driver.

   b. Clean the bearing holder in solvent and dry it thoroughly.

   c. Install the new seal so that the manufacturer marks face out, as shown in **Figure 20**.

   d. Press or drive the seal into the bearing holder with a suitable bearing driver until it is flush with the bearing holder.

   e. Check the seal for proper installation.

   f. Pack the seal's dust lip with grease.

2. Replace the bearing holder O-ring (**Figure 21**) if it has become hardened or if it has flat spots or appears damaged.

Rear Engine Case Inspection

1. Remove all gasket residue from the rear case and crankcase gasket surfaces (A, **Figure 22**) with a suitable scraper or putty knife. Remove gasket residue carefully to avoid damaging the mating surfaces.

2. Inspect the gasket surfaces for damage. Light damage may be smoothed with an oil stone.

3. Inspect the rear case bearings (B, **Figure 22**) and replace them if required, as described in this chapter.

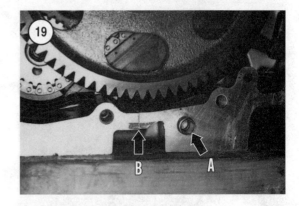

Mainshaft Bearing Inspection/Replacement

1. Turn the inner bearing race (A, **Figure 23**) slowly, checking for any roughness or radial (up and down) play. If roughness or radial play is detected, remove the bearing as follows:

   a. Remove the bearing holder bolts and remove the bearing holders (B, **Figure 23**).

   b. Support the rear case and press or drive the mainshaft bearing out with a suitable bearing driver.

   c. Clean the cover bearings bore with solvent and dry it thoroughly.

   d. Remove all sealer residue from the bearing holder bolts.

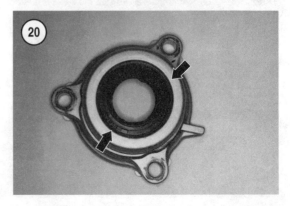

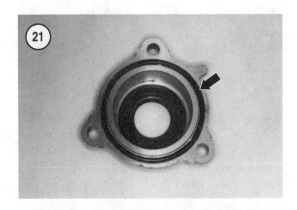

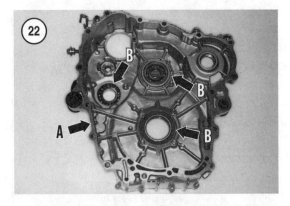

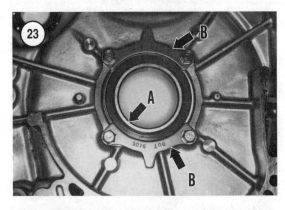

e. Clean the bearing holder bolt holes in the rear case with solvent and dry it with compressed air.

NOTE
Refer to **Bearing Replacement** *in Chapter One for general information on bearing installation.*

2. Install the new mainshaft bearing so that the manufacturer marks face out, as shown in A, **Figure 23**.

3. Support the rear case and press or drive the bearing in until it bottoms out.

4. Check the bearing for proper installation.

5. Place the bearing holder onto the rear case with the OUTSIDE mark on each holder facing out. See B, **Figure 23**.

6. Apply ThreeBond TB1342 or Loctite 242 (blue) onto the bearing holder mounting bolts. Then install and tighten the bolts securely.

Output Shaft Bearing Inspection/Replacement

1. Turn the inner bearing race (**Figure 24**) slowly, checking for any roughness or radial (up and down) play. If roughness or radial play is detected, remove the bearing as follows:

   a. Support the rear case so that the rear side faces up and press or drive the output shaft bearing out with a suitable bearing driver.

   b. Clean the case bearings bore with solvent and dry it thoroughly.

NOTE
Refer to **Bearing Replacement** *in Chapter One for general information on bearing installation.*

2. Install the new output shaft bearing so that the manufacturer marks face out as shown in **Figure 24**.

3. Support the front cover and press or drive the bearing into the cover until it bottoms out.

4. Check the bearing for proper installation.

Rear Case Installation

1. Install the two rear cover dowel pins. See **Figure 18** and A, **Figure 19**.

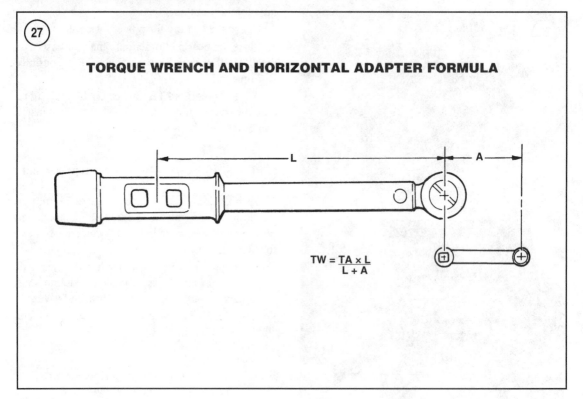

TORQUE WRENCH AND HORIZONTAL ADAPTER FORMULA

$$TW = \frac{TA \times L}{L + A}$$

2. Apply gasket sealer to the crankcase where both crankcase halves mate together. See B, **Figure 19** and **Figure 25**.

3. Install a new gasket, making sure that it aligns with the dowel pins and case halves correctly.

4. Install the rear case (**Figure 17**) over the dowel pins and hold it in position. Check that the gasket is positioned correctly between the rear cover and engine cases.

5. Install all of the rear case mounting bolts finger-tight. Then, tighten the bolts securely in a crisscross pattern.

6. Thread a new nut (**Figure 15**) onto the output shaft.

7. Shift the transmission into gear.

8. Install the mainshaft holder (A, **Figure 16**) onto the mainshaft and the locknut wrench (B, **Figure 16**) onto the output shaft locknut.

NOTE
*The Honda locknut wrench (**Figure 26**) is a horizontal adapter. It effectively lengthens the torque wrench when tightening the output shaft locknut. The torque value indicated*

*on the torque wrench is not the same amount of torque actually applied to the locknut. When using a torque wrench with a horizontal adapter, it is necessary to recalculate the torque reading. Refer to **Figure 27**. TW is the torque setting or dial reading to set on the torque wrench. TA is the actual torque specification in **Table 3**. L is the lever length of the torque wrench from the center of the square drive to the center of the handle. A is the length of the adapter from the center of the square drive to the centerline of the nut or bolt.*

9. Hold the mainshaft securely and using the example in **Figure 27** to compute the torque reading, tighten the output shaft locknut to the torque specification in **Table 3**. Remove the special tools.

10. The output shaft has two notches (**Figure 28**) for staking the locknut to the shaft. Stake the locknut as follows:

    a. Align a punch with one of the output shaft notches (**Figure 29**) and stake the locknut in place with a hammer.

    b. Shift the transmission into NEUTRAL and turn the output shaft to access the opposite notch.

    c. Repeat sub-step a to stake the notch.

11. Apply clean engine oil onto the bearing holder O-ring (**Figure 21**) and install the holder onto the rear cover. Install the bearing holder mounting bolts and tighten the bolts securely.

12. Install the clutch as described in Chapter Six.

13. Install the engine in the frame as described in this chapter.

STARTER CLUTCH

Removal

1. Remove the rear engine case as described in this chapter.

2. Hold the starter clutch with a universal holding tool (**Figure 30**) and loosen the starter clutch bolt.

3. Remove the starter clutch bolt, washer and bearing (**Figure 31**).

4. Remove the starter clutch assembly (**Figure 32**).

Inspection

1. Place the starter clutch on a workbench with the driven gear facing up, as shown in **Figure 33**.

2. Hold the starter clutch and try to turn the driven gear clockwise and then counterclockwise. The gear should only turn clockwise (**Figure 33**). If the gear turns both ways, disassemble and inspect the starter clutch as described in this chapter.

3. Remove the needle bearing (**Figure 34**) and check it for excessive wear or damage.

Disassembly/Inspection/Assembly

If the rollers are corroded or have flat spots, they often will not move in the starter clutch outer housing ramp. This will cause the starter motor to turn without turning the engine or emit a loud screeching sound as the engine turns over.

1. Remove the driven gear (**Figure 35**) and needle bearing (**Figure 34**) from the starter clutch.

2. Rotate the driven gear clockwise while pulling up and remove the driven gear from the starter clutch assembly.

3. Inspect the rollers in the starter clutch for corrosion, flat spots, uneven or excessive wear. Replace the clutch roller assembly, if necessary.

4. Check the driven gear boss and the inner boss in the starter clutch for excessive wear or damage. Replace damaged parts as required.

5. Check the driven gear for worn or damaged teeth.

6. Rotate the driven gear clockwise while pushing down and install the driven gear onto the starter clutch assembly.

7. Install the needle bearing (**Figure 34**) into the starter clutch.

Installation

1. Slide the starter clutch (**Figure 32**) onto the crankshaft.

2. Install the bearing, washer (chamfered side facing out) and mounting bolt (**Figure 31**).

3. Hold the starter clutch with a universal holding tool (**Figure 30**) and tighten the starter clutch mounting bolt to the torque specification in **Table 3**.

4. Install the rear engine cover as described in this chapter.

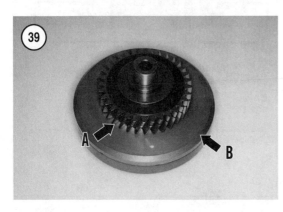

ALTERNATOR CLUTCH ASSEMBLY

Removal

1. Remove the rear engine case as described in this chapter.

2. Remove the starter clutch as described in this chapter.

3. Remove the alternator clutch assembly (**Figure 36**).

4. Remove the primary drive and driven gears as described in this chapter.

5. Remove the bolts securing the alternator drive gear (**Figure 37**) to the crankshaft and remove the gear.

Inspection

1. Turn the outer bearing race (**Figure 38**) by hand. The bearing should turn smoothly with no roughness or noise.

2. Check that the bearing (**Figure 38**) is a tight fit on the driven shaft.

3. Inspect the sub-gear (A, **Figure 39**) for worn or damaged gear teeth.

4. Inspect the flywheel halves (B, **Figure 39**) for damage.

5. If necessary, replace worn or damaged parts as described in the following procedure.

6. Inspect the alternator drive gear (**Figure 40**) for worn or damaged gear teeth. Replace the gear if necessary.

Disassembly/Assembly

Refer to **Figure 41** when performing this procedure.

1. Support the alternator clutch assembly in a press with the bearing (**Figure 38**) facing up.

2. Press the driven shaft out of the bearing.

3. Slide the special washer and the spring washer off the driven shaft.

4. Remove the driven subgear and the gear spring.

5. The flywheels have eight pry points for separating them. Pry the flywheel halves apart in a criss-cross pattern (even movement) and separate the flywheels.

6. Remove the damper springs and spring seats from one flywheel half.

7. Check the spring seats for cracks or damage.

8. Check the damper springs for weakness or damage. Replace the springs as a set if one or more of the springs require replacement.

9. Check the flywheel halves for damage.

10. Apply engine oil to each of the damper springs.

11. Install two spring seats on each spring and install the assembly into one of the flywheel halves.

12. Repeat Step 11 for each spring.

13. Align the bosses on one flywheel with the notches on the opposite flywheel and assemble the flywheel halves. Do not damage the spring seats while assembling the flywheel halves.

14. Install the driven gear spring onto the driven gear.

15. Install the sub-gear, aligning the spring hole with the gear boss on the sub-gear.

16. Install the special washer onto the driven shaft so that its shoulder faces toward the spline shaft end; see 10, **Figure 41**.

17. Install the spring washer onto the driven shaft with the washer's dished side facing toward the driven gears.

18. Align the oil hole in the driven shaft with the oil hole in the flywheel and install the driven shaft.

19. Press a new bearing onto the driven shaft as follows:

   a. Support the driven shaft in the press bed as shown in **Figure 42**. The driven shaft shoulder (**Figure 43**) is placed on the press blocks.

   b. Place bearing drivers on the bearing as shown in **Figure 42**.

   c. Press the bearing (**Figure 38**) onto the driven shaft.

   d. Ensure that the bearing turns smoothly with no sign of roughness or noise.

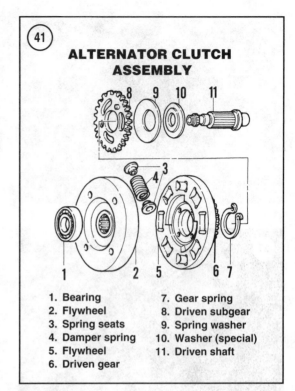

41

ALTERNATOR CLUTCH ASSEMBLY

1. Bearing
2. Flywheel
3. Spring seats
4. Damper spring
5. Flywheel
6. Driven gear
7. Gear spring
8. Driven subgear
9. Spring washer
10. Washer (special)
11. Driven shaft

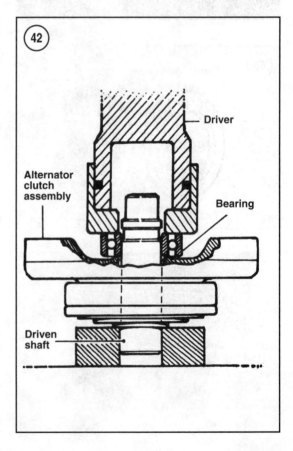

42

Driver

Alternator clutch assembly

Bearing

Driven shaft

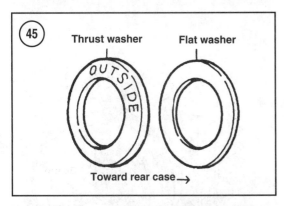

Thrust washer   Flat washer

OUTSIDE

Toward rear case →

Alternator Clutch Bearing Replacement

1. Turn the inner bearing race (**Figure 44**) by hand. Ensure that the bearing turns smoothly with no sign of roughness or noise. If the bearing appears damaged, replace it as follows.

2. Remove the bearing with a blind bearing remover. Discard the bearing.

3. Remove the thrust washer and flat washer from the rear case.

4. Clean the bearing recess with a rag.

5. Install the flat washer (**Figure 45**).

6. Install the thrust washer with the side marked OUTSIDE facing out (**Figure 45**).

7. Align the new bearing with the case so that the bearing's sealed side faces toward the case.

8. Drive the bearing into the case until it bottoms out.

9. Ensure that the inner bearing race turns smoothly with no sign of roughness or noise.

Installation

1. Apply molybdenum disulfide oil to the alternator drive gear bolt head flanges and threads.

2. Install the alternator drive gear (**Figure 37**) onto the crankshaft.

3. Install the alternator drive gear mounting bolts and tighten in a crisscross pattern to the torque specification in **Table 3**.

4. Install the primary drive and driven gears as described in this chapter.

5. Install the alternator clutch assembly (**Figure 36**), aligning the driven and drive gear teeth (**Figure 46**).

6. Install the starter clutch as described in this chapter.

7. Install the rear engine case as described in this chapter.

PRIMARY DRIVE AND DRIVEN GEARS

Removal

1. Remove the starter clutch (**Figure 47**) as described in this chapter.

2. Remove the alternator clutch assembly (**Figure 36**) as described in this chapter.

3. Remove the primary driven gear (**Figure 48**).

4. Remove the spline washer (**Figure 49**).

5. Remove the primary drive gear (**Figure 50**).

6. If necessary, remove the primary driven gear boss as follows:

   a. Install the clutch outer onto the mainshaft and hold it with the Honda clutch outer holder (part No. 07JMB-MN50100). This will prevent the oil pump driven sprocket from rotating. See **Figure 51**.

   b. Remove the oil pump driven sprocket bolt and washer (**Figure 52**).

   c. Remove the clutch outer holder and the clutch outer (**Figure 51**).

   d. Remove the primary driven gear boss, drive chain and driven sprocket as an assembly (**Figure 53**).

Primary Drive and Driven Gear Inspection

1. Clean the gears in solvent and dry them thoroughly.

2. Check the primary drive (**Figure 54**) and primary driven (**Figure 55**) gears for damaged or severely worn gear teeth and splines. Replace damaged parts as required.

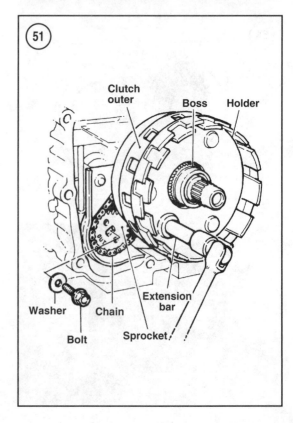

5

Primary Driven Gear Boss Inspection

1. Clean the primary driven gear boss assembly in solvent and dry it thoroughly.

2. Inspect the oil pump driven sprocket (A, **Figure 56**) for damaged or severely worn gear teeth.

3. Inspect the drive chain (B, **Figure 56**) for loose, severely worn or damaged chain pins or links.

4. Inspect the primary driven gear boss (C, **Figure 56**) for damaged or severely worn gear teeth or splines.

5. Inspect the primary driven gear boss needle bearing for excessive play or damage. If necessary, replace the needle bearing as described in the following procedure.

6. Replace worn or damaged parts as required.

Primary Driven Gear Boss
Needle Bearing Replacement

1. Prior to removing the needle bearing, measure its installed position in the primary driven gear boss as shown in **Figure 57**. The bearing should be installed within the listed specifications.

2. Support the primary driven gear boss in a press and press out the needle bearing. Discard the needle bearing.

3. Clean the primary driven gear boss in solvent and dry it thoroughly.

4. Support the primary driven gear boss in a press. Then press in the new needle bearing to the depth specifications listed in **Figure 57**.

5. Check the needle bearing installation.

Installation

1. If removed, install the primary driven gear boss as follows:

    a. Assemble the primary driven gear boss, drive chain and oil pump driven sprocket as shown in **Figure 56**. Assemble the oil pump driven sprocket with the side marked OUT facing out; see **Figure 58**.

    b. Install the primary driven gear boss assembly as shown in **Figure 53**.

    c. Install the clutch outer onto the mainshaft and hold it with the Honda clutch outer holder (part No. 07JMB-MN50100). See **Figure 51**.

    d. Apply Loctite 242 (blue) onto the oil pump driven sprocket mounting bolt. Then install the bolt and washer (**Figure 52**) and tighten it to the torque specification in **Table 3**.

    e. Remove the clutch outer holder and the clutch outer (**Figure 51**).

2. Install the primary drive gear (**Figure 50**) onto the crankshaft.

3. Install the splined washer (**Figure 49**) onto the crankshaft.

4. Align the drive gear serrated teeth with the primary driven gear teeth and install the primary driven gear onto the driven gear boss. See **Figure 48**.

5. Install the starter clutch (**Figure 47**) as described in this chapter.

FINAL DRIVE GEAR

Removal

1. Remove the primary drive gear and the primary driven gear as described in this chapter.

2. Remove the output shaft (**Figure 59**) from the engine.

NOTE
Output shaft service is described in Chapter Seven.

3. The final drive gear locknut (**Figure 60**) is staked to the countershaft in two places. Unstake the nut with a die grinder or drill, working carefully to avoid damaging the countershaft.

4. Shift the transmission into gear.

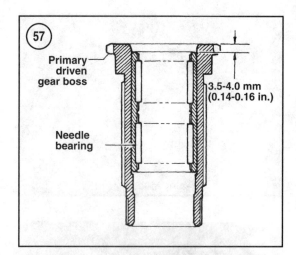

5. Secure the mainshaft with the Honda mainshaft holder (part No. 07JMB-MN50200). See A, **Figure 61**.

NOTE
The final drive gear locknut has left-hand threads.

6. Turn the final drive gear locknut (B, **Figure 61**) clockwise and remove it. Discard the locknut.

7. Remove the mainshaft holder (A, **Figure 61**).

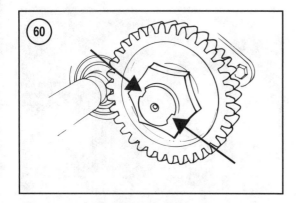

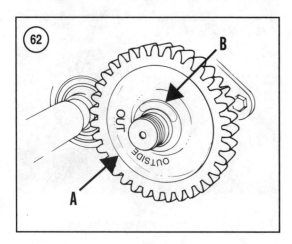

8. Remove the lockwasher and the final drive gear.

Inspection

1. Inspect the final drive gear for worn gear teeth and splines. Replace the gear if necessary.

2. Clean the engine case of all metal shavings that resulted from unstaking the final drive gear locknut.

Installation

1. Apply engine oil to the countershaft and final drive gear splines.

2. Position the final drive gear with the OUT mark (A, **Figure 62**) facing out and install the gear onto the countershaft.

3. Position the lockwasher with the OUTSIDE mark (B, **Figure 62**) facing out and install the lockwasher onto the countershaft.

4. Shift the transmission into gear.

5. Secure the mainshaft with the Honda mainshaft holder (part No. 07JMB-MN50200). See A, **Figure 61**.

6. Apply ThreeBond TB1342, or Loctite 242 (blue) to the threads on the new locknut.

NOTE
The final drive gear locknut has left-hand threads.

7. Install the final drive gear locknut onto the crankshaft by turning it counterclockwise. Then tighten the locknut to the torque specification in **Table 3**.

8. The countershaft is machined with two notches. Stake the locknut directly over the countershaft notches (**Figure 60**).

9. Remove the mainshaft holder.

10. Install the output shaft (**Figure 59**).

11. Install the primary drive gear and the primary driven gear as described in this chapter.

SCAVENGE OIL PUMP

Scavenge Oil Pump Filter
Removal/Installation

1. Remove the clutch cover as described in Chapter Six.

2. Remove the scavenge oil pump filter (**Figure 63**).

3. Check the oil filter for contamination buildup or damage.

4. Replace the oil filter, if necessary.

5. Reinstall by reversing these steps.

Removal

1. Remove the rear engine case as described in this chapter.

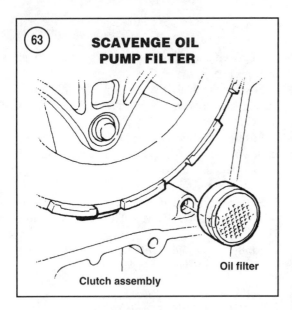

2. Remove the primary driven gear boss as described in this chapter.

3. Remove the bolts holding the drive chain guide (**Figure 64**) to the crankcase. Remove the drive chain guide.

4. Remove the oil pump mounting bolts (A, **Figure 65**) and remove the oil pump (B, **Figure 65**).

5. Remove the dowel pin (A, **Figure 66**).

Disassembly

Refer to **Figure 67** for this procedure.

1. Remove the oil pump body attaching bolt (A, **Figure 68**) and separate the pump body halves.

2. Remove the grommet (B, **Figure 68**) from the pump cover.

3. Remove the dowel pins (A, **Figure 69**).

4. Remove the drive guide (B, **Figure 69**).

5. Remove the inner and outer rotors (**Figure 70**).

6. Remove oil seals from the pump body and cover.

Inspection

Refer to the service specifications in **Table 2**. Replace worn or damaged parts. If several parts require replacement, it is recommended that the entire oil pump be replaced.

1. Clean all of the oil pump components in solvent and place them on a clean, lint-free cloth.

2. Examine the pump body and cover (**Figure 71**) for scoring or other damage in the rotor areas.

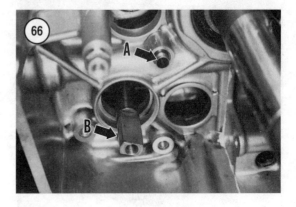

Check the rod on the pump cover for looseness or damage.

3. Examine the rotors for scratches or other damage. If the rotors are damaged, replace the pump.

4. Install the inner and outer rotors into the pump body (**Figure 70**) with the punch mark on both rotors facing up.

5. Measure the clearance between the outer rotor and the body (**Figure 72**) with a flat feeler gauge.

6. Measure the pump side clearance with a straightedge and flat feeler gauge (**Figure 73**).

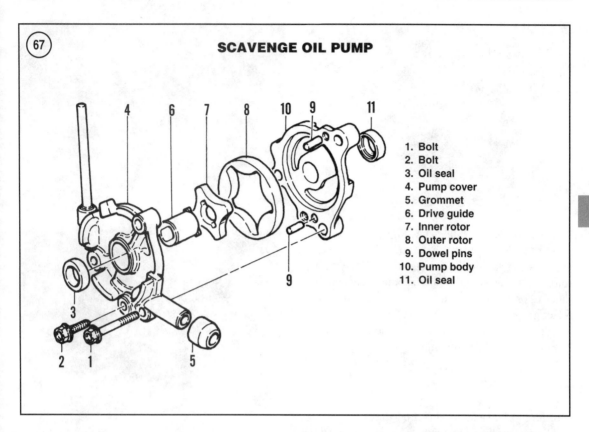

SCAVENGE OIL PUMP

1. Bolt
2. Bolt
3. Oil seal
4. Pump cover
5. Grommet
6. Drive guide
7. Inner rotor
8. Outer rotor
9. Dowel pins
10. Pump body
11. Oil seal

5

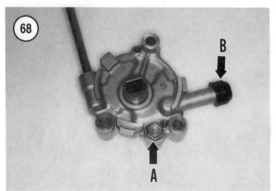

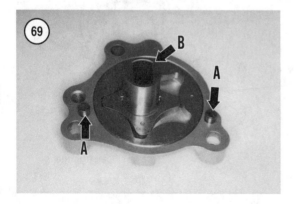

7. Reinstall the drive guide (A, **Figure 74**) into the inner rotor. Then, install the oil pump onto the engine case, engaging the drive shaft with the pump rotor shaft. Measure the tip clearance between the inner rotor tip and the outer rotor ramp with a flat feeler gauge, as shown in **Figure 75**.

8. If the tip clearance is worn to the service limit in **Table 2**, replace the oil pump.

Assembly

Refer to **Figure 67** for this procedure.

1. Clean all of the components with solvent and dry them thoroughly.

2. Install a new seal into the pump body.

3. Install a new seal into the pump cover.

4. Dip the rotors and drive guide in clean engine oil and place them on a clean, lint-free cloth prior to assembly.

5. Install the inner and outer rotors into the pump body (**Figure 70**) with their punch marks facing up (B, **Figure 74**).

6. Install the drive guide (A, **Figure 74**) into the inner rotor.

7. Install the two dowel pins (A, **Figure 69**).

8. Install the pump cover onto the pump body and secure with the mounting bolt (A, **Figure 68**). Tighten the bolt securely.

9. Install the grommet (B, **Figure 68**) onto the pump cover.

Installation

1. Make sure the grommet (B, **Figure 68**) is installed onto the pump cover.

2. Install the dowel pin (A, **Figure 66**) into the crankcase.

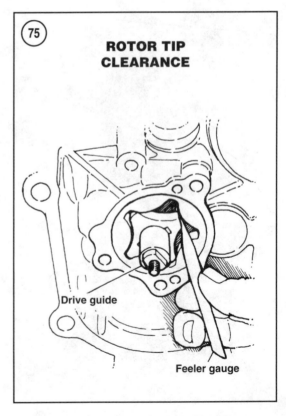

ROTOR TIP CLEARANCE

Drive guide

Feeler gauge

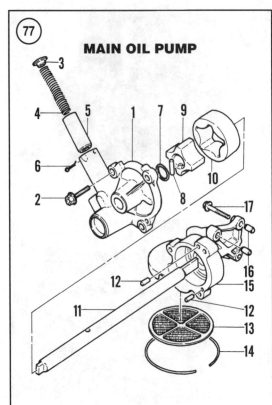

MAIN OIL PUMP

1. Pump cover
2. Bolt
3. Relief valve cap
4. Relief valve spring
5. Relief valve piston
6. Cotter pin
7. Spacer
8. Drive pin
9. Inner rotor
10. Outer rotor
11. Rotor shaft
12. Dowel pins
13. Oil strainer
14. Set ring
15. Pump body
16. Dowel pins
17. Bolt

3. Align the flat on the pump rotor shaft (B, **Figure 66**) with the flat on the drive guide and install the oil pump (B, **Figure 65**). Make sure the grommet on the oil pump slips over the engine tube, as shown in **Figure 76**.

4. Install the oil pump mounting bolts (A, **Figure 65**) and tighten them securely.

5. Install the drive chain guide (**Figure 64**) onto the crankcase. Install and tighten the drive chain guide mounting bolts securely.

6. Install the primary driven gear boss as described in this chapter.

7. Install the rear engine case as described in this chapter.

OIL STRAINER AND MAIN OIL PUMP

The main oil pump is mounted within the crankcase and draws oil from the cylinder block sump. The oil is then delivered under pressure to the bearings and other parts of the engine.

Refer to **Figure 77** for this procedure.

Removal

1. Remove the engine from the frame as described in this chapter.

2. Disassemble the crankcase as described in this chapter.

3. Remove the three bolts (A, **Figure 78**) securing the oil pump and remove the oil pump (B, **Figure 78**).

4. Remove the two oil pump dowel pins (**Figure 79**).

Oil Strainer Cleaning

The oil strainer (**Figure 80**) can be serviced without disassembling the oil pump.

1. Remove the oil pump as described in this chapter.

2. Carefully pry the set ring (**Figure 81**) out of its groove.

3. Remove the oil strainer (**Figure 80**) from the oil pump.

4. Clean the oil strainer in solvent and dry it thoroughly.

5. Inspect the oil strainer screen (**Figure 82**) for damage. Replace the oil strainer if it is damaged or if the screen cannot be thoroughly cleaned.

6. Align the tab on the oil strainer with the notch in the oil pump housing (**Figure 83**) and install the oil strainer.

7. Secure the oil screen with the set ring (**Figure 81**). Make sure the set ring seats within the mounting groove completely.

8. Install the oil pump as described in this chapter.

Oil Pump Relief Valve
Removal/Inspection/Installation

A spring-loaded, piston-type relief valve is incorporated in the oil pump. The relief valve maintains a constant oil pressure by bleeding off excess oil when the oil pressure reaches a specified level; the piston is forced open, allowing some of the oil to return to the sump. The relief valve assembly consists of a spring, piston, cap, cotter pin and the relief valve bore in the oil pump.

The relief valve spring tension controls oil pressure. A weak or damaged spring can reduce oil pressure and cause engine damage. Likewise, a damaged or stuck piston can reduce oil pressure—the piston will be forced open at a lower oil pressure, thus reducing the amount of oil that the engine receives. Whenever the oil pump is removed from the engine, remove and inspect the relief valve assembly as follows.

1. Remove the main oil pump as described in this chapter.

NOTE
When servicing the relief valve assembly in the following steps, place the parts on a clean, lint-free cloth when not handling them. This will

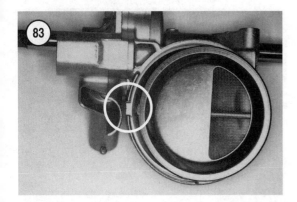

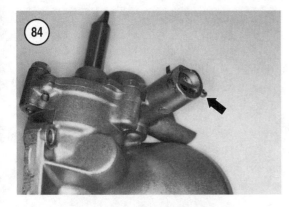

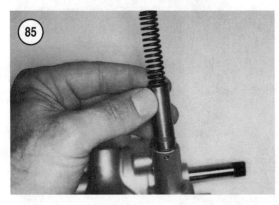

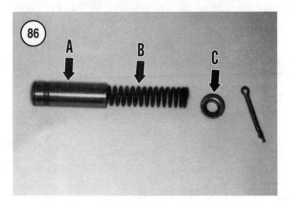

help to prevent dirt from scratching the piston or entering the pump; both conditions will reduce oil pressure.

WARNING
The relief valve spring is under pressure and will fly out when the cotter pin is removed. Use a hand to block the spring and cap when removing the cotter pin. Wear safety glasses to protect eyes.

2. Remove the relief valve cotter pin (**Figure 84**) and remove the relief valve assembly (**Figure 85**). Discard the cotter pin.

3. Wash the piston, spring and cap in solvent and dry them thoroughly.

4. Inspect the piston (A, **Figure 86**) for scratches, scoring or other damage.

5. Inspect the spring (B, **Figure 86**) for distortion or damage. Measure the spring free length with a vernier caliper and check it against the specification in **Table 2**. Replace the spring if its length is less than the wear limit.

6. Inspect the spring cap (C, **Figure 86**) for cracks or damage.

7. Check the relief valve bore in the pump housing for excessive wear, scratches or other damage. The piston must move freely within the bore. Lubricate the piston and the relief valve bore with clean engine oil. Then install the piston in the bore and check its operation. The piston should move through the bore with no binding or sticking.

8. Replace all worn or damaged parts.

9. Coat the piston and spring with clean engine oil. Pour some engine oil into the relief valve bore.

10. Install the piston and spring (**Figure 85**) into the bore.

11. Install the spring cap (**Figure 87**) onto the spring.

12. Compress the relief valve assembly and secure it with a *new* cotter pin (**Figure 84**). Bend the cotter pin over completely to lock it in place.

13. Install the oil pump as described in this chapter.

Main Oil Pump Disassembly

1. Remove the oil strainer as described in this chapter.

2. Remove the relief valve as described in this chapter.

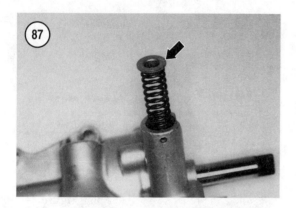

3. Remove bolts securing the pump cover to the pump body. Remove the pump cover (**Figure 88**).

4. Remove the spacer from the rotor shaft.

5. Remove the drive pin from the rotor shaft and remove the shaft.

6. Remove the inner and outer rotors.

Inspection

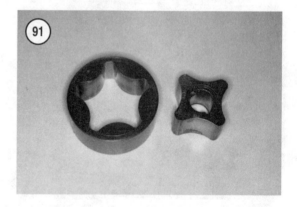

Refer to service specifications in **Table 2**. Replace worn or damaged parts. If several parts require replacement, it is recommended that the entire oil pump be replaced.

1. Clean all of the oil pump components in solvent and place them on a clean, lint-free cloth.

2. Examine the pump body (**Figure 89**) and cover (**Figure 90**) for scoring or other damage, especially in the rotor recess areas.

3. Examine the rotors (**Figure 91**) for scratches and abrasions. Replace the pump if damaged.

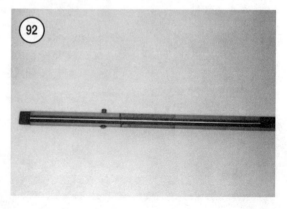

4. Inspect the rotor shaft (**Figure 92**) for bending or damage.

5. Position the outer rotor with the mark facing toward the pump body and install the outer rotor into the pump body.

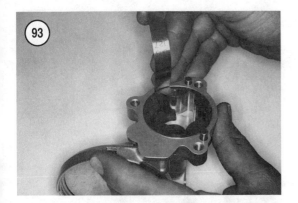

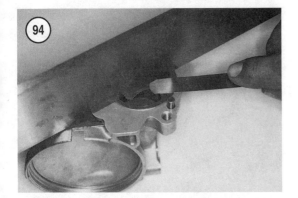

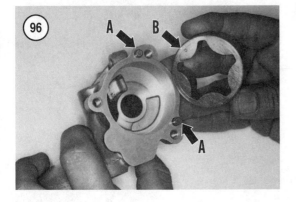

6. Measure the clearance between the outer rotor and the body (**Figure 93**) with a flat feeler gauge.

7. Install the inner rotor into the pump body.

8. Check the pump side clearance with a straight-edge and flat feeler gauge (**Figure 94**).

9. Reinstall the rotor shaft and drive pin.

10. Check the clearance between the inner rotor tip and the outer rotor ramp with a flat feeler gauge, as shown in **Figure 95**.

11. Remove the rotor shaft and inner and outer rotors from the oil pump.

Main Oil Pump Assembly

1. Clean all of the components with solvent and dry them thoroughly.

2. Dip all of the components in clean engine oil and place them on a clean, lint-free cloth prior to assembly.

3. Install the two pump body dowel pins (A, **Figure 96**).

4. Position the outer rotor with the mark (B, **Figure 96**) facing toward the pump body and install the outer rotor into the pump body (**Figure 97**).

NOTE
The mark on the outer rotor ensures that the rotors are in the same relative position to each other when installed.

5. Position the inner rotor with the notched side facing up and install it into the body and outer rotor (**Figure 98**).

6. Slide the rotor shaft through the inner rotor and align the hole in the shaft with the notch in the rotor (**Figure 99**). The end of the rotor shaft closest to the shaft hole should be directly above the rotors.

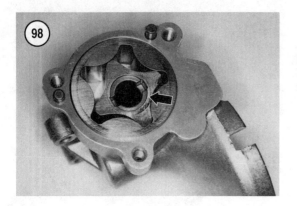

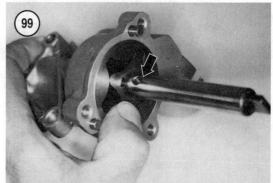

7. Install the drive pin through the rotor shaft and seat the pin in the inner rotor notch (**Figure 100**).

8. Install the spacer (**Figure 101**) onto the rotor shaft and seat it against the inner rotor.

9. Slide the pump cover (**Figure 102**) over the rotor shaft and align it with the two dowel pins. Install and tighten the pump cover mounting bolts securely.

10. Install the relief valve assembly, as described in this chapter.

11. Install the oil strainer as described in this chapter.

Main Oil Pump Installation

1. Install the two oil pump dowel pins (**Figure 79**) into the engine case.

2. Align the oil pump with the dowel pins and install the oil pump (B, **Figure 78**) and its mounting bolts (A, **Figure 78**). Tighten the bolts securely.

3. Reassemble the crankcase as described in this chapter.

4. Install the engine into the frame as described in this chapter.

5. Check the engine oil pressure as described in Chapter Three.

CRANKCASE

The crankcase assembly includes the cylinder bores and is split vertically along the crankcase centerline. The separate cylinder heads attach directly to the crankcase assembly. There is no separate oil pan, as the oil sump is part of the crankcase.

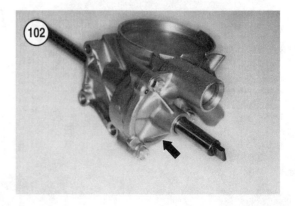

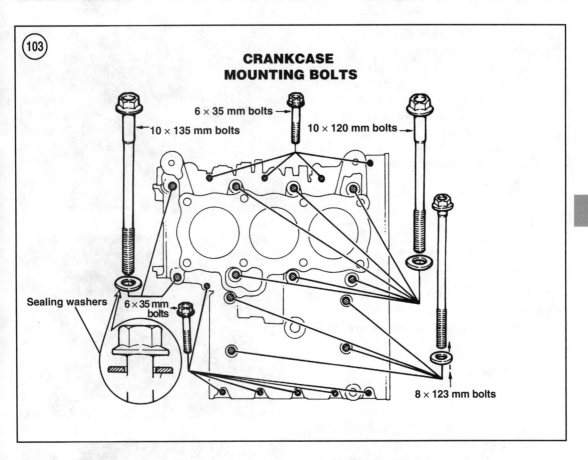

CRANKCASE MOUNTING BOLTS

6 × 35 mm bolts →

←10 × 135 mm bolts

10 × 120 mm bolts →

Sealing washers

6 × 35 mm bolts

8 × 123 mm bolts

5

Disassembly

1. Remove the engine as described in this chapter.

2. Remove the secondary air supply as described in Chapter Eight.

3. Remove the timing belts as described in Chapter Four.

4. Remove the cylinder heads as described in Chapter Four.

5. Remove the clutch as described in Chapter Six.

6. Remove the following components as described in this chapter:

    a. Rear engine case.

    b. Starter clutch.

    c. Alternator clutch assembly.

    d. Primary drive and driven gears.

    e. Final drive gear (and output shaft).

    f. Scavenge oil pump.

    g. Transmission mainshaft and countershaft bearing holders.

7. Remove the engine front cover as described in Chapter Four.

8. Remove the bearing holder as described in Chapter Four.

9. Remove the gearshift linkage (drum center, cam plate and stopper arm) as described in Chapter Seven. The shift spindle and shift arm are removed after disassembling the engine.

10. On the left side of the crankcase, in a crisscross pattern in two or three stages, remove the 6 mm, 8 mm and 10 mm bolts (**Figure 103**) securing the cylinder block halves together.

CAUTION
In the next steps, make sure to protect the cylinder head mating surfaces on the crankcase from damage. If they are gouged or damaged in any way the very expensive crankcase assembly must be replaced.

11. If the engine is not in an engine stand, perform the following:

    a. Clean the cylinder head mating surface of the right crankcase half with contact cleaner.

b. Apply several layers of duct tape to this case half surface to protect it.

c. Place a protective sheet of clean two-ply corrugated cardboard (not too thick, as the engine will not be steady) or similar material on top of the workbench. This is to protect the cylinder head mating surface on the right crankcase.

d. Place wooden block(s) under the oil sump section to help steady the engine.

NOTE
The crankshaft is secured within the right crankcase. Therefore the left crankcase must be removed from the right crankcase.

12. Pull the shift arm (**Figure 104**) away from the shift drum.

13. Set the engine on its right side (**Figure 105**).

NOTE
Due to the size of the cylinder block, the following steps require the aid of an assistant.

14. With the aid of an assistant, gradually pull the left crankcase part way up, then stop.

15. Place wooden blocks between the crankcase halves.

16. Wrap clean shop cloths around the connecting rods and pistons in the left crankcase. This will prevent the pistons from falling onto the transmission gears in the right crankcase when the left crankcase is removed.

CAUTION
In the next step, be sure to pull the left crankcase straight up. If the crankcase does not come off straight, there will be abnormal stress placed on the pistons, piston pins and connecting rods, resulting in expensive damage.

17. Remove the wood blocks from between the crankcase halves.

18. With the aid of an assistant, completely pull the left crankcase straight up and off of the pistons. Place the crankcase on the workbench out of the way.

19. Remove the two dowel pins with O-rings (A, **Figure 106**).

20. Remove the two dowel pins without O-rings. See B, **Figure 106** and **Figure 107**.

21. Remove the shift arm (A, **Figure 108**) and shift spindle as described in Chapter Seven.

22. Remove the main oil pump (B, **Figure 108**) as described in this chapter.

23. Remove the transmission/shift drum assembly as described in Chapter Seven.

24. Remove the left side connecting rod/piston assemblies as described in this chapter.

25. Remove the right side connecting rod/piston assemblies as described in this chapter.

26. Remove the crankshaft as described in this chapter.

Inspection

The following procedure requires the use of specialized measuring tools. If these tools are not readily available, have the measurements performed by a dealership or machine shop.

NOTE
If there is evidence of an oil leak, inspect the crankcase mating halves before cleaning them; oil will generally run into a crack and highlight it.

1. Check the crankcase halves for cracks. Inspect the mating surfaces of both halves. They must be free of gouges, burrs or any damage that could cause an oil leak. If damage is noted, have it inspected by a Honda dealership or machine shop.

2. Check all gasket surfaces for warp with a straightedge and feeler gauge.

3. Check all of the threaded holes in the crankcase halves for deposit buildup or damaged threads. Threaded holes should be cleaned out with compressed air, as dirt buildup in the bottom of the hole may prevent the bolt from being tightened properly. Use a tap to clean the threads and to remove any deposits. Use an aluminum thread tapping fluid or kerosene on the tap threads to prevent thread damage. If a damaged threaded hole is found, check the mating bolt or screw for damage. Replace any damaged bolt or screw.

4. Check the dowel pins for cracks, rust or other damage. Make sure the dowel pins were not damaged during removal. Discard the dowel pin O-rings and install new O-rings during assembly.

5. Inspect the needle bearings for missing or damaged rollers. Check the cage for cracks or other damage. Inspect ball bearings for wear or damage. Slowly rotate the inner bearing race and check for any radial play, axial play or roughness. Replace worn or damaged bearings as described under *Bearing Replacement* in Chapter One.

6. Soak with solvent any old gasket material that may be stuck to the top of the crankcase. Use a broad-tipped dull chisel to gently scrape off all gasket residue. Do not gouge the sealing surface; oil and air leaks will result.

7. Thoroughly clean the inside and outside of both case halves (**Figure 109**) with cleaning solvent to remove all oil, carbon and grease residue. Then hand-wash the case halves with a liquid dishwashing soap and rinse them with cold water. Dry with compressed air. Make sure there is no solvent residue left in the halves, as it will contaminate the new engine oil. Lubricate all of the bearings with new engine oil to prevent rust.

8. After the crankcase has been thoroughly cleaned, place a straightedge across the crank-

5

case-to-cylinder head gasket surfaces (**Figure 110**) at several points. Measure the warpage by inserting a flat feeler gauge between the straightedge and the cylinder block at each location. If the case-to-cylinder head mating surface is warped in any location by more than 0.05 mm (0.002 in.), it must be replaced.

9. Check the cylinder walls (**Figure 111**) for scratches, scoring or light seizure marks. Any excessive damage will require cylinder boring and new pistons and rings. If the cylinders require boring, have a Honda dealership or a machinist bore the cylinders and fit the new oversize pistons.

10. If there is no evidence of cylinder damage or wear, measure the cylinder bore diameter as described under *Piston Clearance Measurement* in this chapter.

11. Replace any worn or damaged engine mounts (**Figure 112**).

12. After the cylinder block has been serviced, wash the cylinder bores in hot soapy water. This is the only way to clean the cylinder walls of the fine grit material left from the boring or honing job. After washing the cylinder bores, run a clean white cloth through each cylinder. The cloth should show no traces of grit or other debris. If the cloth is dirty, the cylinder wall is not clean enough. Wash it again until the cloth comes out of the cylinders clean. After the cylinder bores are clean, lubricate each cylinder with new engine oil to prevent the cylinder bores from rusting.

> *CAUTION*
> *The combination of soap and water described in Step 12 is the only solution that will completely clean the cylinder walls. Solvent and kerosene cannot wash fine grit out of the cylinder crevices. Grit left in the cylinder wall will act as a grinding compound and cause premature wear to the engine components.*

Assembly

The following tools are required to assemble the cylinder blocks:

1. Three Honda piston ring compressors.
2. Honda piston base A.
3. Honda piston base B.

4. Crankcase support blocks. These can be fabricated from wood to the dimensions 40 × 40 × 86 mm (1-1/2 × 1-1/2 × 3-3/8 in.).

> *NOTE*
> *When fabricating the crankcase support blocks, do not use plywood or other soft wood, as small wood slivers may be pulled off when the tools are removed and fall into the engine. Use a hardwood such as birch, oak or walnut.*

1. Clean the cylinder block as described under *Inspection* in this chapter.

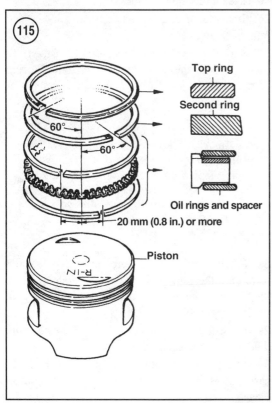

Top ring

Second ring

60°

60°

Oil rings and spacer

20 mm (0.8 in.) or more

Piston

2. Install the transmission/shift drum assembly as described in Chapter Seven.

3. Install the main oil pump (B, **Figure 108**) as described in this chapter.

4. Install the shift arm (A, **Figure 108**) and shift spindle as described in Chapter Seven.

5. Install the crankshaft assembly as described in this chapter.

6. Install the right side rod bearing caps/pistons as described in this chapter.

7. Install the left side rod bearing caps/pistons as described in this chapter.

8. Apply clean engine oil to the piston rings (**Figure 113**) and to the cylinder walls of the left crankcase half.

9. Install the two dowel pins with new O-rings (A, **Figure 106**).

10. Install the two dowel pins without O-rings. See B, **Figure 106** and **Figure 107**.

11. Rotate the crankshaft until the T1.2 drive pulley mark is facing up (**Figure 114**).

12. Cover the transmission with clean shop rags.

13. Stagger the piston rings as shown in **Figure 115**.

14. Install the ring compressors (**Figure 116**) onto the pistons so that the tapered side of each compressor faces up. Stagger the splits in the compressors as shown in **Figure 117**.

NOTE
*Refer to **Figure 118** for cylinder number positions when performing the following.*

15. Install the piston base A under the No. 4 and No. 6 pistons (clutch side). Make sure that both sides of the piston base are parallel (**Figure 119**).

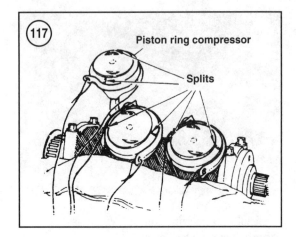

Piston ring compressor

Splits

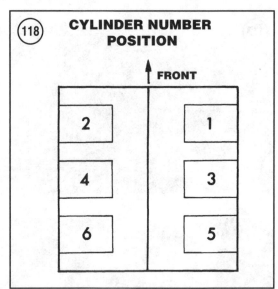

CYLINDER NUMBER POSITION

↑ FRONT

2		1
4		3
6		5

16. Install piston base B under the No. 2 piston (timing belt side) so that its notch faces toward the connecting rod (**Figure 119**).

17. Align the piston ring compressor cables opposite the transmission side to make it easier to remove them later on.

18. Temporarily remove the dowel pin and O-ring shown in **Figure 120**. This will make it easier to use the crankcase support blocks in the following steps.

19. Tie the shift arm with a rubber band or tie wrap (**Figure 121**) so that it is out of the way.

20. Place the crankcase support blocks between the case halves mating surfaces.

CAUTION
In the next step, make sure to install the left case straight down. If the case is not installed straight, there will be abnormal stress on the No. 2 piston. This could cause the ring to break.

21. With the aid of an assistant, align the left case half with the No. 2 piston and lower the cylinder block onto the piston. The case should then rest evenly on the support blocks.

22. Remove piston base B from underneath the No. 2 piston.

23. Slide the No. 2 ring compressor down the piston approximately 13 mm (½ in.).

NOTE
If a ring compressor is knocked off either the No. 3 or No. 5 piston, remove the cylinder block, start over and reinstall both of them.

24. Pull both No. 2 piston ring compressor cables at the same time to separate the compressor halves. Remove the ring compressor from the No. 2 piston.

25. Have the assistant hold the case half in position while turning the crankcase support blocks on their sides. Then align the case with both pistons and set the case on the support blocks.

26. Turn the top edge of piston base A inward and remove piston base A.

27. Slide the No. 6 ring compressor down, then pull both cables at the same time to separate the ring compressor halves. Remove the ring compressor from the engine.

NOTE
The No. 4 cylinder ring compressor is difficult to remove. When removing it in Step 28, have the assistant pivot the left case half away from the transmission as much as possible to gain as much clearance as possible.

28. Pull the No. 4 ring compressor cables back and forth until the compressor halves separate, then remove them from the engine. Rest the cylinder block on the support blocks.

29. Have the assistant hold the case in position, then remove the support blocks.

30. Make sure the mating surfaces of both crankcase halves are clean. Clean them with contact cleaner, if necessary.

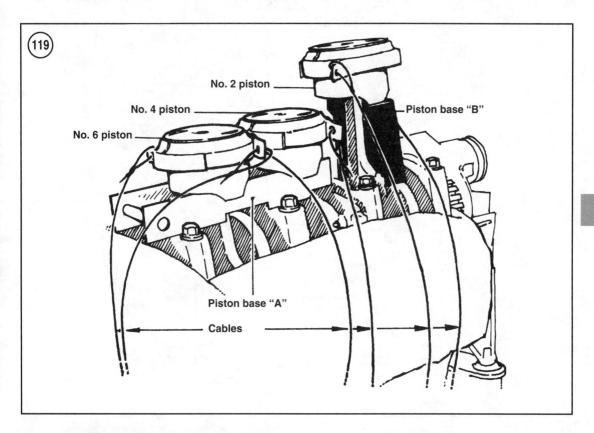

No. 2 piston

No. 4 piston

No. 6 piston

Piston base "B"

Piston base "A"

Cables

5

31. Install the dowel pin and O-ring (**Figure 120**) removed in Step 18.

32. Apply a light coating of gasket sealer, such as ThreeBond No. 1104 or equivalent to the sealing surfaces of both crankcase halves (**Figure 122**). Make the coating as thin as possible for the best seal. Make sure sealant is applied to the difficult to reach areas shown in **Figure 122**.

33. Push the left crankcase down until it seats completely. Check around the entire perimeter to make sure it is seated correctly.

NOTE
The two front 10 mm and the four 8
mm bolts have sealing washers.

34. Apply a light coating of clean engine oil to the threads and under the flanges of the 10 mm bolts. Then install the sealing washers on the 10 mm bolts (**Figure 123**).

35. On the left crankcase, install all the bolts finger-tight.

36. In a crisscross pattern in 2-3 stages, tighten the bolts in the following order:

    a. 10 mm bolts.

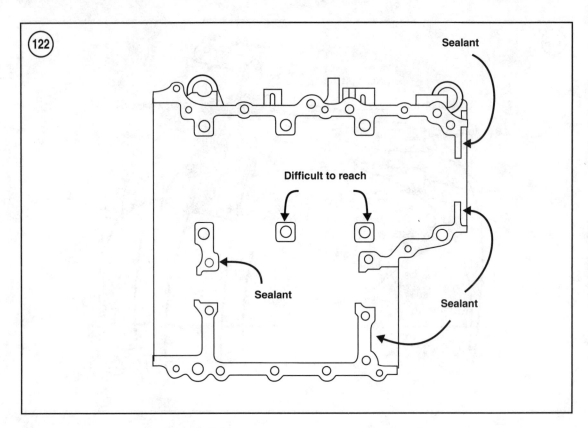

(122)

Sealant

Difficult to reach

Sealant

Sealant

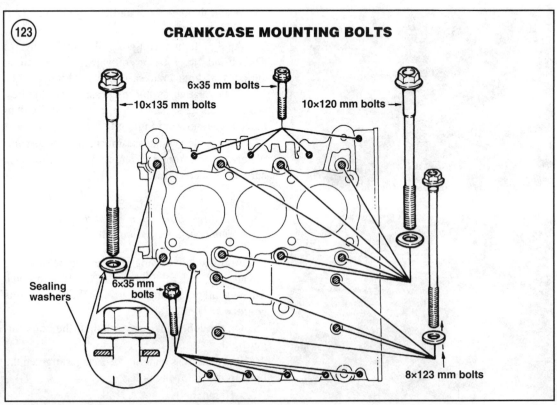

(123)

CRANKCASE MOUNTING BOLTS

6×35 mm bolts

10×135 mm bolts

10×120 mm bolts

Sealing washers

6×35 mm bolts

8×123 mm bolts

b. 8 mm bolts.

c. 6 mm bolts.

Tighten the bolts to the torque specification in **Table 3**.

37. Remove the rubber band from the shift arm (**Figure 124**).

38. Install the gearshift linkage (drum center, cam plate and stopper arm) as described in Chapter Seven.

39. Install the bearing holder as described in Chapter Four.

40. Install the front engine cover as described in Chapter Four.

41. Install the following components as described in this chapter:

a. Scavenge oil pump.

b. Final drive gear and output shaft.

c. Primary drive and driven gears.

d. Alternator clutch assembly.

e. Starter clutch.

f. Rear engine case.

42. Install the clutch as described in Chapter Six.

43. Install the cylinder heads as described in Chapter Four.

44. Install the timing belts as described in Chapter Four.

45. Install the secondary air supply as described in Chapter Eight.

46. Install the engine in the frame as described in this chapter.

47. Refill the engine with the recommended type and quantity of engine oil and coolant as described in Chapter Three.

48. If new components were installed, the engine must be broken in as if it were new. Refer to *Break-in Procedure* at the end of this chapter.

PISTONS AND CONNECTING RODS

5

The engine must be removed from the frame and the crankcase separated to remove the pistons and connecting rods. The pistons and connecting rods for the No. 1, No. 3 and No. 5 cylinders (right side) are removed through the tops of the cylinder bores.

Piston and Connecting Rod Removal

1. Remove the engine as described in this chapter.

2. Separate the crankcase as described in this chapter.

3. Lay a piece of cardboard or some clean shop cloths over the transmission shaft assemblies, to protect the pistons.

4. Mark the piston crown of the three left cylinders (**Figure 113**) with the corresponding cylinder number so the pistons will be reinstalled in the correct cylinders. Refer to **Figure 118** for cylinder numbers.

5. Lay the pistons and connecting rods over onto the cardboard or shop cloths or over onto the other side of the crankcase.

6. Before removing the connecting rods, measure the connecting rod side clearance with a feeler gauge for each rod as shown in **Figure 125**. Record the clearance and compare it with the wear limit in **Table 2**.

7. Prior to disassembly, mark the rods and caps. Number them as identified in **Figure 118**.

8. On the No. 2, No. 4 and No. 6 cylinders, remove the nuts securing the connecting rod caps and remove the caps (**Figure 126**) and connecting rods.

CAUTION
If disassembling a high-milage engine, inspect the tops of the cylinder

*bores on the No. 1, No. 3 and No. 5 cylinders for a ridge where the piston ring reaches the top of its travel (**Figure 127**). Perform Step 9 only if there is a ridge present.*

9. If there is a ridge at the top of any cylinder bore, the ridge must be removed with a ridge reamer. Remove each ridge at a time as follows:
   a. Rotate the crankshaft until the piston to be removed is at the bottom of its travel.
   b. Place an oil-soaked shop cloth down into the cylinder and over the piston to collect the debris. Remove the ridge and/or deposits from the top of the cylinder bore with a ridge reamer.
   c. Turn the crankshaft until that piston is at top dead center and remove the shop cloth and the debris. Make sure to remove all debris, as this material will scratch the cylinder wall during piston removal. Make sure that none of the debris fall into the water jacket surrounding the cylinder bore.

10. Remove the nuts securing the connecting rod caps and remove the caps (**Figure 128**).

11. Mark the piston crowns of the three right pistons with the corresponding cylinder numbers so the pistons will be reinstalled in the correct cylinders. Refer to **Figure 118** for cylinder numbers.

12. Carefully remove the pistons and connecting rods though the tops of the cylinder bores.

13. Mark the back of each bearing insert with the cylinder number and U (upper) or L (lower).

Piston and Pin Removal

The piston pin is pressed into place. Removal of the piston pin from the piston and connecting rod requires the use of a hydraulic press and an expensive Honda special tool. Once the piston pin has been removed, it must be replaced with a new one; it cannot be reinstalled. Installation is also critical since proper alignment is necessary.

Removing the piston/connecting rod assemblies and taking them into a Honda dealership for service can be a considerable savings.

> *WARNING*
> *The edges of all piston rings are very sharp. Be careful when handling the piston.*

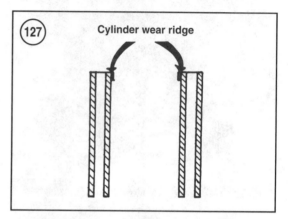

Cylinder wear ridge

Before taking the piston/connecting rod assemblies to the dealership for service, perform this inspection.

1. Place the crankshaft end of the connecting rod in a vise with soft jaws.

2. Rock the piston as shown in **Figure 129**. Any rocking motion (do not confuse with the normal sliding motion) indicates wear on the piston pin, rod bearing surface, or piston pin bore or, more likely, a combination of all three.

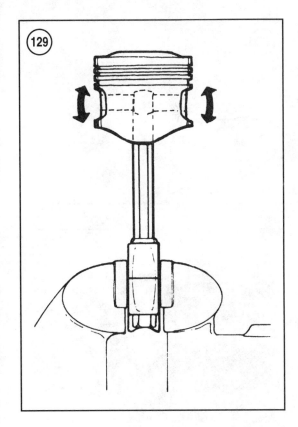

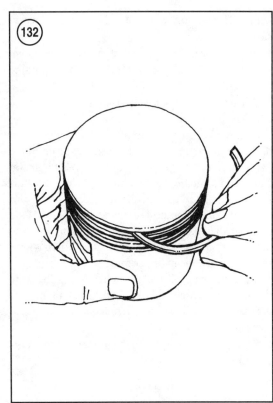

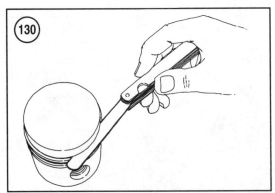

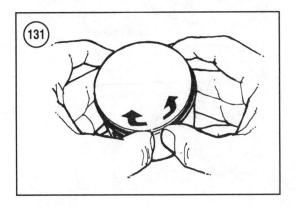

Piston Ring Inspection/Removal/Installation

When measuring the piston rings, compare the actual measurements to the specifications in **Table 2**. Replace worn or damaged parts as described in this section.

1. Measure the side clearance of each ring in its groove with a flat feeler gauge (**Figure 130**) and compare it with dimensions in **Table 2**. If the clearance is greater than specified, replace the rings. If the clearance is still excessive with the new rings, replace the piston and rings.

> *WARNING*
> *The edges of all piston rings are very sharp. Be careful when handling them.*

2. Remove the top ring with a ring expander tool or by spreading the ring ends by hand and lifting the ring up and over the piston (**Figure 131**). Repeat for the remaining rings.

3. Carefully remove all carbon from the ring grooves with a discarded piston ring that has been broken and ground (**Figure 132**). Inspect grooves carefully for burrs, nicks or broken and cracked

lands. Recondition or replace the piston if necessary.

4. Roll each ring around its piston groove as shown in **Figure 133** to check for binding. Minor binding may be cleaned up with a fine-cut file.

5. Measure the rings for wear as shown in **Figure 134**. Place each ring, one at a time, into the cylinder and push it in about 20 mm (3/4 in.) with the crown of the piston to ensure that the ring is square in the cylinder bore. Measure the end gap with a flat feeler gauge and compare it with dimensions in **Table 2**. If the gap is greater than specified, measure the cylinder bore diameter as described in this chapter. If the cylinder diameter is within specifications, replace the ring(s). If the cylinder diameter is not within specifications, the cylinder must be bored and new pistons and rings installed. When installing new rings, measure their end gaps in the same manner. If the gap is less than specified, make sure the correct size rings are installed.

6. Install the piston rings in the order shown in **Figure 135**.

CAUTION
Install compression rings with their markings facing up.

7. Install the piston rings—first the bottom, then the middle, then the top ring—by carefully spreading the ends with two thumbs and slipping the ring over the top of the piston. Remember that the piston rings must be installed with the marks on them facing up toward the top of the piston.

8. Make sure the rings are seated completely in their grooves all the way around the piston and that the end gaps are positioned as shown in **Figure 135**.

9. If new rings are installed, measure the side clearance of each ring in its groove with a flat feeler gauge (**Figure 130**) and compare to dimensions in **Table 2**.

Piston Inspection

1. Remove the piston rings as described in this chapter.

2. Carefully clean the carbon from the piston crown with a chemical remover or with a soft scraper. Do not use a wire brush to clean ring grooves or lands. Large carbon accumulations reduce piston cooling and result in detonation and pis-

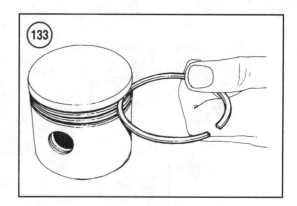

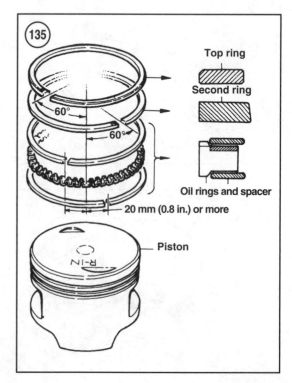

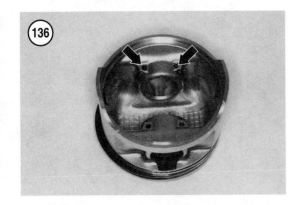

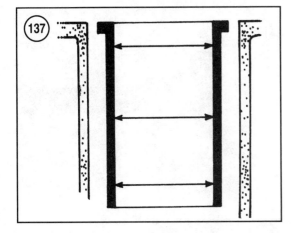

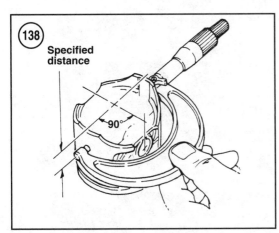

Specified distance

90°

ton damage. Renumber the piston if cleaning has removed the identification mark.

CAUTION
Be careful not to gouge or damage the piston when removing carbon. Never use a wire brush to clean the piston skirt or ring grooves.

3. After cleaning the piston, examine the crown. The crown should show no signs of wear or damage. If the crown appears pecked or spongy-looking, also check the spark plug, valves and combustion chamber for aluminum deposits. If these deposits are found, the engine is overheating.

4. Examine each ring groove for burrs, dented edges and wide wear. Pay particular attention to the top compression ring groove, as it usually wears more than the others. If there is evidence of oil ring groove wear or if the oil ring assembly is tight and difficult to remove, the piston skirt may have collapsed. If so, replace the piston.

5. Measure piston-to-cylinder clearance as described in this chapter. If damage or wear indicates piston replacement, select new pistons as described under *Piston Clearance Measurement* in this chapter.

6. Check the piston skirt for galling and abrasion that may have been caused by piston seizure. If any galling is present, the piston(s) should be replaced.

7. Check the oil hole holes (**Figure 136**) in the underside of the piston for sludge. Clean the holes with wire and clean them with compressed air.

Piston Clearance Measurement

1. Make sure the piston and cylinder walls are clean and dry.

2. Measure the cylinder bores diameter and check for excessive taper and out-of-round using a bore gauge or telescoping gauge. Measure the cylinder bore with an inside micrometer at points near the top, in the middle and toward the bottom as shown in **Figure 137**.

3. To determine if the cylinder is out-of-round, perform the measurements aligned with the piston pin, then at 90° to the piston pin.

4. If the cylinder is excessively worn, tapered or out-of-round, bore the cylinder to the next oversize and replace the piston and rings. Rebore all cylinders even though only one may be worn.

5. Next measure the piston diameter at right angles to the piston pin at a distance 10 mm (0.4 in.) up from the bottom of the piston skirt (**Figure 138**).

6. Subtract the piston diameter from the largest bore diameter, the difference is the piston-to-cylinder clearance. If the clearance is excessive (**Table 2**), bore the cylinders to the next oversize and replace the pistons and rings. Prior to boring

the cylinders oversize, purchase new pistons and measure the oversize pistons to establish the correct finished bore diameter to provide the correct piston clearance (**Table 2**).

7. Honda pistons are available in oversizes of 0.25 mm (0.010 in.), 0.50 mm (0.020 in.), 0.75 mm (0.030 in.) and 1.00 mm (0.039 in.).

Connecting Rod and Piston Pin Inspection

1. Clean the connecting rods and inserts in solvent and dry them with compressed air.

2. Carefully inspect each rod journal (crankpin) on the crankshaft for scratches, ridges, scoring, nicks. Very small nicks and scratches may be removed with fine emery cloth. If damage is serious, the crankshaft must be replaced; it cannot be serviced.

> *NOTE*
> *Measure the pistons, piston pins and connecting rods (**Figure 139**) as a set when performing the following steps.*

3. Measure the diameter of the piston pin end of the connecting rod (A, **Figure 140**) with a telescoping gauge. Then measure the gauge to determine the inside diameter. Replace the connecting rod if the bore diameter exceeds the wear limit in **Table 2**.

4. Measure the piston pin diameter with a micrometer (B, **Figure 140**). Replace the piston pin if its diameter is less than the wear in **Table 2**.

5. Determine the connecting rod-to-piston pin clearance with the measurements obtained in Step 3 and Step 4 and compare to the wear limit in **Table 2**.

6. Measure the piston pin bore diameter (**Figure 141**) with a small hole gauge. Then measure the gauge with an outside micrometer to determine the pin bore diameter. Replace the piston if the pin bore diameter exceeds the wear limit in **Table 2**.

7. Determine the piston pin-to-piston clearance with the measurements obtained in Step 4 and Step 6 and compare to the wear limit in **Table 2**.

Connecting Rod Bearing Clearance Measurement

1. Check the inside and outside surfaces of the bearing inserts (**Figure 142**) for wear, bluish tint (burned), flaking, abrasion and scoring.

2. Check the locking tab (**Figure 143**) on each bearing for damage.

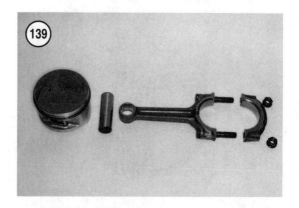

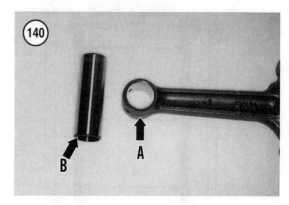

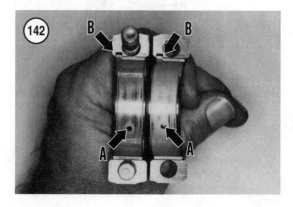

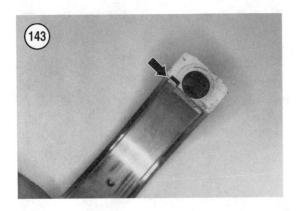

3. If the bearings are good, they may be reused. If any insert is questionable, replace the entire set.

CAUTION
Make sure that old bearings are installed in their exact original locations.

4. Wipe the bearing inserts and crankpins clean. Install the bearing inserts in the rod caps (**Figure 143**).

5. Install the piston and connecting rod assembly onto the crankshaft in the correct location.

6. Place a strip of Plastigage material over the rod bearing journal parallel to the crankshaft (**Figure 144**). Do not place the Plastigage material over an oil hole in the crankshaft.

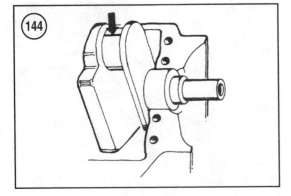

NOTE
Do not rotate the crankshaft while the Plastigage strips are in place.

7. Install the rod cap onto one rod and tighten the nuts to the torque specification in **Table 3**.

8. Remove the rod cap and measure the width of the flattened Plastigage material (**Figure 145**) following the manufacturer's instructions. Measure both ends of the Plastigage strip. A difference of 0.003 mm (0.0001 in.) or more indicates a tapered journal. Confirm with a micrometer. New bearing clearance and service limit specifications are in **Table 2**. Remove all of the Plastigage material from the crankshaft journals and the connecting rods.

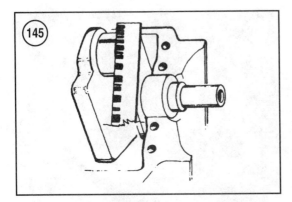

9. If the rod bearing clearance is greater than specified, use the following steps for new bearing selection.

10. The crankshaft rod journals are marked with letters A, B or C (**Figure 146**) on the counterbalance weights. The connecting rod and cap are marked with numbers 1, 2 or 3 or Roman numerals I, II or III (A, **Figure 147**).

11. Select new bearings by cross-referencing the crankshaft rod journal letters (**Figure 146**) in the horizontal column of **Table 4** to the rod bearing number (A, **Figure 147**) in the vertical column. Where the two columns intersect, the new bearing color is indicated. **Table 5** lists the bearing insert color and thickness.

12. After installing the new bearings, recheck clearance by repeating this procedure.

13. Repeat Steps 4-12 for the other five cylinders.

Connecting Rod Replacement (Weight Code)

Each connecting rod is marked with a weight code letter—A, B, C, D or E (B, **Figure 147**). When replacing a connecting rod, replace it with the same weight code as the original rod.

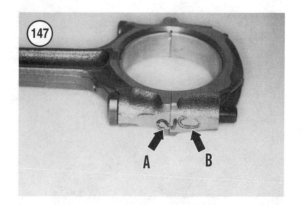

Piston and Pin Installation

The piston pin is pressed into place; this requires a number of special tools and procedures. Refer piston and pin installation to a Honda dealership.

Piston and Connecting Rod Installation

1. Install the piston and piston pins onto their respective connecting rods as described in this chapter.
2. Install the connecting rod bearings as follows:

> *NOTE*
> *Make sure old bearings are installed into their original positions.*

  a. Wipe the bearing inserts and the connecting rod and cap bearing surfaces clean.

  b. Insert the bearing inserts into the rod and cap, aligning the oil hole (A, **Figure 142**) in the bearing with the oil hole in the rod and cap while engaging the bearing tabs with the mating grooves (B, **Figure 142**).

  c. Apply molybdenum disulfide oil to the bearing insert surfaces.

3. Install the piston rings onto the connecting rods as described in this chapter.

4. Apply a light coating of engine oil to the cylinder walls and to the piston rings prior to installation.

5. On the No. 1, No. 3 and No. 5 pistons, perform the following:

  a. Insert short pieces of rubber hose over the threads on each connecting rod bolt.

  b. Install a piston ring compressor (**Figure 148**) onto the piston.

  c. Position the piston/rod assembly so the R-IN mark (**Figure 149**) on the piston crown is pointed up toward the top surface of the cylinder block.

  d. Carefully install the piston and connecting rod assembly into the correct cylinder.

  e. Remove the ring compressor and carefully push the piston and connecting rod assembly all the way in.

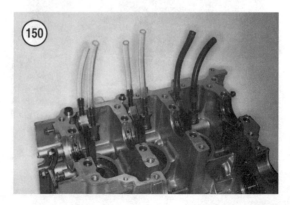

f. Guide the connecting rod onto the crankshaft (if installed) so the bearing surface will not be damaged by the connecting rod during installation.

g. If the crankshaft is installed, remove the hoses from the rod bolts.

h. If the crankshaft is not installed, leave the hoses (**Figure 150**) installed onto the rod bolts.

6. Install the crankshaft, if removed, as described in this chapter.

7. Apply molybdenum disulfide grease to the bearing inserts, crankpins and connecting rod bolt threads. Install the connecting rods and rod caps (**Figure 128**). Tighten the cap nuts evenly in 2-3 steps to the torque specifications in **Table 3**.

8. On the No. 2, No. 4 and No. 6 pistons, position the piston/rod assembly so the L-IN mark on the piston and the oil hole in the connecting rod are pointed up toward the top surface of the cylinder block.

9. Apply molybdenum disulfide grease to the bearing inserts, crankpins and connecting rod bolt threads. Install the connecting rods and rod caps (**Figure 151**). Tighten the cap nuts evenly in 2-3 steps to the torque specifications in **Table 3**.

10. After all rod caps have been installed, rotate the crankshaft several times and make sure there is no binding.

CRANKSHAFT

Handle the crankshaft carefully when removing and servicing it in the following sections. Use a set of V-blocks to support the crankshaft while it is removed from the engine. Place the crankshaft in a safe location where is will not roll off and get damaged.

Removal/Installation

1. Disassemble the cylinder block as described in this chapter.

2. Remove the camshaft drive pulley assembly (**Figure 152**) if not previously removed.

3. Remove and discard the crankshaft seal (**Figure 153**).

4. Remove the pistons and connecting rods from the crankshaft as described in this chapter.

NOTE
*Each main bearing cap (A, **Figure 154**) is identified with the numbers 1, 2, 3 or 4. A dot mark is aligned with one number on each cap, identifying the bearing cap with its position in the engine. In addition, each cap has an arrow that points up toward the top of the engine. Check for these marks before removing the main bearing caps.*

5. Loosen and remove the main bearing cap bolts (B, **Figure 154**) and the bearing cap plates (C, **Figure 154**).

> *NOTE*
> *If the No. 1, No. 3 and No. 5 pistons were not removed, insert a piece of hose over each connecting rod bolt (A, **Figure 155**) to prevent the rod bolts from damaging the crankshaft journals.*

6. Remove the main bearing caps (A, **Figure 154**) and their dowel pins.

7. Lift the crankshaft (B, **Figure 155**) up and out of the cylinder block.

8. Remove the bearing inserts.

Inspection

1. Clean the crankshaft thoroughly with solvent. Clean oil holes with rifle cleaning brushes; flush thoroughly with new solvent and dry with compressed air. Lightly oil all bearing journal surfaces immediately to prevent rust.

2. Carefully inspect each journal (**Figure 156**) for scratches, ridges, scoring, or nicks. Very small nicks and scratches may be removed with fine emery cloth. If damage is serious, the crankshaft must be replaced—it cannot be serviced. If the surface on all journals is satisfactory, perform the following.

3. Measure the journals diameter with a micrometer (**Figure 157**) and check for out-of roundness and taper. See **Table 2** for specifications.

4. Check crankshaft runout as follows:

  a. Set a dial indicator on the center main bearing journals. The arrows in **Figure 158** show the center main bearing journals.

  b. Turn the crankshaft two revolutions and read the runout on the dial indicator.

  c. Divide the total indicator reading in half to determine the runout and compare to the runout service limit in **Table 2**.

  d. Repeat for the other main bearing journal.

5. Replace the crankshaft if the test specifications in Steps 2 and 3 are out of tolerance or if the runout is excessive. Do not attempt to repair the crankshaft.

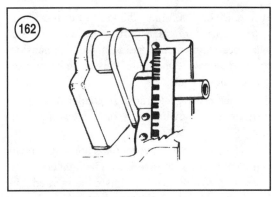

Crankshaft Main Bearing and Journal Inspection

1. Check the inside and outside surfaces of the bearing inserts for wear, bluish tint (burned), flaking, abrasion and scoring; see **Figure 159** and **Figure 160**. If the bearings are good, they may be reused. If any insert is questionable, replace the entire set.

2. Clean the main bearing inserts and the bearing surfaces of the crankshaft. Measure the main bearing clearance by performing the following steps.

3. Install the existing main bearing inserts into the right crankcase half (**Figure 160**).

4. Install the crankshaft into the right crankcase half.

5. Place a strip of material over each main bearing journal parallel to the crankshaft (**Figure 161**). Do not place the Plastigage strip over an oil hole in the crankshaft.

NOTE
Do not rotate the crankshaft while the Plastigage strips are in place.

6. Install the existing bearing inserts into the main bearing caps (**Figure 159**).

7. Install the main bearing caps in their correct positions. See *Crankshaft Installation* in this chapter.

8. Apply oil to the threads of the bolts and install them into the right crankcase   Tighten them evenly in 2-3 steps to the torque specifications in **Table 3**.

9. Remove the main bearing cap bolts.

10. Carefully remove the main bearing caps and measure the width of the flattened Plastigage material following manufacturer's instructions. Measure both ends of the Plastigage strip (**Figure 162**). A

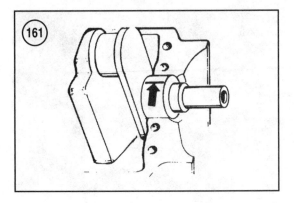

difference of 0.003 mm (0.0001 in.) or more indicates a tapered journal. Confirm with a micrometer. New bearing clearance and wear limit dimensions are in **Table 2**. Remove the Plastigage strips from all bearing journals.

11. If the bearing clearance is greater than specified, use the following steps for new bearing selection.

12. The crankshaft main journals are marked with numbers 1, 2 or 3 (**Figure 163**). The right crankcase (next to the front bearing support) is marked with numbers 1, 2, or 3 or Roman numerals I, II or III (**Figure 164**). The first number toward the top of the crankcase is for the front main bearing and working across is the two center main bearings and then the rear main bearing.

13. Select new main bearings by cross-referencing the main journal number (**Figure 163**) in the horizontal column of **Table 6** to the crankcase bearing number (**Figure 164**) in the vertical column. Where the two columns intersect, the new bearing color is indicated. **Table 7** gives the bearing insert color and thickness. The color code is marked on the side of the bearings (**Figure 165**).

14. After installing the bearings, recheck clearance by repeating this procedure.

Crankshaft Installation

1. Install the crankshaft bearing inserts as follows:

> *NOTE*
> *Make sure old bearings are installed*
> *into their original positions.*

   a. Wipe the bearing inserts and the connecting rod and cap bearing surfaces clean.

   b. Insert the bearing inserts into the case and caps by engaging the bearing tabs with the mating grooves. See **Figure 166** (caps) and **Figure 167** (case).

2. Apply a light coating of molybdenum disulfide grease to the crankshaft bearing surfaces in the cylinder block and to the bearing surfaces of the main bearing caps.

3. Install the two thrust bearings (**Figure 168**) with their grooved sides facing out (**Figure 169**).

4. Place the crankshaft into the cylinder block, as shown in **Figure 170**.

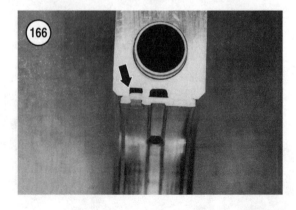

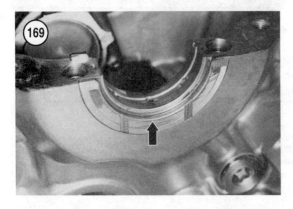

CAUTION
The main bearing caps must be installed in their correct locations, or the engine will be damaged by incorrect bearing oil clearance.

5. Make sure to install the main bearing caps in their correct positions as follows:

    a. Each main bearing cap (A, **Figure 154**) is marked with the numbers 1, 2, 3 or 4. A dot mark is aligned with one number on each cap, identifying the bearing cap with its position in the engine. The cap with the dot over the number 1 is installed at the front of the engine. Then follow with numbers 2, 3 and 4.

    b. The arrows on the bearing caps must point up toward the top surface of the cylinder block.

    c. If removed, install the two dowel pins into each cap (**Figure 159**).

    d. Install the bearing cap plates as shown in C, **Figure 154**.

    e. Apply a light coating of molybdenum disulfide grease to the main bearing cap bolt threads and the surface of the bolts that will contact the main bearing cap.

6. Tighten the main bearing cap bolts to the torque specifications in **Table 3**.

7. Apply a light coating of liquid sealant to the outer edge of the crankshaft seal and install the seal (**Figure 153**).

8. Install the camshaft drive pulley assembly (**Figure 152**) as described in Chapter Four.

9. Reassemble the cylinder block as described in this chapter.

BREAK-IN PROCEDURE

If the rings were replaced, new pistons installed, the cylinders rebored or honed or major lower end work performed, follow the engine break-in procedure, as though it were new. The performance and service life of the engine depend greatly on a careful and sensible break-in.

For the first 1000 km (600 miles), engine speed should not exceed 4000 rpm. Prolonged steady running at one speed, no matter how moderate, is to be avoided as well as hard acceleration.

Increase engine speed by 1000 rpm between 1000 km (600 miles) and 1600 km (1000 miles). Vary engine speed during this mileage interval. Do not exceed 5500 rpm.

5

At 1600 km (1000 miles), full throttle operation can be used. However, never exceed the tachometer redline limit of 5500 rpm at any time.

During engine break-in, oil consumption will be higher than normal. It is therefore important to frequently check and correct oil level. At no time during the break-in or later should the oil level be allowed to drop below the bottom line on the dipstick; if the oil level is low, the oil will become overheated resulting in insufficient lubrication and increased wear.

1000 km (600 mile) Service

It is essential that the oil and filter be changed after the first 1000 km (600 miles). In addition, it is a good idea to change the oil and filter at the completion of the break-in (2414 km/1500 miles) to ensure that all of the particles produced during break-in are removed from the lubrication system. The small additional expense may be considered a smart investment that will pay off in increased engine life.

Table 1 ENGINE WEIGHT (DRY)

Item	kg.	lbs.
49-state and Canada	118.7	261.6
California	119.0	263.3

Table 2 ENGINE LOWER END SERVICE SPECIFICATIONS

	Specifications mm (in.)	Wear mm (in.)
Oil pump (main and scavenge pumps)		
Outer rotor-to-body clearance	0.15-0.22	0.42
	(0.006-0.009)	(0.017)
Pump side clearance	0.02-0.07	0.12
	(0.001-0.003)	(0.005)
Tip clearance	0.15 max.	0.35
	(0.006)	(0.014)
Pressure relief valve		
Relief valve spring free length	90.8	84.0
	(3.57)	(3.31)
Oil pump pressure at switch		
Cold 35° C (95° F)		
Idle speed	127 kPa	–
	(18 psi)	–
At 5000 rpm	490 kPa	–
	(71 psi)	–
Hot 80° C (176° F)		
Idle speed	78 kPa	–
	(11 psi)	–
At 5000 rpm	490 kPa	–
	(71 psi)	–
(continued)		

Table 2 ENGINE LOWER END SERVICE SPECIFICATIONS (continued)

	Specifications mm (in.)	Wear mm (in.)
Cylinders		
Diameter	71.010-71.025	71.1
	(2.7957-2.7963)	(2.80)
Taper	–	0.05
	–	(0.002)
Out-of-round	–	0.15
	–	(0.006)
Warp across		
top of cylinders	–	0.05
	–	(0.002)
Piston-to-cylinder clearance	0.020-0.055	0.10
	(0.0008-0.0022)	(0.004)
Pistons		
Piston diameter at skirt	70.970-70.990	70.85
	(2.7941-2.7948)	(2.789)
Piston pin bore		
inside diameter	18.010-18.016	18.03
	(0.7091-0.7093)	(0.710)
Piston pin		
Diameter at		
sliding surfaces	17.994-18.000	17.99
	(0.7084-0.7087)	(0.708)
Piston pin-to-piston clearance	0.010-0.022	0.05
	(0.0004-0.0009)	(0.002)
Connecting rod-to-piston		
pin clearance	0.015-0.039	–
	(0.0006-0.0015)	–
Piston rings		
Number per piston		
Compression	2	
Oil control	1	
Ring end gap		
Top and second	0.15-0.30	0.5
	(0.006-0.012)	(0.02)
Oil (side rail)	0.20-0.70	0.9
	(0.008-0.028)	(0.04)
Ring side clearance		
Top	0.025-0.055	0.10
	(0.0010-0.0022)	(0.004)
Second	0.015-0.045	0.10
	(0.0006-0.0018)	(0.004)
Oil	–	–
Crankshaft		
Crankpin bearing oil clearance	0.027-0.045	0.06
	(0.0011-0.0018)	(0.002)
Connecting rod side clearance	0.15-0.30	0.40
	(0.006-0.012)	(0.016)
Crank pin and main journal		
Out-of-round	–	0.005
	–	(0.0002)
Taper	–	0.003
	–	(0.0001)
Runout at center journals	–	0.03
	–	(0.001)
Main bearing		
oil clearance	0.020-0.038	0.06
	(0.0008-0.0015)	(0.002)

5

Table 3 ENGINE LOWER END TIGHTENING TORQUES

	N•m	ft.-lb.
Engine mounting fasteners		
Nuts	44	32
Bolts	44	32
Front cross pipe bolt and nut	44	32
Subframe bolts		
8 mm flange bolt	26	19
10 mm flange bolt	40	29
10 mm Allen bolts	44	32
Engine guard bolts and nuts	26	19
Engine crankcase, crankshaft		
and transmission		
Crankcase bolts		
6 mm	12	9
8 mm	25	18
10 mm[1]	34	25
Rear engine case bolts	29	21
Clutch cover bolts	12	9
Starter clutch mounting bolt	74	54
Alternator drive gear mounting bolt[1]	26	20
Output shaft locknut[4]		
Indicated	170	125
Actual	186	137
Oil pump driven sprocket bolt[2]	18	13
Mainshaft locknut[4]	186	137
Countershaft (final drive gear) locknut[2, 4]	186	137
Crankshaft main bearing cap bolt[3]	59	44
Connecting rod cap nut[3]	31	23
Crankshaft drive pulley bolt	74	54
Alternator		
Mounting bolt	29	21
Coupler A mounting nut[2]	57	42
Coupler B mounting nut	57	42
Lubrication system		
Oil pressure switch[5]	12	9
Engine oil drain bolt	35	25
Oil filter boss[2]	18	13
Spark plug	15	11

1. Apply molybdenum disulfide grease, or clean engine oil, to the threads and bolt flange surfaces prior to installation.
2. Apply ThreeBond TB1342 or Loctite 242 (blue) to the threads prior to installation.
3. Apply engine oil to the threads and bolt flange surfaces prior to installation.
4. After tightening fastener, stake in 2 places as described in text.
5. Apply Loctite to the threads prior to installation.

Table 4 CONNECTING ROD BEARING SELECTION

Connecting rod ID	Crankpin journal OD size code letters		
code number	Letter A	Letter B	Letter C
Number 1	Yellow	Green	Brown
Number 2	Green	Brown	Black
Number 3	Brown	Black	Blue

Table 5 CONNECTING ROD BEARING INSERT THICKNESS

Color	mm	in.
Blue	1.503-1.506	0.05917-0.05929
Black	1.500-1.503	0.05906-0.05917
Brown	1.497-1.500	0.05894-0.05906
Green	1.494-1.497	0.05882-0.05894
Yellow	1.491-1.494	0.05870-0.05882

Table 6 MAIN JOURNAL BEARING SELECTION

Crankcase bearing support number	Crankpin journal OD size code letters		
	Letter A	Letter B	Letter C
Number I	Yellow	Green	Brown
Number II	Green	Brown	Black
Number III	Brown	Black	Blue

Table 7 MAIN JOURNAL BEARING INSERT THICKNESS

Color	mm	in.
Blue	2.012-2.015	0.07921-0.07933
Black	2.009-2.012	0.07909-0.07921
Brown	2.006-2.009	0.07898-0.07921
Green	2.003-2.006	0.07886-0.07898
Yellow	2.000-2.003	0.07874-0.07886

5

CHAPTER SIX

CLUTCH

The clutch is a multiplate type that operates immersed in the engine oil. It is mounted at the rear of the engine.

The clutch release mechanism is hydraulic and requires no routine adjustment. The mechanism consists of a clutch master cylinder on the left side of the handlebar, a slave cylinder attached to the clutch cover and a lifter rod that rides within the channel in the transmission .

The clutch is activated by hydraulic fluid pressure and is controlled by the clutch master cylinder. The hydraulic pressure generated by the master cylinder activates the clutch slave cylinder, which in turn pushes the clutch lifter rod. The clutch lifter rod pushes on the lifter piece, thus moving the lifter plate that disengages the clutch mechanism.

Table 1 and **Table 2** are at the end of the chapter.

Servicing Clutch in Frame

The clutch can be removed and installed with the engine installed in the frame; however, access space is very limited. Clutch service in the following steps is shown with the engine removed from the frame for clarity.

Clutch Removal

Refer to **Figure 1** for this procedure.

1. Place the motorcycle on a motorcycle lift. Refer to *Motorcycle Lift* in Chapter One.

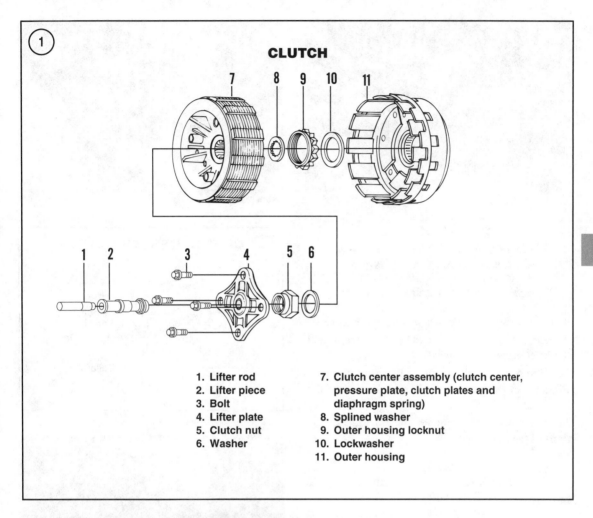

CLUTCH

1. Lifter rod
2. Lifter piece
3. Bolt
4. Lifter plate
5. Clutch nut
6. Washer
7. Clutch center assembly (clutch center, pressure plate, clutch plates and diaphragm spring)
8. Splined washer
9. Outer housing locknut
10. Lockwasher
11. Outer housing

6

2. Drain the engine oil as described in Chapter Three.

3. Remove the front side covers as described in Chapter Fifteen.

4. On California models, remove the carbon canister. See Chapter Eight.

5. Remove the clutch slave cylinder as described in this chapter.

NOTE
Squeeze the clutch lever all the way to the handgrip. Secure the lever to the handgrip with a tie strap or length of wire. This will prevent the clutch slave cylinder piston from moving out of the slave cylinder due to clutch master cylinder reservoir pressure caused by gravity.

6. Place a drain pan underneath the clutch cover to catch the residual oil that will drain out after removing the clutch cover.

7. Remove the bolts securing the clutch cover and remove the cover (A, **Figure 2**) and gasket.

NOTE
Figure 3 *shows only the lower dowel pin. Make sure to remove the upper dowel pin located under the upper right side bolt (B,* ***Figure 2****).*

8. Remove two clutch cover dowel pins (**Figure 3**).

9. Remove the clutch lifter rod (A, **Figure 4**) and the lifter piece (B, **Figure 4**).

10. Remove the bolts securing the lifter plate (C, **Figure 4**) to the pressure plate, then remove the lifter plate.

11. Use a chisel to straighten the two staked portions of the clutch nut.

NOTE
*The Honda clutch center holder (part No. 07HGB-001000A [U.S. models only]) is required to hold the clutch center when removing the clutch nut (**Figure 5**). The tool consists of a holder plate with eight slots and a set of center collars and nuts. The slots in the holder plate are marked with the numbers 4, 5, or 6. These numbers correspond to the number of springs used in a typical Honda clutch assembly. While the clutch does not use individual clutch springs, the pressure plate has four bolt studs. Before using the tool, set the tool collars to the No. 4 holder slot position.*

12. Mount the Honda clutch center holder onto the pressure plate (A, **Figure 6**), then tighten the center collar nuts securely. Install four 6-mm bolts and bolt the tool to the pressure plate.

CAUTION
Install all four bolts to prevent the clutch center holder from slipping

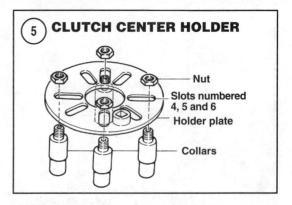

6

and damaging the pressure plate.
Make sure to install these bolts.

13. Hold the clutch center holder with a breaker bar (B, **Figure 6**) and loosen the clutch nut. Remove the clutch nut and the clutch center holder.

14. Remove the flat washer (**Figure 7**).

15. Slide the clutch center assembly—pressure plate, clutch plates and discs—out of the clutch outer housing (**Figure 8**).

16. To remove the clutch outer housing, perform the following:

a. Remove the splined washer (**Figure 9**).

b. The clutch outer nut is staked to a notch (**Figure 10**) machined in the end of the primary driven gear boss. Unstake the locknut with a grinder and small stone. Clean off all grinding residue from the area.

c. Hold the clutch outer with the Honda clutch outer holder A (part No. 07JMB-MN50100) or equivalent.

d. Loosen the clutch outer locknut with the 46 mm Honda clutch locknut wrench (part No. 07JMA-MN50100) or equivalent (**Figure 11**). Discard the locknut.

e. Remove the lockwasher (**Figure 12**).

f. Remove the clutch outer housing (**Figure 13**).

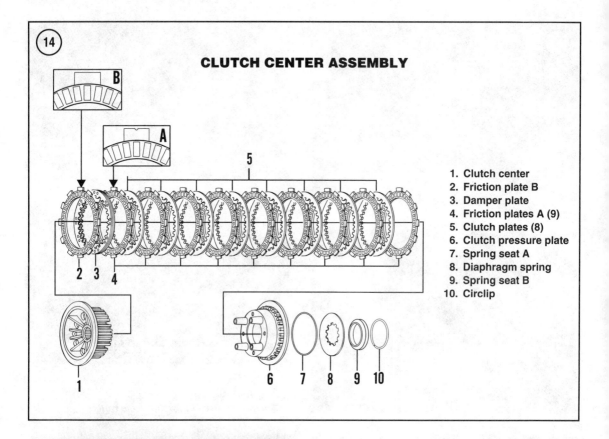

CLUTCH CENTER ASSEMBLY

1. Clutch center
2. Friction plate B
3. Damper plate
4. Friction plates A (9)
5. Clutch plates (8)
6. Clutch pressure plate
7. Spring seat A
8. Diaphragm spring
9. Spring seat B
10. Circlip

Clutch Center Disassembly

The clutch center assembly is shown in **Figure 14**. The assembly is under spring pressure and held together with a circlip (**Figure 15**). In order to disassemble the clutch center assembly, the diaphragm spring must be compressed so the circlip can be removed. The following tools will be required to disassemble and reassemble the clutch center assembly:

   a. Hydraulic press.

   b. Circlip pliers.

   c. The Honda seal driver attachment (part No. 07965-MA10200 [**Figure 16**]) or equivalent. **Figure 17** is a close-up of the tool in place. A large notch is machined in the bottom of the tool to allow access to the circlip when removing it.

1. Place the clutch center on the press bed with the circlip side facing up.

2. Place the driver attachment tool onto the diaphragm spring, aligning the notch in the drive at-

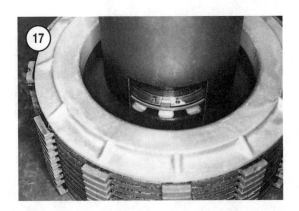

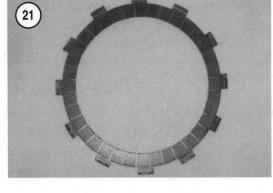

tachment with the open portion of the circlip (**Figure 17**).

3. Bring the press ram into contact with the driver attachment (**Figure 18**).

> *CAUTION*
> *Excessive pressure may cause a loss of diaphragm spring tension.*

4. Compress the diaphragm spring just enough to remove tension from the circlip.

5. Remove the circlip with circlip pliers (**Figure 19**).

6. Release the tension from the press and remove the driver attachment from the clutch center.

7. Remove the clutch center assembly from the press bed.

8. Remove the circlip (A, **Figure 20**) and spring seat B (B, **Figure 20**).

9. Remove the diaphragm spring (C, **Figure 20**) and the pressure plate (D, **Figure 20**).

10. Disassemble the friction disc, clutch plates and damper plate from the clutch center. Keep the parts in the order removed.

Inspection

Refer to **Table 1** for clutch specifications and wear limits.

1. Clean all clutch parts in petroleum-based solvent such as kerosene and dry them thoroughly with compressed air.

2. The friction plate (**Figure 21**) material is bonded onto an aluminum plate for warp resistance and durability. Measure the thickness of each friction plate at several places around the plate(**Figure 22**). Compare the thickness to the specifications in **Table 1**.

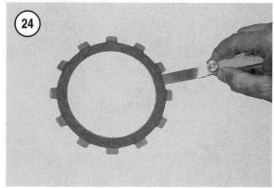

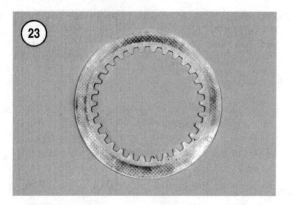

Replace the friction plates as a set if any one plate is worn or damaged.

3. The clutch assembly consists of eight steel clutch plates (**Figure 23**). Check the clutch plates for warpage on a surface plate using a feeler gauge, as shown in **Figure 24**. Compare to the specifications in **Table 1**. Replace the clutch plates as a set if any plate is warped to the wear limit.

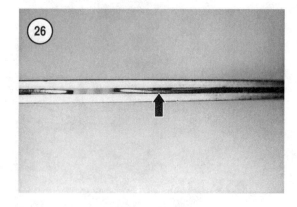

4. Check the clutch damper plate (**Figure 25**) wave spring for damage. **Figure 26** shows the wave spring installed between the clutch damper plate halves. Replace as an assembly, if necessary.

5. Check the diaphragm spring (**Figure 27**) for cracks or spline damage. If the spring appears good, measure the height of the diaphragm spring with a vernier caliper on a flat surface (**Figure 28**) and compare to the specifications in **Table 1**. Replace the spring if it has sagged to the less than the service limit.

6. Inspect the slots in the clutch outer housing (**Figure 29**) for cracks, nicks or galling where they contact the friction disc tabs. Remove minor damage with an oilstone. If any severe damage is evident, replace the outer housing.

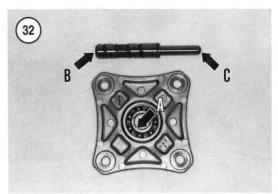

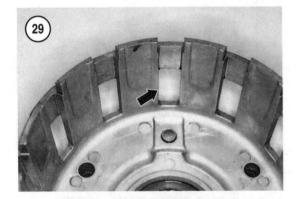

7. Inspect the inner splines and outer grooves of the clutch center (**Figure 30**). If worn or damaged, replace the clutch center.

8. Inspect the outer grooves and raised posts of the pressure plate (**Figure 31**). Replace if necessary.

9. Turn the lifter guide bearing (A, **Figure 32**) inner race by hand. The bearing should turn smoothly with no sign of roughness or damage.

10. The lifter guide bearing (A, **Figure 32**) should fit tightly in the lifter guide. If the bearing can be removed rather easily, or if it drops out, replace the lifter guide.

11. To replace the lifter guide bearing (A, **Figure 32**):

   a. Support the lifter guide and drive the bearing out with a bearing driver or socket.

   b. Check the lifter guide bearing bore for cracks or damage.

   c. Install the new bearing with its manufacturer's mark facing out. Use a driver placed on the outer bearing race. Drive the bearing into the lifter guide until it bottoms out.

12. Check the lifter piece (B, **Figure 32**) for wear or damage.

13. Check the lifter rod (C, **Figure 32**) for bending or damage.

Clutch Outer Housing Installation

The clutch outer housing must be installed before assembling the clutch center assembly. Refer to **Figure 33** for this procedure.

1. Clean the new clutch outer housing locknut threads with contact cleaner.

2. Slide the clutch outer (**Figure 34**) over the mainshaft.

NOTE
*The clutch outer lockwasher (**Figure 35**) is a directional cone-type lockwasher. To*

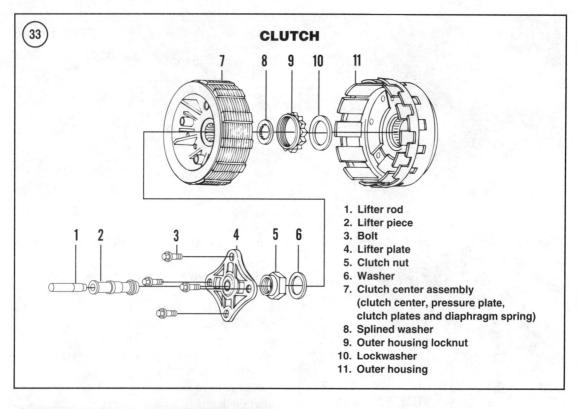

CLUTCH

1. Lifter rod
2. Lifter piece
3. Bolt
4. Lifter plate
5. Clutch nut
6. Washer
7. Clutch center assembly
   (clutch center, pressure plate,
   clutch plates and diaphragm spring)
8. Splined washer
9. Outer housing locknut
10. Lockwasher
11. Outer housing

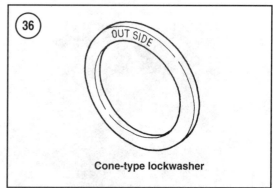

Cone-type lockwasher

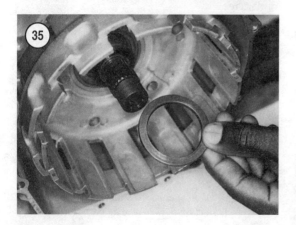

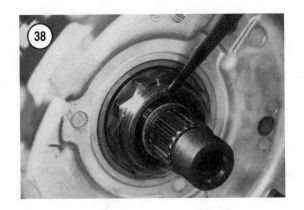

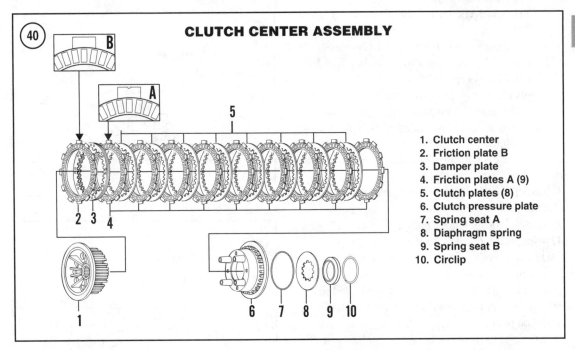

CLUTCH CENTER ASSEMBLY

1. Clutch center
2. Friction plate B
3. Damper plate
4. Friction plates A (9)
5. Clutch plates (8)
6. Clutch pressure plate
7. Spring seat A
8. Diaphragm spring
9. Spring seat B
10. Circlip

6

prevent the nut from loosening, install the lockwasher as described in Step 3.

3. Position the clutch outer lockwasher (**Figure 35**) with the side marked OUTSIDE facing out (**Figure 36**) and install the lockwasher onto the transmission mainshaft. If the lockwasher is not marked, install the washer so that the convex side faces out.

4. Apply ThreeBond TB1342 or Loctite 242 (blue) to the threads of the new locknut prior to installation. Thread the locknut (**Figure 37**) onto the transmission mainshaft.

5. Using the same tools to hold the clutch outer as during disassembly, tighten the clutch outer locknut to the torque specification in **Table 2**.

6. Using a punch (**Figure 38**), stake the locknut in two places into the driven gear boss notches on the transmission mainshaft.

7. Install the splined washer (**Figure 39**).

Clutch Center Assembly

Refer to **Figure 40** when performing this procedure.

1. Using **Figure 40** to identify the parts, lay the clutch plates and discs out in order. Note the following:

   a. There are two different types of friction plates (**Figure 21**). The nine friction plates A have a notch in three of the tabs. The single friction plate B does not have any notches.

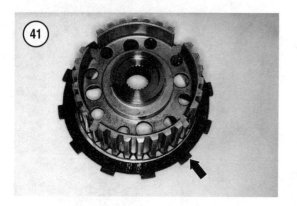

b. There are eight steel clutch plates (**Figure 23**).

c. The clutch damper plate assembly consists of two steel plates and a wave spring. See **Figure 25** and **Figure 26**.

2. Apply clean engine oil to all sliding components. If installing new friction plates, apply a liberal coat of clean engine oil to both sides of each plate. Coat all of the clutch plates and friction plates with clean engine oil. This will eliminate clutch lock-up on initial engine startup.

3. Install friction plate B (**Figure 41**) onto the clutch center.

4. Install the clutch damper plate (**Figure 42**)—align the O mark on the clutch damper with the O mark on the clutch center (**Figure 43**).

5. Continue to install a friction plate, then a clutch plate and alternate them until all are installed in the order shown in **Figure 40**. The last item installed is a friction plate.

6. Align the O mark on the pressure plate with the clutch center O mark (**Figure 44**) and install the pressure plate (**Figure 45**) onto the clutch center.

NOTE
The following steps describe procedures to align and assemble the clutch center assembly.

7. First, install the clutch center into the clutch outer housing (**Figure 46**) to align the clutch friction plate tabs (**Figure 47**).

NOTE
Do not disturb the friction plate tab alignment in the next step. After the clutch center is completely assembled, it is very difficult to make any adjustment to the tab alignment. The

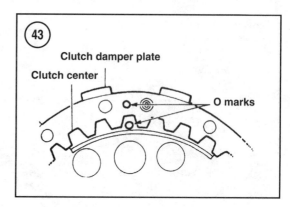

Clutch damper plate
Clutch center
O marks

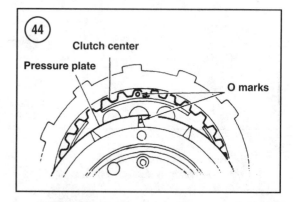

Clutch center
Pressure plate
O marks

*tabs must be correctly aligned so the assembly can be installed back into the clutch outer housing as described in **Installation** Step 3.*

8. Hold onto the posts of the pressure plate and carefully remove the clutch center assembly from the clutch outer housing without disturbing the alignment of the friction plate tabs.

9. Set the clutch center assembly down with the pressure plate facing up (**Figure 45**).

10. If removed, install spring seat A (**Figure 48**).

11. Position the diaphragm spring with the convex side facing up and install the spring (A, **Figure 49**).

12. Install spring seat B so that its shoulder faces up (B, **Figure 49**).

NOTE
In the following step, position the circlip with the sharp side is facing out.

13. Place the circlip onto the spring seat. Center spring seat B and the circlip onto the clutch center (**Figure 50**).

14. Place the clutch center on the press bed and place the same tool used to compress the spring on top of the spring as shown in **Figure 51**.

CAUTION
To avoid loss of diaphragm spring tension, do not press the spring any more than necessary to install the circlip.

15. Slowly press the diaphragm spring so the circlip groove is visible above the diaphragm spring.

16. Insert the circlip pliers through the hole in the special tool and install the circlip onto the groove in

the clutch center (**Figure 52**). Make sure the circlip is seated correctly in the groove.

17. Release the press pressure and remove the special tool.

18. After removing the special tool, confirm that the circlip is properly seated in the groove in the clutch center (**Figure 53**).

Installation

Refer to **Figure 33** for this procedure.

1. Install the clutch outer housing as described in this chapter.

2. Assemble the clutch center as described in this chapter.

3. Install the clutch center into the clutch outer housing (**Figure 46**).

4. Install the flat washer (**Figure 54**).

5. Install the clutch nut and tighten it to the torque specification in **Table 2**. Use the same tools and procedures to prevent the clutch center from turning as during the removal sequence.

6. Stake the locknut in two places into the transmission mainshaft.

7. Install the lifter plate (A, **Figure 55**) onto the pressure plate and secure it with its four bolts. Tighten the bolts in a crisscross pattern to the torque specification in **Table 2**.

> *NOTE*
> *A clip installed on the end of the lifter piece spaces the lifter piece in the mainshaft for proper pushrod operation. Make sure the clip is properly installed before installing the lifter piece in the following steps.*

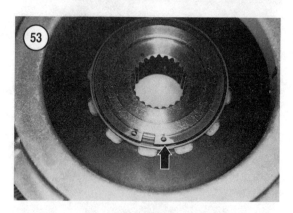

8. Apply a light coating of grease to the lifter rod and lifter piece. Install the lifter rod into the lifter piece (B, **Figure 55**).

9. Insert the lifter piece into the mainshaft until the clip on the lifter piece seats against the mainshaft.

10. Install a new gasket and the two locating dowels on the crankcase.

11. Install the clutch cover and its mounting bolts. Tighten the bolts to the specification in **Table 2**.

12. Install the clutch slave cylinder as described in this chapter.

13. Refill the engine with oil as described in Chapter Three.

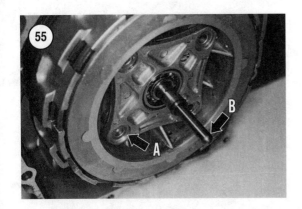

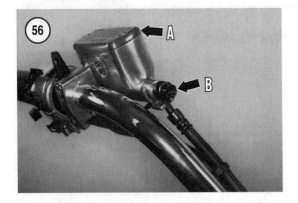

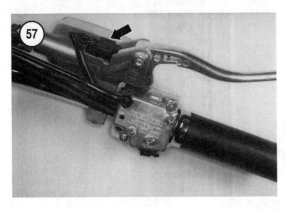

14. On California models, install the carbon canister. See Chapter Eight.

15. Install the front side covers as described in Chapter Fifteen.

16. If necessary, bleed the clutch as described in this chapter.

CLUTCH HYDRAULIC SYSTEM

The clutch is actuated by hydraulic fluid pressure and is controlled by the hand lever on the clutch master cylinder. As clutch components wear, the fluid level drops in the reservoir and automatically adjusts for wear. There is no routine clutch adjustment necessary or possible.

When working on the clutch hydraulic system, it is necessary that the work area and all tools be absolutely clean. Any tiny particles of debris that enter the clutch slave cylinder or the clutch master cylinder can damage the components. Also, do not use sharp tools inside the slave cylinder or on the piston. If there is any doubt about the ability to correctly and safely carry out service on the clutch hydraulic components, have a Honda dealership or other qualified specialist perform the procedures.

WARNING
Use only DOT 4 brake fluid in the clutch hydraulic system. Do not use other types of fluids, as they are not compatible. Do not intermix silicone-based (DOT 5) brake fluid, as it can cause clutch component damage leading to clutch system failure.

CLUTCH MASTER CYLINDER

Removal

CAUTION
Cover the instrument cluster, fuel tank and front fairing (GL1500CF models) with a heavy cloth or plastic tarp to protect them from accidental brake fluid spills. Wash fluid off any painted or plated surfaces immediately, as it will destroy the finish. Use soapy water and rinse completely.

1. Unscrew and remove the rearview mirror.

2. Remove the master cylinder cover (A, **Figure 56**), diaphragm and float.

3. Using a syringe, empty the reservoir of all brake fluid. Discard the fluid.

4. Disconnect the electrical connectors at the clutch master cylinder (**Figure 57**).

5. Place a shop rag under the banjo bolt to catch the residual clutch fluid that will drain out in the next step.

6. Remove the banjo bolt and washers (B, **Figure 56**) securing the clutch hose to the clutch master cylinder and remove the clutch hose. Tie the hose up and cover the end to prevent debris from entering.

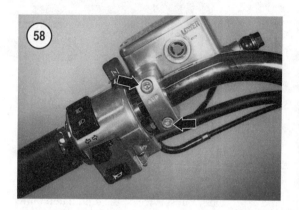

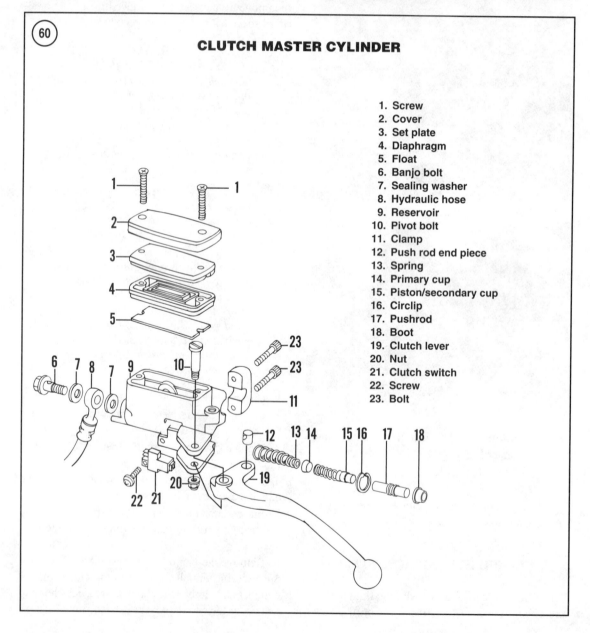

CLUTCH MASTER CYLINDER

1. Screw
2. Cover
3. Set plate
4. Diaphragm
5. Float
6. Banjo bolt
7. Sealing washer
8. Hydraulic hose
9. Reservoir
10. Pivot bolt
11. Clamp
12. Push rod end piece
13. Spring
14. Primary cup
15. Piston/secondary cup
16. Circlip
17. Pushrod
18. Boot
19. Clutch lever
20. Nut
21. Clutch switch
22. Screw
23. Bolt

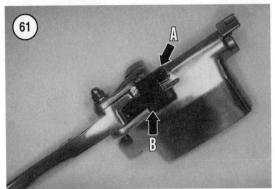

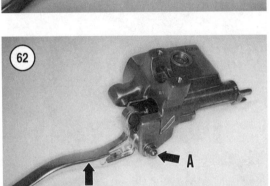

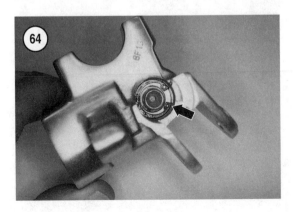

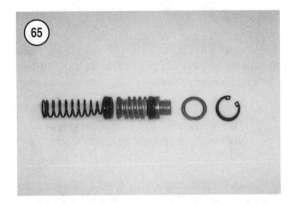

7. Remove the master cylinder clamp bolts (**Figure 58**). Then remove the bolts, clamp and the master cylinder.

Installation

1. Install the clamp onto the master cylinder and install the two mounting bolts. Align the end of the master cylinder with the index mark on the handlebar (**Figure 59**). Tighten the upper bolt first, then the lower bolt to the torque specification in **Table 2**.
2. Install the clutch hose onto the clutch master cylinder. Install a *new* sealing washer on each side of the fitting and install the banjo bolt (B, **Figure 56**). Tighten the banjo bolt to the torque specification in **Table 2**.
3. Attach the electrical connectors to the switch mounted on the bottom of the clutch master cylinder (**Figure 57**).
4. Bleed the clutch as described in this chapter.

Disassembly

Refer to **Figure 60** for this procedure.
1. Remove the master cylinder as described in this chapter.
2. Remove the screw (A, **Figure 61**) securing the clutch switch (B, **Figure 61**) and remove the switch.
3. Remove the clutch lever nut and bolt (A, **Figure 62**) and remove the clutch lever (B, **Figure 62**).
4. Remove the pushrod and boot (**Figure 63**).
5. Support the master cylinder securely and compress the piston assembly with a screwdriver. Then remove the circlip (**Figure 64**) from the piston bore and allow the piston assembly to extend out slowly.
6. Remove the circlip, washer, piston assembly and spring from the master cylinder (**Figure 65**).

Inspection

1. Clean all parts in fresh DOT 4 brake fluid. Place the master cylinder components on a clean lint-free cloth after cleaning them.

NOTE
Do not lose the protector plate (Figure 66) in the master cylinder reservoir.

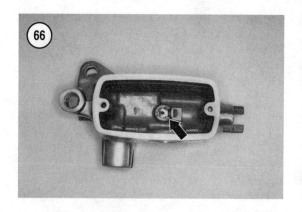

2. Check the piston assembly for the following defects:
   a. Sagged or damaged spring (A, **Figure 67**).
   b. Primary (B) and secondary (C) cups that are damaged, swollen or show signs of deterioration. Do not attempt to remove the secondary cup (C) from the piston, as this will damage it.
   c. Damaged or scored piston (D). Also check the end of the piston for wear or damage caused by the pushrod.
   d. Measure the piston diameter with a micrometer, as shown in **Figure 68**. Replace the piston if the diameter is less than the service limit in **Table 1**.
   e. The piston, piston cups and spring must be replaced as a set.

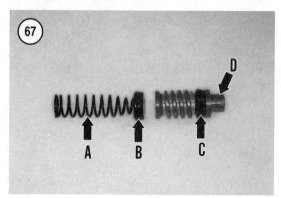

3. Check the master cylinder bore (**Figure 69**) for severe wear, cracks or scoring.

4. Measure the cylinder bore inner diameter with a bore gauge (**Figure 70**). Replace the master cylinder if the bore exceeds the service limit in **Table 1**.

5. Make sure the passages in the fluid reservoir are clear.

6. Check the reservoir cover, set plate, diaphragm and float for damage.

7. Check the reservoir housing banjo bolt threads. If the threads are damaged or partially stripped, replace the master cylinder.

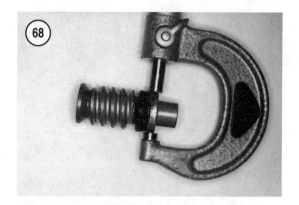

8. Flush the banjo bolt with clean brake fluid. Replace the sealing washers if crushed or damaged.

9. Check the clutch lever pivot hole (A, **Figure 71**) for wear or damage. Inspect the pushrod receptacle (**Figure 72**) for wear or damage. Replace the lever, if required.

10. Check the clutch lever pivot bolt and nut (B, **Figure 71**) for damage. Replace the bolt and nut if required.

11. Inspect the pushrod and boot (**Figure 73**) for damage. Replace the parts if necessary.

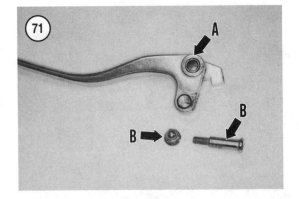

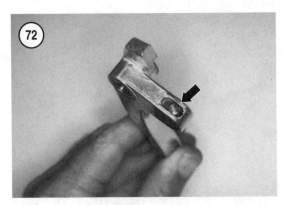

Assembly

Refer to **Figure 60** for this procedure.

1. Soak new cups in fresh DOT 4 brake fluid for at least 15 minutes to make them pliable. Coat the master cylinder bore with brake fluid.

> *CAUTION*
> *When installing the piston assembly, do not allow the cups to turn inside out. This will damage the cups and allow brake fluid to leak within the cylinder bore.*

2. Install the spring/primary cup and the piston/secondary cup into the master cylinder in the order shown in **Figure 74**.
3. Support the master cylinder so that the piston assembly faces up.
4. Install the flat washer onto the end of the piston.
5. Compress the piston and install the circlip (**Figure 64**) into the master cylinder bore groove. Release the piston and check that the circlip seats in the groove completely.
6. Install the pushrod and boot into the end of the master cylinder (**Figure 75**). Seat the boot lip in the piston bore (**Figure 63**).
7. Install the clutch lever as follows:
   a. Apply a light coat of silicone grease to the clutch lever pivot bolt, the pushrod end piece and the clutch lever pivot bolt hole.
   b. Move the clutch lever into position (**Figure 76**) and index the pushrod end piece into the clutch lever receptacle (**Figure 77**).
   c. Install the clutch lever pivot bolt and nut (A, **Figure 62**). Tighten the nut securely.
   d. Operate the clutch lever, making sure it pivots smoothly and that the pushrod engages the pushrod end piece correctly.

8. Install the clutch switch (B, **Figure 61**) and tighten the screw (A, **Figure 61**) securely.

9. Operate the clutch lever, making sure it pivots smoothly and contact the clutch switch correctly.

10. Install the master cylinder as described in this chapter.

SLAVE CYLINDER

The clutch slave cylinder can be serviced with the engine mounted in the frame.

Removal

This procedure describes removal of the slave cylinder. If disassembling the slave cylinder, refer to *Disassembly* in this section.

Refer to **Figure 78** for this procedure.

1. Place the motorcycle on a motorcycle lift. Refer to *Motorcycle Lift* in Chapter One.

2. Remove both frame rear side covers as described in Chapter Fifteen.

3. On California models, remove the carbon canister as described in Chapter Eight.

4. Place a piece of wood between the clutch lever and the hand grip to hold the lever in the released position. Secure the piece of wood with a rubber band or tape. This will prevent the clutch lever from being applied accidentally after the clutch slave cylinder is removed from the clutch cover.

5. Remove the bleed pipe banjo bolt and sealing washers (**Figure 79**) at the top of the slave cylinder. Move the bleed pipe out of the way.

6. Remove the banjo bolt and two sealing washers (A, **Figure 80**) securing the hydraulic hose to the slave cylinder.

7. Remove the bolts securing the clutch slave cylinder (B, **Figure 80**) to the clutch cover and withdraw the unit from the clutch cover.

8. Remove the dowel pins from the clutch cover.

> *CAUTION*
> *Wash any spilled hydraulic fluid off any painted or plated surface immediately, as it will destroy the finish.*

Disassembly

Refer to **Figure 81** for this procedure.

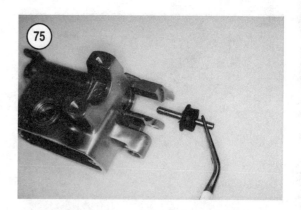

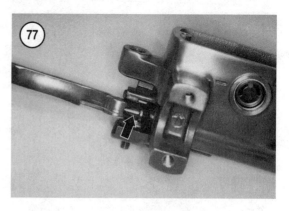

1. Remove both rear side covers as described in Chapter Fifteen.

2. On California models, remove the carbon canister as described in Chapter Eight.

3. Remove the bleed pipe mounting bolt at the top of the clutch cover.

4. Remove the bolts securing the clutch slave cylinder (B, **Figure 80**) to the clutch cover and withdraw the unit from the clutch cover.

5. Operate the clutch lever to force the piston out of the slave cylinder. Remove the piston and spring.

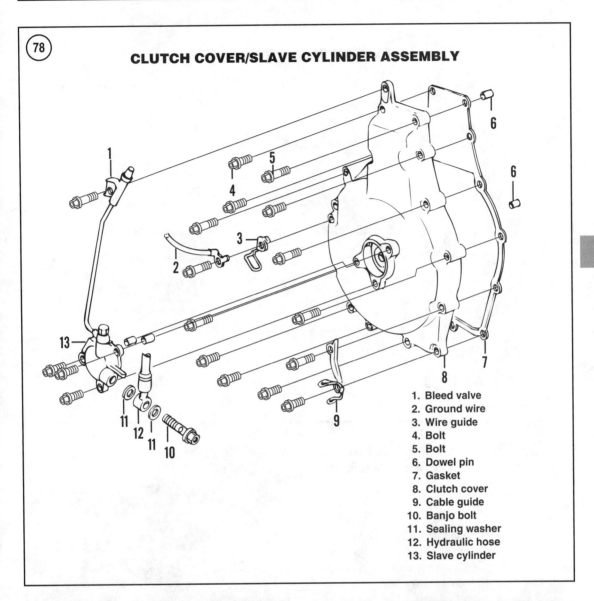

CLUTCH COVER/SLAVE CYLINDER ASSEMBLY

1. Bleed valve
2. Ground wire
3. Wire guide
4. Bolt
5. Bolt
6. Dowel pin
7. Gasket
8. Clutch cover
9. Cable guide
10. Banjo bolt
11. Sealing washer
12. Hydraulic hose
13. Slave cylinder

6

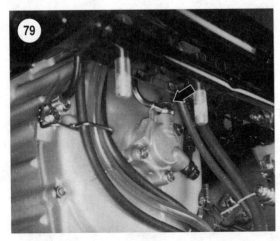

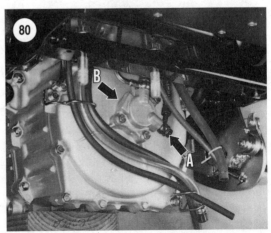

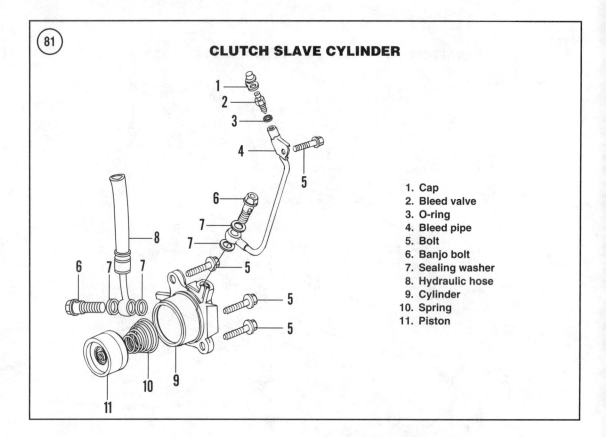

CLUTCH SLAVE CYLINDER

1. Cap
2. Bleed valve
3. O-ring
4. Bleed pipe
5. Bolt
6. Banjo bolt
7. Sealing washer
8. Hydraulic hose
9. Cylinder
10. Spring
11. Piston

6. Place a container under the clutch hose at the clutch slave cylinder to catch any remaining fluid.

Inspection

1. Remove the spring (**Figure 82**) from the piston.
2. Clean all parts in fresh DOT 4 brake fluid. Place the slave cylinder components on a clean lint-free cloth after cleaning them (**Figure 83**).

> *NOTE*
> *Do not remove the piston seal or the piston oil seal unless they are going to be replaced.*

3. Inspect the piston cup seal (**Figure 84**) for cuts or other damage. If necessary, install a new piston cup seal so that the lip faces in the direction shown in **Figure 84**.
4. Inspect the piston oil seal (**Figure 85**) for damage. Remove the oil seal by prying it out with a screwdriver, being careful not to damage the piston. Tap the new oil seal into the piston making sure it seats correctly.
5. Check the piston surface for scoring or damage.

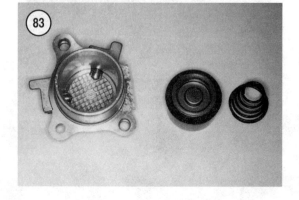

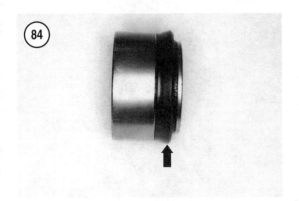

6

6. Check the slave cylinder bore surface (**Figure 86**) for scoring or damage.

7. Remove the bleed valve (**Figure 87**) from the bleed pipe. Clean the bleed valve and bleed pipe with compressed air.

8. Replace the bleed valve O-ring (**Figure 88**) if worn or damaged. Coat a new O-ring with DOT 4 brake fluid and install it onto the valve.

9. Clean the banjo bolt with compressed air. Replace the washers if crushed or damaged.

Assembly

Refer to **Figure 81** for this procedure.

1. The piston spring has a small and large end. Insert the small spring end into the piston as shown in **Figure 82**.

2. Apply a small amount of high-temperature silicone grease onto the piston oil seal.

3. Apply DOT 4 brake fluid to the piston cup seal and cylinder bore.

4. Install the spring and piston into the cylinder bore as shown in **Figure 89**. Push the piston all the way into the cylinder (**Figure 90**).

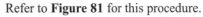

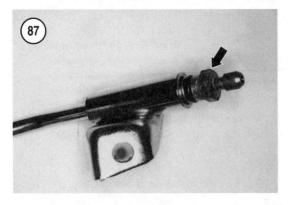

5. Apply DOT 4 brake fluid to the bleed valve O-ring (**Figure 88**) and thread the valve into the bleed pipe (**Figure 87**).

6. Install the slave cylinder onto the clutch cover as described in this chapter.

Installation

Refer to **Figure 78** for this procedure.

1. If the slave cylinder was not disassembled, apply a light coat of high-temperature silicone grease (or brake fluid) to the piston cup seal and the oil seal prior to installing the assembly.

2. Install the two slave cylinder-to-clutch cover dowel pins.

3. Install the slave cylinder onto the clutch cover, making sure the clutch pushrod is inserted correctly into the receptacle in the slave cylinder piston.

> *NOTE*
> *After being positioned correctly into the clutch cover, the slave cylinder assembly may stick out approximately 3/8 in. (9.5 mm) from the clutch cover mating surface. This is due either to the pressure within the clutch hydraulic system or to spring pressure.*

4. Install the bolts securing the slave cylinder (B, **Figure 80**). Gradually tighten the bolts in a criss-cross pattern. Continue to tighten them until the slave cylinder has bottomed out on the clutch cover mating surface. Tighten the bolts securely.

5. If the slave cylinder was disassembled or the banjo bolts removed, perform the following:

   a. Install the clutch hose onto the slave cylinder, installing a washer on both sides of the hose fitting. Install and tighten the banjo bolt (A, **Figure 80**) to the torque specification in **Table 2**.

   b. Install the bleed pipe onto the slave cylinder, installing a washer on both sides of the hose fitting. Install and tighten the banjo bolt (A, **Figure 79**) to the torque specification in **Table 2**.

   c. Tighten the bleed valve securely. Insert the rubber cap onto the end of the bleed valve.

6. Bleed the clutch as described in this chapter.

7. On California models, install the carbon canister as described in Chapter Eight.

8. Install both front side covers as described in Chapter Fifteen.

Hose Replacement

Inspect the clutch hose at the recommended service interval. Replace the clutch hose assembly if it shows signs of cracking or damage. The clutch hose assembly consists of two flexible hoses and one metal hose. The rear flexible hose is permanently attached to the section of metal tubing. The entire hose assembly (two pieces) is sold as a set.

> *CAUTION*
> *Cover the front wheel, fender and frame with a heavy cloth or plastic tarp to protect them from accidentally spilled brake fluid. Wash the fluid off of any painted or plated surface immediately, as it will destroy the finish. Use soapy water and rinse completely.*

1. Remove the seat as described in Chapter Fifteen.

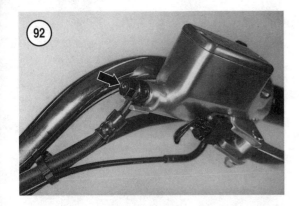

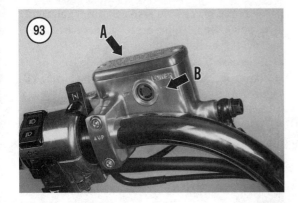

2. Remove the fuel tank as described in Chapter Eight.

3. Attach a hose to the bleed valve on the clutch slave cylinder bleed pipe (**Figure 91**).

4. Drain the fluid from the entire system. Place the loose end of the hose into a container and open the bleed valve. Operate the clutch lever until all fluid is pumped out of the system. Close the bleed valve and remove the hose.

WARNING
Dispose of this fluid—never reuse brake fluid. Contaminated fluid can cause clutch failure.

5. Remove the banjo bolt (**Figure 92**) securing the clutch hose to the clutch master cylinder. Remove the clutch hose; tie the hose up and cover the end to prevent the entry of debris.

6. Place a container under the clutch hose at the clutch slave cylinder to catch any remaining fluid. Remove the banjo bolt and sealing washers securing the clutch hose to the clutch slave cylinder. Remove the clutch hose and let any remaining fluid drain out into the container.

7. Remove any clamps, bolts or guides securing the clutch hose to the frame or engine.

8. Remove the clutch hose assembly from the frame.

CAUTION
Wash any spilled brake fluid off of any painted or plated surface immediately; it will destroy the finish.

9. Install the hose assembly, sealing washers and banjo bolts in the reverse order of removal. Make sure to install new sealing washers in the correct position on each side of each banjo bolt.

10. Tighten all banjo bolts to the torque specification in **Table 2**.

11. Refill the clutch master cylinder to the upper line with fresh brake fluid marked DOT 4. Bleed the clutch system as described in this chapter.

12. Reinstall all removed items.

BLEEDING THE CLUTCH SYSTEM

This procedure is not necessary unless the clutch feels spongy (air in the line), there has been a leak in the system, a component has been replaced or the hydraulic fluid has been replaced. If the clutch operates correctly when the engine is cold or in cool weather, but operates erratically (or not at all) after the engine warms up or in hot weather, there is air in the line and the clutch must be bled.

This procedure uses a brake bleeder that is available from motorcycle or automotive supply dealers.

WARNING
Use only DOT 4 hydraulic brake fluid. Do not use other fluids as they are not compatible. Do not intermix silicone-based (DOT 5) brake fluid as it can cause clutch component damage leading to clutch system failure.

1. Clean the clutch master cylinder cover (A, **Figure 93**) of all dirt and foreign matter. Remove screws securing the cover and remove the cover and the diaphragm.

2. Fill the reservoir almost to the top line. Insert the diaphragm and install the cover. Install the screws loosely.

WARNING
Use brake fluid marked DOT 4 only. Others may vaporize and cause clutch failure. Always use the same brand name; do not intermix, as many brands

*are not compatible. Do not intermix sil-
icone-based (DOT 5) brake fluid, as it
can cause clutch component damage
leading to clutch system failure.*

3. Remove the dust cap from the bleed valve on the
clutch slave cylinder (**Figure 91**).

4. Connect the brake bleeder and wrench to the
bleed valve.

5. Open the bleed valve about one-half turn and
pump the brake bleeder (**Figure 94**).

> *NOTE*
> *If air is entering the brake bleeder
> hose from around the bleed valve, re-
> move the hose and apply several lay-
> ers of Teflon tape to the bleed valve.*

6. Continue to pump the lever on the bleeder until
the fluid emerging from the hose is free of bubbles.

> *NOTE*
> *Do not allow the reservoir to empty
> during the bleeding operation or air
> will enter the system. If this occurs,
> repeat the procedure.*

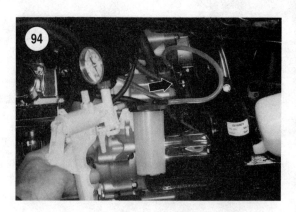

7. When the brake fluid is free of air, retighten the
bleed valve. Remove the brake bleeder tube and install the bleed valve dust cap.

8. If necessary, add fluid to correct the level in the
reservoir. It should be to the upper level line (B,
Figure 93).

9. Install the diaphragm and cover.

10. Test the feel of the clutch lever. It should be
firm and offer the same resistance each time it is operated. If it feels spongy, it is likely that there is air
in the system and it must be bled again. When all air
has been bled from the system and the fluid level is
correct in the reservoir, recheck for leaks and
tighten all the fittings and connections.

Table 1 CLUTCH SPECIFICATIONS

	Standard mm (in.)	Service limit mm (in.)
Steel plate warpage	– –	0.30 (0.012)
Friction plate thickness	3.73-3.88 (0.147-0.153)	3.5 (0.14)
Diaphragm spring free length	5.38 (0.212)	5.1 (0.20)
Clutch master cylinder		
Piston diameter	15.827-15.854 (0.6231-0.6242)	15.82 (0.623)
Cylinder inner diameter	15.870-15.913 (0.6248-0.6264)	15.93 (0.627)

Table 2 CLUTCH TIGHTENING TORQUES

	N•m	in.-lb.	ft.-lb.
Banjo bolts	30	–	22
Bleed pipe bolt [1]	12	106	–
Bleed pipe mounting bolts	12	106	–
Clutch cover	12	106	–
Clutch lifter plate	10	88	–
Clutch outer locknut [1,2]	186	–	137
Clutch nut [2]	127	–	94
Master cylinder mounting bolts	12	106	–
Slave cylinder bleed valve	9	62	–

1. Apply Loctite 242 (blue) to the threads prior to installation.
2. After tightening nut, stake in two places as described in text.

6

CHAPTER SEVEN

TRANSMISSION AND GEARSHIFT MECHANISM

This chapter describes service procedures for the shift mechanism, transmission, primary drive gears and the output shaft.

Tables 1-4 are at the end of the chapter.

EXTERNAL SHIFT MECHANISM

The external shift mechanism (A, **Figure 1**) is located at the front of the engine under the engine front cover. Most of the parts can be removed while the engine is in the frame. To remove the gearshift arm (B, **Figure 1**) and gearshift spindle, it is necessary to remove the engine and separate the crankcase.

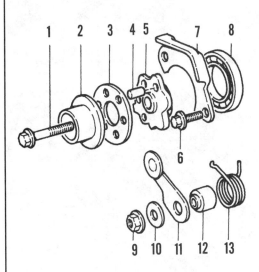

**EXTERNAL SHIFT
MECHANISM**

1. Drum center bolt
2. Drum center
3. Stopper plate
4. Dowel pins (4)
5. Cam plate
6. Bolt
7. Bearing stopper
   plate
8. Bearing
9. Nut
10. Washer
11. Stopper arm
12. Collar
13. Spring

To remove the shift drum and shift forks, it is necessary to remove the engine and separate the crankcase. This procedure is covered under *Internal Shift Mechanism* in this chapter.

Refer to **Figure 2** for this procedure.

Removal

1. Remove the engine front cover as described in Chapter Four.

2. Remove the bolt (A, **Figure 3**) securing the gearshift drum center to the shift drum. Remove the gearshift drum center (B, **Figure 3**).

3. Lift the shift arm (A, **Figure 4**) up and set it on the bearing plate.

4. Remove the stopper plate (B, **Figure 4**).

5. Remove the cam plate and the four dowel pins (**Figure 5**).

6. Remove the shift drum dowel pin (A, **Figure 6**).

7. Remove the stopper arm assembly (B, **Figure 6**) as follows:

   a. Remove the nut and washer securing the gearshift drum stopper arm.

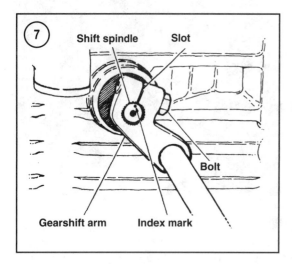

b. Disconnect the spring from the gearshift drum stopper arm.

c. Remove the gearshift drum stopper arm and spring from the spacer.

d. Remove the spacer from the threaded stud.

8. If necessary, remove the bearing stopper plate (C, **Figure 6**) and the shift drum bearing (D, **Figure 6**) from the crankcase.

9. To remove the gearshift arm and gearshift spindle, perform the following:

a. Remove the engine from the frame and separate the crankcase as described in Chapter Five.

b. If not already removed, remove the bolt securing the gearshift arm to the shift spindle and remove the gearshift arm (**Figure 7**). Reinstall the bolt onto the arm to avoid misplacing it.

c. Straighten the tab on the lockwasher (A, **Figure 8**).

d. Remove the bolt (B, **Figure 8**) and lockwasher securing the shift lever to the gearshift arm. Discard the lockwasher.

e. Partially remove the gearshift arm (A, **Figure 9**) and then catch the shift lever (B, **Figure 9**) as the gearshift arm is withdrawn.

f. Remove the gearshift arm from the crankcase (**Figure 10**). Do not lose the washer (**Figure 11**) on the gearshift arm.

g. Remove the gearshift spindle (**Figure 12**) from the crankcase.

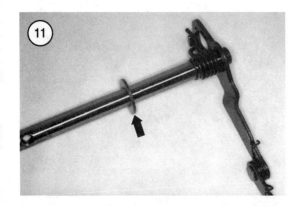

7

Inspection

1. Inspect the stopper arm spring. Replace if weak or damaged.

2. Inspect the stopper arm roller for wear or damage. If damaged, replace the stopper arm.

3. Inspect the two return springs on the gearshift arm; see **Figure 13** and **Figure 14**. Replace weak or damaged springs.

4. Inspect the gearshift spindle shaft (**Figure 15**) and gearshift arm (**Figure 16**) for bending, wear or other damage; replace either part if necessary.

5. Inspect the shift spindle seal (**Figure 17**) and the needle bearings for damage. Note the following:

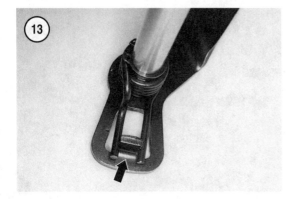

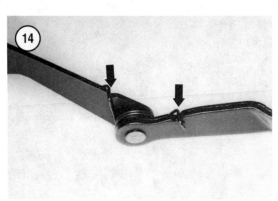

   a. Insert the shift spindle into the bearings (**Figure 12**) and turn the shift spindle by hand. The shift spindle should turn smoothly. Replace the bearings if the shift spindle turns roughly or if there is excessive play. Remove the shift spindle.

   b. Remove the seal (**Figure 17**) with a flat blade screwdriver. Place a rag underneath the seal to avoid damaging the case.

c. Replace the bearings (**Figure 18**) with suitable bearing drivers. Only remove the bearings if they are going to be replaced.

d. Prior to installing the new seal, pack the seal cavity with multi-purpose grease. Install the oil seal with the manufacturer's mark facing out (**Figure 17**).

e. If the seal was damaged, check the shift spindle shaft and splines (**Figure 15**) for any defects that could damage the new seal.

6. Check the two shift arm needle bearings for wear or damage; see **Figure 19** and A, **Figure 20**. Note the following:

a. Install the shift arm into the case (**Figure 10**). Move the shift arm in the bearings and check bearing play. Remove the shift arm.

b. Do not remove the bearings unless they require replacement.

c. Measure the position of each bearing in the case to ensure that the new bearings will be installed in the same position.

d. Install the bearings with the manufacturer's mark facing out.

e. Replace the bearings with suitable bearing drivers.

7. Check the shift arm pin (B, **Figure 20**) for excessive wear or looseness. If loose, remove the pin and apply TB1342 or Loctite 242 (blue) to the pin threads, then install and tighten the pin securely.

Installation

1. To install the gearshift arm and gearshift spindle, perform the following:

a. Install the gearshift spindle (**Figure 12**) into the crankcase.

b. Make sure the circlip is seated properly in the shift arm and that both shift arm return springs are positioned as shown in **Figure 13** and **Figure 14**.

c. Slide the washer onto the shift arm (**Figure 11**).

d. Position the shift lever into the case as shown in A, **Figure 21** and insert the shift arm (**Figure 10**) through it (B, **Figure 21**). The shift lever must engage the shift spindle as shown in C, **Figure 21**.

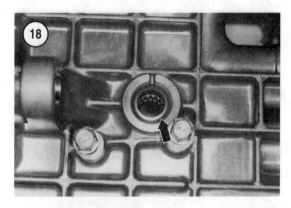

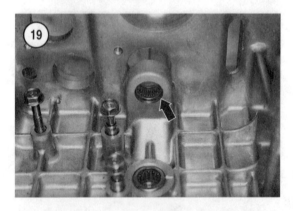

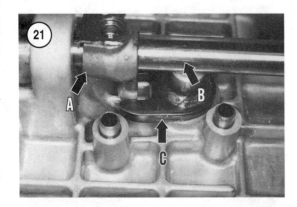

NOTE
When installing the shift arm, make sure the shift arm return spring aligns with the pin as shown in Figure 22.

e. Align the shift lever hole with the threaded hole in the shift arm. Install a new lockwasher and thread the bolt (B, **Figure 8**) into the shift arm. Tighten the shift lever bolt to the torque specification in **Table 4**.

f. Bend one of the tabs (A, **Figure 8**) so that it is up against a flat on the bolt.

g. Assemble the crankcase and install the engine in the frame as described in Chapter Five.

h. Align the punch marks on the gearshift spindle and the gearshift lever and install the lever. Tighten the bolt securely (**Figure 7**).

2. Install the stopper arm assembly as follows:

a. Install the collar onto the threaded stud so that the shoulder on the collar faces out (**Figure 23**).

b. Install the spring onto the collar, engaging the end of the spring with the case tab as shown in **Figure 24**.

c. Install the stopper arm onto the collar shoulder so that the roller wheel faces out (A, **Figure 25**). Engage the spring with the roller (B, **Figure 25**).

d. Install the washer onto the threaded stud.

e. Apply ThreeBond TB1342 or Loctite 242 (blue) onto the flange nut threads, then install and tighten the nut (A, **Figure 26**) securely.

3. Install the shift drum dowel pin (B, **Figure 26**).

NOTE
The stopper arm must be pushed down when installing the cam plate in Step 4.

4. Align the hole in the back of the cam plate with the shift drum dowel pin (B, **Figure 26**) and install the cam plate (A, **Figure 27**) onto the shift drum/bearing assembly. Then release the stopper arm and allow it to rest against the cam plate.

5. Install the four cam plate dowel pins (B, **Figure 27**).

6. Install the stopper plate (**Figure 28**) over the cam plate dowel pins. Make sure that none of the dowel pins fall out during installation.

7. Align the holes in the back of the drum center with the four cam plate dowel pins and install the drum center (A, **Figure 29**). Install and tighten the drum center bolt (B, **Figure 29**) to the torque specification in **Table 4**.

8. Engage the shift arm with the dowel pins (C, **Figure 29**).

9. Check the shift mechanism operation. Position the shift drum in the NEUTRAL position.

10. Install the engine front cover as described in Chapter Four.

TRANSMISSION

The transmission is located within the crankcase assembly. To access the transmission and internal shift mechanism, it is necessary to remove the engine and separate the crankcase as described in Chapter Five.

Specifications for the transmission components are listed in **Table 1** and **Table 2**.

Preliminary Inspection

After the transmission shaft assemblies have been removed from the crankcase, clean and inspect the assemblies prior to disassembling them. Place the assembled shaft or the individual gears into a large can or plastic bucket and clean thoroughly with solvent and a stiff brush. Dry with compressed air or set them on rags to drip dry.

1. After they have been cleaned, visually inspect the components of the assemblies for excessive wear. Any burrs, pitting or roughness on the teeth of a gear will cause wear on the mating gear.

NOTE
Replace defective gears. It is recommended to replace the mating gear on

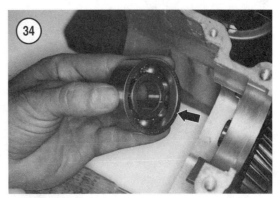

the other shaft even though it may not show as much wear or damage.

2. Carefully check the engagement dogs. If any are chipped, worn, rounded or missing, the affected gear must be replaced.

3. Rotate the transmission and shift drum bearings in the cylinder block by hand. Check for roughness, noise and radial play. Any bearing that is suspect should be replaced as described in Chapter Five.

Transmission/Internal Shift Mechanism Removal

1. Separate the crankcase as described in Chapter Five.

2. Lift the mainshaft (A, **Figure 30**) up, disengage the front shift fork (B, **Figure 30**), and remove the shaft from the engine.

3. Remove the gearshift linkage assembly as described in this chapter.

4. Remove the shift drum bearing set plate bolts and remove the plate (**Figure 31**).

> *NOTE*
> *The shift forks are not identical and on some models they are not marked. Prior to removing the shift forks mark them with a F (front), C (center) and R (rear) as shown in **Figure 33** to indicate their operating positions.*

5. Remove the shift fork shaft (**Figure 32**) and the three shift forks (**Figure 33**).

6. Remove the final drive gear, as described in this chapter, if it was not previously removed.

7. Remove the countershaft front bearing (**Figure 34**).

> *CAUTION*
> *In Step 8, when the countershaft is withdrawn, the gears will slide off the end of the shaft. Be prepared to catch them as the shaft is removed.*

8. Carefully and slowly withdraw the countershaft (**Figure 35**). Remove each gear as the shaft is removed (**Figure 36**).

9. Remove the countershaft washer (**Figure 37**) from the rear bearing .

10. Remove the front shift drum bearing (**Figure 38**) and remove the shift drum (**Figure 39**).

Mainshaft Disassembly

Refer to **Figure 40** for this procedure.

> *NOTE*
> *Use a large egg flat (the type restaurants get their eggs in) to hold the parts during transmission disassembly. As a part is removed from the shaft, set it in one of the depressions in the same position from which it was removed.*

1. Clean the shaft as described under *Preliminary Inspection* in this chapter.

2. To remove the mainshaft nut (**Figure 41**), perform the following:

 a. The mainshaft nut is staked to the mainshaft. Remove the staked portion from the nut with a grinder or drill bit. Work carefully to prevent damaging the gear and shaft.

 b. Support the mainshaft (A, **Figure 42**) in a vise with the Honda mainshaft holder (part

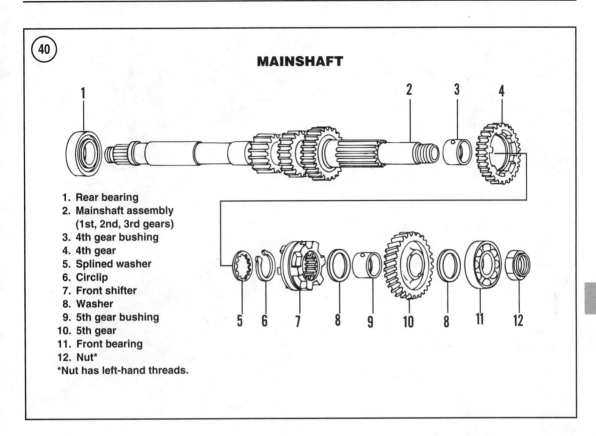

MAINSHAFT

1. Rear bearing
2. Mainshaft assembly
   (1st, 2nd, 3rd gears)
3. 4th gear bushing
4. 4th gear
5. Splined washer
6. Circlip
7. Front shifter
8. Washer
9. 5th gear bushing
10. 5th gear
11. Front bearing
12. Nut*
*Nut has left-hand threads.

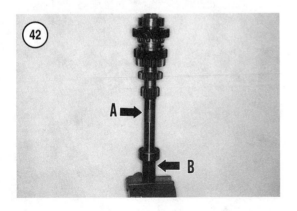

No. 07JMB-MN50200) or equivalent. See B, **Figure 42**.

> *CAUTION*
> *The mainshaft nut torque specification is 186 N•m (137 ft.-lb.). Do not attempt to loosen the nut without properly securing the mainshaft in a vise as described in substep b or the mainshaft splines may be damaged.*

> *NOTE*
> *The mainshaft nut has left-hand threads.*

   c. Loosen the mainshaft nut with a socket and breaker bar. Turn the mainshaft nut *clockwise* to loosen it.

   d. Remove the mainshaft from the vise and remove the special tool.

   e. Remove and discard the mainshaft nut (A, **Figure 43**).

3. Remove the front bearing (B, **Figure 43**).
4. Remove the rear bearing.
5. Remove the washer.
6. Slide off fifth gear and the gear bushing.

7. Remove the washer.

8. Slide off the front shifter.

9. Remove the circlip and the splined washer.

10. Slide off fourth gear and the gear bushing.

11. The first, second and third gear cluster is an integral part of the mainshaft.

12. Inspect the mainshaft assembly as described in this chapter. Replace all worn or defective parts. Thoroughly clean all parts before assembly.

Mainshaft Assembly

Refer to **Figure 40** for this procedure.

1. Prior to assembly, apply clean engine oil to all sliding gear and shaft surfaces.

2. Install the fourth gear bushing and fourth gear (**Figure 44**).

3. Slide on the splined washer and install the circlip. Make sure the circlip is seated correctly in the mainshaft groove.

4. Slide the front shifter with the shifter knobs facing in the direction shown in **Figure 45**.

5. Slide on the washer.

6. Slide on the fifth gear bushing.

7. Slide on fifth gear so that the gear teeth face in the direction shown in **Figure 46**.

8. Install the washer (**Figure 47**).

9. Position the front bearing with the manufacturer's mark facing out and install the front bearing (B, **Figure 43**).

10. Position the rear bearing with the manufacturer's mark facing out and install the rear bearing (**Figure 48**).

NOTE
The mainshaft nut has left-hand threads.

11. Thread a *new* nut onto the mainshaft, turning it *counterclockwise* and hand-tighten it.

12. Refer to **Figure 49** for the correct placement of each gear. Make sure the circlip is correctly seated in the mainshaft groove.

13. Tighten the mainshaft nut to the correct torque as follows:

    a. Support the mainshaft (A, **Figure 42**) in a vise with the Honda mainshaft holder (part No. 07JMB-MN50200) or equivalent. See B, **Figure 42**.

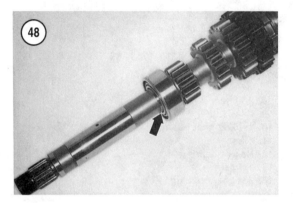

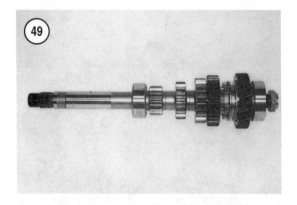

CAUTION
The mainshaft nut torque specification is 186 N•m (137 ft.-lb.). Do not attempt to tighten the nut without properly securing the mainshaft in a vise as described in substep a or the mainshaft splines will be damaged.

NOTE
The mainshaft nut has left-hand threads.

   b. If not already in place, install a *new* mainshaft nut onto the mainshaft, turning it *counterclockwise* until it stops.

   c. Tighten the mainshaft nut with a torque wrench to the torque specification in **Table 4**.

   d. Stake the new nut in two places in the mainshaft end grooves (**Figure 50**) with a flat punch or drift (**Figure 51**).

14. Rotate both bearings by hand. Make sure they rotate freely with no binding or roughness.

Countershaft Assembly

The countershaft (**Figure 52**) is assembled as it is installed into the cylinder block; see *Transmission Installation* in this section. Inspect the countershaft assembly as described under *Inspection* in this section.

Main and Countershaft Inspection

1. Clean the transmission parts in solvent and dry with compressed air.

2. Check each gear for excessive wear, burrs, pitting or chipped or missing teeth. Make sure the gear lugs (**Figure 53**) are in good condition.

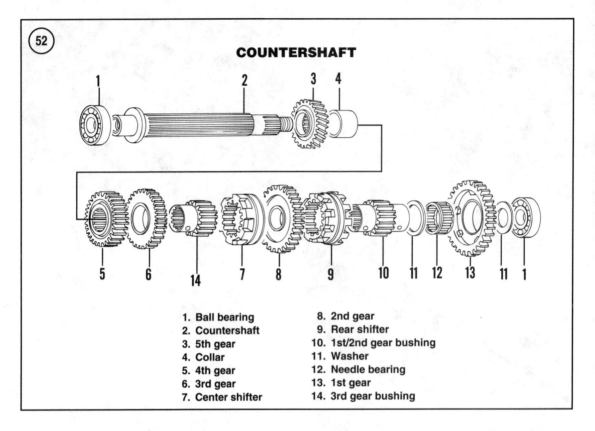

COUNTERSHAFT

1. Ball bearing
2. Countershaft
3. 5th gear
4. Collar
5. 4th gear
6. 3rd gear
7. Center shifter
8. 2nd gear
9. Rear shifter
10. 1st/2nd gear bushing
11. Washer
12. Needle bearing
13. 1st gear
14. 3rd gear bushing

3. Check the bushing surface (**Figure 54**) for wear, cracks or other damage in the applicable gears.

> *NOTE*
> *Replace defective gears. It is recommended to replace gears that mate as a set.*

> *NOTE*
> *The first, second and third mainshaft gears (**Figure 55**) are part of the mainshaft. If any one gear is defective, the shaft must be replaced.*

4. Make sure that all gears and bushings slide smoothly on their respective shaft splines.

5. Measure the inside diameter of the mainshaft fourth and fifth gears and the countershaft second and third gears (**Figure 56**). Replace any gear that exceeds the service limit in **Table 2**. If the gear inside diameter is within specification, record the dimension for use later.

6. Measure the inside diameter and the outside diameter of the mainshaft fourth and fifth gear bushings (**Figure 57**). Replace the bushing if the inside or outside diameter is worn to the service limit in

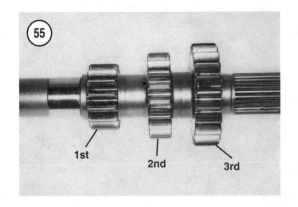

1st   2nd   3rd

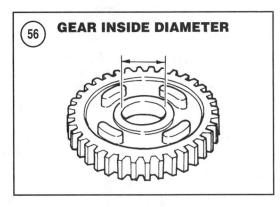

GEAR INSIDE DIAMETER

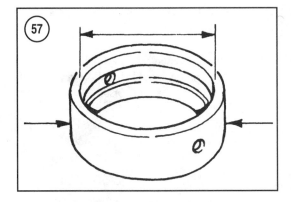

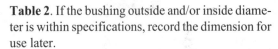

Table 2. If the bushing outside and/or inside diameter is within specifications, record the dimension for use later.

7. Measure the outside diameter of the countershaft second and third gear bushings (**Figure 58**). Replace the bushing(s) if the diameter is less than the service limit in **Table 2**. If the bushing outside diameter is within specifications, record the dimension for use later.

8. The bushings and gears must operate within a specified running clearance. Subtract the bushing outside diameter (Step 6 and 7) from the gear inside diameter (Step 5). Replace the gear and bushing combination if the clearance is worn to the service limit listed in **Table 2**.

9. Check the groove in each shifter (**Figure 59**) for severe wear or damage. Replace the shifter if necessary.

10. Check the countershaft first gear needle bearing (**Figure 60**) for damage or wear.

11. Check the mainshaft and countershaft for damaged splines, threads or other wear. Clean the oil holes in both shafts and countershaft bushings with compressed air.

12. Inspect the shift forks and shift fork shaft as described under *Internal Shift Mechanism* in this chapter.

Transmission Installation

> *NOTE*
> *Install the shift drum as an assembled unit; the rear bearing and set collar must be installed and bolted onto the shift drum. Refer to **Internal Shift Mechanism** in this chapter.*

1. Install the shift drum (**Figure 39**) and the front shift drum bearing (**Figure 38**).

> *NOTE*
> *When assembling and installing the countershaft assembly in Step 2, align the oil holes in the bushings and shifters with the countershaft oil holes (**Figure 61**, typical). This alignment is necessary for proper oil flow.*

2. If removed, install the countershaft rear bearing. Position the bearing set plate with the OUTSIDE mark facing out and install it onto the cylinder block. Apply ThreeBond TB1342 or Loctite 242 (blue) to the bolt threads prior to installation. Install the bolts and tighten them securely.

3. Assemble and install the countershaft assembly as follows:

    a. Identify and lay out all of the countershaft components in the order shown in **Figure 52**. Install all gears in the order shown in **Figure 62**.

    b. Apply oil to the countershaft washer and place the washer against the rear countershaft bearing (**Figure 62**).

    c. Apply engine oil to the countershaft splines.

    d. Slide the countershaft partway through the case opening (**Figure 63**).

    e. Position fifth gear with the shoulder facing toward the outside of the cylinder block. Push the countershaft through fifth gear.

    f. Slide the collar onto the countershaft and up against fifth gear.

    g. Slide on fourth gear and seat it against the collar.

    h. Assemble third gear, the third gear bushing and the center shifter as shown in **Figure 64**. Then slide on the third gear assembly so that

third gear seats next to fourth gear. Push the countershaft through this assembly.

    i. Assemble second gear, first/second gear bushing, rear shifter, washer, needle bearing and first gear as shown in **Figure 65**. Note that the longer bushing shoulder faces toward first gear.

    j. Position the first and second gear assembly (assembled in substep i) so that second gear faces toward the center shifter. Push the countershaft through this assembly.

    k. Push the countershaft through the washer and into the rear bearing in the crankcase. Push the countershaft in until it bottoms in the rear bearing.

    l. The front countershaft bearing has a shoulder (**Figure 66**) on one side that fits over and supports the countershaft. Install the bearing so the shoulder side faces in and meshes properly with the countershaft raised rib. **Figure 67** shows the bearing properly installed.

> *NOTE*
> *To prevent the countershaft from sliding out of the engine case, temporarily install the final drive gear and nut onto the rear of the countershaft. Tighten the nut finger-tight (**Figure 68**).*

4. Apply molybdenum disulfide oil to each mainshaft and countershaft shifter groove (**Figure 59**).

> *NOTE*
> *The shift forks are marked with an F (front), C (center) or R (rear) as shown in **Figure 69**.*

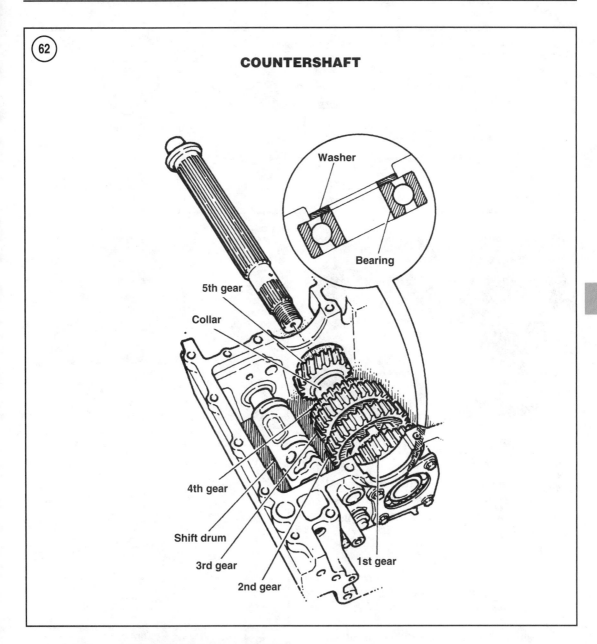

COUNTERSHAFT

Washer

Bearing

5th gear

Collar

4th gear

Shift drum

3rd gear

2nd gear

1st gear

7

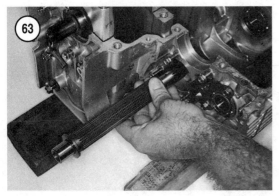

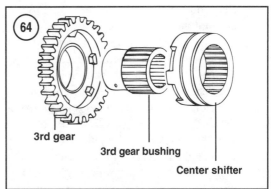

3rd gear

3rd gear bushing

Center shifter

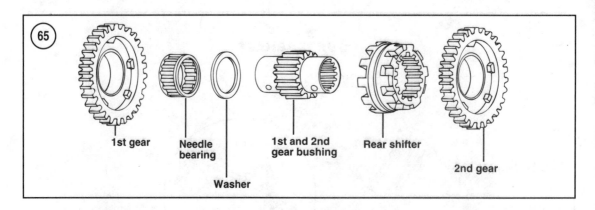

65 1st gear   Needle bearing   1st and 2nd gear bushing   Rear shifter   2nd gear   Washer

5. Install the shift forks and the shift fork shaft as follows:

   a. Apply engine oil to the shift fork shaft and to the inner sliding surfaces of the shift forks.

   b. Insert the shift fork shaft partially into the cylinder block.

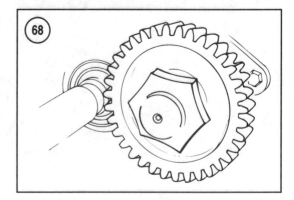

NOTE
The F shift fork meshes with the front shifter groove on the mainshaft that will be installed later in this procedure.

   c. Position the F (front) shift fork in place as shown in F, **Figure 70** and push the shift fork shaft through it.

   d. Position the C (center) shift fork with the mark facing toward the front of the engine (C, **Figure 70**). Install the shift fork into the countershaft center shifter groove and the shift fork guide pin into the center groove in the shift drum (C, **Figure 71**). Push the shift fork shaft through the C shift fork.

   e. Position the R (rear) shift fork with the mark facing toward the front of the engine (R, **Figure 70**). Install the shift fork into the

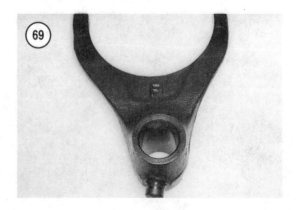

7

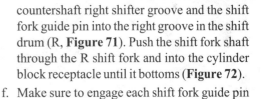

countershaft right shifter groove and the shift
fork guide pin into the right groove in the shift
drum (R, **Figure 71**). Push the shift fork shaft
through the R shift fork and into the cylinder
block receptacle until it bottoms (**Figure 72**).

   f. Make sure to engage each shift fork guide pin
with its respective shift drum groove. See F, C
and R in **Figure 71**.

   g. Apply ThreeBond TB1342 or Loctite 242
(blue) to the shift fork guide plate bolts. Then
install the plate (**Figure 73**) and mounting
bolts and tighten the bolts securely.

6. Lift up on the F shift fork and partially install the
mainshaft (**Figure 74**). Lower the mainshaft while
engaging the F shift fork with the front shifter
groove (**Figure 75**). Lower the mainshaft onto the
crankcase.

NOTE
Step 7 is best performed with the aid
of an assistant, as the assemblies are
loose and will not rotate very easily.
Have the assistant rotate the trans-
mission shafts while turning the shift
drum through all the gears.

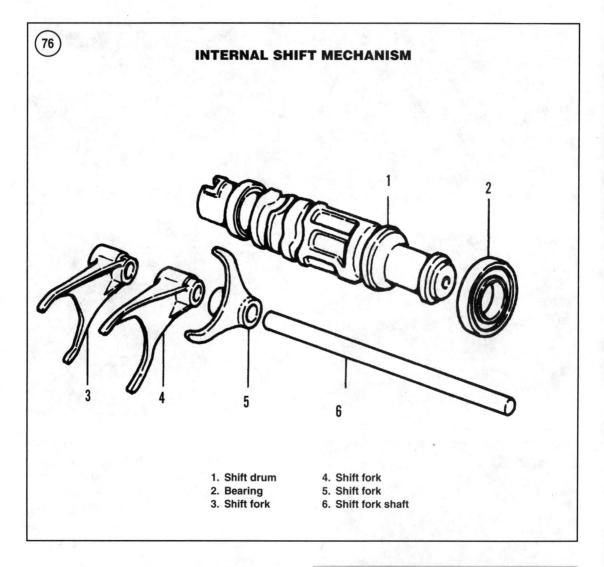

INTERNAL SHIFT MECHANISM

1. Shift drum   4. Shift fork
2. Bearing   5. Shift fork
3. Shift fork   6. Shift fork shaft

7. Rotate the transmission shafts and shift through the gears using the shift drum. Make sure the transmission can be shifted through all of the gears.

8. Assemble the crankcase as described in Chapter Five. If any difficulty is encountered, determine the cause *before* continuing.

INTERNAL SHIFT MECHANISM

The internal shift mechanism consists of the shift drum, shift forks and shift fork shaft (**Figure 76**). The shift fork shaft and shift forks are removed and installed during the removal and installation of the transmission.

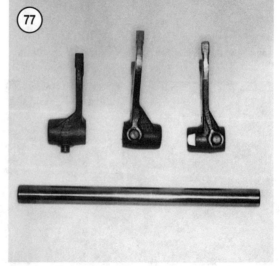

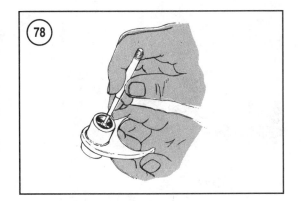

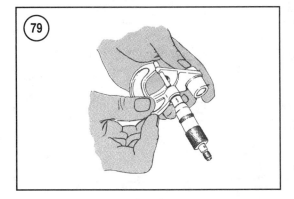

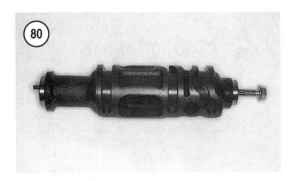

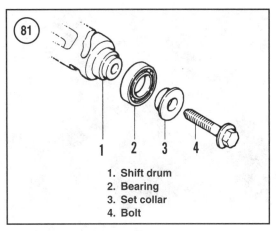

1. Shift drum
2. Bearing
3. Set collar
4. Bolt

Inspection

Refer to **Table 2** for shift fork, shift fork shaft and shift drum specifications.

1. Clean all parts in solvent and dry them thoroughly with compressed air.

2. Inspect each shift fork (**Figure 77**) for signs of wear or cracking. Check for bending and make sure each fork slides smoothly on the shaft. Replace any worn or damaged forks.

3. Check for any arc-shaped wear or burned marks on the shift forks. This indicates that the shift fork has come in contact with the gear. If fork fingers are excessively worn, replace the fork.

4. Measure the inside diameter of each shift fork with an inside micrometer or snap gauge (**Figure 78**). Replace any shift fork if the bore exceeds the service limit in **Table 2**.

5. Measure the shift fork finger thickness with a micrometer (**Figure 79**). Replace any that are worn to less than the service limit in **Table 2**.

6. Check the shift drum guide pin on each shift fork for wear or damage; replace the shift fork as necessary.

7. Roll the shift fork shaft on a surface plate and check for any bends. If the shaft is bent, it must be replaced.

8. Measure the outside diameter of the shift fork shaft at each of the three shift fork operating positions with a micrometer. Replace any shift fork if the diameter is less than the service limit in **Table 1**.

9. Check the grooves in the shift drum (**Figure 80**) for wear or roughness. If any of the groove profiles show excessive wear or damage, replace the shift drum.

10. Inspect the shift drum bearings. Each bearing must rotate smoothly with no roughness or noise. Replace damaged bearings.

11. To replace the rear shift drum bearing perform the following:

   a. Remove the set collar bolt and remove the set collar and bearing (**Figure 81**).

   b. Install a new bearing onto the shift drum.

   c. Install the set collar into the bearing.

   d. Apply ThreeBond TB1342 or Loctite 242 (blue) onto the set collar bolt. Then install and tighten the set collar bolt to the torque specification in **Table 4**.

7

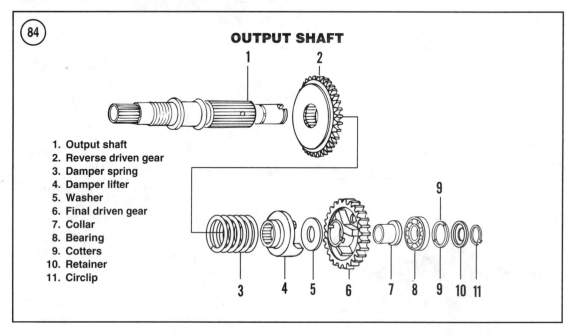

OUTPUT SHAFT

1. Output shaft
2. Reverse driven gear
3. Damper spring
4. Damper lifter
5. Washer
6. Final driven gear
7. Collar
8. Bearing
9. Cotters
10. Retainer
11. Circlip

OUTPUT SHAFT

Excessive output shaft (A, **Figure 82**) noise is an indication of worn or damaged parts. Possible problem areas are:

1. Worn or damaged final drive (B, **Figure 82**) and driven (A, **Figure 83**) gears.

2. Excessive final drive and driven gear backlash.

3. Worn or damaged output shaft bearing (B, **Figure 83**).

A thorough inspection requires disassembly of the output shaft.

The output shaft is mounted behind the rear cover. The final driven gear is mounted on the output shaft. Final drive gear service is in Chapter Five.

NOTE
The output shaft assembly is identical to the output shaft used on the GL1500 Gold Wing equipped with reverse. A reverse gear is on the GL1500 Valkyrie output shaft even though this model is not equipped with reverse.

Removal

1. Remove the engine from the frame as described in Chapter Five.

2. Remove the rear engine case as described in Chapter Five.

3. Remove the alternator drive gear as described in Chapter Five.

4. Remove the output shaft assembly from the engine. See A, **Figure 82**.

Disassembly

A hydraulic press is required to overhaul the output shaft assembly. Refer to **Figure 84** for this procedure.

> *WARNING*
> *Because the output shaft (**Figure 83**) is under considerable spring pressure, do not try to disassemble the output shaft without a hydraulic press. If necessary, refer service to a Honda dealership.*

1. Remove the output shaft from the engine as described in this chapter.

2. Prior to disassembling the output shaft, perform the following:

    a. Turn the output shaft outer bearing race (**Figure 85**) by hand. The race should turn smoothly with no binding or excessive noise.

    b. Hold the outer bearing race and try to move the bearing axially on the output shaft. The inner bearing race should fit tightly on the output shaft.

    c. If the output shaft bearing is worn, damaged or if the inner bearing race is loose on the shaft, install a new bearing during assembly.

3. Remove the circlip and the retainer from the output shaft (**Figure 86**).

4. Tap the cotters out with a screwdriver (**Figure 87**).

5. Support the final driven gear in a press as shown in **Figure 88** and press the output shaft out of the bearing.

6. Disassemble the output shaft in the order shown in **Figure 84**.

Inspection

Refer to **Figure 84** for this procedure. Refer to **Table 3** for output shaft specifications.

1. Clean all parts in solvent and dry them thoroughly with compressed air.

2. Check the damper lifter for damaged splines or worn or damaged gear lugs.

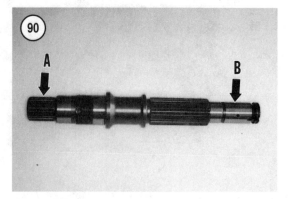

3. Measure the damper spring free length with a vernier caliper. Replace the spring if it has sagged to the service limit in **Table 3**.

4. Check the collar (A, **Figure 89**) for scoring, wear or cracks. Then measure the collar inside diameter and outside diameter. Replace the collar if the diameter is greater or less than the service limit in **Table 3**.

5. Check the final driven gear (B, **Figure 89**) for worn, broken or chipped teeth. Measure the final driven gear inside diameter and compare to the specification in **Table 3**.

6. Check the output shaft (A, **Figure 90**) for worn or damaged splines. Place the output shaft on a set of V-blocks and check runout with a dial indicator; replace the shaft if it is bent.

7. Measure the output shaft outside diameter where the collar makes contact (B, **Figure 90**). Replace the shaft if the outside diameter is less than the service limit in **Table 1**.

8. Inspect the reverse driven gear for worn, broken or chipped teeth.

9. Discard all worn or damaged parts.

Assembly

Refer to **Figure 84** for this procedure.

1. Prior to assembly, perform the *Inspection* procedures to make sure all worn or defective parts have been replaced. Thoroughly clean all parts before assembly.

2. Apply engine oil to all bearing surfaces prior to assembly.

3. Slide on the reverse driven gear so that the flat side seats against the output shaft shoulder; see **Figure 91**. Refer to the previous NOTE relating to the reverse system.

4. Slide on the damper spring (A, **Figure 92**).

5. Slide on the damper lifter so that the arms face away from the spring (B, **Figure 92**).

6. Slide on the washer (**Figure 93**) and seat it against the damper lifter.

7. Slide on the final driven gear (**Figure 94**) so that the dished side of the gear faces toward the damper lifter. Engage the damper lifter arms with the final driven gear as shown in **Figure 95**.

8. Slide on the collar and insert it through the final driven gear (**Figure 96**).

9. Support the output shaft in a press (**Figure 97**).

NOTE
Install a new output shaft bearing during reassembly.

10. Place a new output shaft bearing over the end of the output shaft so that the sealed bearing side faces up (A, **Figure 98**).

11. Place a bearing installer over the inner bearing race (B, **Figure 98**) and press the bearing onto the shaft until the inner bearing race is approximately even with the lower cotter shoulder (**Figure 99**).

12. Install the two cotters (**Figure 100**) onto the bearing and fit them around the end of the output shaft. The cotters should fit snugly when properly installed. If the cotters are loose, support the final driven gear in a press (as during disassembly) and reposition the shaft.

13. Fit the retainer (**Figure 86**) over the output shaft and turn it so that the retainer tab is 180° opposite the output shaft keyway (**Figure 101**).

14. Install a new circlip so that the chamfered circlip surface faces toward the retainer.

15. Turn the outer bearing race by hand. The bearing should turn smoothly with no sign of roughness or excessive noise.

Installation

1. Install the output shaft assembly into the cylinder block (A, **Figure 82**).

2. Install the alternator drive gear as described in Chapter Five.

3. Install the rear engine case as described in Chapter Five.

4. Install the engine in the frame as described in Chapter Five.

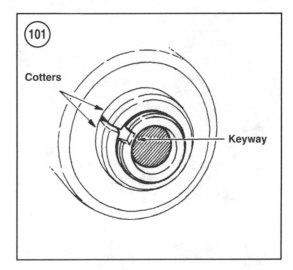

Table 1 GENERAL TRANSMISSION SPECIFICATIONS

Type	5-speed, constant mesh
Shift pattern (with left foot)	1-N-2-3-4-5 (OD)
Primary reduction ratio	1.592 (78/49)
Secondary reduction ratio	0.971 (34/35)
Gear ratio	
1st	2.666 (40/15)
2nd	1.722 (31/18)
3rd	1.291 (31/24)
4th	1.000 (30/30)
5th (overdrive)	0.804 (29/36)
Final reduction ratio	2.833 (34/12)

Table 2 TRANSMISSION SERVICE SPECIFICATIONS

	Specification mm (in.)	Service limit mm (in.)
Mainshaft gear inside diameter		
Fourth gear	31.000-31.025 (1.2205-1.2215)	31.04 (1.222)
Fifth gear	30.000-30.021 (1.1811-1.1819)	30.04 (1.183)
Countershaft gear inside diameter		
Second and third gears	34.000-34.016 (1.3386-1.3392)	34.04 (1.340)
Gear bushing outside diameter		
Mainshaft fourth gear	30.950-30.975 (1.2185-1.2195)	30.93 (1.218)
Mainshaft fifth gear	29.955-29.980 (1.1793-1.1803)	29.93 (1.178)
Countershaft second and third gears	33.940-33.965 (1.3362-1.3372)	33.92 (1.335)
Gear bushing inside diameter		
Mainshaft fourth gear	28.000-28.021 (1.1024-1.1032)	28.04 (1.104)
Mainshaft fifth gear	23.000-23.021 (0.9055-0.9063)	23.03 (0.907)
Gear-to-bushing clearance		
Mainshaft fourth gear	0.025-0.076 (0.0010-0.0030)	0.10 (0.004)
Mainshaft fifth gear	0.020-0.066 (0.0008-0.0026)	0.09 (0.004)
Countershaft second and third gears	0.035-0.076 (0.0014-0.0030)	0.10 (0.004)
Bushing-to-shaft clearance		
Mainshaft fourth and fifth gears	0.013-0.047 (0.0005-0.0019)	0.08 (0.003)
Mainshaft outside diameter		
At fourth gear bushing location	27.974-27.987 (1.1013-1.1018)	27.95 (1.100)
At fifth gear bushing location	22.974-22.987 (0.9045-0.9050)	22.95 (0.904)
Shift fork shaft outside diameter	13.966-13.984 (0.5498-0.5506)	13.90 (0.547)
Shift fork		
Inside diameter	14.000-14.021 (0.5512-0.5520)	14.04 (0.553)
Finger thickness	5.93-6.00 (0.233-0.236)	5.6 (0.22)

Table 3 OUTPUT SHAFT SPECIFICATIONS

	Specification mm (in.)	Wear mm (in.)
Driven gear inside diameter	26.000-26.016 (1.0236-1.0242)	26.03 (1.025)
Output shaft outside diameter	22.008-22.021 (0.8665-0.8670)	21.99 (0.866)

(continued)

Table 3 OUTPUT SHAFT SPECIFICATIONS (continued)

	Specification mm (in.)	Wear mm (in.)
Collar		
Inside diameter	22.026-22.041 (0.8672-0.8678)	22.05 (0.868)
Outside diameter	25.959-25.980 (1.0220-1.0228)	25.95 (1.022)
Damper spring free length	60.82 (2.394)	57.0 (2.24)

Table 4 TRANSMISSION TIGHTENING TORQUES

	N•m	ft.-lb.
Drum center bolt	27	20
Mainshaft locknut*	186	137
Countershaft		
(final drive gear) locknut*	186	137
Set collar bolt	12	9
Shift lever bolt	25	18
* After tightening nut, stake in two places as described in text.		

CHAPTER EIGHT

FUEL AND EMISSION CONTROL SYSTEMS

The fuel system consists of a fuel tank, shutoff valve, six constant velocity carburetors and the air filter.

Adjustment procedures and service intervals are covered in Chapter Three.

This chapter includes service procedures for all parts of the fuel and emission control systems.

Carburetor specifications are in **Table 1**. **Table 1** and **Table 2** are at the end of this chapter.

The carburetors on all U.S. models are engineered to meet Environmental Protection Agency (EPA) regulations. The carburetors are flow-tested and preset by the manufacturer for maximum performance and efficiency. Do not alter the preset carburetor jet needle and pilot screw adjustments.

Failure to comply with EPA regulations may result in heavy fines.

WARNING
Because of the explosive and flammable conditions that exist around gasoline, always observe the following precautions.

1. Disconnect the negative battery cable before working on the fuel system. Refer to Chapter Three.

2. Gasoline dripping onto a hot engine component may cause a fire. Always allow the engine to cool completely before working on any fuel system component.

3. Spilled gasoline should be wiped up immediately with dry rags. Then store the rags in a suitable

metal container until they can be cleaned or disposed of.

4. Do not service any fuel system component while in the vicinity of open flames, sparks or while anyone is smoking next to the motorcycle.

5. Always have a fire extinguisher available when working on the fuel system.

FUEL SYSTEM IDENTIFICATION

There will be a number of fuel lines and hoses disconnected when removing many of the fuel system components for service. Thus it is important to identify the hoses prior to disconnecting them. Many of the hoses are coded by number and/or color. Look for these marks. If a hose is not labeled, identify and tag the hose. As a hose is disconnected, record the part and connection point on the tag and immediately attach the tag to the hose. Tags can be made with strips of masking tape and a fine-point permanent marking pen. This preparation will prevent considerable inconvenience during reassembly.

AIR FILTER CASE

Air filter service is described in Chapter Three. The following section describes air filter case removal/installation.

Removal/Installation

1. Remove the fuel tank as described in this chapter.

2. Remove the air filter element as described in Chapter Three.

3. On the right side, disconnect the crankcase breather storage tank hose from the air filter case.

4. On the left side, perform the following:
    a. Remove the No. 1 and No. 2 cylinders ignition coil as described in Chapter Nine.
    b. Disconnect the secondary air supply hose (A, **Figure 1**) from the air filter case.
    c. Disconnect the air filter housing drain tube (B, **Figure 1**) from the air filter case.

5. Loosen all six screws on the connecting tube clamps (**Figure 2**).

6. Remove the bolt (A, **Figure 3**) securing the air filter air box to the frame.

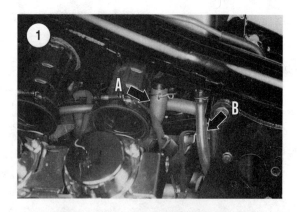

7. Carefully pull the air box (B, **Figure 3**) toward the rear and up and out of the frame. Do not damage the connecting tubes during removal.

8. Cover the carburetor openings with clean lint-free shop cloths.

9. Inspect and service the air filter element, as described in Chapter Three.

10. Check the air filter case (**Figure 4**) and the connecting tube seals (**Figure 5**) for cracks or damage.

11. Install the air filter case by reversing these steps. Make sure all of the connecting tubes and all hoses are connected and secured properly.

CARBURETOR OPERATION

Understanding the function of each of the carburetor components and their relationships to one another is a valuable aid for pinpointing carburetor trouble.

The carburetor's purpose is to supply and atomize fuel and mix it in correct proportions with air that is drawn in through the air intake. At the primary throttle opening (idle), a small amount of fuel is siphoned through the slow jet by the incoming air. As the throttle is opened further, the air stream begins to siphon fuel through the main jet and main jet holder. The tapered needle increases the effective flow capacity of the main jet holder as it is lifted, in that it occupies less of the jet area.

At full throttle, the carburetor venturi is fully open and the needle is lifted far enough to permit the main jet to flow at full capacity.

The starting enrichment (SE) circuit is a starting jet system in which the choke lever operate the SE valve rather than closing an air restricting butterfly. In the open position, the pilot jet discharges an additional stream of fuel into the carburetor venturi to enrich the mixture when the engine is cold.

CARBURETOR SERVICE

Carburetor Assembly Removal

1. Place the motorcycle on a lift. See *Motorcycle Lift* in Chapter One.

2. Disconnect the negative battery lead as described in Chapter Three.

3. Drain the cooling system as described in Chapter Three.

4. On GL1500CF models, remove the right and left side radiator covers as described in Chapter Fifteen.

5. Remove the fuel tank and the air filter case as described in this chapter.

6. Remove the three screws and the linkage covers (**Figure 6**) on both sides.

7. Open the drain screw (**Figure 7**) and drain the fuel from all six carburetors. Dispose of the fuel safely. Close all six drain screws.

8. On the left side, loosen the choke cable locknuts (A, **Figure 8**) and disconnect the choke cable end from the choke linkage (B, **Figure 8**).

8

NOTE
The throttle push cable is located at the top position on the throttle drum and the pull cable is located at the lower position. Both cables must be reinstalled in the correct location during installation.

9. On the right side, loosen the throttle cable locknuts (**Figure 9**) and disconnect the throttle cables at the carburetor throttle drum (**Figure 10**).

10. At the PAIR control valve assembly, refer to **Figure 11** and perform the following:

   a. Disconnect the No. 10 vacuum tube (A).

   b. Remove the two screws (B) securing the PAIR valve.

   c. Disconnect the two No. 16 hoses (C).

   d. Remove the PAIR valve and bracket (D) from the engine.

11. On California models only, refer to **Figure 12** and perform the following:

   a. Remove the No. 5 purge control tube (A).

   b. Remove the two screws (B) securing the evaporative emission (EVAP) purge control valve and the EVAP carburetor air vent (CAV) control valve.

   c. Disconnect both No. 6 air vent tubes (C) from the control valve.

   d. Disconnect the No. 6 vacuum tube from the three-way joint.

   e. Disconnect the No. 11 vacuum tube from the EVAP purge control valve.

   f. Disconnect the No. 4 purge control tube from the three-way joint.

   g. Remove the evaporative emission (EVAP) purge control valve and the EVAP carburetor air vent (CAV) control valve and the mounting bracket.

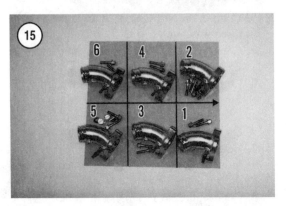

12. Loosen the clamp screw (A, **Figure 13**) and remove both bolts (B, **Figure 13**) securing the intake manifolds to the cylinder head and carburetor assembly.

13. Remove all six intake manifolds (**Figure 14**) and keep them in order of removal (**Figure 15**).

14. Cover the intake ports in the cylinder head with duct tape (**Figure 16**).

15. Remove the bolts securing the upper rear engine mounting brackets (**Figure 17**). Remove both brackets.

16. Disconnect the carburetor drain tube from the drain tube joint.

17. On the right side, unhook the wiring harness and hose from the frame clamps (**Figure 18**).

18. To gain more vertical room, attach the wiring harness and hose to the frame and secure them with tie wraps (**Figure 19**).

> *WARNING*
> *Do not hold onto the throttle linkage while removing the carburetor assembly, this may bend the linkage. If this occurs, throttle operation will be in-*

correct, as the carburetor will be out of synchronization.

19. Carefully remove the carburetor assembly from the engine and frame.

20. Check all of the hoses for cracks, age deterioration or other damage. Replace damaged hoses.

Carburetor Assembly Installation

> *WARNING*
> *Do not hold onto the throttle linkage while installing the carburetor assembly, this may bend the linkage. If this occurs, throttle operation will be incorrect, as the carburetors will be out of synchronization.*

1. Carefully install the carburetor assembly onto the engine and frame.

2. On the right side, remove the tie wraps and hook the wiring harness and hose onto the frame clamps (**Figure 18**).

3. Connect the carburetor drain tube onto the drain tube joint.

4. Install both upper rear engine mounting brackets (**Figure 17**). Tighten the bolts to the torque specification in **Table 3**. Note there are two different torque specifications for the different size bolts.

5. Remove the duct tape (**Figure 16**) from the intake ports in the cylinder head. Remove any tape residue from the sealing surface of the cylinder head with solvent and thoroughly dry.

6. Install a new O-ring (**Figure 20**) into each of the six intake manifolds.

7. Align the intake manifold lug (**Figure 21**) with the groove in the carburetor insulator.

8. Install the six intake manifolds (**Figure 14**) in the same order as removal (**Figure 15**). Make sure they are seated correctly within the carburetor insulator and on the cylinder head mating surface. Tighten both bolts (B, **Figure 13**) and the clamp screw (A, **Figure 13**) on each intake manifold. Tighten the bolts and clamp screws securely.

9. On California models only, refer to **Figure 12** and perform the following:

   a. Install the evaporative emission (EVAP) purge control valve and the EVAP carburetor air vent (CAV) control valve and the mounting bracket onto the engine.

   b. Connect the No. 4 purge control tube onto the three-way joint.

   c. Connect the No. 11 vacuum tube onto the EVAP purge control valve.

   d. Connect the No. 6 vacuum tube onto the 3-way joint.

   e. Connect both No. 6 air vent tubes (C) onto the control valve.

   f. Install the two screws (B) securing the evaporative emission (EVAP) purge control and tighten them securely.

   g. Connect the No. 5 purge control tube (A).

10. At the PAIR control valve assembly, refer to **Figure 11** and perform the following:

   a. Install the PAIR valve and bracket (D) onto the engine.

   b. Connect the two No. 16 hoses (C).

   c. Install the two screws (B) securing the PAIR valve and tighten them securely.

   d. Connect the No. 10 vacuum tube (A).

> *NOTE*
> *Make sure to install the cables in the correct location on the throttle drum. The pull cable has two locknuts (A,*

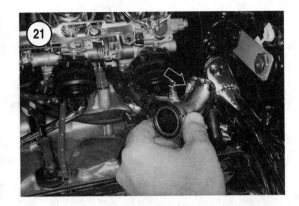

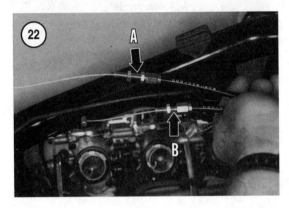

*Figure 22) and the push cable has
one locknut (B, Figure 22).*

11. On the right side, connect the throttle cables to
the carburetor throttle drum (**Figure 10**). The throttle push cable is located at the top position on the
throttle drum and the pull cable is located at the
lower position.

12. Install the throttle cable onto the cable bracket
and temporarily tighten the locknuts (**Figure 9**).

13. On the left side, connect the choke cable end
onto the choke linkage (B, **Figure 8**) at the carburetor plate. Install the choke cable onto the cable
bracket and temporarily tighten the choke cable
locknuts (A, **Figure 8**).

14. Install the linkage covers (**Figure 6**) on both
sides and tighten the screws securely.

NOTE
*Prior to installing the air filter case,
make sure the fuel hose and the No. 10
vacuum hose are routed so they can
reach the fuel tank. Do not pull too
hard on the No. 10 vacuum hose; it
may disconnect from the fitting.*

15. Install the air filter case and fuel tank as described in this chapter.

16. On GL1500CF models, install the right and left
side radiator covers as described in Chapter Fifteen.

17. Refill the cooling system as described in Chapter Three.

18. Connect the negative battery lead as described
in Chapter Three.

19. Remove the motorcycle from the lift.

20. Adjust the throttle cables as described in Chapter Three.

21. Adjust the choke cable as described in Chapter
Three.

22. Install the air filter case as described in this
chapter.

23. Install the fairing inner covers as described in
Chapter Fifteen.

24. Reconnect the negative battery lead as described in Chapter Three.

WARNING
*Do not ride the motorcycle until the
throttle cables are adjusted properly.*

Carburetor Separation

Separating the carburetors is not necessary to service the individual carburetors. All service procedures can be accomplished with the six carburetors
in place. It is not recommended that the carburetor
assembly be separated, but this procedure is included if the task is necessary.

If only one carburetor body, or more, requires replacement, perform only the tasks necessary to remove that carburetor(s). It may not be necessary to
completely disassemble the entire assembly.

Refer to **Figure 23** for this procedure.

1. Label all of the hoses and fittings, then disconnect the hoses from the carburetors. Use **Figure 24**
and **Figure 25** as a reference. The carburetor assembly being worked on may have a slightly different
hose layout.

2. Disconnect the interconnecting choke cable (A,
Figure 26).

3. Remove the screws, washers, set collars and
springs and remove the choke linkage (B, **Figure 26**)
from each side.

4. Remove the cotter pin, small metal washer, plastic
washer, large metal washer and the throttle link plate
from each side. Refer to **Figure 27** and **Figure 28**.

8

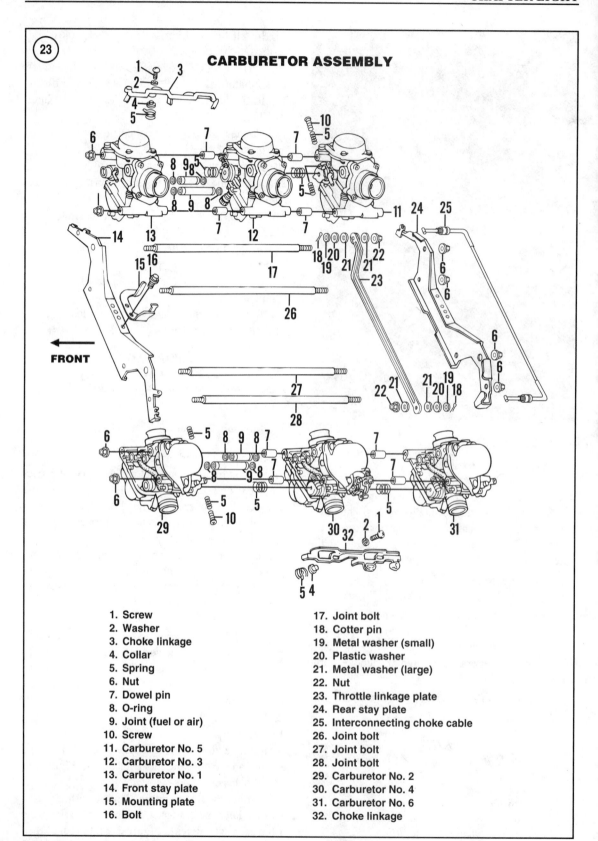

CARBURETOR ASSEMBLY

1. Screw
2. Washer
3. Choke linkage
4. Collar
5. Spring
6. Nut
7. Dowel pin
8. O-ring
9. Joint (fuel or air)
10. Screw
11. Carburetor No. 5
12. Carburetor No. 3
13. Carburetor No. 1
14. Front stay plate
15. Mounting plate
16. Bolt
17. Joint bolt
18. Cotter pin
19. Metal washer (small)
20. Plastic washer
21. Metal washer (large)
22. Nut
23. Throttle linkage plate
24. Rear stay plate
25. Interconnecting choke cable
26. Joint bolt
27. Joint bolt
28. Joint bolt
29. Carburetor No. 2
30. Carburetor No. 4
31. Carburetor No. 6
32. Choke linkage

FRONT

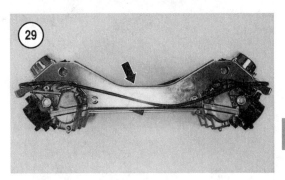

8

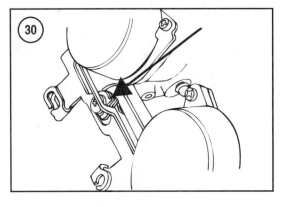

5. Remove the nuts securing the front and rear stay plates (**Figure 29**) to the long joint bolts. Remove the front and rear stay plates.

6. Carefully separate the individual carburetors from each other. Note the locations of all of the fuel joints, air joints, thrust springs, synchronizing springs, dowel pins and three-way joints.

7. Assemble by reversing these steps while noting the following:

    a. Install new O-ring seals on all fuel and air joints.

    b. Hook the choke linkage spring ends to the carburetor body and choke linkage as shown in **Figure 30**.

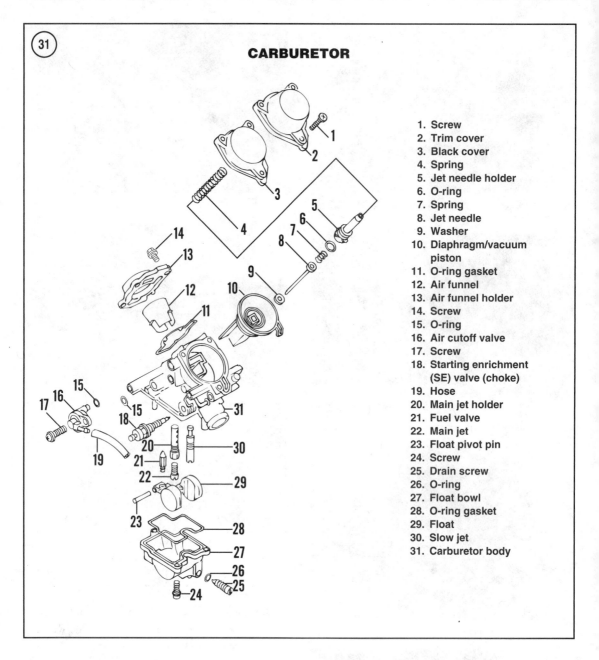

CARBURETOR

1. Screw
2. Trim cover
3. Black cover
4. Spring
5. Jet needle holder
6. O-ring
7. Spring
8. Jet needle
9. Washer
10. Diaphragm/vacuum piston
11. O-ring gasket
12. Air funnel
13. Air funnel holder
14. Screw
15. O-ring
16. Air cutoff valve
17. Screw
18. Starting enrichment (SE) valve (choke)
19. Hose
20. Main jet holder
21. Fuel valve
22. Main jet
23. Float pivot pin
24. Screw
25. Drain screw
26. O-ring
27. Float bowl
28. O-ring gasket
29. Float
30. Slow jet
31. Carburetor body

Carburetor Disassembly

Refer to **Figure 31** for this procedure.

NOTE
Do not interchange parts between any of the six carburetors. Work only on one carburetor at a time.

1. Remove the screws securing the cover assembly and remove the cover (**Figure 32**) and spring. Separate the trim cover from the black cover.

2. Carefully withdraw the diaphragm/vacuum piston (**Figure 33**) from the carburetor.

3. Remove the screws securing the air funnel holder (**Figure 34**) and remove it.

4. Remove the air funnel (**Figure 35**) and the O-ring seal (**Figure 36**).

5. Remove the screws securing the float bowl to the main body and remove the float bowl (**Figure 37**).

6. Pull out the float pin (**Figure 38**) and remove the float and the fuel valve (**Figure 39**).

7. Unscrew and remove the main jet (**Figure 40**).

8. Remove the main jet holder (**Figure 41**).

9. Remove the slow jet (**Figure 42**).

NOTE
Step 10 describes removal of the pilot screw, it should not be removed unless the carburetor is being overhauled.

CAUTION
When seating the pilot screw in Step 10, do not tighten it against the seat.

The tip on the pilot screw is very thin and can break off, thus damaging the pilot screw and the pilot screw seat in the carburetor.

10. Lightly seat the pilot screw (A, **Figure 43**), counting the number of turns required for reassembly reference, then back the screw out and remove it from the carburetor along with the spring, washer and O-ring.

11. The needle jet (B, **Figure 43**) is pressed into place and cannot be removed.

12. Remove the screw (A, **Figure 44**) and the air cutoff valve (B, **Figure 44**).

13. To disassemble the diaphragm/vacuum piston, perform the following:

CAUTION
Do not damage the diaphragm while installing the 4 mm screw. Do not try to push the jet needle out of the vacuum piston by pushing on the jet needle.

a. Screw the 4 mm screw (**Figure 45**) from the cover into the jet needle holder.

b. Pull on the 4 mm screw and withdraw the jet needle holder (**Figure 46**) from the vacuum piston. Remove the 4 mm screw.

c. Remove the spring, jet needle and washer (**Figure 47**) from the vacuum piston.

NOTE
Further disassembly is not recommended. If the throttle plate and shaft are damaged, the carburetor body must be replaced.

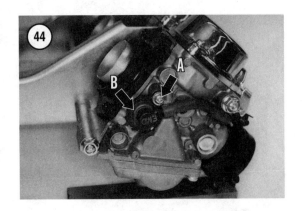

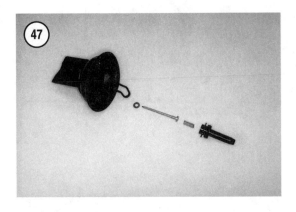

8

Cleaning and Inspection

The following steps list step-by-step cleaning and inspection procedures for the carburetors. If the motorcycle has been in storage for more than a month and the float bowls were not drained, the carburetor passages and jets must be cleaned thoroughly to remove any varnish residue that is left from evaporating gasoline.

CAUTION
Do not clean the float or O-rings in a carburetor cleaner or other solution that can damage them.

1. Initially clean all parts in a petroleum-based solvent, or an aerosol-type carburetor cleaner, then clean them in hot, soapy water. Rinse the parts with clean water and blow dry with compressed air,
2. Inspect the float bowl O-ring (**Figure 48**) gasket. Replace the O-ring if it is hard or is starting to deteriorate.
3. Make sure the float bowl drain screw is in good condition and does not leak. If necessary, replace the drain screw and O-ring seal.
4. Inspect the end of the fuel valve (**Figure 49**) and fuel valve seat for uneven wear or damage. Insert the needle valve into the valve seat (**Figure 50**) and slowly move it in and out to check for smooth operation. If the fuel valve is worn, the seat may also be worn. The fuel valve can be replaced, but the valve seat is an integral part of the carburetor body and cannot be replaced.
5. If removed, inspect the pilot screw for wear or damage that may have occurred during removal.

CAUTION
*Do **not** use a piece of wire to clean the jets; minor gouges in a jet can alter the air/fuel mixture.*

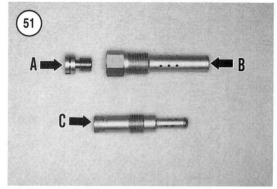

6. Inspect the main jet (A, **Figure 51**), the needle jet holder (B) and the slow jet (C). Make sure all holes are open and none of the parts are either worn or damaged.

7. Check the vacuum piston diaphragm (A, **Figure 52**) for tearing, pin holes, age deterioration or other damage.

8. Check the vacuum piston (B, **Figure 52**) for nicks, scoring or damage. Install the vacuum piston into the carburetor body and move it up and down in the bore. The vacuum piston should move smoothly without excessive play. If there is excessive play, the vacuum piston and/or the carburetor body must be replaced.

9. Inspect the jet needle (**Figure 53**) for excessive wear at the tip or other damage on the needle.

10. Inspect the float (**Figure 54**) for deterioration or damage. If the float is suspected of leakage, place it in a container of water and push it down. If the float sinks or if bubbles appear (indicating a leak), the float must be replaced.

11. Make sure all passages in the carburetor body are clear. Refer to **Figure 55** and **Figure 56**. Clean all openings with compressed air.

12. Inspect the black top cover (**Figure 57**) for cracks or damage. Replace if necessary.

13. Inspect the carburetor body for internal and external damage. If damaged, the carburetor body cannot be replaced separately.

14. Replace all O-rings and gaskets upon assembly. O-ring seals harden after prolonged use and exposure to heat and therefore lose their ability to seal properly.

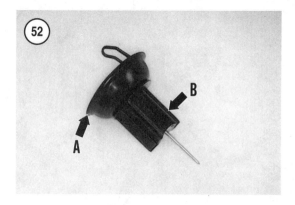

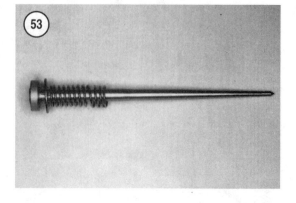

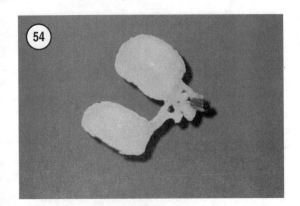

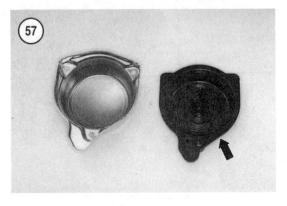

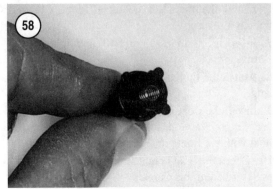

Assembly

Refer to **Figure 31** for this procedure.

1. If the pilot screw (A, **Figure 43**) was removed or replaced, install it as follows:

    a. Slide the spring, washer and a new O-ring onto the pilot screw.

NOTE
The pilot screw must be installed into the carburetor from which it was removed.

    b. When installing the original pilot screw, screw the pilot screw into the carburetor body until it lightly seats, then back out the number of turns noted during disassembly.

    c. When installing a new pilot screw, screw the pilot screw into the carburetor body until it lightly seats, and then back it out the number of turns in **Table 1**.

2. To assemble the diaphragm/vacuum piston, perform the following:

    a. Install the washer, jet needle and spring into the vacuum piston (**Figure 47**).

    b. Align the square shoulder of the jet needle holder (**Figure 58**) with the square opening in the top of the vacuum piston. Install the jet needle holder and push it down until it bottoms out (**Figure 59**).

3. Install a new O-ring seal onto the carburetor post (A, **Figure 60**) and onto the air cut-off valve post (B, **Figure 60**).

4. Install the air cutoff valve (B, **Figure 44**) and tighten the screw securely (A).

5. Install the slow jet (**Figure 42**) and tighten it securely.

6. Install the main jet holder (**Figure 41**) and tighten it securely.

7. Install the main jet (**Figure 40**) and tighten it securely.

8. Attach the fuel valve (**Figure 39**) onto the float tang.

9. Install the float into the carburetor body, inserting the fuel valve needle into its seat. Secure the float with the float pin (**Figure 38**).

10. Check the float height and adjust it if necessary as described in this chapter.

11. Install the O-ring (**Figure 61**) onto the float bowl.

12. Install the float bowl (**Figure 37**) onto the carburetor body. Install and tighten the float bowl screws in a crisscross pattern.

13. Install the air funnel (**Figure 62**) and align the tabs with the grooves in the carburetor body (A, **Figure 63**). Push the air funnel in until it bottoms out.

14. Install the O-ring gasket (B, **Figure 63**).

15. Align the dowel pin in the air funnel holder with the dowel pin holes in the carburetor body and install the air funnel holder (**Figure 34**). Install the screws and tighten them securely.

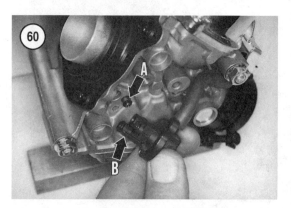

NOTE
Make sure the diaphragm bead is clean and that the groove in the carburetor body is clean. Both areas must be free of all dirt and lint. This is necessary so the diaphragm can seat properly and to prevent it from tearing as it moves up and down during use.

CAUTION
To keep the rubber diaphragm from tearing and also to make sure the diaphragm bead is properly seated, hold the vacuum piston in the raised position until the top cover is installed.

16. Insert a finger into the carburetor throat and hold the vacuum piston up in its bore.

17. Align the tab on the diaphragm with the opening (**Figure 64**) in the carburetor body. Make sure the diaphragm bead is properly seated in the groove in the carburetor body.

18. Install the vacuum piston compression spring into the vacuum piston and index it onto the boss on the top cover (**Figure 65**).

19. Install the top cover (**Figure 32**) and tighten the screws securely.

CARBURETOR ADJUSTMENT

Float Level Inspection

The carburetor assembly must be removed and partially disassembled for this inspection.

1. Remove the carburetor assembly as described in this chapter.

2. Remove the screws securing the float bowl (**Figure 66**) and remove the float bowl.

3. Hold the carburetor assembly with the float arm is just touching the float needle. Use a float level gauge, or steel ruler, and measure the distance from the carburetor body to the float (**Figure 67**). The correct float height is in **Table 1**.

4. The float cannot be adjusted. If the float level is incorrect, replace the float.

5. If the float level is too high, the result will be a rich fuel-air mixture. If it is too low, the mixture will be too lean.

> *NOTE*
> *The float on each carburetor must be at the same height to ensure the air/fuel mixture is identical for each cylinder.*

6. Make sure the O-ring (**Figure 61**) is in place on the float bowl.

7. Install the float bowl (**Figure 66**) onto the carburetor body. Install and tighten the float bowl screws in a crisscross pattern.

8. Install the carburetor assembly.

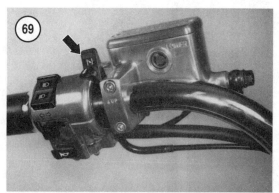

Needle Jet Adjustment

The needle jet is non-adjustable on all models.

Choke Adjustment

Make sure the choke operates smoothly with no binding. The choke cable is attached to the lever next to the left switch assembly on the handlebar. If the cable binds, lubricate it as described in Chapter Three. If the cable still does not operate smoothly, it must be replaced.

1. Place the motorcycle on the sidestand.

2. On GL1500CF models, remove the left and right side radiator cover as described in Chapter Fifteen.

3. Remove the three screws and the linkage cover (**Figure 68**) on both sides.

4. Operate the choke lever (**Figure 69**) and check for smooth operation of the cable and choke mechanism at the carburetor assembly.

5. Move the choke lever in the closed (OFF) position, check that the starting enrichment (SE) valves are fully closed. Refer to **Figure 70** and **Figure 71**. Move the choke lever in the open (ON) position, check that the SE valves are fully open. Check the SE valves on each carburetor.

6. If the SE valves do not open or close correctly, the choke cable must be adjusted as described in Step 7.

7. To adjust the choke cable, perform the following:

    a. Loosen the locknut (A, **Figure 72**) on the choke cable.

    b. Turn the adjuster (B, **Figure 72**) in either direction until the amount of movement at the choke valve (**Figure 70**) is correct.

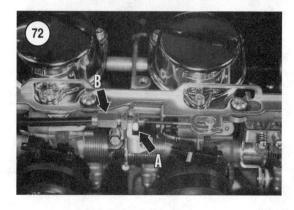

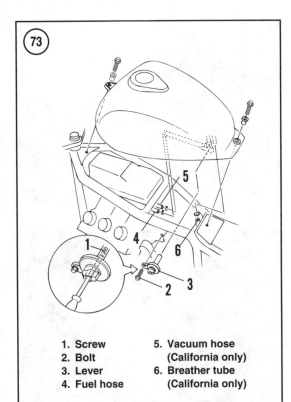

1. Screw
2. Bolt
3. Lever
4. Fuel hose
5. Vacuum hose (California only)
6. Breather tube (California only)

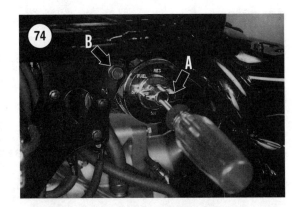

c. Tighten the locknut and recheck the choke valve operation.

8. Install both linkage covers (**Figure 68**) and tighten the screws securely.

9. On GL1500CF models, install the left and right side radiator cover as described in Chapter Fifteen.

FUEL TANK

Removal/Installation

Refer to **Figure 73** for this procedure.

1. Some fuel may spill in the following procedure. Read the *WARNING* at the beginning of this chapter and keep a B:C rated fire extinguisher near by.

2. Place the motorcycle on a lift. See *Motorcycle Lift* in Chapter One.

3. Remove the seat as described in Chapter Fifteen.

4. Disconnect the battery negative cable as described in Chapter Three.

5. Insert a long Phillips screwdriver into the valve lever (A, **Figure 74**) and remove the lever screw.

6. Remove the lever mounting bolt (B, **Figure 74**) and remove the lever (**Figure 75**).

7. Remove the mounting bolt and collar at the front (**Figure 76**) and rear (**Figure 77**) of the fuel tank.

8. Disconnect the fuel hose (A, **Figure 78**) from the fuel valve and insert a suitable plug such as a golf tee into the hose to prevent the loss of fuel and the entry of foreign matter.

9. Raise the rear of the fuel tank and support it with a wooden block.

10. On California models, perform the following:

    a. Disconnect the No. 10 vacuum hose (B, **Figure 78**) from the fuel valve.

    b. Disconnect the No. 1 breather hose (**Figure 79**) from the fuel tank fitting.

8

c. Insert a plug into both hoses to prevent the entry of foreign matter.

11. On GL1500CF models, disconnect the fuel level sensor electrical connector from the fuel tank.

12. Remove the fuel tank from the frame.

13. Pour the gasoline from the tank into an appropriate gasoline storage container.

14. If the fuel tank requires repair, refer all service work to a Honda dealership.

15. Install the fuel tank by reversing these removal steps while noting the following:

   a. Replace missing or damaged fuel tank dampers.

   b. Install the fuel tank carefully; do not pinch or bend any wires or cables below the tank.

   c. Make sure all of the wiring, hoses and cables are correctly connected and are tight.

   d. Turn the fuel on and check for any fuel leaks. Correct any fuel leaks before starting the engine.

FUEL VALVE

Removal/Installation

1. Remove the fuel tank as described in this chapter.

2. Unscrew the fitting (**Figure 80**) securing the fuel valve to the base of the fuel tank.

3. Install a new O-ring seal on the base of the filter.

4. Installation is the reverse of these steps. Tighten the fitting securely.

SECONDARY AIR SUPPLY SYSTEM

The air supply system, known as the secondary air supply system is installed on all models to help reduce engine emissions. The emission control label (**Figure 81**) is located under the left side rear frame cover. This label indicates which system is used on the motorcycle.

System Inspection

1. Start the engine and let it reach normal operating temperature. Approximately 10-15 minutes of riding is sufficient.

2. Shut the engine off and place the motorcycle on the side stand.

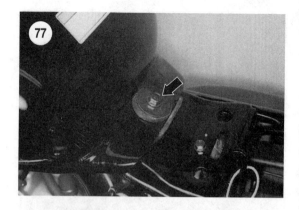

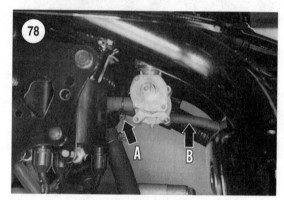

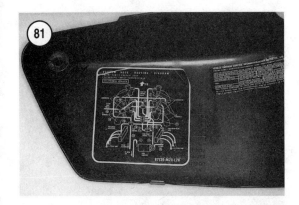

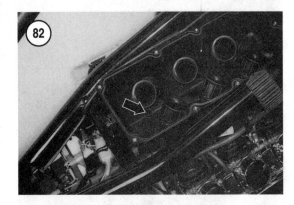

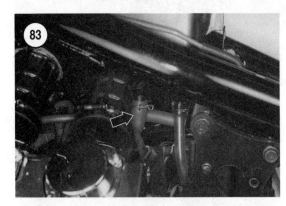

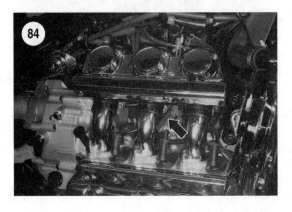

3. Remove the air filter element as described in Chapter Three.

4. Check that the opening of the secondary air intake port (**Figure 82**) is clean and free of carbon deposits. Clean it off if necessary. If the hole is severely clogged, remove the air filter case as described in this chapter and clean it out with solvent and dry it with compressed air.

5. If the air intake port is clogged with carbon, inspect the pulse secondary air injection (PAIR) check valves as described in the following procedure.

6. Install the air filter element as described in Chapter Three.

7. On the left side, disconnect the air filter case-to-control valve hose No. 15 (**Figure 83**) from the air filter case.

8. On the right side, disconnect the vacuum hose from the No. 3 cylinder intake manifold (**Figure 84**). Plug the vacuum port on the No. 3 intake manifold to prevent a vacuum leak.

9. Connect a hand held vacuum pump to the No. 3 vacuum hose. Do not apply any vacuum at this time.

10. Clamp off the No. 4 cylinder vacuum hose with a hemostat.

11. Start the engine and open the throttle slightly and check that air is being drawn into the No. 15 hose, disconnected in Step 7. Air should be drawn into the hose.

12. If no air is being drawn in, disconnect the No. 15 hose and check if the hose is clogged.

Disconnect and clean out if necessary.

13. With the engine running, gradually apply vacuum (400 mm/15.7 Hg) to the No. 3 vacuum hose. Check that the No. 15 hose is not drawing in air and that the vacuum does not bleed.

14. If air is being drawn into the No. 15 hose, or if the specified vacuum is not maintained, install a new PAIR valve as described in this chapter.

15. Shut off the engine.

16. Disconnect the hand-held vacuum pump and reconnect all hoses to the correct fittings.

PAIR Check Valve Inspection

1. Remove the carburetor assembly as described in this chapter.

2. Disconnect the hose and the air feed pipes (A, **Figure 85**) from the three fittings on the reed valve case.

3. Remove the two screws securing the check valve case (B, **Figure 85**) to the engine.

4. Remove the mounting screws and separate the cover from the case (**Figure 86**).

5. Repeat Steps 2-4 for the other reed valve case.

CAUTION
The reed valves must not be serviced or disassembled. Do not try to bend the stopper. If any part of the valve is faulty, the valve assembly must be replaced.

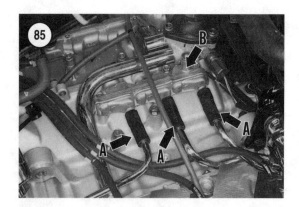

6. Inspect each valve reed for fatigue or damage. If either is found, the valve(s) must be replaced.

7. Check the rubber seal for deterioration or cracking. If either is found, the valve(s) must be replaced.

8. Make sure there is no clearance between the valve and the rubber seal. If there is any gap, the valve(s) must be replaced.

9. Check the air feed pipes (**Figure 87**) for cracks or damage.

10. Install by reversing these removal steps.

PAIR Control Valve Replacement

1. Place the motorcycle on a lift. See *Motorcycle Lift* in Chapter One.

2. Disconnect the negative battery lead as described in Chapter Three.

3. Remove the fuel tank and the air filter case as described in this chapter.

4. At the PAIR control valve assembly, refer to **Figure 88** and perform the following:

   a. Disconnect the No. 10 vacuum tube (A).

   b. Remove the two screws (B) securing the PAIR valve.

   c. Disconnect the two No. 16 hoses (C).

   d. Remove the PAIR valve and bracket (D) from the engine.

5. To install the PAIR control valve assembly, refer to **Figure 88** and perform the following:

   a. Install the PAIR valve and bracket (D) onto the engine.

   b. Connect the two No. 16 hoses (C).

   c. Install the two screws (B) securing the PAIR valve and tighten them securely.

   d. Connect the No. 10 vacuum tube (A).

6. Install the air filter case and fuel tank as described in this chapter.

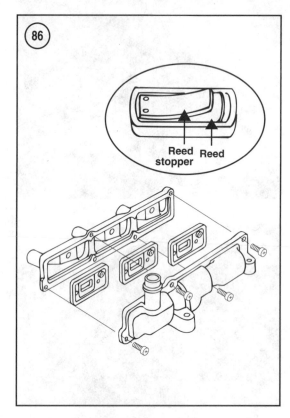

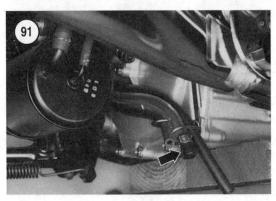

7. Connect the negative battery lead as described in Chapter Three.

8. Remove the motorcycle from the lift.

CRANKCASE BREATHER SYSTEM (U.S. ONLY)

To comply with clean air standards, GL1500 models are equipped with a crankcase breather system. The system draws blow-by gasses from the crankcase and recirculates them into the fuel-air mixture and into the engine to be burned.

Inspection/Cleaning

Perform this cleaning procedure more frequently if a considerable amount of riding is done at full throttle or in the rain.

1. Remove the left side rear frame cover as described in Chapter Fifteen.

2. On the left side, remove the crankcase breather hose (**Figure 89**) from the air filter case and crankcase.

3. On the right side, disconnect the crankcase breather storage tank hose (**Figure 90**) from the air filter case.

4. Clean out the hoses removed in Step 2 and Step 3 with solvent and thoroughly dry them with compressed air. Reinstall both hoses.

5. Remove the plug (**Figure 91**) from the drain hose and drain the hose. Reinstall the drain plug.

EVAPORATIVE EMISSION CONTROL SYSTEM (CALIFORNIA ONLY)

Fuel tank vapor is routed into a charcoal canister. This vapor is stored when the engine is not running. When the engine is running, this vapor is drawn through a purge control valve (PCV) and into the carburetor.

Make sure all hose clamps are tight. Check all hoses for deterioration and replace them as necessary.

Refer to the emission control decal on the motorcycle for the vacuum hose diagram.

8

Charcoal Canister Replacement

1. Place the motorcycle on a lift. See *Motorcycle Lift* in Chapter One.

2. Disconnect both hoses (A, **Figure 92**) from the canister.

3. Remove the canister mounting bolts (B, **Figure 92**) and remove the canister from the frame.

4. Installation is the reverse of these steps.

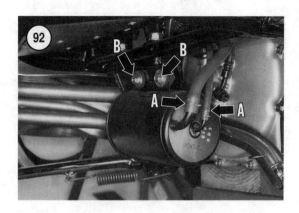

Table 1 CARBURETOR SPECIFICATIONS

Item	Specification
Carburetor model No.	
49-state	
GL1500 C & CT	
1997	VPK0A
1998-on	VPK0J
GL1500 CF	VPK1B
California	
GL1500 C & CT	
1997	BPK0B
1998-on	VPK0K
GL1500 CF	VPK1C
Throttle valve bore	28 mm (1.1 in.)
Main jet	No. 100
Slow jet	No. 35
Jet needle	
1997	No. J6KG
1998-on	No. J6KJ
Float level	13.2-14.2 mm (0.52-056 in.)
Pilot screw initial adjustment	
GL1500C & CT	
1997	
49-state	1-3/4 turns out
California	2 turns out
1998-on	
49-state	2-1/4 turns out
California	2-3/8 turns out
GL1500CF	
49-state	2-1/4 turns out
California	2-3/8 turns out
Pilot screw high-altitude initial adjustment	
All models	½ turn in

Table 2 FUEL SYSTEM SPECIFICATIONS

Throttle grip free play	2-6 mm (1/12-1/4 in.)
Carburetor vacuum difference	
(Synchronization all cylinders)	Within 40 mm (1.6 in. HG) of each other
Idle speed	800-1000 rpm

Table 3 TIGHTENING TORQUES

Item	N•m	ft.-lb.
Upper rear engine mount		
Upper bracket to frame bolts	26	20
Lower mounting bolts to engine	44	33

8

CHAPTER NINE

ELECTRICAL SYSTEM

All GL1500 models are equipped with a 12-volt, negative-ground electrical system. Many electrical problems can be traced to a simple cause such as a blown fuse, a loose or corroded connection or a frayed wire.

The electrical system consists of the following:

1. Charging system.
2. Ignition system.
3. Starting system.
4. Lighting system.
5. Electrical components.
6. Switches.
7. Horn.
8. Fuses and relays.

Tables 1-7 are located at the end of this chapter. Wiring diagrams are at the end of the manual.

Before starting any work, refer to Chapter One and review the service hints and the electrical testing equipment information.

Figure 1 shows the basic locations of the electrical components.

BASIC INFORMATION

Electrical Component Resistance Testing

To get accurate resistance measurements of an electrical component, the component, or the specific coil portion of a component must be at approx-

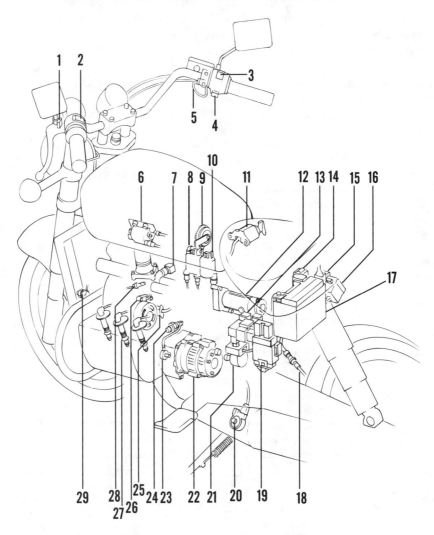

ELECTRICAL COMPONENT LOCATION

1. Clutch switch
2. Headlight dimmer switch
3. Engine stop switch
4. Start button
5. Front brake light switch
6. Ignition coil No. 1 and No. 2
7. Engine coolant sensor
8. Ignition coil No. 3 and No. 4
9. Horn
10. Ignition coil No. 5 and No. 6
11. Ignition switch
12. Starter motor
13. Bank angle sensor relay
14. Alternator fuse (55A)
15. Main fuse (30A) and starter relay switch
16. Diode and fuse box
17. Battery
18. Rear brake light switch
19. Ignition control module
20. Side stand switch
21. Bank angle sensor
22. Alternator
23. Neutral switch
24. Neutral switch
25. Ignition pulse generator
26. Ignition pulse generator
27. Spark plug
28. Thermo switch
29. Cooling fan switch

9

imately 20° C (68° F). The manufacturer performs its tests at this temperature and base their resistance specifications on tests performed at this specific temperature. Readings taken on a hot engine will show increased resistance caused by engine heat and may lead to replacing parts that are not defective.

If the component is too hot, allow it to cool to this temperature. Any temperature variation, other than that specified, will change the resistance reading of the component.

NOTE
With the exception of certain semiconductors, the resistance of a conductor increases as its temperature increases. In general, the resistance of a conductor changes 10 ohms per each degree of temperature change. The opposite is true if the temperature drops.

Resistance tests are performed after disconnecting the component from the main wiring harness. Do not remove the part to test it, but instead locate its wiring connectors and then disconnect them.

NOTE
When using an analog ohmmeter and switching between ohmmeter scales, always cross the test leads and zero the needle to ensure a correct reading. This is not necessary when using a digital ohmmeter.

Electrical Component Replacement

Most motorcycle dealerships and parts suppliers do not accept returns on electrical parts. If testing has not determined the exact cause of an electrical system failure, have a Honda dealership retest the electrical system to verify the test results. If a new part is installed, and the system still does not work properly, in most cases the electrical unit cannot be returned for a refund.

Electrical Connection Location

The electrical connection varies with the different years. Also if someone else has serviced the motorcycle, they may have repositioned the connector differently than the original location. The photo-

graphs shown in this chapter are of a 1999 GL1500C, but the electrical connector location on the motorcycle being worked on may vary. Always check the wire colors referred to in the procedure to make sure the correct connector and circuit is being serviced. To verify, follow the circuit from the specific component to where it connects to the wiring harness or to another component within the system. Also refer to the specific wiring diagrams in this chapter and/or to the complete wiring diagrams at the end of this manual.

ELECTRICAL CONNECTORS

The motorcycle is equipped with a multitude of electrical components, connectors and wires. Corrosion-causing moisture can enter these electrical connectors and cause poor electrical connections, which leads to component failure. Troubleshooting an electrical circuit with one or more corroded electrical connectors can be time-consuming and frustrating.

Most of the electrical connectors are packed with a special Honda sealing compound that looks like a cream-colored grease. This sealing compound is called *Hondaline Dielectric Compound* and is available at most Honda dealerships. This dielectric compound is specially formulated to seal and waterproof electrical connectors and will not interfere with the current flow through the electrical connectors. Use only this compound or equivalent dielectric grease. Do not use a substitute that may interfere with the current flow within the electrical connector.

After cleaning both the male and female connector, make sure they are thoroughly dry. Using a dielectric compound, pack the interior of one of the connectors prior to connecting the two-connector halves. On multipin connectors, pack the male side and on single-wire connectors, pack the female side. For best results, the compound should fill the entire inner area of the connector. On multipin connectors, also pack the backside of both the male and female side with the compound to prevent moisture from entering the connector. After the connector is fully packed, wipe the exterior of all excessive compound.

Clean and seal all electrical connectors each time they are unplugged.

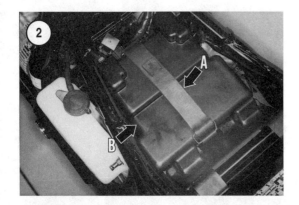

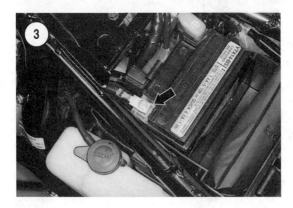

BATTERY CABLE

The battery is mounted under the driver's seat.

To prevent accidental shorts that could blow a fuse when working on the electrical system, always disconnect the negative ground cable from the negative battery terminal as follows.

1. Turn the ignition switch to the OFF position.

2. Remove the driver's seat as described in Chapter Fifteen.

3. Unhook the rubber strap (A, **Figure 2**) and remove the battery cover (B, **Figure 2**).

4. Remove the negative battery terminal bolt and disconnect the negative ground cable (**Figure 3**). Position the cable away from the battery so that it cannot accidentally move back and make contact with the negative battery terminal.

5. If removal of the battery is necessary, remove it as described in Chapter Three.

6. Reconnect the negative cable to the battery and tighten the bolt securely.

7. Install the battery cover and reconnect the strap securely.

8. Install the driver's seat as described in Chapter Fifteen.

CHARGING SYSTEM

Alternating current generated by the alternator is rectified to direct current. The voltage regulator maintains a constant voltage to the battery and additional electrical loads, such as the lights and ignition, regardless of variations in engine speed and load.

The charging system (**Figure 4**) consists of the following components:

1. Battery.

2. Starter relay switch.

3. Alternator with integral IC regulator and rectifier.

4. Ignition switch.

5. Main fuse (30A).

6. Fuse (10A).

Precautions

A malfunction in the charging system generally causes the battery to be undercharged. To prevent damage to the alternator and the regulator/rectifier when testing and repairing the charging system, note the following precautions:

1. Always disconnect the negative battery cable before removing a component in the charging system.

2. Remove the battery from the motorcycle before charging it; see Chapter Three.

3. Inspect the battery; look for bulges or cracks in the case, leaking electrolyte or corrosion build-up.

4. Check the wiring in the charging system for signs of chafing, deterioration or other damage.

5. Check the wiring for corroded or loose connections. Clean, tighten or reconnect as required.

6. Before disconnecting the white wire terminal from the alternator, disconnect the negative battery cable first.

Leakage Test

Perform this test before performing the output test.

1. Turn the ignition switch to the OFF position.

2. Disconnect the negative battery lead (**Figure 3**) as described in this chapter.

CAUTION
Before connecting the ammeter into the circuit in Step 3, set the meter to its highest amperage scale. This will prevent a large current flow from damag-

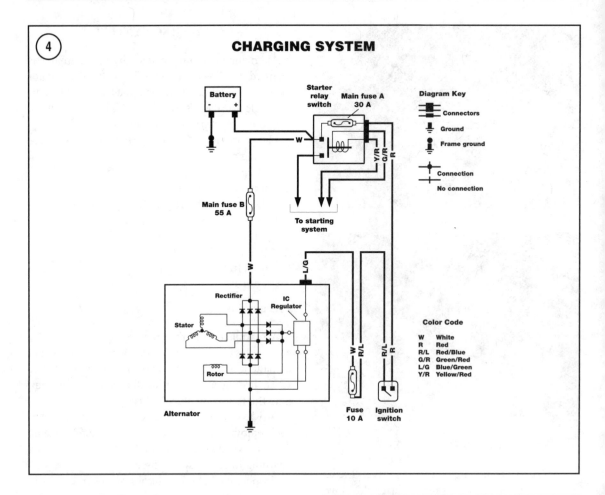

④ **CHARGING SYSTEM**

Diagram Key

- Connectors
- Ground
- Frame ground
- Connection
- No connection

Color Code

W	White
R	Red
R/L	Red/Blue
G/R	Green/Red
L/G	Blue/Green
Y/R	Yellow/Red

Battery

Starter relay switch

Main fuse A 30 A

Main fuse B 55 A

To starting system

Rectifier

IC Regulator

Stator

Rotor

Alternator

Fuse 10 A

Ignition switch

ing the meter or blowing the meter's fuse, if so equipped.

3. Connect an ammeter between the battery ground cable and the negative terminal on the battery (**Figure 5**).

4. Switch the ammeter from its highest to lowest amperage scale while reading the meter scale. The standard current leakage value is 0.1 mA maximum.

5. A higher current leakage value indicates a continuous battery discharge. This could be caused by dirt and/or electrolyte that has collected on top of the battery or a crack in the battery case. These conditions provide a path for battery current. Remove, clean and inspect the battery as described in Chapter Three. Then reinstall the battery and retest.

6. If the current leakage rate is still excessive, the probable causes are:

    a. Damaged battery.

    b. Short circuit in the system.

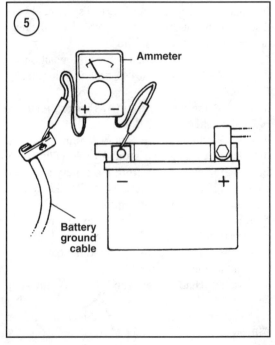

⑤

Ammeter

Battery ground cable

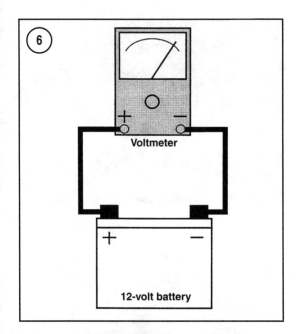

Voltmeter

12-volt battery

c. Loose, dirty or defective electrical connectors in the charging circuit.

d. Accessory system drawing current.

7. Disconnect the ammeter and reconnect the negative battery lead as described in this chapter.

Regulated Voltage Inspection

This procedure tests charging system operation. The test does not measure maximum charging system output. Charging system specifications are in **Table 1**.

1. Prior to making this test, check that the battery is fully charged. Refer to Chapter Three.

2. Prior to starting this test, start the motorcycle and let it reach normal operating temperature, then shut off the engine.

3. Remove the driver's seat as described in Chapter Fifteen.

4. Unhook the rubber strap (A, **Figure 2**) and remove the battery cover (B, **Figure 2**).

> *NOTE*
> *Do not disconnect the battery cables.*

5. Connect the voltmeter between the negative battery and positive leads (**Figure 6**).

6. Restart the engine and allow it to idle. Turn the headlight switch to HIGH BEAM.

> *NOTE*
> *The exact engine speed at which the voltage starts to increase cannot be checked, as this varies with engine temperature and the alternator load.*

7. Gradually increase engine speed from idle to 5000 rpm. At this engine speed, the regulated voltage should be 15.5 V.

8. If the regulated voltage is below specification, the probable cause(s) is the following:

    a. Open or shorted circuit in the charging system wiring harness.

    b. Improperly connected electrical connector in the charging system.

    c. Open or shorted alternator.

    d. Defective voltage regulator/rectifier. Check the voltage regulator/rectifier as described in this chapter.

9. If the regulated voltage is above specification, the probable cause is a defective voltage regulator/rectifier. Check the voltage regulator/rectifier as described in this chapter.

10. Turn off the engine.

11. Disconnect the voltmeter.

12. Install the battery cover and secure the rubber strap.

13. Install the driver's seat as described in Chapter Fifteen.

Wiring Harness Test

> *CAUTION*
> *The negative battery cable is disconnected in Step 1 to prevent the white wire terminal from grounding when it is disconnected.*

1. Disconnect the negative battery cable as described in this chapter.

2. Remove the left frame rear side cover and the center cover as described in Chapter Fifteen.

3. On GL1500CF models, remove the driver's seat as described in Chapter Fifteen.

4. Remove the bolt and washer (A, **Figure 7**) securing the alternator cover and remove the cover (B, **Figure 7**).

5. Move the rubber boot up and disconnect the main electrical white wire connector from the alternator (**Figure 8**).

6. Disconnect the two-pin white electrical connector containing the black/green wire from the rear of the alternator.

7. Reconnect the negative battery cable to the battery.

8. Check the battery charging lead as follows:

   a. Connect the positive voltmeter lead to the alternator white terminal and the negative voltmeter lead to a good engine ground.

   b. With the ignition switch turned OFF, the voltmeter should show battery voltage.

   c. Disconnect the voltmeter leads.

9. Check the battery voltage input lead as follows:

   a. Connect the positive voltmeter lead to the alternator black/green connector and the negative voltmeter lead to a good engine ground (**Figure 9**).

   b. With the ignition switch turned ON, the voltmeter should show battery voltage.

   c. Disconnect the voltmeter leads.

10. If the voltmeter did not show the specified test results as described in Step 8 or Step 9, troubleshoot the charging system as described in Chapter Two.

11. Disconnect the negative battery cable.

12. Reconnect the white wire terminal and the black/green connector at the alternator (**Figure 9**).

13. Connect the negative battery cable to the battery.

14. Install the center cover and the left frame rear side cover as described in Chapter Fifteen.

ALTERNATOR

The alternator is a three-phase current generator consisting of stationary conductors (stator), a rotating field (rotor) and a rectifying bridge of silicon diodes. The alternator generates alternating current that is converted to direct current by the silicon diodes for use in the Valkyrie's electrical system. Alternator output is regulated by a voltage regulator to

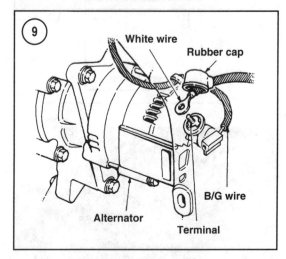

keep the battery charged. The alternator is mounted at the back of the engine on the left side.

Make sure the electrical connectors are not reversed when working on the alternator. Reverse current flow will damage the diodes, requiring alternator replacement.

CAUTION
Always disconnect the negative battery cable before disconnecting any alternator wire as described in this chapter.

Removal

Refer to **Figure 10** for this procedure.

1. Disconnect the negative battery cable as described in this chapter.

2. Remove the left side cover and the center cover as described in Chapter Fifteen.

3. On GL1500CF models, perform the following:

   a. Remove the seat as described in Chapter Fifteen.

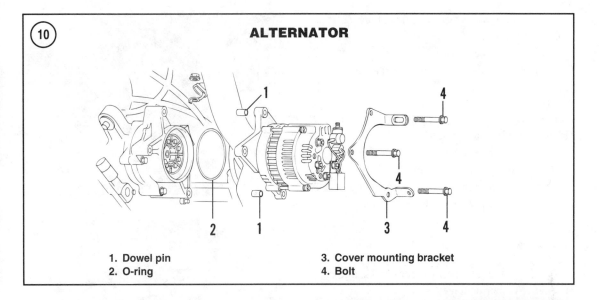

ALTERNATOR

1. Dowel pin
2. O-ring
3. Cover mounting bracket
4. Bolt

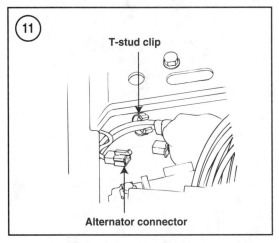

T-stud clip

Alternator connector

CAUTION
Unfasten but do not remove the T-clip from the frame. If removed, it will be damaged and cannot be re-used. If removed, a new T-clip must be installed.

  b. Unfasten the T-stud clip from the frame and disconnect the two-pin white electrical connector containing the black/green wire (**Figure 11**).

4. Remove the bolt and washer (A, **Figure 7**) securing the alternator cover and remove the cover (B, **Figure 7**).

5. Move the rubber boot up and disconnect the main electrical white wire connector from the alternator.

6. Remove the alternator mounting bolts (**Figure 12**) and remove the alternator cover mounting plate (**Figure 13**).

7. Partially remove the alternator from the engine and frame. On GL1500C and GL1500CT models, disconnect the two-pin white electrical connector

containing the black/green wire from the rear of the alternator (**Figure 9**).

8. Remove the alternator from the frame.

9. Remove the dowel pins from the rear case cover, if used.

10. If necessary, remove the alternator rubber dampers (A, **Figure 14**) and alternator coupler A (B, **Figure 14**) as follows:

   a. Remove the rubber dampers (A, **Figure 14**).

   b. Shift the transmission into gear.

   c. Loosen and remove the alternator coupler A nut (C, **Figure 14**), washer and the coupler.

Inspection

1. Inspect the rubber dampers for cracks, age deterioration or other damage.

2. Check the alternator coupler A for cracks or other damage.

3. Check the alternator O-ring (A, **Figure 15**) for flat spots or damage.

4. Replace worn or damaged parts.

Installation

1. If removed, install the alternator coupler A and the rubber dampers as follows:

   a. Apply engine oil to the alternator driven gear shaft splines.

   b. Install the alternator coupler A (B, **Figure 14**) onto the alternator driven gear shaft.

   c. Install the coupler A washer.

   d. Shift the transmission into gear.

   e. Apply ThreeBond TB1342 or Loctite 242 (blue) to the coupler A nut threads.

   f. Install the coupler A nut (C, **Figure 14**) and tighten to the torque specification in **Table 6**.

   g. Install the rubber dampers (B, **Figure 14**) into coupler A.

2. Install the alternator dowel pins.

3. Apply engine oil to the alternator O-ring and install the O-ring into the alternator groove (A, **Figure 15**).

CAUTION
Prior to reconnecting the electrical connectors at the alternator, make sure the negative battery cable is disconnected.

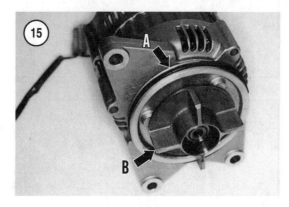

4. Clean all of the alternator connectors with electrical contact cleaner. Then apply dielectric grease to the connectors

5. On GL1500C and GL1500CT models, connect the two-pin white electrical connector containing the black/green wire onto the rear of the alternator (**Figure 9**).

6. Align the alternator coupler B tabs (B, **Figure 15**) with the rubber damper grooves, then install the alternator partially onto the engine.

7. Install the alternator cover mounting plate (**Figure 13**).

8. Push the alternator into place and install the alternator mounting bolts (**Figure 12**). Tighten the alternator mounting bolts securely.

9. On GL1500CF models, perform the following:

   a. Connect the two-pin white electrical connector containing the black/green wire (**Figure 11**).

CAUTION
If the T-clip was removed from the frame it was damaged and a new T-clip must be installed.

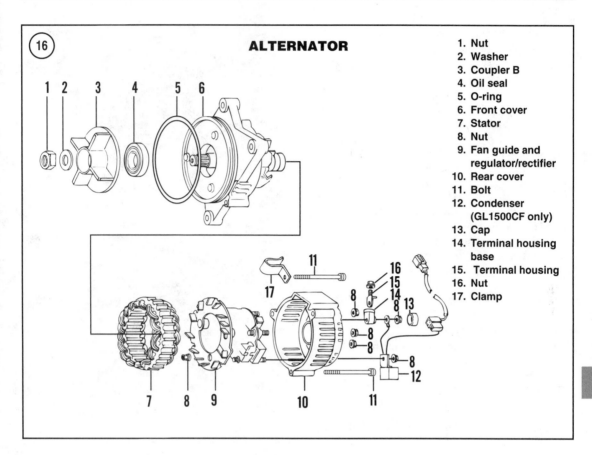

16 ALTERNATOR

1. Nut
2. Washer
3. Coupler B
4. Oil seal
5. O-ring
6. Front cover
7. Stator
8. Nut
9. Fan guide and regulator/rectifier
10. Rear cover
11. Bolt
12. Condenser (GL1500CF only)
13. Cap
14. Terminal housing base
15. Terminal housing
16. Nut
17. Clamp

b. Fasten the T-stud clip onto the frame.

10. Install the main electrical white wire connector onto the alternator and move the rubber boot back into position.

11. Install the alternator cover boss into the rubber grommet and align the bolt hole. Install the bolt and washer (A, **Figure 7**) and tighten securely.

12. Reconnect the negative battery cable as described in this chapter.

13. On GL1500CF models, install the seat as in Chapter Fifteen.

14. Install the center cover and left side rear cover as described in Chapter Fifteen.

Alternator Drive and Driven Gears

Refer to Chapter Five for the service procedures.

Alternator Disassembly

The GL1500 alternator is shown in **Figure 16**. Complete alternator disassembly is required to fully

test all of the alternator components. If the tools and the skills to properly overhaul the alternator are not available, refer service to a Honda dealership. The following tools are required to test and overhaul the alternator:

a. Hydraulic press and suitable adapters.

b. Ohmmeter.

NOTE
An analog ohmmeter is required for condenser testing (GL1500CF only).

c. Soldering iron and rosin core solder.

d. Heat sink.

1. Rotate the alternator coupler B (A, **Figure 17**) by hand. The alternator shaft should turn smoothly.

2. Secure coupler B with a universal holder and remove the coupler B nut (B, **Figure 17**), washer and coupler B (A, **Figure 17**).

3. Make alignment marks on the front and rear covers for reference during assembly.

4. Mark the position of the wire clamp (A, **Figure 18**) before removing the cover screws.

5. Remove the cover screws (B, **Figure 18**) and wire clamp from the alternator.

6. Remove the nuts from the alternator rear cover.

NOTE
The GL1500CF is the only model equipped with a condenser.

7. On GL1500 CF models, remove the terminal housing and condenser (C, **Figure 18**).

CAUTION
Pry the front cover at the screw thread locations. Use these pry points, making sure not to damage the stator coil when prying the front cover away from the stator coil.

8. Carefully and slowly pry the front cover/rotor assembly away from the rear cover/stator coil assembly at the three pry points.

9. Carefully separate the stator coil from the rear cover.

CAUTION
Handle the stator coil carefully to avoid damaging it and/or the regulator/rectifier.

10. Perform the following test procedures as required.

Cleaning

Do not use solvent to clean the rotor, stator, rectifier assembly or bearings. Solvent may damage the parts, requiring their replacement. Wipe the parts with a clean lint-free cloth.

Condenser Testing (GL1500CF Models Only)

An analog ohmmeter must be used to perform this test.

1. Take the condenser eyelet and short each one against the condenser housing (**Figure 19**).

2. Connect one ohmmeter lead to the condenser housing and the other ohmmeter to one of the condenser connector pins (**Figure 20**). The ohmmeter needle should swing momentarily toward 0, then swing back to infinity.

3. Repeat Step 2 for each condenser connector pin, including the eyelet connector.

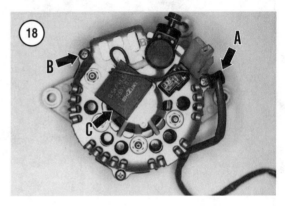

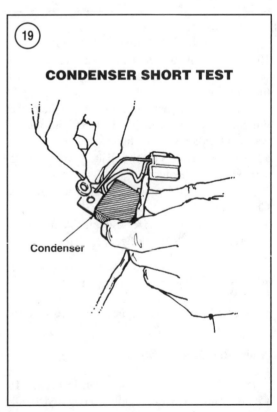

CONDENSER SHORT TEST

Condenser

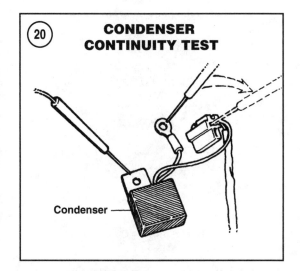

CONDENSER CONTINUITY TEST

Condenser

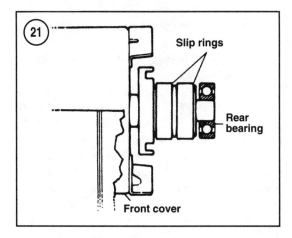

Slip rings

Rear bearing

Front cover

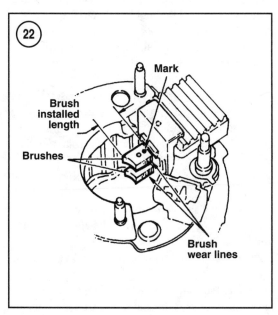

Mark

Brush installed length

Brushes

Brush wear lines

4. If the ohmmeter needle did not operate as described, or if continuity is recorded, the condenser is defective and must be replaced.

Rotor Coil Inspection and Testing

1. Check the slip rings (**Figure 21**) for discoloration, severe wear or damage. If the slip rings require cleaning, polish them with 00 sandpaper or a 400-grain polishing cloth. Slip rings that are rough or pitted can be generally trued on a lathe, removing only enough material to clean up the marks. However, because the rotor on the GL1500 alternator is an integral part of the front cover, the front cover assembly must be replaced if either slip ring is damaged.

2. Measure the slip ring outer diameter with a micrometer. If the outer diameter is worn to the wear limit specified in **Table 1**, replace the front cover assembly. If the slip ring outer diameter is within specifications, continue with Step 3.

3. To test the rotor for an open circuit:
   a. Switch an ohmmeter to R × 1 and zero the test leads.
   b. Touch the ohmmeter leads to the two slip rings.
   c. The ohmmeter should read 2.9-4.0 ohms. A higher reading indicates an open circuit. An open circuit can be caused by a bad connection at the slip ring or a shorted winding.

4. To test the rotor for a short circuit:
   a. Switch an ohmmeter to R × 1 and zero the test leads.
   b. Touch one ohmmeter lead to the rotor shaft and the other test lead to one slip ring and then to the other.
   c. The ohmmeter should show infinity (no reading). If there is a reading, there is a short circuit between the rotor shaft, windings or slip rings.

5. If the rotor fails either test, replace the front cover assembly.

Brush Inspection

1. The brushes are installed at a fixed length. Each brush has a wear line for visual inspection (**Figure 22**). Replace the brushes as a set if either brush is worn down to or close to its wear line.

9

2. If the brushes are not worn down to the wear line, inspect them for cracks or other damage.

3. If necessary, replace the brushes as described in the following procedure.

Brush Replacement

The brushes should always be replaced as a set. Prior to replacing the brushes, note the following:

   a. Use a soldering iron of approximately 32 W for brush replacement.

   b. Use a low-temperature (82-93° C [180-200° F]), rosin core solder when soldering the new brushes.

   c. When soldering the new brushes to the brush holder, keep solder out of the brush holder or the brushes will not move freely and will not operate properly.

1. Melt the solder securing the brush wire to the end of the brush holder, and pull the brush and wire out.

2. Each brush has one side marked for alignment. Install both brushes into the brush holder so that their marked side faces toward the rear cover (**Figure 22**). Insert the brush wires through the brush holder surface, as shown in **Figure 23**.

3. Position the brushes in the brush holder so that their installed length (measured from the tip of the brush to the brush holder) is 18.0 mm (0.71 in.). See **Figure 22**.

4. Solder the new brush wire to the brush holder surface. Make sure to align the brush wire with the holder surface as shown in **Figure 23**.

5. Cut off the surplus brush wire so that the brush wire joint is flush with the holder surface as shown in **Figure 23**.

Regulator/Rectifier Removal/Installation

Test specifications for the regulator/rectifier assemblies are not available. If all of the other alternator test procedures have not identified the damaged component, replace the regulator/rectifier assembly.

Prior to unsoldering the regulator/rectifier-to-stator coil wires, note the following. Improper use of a solder iron can damage a good regulator/rectifier unit.

   a. To help dissipate heat away from the regulator/rectifier when melting the solder, hold the

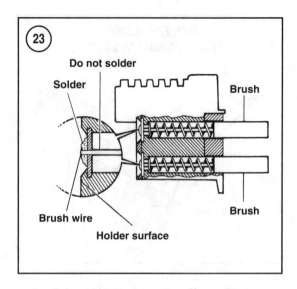

stator coil wires with needlenose pliers or use a heat sink.

   b. Work quickly to protect the regulator/rectifier from heat damage.

   c. Use a high-amperage soldering iron (approximately 110 W) and a high-temperature (300° C [572° F]), high-lead content solder to solder the stator coil wires to the regulator/rectifier.

1. Noting the placement of the stator coil wires through the fan guide and the regulator/rectifier mounting position on the stator coil, make a drawing so they can be properly realigned on assembly.

2. Hold one of the stator coil wires with a pair of needlenose pliers and melt the solder connecting the stator coil wire to the regulator/rectifier diode. Pull the wire out of the diode when the solder is sufficiently melted. Repeat for the remaining wires.

3. Lift the regulator/rectifier assembly off of the stator coil.

4. To replace the regulator/rectifier assembly, remove the nuts securing the fan guide to the regulator/rectifier and remove the fan.

5. Replace the fan guide if it is cracked or damaged.

6. Clean the fan guide thoroughly before reinstalling it.

7. Install the fan guide onto the regulator/rectifier assembly and secure it with the three mounting nuts. Tighten the nuts securely.

8. Position the regulator/rectifier and fan onto the stator coil.

9. Route the stator coil wires around the fan guide grooves and insert the end of the wires through the

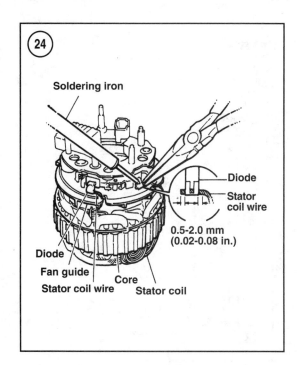

(24)

Soldering iron

Diode

Stator coil wire

0.5-2.0 mm (0.02-0.08 in.)

Diode

Fan guide

Stator coil wire

Core

Stator coil

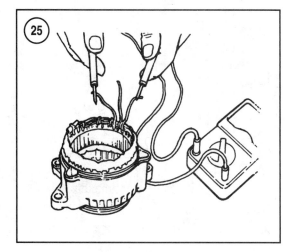

(25)

diodes, maintaining the specifications shown in **Figure 24**.

10. Solder the stator coil wires to the diodes.

Stator Coil Testing

1. To test the stator coil, the regulator/rectifier assembly must be removed from the stator coil as described under *Regulator/Rectifier Removal/Installation* in this chapter.

2. To check stator coil wire resistance:

a. Switch an ohmmeter to R × 1 and zero the test leads.

b. Touch one ohmmeter lead to one stator coil wire and the other lead to another stator coil wire and then to the other (**Figure 25**).

c. The ohmmeter should read 0.1-0.3 ohms. A higher reading indicates an open circuit.

NOTE
The green portion of the stator core is insulated. Place the test lead to the silver colored portion of the stator core.

3. To check the stator coil for grounding:

a. Switch an ohmmeter to R × 1 and zero the test leads.

b. Touch one ohmmeter lead to the stator core (silver part) and the other lead to one stator coil wire and then to the other two wires separately.

c. The ohmmeter should show infinity (no reading). If there is a reading, there is a short circuit between the stator coil and the stator core.

4. If the stator coil fails either test, replace it.

5. Re-solder the regulator/rectifier assembly to the stator coil; refer to *Regulator/Rectifier Removal/Installation* in this chapter.

Rotor Bearings Inspection

The front and rear bearings are pressed onto the rotor shaft. The rear bearing (**Figure 21**) can be replaced separately. The front bearing is an integral part of the front cover and rotor assembly. If the front bearing is damaged, the front cover assembly must be replaced.

1. Turn the rotor shaft to check the front bearing.

2. Turn the rear outer bearing race (**Figure 21**) by hand.

3. Both bearings should turn smoothly with no sign of roughness or noise.

4. Check that both bearing inner races are a tight fit on the rotor shaft.

5. If necessary, replace the rear bearing (**Figure 21**) as described in this chapter.

9

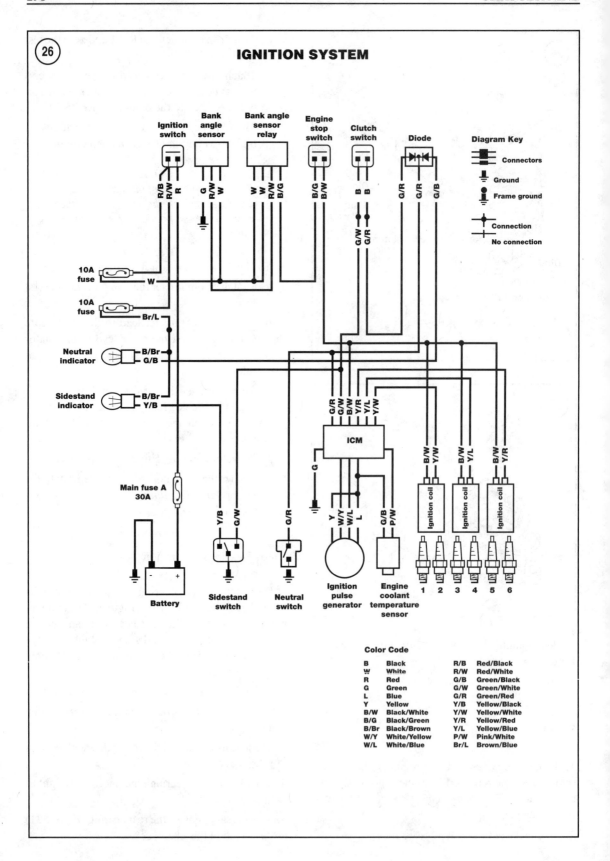

Rear Rotor Bearing Replacement

1. Mount a bearing puller onto the rear bearing (**Figure 21**) and pull the bearing off of the shaft.
2. Support the front cover in a press.
3. Align the new bearing with the rotor shaft.
4. Install a pilot over the inner bearing race as described under *Bearing Replacement* in Chapter One and press the new bearing onto the shaft.
5. Spin the bearing outer race to check that the bearing has been installed correctly.

Front Cover Seal Inspection/Replacement

1. Inspect the front cover seal for leaking or damage.

NOTE
The front seal must be removed with the rotor installed in the front cover. Do not disassemble the front cover assembly (front cover, rotor and bearing), since these parts are not available separately.

2. Remove the seal from the front cover with a tool that can pull the seal out without damaging the cover or rotor shaft.
3. Clean the seal recess with a clean, lint-free cloth.
4. Wipe the new seal lips with grease.
5. Position the new seal with the open side facing out and align it on the front cover.
6. Press the new seal into the front cover until the seal surface is flush with the front cover.

Alternator Assembly

Refer to **Figure 16** for this procedure.
1. Position the stator coil and regulator/rectifier assembly over the front cover and rotor assembly. Then press the brushes into the brush holder and slide the assembly over the rotor.

CAUTION
When aligning the cover marks in Step 2, do not move the rear cover as the stator coil wires may be damaged.

2. Move the stator coil assembly to align the marks made prior to disassembly.

3. On GL1500CF models, install the condenser (C, **Figure 18**) onto the rear cover and secure it with its mounting nut.
4. Install the remaining mounting nuts and tighten them securely.
5. Install the wire clamp (A, **Figure 18**) and the cover screws (B, **Figure 18**) into the alternator. Tighten the screws securely.
6. Install the alternator coupler B (A, **Figure 17**) onto the rotor shaft. Then install the washer and nut (B, **Figure 17**).
7. Hold the coupler B with the same tool used during disassembly and tighten the coupler B nut to the torque specification in **Table 6**.
8. After installing the alternator onto the motorcycle, perform the charging system output test as described in this chapter.

IGNITION SYSTEM

The ignition system consists of three ignition coils, ignition control module (ICM), engine coolant temperature sensor (ETC), bank angle sensor and relay, neutral switch, clutch switch, engine stop switch, side stand switch, two ignition pulse generators and six spark plugs (**Figure 26**).

The Valkyrie GL1500 is equipped with a capacitor discharge ignition (CDI) system. This solid-state system uses no breaker points or other moving parts. This system provides a longer life for components and delivers a more efficient spark throughout the entire speed range of the engine. Ignition timing does not require adjustment and cannot be adjusted. If ignition timing is incorrect, it is due to a defect within the ignition system.

The ICM electronically varies the ignition timing according to engine speed and coolant temperature. Direct current charges the capacitor. As the piston approaches the firing position, a pulse from the pulse generator coil triggers the silicon-controlled rectifier. The rectifier, in turn, allows the capacitor to discharge quickly into the primary circuit of the ignition coil, where the voltage is increased in the secondary circuit to a value sufficient to fire the spark plugs. The distribution of the pulses from the pulse generator is controlled by the rotation of the pulse generator plate that is attached to the pulse generator rotor on the end of the crankshaft.

9

NOTE
*The following sections describe testing
and removal/installation procedures
for the ignition system components.
When troubleshooting the ignition system, first refer to the troubleshooting
procedures in Chapter Two, then refer
back to the related testing procedure in
this chapter.*

CDI Precautions

Observe the following precautions to protect the capacitor discharge system when performing service and troubleshooting procedures to prevent damage to the semiconductors in the system.

1. Never connect the battery backwards. If the battery polarity is reversed, damage will occur to the voltage regulator/rectifier and alternator.

2. Do not disconnect the battery while the engine is running. A voltage surge will occur which will damage the voltage regulator/rectifier and possibly burn out the lights.

3. Keep all connections between the various units clean and tight. Be sure that the wiring connections are pushed together firmly and packed with dielectric grease to seal out moisture.

4. Do not substitute another type of ignition coil.

5. Each component is mounted within a rubber vibration isolator. Always be sure the isolator is in place when installing any units in the system.

6. Prior to inspecting or troubleshooting the ignition system, check that the battery is fully charged as described in Chapter Three. For the following test results to be accurate, the battery must be fully charged.

7. Do not turn the engine over unless all of the spark plugs are securely rounded against the engine.

IGNITION SYSTEM ELECTRICAL COMPONENTS

Ignition Control Module (ICM) Replacement

1. Disconnect the negative battery cable as described in this chapter.

2. Remove the left side cover as described in Chapter Fifteen.

3. Remove the coolant reservoir as described in Chapter Ten.

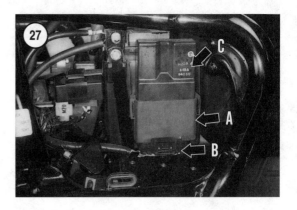

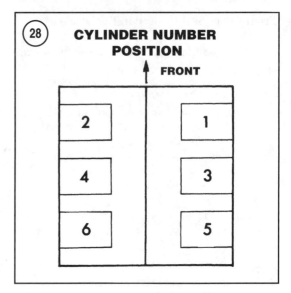

CYLINDER NUMBER POSITION

4. Carefully remove the ignition control module and rubber strap (A, **Figure 27**) from the frame mounting tabs.

5. Disconnect the electrical connector (B, **Figure 27**) from the ignition control module.

6. Remove the ignition control module (C, **Figure 27**) from the frame.

7. Install by reversing these removal steps. Make sure the electrical connector is tight and free of corrosion.

Ignition Coils

The ignition coil is a form of transformer that develops the high voltage required to jump the spark plug gap. Maintenance consists of keeping the electrical connections clean and tight and making sure the coils are mounted securely.

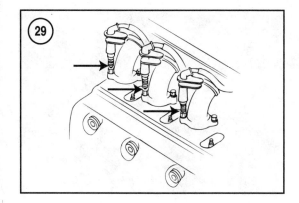

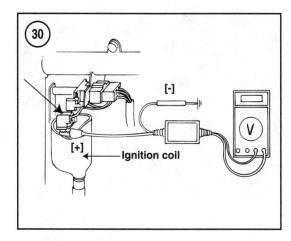

Ignition coil

There are three ignition coils: The first coil provides spark for plugs one and two, the second for plugs three and four, and the third for plugs five and six. **Figure 28** identifies the cylinders and plugs.

Ignition Coil Dynamic Test

Disconnect the high voltage lead from one of the spark plugs. Remove the spark plug from the cylinder head. Connect a new or known good spark plug to the high voltage lead and ground the spark plug base to the cylinder head. Position the spark plug so the electrodes are visible.

> *WARNING*
> *If it is necessary to hold the high voltage lead, do so with insulated pliers. The high voltage generated could produce a fatal shock.*

> *WARNING*
> *Turning the engine over with a spark plug removed will allow fuel to be*

ejected through the spark plug hole. When making a spark test, do not place the spark plug next to the open spark plug hole because the air/fuel mixture in the cylinders may ignite.

With the engine stop switch in the RUN position, push the starter button to turn the engine over a couple of times. If a fat blue spark occurs, the coil is in good condition; if not it must be replaced. Make sure that a known good spark plug is used for this test. If the spark plug used is defective the test results will be incorrect.

Reinstall the spark plug in the cylinder head.

Ignition Coil Primary Voltage Test

A special tool, a peak voltage tester, or a peak voltage adapter and a digital multimeter with a minimum impedance of 10 M ohm/DCV, is required to test the ignition coil primary voltage.

1. Place the motorcycle on the sidestand.
2. Remove the fuel tank as described in Chapter Eight.
3. Remove the spark plugs as described in Chapter Three.
4. Reconnect the plug caps to the spark plugs and securely ground the plugs against the cylinder head, as shown in **Figure 29**.
5. Turn the ignition switch to the ON position.
6. Turn the engine stop switch to the RUN position.
7. Connect the peak voltage tester to the different ignition coils as follows (**Figure 30**):
   a. Ignition coil No. 1 and No. 2: positive test lead to yellow/white terminal, negative test lead to ground.
   b. Ignition coil No. 3 and No. 4: positive test lead to yellow/blue terminal, negative test lead to ground.
   c. Ignition coil No. 5 and No. 6: positive test lead to yellow/red terminal, negative test lead to ground.
8. In Step 7 there should be battery voltage at each substep. If there is no battery voltage, one of the following may be the probable cause:
   a. Defective engine stop switch.
   b. Short to ground in the black/white wire between the ignition coil and engine stop switch.
   c. Loose primary terminal or an open circuit in the primary coil portion of the coil.

9

d. Defective ignition control module (ICM): when the initial voltage is normal while disconnecting the ICM electrical connector.

9. Shift the transmission into NEUTRAL.

10. Crank the engine over several times with the starter and check for primary voltage. The peak voltage should be 100 V minimum. If the peak voltage is less than specified, refer to the following steps.

11. If the initial voltage is normal but it drops down 2-4 volts while cranking the engine, one of the following may be the probable cause:

a. Incorrect peak voltage adapter connections.

b. Battery is undercharged.

c. No voltage between the black/white wire (power) and ground of the ICM connector or loose ICM connection.

d. An open circuit at the green wire (ground) of the ICM.

e. An open circuit in the primary coil portion of the coil

f. Defective side stand switch, clutch interlock switch or neutral switch.

g. An open circuit or loose connection within the side stand switch, clutch interlock switch or neutral switch circuit(s).

h. A defective ignition pulse generator.

i. If a problem was not detected in the previous substeps, consider the ICM to be defective by process of elimination.

12. If the initial voltage is normal, but no peak voltage while cranking the engine, one of the following may be the probable cause:

a. Incorrect peak voltage adapter connections.

b. Defective peak voltage adapter.

c. If a problem was not detected in the previous substeps, consider the ICM to be defective by process of elimination.

13. If the initial voltage is normal, but no peak voltage is lower than standard value, one of the following may be the probable cause:

a. The multimeter impedance is too low; below 10M ohms/DCV.

b. Cranking speed is too slow (battery is under charged).

c. The sample timing of the tester and the measured pulse were not synchronized (system is normal if the measured voltage is over the standard voltage at least once).

d. If a problem was not detected in the previous substeps, consider the ICM to be defective by process of elimination.

14. If the initial and peak voltage is normal, but no spark is present, one of the following may be the probable cause:

a. Defective spark plug(s) or leaking ignition coil secondary current.

b. Defective ignition coil(s)

15. Turn the ignition switch to the OFF position.

16. If the coil(s) fail any portion of these tests, the coil is defective and must be replaced as described in the following procedure.

17. Install the spark plugs as described in Chapter Three.

18. Install the fuel tank as described in Chapter Eight.

Ignition Coils and Spark Plug Wires Removal

This procedure includes the removal and installation of the ignition coils as well as the spark plug wires. The spark plug wire and cap assemblies are available for each specific cylinder. The individual

assemblies are so marked next to the spark plug cap (**Figure 31**). If only the ignition coil(s) is to be removed, perform only those steps.

1. Place the motorcycle on the sidestand.

2. Disconnect the negative battery cable as described in this chapter.

3. Remove the fuel tank as described in Chapter Eight.

4. Disconnect the spark plug caps (**Figure 32**) from the spark plugs.

5A. To remove the cylinder No. 1 and No. 2 ignition coil, perform the following:
   a. Disconnect the primary wires (A, **Figure 33**) from the ignition coil.
   b. Remove the mounting bolts (B, **Figure 33**).
   c. Remove the ignition coil (C, **Figure 33**) from the mounting bracket.

5B. To remove the cylinder No. 3 and No. 4 and the No. 5 and No. 6, ignition coil assembly perform the following:
   a. Remove the two bolts (A, **Figure 34**) and single collar (B, **Figure 34**) securing the coil assembly to the frame bracket.
   b. Carefully pull the ignition coil assembly down away from the frame bracket.
   c. Disconnect the primary wires (**Figure 35**) from both ignition coils.

6. Disconnect the spark plug wires from the clamps.

NOTE
Make a drawing of the location of the spark plug wires routing under the carburetor assembly. The wires must be installed in exactly the same location.

7. Carefully withdraw the spark plug wires from under the carburetor assembly and remove the ignition coil(s) and spark plugs from the engine.

Ignition Coils and
Spark Plug Wires Installation

1. Carefully install the spark plug wires under the carburetor assembly and correctly position the ignition coil(s) in the frame mounting area.

2. Connect the spark plug wires onto the clamps.

3A. To install the cylinder No. 1 and No. 2 ignition coil, perform the following:
   a. Position the ignition coil onto the frame mounting bracket.
   b. Install the mounting bolts (B, **Figure 33**) and tighten securely.
   c. Connect the primary wires (A, **Figure 33**) onto the ignition coil primary terminals, matching the terminal and wire harness wire colors as in **Table 3**.

3B. To install the cylinder No. 3 and No. 4 and the No. 5 and No. 6, ignition coil assembly perform the following:

9

a. Position the ignition coil onto the frame mounting area.

b. Connect the primary wires (**Figure 35**) onto the ignition coil primary terminals, matching the terminal and wire harness wire colors as in **Table 3**

d. Move the ignition coil assembly into position and install the lower bolt (A, **Figure 36**) through the frame mounting bracket, then install the single collar (B, **Figure 36**) onto the bolt.

e. Align the ignition coil assembly bolt holes with the frame and install the lower and upper bolt (**Figure 34**) and tighten it securely.

4. Make sure all electrical connections are tight and free of corrosion.

5. Connect all six spark plug caps (**Figure 32**) onto to the correct plugs. Each spark plug wire is numbered adjacent to the spark plug rubber boot (**Figure 31**). The cylinders are numbered as shown in **Figure 28**.

6. Install the fuel tank as described in Chapter Eight.

7. Connect the negative battery cable as described in this chapter.

Pulse Generator Peak Voltage Test

Testing the pulse generators requires a special tool, a peak voltage tester, or a peak voltage adapter and a digital multimeter (impedance 10 M ohm/DCV minimum).

1. Disconnect the negative battery cable as described in this chapter.

2. Remove the left side cover as described in Chapter Fifteen.

3. Remove the coolant reservoir as described in Chapter Ten.

4. Carefully remove the ignition control module and rubber strap (A, **Figure 37**) from the frame mounting tabs.

5. Disconnect the electrical connector (B, **Figure 37**) from the ignition control module.

6. Connect the negative battery cable.

7. Connect the peak voltage tester to the wiring harness side of the ignition control module connectors. Connect the tester's positive test lead to the white/yellow terminal, and the negative test lead to green/black terminal.

8. Crank the engine over several times with the starter and note the reading. The minimum peak voltage is 0.7 volts.

9. Connect the peak voltage tester to the wiring harness side of the ignition control module connectors. Positive test lead to white/blue terminal, negative test lead to green/black terminal.

10. Crank the engine over with the starter several times and note the reading. The minimum peak voltage is 0.7 volts.

11. If the peak voltage is not as specified, measure the peak voltage at the ignition pulse generator electrical connector.

12. Connect the electrical connector (B, **Figure 37**) onto the ignition control module.

13. Carefully install the ignition control module and rubber strap (A, **Figure 37**) onto the frame mounting tabs.

14. Remove the fuel tank as described in Chapter Eight.

15. Remove the right side steering head cover as described in Chapter Fifteen.

16. Disconnect the ignition pulse generator white four-pin electrical connector (**Figure 38**). The four

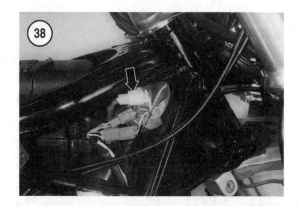

a. The multimeter impedance is too low; less than 10M ohms/DCV.

b. Cranking speed is too slow (battery is undercharged).

c. The sample timing of the tester and the measured pulse were not synchronized (system is normal if the measured voltage is over the standard voltage at least once).

d. If a problem was not detected in the previous substeps, assume the ICM is defective by process of elimination.

23. If there is no peak voltage, one of the following may be the probable cause:

a. Defective peak voltage adapter.

b. Defective ignition pulse generator(s).

24. Install the right side steering head cover as described in Chapter Fifteen.

25. Install the fuel tank as described in Chapter Eight.

26. Install the coolant reservoir as described in Chapter Ten.

27. Install the left side cover as described in Chapter Fifteen.

28. Connect the negative battery cable as described in this chapter.

Pulse Generator Removal/Installation

The pulse generators (A, **Figure 39**) and pulse rotor (B, **Figure 39**) are mounted at the front of the engine behind the timing belt cover. To remove the pulse generators and the pulse rotor, refer to *Camshaft Timing Belts and Driven Pulleys* in Chapter Four.

STARTING SYSTEM

The starting system consists of the starter motor, starter relay switch, start switch, engine stop switch, neutral switch, sidestand switch, bank angle sensor and relay, clutch switch, neutral switch and ignition switch (**Figure 40**).

When the starter button is pressed, it engages the starter relay switch coil that completes the circuit allowing electricity to flow from the battery to the starter motor.

CAUTION
Do not operate the starter for more than five seconds at a time. Wait ap-

wires are blue, white/blue, white/yellow, and yellow.

17. Connect the peak voltage tester to the pulse generator side of the electrical connector with the positive test lead to white/yellow terminal, negative test lead to yellow terminal.

18. Crank the engine over with the starter several times and note the reading. The minimum peak voltage is 0.7 volts.

19. Connect the peak voltage tester to the pulse generator side of the electrical connector. Positive test lead to white/blue terminal, negative test lead to blue terminal.

20. Crank the engine over with the starter several times and note the reading. The minimum peak voltage is 0.7 volts.

21. If the peak voltage measured at the ignition control module electrical connector and the pulse generator electrical connector are within specification, the wiring harness has an open circuit or loose connection.

22. If the peak voltage is lower than standard value, one of the following may be the probable cause:

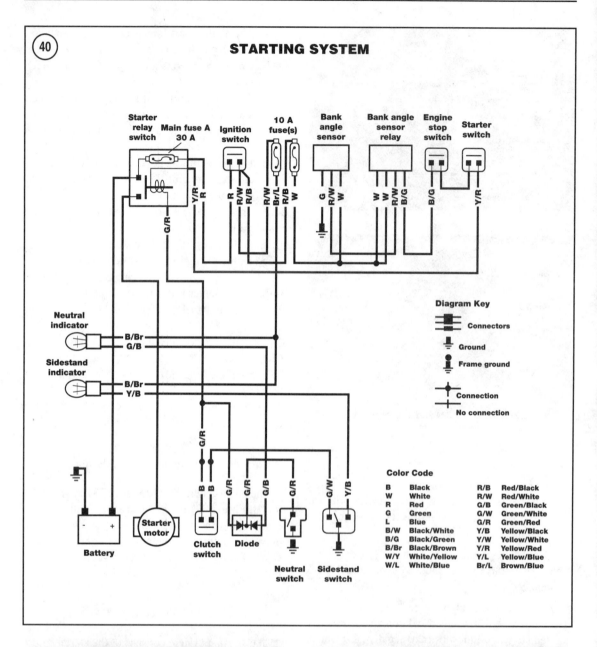

40　　　　　　　　　　**STARTING SYSTEM**

Diagram Key

- Connectors
- Ground
- Frame ground
- Connection
- No connection

Color Code

B	Black	R/B	Red/Black
W	White	R/W	Red/White
R	Red	G/B	Green/Black
G	Green	G/W	Green/White
L	Blue	G/R	Green/Red
B/W	Black/White	Y/B	Yellow/Black
B/G	Black/Green	Y/W	Yellow/White
B/Br	Black/Brown	Y/R	Yellow/Red
W/Y	White/Yellow	Y/L	Yellow/Blue
W/L	White/Blue	Br/L	Brown/Blue

41

42

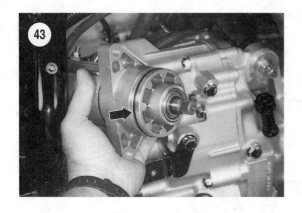

proximately 10 seconds before operating it again.

The starter clutch and the starter drive gear are described in Chapter Five.

Starter Motor Removal/Installation

1. Remove the seat and the center cover as described in Chapter Fifteen.
2. Move the rubber cap from the electrical cable connector.
3. Remove the nut and disconnect the electrical cable from the starter motor (**Figure 41**).
4. Remove the bolts (**Figure 42**) securing the starter motor to the crankcase and remove the starter motor.
5. Apply engine oil to the starter O-ring (**Figure 43**) prior to installing the starter onto the engine.
6. Make sure the crankcase mating surface is clean prior to installing the starter onto it.
7. Install the starter onto the crankcase and align the bolt holes.
8. Install the two mounting bolts (**Figure 42**) and tighten securely.
9. Connect the electrical cable onto the starter motor (**Figure 41**) and the nut. Tighten the nut securely.
10. Move the rubber cap back into position over the electrical cable connector.
11. Install the center cover and seat as described in Chapter Fifteen.

Starter Motor Disassembly

Refer to **Figure 44** for this procedure.

1. Note the alignment marks on the case and the rear cover (**Figure 45**). If there are no marks, make an alignment mark across both parts.
2. Unscrew and remove the long bolts (**Figure 46**) securing the starter motor assembly to the reduction gearcase and separate the two assemblies. If the reduction gearcase requires service, refer to *Reduction Gearcase Disassembly* in this chapter.
3. Remove the rear cover (**Figure 47**) from the housing.
4. Remove the washer (**Figure 48**) from the armature shaft.
5. Remove the gear holder (A, **Figure 49**) and washer (B, **Figure 49**).

> *CAUTION*
> *The armature coils may be damaged if the magnets within the housing pull the armature against the housing during armature removal.*

6. Hold tightly onto the armature and slowly and carefully slide the armature out of the housing (**Figure 50**).
7. To replace the brushes, refer to *Brush Replacement* in this chapter.

Inspection

> *CAUTION*
> *Do not immerse the brushes or the armature in solvent as the insulation may be damaged. Wipe the windings with a cloth lightly moistened with solvent and then dry thoroughly with compressed air.*

1. Clean all grease, dirt and carbon from the armature, rear cover and housing.
2. Check each brush (**Figure 51**) for cracks or damage. Then measure the length of each brush (**Figure 52**) with a vernier caliper. If the length is worn to the service limit in **Table 4**, or if the brush is damaged, replace the brushes as a set as described in this chapter.
3. Use an ohmmeter to perform the following continuity checks:
   a. Check for continuity between the cable terminal and the brushes with insulated wires (**Figure 53**). There should be continuity.

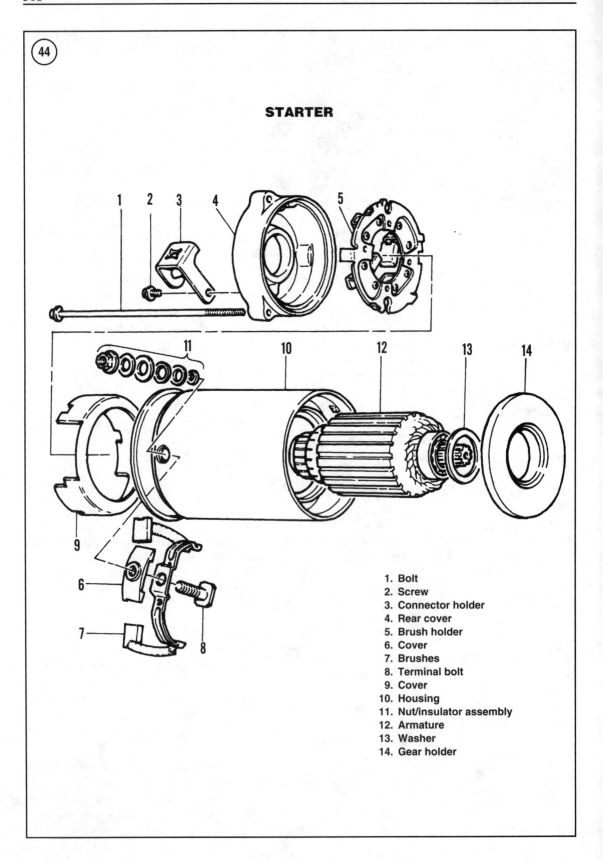

STARTER

1. Bolt
2. Screw
3. Connector holder
4. Rear cover
5. Brush holder
6. Cover
7. Brushes
8. Terminal bolt
9. Cover
10. Housing
11. Nut/insulator assembly
12. Armature
13. Washer
14. Gear holder

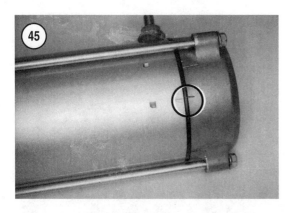

9

b. Check for continuity between the housing and the cable terminal (**Figure 54**). There should be no continuity.

4. Inspect for weak or damaged brush springs on the brush holder.

5. Inspect the individual commutator bars (**Figure 55**) for discoloration. If a pair of bars is discolored, the armature coils are grounded.

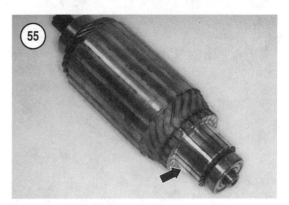

6. Inspect the mica between the commutator bars. On a good commutator, the mica is below the surface of the copper bars. On a worn commutator the mica and copper bars may be worn to the same level (**Figure 56**). If necessary, have the commutator serviced by a Honda dealership or electrical repair shop.

7. Use an ohmmeter to perform the following:

a. Check for continuity between the commutator segments (**Figure 57**); there should be continuity between pairs of bars.

b. Check for continuity between the commutator segments and the shaft (**Figure 58**); there should be no continuity.

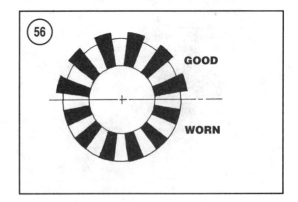

8. Turn the armature bearings (**Figure 59**) by hand. The bearings must turn smoothly without excessive play or noise. Also check that the bearings are a press fit on the shaft. If the bearings are damaged or loose, replace the starter motor. The bearing cannot be replaced separately.

9. Inspect the field coil assembly within the housing (**Figure 60**) for wear or damage. If it is damaged, replace the starter motor; this part is not available separately.

10. Inspect the cable/brush terminal set (**Figure 61**) for wear or damage.

11. Inspect the brush holder assembly (**Figure 62**) for wear or damage.

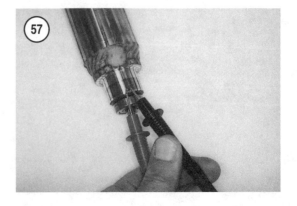

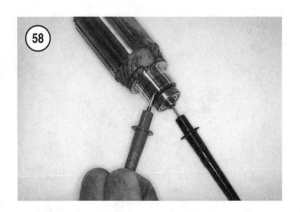

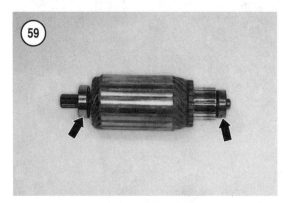

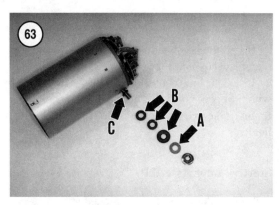

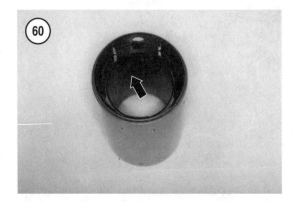

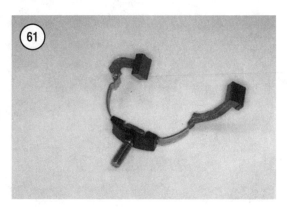

Brush Replacement

Refer to **Figure 44** for this procedure.

NOTE
*The cable terminal assembly securing the brushes to the housing consists of a number of insulated and steel washers and nuts. Remove the parts and lay them out in the order of removal (**Figure 63**). They must be reinstalled in the exact same order to insulate the brushes from the housing.*

1. Remove the terminal nut from the cable/brush terminal set.

2. Remove the steel washer (A, **Figure 63**), then three fiber washers (B, **Figure 63**) and the O-ring (C, **Figure 63**) from the terminal bolt.

3. Remove the terminal bolt and cable/brush terminal set (A, **Figure 64**), the brush assembly (B, **Figure 64**) and cover (C, **Figure 64**) from the housing.

4. Separate the terminal bolt and cable/brush terminal set from the brush assembly.

5. Install the cover (A, **Figure 65**) and new cable/brush terminal set (B, **Figure 65**) into the hous-

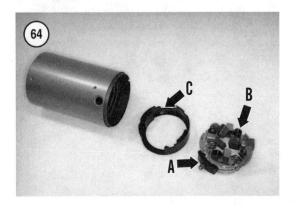

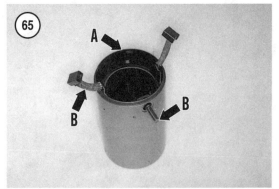

ing. Align the brush cables with the notches in the cover.

6. Install the brush terminal insulator assembly in the order shown in **Figure 63**.

7. Install the brush holder and align the locating tab with the cover notch (**Figure 66**).

8. Insert the two brushes into the receptacles in the holder.

Starter Motor Assembly

Refer to **Figure 44** for this procedure.

1. If removed, install the brushes as described under *Brush Replacement* in this chapter.

2. To keep spring pressure off the four brushes, insert small strips of plastic between each brush and its spring (**Figure 67**).

> CAUTION
> *The armature coils may be damaged if the magnets within the housing pull the armature against the housing during armature installation.*

3. Hold tightly onto the armature while slowly and carefully inserting the armature into the housing (**Figure 50**). Push the armature all the way in past the brush assembly.

4. Slowly remove the small strips of plastic from between each brush and its spring (**Figure 68**). Make sure all four brushes are located correctly against the commutator (**Figure 69**).

5. Install a new O-ring (**Figure 70**) onto the housing.

6. Apply a *small* amount of grease onto the washer and install it into the rear cover (**Figure 71**).

7. Align the slot in the rear cover (A, **Figure 72**) with the locating tab on the brush holder (B, **Figure**

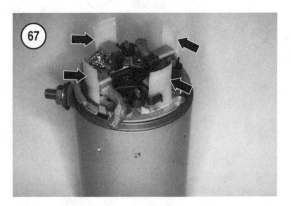

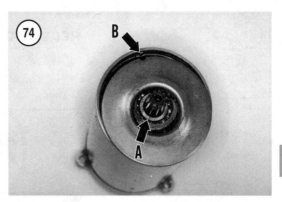

9

72) and install the rear cover. Carefully press it on until it bottoms.

8. Make sure marks on the case and the rear cover (**Figure 73**) are correctly aligned. Reposition if necessary.

9. Install the washer (A, **Figure 74**) onto the armature shaft.

10. Align the notch in the gear holder with the housing locating tab (B, **Figure 74**) and install the gear holder. Push it on until it is completely seated.

11. Align the notch in the reduction gearcase with the housing location tab (**Figure 75**) and install the reduction gearcase onto the starter motor (**Figure 76**).

12. Install the long bolts (**Figure 46**) securing the starter motor assembly to the reduction gearcase and tighten securely.

Reduction Gearcase Disassembly

Refer to **Figure 77** for this procedure.

1. Remove the reduction gearcase from the starter motor as previously described in this chapter.

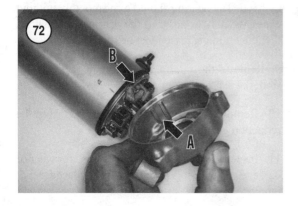

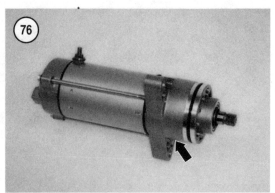

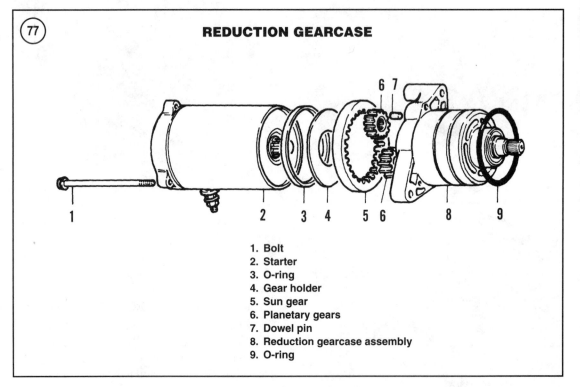

REDUCTION GEARCASE

1. Bolt
2. Starter
3. O-ring
4. Gear holder
5. Sun gear
6. Planetary gears
7. Dowel pin
8. Reduction gearcase assembly
9. O-ring

2. Remove the gear holder and O-ring (**Figure 78**) from the gearcase.

3. Remove the starter reduction planetary gears (A, **Figure 79**) and the sun gear (B, **Figure 79**) from the gearcase.

4. Remove the dowel pin (C, **Figure 79**) from the gearcase.

5. Check the starter reduction gears (**Figure 80**) for excessive wear or damage.

6. Check the needle bearing in each planetary gear for wear or damage.

7. Check the planetary gear bosses in the reduction gearcase for severe wear or damage.

8. Turn the starter shaft in the reduction gearcase by hand. The bearing should turn smoothly without excessive play or noise. If the bearing is damaged, the reduction gearcase must be replaced.

9. Remove the circlip and washers (**Figure 81**) from the starter shaft.

10. Remove the starter shaft (**Figure 82**) from the reduction gearcase.

11. Inspect the dust seal of the gearcase for wear or damage. The dust seal cannot be replaced separately.

9

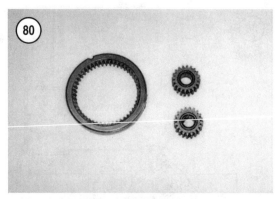

12. Replace all worn or damaged parts as required. Some individual parts cannot be ordered separately. See a Honda dealership for the availability of parts.

13. After all worn or damaged parts have been replaced and the parts washed and dried thoroughly, continue with Step 14 to assemble the reduction gearcase.

14. Apply grease to the gears, gear bosses and needle bearings.

15. Install the starter shaft (**Figure 82**) into the reduction gearcase. Push it in until it bottoms out.

16. Install the washers and circlip (**Figure 81**) onto the starter shaft. Make sure the circlip is properly seated in the shaft (**Figure 83**).

17. Install the dowel pin (C, **Figure 79**) into the reduction gearcase groove.

18. Install the sun gear (B, **Figure 79**), aligning the notch in the gear with the dowel pin installed in Step 17.

19. Install the two planetary gears (A, **Figure 79**) onto the gear bosses.

20. Align the notch in the gear holder with the dowel pin installed in Step 17 and install the gear holder (A, **Figure 84**).

21. Install a new O-ring seal (B, **Figure 84**).

22. Turn the starter shaft to make sure the gears and bearing turn smoothly.

STARTER SYSTEM ELECTRICAL COMPONENTS

This section describes service to electrical components (except switches) that are a part of the starting system. Starting system troubleshooting procedures are described in Chapter Two.

Starter Relay Switch

Operation test

1. Remove the right side rear cover as described in Chapter Fifteen.

2. Check the starter relay switch operation as follows:

   a. Locate the starter relay switch next to the battery (**Figure 85**).

   b. With the ignition switch on, the starter relay switch should click when the starter button is pressed.

3. Check the starter relay switch continuity as follows:

   a. Disconnect the negative battery cable at the battery.

   b. Disconnect the connector from the starter relay switch and remove it.

   c. Connect a 12-volt battery with jumper wires to the two terminals on the relay switch as shown in **Figure 86**.

   d. Connect the test leads of an ohmmeter to the two terminals on the relay, as shown in **Figure 86**.

   e. There should be continuity when the voltage is applied.

4. If the starter relay switch fails any part of this test, replace the relay.

5. Install by reversing these removal steps.

Ground circuit test

1. Disconnect the connector from the starter relay switch.

2. Check for continuity with an ohmmeter between the green/red wire terminal and ground (**Figure 87**).

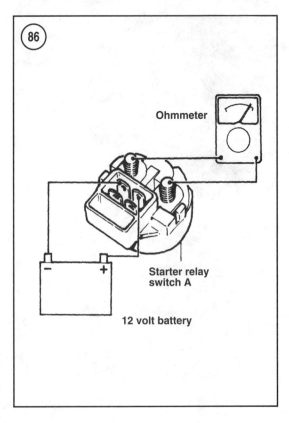

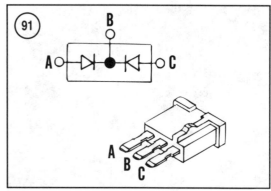

3. With the transmission in NEUTRAL, there will be a slight resistance indicated due to the diode in the circuit.

4. With the clutch lever applied and with the side stand in the raised position, there should be continuity.

Starter relay voltage test

1. Fasten the connector onto the starter relay switch.

2. Shift the transmission into NEUTRAL.

3. Use a voltmeter to measure the voltage between the yellow/red and ground at the starter relay switch connector (**Figure 88**).

4. Battery voltage should be present with the following conditions:
   a. The ignition switch is in the ON position.
   b. The engine stop switch is in the RUN position.
   c. The starter button is pressed.

5. If battery voltage is not present, one of the switches in Step 4 may be defective or there is an open in the circuit.

Neutral Switch Diode Testing/Replacement

1. Remove the right side rear cover as described in Chapter Fifteen.

2. Open the fuse box cover (**Figure 89**).

3. Remove the diode (**Figure 90**) from the fuse box.

4. Check for continuity between two terminals on the diode (**Figure 91**) with an ohmmeter. There should be continuity with the test leads connected in one direction and no continuity with the leads reversed.

5. Replace any diode that fails this test.

6. If the diode tests good, install it into the fuse box and close the cover.

7. Install the right side rear cover as described in Chapter Fifteen.

9

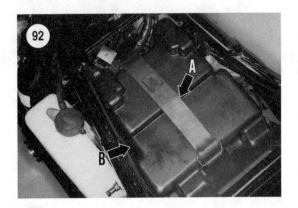

Bank Angle Sensor Testing/Replacement

This test requires a special Honda electrical test Inspection Adapter (part No. 07GMJ-ML80100) and a voltmeter.

1. Remove the seat as described in Chapter Fifteen:
2. Unhook the rubber strap (A, **Figure 92**) and remove the battery cover (B, **Figure 92**).
3. Locate and disconnect the bank angle sensor white three-pin electrical connector (A, **Figure 93**). Make sure the wires are green, red/white, and white.
4. Connect the inspection adapter to each end of the three-pin electrical connector (**Figure 94**).
5. Turn the ignition switch ON, connect a voltmeter and measure voltage between the following terminals of the adapter:

    a. Green (+) and red (–): 0-1 volt.
    b. White (+) and red (–): 10-14 volts.

6. Turn the ignition switch to the OFF position.
7. Disconnect the inspection adapter and reconnect the white 3-pin electrical connector to the bank angle sensor.
8. Remove the center cover as described in Chapter Fifteen.
9. Remove the two mounting screws and remove the bank angle sensor from its mount.
10. Hold the bank angle sensor in its normal operating position (horizontal) (**Figure 95**) and turn the ignition switch ON. The red/white wire at the sensor relay should have battery voltage and the relay should click.
11. Turn the ignition switch OFF.
12. Angle the bank angle sensor approximately 50°, then turn the ignition switch ON. The red/white wire at the sensor relay should show zero volts and the relay should click..

NOTE
If this test is going to be repeated, first turn the ignition switch OFF, then back ON.

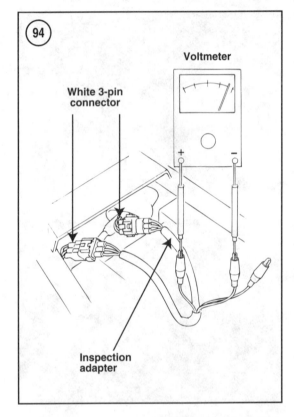

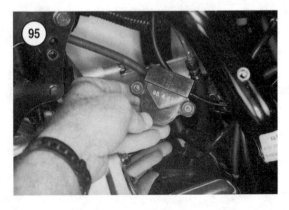

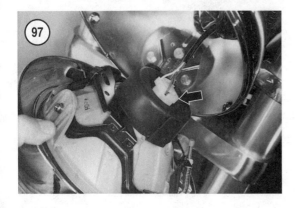

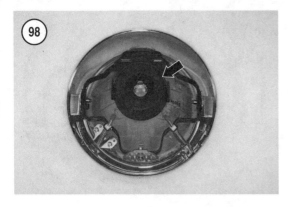

13. Turn the ignition switch OFF and remove the voltmeter.

14. If the bank angle sensor fails any part of this test, replace the bank angle sensor.

15. Install by reversing the removal steps. Make sure all electrical connectors are tight.

Bank Angle Sensor Relay Test

1. Remove the seat as described in Chapter Fifteen.

2. Unhook the rubber strap (A, **Figure 92**) and remove the battery cover (B, **Figure 92**).

3. Locate the bank angle sensor relay (B, **Figure 93**) and disconnect it from the battery box bracket.

4. Disconnect the four-pin electrical connector from the relay.

5. Connect a 12-volt battery with jumper wires to the white and the red/white terminals on the relay.

6. Connect the test leads of an ohmmeter to the white and black/green terminals on the relay.

7. There should be continuity when voltage is applied.

8. There should be no continuity when there is no voltage applied.

9. If the bank angle sensor relay switch fails any part of this test, replace the relay.

10. Install by reversing these removal steps.

LIGHTING SYSTEM

The lighting system consists of a headlight, taillight/brake light combination, license plate light, turn signals, turn signal relay, indicator lights and speedometer and tachometer illumination lights. The meter illumination bulbs are covered in *Meters* in this chapter. **Table 5** lists replacement bulbs for these components.

Always use the correct wattage bulb as indicated in this section. Using a larger wattage bulb will give a dim light and a smaller wattage bulb will burn out prematurely.

Headlight Bulb Replacement

GL1500C and GL1500CT models

1. Remove the screw (**Figure 96**) on each side of the headlight case.

2. Carefully pull the headlight lens assembly out of the headlight case and disconnect the electrical connector (**Figure 97**) from the headlight bulb.

3. Remove the rubber dust cover (**Figure 98**) from the headlight lens.

4. Release the bulb spring retainer (**Figure 99**) and remove headlight bulb (**Figure 100**).

CAUTION
Carefully read all instructions with the replacement quartz halogen bulb. Do not touch the bulb glass. Any trace of oil on the glass will reduce the life of the bulb. Clean any oil from the

*bulb with a cloth moistened in alcohol
or lacquer thinner.*

5. Align the locating tabs and install the new bulb
(**Figure 101**).

6. Lock the bulb spring retainer (**Figure 99**) into
place over the bulb to hold it in place.

7. Install the rubber dust cover (**Figure 98**) so that
the TOP mark (**Figure 102**) on the cover faces toward the top of the headlight lens assembly.

8. Connect the headlight electrical connector (**Figure 97**).

9. Install the headlight lens assembly into the headlight case and secure with the screw (**Figure 96**) on
each side.

10. Turn the ignition switch to the ON position and
check the headlight operation in the HI and LO positions.

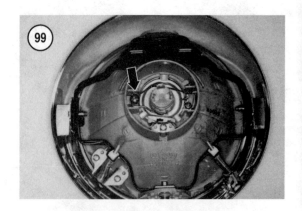

GL1500CF models

Refer to **Figure 103** for this procedure.

> *NOTE*
> *For additional working room, turn the
> handlebar away from the headlight
> assembly being serviced.*

1. Disconnect the electrical connector from the
headlight bulb. Access the connector through the
fairing.

2. Remove the rubber dust cover from the headlight lens.

3. Release the bulb spring retainer and remove the
headlight bulb.

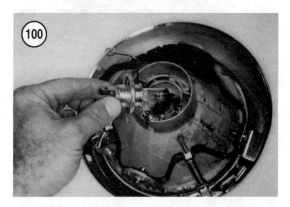

> *CAUTION*
> *Carefully read all instructions with
> the replacement quartz halogen bulb.
> Do not touch the bulb glass. Any trace
> of oil on the glass will reduce the life
> of the bulb. Clean any traces of oil
> from the bulb with a cloth moistened
> in alcohol or lacquer thinner.*

4. Align the locating tabs and install the new bulb
(**Figure 101**).

5. Lock the bulb spring retainer (**Figure 99**) into
place over the bulb to hold it in place.

6. Install the rubber dust cover (**Figure 98**) so that
the TOP mark (**Figure 102**) on the cover faces toward the top of the headlight lens assembly.

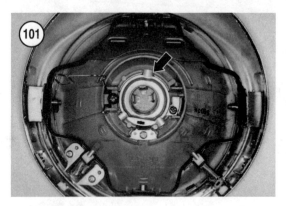

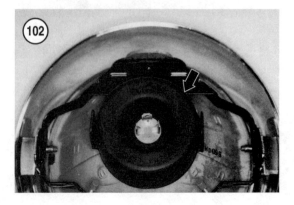

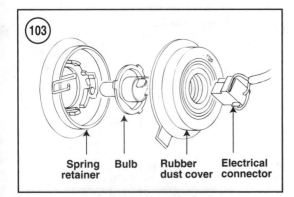

Spring retainer | Bulb | Rubber dust cover | Electrical connector

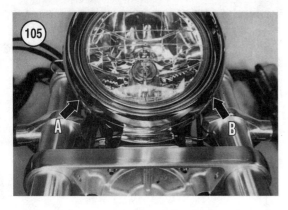

7. Connect the headlight electrical connector (**Figure 97**).

8. Turn the ignition switch to the ON position and check both headlights' operation in the HI and LO positions.

Headlight Case Removal/Installation (GL1500C and GL1500CT Models)

NOTE
The headlight case on GL1500CF models is part of the front fairing and

that procedure is covered in Chapter Fifteen.

1. Remove the headlight lens assembly as described under *Headlight Bulb Replacement GL1500C and GL1500CT Models* in this chapter.

2. Disconnect the electrical connectors within the headlight case.

3A. On GL1500C models, remove the two bolts and nuts (**Figure 104**) and remove the headlight case from the lower fork bridge.

3B. On GL1500CT models, perform the following:

  a. Remove the windshield as described in Chapter Fifteen.

  b. Remove the two nuts and secure the lower bracket, then remove the lower bracket and the headlight case from the lower fork bridge.

4. Install by reversing these removal steps while noting the following:

  a. Make sure all electrical connections are free of corrosion and are tight.

  b. Adjust the headlight as described in this chapter.

Headlight Aim Adjustment

Adjust the headlight(s) horizontally and vertically according to Department of Motor Vehicles regulations in the local area.

1A. On GL1500C and GL1500CT models, perform the following:

  a. To adjust the headlight vertically, turn the right side adjust screw (A, **Figure 105**) in either direction as required.

  b. To adjust the headlight horizontally, turn the left side adjust screw (B, **Figure 105**) in either direction as required.

1B. On GL1500CF models, perform the following:

  a. To adjust the headlight(s) vertically, turn the upper knob(s) (**Figure 106**) in either direction as required.

  b. To adjust the headlight(s) horizontally, turn the lower adjust screw(s) (**Figure 106**) in either direction as required.

9

Front and Rear Turn Signal Bulb Replacement

1A. On GL1500C and GL1500CT models, remove the screws securing the turn signal lens and remove the lens.

1B. On GL1500CF models, remove the lower screw, securing the turn signal lens and remove the lens.

2. Push in on the bulb, turn it counterclockwise and remove it (A, **Figure 107**).

3. Wash the inside and outside of the lens with a mild detergent and wipe it dry.

4. Install a new bulb and make sure it is secure in the socket.

5. Check the lens gasket (B, **Figure 107**) for deterioration or damage. Replace if necessary.

6A. On 1997-1999 GL1500C and GL1500CT models, align the lens tab with the housing groove and install the lens and the screws. Do not overtighten the screws as the lens may crack.

6B. On GL1500C and GL1500CT models since 2000 and all GL1500CF models, align the lens slot with the housing tab and install the lens and lower screw. Do not overtighten the screw as the lens may crack.

Turn Signal Relay Testing/Replacement

1. Remove the seat and frame left rear side cover as described in Chapter Fifteen.

2. Remove the coolant reservoir tank as described in Chapter Ten.

3. Unhook the turn signal relay and rubber mount (**Figure 108**) from the battery case mounting tab.

4. Disconnect the three-pin black electrical connector from the relay. Make sure the three wires are green, black, and gray.

5. Connect a jumper wire from the black wire terminal to the gray wire terminal on the wiring harness side of the connector.

6. Turn the ignition switch to the ON position.

7. Operate the turn signal switch to either position and ensure that the turn signal is operating.

8. If the turn signal does not operate, check for a break in the black and gray wires.

9. If the turn signal operates correctly, check for continuity between the green wire terminal and ground with an ohmmeter as follows:

    a. If there is no continuity, check for an open circuit in the green wire.

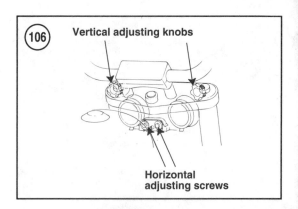

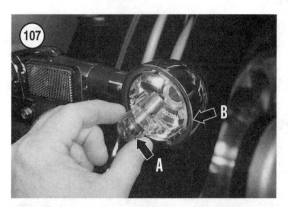

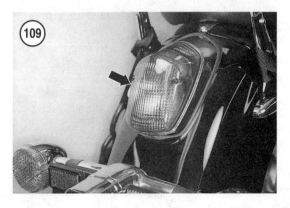

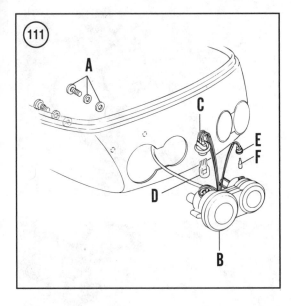

2. Push in on the bulb, turn it counterclockwise and remove it (A, **Figure 110**).

3. Wash the inside and outside of the lens with a mild detergent and wipe dry.

4. Check the lens gasket (B, **Figure 110**) for deterioration or damage. Replace if necessary.

5. Install a new bulb and make sure it is secure in the socket.

6. Install the lens and screws. Do not overtighten the screws; the lens may crack.

Brake and Taillight Bulb and Accessory Bulb Replacement (GL1500CF Models)

1. Open the trunk lid.

2. Remove the two screws, two metal washers and two rubber sealing washers (A, **Figure 111**) securing the brake and taillight assembly to the trunk.

3. Partially withdraw the brake and taillight assembly (B) from the trunk to gain access to the bulb sockets.

4. Turn the brake and taillight bulb socket (C) counterclockwise and remove it from the assembly.

5. Carefully pull the brake and taillight bulb (D) straight out of the socket and replace the defective bulb.

6. Pull the accessory socket (E) straight up and out of the assembly.

7. Carefully pull the accessory bulb (F) straight out of the socket and replace the defective bulb.

8. Install the socket(s) into the assembly.

9. Install the brake and taillight assembly (B) into the trunk. Push it in until it bottoms.

10. Hold the assembly in place and install the two rubber sealing washers, two metal washers and the two screws. Do not overtighten the screws as the assembly may crack.

11. Close the trunk lid.

License Light Bulb Replacement

1. Remove the license plate.

2. Remove the bolts securing the rear reflector assembly (**Figure 112**) and remove the assembly.

3. Working under the rear fender, remove the nuts and washers securing the license plate light and rear turn signal assembly (**Figure 113**) to the rear fender. Carefully lower the assembly and rest it on the rear fender.

b. If there is continuity, check the connector terminals for loose or poor contacts. If the connector terminals are good, replace the turn signal relay.

10. Remove the jumper wire installed in Step 5.

11. Connect the three-pin black electrical connector onto the relay.

12. Install the turn signal relay and rubber mount (**Figure 108**) onto the battery case mounting tab.

13. Install the coolant reservoir tank as described in Chapter Ten.

14. Install the rear cover and seat as described in Chapter Fifteen.

Brake and Taillight Bulb Replacement (GL1500C, and GL1500CT Models)

1. Remove the screws securing the brake and taillight lens and remove the lens (**Figure 109**).

4. Remove the screws (**Figure 114**) securing the stay cover and remove the cover.

5. Remove the license plate light assembly from the rear turn signal assembly.

6. Disconnect the electrical wire connectors from the main harness.

7. Remove the nuts (**Figure 115**) securing the mounting bracket to the license plate light assembly and separate the socket base from the lens/cover.

8. Push in on the bulb (**Figure 116**), turn it counter-clockwise and remove it from the socket.

9. Replace the bulb.

10. Wash the inside and outside of the lens/cover with a mild detergent and wipe dry.

11. Install by reversing these removal steps.

COOLING SYSTEM ELECTRICAL COMPONENTS

This section contains procedures for testing the coolant temperature indicator and coolant thermosensor.

Coolant Temperature Indicator Inspection (GL1500C and GL1500CT Models)

Coolant temperature light comes on when the ignition switch is turned ON

1. Remove the radiator as described in Chapter Ten.

2A. On 1997-1999 models, disconnect the electrical connector from the thermosensor (**Figure 117**).

2B. On 2000 models, disconnect the electrical connector from the thermostatic switch (**Figure 117**).

3. Turn the ignition switch to the ON position and check the indicator.

4A. On 1997-1999 models, check the following:

  a. If the indicator does not come on, check the thermosensor. If the thermosensor is good, replace the coolant temperature indicator unit.

  b. If the indicator comes on, remove the coolant reservoir without disconnecting the siphon tube. Disconnect the two-pin electrical connector from the coolant temperature indicator unit (A, **Figure 118**). Turn the ignition switch to the ON position and check the light.

  c. If the light does not come on, repair the short circuit in the green/blue wire between

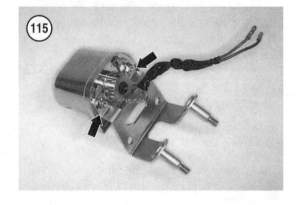

ter nine-pin electrical connector and the indicator four-pin electrical connector. If the green/black wire is good, replace the tachometer assembly.

g. Reconnect all electrical connectors and install all components removed.

4B. On 2000 models, check the following:

a. If the light does not come on, replace the thermostatic switch.

b. If the light comes on, check for a short circuit in the green/blue wire between the thermostatic switch and the tachometer nine-pin electrical connector. If the wire is good, replace the tachometer assembly.

5. Install the radiator as described in Chapter Ten.

Coolant temperature is too high, but the coolant temperature light does not come on

1. Check that the oil pressure and side stand indicators function properly when the ignition switch is in the ON position.

2. If they do not function properly, perform the wire harness inspection at the tachometer nine-pin electrical connector as described under *Meters (GL1500C and GL1500CT models)* in this chapter.

3. If they do function properly, perform the following:

a. On 1997-1999 models, disconnect the electrical connector from the thermosensor (**Figure 117**).

b. On 2000 models, disconnect the electrical connector from the thermostatic switch (**Figure 117**).

c. Use a jumper wire and ground the electrical connector. Turn the ignition switch to the ON position.

4A. On 1997-1999 models, check the following:

a. If the indicator comes on, check the thermosensor (**Figure 117**). If the thermosensor is good, replace the coolant temperature indicator unit.

b. If the indicator does not come on, check for an open circuit in the green/blue wire between the thermosensor and the indicator two-pin electrical connector.

c. If the green/blue wire is good, remove the coolant reservoir without disconnecting the

the indicator units two-pin electrical connector and the thermosensor.

d. If the light comes on, disconnect the four-pin electrical connector from the temperature indicator unit (B, **Figure 118**). Turn the ignition switch to the ON position and check the light.

e. If the light does not come on, replace the indicator unit.

f. If the light comes on, check for a short circuit in the green/black wire between the tachome-

siphon tube. Disconnect the four-pin electrical connector (B, **Figure 118**) from indicator unit and ground the green/black wire terminal. Turn the ignition switch to the ON position and check the indicator.

d. If the indicator does not come on, check for an open circuit in the green/black wire between the tachometer nine-pin electrical connector and the indicator unit four-pin electrical connector. If the green/black wire is good, replace the tachometer assembly.

e. If the indicator comes on, measure the voltage between the black/brown and the green/black wire terminals of the indicator unit's four-pin electrical connector (B, **Figure 118**). Turn the ignition switch to the ON position, there should be battery voltage.

f. If there is battery voltage, replace the indicator unit.

g. If there is no battery voltage, check for an open circuit in the wire harness.

4B. On 2000 models, check the following:

a. If the indicator comes on, replace the thermostatic switch.

b. If the indicator does not come on, check for an open circuit in the green/blue wire between the thermostatic switch and the tachometer nine-pin electrical connector.

c. If the wires are good, replace the tachometer assembly.

Coolant Temperature Indicator Inspection (GL1500CF Models)

Coolant temperature light does not come on when the ignition switch is turned ON

1. Check that the speedometer, tachometer and LCD function properly when the ignition switch is in the ON position. If they do not function properly, perform the wire harness inspection at the tachometer nine-pin electrical connector as described under *Combination Meter (GL1500CF models)* in this chapter.

2. If the speedometer, tachometer and LCD indicators function properly when the ignition switch is in the ON position, replace the combination meter/LCD assembly.

Coolant temperature light remains on with the ignition switch in the ON position

1. Remove the radiator as described in Chapter Ten.
2. Disconnect the electrical connector from the thermosensor (**Figure 117**).
3. Turn the ignition switch to the ON position and check the coolant temperature indicator light.
4. If the indicator light comes on for two seconds and then goes off, replace the thermosensor as described in Chapter Ten.
5. If the indicator light comes on and remains on, check for continuity between the thermosensor green/blue wire and ground with an ohmmeter. There should be continuity.
6. If there is continuity, check for a short circuit in the green/blue wire between the coolant temperature indicator unit and the thermosensor.
7. If there is no continuity, replace the combination meter/LCD assembly.
8. Install the radiator as described in Chapter Ten.

Coolant temperature is too high, but the coolant temperature indicator does not come on

1. Turn the ignition switch to the ON position. The coolant temperature indicator light should come on for two seconds then go off. Turn the ignition switch off.
2. Remove the radiator as described in Chapter Ten.
3. Disconnect the electrical connector from the thermosensor (**Figure 117**).
4. Use a jumper wire to ground the thermosensor electrical connector, then turn the ignition switch to the ON position.
5. If the coolant temperature indicator light comes on, replace the thermosensor as described in Chapter Ten.
6. If the coolant temperature indicator light did not come on for two seconds and then go off, check the following.

a. Remove the seat and left side rear cover as described in Chapter Fifteen.

b. Remove the coolant reservoir tank as described in Chapter Ten.

c. Check the green/blue wire for continuity between the thermosensor and the combination meter with an ohmmeter. There should be continuity.

(119) HORN SWITCH

	B/Br	G
PUSH	•———————•	
FREE		

d. If there is continuity, replace the combination meter/LCD assembly.

e. Install the coolant reservoir tank as described in Chapter Ten.

f. Install the left side rear cover and seat as described in Chapter Fifteen.

7. Install the radiator as described in Chapter Ten.

Coolant Thermosensor Testing (1997-1999)

1. Remove the coolant thermosensor (**Figure 117**) from the thermostat housing as described in Chapter Ten.

2. Fill a pan with water and place on a stove or hot plate.

3. Position the coolant thermosensor so that the temperature sensing tip and the threaded portion of the body are submerged. Keep the tip away from the bottom of the pan by at least 40 mm (1.57 in.).

NOTE
The thermometer and the coolant thermosensor must not touch the pan sides or bottom. If either does, it will result in a false reading.

4. Place a thermometer in the pan of water (use a cooking or candy thermometer that is rated higher than the test temperature).

5. Attach one ohmmeter lead to the coolant thermosensor terminal and the other to the body.

6. Gradually heat the water for approximately three minutes before performing the test.

7. Check the resistance as follows:
   a. When the temperature reaches 175° F (80° C), the resistance reading should be between 47-57 ohms.

b. When the temperature reaches 248° F (120° C), the resistance reading should be between 14-18 ohms.

8. Replace the temperature sensor if it is out of specification by more than 10 % in Step 7.

9. If the coolant temperature sensor tests good, install the sensor into the thermostat housing as described in Chapter Ten.

SWITCHES

This section contains procedures for testing and replacing switches.

Basic Switch Testing

Test the switches using an ohmmeter (see Chapter One) or a self-powered test light at the switch electrical connector plug, operating the switch in each of its operating positions and comparing the results with the switch continuity diagram. For example, **Figure 119** shows a continuity diagram for a typical horn button. It indicates which terminals should show continuity when the horn button is in a given position.

When the horn button is pushed, there should be continuity between the green and black/brown wire terminals. This is indicated by the line on the continuity diagram. An ohmmeter connected between these two terminals should indicate little or no resistance when the horn button is pushed. When the button is free, there should be no continuity between the same wire terminals.

When testing switches, note the following.

1. First check the fuses as described in this chapter.

2. Disconnect the negative battery cable if the switch connectors have not been disconnected from the circuit.

CAUTION
Do not attempt to start the engine with the negative battery cable disconnected or the wiring will be damaged.

3. When separating two connectors, pull on the connector blocks and not on the wires. See **Figure 120**.

4. After locating a defective circuit, check the connector blocks for dirty or loose-fitting (**Figure 121**)

9

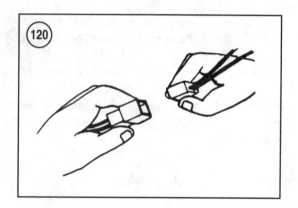

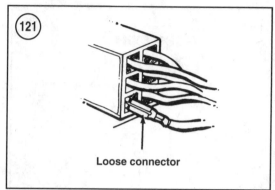

Loose connector

terminals. Check all wires going into a connector block to make sure each wire is properly positioned.

5. To properly reconnect two connector halves, push them together until they click and are locked into place. See **Figure 122**.

6. When replacing a switch assembly, make sure the cable wiring harness is routed correctly.

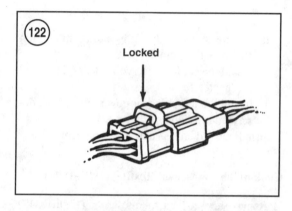

Locked

Ignition Switch Continuity Test

1. Remove the fuel tank as described in Chapter Eight.

2A. On GL1500C and GL1500CT models, disconnect the ignition switch four-pin white connector and the additional yellow/black connector (**Figure 123**).

2B. On GL1500CF models, disconnect the ignition switch four-pin white connector containing four wires (1 red, 1 red/black, 1 blue/orange, 1 red/white) and an additional single yellow/black connector (**Figure 123**).

3. Refer to **Figure 124** for GL1500C and GL1500CT models, or **Figure 125** for GL1500CF models, and connect the test leads to the indicated wire colors with the ignition switch in the indicated positions. Test as described under *Basic Switch Testing* in this chapter.

4. If the ignition switch fails any one of the tests, the electrical contact portion of the switch must be replaced.

5. Install by reversing these steps.

Ignition Switch Replacement

1. Remove the fuel tank as described in Chapter Eight.

2. Disconnect the negative battery cable.

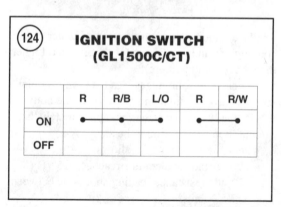

IGNITION SWITCH (GL1500C/CT)

	R	R/B	L/O	R	R/W
ON	●—	—●	●	●—	—●
OFF					

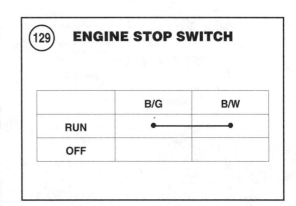

(125) IGNITION SWITCH (GL1500CF)						
	Y/B	R	R/B	L/O	R	R/W
ON		●——●——●			●——●	
OFF						
ACC	●——●					

(129) ENGINE STOP SWITCH		
	B/G	B/W
RUN	●————●	
OFF		

3. Remove the single screw and the ignition switch cover (**Figure 126**).

4A. On GL1500C and GL1500CT models, disconnect the ignition switch four-pin white connector (**Figure 123**).

4B. On GL1500CF models, disconnect the ignition switch four-pin white connector and the additional single yellow/black connector (**Figure 123**).

5. Disconnect the wire harness holder clamps from the ignition switch.

6. Remove the Torx bolts securing the ignition switch to the switch base and remove the switch.

7. Assemble and install the ignition switch by reversing these steps. Test the ignition switch as described in this chapter.

Engine Stop Switch Testing

The engine stop switch (A, **Figure 127**) is an integral part of the right switch housing.

1A. On GL1500C and GL1500CT models, perform the following:

  a. Remove the headlight lens assembly as described in this chapter.

  b. Disconnect the engine stop switch nine-pin black electrical connector containing eight wires within the headlight case (**Figure 128**).

1B. On GL1500CF models, perform the following:

  a. Remove the front fairing left side inner fairing as described in Chapter Fifteen.

  b. Disconnect the engine stop switch nine-pin red electrical connector containing seven wires located next to the fork leg.

2. Refer to **Figure 129** and connect the test leads to the indicated wire colors with the engine stop switch in the indicated positions. Test as described under *Switch Testing* in this chapter.

9

3. If the engine stop switch fails any one of the tests, replace the right switch housing assembly.

4. Install by reversing these steps.

Starter Switch Testing

The starter switch (B, **Figure 127**) is an integral part of the right-hand switch assembly.

1. Remove the headlight lens assembly as described in this chapter.

2A. On GL1500C and GL1500CT models, disconnect the engine stop switch nine-pin black electrical connector containing eight wires within the headlight case (**Figure 128**).

2B. On GL1500CF models, perform the following:

   a. Remove the front fairing left side inner fairing as described in Chapter Fifteen.

   b. Disconnect the engine stop switch nine-pin red electrical connector containing seven wires.

3. Refer to **Figure 130** and connect the test leads to the indicated wire colors with the starter switch in the indicated positions. Test as described under *Switch Testing* in this chapter.

4. If the starter switch fails any one of the tests, replace the right switch housing assembly as described in Chapter Twelve.

5. Install by reversing these steps.

Clutch Switch Testing/Replacement

The clutch switch (**Figure 131**) is mounted on the clutch master cylinder next to the clutch lever.

1. Disconnect the clutch switch wires at the clutch switch.

2. Check for continuity between the two terminals on the clutch switch with an ohmmeter. There should be no continuity with the clutch lever released. With the clutch lever pulled in, there should be continuity.

3. If the clutch switch fails either of these tests, the switch must be replaced.

4. Remove the screw securing the clutch switch (**Figure 131**) and remove the clutch switch from the clutch master cylinder.

5. Install a new switch by reversing these removal steps.

6. Make sure all electrical connectors are tight and corrosion free.

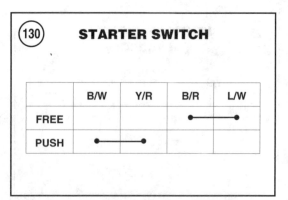

	B/W	Y/R	B/R	L/W
FREE			●———●	
PUSH	●———●			

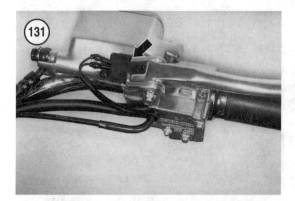

Sidestand Switch Testing

The sidestand switch is mounted on the left side of the motorcycle, adjacent to the sidestand.

1. Remove the seat as described in Chapter Fifteen.

2. Remove the left side rear frame cover as described in Chapter Fifteen.

3A. On GL1500C and GL1500CT models, disconnect the sidestand switch three-pin green connector in front of the battery (**Figure 132**) from the wiring harness.

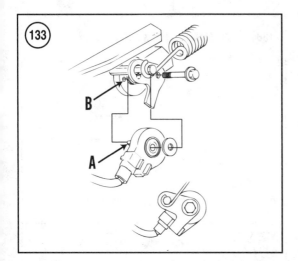

3B. On GL1500CF models, disconnect the sidestand switch two-pin green connector in front of the battery (**Figure 132**) from the wiring harness.

4. Check for continuity at the indicated wire positions with an ohmmeter.

5. Connect one ohmmeter lead to the green/white wire and the other lead to the green wire. Perform the following:

    a. With the sidestand lowered, there should be no continuity.

    b. With the sidestand raised, there should be continuity.

6. On GL1500C and GL1500CT models only, connect one ohmmeter lead to the yellow/black wire and the other lead to the green wire. With the sidestand lowered, there should be continuity.

7. If the sidestand switch fails any part of this test, replace the sidestand switch.

Sidestand Switch Replacement

1. Disconnect the sidestand switch electrical connector.

2. Place the motorcycle securely on a lift.

3. Disconnect the side stand switch wires from the harness as described in the previous procedure.

4. Remove the clamps from the sidestand switch wiring harness.

5. Remove the bolt and washer securing the side stand switch to the side stand pivot.

6. Remove the switch and wiring harness from the frame.

7. Installation is the reverse of these steps while noting the following:

    a. Install the new switch. Align the switch pin (A, **Figure 133**) with the hole in the side stand (B, **Figure 133**).

    b. Make sure the switch is aligned with the setting plate

    c. Apply ThreeBond TB1324, or Loctite 242, to the bolt threads prior to installation and tighten the bolt securely.

Dimmer Switch, Turn Signal Switch and Horn Switch Testing

The headlight dimmer (A, **Figure 134**), turn signal (B, **Figure 134**) and horn switch (C, **Figure 134**) are integral parts of the left side switch assembly.

1A. On GL1500C and GL1500CT models, perform the following:

    a. Remove the headlight lens assembly as described in this chapter.

    b. Disconnect the left side combination switch nine-pin red electrical connector and the single blue/white connector within the headlight case (**Figure 128**).

1B. On GL1500CF models, perform the following:

    a. Remove the front fairing left side inner fairing as described in Chapter Fifteen.

    b. Disconnect the left side combination switch four-pin green electrical connector containing eight wires next to the fork leg.

2. Refer to **Figure 135**, **Figure 136** or **Figure 137** and connect the tests leads to the indicated wire colors with the dimmer, hazard, turn signal or horn switch in the indicated positions. Test as described under *Basic Switch Testing* in this chapter.

9

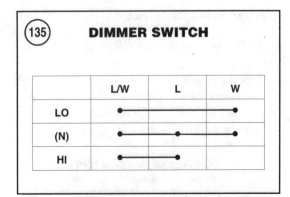

DIMMER SWITCH (135)

	L/W	L	W
LO	●———————●		
(N)	●———————●———————●		
HI	●———————●		

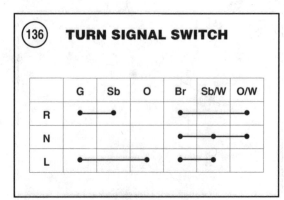

TURN SIGNAL SWITCH (136)

	G	Sb	O	Br	Sb/W	O/W
R	●———●			●———————●———————●		
N				●———————●———————●		
L	●———————●———————●		●———————●		

3. If any single switch tests incorrectly, replace the left side combination switch housing assembly as described in Chapter Twelve.

4. Install by reversing these steps.

Front Brake Light Switch Testing/Replacement

The front brake light switch is mounted on the front brake master cylinder.

1. Disconnect the electrical wires (**Figure 138**) at the brake light switch.

2. Check for continuity between the two terminals on the brake light switch with an ohmmeter. There should be no continuity with the brake lever released. With the brake lever applied there should be continuity. If the switch fails either of these tests the switch must be replaced.

3. Remove the screw securing the brake switch (**Figure 139**) and remove the brake switch from the brake master cylinder.

4. Install a new switch by reversing these removal steps. Make sure all electrical connections are tight and corrosion free.

Rear Brake Light Switch Testing/Replacement

The rear brake light switch (**Figure 140**) is mounted below the rear brake master cylinder.

1. Remove the seat as described in Chapter Fifteen.

2. Remove the frame right side rear cover as described in Chapter Fifteen.

NOTE
The wiring color changes at the two-pin electrical connector. On the brake switch side of the connector there are two black wires; on the wir-

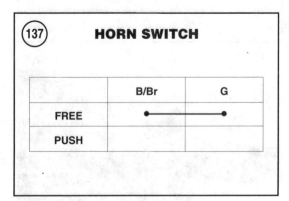

HORN SWITCH (137)

	B/Br	G
FREE	●———————●	
PUSH		

(138)

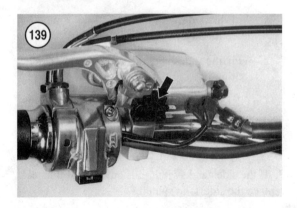

(139)

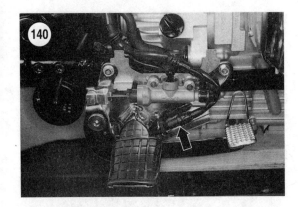

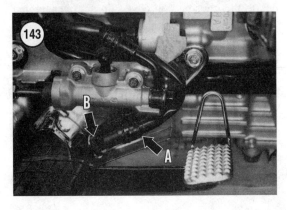

ing harness side, there is one black and one green/yellow wire.

3. Disconnect the two-pin yellow electrical connector (**Figure 141**).

4. Check for continuity between the two terminals on the brake light switch side of the connector (two black wires) with an ohmmeter. There should be no continuity with the brake pedal released. With the brake pedal applied, there should be continuity. If the switch fails either of these tests, replace the switch.

5. Remove the screws securing the rear master cylinder cover (**Figure 142**) and remove the cover.

6. Unhook the return spring and remove the end of the switch.

7. Remove the switch (A, **Figure 143**) and the wiring harness from the bracket.

8. Install a new switch by reversing these removal steps while noting the following:

   a. Make sure all electrical connections are tight and corrosion-free.

   b. Adjust the switch as described in this chapter.

Rear Brake Light Switch Adjustment

1. Turn the ignition switch on.

2. Apply the brake pedal. The light should come on just as the brake begins to engage.

3. Remove the screws securing the rear master cylinder cover (**Figure 142**) and remove the cover.

4. To adjust when the light comes on, hold the switch body and turn the adjusting nut (B, **Figure 143**) clockwise or counterclockwise as viewed from the top.

5. Turn the ignition switch off.

6. Install the rear master cylinder cover and tighten the screws securely.

Oil Pressure Switch and Indicator Testing

The oil pressure switch (**Figure 144**) is mounted on the front cover directly above the oil filter. If the oil pressure indicator light does not come on with the ignition switch in the ON position, perform the following.

1. Place the motorcycle on the side stand.

2. Check that the coolant temperature indicator is working properly as described in this chapter.

3A. If the coolant temperature indicator does not work properly, refer to *Meters* in this chapter.

3B. If the coolant temperature indicator works properly, perform the following:

    a. Pull back the rubber boot (A, **Figure 145**) and remove the screw securing the electrical connector to the oil pressure switch (B, **Figure 145**).

    b. Use a jumper wire and ground the electrical wire connector.

    c. Turn the ignition switch to the ON position. The oil pressure indicator should come on. If it comes on, replace the oil pressure switch as described in this chapter.

    d. On GL1500C and GL1500CT models, if the oil pressure indicator does not come on, check for an open circuit of the blue/red wire between the tachometer and the oil pressure switch. If the blue/red wire is good, replace the tachometer unit.

    e. On GL1500CF models, if the oil pressure indicator does not come on, check for an open circuit of the blue/red wire between the combination meter and the oil pressure switch. If the blue/red wire is good, replace the combination meter unit.

If the oil pressure indicator light stays on, with the engine running, perform the following.

1. Place the motorcycle on the side stand.

2. Pull back the rubber boot (A, **Figure 145**) and remove the screw securing the electrical connector to the oil pressure switch (B, **Figure 145**).

3. Check for continuity between the wire connector and ground with an ohmmeter.

    a. If there is continuity, check for a short circuit in the blue/red wire between the tachometer or combination meter and the oil pressure switch.

    b. If there is no continuity, check the oil level (Chapter Three) and oil pressure (Chapter Two). If it is satisfactory, replace the oil pressure switch.

Oil Pressure Switch Replacement

1. Place the motorcycle on the side stand.

2. Pull back the rubber boot (A, **Figure 145**) and remove the screw securing the electrical connector to the oil pressure switch (B, **Figure 145**).

3. Unscrew the oil pressure switch from the engine front cover.

> *CAUTION*
> *Do not apply sealant to within 3-4 mm (0.1-0.2 in.) of the open end of the switch threads. If applied to this area, it could seal off the switch opening and render the switch ineffective.*

4. Apply a light coating of sealant to the threads of the new switch. Screw the switch in and tighten it to the torque specification in **Table 6**. To prevent damage to the transmission cover, do not over tighten the switch.

5. Install the electrical connector to the switch and tighten the screw securely. Make sure the electrical connection is tight and free of corrosion.

6. Pull the rubber boot back into position.

Neutral Switch Testing

1. Remove the fuel tank as described in Chapter Eight.

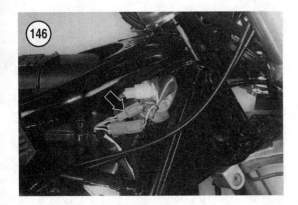

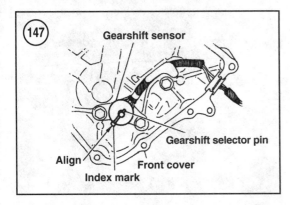

Gearshift sensor

Gearshift selector pin

Align

Front cover

Index mark

7. If the switch fails either of these tests, replace the switch as described in this chapter.

Neutral Switch Replacement

1. Remove the engine front cover as described in Chapter Four.
2. Carefully disengage the rubber grommet from the front cover.
3. Remove the bolt and electrical harness retainer.
4. Remove the two bolts securing the neutral switch to the front cover and remove the switch and electrical harness.
5. Shift the transmission into NEUTRAL.
6. Install the new switch into position and tighten the two mounting bolts.
7. Correctly position the wiring harness within the front cover and install the harness retainer and bolt. Tighten the bolt securely.
8. Apply a light coating of sealant to the grommet prior to installation, then press the grommet into the front cover. Make sure it is seated correctly and is flush with the sealing surface of the front cover.

NOTE
The alignment in the next step is necessary for the neutral indicator on the instrument panel to operate properly.

9. Align the long side of the gearshift sensor pin with the switch body index mark as shown in **Figure 147**.
10. Install the engine front cover as described in Chapter Four.

METERS
(GL1500C, GL1500CT)

Indicator Bulb Replacement

1. Remove the headlight lens assembly as described under *Headlight Bulb Replacement GL1500C and GL1500CT Models* in this chapter.
2. Use a pry bar to carefully pry the lens (**Figure 148**) out of the rubber shoulder of the socket assembly on top of the headlight case.
3. Working within the headlight case, carefully pull the socket and bulb assembly (**Figure 149**) down and out of the headlight case.
4. Carefully pull the indicator bulb out of the socket (**Figure 150**).

2. Remove the right side steering head cover as described in Chapter Fifteen.

3. Disconnect the four-pin red electrical connector (**Figure 146**).

4. Check for continuity between the green/red wire and ground on the wiring harness side of the electrical connector with an ohmmeter.

5. Shift the transmission into NEUTRAL; there should be continuity.

6. Shift the transmission into gear; there should be no continuity.

5. Install a new bulb and reinstall the socket assembly into the headlight case. Press the socket completely through the case opening until the rubber shoulder has passed through the opening.

6. Install the lens (A, **Figure 151**) into the socket (B, **Figure 151**) until it bottoms.

7. Install the headlight lens assembly as described in this chapter.

Speedometer and Tachometer Illumination Bulb Replacement

1. Place a shop cloth over the headlight case.

2. On the speedometer only, remove the screw securing the trip meter reset knob (**Figure 152**) and remove the knob.

3. Remove the mounting screw (A, **Figure 153**) and carefully remove the meter cover (B, **Figure 153**).

4. Carefully withdraw the bulb and socket assembly (**Figure 154**) out of the back of the meter housing.

5. Carefully pull the illumination bulb out of the socket.

6. Install a new bulb and reinstall the socket assembly into the meter housing. Press the socket in until it bottoms.

7. Repeat for the other meter if necessary.

8. Install the meter cover being careful not to damage any of the wiring. Push the cover on until it is up against the meter face bezel. Install the mounting screw and tighten it securely. Do not overtighten, as the screw may damage the threads in the plastic meter housing.

9. On the speedometer only, install the trip meter reset knob. Apply a small amount of ThreeBond TB1342 to the set screw threads prior to installation. Tighten the screw securely.

Wiring Harness Inspection

1. Remove the headlight lens assembly as described in this chapter.

2. Disconnect the tachometer nine-pin white electrical connector containing six wires within the headlight case (**Figure 155**).

3. Turn the ignition switch to the ON position.

4. Check between the black/brown wire terminal and ground on the wiring harness side of the connector with a voltmeter. There should be battery voltage.

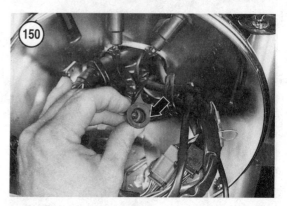

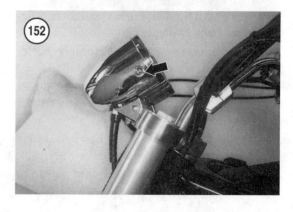

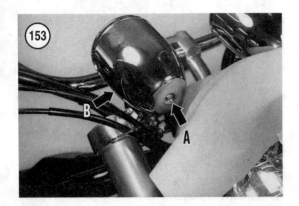

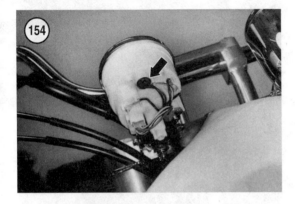

5. Check for continuity between the green wire terminal and ground on the wiring harness side of the connector with an ohmmeter. There should be continuity.

6. If there is no battery voltage or continuity, check for an open circuit within the wiring harness.

7. Reconnect the nine-pin electrical connector and install the headlight lens assembly.

Tachometer Inspection

1. Place the motorcycle on the side stand.

2. Turn the ignition switch to the ON position.

3. Check that the coolant temperature, oil pressure and sidestand indicators are working properly as described in this chapter.

4A. If the indicators do not work properly, perform *Wiring Harness Inspection* in this chapter.

4B. If the indicators work properly, perform the following:

  a. Remove the headlight lens assembly, as described under *Headlight Bulb Replacement GL1500C and GL1500CT Models* in this chapter.

  NOTE
  Do not disconnect the nine-pin white electrical within the headlight case (Figure 155).

  b. Connect a peak voltage tester positive test lead to the yellow/green wire terminal within the nine-pin white electrical connector. Connect the negative test lead to the green wire terminal within the same nine-pin white electrical connector.

  c. Start the engine and measure the tachometer signal peak voltage. There should be a minimum of 10.5 volts.

  d. If the measured peak voltage is more than 10.5 volts, replace the tachometer assembly as described in this chapter.

  e. If the measured peak voltage is less than 10.5 volts, replace the ignition control module (ICM), as described in this chapter.

5. If there is no peak voltage, perform the following:

  a. Disconnect the negative battery cable as described in this chapter.

  b. Remove the left side cover as described in Chapter Fifteen.

  c. Remove the coolant reservoir as described in Chapter Ten.

  d. Carefully remove the ignition control module and rubber strap (A, **Figure 156**) from the frame mounting tabs.

  e. Disconnect the electrical connector (B, **Figure 156**) from the ignition control unit.

  f. Check the yellow/green wire for continuity between the ignition control module and the tachometer with an ohmmeter. There should be continuity. If there is no continuity, check for an open circuit within the wiring harness.

9

6. Install by reversing these removal steps. Make sure the electrical connector is clean and tight.

Speedometer and Tachometer Removal/Installation

The meters are separate and can be removed individually. This procedure describes the removal and installation of both meters.

1. Remove the headlight lens assembly as described under *Headlight Bulb Replacement GL1500C and GL1500CT Models* in this chapter.

2. Cover the headlight case with a shop cloth to protect the finish.

3A. To remove the speedometer, perform the following:

    a. Working within the headlight case, disconnect the speedometer two-pin white electrical connector.

    b. Carefully withdraw the electrical harness from the backside of the headlight case.

    c. Unscrew the knurled connector and disconnect the speedometer cable (**Figure 157**) from the base of the meter.

    d. Remove the bolt and nut (A, **Figure 158**) and the nut and washer (B, **Figure 158**) securing the speedometer to the mounting bracket.

    e. Remove the speedometer assembly from the mounting bracket and upper fork bridge.

3B. To remove the tachometer, perform the following:

    a. Working within the headlight case, disconnect the speedometer nine-pin white electrical connector containing six wires and the single yellow/green connector.

    b. Carefully withdraw the electrical harness from the backside of the headlight case.

NOTE
Figure 159 *is shown with the meter cover removed.*

    c. Remove the bolt and nut (A, **Figure 159**) and the nut and washer (B, **Figure 159**) securing the tachometer to the mounting bracket.

    d. Remove the tachometer assembly from the mounting bracket and upper fork bridge.

4. Install by reversing these removal steps. Make sure the electrical connector(s) is clean and tight.

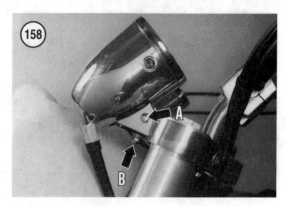

COMBINATION METER (GL1500CF)

Removal/Installation

1. Remove the left and right side front inner fairing panels as described in Chapter Fifteen.

2. Remove the two screws (A, **Figure 160**), four bolts and collars (B, **Figure 160**) securing the combination meter to the front fairing mounting bracket.

3. Carefully pull the combination meter (C, **Figure 160**) partially out and disconnect the 20-pin white

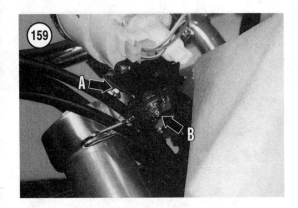

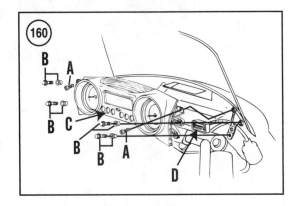

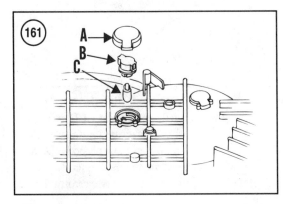

electrical connector from the main wiring harness (D, **Figure 160**).

4. Remove the combination meter from the frame.

5. Install by reversing these removal steps. Make sure the electrical connector is clean and tight.

Bulb Replacement

1. Remove the combination meter panel as described in this chapter.

2. Place the panel face down on clean shop towel.

3. Remove the rubber cap (A, **Figure 161**) above the bulb socket.

4. Turn the bulb socket (B, **Figure 161**) 45° counterclockwise and remove the socket from the meter lower case.

5. Pull the defective bulb (C, **Figure 161**) out of the socket and install a new one.

6. Install the socket into the meter lower case. Turn the bulb socket (B, **Figure 161**) 45° clockwise and lock the socket into place in the meter lower case.

7. Install the rubber cap (A, **Figure 161**) above the bulb socket. Press it in until it seats correctly.

8. Install the combination meter panel as described in this chapter.

Meter Case Disassembly/Assembly

Refer to **Figure 162** for this procedure.

If either the speedometer, tachometer or the LCD portion of the combination meter is defective the meter assembly can be replaced separately from all of the case components.

1. Remove the combination meter from the frame as described in this chapter.

2. Remove the four self-tapping screws securing the visor and remove the visor.

3. Remove the five self-tapping screws and remove the upper case and lens panel from the lower case.

4. On the backside of the lower case, perform the following:

   a. Carefully remove the rubber caps (A, **Figure 161**) above the bulb socket.

   b. Turn the bulb socket (B, **Figure 161**) 45° counterclockwise and remove the socket and bulb from the lower case.

5. Remove the five screws, washers, and six self-tapping screws. Remove the meter assembly from the lower case.

6. Assemble by reversing these disassembly steps. Do not overtighten the self-tapping screws; they will damage the plastic case.

Wiring Harness Inspection

1. Remove the combination meter as described in this chapter.

2. Turn the ignition switch to the ON position.

3. Connect a positive voltmeter test lead to the black/brown wire terminal on the wiring harness side of the 20-pin connector (**Figure 163**). Connect

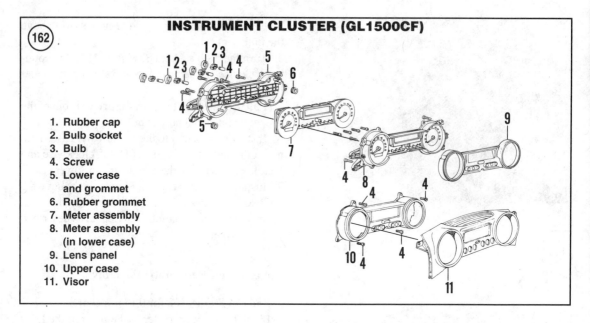

INSTRUMENT CLUSTER (GL1500CF)

1. Rubber cap
2. Bulb socket
3. Bulb
4. Screw
5. Lower case
   and grommet
6. Rubber grommet
7. Meter assembly
8. Meter assembly
   (in lower case)
9. Lens panel
10. Upper case
11. Visor

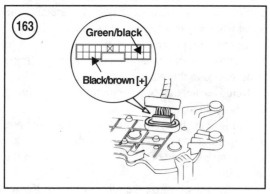

Green/black

Black/brown [+]

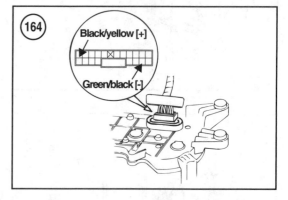

Black/yellow [+]

Green/black [-]

the negative test lead to ground. There should be battery voltage.

4. Check for continuity between the green/black wire terminal on the wiring harness side of the 20-pin connector (**Figure 163**) and ground with an ohmmeter. There should be continuity.

5. If there is no battery voltage or continuity, check for an open circuit within the wiring harness.

6. Turn the ignition switch to the OFF position.

7. Install the combination meter as described in this chapter.

**Speedometer and
Speed Sensor System Inspection**

1. Place the motorcycle securely on a stand with the front wheel off the ground.

2. Turn the ignition switch to the ON position.

3. Check that the tachometer and LCD indicators are working properly, as described in this chapter.

4A. If the indicators do not work properly, perform *Wiring Harness Inspection* in this chapter.

4B. If the indicators work properly, perform the following:

   a. Remove the combination meter as described in this chapter.

   b. Turn the ignition switch to the ON position.

   c. Connect a positive voltmeter test lead to the black/yellow wire terminal on the wiring harness side of the 20-pin connector (**Figure 164**). Connect the negative test lead to the green/black terminal on the same connector.

   d. Slowly rotate the front wheel by hand in the normal forward direction.

   e. The meter reading should pulse from zero to five volts.

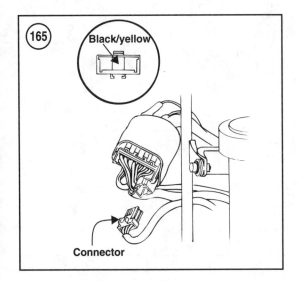

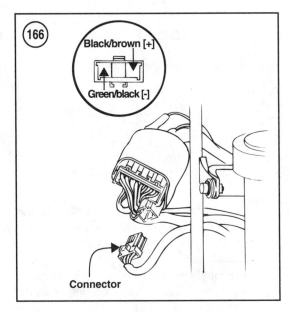

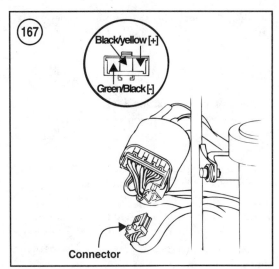

6. Install by reversing these removal steps. Make sure the electrical connector is tight and clean.

Speed Sensor Inspection

1. Place the motorcycle securely on a stand with the front wheel off the ground.
2. Remove the front fairing left side inner fairing as described in Chapter Fifteen.
3. Disconnect the three-pin green electrical connector.
4. Connect a voltmeter positive test lead to the black/brown wire terminal on the wiring harness side of the three-pin connector (**Figure 166**). Connect the negative test lead to the green/black terminal on the same connector.
5. Turn the ignition switch to the ON position. There should be battery voltage.
6. If there is no battery voltage, check for an open circuit within the wiring harness.
7. Turn the ignition switch to the OFF position.
8. Connect the three-pin green electrical connector.
9. Connect a voltmeter positive test lead to the black/yellow wire terminal on the backside of the 3-pin connector (**Figure 167**). Connect the negative test lead to the green/black terminal on the same connector.
10. Slowly rotate the front wheel by hand in the normal forward direction.
11. There should be a zero to five volt pulse.
12. If there is not a zero to five volt pulse, replace the speed sensor as described in this chapter.
13. Turn the ignition switch to the OFF position.

5A. If there is a zero to five volt pulse, replace the meter assembly portion of the combination meter.

5B. If there is not a zero to five volt pulse, perform the following:

    a. Remove the front fairing left side inner fairing as described in Chapter Fifteen.

    b. Disconnect the three-pin green electrical connector.

    c. Check for an open or short circuit in the black/yellow wire between the combination meter and the speed sensor connector (**Figure 165**).

    d. If the black/yellow wire checks good, inspect the speed sensor as described in this chapter.

14. Install by reversing these removal steps. Make sure the electrical connector is tight and clean.

Speed Sensor Replacement

1. Remove the front fairing left side inner fairing as described in Chapter Fifteen.
2. Disconnect the three-pin green electrical connector.
3. Remove the speed sensor electrical harness from the clamps on the front brake caliper, front fender and lower fork bridge.
4. Remove the set screw and remove the speed sensor from the speedometer gear box (**Figure 168**).
5. Install by reversing these removal steps while noting the following:
   a. Make sure O-ring seal is in place on the new speed sensor prior to installation on the gear box.
   b. Make sure the electrical connector is tight and clean.

Tachometer System Inspection

1. Place the motorcycle on the side stand.
2. Turn the ignition switch to the ON position.
3. Check that the tachometer and LCD indicators are working properly, as described in this chapter.
4A. If the indicators do not work properly, perform *Wiring Harness Inspection* in this chapter.
4B. If the indicators work properly, perform the following:
   a. Remove the combination meter as described in this chapter.
   b. Turn the ignition switch to the ON position.
   c. Connect a peak voltage tester positive test lead to the yellow/green wire terminal to the wiring harness side of the 20-pin connector (**Figure 169**). Connect the negative test lead to the green/black terminal on the same connector.
   d. Start the engine and measure the tachometer peak voltage. The peak voltage should be 10.5 volts.
5A. If the measured peak voltage is more than the 10.5 volts, replace the meter assembly portion of the combination meter.
5B. If the measured peak voltage is less than 10.5 volts, replace the ignition control module.
6. If there is no voltage, perform the following:
   a. Disconnect the negative battery cable as described in this chapter.

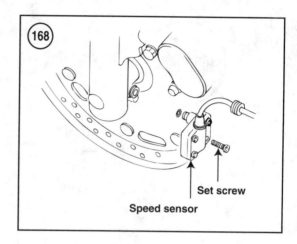

Set screw

Speed sensor

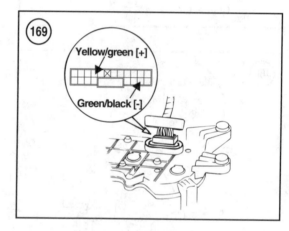

Yellow/green [+]

Green/black [-]

   b. Remove the left side cover as described in Chapter Fifteen.
   c. Remove the coolant reservoir as described in Chapter Ten.
   d. Carefully remove the ignition control module and rubber strap (A, **Figure 156**) from the frame mounting tabs.
   e. Disconnect the electrical connector (B, **Figure 156**) from the ignition control module.
   f. Check the yellow/green wire for continuity between the ignition control module and the tachometer with an ohmmeter. There should be continuity (low resistance). If there is no continuity, check for an open circuit within the wiring harness.
7. Install by reversing these removal steps. Make sure the electrical connector is tight and clean.

Fuel Sensor Inspection

1. Turn the ignition switch to the ON position.

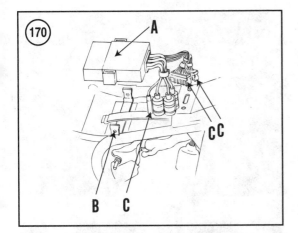

2. The fuel gauge segments on the LCD should appear within the combination meter.

3. If the segments do not appear properly, perform *Wiring Harness Inspection (GL1500CF Models)* in this chapter.

4. If the power ground circuit is okay, replace the combination meter as described in this chapter.

RADIO (GL1500CF)

Removal/Installation

1. Remove the seat as described in Chapter Fifteen.

2. Carefully pull the radio (A, **Figure 170**) and its rubber mount up and off the frame mounting tabs (B).

3. Disconnect the 18-pin green, 20-pin blue and individual electrical connectors (C, **Figure 170**) from the radio and remove it.

4. Install by reversing these removal steps. Make sure the electrical connectors are tight and clean.

HORN

Removal/Installation

1. On GL1500CF models, remove the right side radiator cover as described in Chapter Fifteen.

2. Disconnect the electrical connectors (A, **Figure 171**) from the horn.

3. Remove the horn mounting screw and remove the horn and mounting bracket (B, **Figure 171**).

4. Install by reversing these steps. Make sure the electrical connections are tight and clean.

Testing

1. Remove the horn, as described in this chapter.

2. Connect a 12-volt battery across the horn terminals. The horn should sound. If not replace it.

3. Install by reversing these steps.

FUSES

Table 7 lists fuse ratings for Valkyrie GL1500 models covered in this manual. Whenever a fuse blows, find out the reason for the failure before replacing the fuse. Usually the trouble is a short circuit in the wiring. This may be caused by worn-through insulation or a disconnected wire shorted to ground.

When replacing a blown fuse, make sure to purchase additional spare fuses as necessary and store them in their appropriate cover.

> *CAUTION*
> *Never substitute aluminum foil or wire for a fuse. Never use a higher amperage fuse than specified. An overload could cause a fire and result in the complete loss of the motorcycle.*

> *CAUTION*
> *When replacing a fuse, make sure the ignition switch is in the OFF position. This will lessen the chance of a short circuit.*

Fuse Box

The fuse box is mounted on the right side of the motorcycle behind the frame side cover.

To replace a fuse:

9

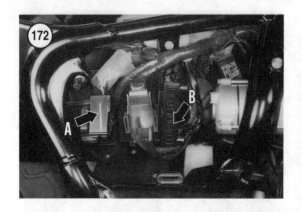

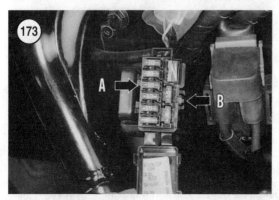

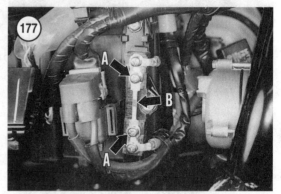

1. Remove the right side rear frame cover as described in Chapter Fifteen.

2. Hinge open the fuse cover (A, **Figure 172**).

3. Remove the old fuse (A, **Figure 173**) and install a new one of the correct amperage.

NOTE
*Extra fuses are installed along the side of the fuse carrier (B, **Figure 173**).*

4. Reinstall by reversing these steps.

Main Fuse A

Main fuse A (30A) is attached to the starter solenoid switch.

1. Remove the right side rear frame cover as described in Chapter Fifteen.

2. Carefully pull the starter solenoid switch (**Figure 174**) and its rubber mount off the frame mounting tabs.

3. Disconnect the electrical connector (**Figure 175**) from the top of the starter solenoid switch.

4. Remove the main fuse A (**Figure 176**) and replace it with the spare fuse.

5. Install by reversing these steps.

Main Fuse B (Alternator)

Main fuse B (55A) is mounted near the battery.

1. Remove the right side rear frame cover as described in Chapter Fifteen.

2. Remove the main fuse B cover (B, **Figure 172**).

3. Remove the two screws (A, **Figure 177**) and remove main fuse B (B, **Figure 177**).

4. Install the spare fuse (**Figure 178**), located in the main fuse B cover.

5. Install by reversing these steps.

Table 1 ALTERNATOR SPECIFICATIONS

Charging system starting rpm	800-1000 rpm
Stator coil resistance	0.1-0.3 ohms
Rotor coil resistance	2.9-4.0 ohms
Slip ring outer diameter	
New	27.0 mm (1.06 in.)
Wear limit	26.0 mm (1.02 in.)

Table 2 IGNITION SYSTEM TEST SPECIFICATIONS*

Ignition coil primary peak voltage
  Terminals
    Cylinder No. 1 and 2 coil: yellow/white (+) to ground (-)
100 volts minimum
    Cylinder No. 3 and 4 coil: yellow/blue (+) to ground (-)
100 volts minimum
    Cylinder No. 5 and 6 coil: yellow/red (+) to ground (-)
100 volts minimum
Ignition pulse generator peak voltage
  Terminal wire colors
    White/yellow (+) to green/black (-)
0.7 volts minimum
    White/blue (+) to green/black(-)
0.7 volts minimum

* Measure at an ambient temperature of 20° C (68° F).

Table 3 IGNITION COIL WIRE CONNECTIONS

Coil number	Green terminal	Black terminal
Cylinder No. 1 and 2	Yellow/white wire	Black/white wire
Cylinder No. 3 and 4	Yellow/blue wire	Black/white wire
Cylinder No. 5 and 6	Yellow/red wire	Black/white wire

Table 4 STARTER MOTOR SERVICE SPECIFICATIONS

Starter motor brush length	
New	12.5 mm (0.49 in.)

Table 5 REPLACEMENT BULBS

Item	Wattage
Headlight	
GL1500C, GL1500CT	12V 60/55W × 2
GL1500CF	12V 45/45W × 2
Tail/stoplight	12V 32/3cp
GL1500C, GL1500CT	12V 32/3cp
GL1500CF	12V 21/5 × 2
License light	12V 4 cp
Turn signal	
Front/running light	12V 32/3cp
Rear	12V 32cp
Meter lights	12V 1.7W
Indicator light	
GL1500C, GL1500CT	12V 3.4W × 4
Trunk accessory light	
GL1500CF	12V 3W (2)

Table 6 ELECTRICAL SYSTEM TIGHTENING TORQUES

	N•m	in-lb.	ft.-lb.
Alternator			
Coupler A nut [1]	57	–	42
Coupler B nut	57	–	42
Thermostatic fan			
motor switch	28	–	21
Starter motor			
mounting bolt	28	–	21
Oil pressure switch [2]	12	106	–

1. Apply ThreeBond TB1432, or Loctite 242 (blue) to threads.
2. Apply sealant to threads prior to installation.

Table 7 REPLACEMENT FUSES

Item	Amperage	Quantity
Main fuse A	30A	1
Main fuse B (alternator)	55A	1
Sub-fuses		
GL1500C, GL1500CT	10A	5
	5A	1
GL1500CF	15A	3
	10A	2
	5A	3

CHAPTER TEN

COOLING SYSTEM

This chapter describes repair and replacement of cooling system components. For routine maintenance, refer to Chapter Three.

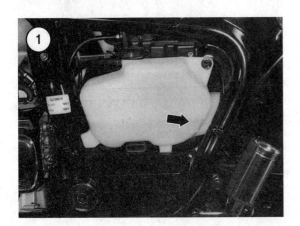

The pressurized cooling system consists of the radiator, coolant pump, thermostat, electric cooling fan and a coolant reservoir. The coolant pump requires no routine maintenance and is replaced as a complete unit if it is defective.

It is important to keep the coolant level between the two marks on the coolant reservoir (**Figure 1**). During periodic maintenance, add coolant to the reservoir, not to the radiator. If the cooling system requires repeated refilling, inspect the system for a leak. Perform the *Cooling System Inspection* in Chapter Three.

Tables 1 and **2** are at the end of the chapter.

CAUTION
Drain and flush the cooling system at least every two years. Refill with a

mixture of ethylene glycol antifreeze (formulated for aluminum engines) and distilled water. Do not reuse the old coolant, as it deteriorates with use. Do not operate the cooling system with only distilled water (even in climates where antifreeze protection is not required). This is important because the engine is aluminum; it will oxidize internally and require replacement. Refer to Chapter Three.

CAUTION
Use only a high-quality ethylene glycol coolant specifically labeled for use with aluminum engines. Do not use an alcohol-based coolant or a coolant with silicate inhibitors, as it will cause premature wear of the coolant pump seal and/or block radiator passages.

WARNING
Coolant is classified as an environmental toxic waste by the EPA and cannot be legally disposed of by flushing down a drain or pouring it onto the ground. Place coolant in a suitable container and dispose of it according to local EPA regulations. Do not store coolant where it is accessible by children or animals.

HOSES AND HOSE CLAMPS

Hoses deteriorate with age and should be inspected periodically and replaced whenever they are cracked or leaking. The spray of hot coolant from a cracked hose can injure the rider and passenger. Loss of coolant can also cause the engine to overheat and cause damage.

Whenever any component of the cooling system is removed, inspect the coolant hoses and determine if replacement is necessary.

The small diameter hoses are usually very stiff and can be difficult to install. Prior to installing the hoses, soak the ends in hot water to make them pliable. Do not apply any type of lubricant to the inner surface of the hoses as the hose may slip off even with the hose clamp in place.

Always use the screw-type clamps on the large diameter coolant hoses. This type of clamp is supe-

rior in its holding ability and is easily released with a screwdriver.

1. Make sure the cooling system is cool before replacing any hoses.
2. Make sure to replace the hoses with Honda replacement hoses since they are formed to a specific shape and of the correct length and inner diameter to fit correctly.
3. Loosen the hose clamp on the hose that is to be replaced, slide the clamp back off the fitting.

CAUTION
Do not use excessive force when attempting to remove a stubborn hose from the radiator. The radiator inlet and outlet are fragile and easily damaged.

4. Twist the hose to release it from the fitting. If the hose has been on for some time, it may be difficult to break loose. If so, carefully insert a small screwdriver or pick between the hose and fitting. Work the tool around the inside diameter of the hose. Carefully remove the hose from the fitting.

CAUTION
If the hose does not come off, cut the hose parallel to the fitting and pry it loose.

5. Examine the fitting for cracks or other damage. Repair or replace as necessary. If the fitting is in good condition, use a wire brush and clear any hose residue that may have transferred to the fitting. Wipe it clean with a cloth.
6. Inspect the hose clamps and replace if necessary. The hose clamps are as important as the hoses. If they do not hold the hose in place tightly there will be a coolant leak. For best results, always use the screw-type clamps.
7. With the hose installed correctly on each fitting, position the hose clamp back away from the end of the hose by about 0.5 in. (12.7 mm). Make sure the hose clamps are still positioned over the fitting and tighten the clamp securely.

COOLING SYSTEM CHECK

If a cooling system fault is suspected, two checks should be made before disassembling the system.
1. Run the engine until it reaches operating temperature. While the engine is running, a pressure surge should be felt when the radiator upper hose is squeezed.

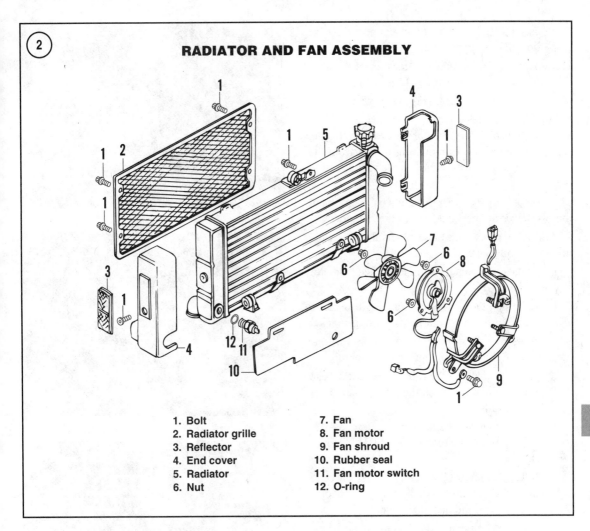

② **RADIATOR AND FAN ASSEMBLY**

1. Bolt
2. Radiator grille
3. Reflector
4. End cover
5. Radiator
6. Nut
7. Fan
8. Fan motor
9. Fan shroud
10. Rubber seal
11. Fan motor switch
12. O-ring

10

2. If a substantial coolant loss is noted, one of the head gaskets may be leaking. In extreme cases, enough coolant will leak into a cylinder(s) while the motorcycle is left standing for several hours so that the engine cannot be turned over with the starter. White smoke (steam) might also be observed at the muffler(s) when the engine is running. In severe cases, coolant may also leak into the oil. If the oil has a white, foamy appearance, coolant has mixed with the oil. Any internal coolant leakage must be corrected immediately. If this condition is not corrected, extensive engine damage will result.

CAUTION
After the cooling system problem is corrected, drain and thoroughly flush out the engine oil system to eliminate all coolant residue. Refill with fresh engine oil; refer to Chapter Three.

RADIATOR

Refer to **Figure 2** for this procedure.

Removal/Installation

1. Remove the fuel tank as described in Chapter Eight.
2. Remove the right side steering head cover as described in Chapter Fifteen:
3. Drain the cooling system as described under *Coolant Change* in Chapter Three.
4. On GL1500CF models, remove the radiator cover on both sides as described in Chapter Fifteen.
5. Disconnect the fan motor switch and the fan motor two-pin black electrical connector (**Figure 3**).
6. Disconnect the siphon hose from the radiator filler neck (A, **Figure 4**).

7. Loosen the hose clamp and disconnect the hose from the radiator upper fitting (B, **Figure 4**).

8. Loosen the hose clamp and disconnect the hose from the radiator lower fitting (**Figure 5**).

9. Remove the upper bolt (**Figure 6**) securing the radiator to the frame.

10. Carefully slide the radiator toward the left side, releasing the two lower mounting bosses from the mounting bracket posts. Remove the radiator from the frame.

11. Account for the rubber cushions and collars in the two lower mounting bosses of the radiator.

12. Install by reversing these removal steps while noting the following:

   a. Replace damaged or deteriorated radiator hoses.

   b. Make sure the two lower mounting bosses are indexed correctly into the mounting bracket posts.

   c. Tighten the upper mounting bolt securely.

   d. Correctly position the rubber seal at the base of the radiator between the timing belt cover and the radiator.

   e. Pressure check the cooling system as described under *Coolant Change* in Chapter Three.

   f. Refer to *Coolant Change* in Chapter Three to refill the cooling system with the recommended type and quantity of coolant.

   g. Start the engine and check for coolant leaks. Correct any coolant leak immediately.

Inspection

1. Remove the radiator grill from the front of the radiator.

2. Flush off the exterior of the radiator with a garden hose on low pressure. Spray both the front and the back to remove all road dirt and bugs. Carefully use a whisk broom or stiff paint brush to remove any stubborn dirt.

CAUTION
Do not press too hard, or the cooling fins and tubes may be damaged.

3. Carefully straighten out any bent cooling fins with a broad-tipped screwdriver or putty knife.

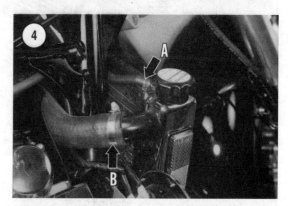

NOTE
If the radiator has been damaged across approximately 20% or more of the frontal area, the radiator should be re-cored or replaced.

4. Check for cracks or leakage (usually a moss green-colored residue) at the filler neck, the inlet and outlet hose fittings and the tank seams on each side.

5. If the condition of the radiator is doubtful, have it pressure-checked as described under *Coolant*

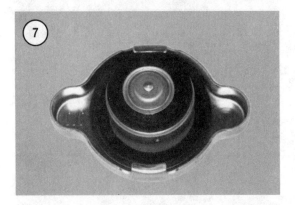

Change in Chapter Three. The radiator can be pressure-checked while removed or when mounted on the motorcycle.

6. If paint has been worn off in any area of the radiator, repaint it with black spray paint. Do not apply too much paint to the cooling fin area, as this will cut down on the cooling capabilities of the radiator.

7. Make sure the lower mounting boss rubber grommets are in good condition. Replace if necessary.

8. Inspect the rubber seals on the radiator fill cap (**Figure 7**). Replace the cap if they are hardened or starting to deteriorate.

COOLING FAN

Fan and Shroud Removal/Installation

Refer to **Figure 2** for this procedure.

1. Remove the radiator as described in this chapter.

2. Place the radiator on several towels or a blanket on the workbench with the fan assembly facing up.

3. Disconnect the electrical connector from the thermostatic fan motor switch.

4. Remove the fan shroud mounting bolts. Note the location of the ground wire connector under the lower left side bolt.

5. Lift the fan shroud up and remove the fan and shroud assembly from the backside of the radiator.

6. Do not lose the rubber cushions at the top and bottom of the radiator.

7. Check for cracked or damaged fan blades. If necessary, replace the fan blade assembly as described in this chapter.

8. Check all of the fan motor mounting bolts for tightness.

9. Check for a loose fan blade nut (**Figure 8**). Tighten if necessary.

10. If the fan is suspected of not operating properly, test it as described later in this chapter.

11. Install by reversing these removal steps.

Fan Motor Removal/Testing/Installation

Refer to **Figure 2** for this procedure.

1. Remove the cooling fan and shroud assembly from the radiator as previously described in this chapter.

2. Remove the fan blade mounting nut (**Figure 8**) and remove the fan blade.

3. Test the fan motor as follows:
   a. Connect a 12-volt battery to the fan motor two-pin electrical connector.
   b. The fan motor should operate with no grinding or excessive noise.
   c. Disconnect the battery from the fan.

4. Replace worn or damaged parts as required.

5. Install by reversing these removal steps.

COOLANT RESERVOIR

Removal/Installation

1. Remove the left frame rear side cover as described in Chapter Fifteen.

2. Disconnect the vent tube (A, **Figure 9**) from the top of the reservoir.

3. Remove the reservoir mounting bolt and collar (B, **Figure 9**). Lift up and partially remove the reservoir from the frame.

4. Disconnect the siphon tube from the base of the reservoir. Plug the siphon tube fitting on the reservoir to prevent coolant from flowing out of the reservoir.

5. Plug the siphon tube to prevent coolant from flowing out of the tube.

6. Remove the filler cap (C, **Figure 9**) and drain the coolant from the reservoir.

7. Flush the reservoir with clean water. Check the reservoir for cracks or other damage.

8. Install the reservoir by reversing these steps while noting the following:

    a. When installing the reservoir, insert the reservoir bosses into the frame receptacles (**Figure 10**).

    b. Fill the reservoir as described under *Coolant Change* in Chapter Three.

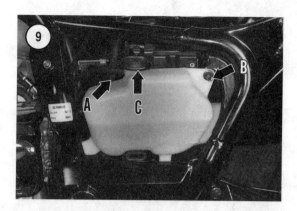

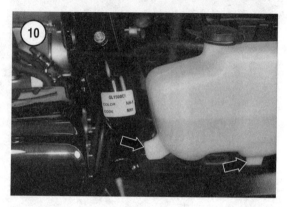

ENGINE COOLANT TEMPERATURE (ECT) SENSOR

The engine coolant temperature sensor adjusts the ignition timing according to coolant temperature.

Refer to **Figure 11** for this procedure.

Removal/Installation

> *NOTE*
> *This procedure is shown with the carburetor assembly removed instead of the radiator to better illustrate the steps. It is not necessary to remove the carburetor assembly.*

1. Remove the radiator as described in this chapter.

2. Disconnect the two-pin green electrical connector (A, **Figure 12**) from the engine coolant temperature sensor.

3. Unscrew and remove the engine coolant temperature sensor (B, **Figure 12**) and sealing washer from the thermostat housing. Discard the sealing washer.

4. Install the engine coolant temperature sensor and *new* sealing washer onto the thermostat housing.

5. Tighten the sensor to the torque specification listed in **Table 2**.

6. Install the radiator as described in this chapter.

7. Start the engine and check for coolant leaks. Correct any coolant leak immediately.

ENGINE COOLANT THERMOSENSOR (1997-1999) AND ENGINE COOLANT THERMOSTATIC SWITCH (SINCE 2000)

The engine coolant thermosensor provides the signal to the temperature indicator on the meter panel.

Refer to **Figure 11** for this procedure.

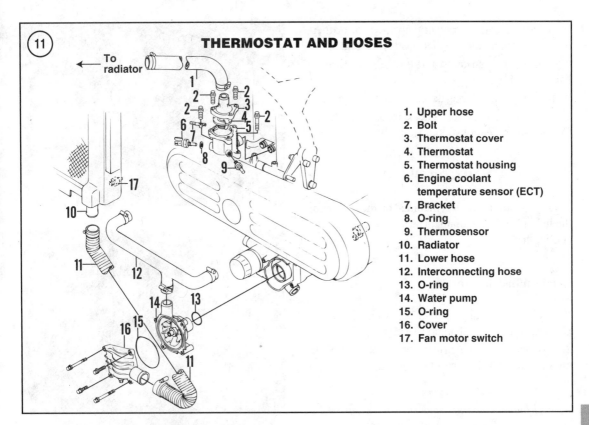

THERMOSTAT AND HOSES

1. Upper hose
2. Bolt
3. Thermostat cover
4. Thermostat
5. Thermostat housing
6. Engine coolant temperature sensor (ECT)
7. Bracket
8. O-ring
9. Thermosensor
10. Radiator
11. Lower hose
12. Interconnecting hose
13. O-ring
14. Water pump
15. O-ring
16. Cover
17. Fan motor switch

10

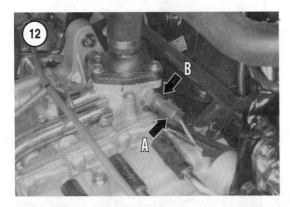

Removal/Installation

NOTE
This procedure is shown with the carburetor assembly removed instead of the radiator to better illustrate the steps. It is not necessary to remove the carburetor assembly.

1. Remove the radiator as described in this chapter.

2. Disconnect the single electrical connector (A, **Figure 13**) from the engine coolant thermosensor, or thermostatic switch.

3. Unscrew and remove the engine coolant thermosensor (B, **Figure 13**) from the thermostat housing.

4. If necessary, test the coolant thermosensor or thermostatic switch as described under *Cooling System Electrical Components* in Chapter Nine.

5. Clean the coolant thermosensor threads of all sealer residue.

6. Apply a light coating of sealant to the threads of the thermosensor or thermostatic switch prior to installation.

7. Install the engine coolant thermosensor or thermostatic switch onto the thermostat housing.

8. Tighten the sensor to the torque specification listed in **Table 2**.

9. Install the radiator as described in this chapter.

10. Start the engine and check for coolant leaks. Correct any coolant leak immediately.

FAN MOTOR SWITCH

The fan motor switch is mounted on the bottom of the left side of the radiator. The switch controls the cooling fan.

Removal/Installation

1. Drain the cooling system as described under *Coolant Change* in Chapter Three.

2. Disconnect the electrical connector at the fan motor switch (A, **Figure 14**).

> *NOTE*
> *Place a container underneath the left side of the radiator to catch any remaining coolant as it drains out when the switch is removed in Step 3.*

3. Unscrew and remove the fan motor switch (B, **Figure 14**).

4. Remove and discard the O-ring on the switch.

5. Test the fan motor switch as described under *Cooling System Electrical Components* in Chapter Nine.

6. Install by reversing these steps while noting the following:

    a. Install a new O-ring on the fan motor switch. Install and tighten the switch to the torque specification listed in **Table 2**.

    b. Fill and bleed the cooling system as described under *Coolant Change* in Chapter Three.

    c. Start the engine and check for coolant leaks. Correct any coolant leak immediately.

THERMOSTAT

Removal/Installation

Refer to **Figure 11** for this procedure.

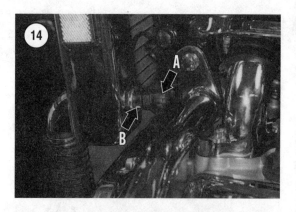

> *NOTE*
> *This procedure is shown with the carburetor assembly removed instead of the radiator to better illustrate the steps. It is not necessary to remove the carburetor assembly.*

1. Drain the cooling system as described under *Coolant Change* in Chapter Three.

2. Remove the radiator as described in this chapter.

3. Disconnect the upper water hose at the thermostat cover.

4. Remove the thermostat cover mounting bolts and remove the thermostat cover (A, **Figure 15**) and the O-ring.

5. Remove the thermostat from the housing.

6. Install by reversing these removal steps while noting the following:

    a. Position the thermostat with the hole facing toward the rear of the engine.

    b. Make sure the O-ring seal in the thermostat housing cover is in good condition. If it is starting to deteriorate or harden, replace it.

    c. Refill the cooling system with the recommended type and quantity of coolant as de-

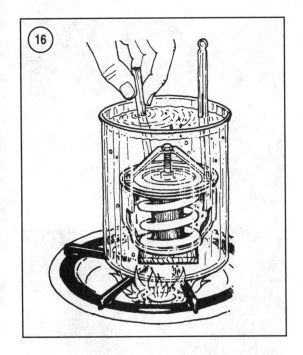

scribed under *Coolant Change* in Chapter Three.

   d. Start the engine and check for coolant leaks. Correct any coolant leak immediately.

Testing

Test the thermostat to ensure proper operation. Replace the thermostat if it remains open at normal room temperature or stays closed after the specified temperature has been reached during the test procedure.

Place the thermostat on a small piece of wood in a pan of water (**Figure 16**). Place a thermometer in the pan of water (use a cooking or candy thermometer that is rated higher than the test temperature). Gradually heat the water and continue to gently stir the water until it reaches 80-84° C (176-183° F). At this temperature, the thermostat valve should start to open. At 93-97° C (199-206° F), the thermostat valve should be fully open (minimum 8 mm [0.31 in.] valve lift).

NOTE
It may take 3-5 minutes for the thermostat to heat up and operate properly.

If the thermostat fails to operate at the listed temperatures, or if the valve lift is below minimum, replace the thermostat (it cannot be serviced). Be sure to replace it with one that has the same temperature rating.

THERMOSTAT HOUSING

Removal/Installation

Refer to **Figure 11** for this procedure.

1. Remove the thermostat cover and thermostat (A, **Figure 15**) as described in this chapter.

2. Disconnect the electrical connectors from the engine coolant thermosensor and the engine coolant temperature sensor (ECT) as described in this chapter.

3. Remove the thermostat housing (B, **Figure 15**) mounting bolts. Note the location of the ground strap on the right side bolt.

4. Pull the thermostat housing straight out of the coolant pipes. Remove the O-rings from the coolant pipes.

5. Lubricate and install new O-ring seals onto the coolant pipes.

6. Push the thermostat housing straight onto the coolant pipes until the mounting bolt holes align.

7. Install the ground strap under the right side bolt and install both mounting bolts. Tighten the bolts securely.

8. Connect the electrical connectors onto the engine coolant thermosensor and the engine coolant temperature sensor as described in this chapter.

9. Install the thermostat and cover as described in this chapter.

10. Start the engine and check for coolant leaks. Correct any coolant leak immediately.

COOLANT PUMP

The coolant pump (**Figure 11**) is mounted at the front of the engine, next to the oil filter.

The coolant pump is available as a complete unit only. If any component is damaged, replace the entire coolant pump assembly. The two coolant pump O-rings can be replaced separately.

10

Pre-inspection

If the coolant level has been dropping, check the weep hole (**Figure 17**) at the bottom of the coolant pump housing. If coolant leaks from the hole, the internal coolant pump seal is damaged; replace the coolant pump as a unit.

If coolant is not leaking from the weep hole, pressure test the cooling system as described under *Coolant Change* in Chapter Three.

Removal

1. Drain the engine coolant as described under *Coolant Change* in Chapter Three.
2. Drain the engine oil as described under *Engine Oil and Filter Change* in Chapter Three.
3. Disconnect the lower radiator hose from the coolant pump cover (A, **Figure 18**).
4. Remove the bolts securing the coolant pump and cover to the engine.
5. Remove the cover (B, **Figure 18**) from the coolant pump.
6. Disconnect the interconnecting hose (A, **Figure 19**) from the coolant pump housing.
7. Pull the coolant pump (B, **Figure 19**) out of the engine.
8. Inspect the coolant pump as described in this chapter.

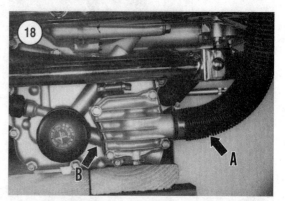

Installation

1. Lubricate and install a new O-ring (**Figure 20**) on the coolant pump.

> *NOTE*
> *When properly installed, the coolant pump rotor shaft slot (A, **Figure 21**) will align with the oil pump shaft notch (B, **Figure 21**).*

2. Install the coolant pump up against the crankcase and rotate the rotor until the coolant pump shaft slot is correctly engaged with the oil pump shaft notch. When the coolant pump is flush with the crankcase, it is properly installed. If there is gap between the two surfaces, continue to rotate the impeller until the two parts are aligned correctly. Align the mounting bolt holes.
3. Connect the interconnecting hose (A, **Figure 19**) onto the coolant pump housing.

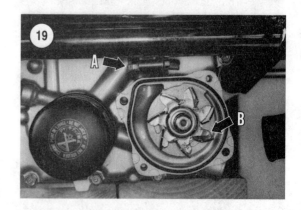

4. If the coolant pump cover was removed from the coolant pump, install a new coolant pump O-ring.

5. Make sure the O-ring seal (**Figure 22**) is still in place on the coolant pump prior to installing the cover.

6. Install the cover (B, **Figure 18**) and align the bolt holes.

7. Install the bolts securing the coolant pump and cover to the engine. Tighten the bolts to the torque specification in **Table 2**.

8. Connect the lower radiator hose onto the coolant pump cover (A, **Figure 18**).

9. Refill the engine oil as described under *Engine Oil and Filter Change* in Chapter Three.

10. Fill and bleed the cooling system as described under *Coolant Change* in Chapter Three.

11. Start the engine and check for coolant leaks. Correct any coolant leak immediately.

Inspection

1. Separate the coolant pump assembly.

2. Check the O-rings for flat spots or damage.

3. Check the impeller blades (**Figure 23**) for corrosion or damage. If the corrosion buildup on the blades is minor, clean the blades. If the corrosion is severe or if the blades are cracked or broken, replace the coolant pump assembly.

4. Turn the impeller shaft and check the pump bearing for excessive noise or roughness. If the bearing operation is rough or abnormal, replace the coolant pump assembly.

COOLANT PIPES

Removal/Installation

1. Drain the engine coolant as described under *Coolant Change* in Chapter Three.

2. Remove the carburetor assembly as described in Chapter Eight.

3. Remove the insulator panel located behind the thermostat housing.

4. Remove the bolt securing the coolant pipe to the top surface of the cylinder block.

5. Carefully disconnect the coolant pipe from the backside of the thermostat housing and the cylinder head. Remove and discard the O-ring seal from each end of the coolant pipe.

6. Repeat Step 4 and Step 5 for the other coolant pipe if necessary.

7. Lubricate and install a new O-ring on each end of the coolant pipe.

8. Carefully insert the coolant pipe into the fitting on the backside of the thermostat housing and into the cylinder head. Push the coolant pipe into each fitting making sure the O-ring seal remains seated in the coolant pipe groove. If the O-ring becomes unseated it will result in a coolant leak.

9. Install the mounting bolt and tighten it securely.

10

10. Install the insulator panel located behind the thermostat housing.

11. Install the carburetor assembly as described in Chapter Eight.

12. Refill the engine coolant as described under *Coolant Change* in Chapter Three.

13. Start the engine and check for coolant leaks. Correct any coolant leak immediately.

Table 1 COOLING SYSTEM SPECIFICATIONS

Coolant capacity	
Radiator and engine	3.7 L (3.9 U.S. qt/3.3 lmp. qt)
Reserve tank capacity	1.0 L (1.1 U.S qt./0.9 lmp.qt.)
Radiator cap relief pressure	108-137 kPa (16-20 psi)
Thermostat	
Begins to open	80-84° C (176-182° F)
Fully opened	93-97° C (199-206° F)
Valve lift	Minimum of 8 mm (0.32 in.) @ 95° C (203° F)
Thermostatic fan motor switch	
Starts to close temperature (ON)	112-118° C (234-244° F)
Stops opening (OFF)	108° C (226° F)
Fan motor switch	
Starts to close temperature (ON)	98-102° C (208-216° F)
Stops opening (OFF)	93-97° C (199-207° F)
Coolant temperature thermosensor resistance (1997-1999)	
at 80° C (176° F)	47-57 ohms
at 120° C (248° F)	14-18 ohms

Table 2 COOLING SYSTEM TORQUE SPECIFICATIONS

	N•m	in.-lb	ft.-lb.
Coolant thermo sensor			
(at thermostat housing)	10	88	–
Thermostatic fan motor switch	18	–	13
Water pump			
Assembly bolt	13	115	–
Drain bolt	13	115	–
Engine coolant temperature (ECT) sensor			
(at thermostat housing)	27	–	20

WHEELS, TIRES AND FINAL DRIVE

11

This chapter describes repair and maintenance procedures for the front and rear wheels, tires and final drive.

Power from the engine is transmitted to the rear wheel by a drive shaft and the final drive unit.

Table 1 and **Table 2** are located at the end of this chapter.

FRONT WHEEL

Removal

1A. On GL1500C and GL1500CT models, remove the setscrew and disconnect the speedometer cable from the left side fork slider. Pull the speedometer cable free from the speedometer gearbox.

1B. On GL1500CF models, remove the setscrew and disconnect the speed sensor from the left side fork slider. Move the sensor and electrical cable out of the way.

> *NOTE*
> *It is only necessary to remove one of the brake calipers in Step 2.*

2. Remove one of the front caliper assemblies as described in Chapter Fourteen.

3. On the right side, perform the following:

   a. Remove the caps from the axle pinch bolts, then loosen the pinch bolts (A, **Figure 1**).

   b. Loosen the front axle bolt (B, **Figure 1**). Do not remove it at this time.

4. On the left side, remove the caps from the axle pinch bolts then loosen the pinch bolts (**Figure 2**).

> *CAUTION*
> *Due to the weight of the motorcycle, do not try to lift and support it by any other type of jacking equipment other than the recommended motorcycle lift. The motorcycle lift is very stable and is designed specifically for this type of procedure.*

5. Place the motorcycle on a level firm surface. Do not perform this procedure on a surface that may shift under the weight of the vehicle.

6. Park the motorcycle on level ground and on a motorcycle lift with the front wheel off the ground. Refer to *Motorcycle Lift* in Chapter One.

7. On the right side, unscrew the axle bolt (B, **Figure 1**) about one-half way.

> *CAUTION*
> *To avoid damage to the axle bolt, there must be sufficient thread engagement into the front axle.*

8. Use a soft-faced mallet, gently tap the axle bolt and partially drive the front axle out of the left side fork slider.

9. Remove the front axle bolt (B, **Figure 1**), support the front wheel and withdraw the front axle (**Figure 3**) from the left side.

10. Carefully remove the front wheel from the fork assembly and the remaining brake caliper.

11. Remove the right side axle spacer (**Figure 4**).

12. Remove the speedometer drive gear (**Figure 5**) from the left side.

> *NOTE*
> *Insert a piece of vinyl tubing or wood between the brake pads. If the brake lever is inadvertently squeezed, the pistons will not be forced out of the cylinder. If this does occur the caliper will have to be disassembled to reseat the pistons and the system will have to be bled.*

> *CAUTION*
> *Do not set the wheel down on the disc surface, as it may be scratched or warped. Set the sidewall on wooden blocks*

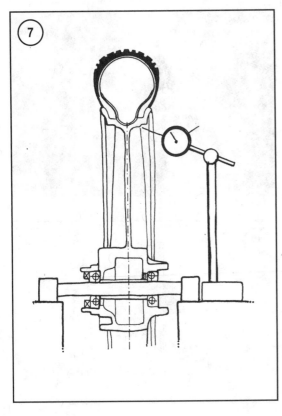

13. Install the right side spacer and speedometer gearbox onto the front axle to avoid misplacing them.

Inspection

1. Clean the axle bolt and axle in solvent and dry thoroughly.

2. Check the axle bolt and axle threads for deposit buildup or damage. Clean the threads thoroughly. Clean the axle threads with compressed air, if available.

3. Check the front axle for wear and straightness. Check axle runout with a dial indicator and V-blocks as shown in **Figure 6**. Rotate the axle slowly and check runout—runout is ½ of the total indicator reading. Replace the front axle if the runout meets or exceeds the service limit in **Table 1**.

> *WARNING*
> *Do not attempt to straighten a bent axle. If the axle is bent, it must be replaced.*

4. Place the wheel in a truing stand. Then place a dial indicator against the wheel (**Figure 7**) and measure axial (side to side) and radial (up and down) runout. The maximum axial and radial runout is in **Table 1**. If the runout meets or exceeds this dimension, check the wheel bearings as described in *Front Hub* in this chapter. Note the following.

5. Replace the wheel if the wheel bearings are acceptable, as it cannot be serviced. Inspect the wheel for signs of cracks, fractures, dents or other damage.

> *WARNING*
> *Do not attempt to repair a damaged alloy wheel; it will result in an unsafe riding condition.*

Installation

1. Make sure the front axle and the fork slider axle bearing surfaces are free from burrs and nicks.

2. Position the right side axle spacer as shown in **Figure 8** and install it into the hub (**Figure 4**).

3. Install the speedometer drive gear by aligning the two notches in the speedometer drive gear (A, **Figure 9**) with the two hub retainer tabs (B, **Figure 9**).

11

4. Position the wheel between the fork legs, sliding the brake disc through the brake caliper. The speedometer drive gear (**Figure 5**) must be on the left side.

5. Position the speedometer housing tang behind the raised boss on the left side fork slider (**Figure 10**).

6. Install the front axle from the left side (**Figure 3**). Push it in until it bottoms.

7. Install and tighten the left axle pinch bolts (**Figure 2**) to the torque specification in **Table 2**. Install the trim caps onto the bolts.

8. On the right side, install the front axle bolt (**Figure 11**).

9. Secure the front axle on the left side with a 17 mm Allen wrench, then tighten the front axle bolt (B, **Figure 1**) on the right side to the torque specification in **Table 2**.

10. Install the brake caliper as described in Chapter Fourteen.

11A. On GL1500C and GL1500CT models, slowly rotate the front wheel and insert the speedometer cable into the speedometer gearbox. Install the setscrew and tighten it securely.

11B. On GL1500CF models, install the speed sensor onto the left fork slider and install the setscrew. Tighten the screw securely.

12. Remove the motorcycle from the lift and place it securely on the sidestand.

13. Sit on the motorcycle, apply the front brake and pump the front fork several times to center the front axle within the fork sliders.

14. Tighten the right side axle pinch bolts (A, **Figure 1**) to the torque specification in **Table 2**. Install the trim caps onto the bolts.

15. Check the caliper bracket-to-disc clearance on both sides as follows:

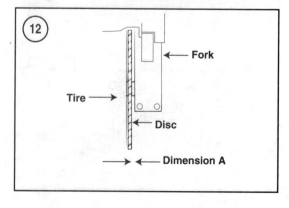

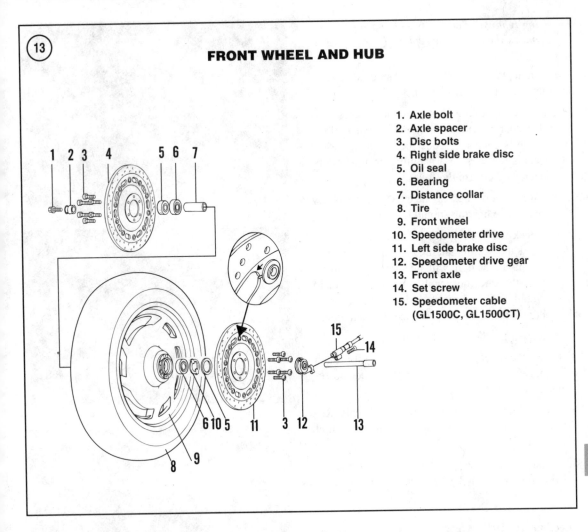

FRONT WHEEL AND HUB

1. Axle bolt
2. Axle spacer
3. Disc bolts
4. Right side brake disc
5. Oil seal
6. Bearing
7. Distance collar
8. Tire
9. Front wheel
10. Speedometer drive
11. Left side brake disc
12. Speedometer drive gear
13. Front axle
14. Set screw
15. Speedometer cable
     (GL1500C, GL1500CT)

a. Insert a 0.70 mm (0.027 in.) flat feeler gauge between the left-hand brake disc and the brake caliper bracket (**Figure 12**).

b. A feeler gauge must move freely when inserted at the points shown in **Figure 12**.

c. If the clearance is insufficient, loosen the axle pinch bolts on that side. Then move the fork slider out until the correct clearance is obtained. Tighten the axle pinch bolts to the torque specification in **Table 2**.

d. Recheck the clearance again. Readjust if necessary.

e. Repeat for the other side if necessary.

16. After the wheel is completely installed, push the motorcycle back and forth several times and apply the brake a couple of times. Make sure that the wheel rotates freely and that the brake pads are contacting the discs correctly.

WARNING
Do not ride the motorcycle until the brakes are operating correctly with full hydraulic advantage. If necessary, bleed the brakes as described in Chapter Fourteen.

FRONT HUB

Refer to **Figure 13** for this procedure.

Inspection

CAUTION
Do not reuse bearings that have been removed from a hub. Do not remove the wheel bearings for inspection purposes, as they may be damaged dur-

ing removal. Remove wheel bearings only if they are to be replaced.

1. If still in place, remove the right side axle spacer and the speedometer drive gear.

2. The condition of the front wheel bearings is critical to the steering and handling performance of the motorcycle. Check the wheel bearings whenever the wheel is removed or a handling or noise problem develops. Perform the following:

    a. Turn the inner bearing race (A, **Figure 14**) by hand. The bearing should turn smoothly.

    b. Check the bearing fit in the hub by trying to move the bearing laterally by hand. The bearing should be tight with no sign of play. Bearings that are loose will allow the wheel to wobble. If the bearing is loose, the bearing bore in the hub is probably worn or damaged.

    c. Repeat for the opposite bearing.

3. Check the speedometer drive retainer for broken or damaged tabs (B, **Figure 14**). Replace the retainer as described in this chapter.

4. Check for severely worn or damaged seals. Refer to C, **Figure 14** (left side) and **Figure 15** (right side).

5. Replace worn or damaged parts as described under *Bearing and Seal Replacement* in this chapter.

**Speedometer Drive Gear
Inspection/Gear Replacement**

1. Check for a severely worn or damaged speedometer drive gear (**Figure 16**). The drive gear notches that engage the retainer tabs must not be severely worn or damaged.

2. To replace the speedometer drive gear:

    a. Pull the seal from the hub.

    b. Pull the drive gear out of the housing.

    c. Coat the new speedometer drive gear with grease and install it into the drive gear housing.

    d. Install a new seal.

3. Inspect the speedometer cable drive mechanism. If damaged, replace the speedometer drive gear housing.

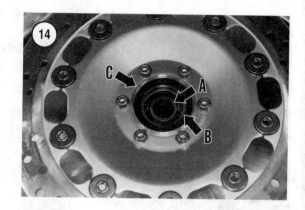

REAR WHEEL

Removal

> *NOTE*
> *The rear wheel is large and heavy. Use an assistant to remove and install the rear wheel.*

1. Remove the exhaust system as described in Chapter Four.

2. On models so equipped, remove the saddlebag and saddlebag bracket from each side, as described in Chapter Fifteen.

3. Remove the rear fender as described in Chapter Fifteen.

> *CAUTION*
> *Due to the weight of the motorcycle, do not try to lift and support the motorcycle by any other type of jacking equipment other than the recommended motorcycle lift. The motorcycle lift is very stable and is designed specifically for this type of procedure.*

4. Place the motorcycle on a level firm surface. Do not perform this procedure on a dirt surface or one that may shift under the weight of the motorcycle.

5. Park the vehicle on level ground and on a motorcycle lift. Refer to *Motorcycle Lift* in Chapter One.

6. On the left side, loosen and remove the axle nut (A, **Figure 17**).

7. Loosen and remove the rear brake caliper stopper bolt (B, **Figure 17**).

8. On the right side, pull the rear axle (**Figure 18**) out sufficiently to remove the rear brake caliper mounting bracket.

> *NOTE*
> *Insert a piece of vinyl tubing or a wooden spacer between the brake pads. If the brake pedal is inadvertently applied, the pistons will not be forced out of the caliper. If this does occur, the caliper will have to be disassembled to reseat the pistons and the system will have to be bled.*

9. Carefully remove the rear brake caliper and mounting bracket up and off the rear disc. Suspend the caliper with a bungee cord or piece of wire on the grab rail. Do not twist the brake hose.

10. Support the rear wheel with a small jack or wooden block(s).

11. Remove the left axle spacer (**Figure 19**) from the hub.

12. On the right side, completely remove the rear axle (**Figure 18**).

> *CAUTION*
> *While moving the rear wheel toward the left side, check that the final driven flange is also moving toward the left side with the wheel. If the driven flange partially separates from the hub and stays with the final drive unit, the rear wheel **cannot be re-***

11

moved. If this occurs, insert a long screwdriver into the hub and force the driven flange back onto the rear hub.

13. Slide the wheel and the driven flange to the left to disengage it from the final drive unit splines.

14. Remove the jack or block(s) from under the rear wheel and remove the rear wheel down and out of the swing arm (**Figure 20**).

NOTE
*It is possible to remove the rear wheel without removing the exhaust system, rear fender and saddle bag mounts by removing both shocks and installing a fabricated strut rod (**Figure 21**). The brackets will still require removal. To use the strut, raise the wheel and install the strut in place of the left shock so holes A and B are engaged. Removed the axle and brake caliper stopper bolts. Lower the wheel and engage holes A and C. Remove the brake caliper and rear wheel.*

Inspection

1. Check the rear axle for wear and straightness. Check axle runout with a dial indicator and V-blocks as shown in **Figure 6**. Rotate the axle slowly and check runout—runout is ½ of the total indicator reading. Replace the rear axle if the runout exceeds the service limit specification in **Table 1**.

WARNING
Do not attempt to straighten a bent axle. If the axle is bent, replace it.

2. Place the wheel in a truing stand and place a dial indicator against the wheel, as shown in **Figure 7**, and measure axial (side to side) and radial (up and down) runout. The maximum axial and radial runout is in **Table 1**. If the runout exceeds this dimension, check the wheel bearings as described in *Rear Hub* in this chapter.

3. The wheel must be replaced if the wheel bearings are acceptable, as it cannot be serviced. Inspect the wheel for signs of cracks, fractures, dents or other damage.

WARNING
Do not attempt to repair a damaged alloy wheel, as it will result in an unsafe riding condition.

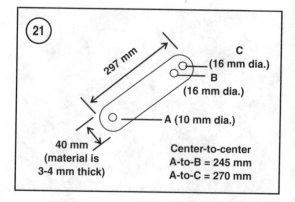

Installation

1. Loosen all four nuts (**Figure 22**) (only three nuts shown) securing the final drive unit to the swing arm. This will make rear axle installation easier.

2. Remove the old O-ring seal and install a new one in the final driven flange (A, **Figure 23**).

3. Apply molybdenum disulfide grease, or equivalent, onto the driven flange splines (B, **Figure 23**). Make sure the final driven flange is seated completely into the rear hub

4. Apply molybdenum disulfide grease, or equivalent, onto the drive flange splines (A, **Figure 24**) on the final drive unit.

5. The spacer within the final drive unit may move out during axle and wheel removal. If so, push it back into place (B, **Figure 24**). If the spacer is removed, reinstall it into the hub with the narrow end in first.

6. Position the left side axle spacer with the flange side facing out and install it into the hub (**Figure 25**).

7. Move the wheel into position, raise it up and place the same jack or wooden block(s) under it that were used during removal.

8. Position the rear wheel so that the splines of the final driven flange and the final drive unit align. Slowly move the wheel back and forth and push the wheel to the right until it seats completely.

9. On the right side, partially insert the rear axle (**Figure 18**) through the final drive unit and rear wheel hub. Do not push it in all the way since the rear brake caliper mounting bracket must be installed in the following steps.

NOTE
Remove the spacer from between the brake pads, if used, prior to installing the rear caliper assembly in Step 10.

NOTE
*Make sure the axle spacer (**Figure 20**) is still in place on the left side of the wheel hub.*

10. Untie the rear caliper assembly from the grab rail and carefully install it over the brake disc (**Figure 19**). Be careful not to damage the leading edges of the brake pads during installation. Align the hole in the caliper assembly with the swing arm hole and rear wheel.

11. On the right side, push the rear axle the rest of the way through the rear wheel, axle spacer, brake caliper bracket and the swing arm. Push the rear axle in until it bottoms in the final drive unit.

12. Install the axle nut (A, **Figure 17**) only finger-tight.

13. Install the rear brake caliper mounting bracket stopper bolt (B, **Figure 17**) and tighten it to the torque specification in **Table 2**.

14. Tighten the rear axle nut (A, **Figure 17**) to the torque specification in **Table 2**.

15. Remove the jack or wooden block(s) from under the rear wheel.

16. After the wheel is installed, completely rotate it and apply the brake several times to make sure it rotates freely and that the rear brake works properly.

17. Remove the motorcycle from the lift and place it on the sidestand.

18. Install the rear fender as described in Chapter Fifteen.

19. On models so equipped, install the saddlebag bracket and saddlebag from each side as described in Chapter Fifteen.

20. Install the exhaust system as described in Chapter Four.

11

REAR HUB

Refer to **Figure 26** for this procedure.

Driven Flange and Damper

Removal

1. Pull the final driven flange (C, **Figure 23**) out of the rear hub. If the final driven flange is tight, use a pry bar with a block of wood under it and work the final driven flange out of the rear hub.

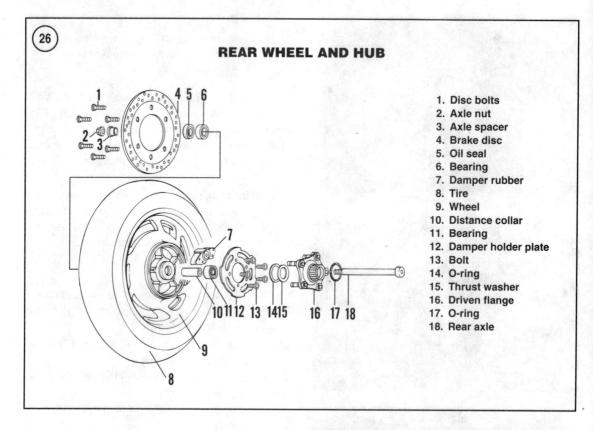

REAR WHEEL AND HUB

1. Disc bolts
2. Axle nut
3. Axle spacer
4. Brake disc
5. Oil seal
6. Bearing
7. Damper rubber
8. Tire
9. Wheel
10. Distance collar
11. Bearing
12. Damper holder plate
13. Bolt
14. O-ring
15. Thrust washer
16. Driven flange
17. O-ring
18. Rear axle

2. Remove the thrust washer (**Figure 27**). The thrust washer may come out with the final driven flange or remain with the hub.

3. Remove the bolts (**Figure 28**) securing the damper holder to the wheel.

4. Turn the damper holder in either direction until the arrow mark (A, **Figure 29**) on the damper holder is located between the hub projections (B, **Figure 29**).

5. Lift the damper holder out of the wheel hub.

6. Remove the rubber dampers (**Figure 30**).

7. Inspect the components as described in the following procedure.

Inspection

> *CAUTION*
> *Do not reuse bearings that have been removed from a hub. Do not remove the wheel bearings for inspection purposes, as they will be damaged during removal. Remove wheel bearings only if they are to be replaced.*

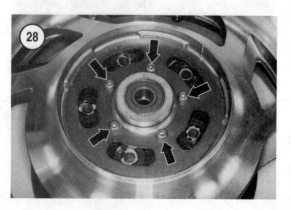

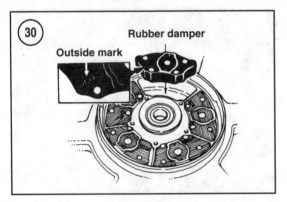

Rubber damper

Outside mark

1. The condition of the rear wheel bearings is critical to the handling and performance of the motorcycle. Check the wheel bearings whenever the wheel is removed and if handling or noise problems arise. Perform the following:

  a. Turn the inner bearing race (**Figure 31**) by hand. The bearing should turn smoothly.

  b. Check the bearing fit in the hub by trying to move the bearing laterally by hand. The bearing should be tight with no sign of play. Bearings that are loose will allow the wheel to wobble. If the bearing is loose, the bearing bore in the hub is probably worn or cracked.

  c. Repeat for the opposite bearing.

2. Inspect the final driven flange splines (**Figure 32**) and posts (**Figure 33**) for wear and damage. Replace the final driven flange, if necessary.

> *CAUTION*
> *Do not attempt to remove the final driven flange pins and nuts (**Figure 34**).*

3. Inspect the six individual rubber dampers (**Figure 30**) for wear, damage or deterioration.

11

NOTE
The driven flange inner O-ring is larger than the outer O-ring.

4. Remove both O-rings from the driven flange and install new ones.

Installation

1. Install the rubber dampers into the hub with the OUTSIDE mark facing out. See **Figure 30**.
2. Install the damper holder into the hub. Turn the damper holder in either direction until the bolt holes are aligned.
3. Install the damper holder bolts (**Figure 28**) and tighten them to the torque specification in **Table 2**.
4. Apply a light coating of molybdenum disulfide grease to both sides of the thrust washer (**Figure 27**) and install it onto the hub center.
5. Apply a light coating of molybdenum disulfide grease to the driven flange pins (**Figure 33**).
6. Install the final driven flange into the rear wheel hub. Tap the flange in with a soft-faced mallet and make sure it is completely seated in the hub (C, **Figure 23**).

BEARING AND SEAL REPLACEMENT

This procedure is for both the front and rear hubs. Where differences occur they are identified.

Disassembly

Refer to the following illustrations:
 a. **Figure 13**: front wheel and hub.
 b. **Figure 26**: rear wheel and hub.
1A. On front wheels perform the following:
 a. If necessary, remove the bolts securing both brake discs and remove the discs (A, **Figure 35**) from the wheel.
 b. Use a wide-blade screwdriver and pry the right side seal (B, **Figure 35**) out of the hub. Place a rag underneath the screwdriver to prevent hub damage.
 c. Remove the left seal (A, **Figure 36**) the same way.
 d. Remove the speedometer retainer ring (B, **Figure 36**).
1B. On rear wheels, perform the following:
 a. Remove the driven flange assembly, as described in this chapter.

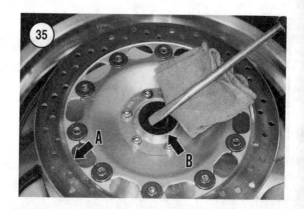

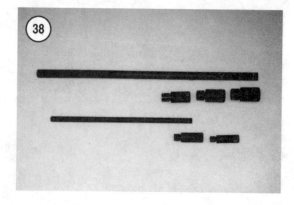

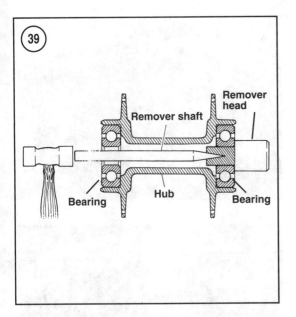

b. If necessary, remove the bolts (A, **Figure 37**) securing the brake disc to the rear hub and remove the brake disc.

c. Use a wide-blade screwdriver to pry the left side seal (B, **Figure 37**) out of the hub. Place a rag underneath the screwdriver to prevent hub damage.

NOTE
On the rear wheel only, the left side and right side bearings are different. Identify the bearings as they are removed to ensure correct installation of the new bearings.

NOTE
The Kowa Seiki Wheel Bearing Remover set can be used to remove the wheel bearings. This tool set is shown

in **Figure 38** *and can be ordered through a Honda dealership.*

2. To remove the wheel bearings with the Kowa Seiki Wheel Bearing Remover set, perform the following:

   a. Select the correct size remover head tool and insert it into the outside bearing (**Figure 39**).

   b. From the opposite side of the wheel, insert the remover shaft into the slot in the backside of the remover head (**Figure 39**). Position the wheel so that the remover head tool is resting against a solid surface, then tap the remover shaft to force it into the slot in the remover head. This will tighten the remover head against the bearing's inner race.

   c. Reposition the wheel. Using a hammer (**Figure 39**), tap against the remover shaft to drive the bearing out of the wheel. Slide the bearing and tool assembly out of the hub. Tap on the remover head to release it from the bearing.

   d. Remove the distance collar from the wheel.

   e. Repeat for the bearing on the other side of the wheel.

3. Discard both bearings.

4. Clean the inner hub area with solvent. Dry with compressed air.

Assembly

1. On non-sealed bearings and single-sealed bearings, pack the bearings with high-quality bearing grease. Work the grease into the bearings thoroughly; turn the bearing by hand a couple of times to make sure the grease is distributed evenly inside the bearing.

2. Clean any dirt or foreign matter out of the hub prior to installing the bearings.

3. Pack the hub with multipurpose grease.

4. Install the standard bearings as follows:

   a. Install double-sealed bearings so that the manufacturer's name and size code faces out.

   b. Install single-sealed bearings so that the sealed side faces out.

   c. Install non-sealed bearings so that the manufacturer's name and size code faces out.

CAUTION
Improper bearing installation will damage the bearing. Use a bearing driver or socket (**Figure 40**) *that matches the outer race diameter. Tap the bearings squarely into place and*

11

*tap on the outer race only (**Figure 41**). Do not tap on the inner race, or the bearing will be damaged. Be sure that both bearings are completely seated in the hub.*

5. Install the right side bearing into the hub.

6. Turn the hub over.

7. Install the distance collar into the hub from the left side.

8. Install the right side bearing into the hub.

9. Pack the seal lip cavity with grease. Repeat for both seals.

NOTE
Wipe off all grease from the outside of the seal after installing it.

10. Install new left- and right-side seals so that the closed side faces out. Drive the seals into the hub squarely with a bearing driver or socket placed on the seal (**Figure 42**).

11. Install the brake discs as described in Chapter Fifteen.

TUBELESS TIRE CHANGING

Proper tire service includes frequent inflation checks and adjustment as well as tire inspection, removal, repair and installation practices. By maintaining a routine tire maintenance schedule, tire damage or other abnormal conditions can be detected and repaired before they affect the operation and handling of the motorcycle. Refer to Chapter Three for general tire inspection and inflation procedures.

WARNING
Proper tire maintenance and service is a critical part of the vehicle's operating safety. If the correct tools and/or experience is not available, refer all inspection and service to a Honda dealership, or qualified motorcycle technician.

NOTE
The manufacturer recommends that the tires be removed from the wheel with a tire changer. The tight tire-to-rim fit makes removal difficult with tire irons. This procedure is pro-

vided for those who prefer to perform this task.

Inspection

Visually inspect the tires for tread wear, cracks, cuts, aging and other damage. Check the tire for areas where the tread has broken or torn out. Carefully remove stones from the tread with an appropriate tool. Check the tread closely for damage after removing the stone or other foreign objects. Improper inflation pressure, vehicle overloading or an unbalanced tire can cause uneven tread wear.

Run a hand along the sidewall and check for bulges or knots. If a bulge is noted, mark the area with chalk and then remove the tire from the rim; check the inside and outside of the tire carefully, looking for broken or separated piles. This type of damage can cause the tire to blow out. Likewise, if a tire is damaged on the outside, the tire should be removed from the rim and the inside checked carefully for broken or separated piles or other damage.

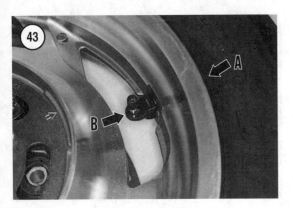

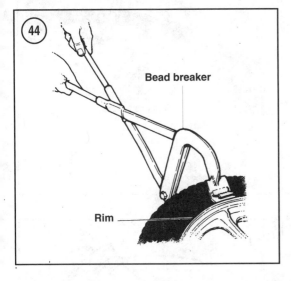

Bead breaker

Rim

WARNING
If damage is evident the tire should be removed from the wheel rim and examined closely, both inside and out. Have a Honda dealership or a qualified motorcycle technician inspect tires with bulges or other questionable damage before returning the tire to use. A damaged or deformed tire can fail and cause loss of control and severe personal injury to the rider and passenger.

Service Notes

Before changing tires, note the following:
1. Tire changing should only be undertaken when there is access to the proper tools and adequate experience using them:
   a. At least two motorcycle tire irons.
   b. Rim protectors.

   c. A bead breaker is required for breaking tires from the alloy rims.
   d. Accurate tire gauge.
   e. Water and liquid soap solution or a special tire mounting lubricant.
   f. Inflatable band (bead expander).
   g. Air compressor.
2. The original equipment cast wheel is aluminum and the exterior appearance can be easily damaged. Special care must be taken with tire irons when changing a tire to avoid scratches and gouges to the outer rim surface. Insert rim protectors between the tire irons and rim to protect the rim from damage.
3. When removing the tire, take care not to damage the tire beads, inner liner of the tire or the wheel rim flange. Use quality tire levers or flat handled tire irons with rounded ends—do not use screwdrivers or similar tools to remove tires.

Removal

NOTE
To avoid scratching or damaging the brake disc or wheel when changing the tire, place the wheel sidewall on wooden block(s).

1. Remove the wheel from the motorcycle and place it on a suitable stand or surface.
2. Place a chalk mark on the tire (A, **Figure 43**) where the tire and valve stem align (B, **Figure 43**). This will maintain tire and wheel balance during installation.
3. Remove the valve stem cap (B, **Figure 43**) and deflate the tire. Remove the valve core and store it with the valve cap.

NOTE
*Removal of tubeless tires from their rims is very difficult because of the tight bead/rim seal. Breaking the bead seal will usually require the use of a special tool (**Figure 44**). If the seal of the bead cannot be broken loose, take the wheel to a Honda dealership or qualified motorcycle technician and have them break it loose on a tire-changing machine.*

CAUTION
The inner rim and bead area are the sealing surfaces on the tubeless tire.

11

Do not scratch the inside surface of the rim or damage the tire bead.

4. Press the entire bead on both sides of the tire into the center of the rim. If the bead is tight, use a bead breaker (**Figure 44**).

> **CAUTION**
> *Do not attempt to insert the tire irons between the tire bead and rim flange to break the bead. This can permanently damage both the tire and rim.*

5. Lubricate the beads with a tire lubricant or soapy water.
6. Place rim protectors (**Figure 45**) along the rim near the valve stem and insert the tire iron under the bead next to the valve stem (**Figure 46**), making sure the tire iron contacts the rim strip and not the rim. Press on the side of the tire opposite the valve stem with a knee and pry the bead over the rim with the tire iron.

> **CAUTION**
> *Do not use excessive force when prying the tire over the rim, as this may stretch or break the bead wires in the tire*

7. Insert a second tire iron next to the first to hold the bead over the rim. Then work around the tire with the first tool prying the bead over the rim (**Figure 47**).
8. Stand the tire upright. Insert a tire iron between the back bead and the side of the rim that the top bead was pried over (**Figure 48**). Force the bead on the opposite side from the tire iron into the center of the rim. Pry the back bead off the rim, working around as with the first side.

Inspection

1. Clean the rim thoroughly to remove all dust and dirt residue.

> **CAUTION**
> *Work carefully when removing burrs or other rough spots from the wheel rim flange. Damaged air sealing surfaces will require wheel replacement.*

2. Mount the wheel on a truing stand (if available) and check the rim-to-tire mating surface for dents,

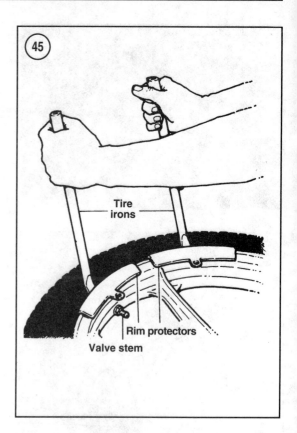

Tire irons
Rim protectors
Valve stem

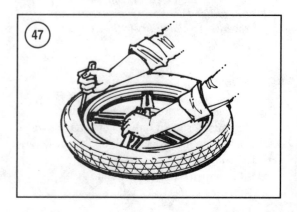

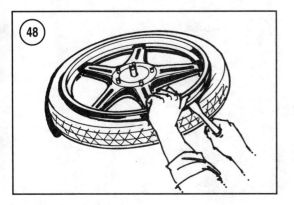

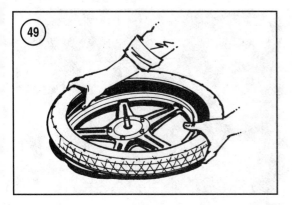

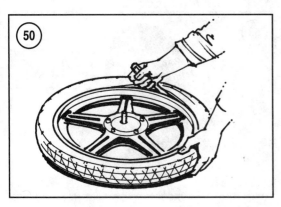

burrs or other rough spots. Emery cloth can be used to remove burrs.

3. Check the wheel for dents or other damage. If the wheel has been damaged from impact, it should be replaced.

> *WARNING*
> *Never operate the motorcycle with a bent wheel that has been straightened. The wheel may fail while in use, resulting in the loss of control.*

4. Check wheel runout as described in this chapter.

5. Blow compressed air inside of the tire casing to remove all dust and dirt. Run a hand along the tire casing and check for small nails, cracks or other damage.

6. If a tire has been punctured, refer to *Tire Repairs* in this chapter.

7. Replace a worn or damaged valve stem (B, **Figure 43**).

Installation

1. A new tire may have rubber balancing weights inside. These are not patches and should not be disturbed. A colored spot near the bead indicates a lighter point on the tire. Place this spot next to the valve stem (A, **Figure 43**).

2. Align the tire with the rim so that the directional arrows molded in the tire's side wall face in the normal rotation position.

3. Lubricate both beads of the tire with soapy water.

4. With the tire properly aligned with the wheel, press the first bead over the rim (**Figure 49**). If necessary, use a tire iron (with rim protectors) for the last few inches of bead.

5. Lubricate the upper bead with soapy water if necessary.

6. Starting 180° away from the valve stem, press the upper bead into the rim. Using tire tools and rim protectors, work around the rim to the valve (**Figure 50**).

7. Check the bead on both sides of the tire for an even fit around the rim.

8. Lubricate both tire beads.

> *WARNING*
> *When seating the tire beads in Step 9, never inflate the tire beyond the tire manufacturer's maximum pressure specification listed on the tire's sidewall. Exceeding this pressure could cause the tire or rim to burst causing severe personal injury. If the beads fail to seat properly, deflate the tire and lubricate the beads. Never stand directly over a tire while inflating it.*

9. Place an inflatable band around the circumference of the tire. Slowly inflate the band until the tire beads are pressed against the rim. Inflate the tire

11

enough to seat it, deflate the band and remove it. The tire is properly seated when the wheel rim and tire side wall lines are parallel (**Figure 51**). Inflate the tire to the pressure reading listed in Chapter Three. Screw on the valve cap.

10. Balance the wheel assembly as described in this chapter.

TIRE REPAIRS

Patching a tubeless tire on the road is very difficult. If both beads are still in place against the rim, a can of pressurized tire sealant may inflate the tire and seal the hole. The beads must be against the wheel for this method to work. Because an incorrectly patched tire might blow out and cause an accident, refer all tire repair to a qualified motorcycle technician.

WHEEL BALANCE

An unbalanced wheel results in unsafe riding conditions. Depending on the degree of unbalance and the speed of the motorcycle, the rider may experience anything from a mild vibration to a violent shimmy, which may result in loss of control.

Before attempting to balance the wheel, check to be sure that the wheel bearings are in good condition and properly lubricated and that the brakes do not drag. The wheel must rotate freely.

Weights are attached to the rims as shown in **Figure 52**.

This procedure describes static wheel balancing using a truing or wheel balancing stand.

For best results, have the wheels dynamically balanced by a Honda dealership.

Before attempting to balance the wheels, check to be sure that the wheel bearings are in good condition and properly lubricated. The wheel must rotate freely.

1. Remove the wheel to be balanced.

2. Mount the wheel on a fixture such as the one in **Figure 53** so it can rotate freely.

3. Spin the wheel and let it coast to a stop. Mark the tire at the lowest point.

4. Spin the wheel several more times. If the wheel keeps coming to rest at the same point, it is out of balance.

5. Tape a test weight to the upper, or light, side of the wheel.

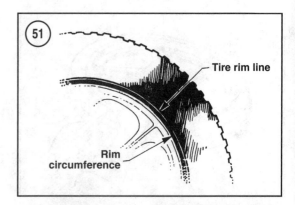

Tire rim line

Rim circumference

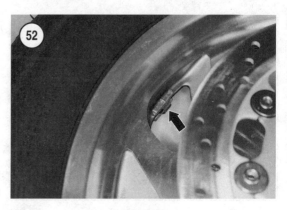

6. Experiment with different weights until the wheel, when spun, comes to rest at a different position each time.

7. Remove the test weight and install the correct size weight.

8. When adding weights, do not exceed the following weight limits:

   a. Front: 60 grams.

   b. Rear: 70 grams.

FINAL DRIVE UNIT AND DRIVE SHAFT

Removal

1. Remove the rear wheel as described in this chapter.
2. Drain the final drive unit oil as described in Chapter Three.
3. Remove all four nuts (A, **Figure 54**) (only three nuts shown) securing the final drive unit to the swing arm.
4. Remove the lower bolt (B, **Figure 54**) securing the shock absorber to the final drive unit. It is not necessary to remove the shock, just move it out of the way.
5. Pull the final drive unit and drive shaft straight back until it is disengaged from the splines on the universal joint.
6. Turn the drive shaft by hand (**Figure 55**). The drive pinion and ring gear should turn smoothly.

Disassembly/Inspection/Assembly

The final drive unit requires a considerable number of special Honda tools for disassembly and as-

sembly. The cost of these tools will exceed the cost of having the repairs performed by a Honda dealership.

Figure 56 shows all internal components of the final drive unit.

1. Install the rear axle into the final drive unit from the spline side (opposite of the normal way).
2. Place the axle in a vise with soft jaws.
3. Using a circular motion, carefully pull the drive shaft from the final drive unit (**Figure 57**). Remove the rear axle.
4. Check that the dust cover flange bolt (A, **Figure 58**) is in place and is tight.
5. Inspect the splines on the final driven ring gear (B, **Figure 58**). If they are damaged or worn, the ring gear must be replaced.

NOTE
If these splines are damaged, also inspect the splines on the rear wheel final driven flange.

6. Make sure the bearing retainer adjust locktab and bolt (A, **Figure 59**) are in place and that the bolt is tight.
7. Check the mounting stud threads (B, **Figure 59**) for damage. If damage is minimal, clean it up with a tap. If damage is severe, replace the stud(s).
8. Inspect the housing for any external damage. Make sure the oil filler cap (A, **Figure 60**) and drain bolt (B, **Figure 60**) are in good condition.
9. Inspect the splines (A, **Figure 61**) on the final drive unit end of the drive shaft. Replace the drive shaft if they are damaged or worn.
10. Inspect the splines (A, **Figure 62**) on the universal joint end of the drive shaft. Replace the driveshaft if they are damaged or worn.

NOTE
If these splines are damaged, inspect the splines on the final drive unit and universal joint.

11. Check the damper spring (B, **Figure 62**). Replace as follows:
   a. Remove the circlip (C, **Figure 62**) and the damper spring.
   b. Install a new damper spring and a new circlip.
   c. Make sure the circlip seats in the drive shaft groove completely.
12. Remove the stopper ring (B, **Figure 61**) from the groove in the end of the drive shaft splines and

11

FINAL DRIVE UNIT AND SWING ARM

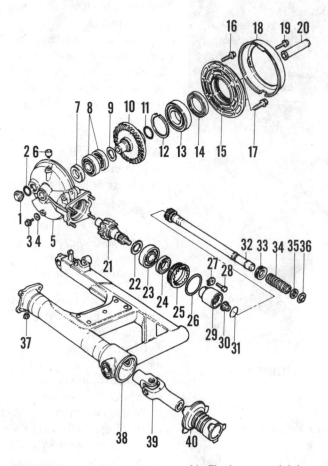

1. Filler cap
2. O-ring
3. Drain bolt
4. Washer
5. Housing
6. Breather cap
7. Oil seal
8. Bearings
9. Washer
10. Final gear set (ring gear)
11. O-ring
12. Spacer
13. Bearing
14. Oil seal
15. Gearcase cover
16. Bolt
17. Bolt
18. Dust guard
19. Bolt
20. Distance collar
21. Final gear set (pinion gear)
22. Pinion gear shim
23. Bearing
24. Oil seal
25. Bearing retainer
26. O-ring
27. Locknut
28. Bolt
29. Pinion joint
30. Nut
31. Stopper ring
32. Drive shaft
33. Oil seal
34. Spring
35. Spring seat
36. Circlip
37. Nut
38. Swing arm
39. Universal joint
40. Boot

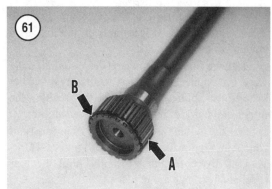

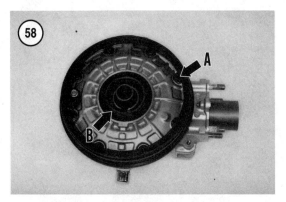

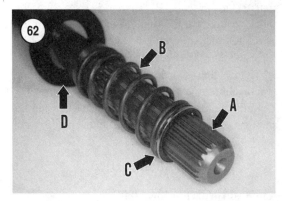

install a new one. The stopper ring must be replaced every time the drive shaft is removed from the final drive unit.

13. Replace the seal on the drive shaft (D, **Figure 62**). The seal must be replaced every time it is removed from the drive shaft. Pack the seal with 0.5 g (0.02 oz.) of grease.

14. Check that gear oil has not been leaking from either side of the unit (ring gear side or pinion joint side). If there are traces of oil leakage, take the unit to a dealer for seal replacement.

15. Do not install a new stopper ring into the groove in the end of the drive shaft splines. It is used only during manufacturing and does not need to be replaced.

Installation

1. Apply a light coating of molybdenum disulfide grease to the splines of the drive shaft and install the drive shaft into the final drive unit. Using a soft-faced mallet, tap on the end of the drive shaft to make sure the drive shaft is completely seated into the final drive unit splines. Work carefully so as not to damage the drive shaft seal (**Figure 63**).

11

2. Apply a light coating of molybdenum disulfide grease to the splines (**Figure 64**) on the universal joint end of the drive shaft.

3. Install the final drive unit and drive shaft into the swing arm. It may be necessary to slightly rotate the final driven spline back and forth to align the splines of the drive shaft and the universal joint.

4. Insert the mounting studs into the swing arm and tighten the final drive unit nuts (A, **Figure 54**) finger-tight. Do not tighten the nuts until the rear wheel and rear axle are in place.

5. Move the shock absorber into position and install the lower bolt (B, **Figure 54**) securing the shock absorber to the final drive unit. Tighten the lower bolt to the torque specification in **Table 2**.

6. Install the rear wheel as described in this chapter.

7. Tighten the final drive unit nuts to the torque specification in **Table 2**.

8. Refill the final drive unit with the correct amount and type of gear oil. Refer to Chapter Three.

UNIVERSAL JOINT

Removal/Inspection/Installation

Refer to **Figure 56** for this procedure.

1. Remove the swing arm as described in Chapter Thirteen.

2. Remove the universal joint from the engine output shaft.

3. Clean the universal joint (**Figure 65**) with solvent and dry it thoroughly with compressed air.

4. Inspect the universal joint pivot points (**Figure 66**) for play. Rotate the joint in both directions. If there is noticeable side play, the universal joint must be replaced.

5. Inspect the splines at each end of the universal joint. If they are damaged or worn, the universal joint must be replaced.

> *NOTE*
> *If these splines are damaged, inspect the splines in the final drive unit and the engine output shaft; they may also need to be replaced.*

6. Apply a light coating of molybdenum disulfide grease to both splines.

7. Install the universal joint onto the engine output shaft so that the long spline side faces to the front.

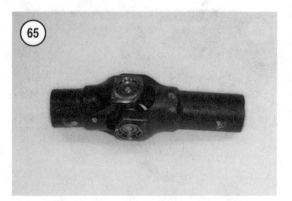

Table 1 WHEEL SERVICE SPECIFICATIONS

	Service limit mm (in.)
Axle runout	0.2 (0.008)
Wheel rim runout	
Axial	2.0 (0.08)
Radial	2.0 (0.08)
Tires size	
Front tire	150/80R17 72H
Rear tire	180/70R15 77H
Dunlop tire size	
Front/rear	D206F/D206

Table 2 WHEEL AND FINAL DRIVE TIGHTENING TORQUES

	N•m	in.-lb.	ft.-lb.
Front axle pinch bolt	22	–	16
Front axle bolt	90	–	66
Front brake caliper mounting bolts*	30	–	22
Rear axle nut	110	–	81
Rear caliper stopper bolt	69	–	51
Damper holder bolts	20	–	15
Shock absorber (right side)			
Upper bolt	26	–	19
Lower bolt	23	–	17
Final drive unit			
Gear case filler cap	12	106	–
Gear case drain bolt	20	–	15
Final drive unit nuts	64	–	47
Dust plate guard bolt	10	88	–
Gearcase cover bolts			
8 mm	25	–	18
10 mm	62	–	46

* Replace with a new original equipment bolt

11

CHAPTER TWELVE

FRONT SUSPENSION AND STEERING

This chapter describes repair and maintenance procedures for the front fork and steering components.

Tables 1-3 are located at the end of this chapter.

HANDLEBAR

Removal

1. Park the motorcycle on level ground and on a lift. Refer to *Motorcycle Lift* in Chapter One.

2. Disconnect the negative battery cable, as described in Chapter Three.

3. Remove the wire clips securing the hoses and cables to the handlebar.

CAUTION
Cover the instruments and front fairing (GL1500CF models) with a heavy cloth or plastic tarp to protect it from the accidental spillage of brake fluid. Wash any spilled brake fluid off any painted or plated surface immediately, as it will destroy the finish. Use soapy water and rinse it thoroughly.

4. Remove the two screws (A, **Figure 1**) securing the right side switch and throttle assembly together. Separate the switch and disconnect the throttle cables (**Figure 2**) from the throttle grip. Set the switch and throttle cable assembly aside. Be careful that the cables do not get crimped or damaged.

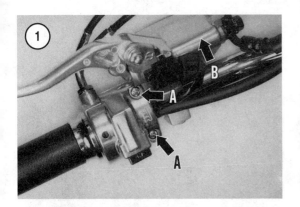

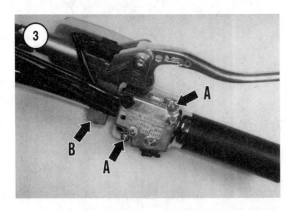

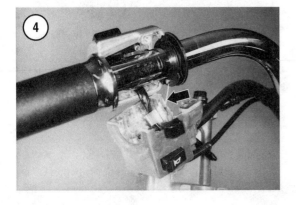

5. Remove the front brake master cylinder (B, **Figure 1**) as described in Chapter Fourteen. It is not necessary to disconnect the hydraulic brake line. Support the reservoir so that it is upright and in the same approximate position to avoid brake fluid loss and to keep air from entering the brake system.

6. Remove the two screws (A, **Figure 3**) securing the left side switch assembly together.

7. Disconnect the choke cable (**Figure 4**) and carefully set the left side switch assembly aside. Be careful that the cable does not get crimped or damaged.

8. Remove the clutch master cylinder (B, **Figure 3**) as described in Chapter Six. It is not necessary to disconnect the hydraulic brake line. Support the reservoir so that it is upright and in the same approximate position to avoid brake fluid loss and to keep air from entering into the system.

9. Remove the caps and bolts (**Figure 5**) securing the handlebar upper holder. Remove the upper holder and then remove the handlebar.

10. To properly secure the handlebar and to prevent it from slipping, clean the knurled section of the handlebar with a wire brush. Clean the handlebar holders of any metal debris that may have been gouged loose by handlebar slippage.

Installation

1. Position the handlebar on the upper fork bridge so the punch mark on the handlebar is aligned with the top surface of the raised portion of the upper fork bridge.

2. Position the handlebar upper holder with the punch marks (**Figure 6**) facing toward the front of the motorcycle.

3. Install the handlebar upper holder (**Figure 5**) and install the bolts. Tighten the forward bolts first and

12

then the rear bolts to the torque specification in **Table 4**.

4. After installation is complete, recheck the alignment of the handlebar punch marks. Readjust handlebar position if necessary.

5. Install the clutch master cylinder (B, **Figure 3**) as described in Chapter Six.

6. To install the left switch housing:
   a. Insert the choke cable onto the choke cable holder (**Figure 4**).
   b. Bring the left switch up to the handlebar, then insert the pin on the bottom half of the left switch assembly into the hole in the handlebar (**Figure 7**).
   c. Insert the choke cable holder securely in the switch housing groove.
   d. Close the switch housing assembly, making sure the pin is inside the handlebar hole. Then install the housing screws (A, **Figure 3**)
   e. Tighten the forward screw first, then the rear.

> *WARNING*
> *After installation is complete make sure the clutch lever does not contact the hand grip assembly when it is pulled on fully. If it does, the hydraulic fluid may be low in the reservoir; refill as necessary. Refer to Chapter Three.*

7. Apply a light coating of multipurpose grease to both throttle cable ends prior to installing the throttle grip assembly. Connect the throttle cables (**Figure 2**) onto the throttle grip.

8. To install the right switch housing:
   a. Insert the pin on the bottom half of the right switch assembly into the hole in the handlebar (**Figure 8**).
   b. Position the throttle grip into the switch housing groove and connect the throttle cables to the grip. Close the switch housing and install the housing screws.
   c. Tighten the forward screws first, then the rear.

9. Install the front master cylinder as described in Chapter Fourteen.

> *WARNING*
> *After installation is complete, make sure the brake lever does not come in contact with the throttle grip assembly when it is pulled on fully. If it does the brake fluid may be low in the res-*

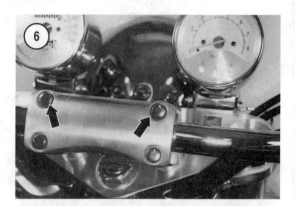

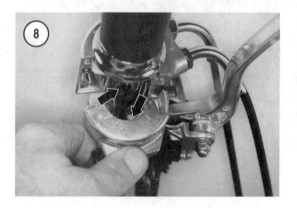

ervoir; refill as necessary. Refer to Chapter Three.

10. Install the wire clips securing the hoses and cables to the handlebar.

11. Connect the negative battery cable as described in Chapter Three.

12. Remove the motorcycle from the lift.

13. Adjust the throttle cables as described in Chapter Three.

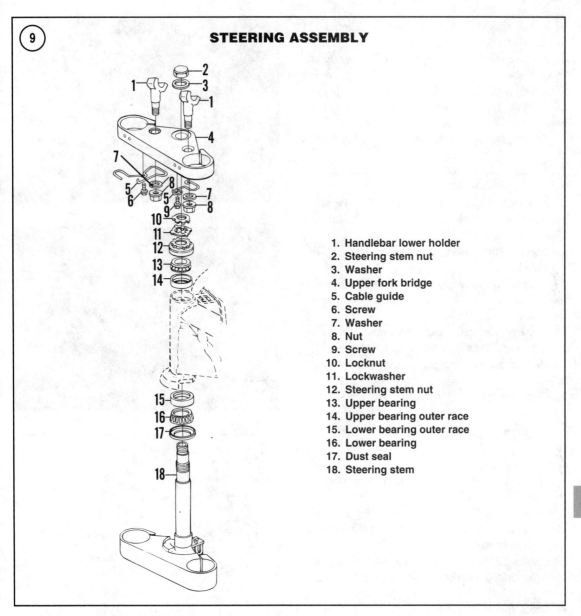

STEERING ASSEMBLY

1. Handlebar lower holder
2. Steering stem nut
3. Washer
4. Upper fork bridge
5. Cable guide
6. Screw
7. Washer
8. Nut
9. Screw
10. Locknut
11. Lockwasher
12. Steering stem nut
13. Upper bearing
14. Upper bearing outer race
15. Lower bearing outer race
16. Lower bearing
17. Dust seal
18. Steering stem

12

STEERING HEAD AND STEM

Refer to **Figure 9**.

Disassembly

1A. On GL1500C and GL1500CT models, perform the following:

    a. Remove the meters as described in Chapter Nine.

    b. Remove the headlight and headlight case assembly as described in Chapter Nine.

1B. On GL1500CF models, perform the following:

    a. Remove the front fairing and fairing bracket as described in Chapter Fifteen.

    b. Remove the combination meter as described in Chapter Nine.

2. Remove the front wheel as described in Chapter Eleven.

3. Remove the front fender as described in Chapter Fifteen.

4. Disconnect the cables from the wire guides on the upper fork bridge.

5. Remove both fork leg assemblies as described in this chapter.

6. Remove the bolts (A, **Figure 10**) securing the front brake interconnecting pipe (B, **Figure 10**) from the lower fork bridge. Move the assembly out of the way, it is not necessary to disconnect the brake hoses from the pipe.

7. Remove the handlebar assembly (A, **Figure 11**) as described in this chapter.

8. Loosen and remove the steering stem nut and washer (B, **Figure 11**).

9. Remove the upper fork bridge (C, **Figure 11**).

10. Bend down the lockwasher tabs in the locknut grooves (**Figure 12**).

11. Remove the locknut and the lockwasher. Discard the lockwasher.

12. Loosen the steering stem adjust nut. To loosen the nut, use a large drift and hammer or a spanner wrench.

13. Have an assistant hold onto the steering stem and remove the steering stem adjust nut (**Figure 13**).

14. Lower the steering stem out of the steering head.

15. Remove the upper bearing from the steering head.

Inspection

1. Clean the bearing races in the steering head and the bearings with solvent.

2. Check the welds around the steering head for cracks. If any are found, have them repaired by a frame shop or welding service.

3. Check the bearings (**Figure 14**) for pitting, scratches or discoloration indicating wear or corrosion.

4. Check the races for pitting, galling and corrosion. If any of these conditions exist, replace the races as described in this chapter.

5. Check the steering stem for cracks and check its race for damage or wear. Replace if necessary.

6. Thread the steering stem adjust nut onto the steering stem. Make sure it screws on easily with no roughness. Unscrew the steering stem adjust nut. If necessary, clean the threads in both parts.

Assembly/Steering Adjustment

1. Make sure both steering head bearing outer races are properly seated in the steering head tube.

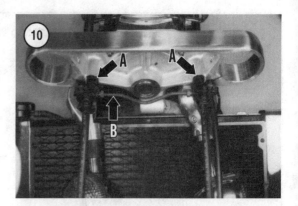

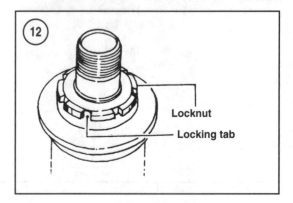

Locknut

Locking tab

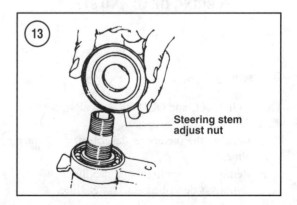

Steering stem adjust nut

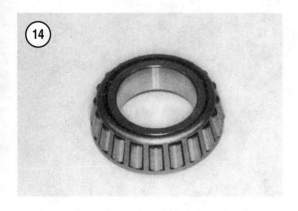

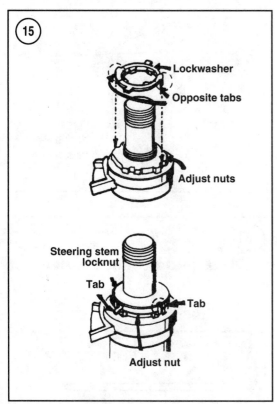

NOTE
The torque specification given in Step 6 is used to seat the steering bearings only. It is not the final steering stem adjust nut torque specification.

6. Install the steering stem adjust nut (**Figure 13**) and tighten it to 40 N•m (29 ft.-lb.).

7. Turn the steering stem from lock-to-lock 5-6 times to seat the bearings.

8. Loosen the steering stem adjust nut until it is hand-tight.

9. Tighten the steering stem adjust nut to the torque specification in **Table 4**.

10. Repeat Steps 7-9 two more times.

11. If necessary, retighten the steering stem adjust nut to the torque specification in **Table 4**. Make sure the steering stem moves smoothly, without play or binding.

12. Install a *new lockwasher* and insert two opposite tabs of the lockwasher into the notches in the steering stem adjust nut as shown in **Figure 15**.

13. Install the steering stem locknut and hand-tighten it. Hold the steering stem adjust nut and tighten the steering stem locknut within 1/4 turn (90°) to a point where two of its opposite grooves align with the two remaining lockwasher tabs. Then bend the two lockwasher tabs up and into the two steering stem locknut grooves, as shown in **Figure 15**.

NOTE
If the grooves in the locknut will not align with two of the tabs of the lockwasher, remove the locknut, turn it over and reinstall the locknut. Repeat Step 13.

14. Install the upper fork legs and the steering stem washer and nut. Tighten the nut only finger-tight at this time.

15. Temporarily install both fork tubes and secure them by tightening the lower fork tube pinch bolts (**Figure 16**), but do not tighten the top bolts at this time.

16. Tighten the steering stem nut to the torque specification in **Table 4**.

17. Install the front brake interconnecting pipe (B, **Figure 10**) and the bolts (A, **Figure 10**) onto the lower fork bridge.

18. Loosen the lower pinch bolts, then correctly install the fork, as described in this chapter.

2. Pack the bearing cavities of both roller bearings (**Figure 14**) with bearing grease. Coat the outer bearing races within the steering head with bearing grease.

3. Apply a light coat of motor oil to the threads of the steering stem and steering stem adjust nut.

4. Install the steering stem, with the lower bearing in place, into the steering head tube and hold it firmly in place.

5. Install the upper roller bearing assembly.

12

19. Install the front fender as described in Chapter Fifteen.

20. Install the front wheel as described in Chapter Eleven.

21. Check the steering head bearing pre-load as follows:

   a. Attach a spring scale to one of the fork legs, as shown in **Figure 17**.

   NOTE
   Wire harness or cable interference must be minimized to obtain an accurate measurement in the next step.

   b. Center the wheel. Pull the spring scale and note the reading on the scale when the steering stem begins to turn. The correct preload adjustment reading for left and right turns is listed in **Table 2**. If any other reading is obtained, readjust the steering adjust nut as previously described.

22. Install the handlebar as described in this chapter.

23A. On GL1500C and GL1500CT models, perform the following:

   a. Install the headlight and headlight case assembly as described in Chapter Nine.

   b. Install the meters as described in Chapter Nine.

23B. On GL1500CF models, perform the following:

   a. Install the combination meter as described in Chapter Nine.

   b. Install the front fairing bracket and fairing, as described in Chapter Fifteen.

   b. Remove the combination meter as described in Chapter Nine.

STEERING HEAD BEARING RACE

The headset and steering stem bearing races are pressed into place. Because they are easily damaged, do not remove them unless they are worn and require replacement.

The top and bottom races are not the same size. The lower race has a larger inside diameter than the upper race (**Figure 18**).

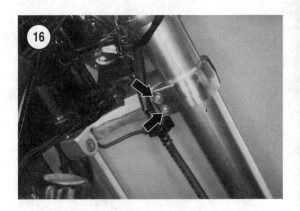

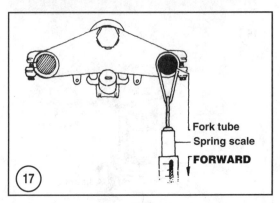

Fork tube
Spring scale
FORWARD

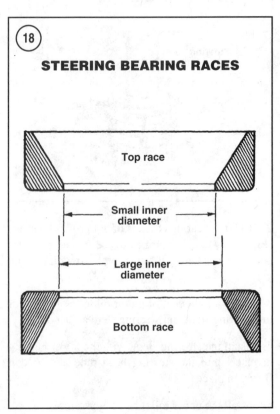

STEERING BEARING RACES

Top race

Small inner diameter

Large inner diameter

Bottom race

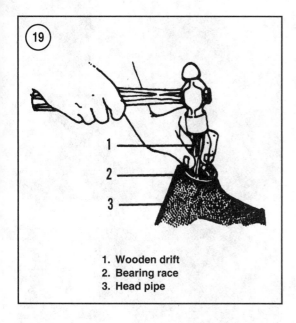

19

1
2
3

1. Wooden drift
2. Bearing race
3. Head pipe

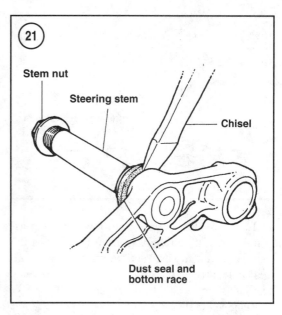

21

Stem nut

Steering stem

Chisel

Dust seal and
bottom race

20

Wooden
block

Race

Head
tube

Steering Head Bearing
Outer Race Replacement

To remove the headset race, insert a hardwood stick or soft punch into the head tube (**Figure 19**) and carefully tap the race out from the inside. After it is started, tap around the race so that neither the race nor the steering head tube is damaged.

The inside diameters of the inner races are different. The lower bearing race has a larger inside diameter than the upper.

To install the steering head bearing race, tap it in slowly with a block of wood, a suitably sized socket or a bearing driver (**Figure 20**). Make sure that the race is squarely seated in the steering head race bore before tapping it into place. Tap the race in until it is flush with the steering head surface.

Steering Stem Lower Bearing Assembly and
Dust Seal Removal/Installation

NOTE
Do not remove the steering stem lower bottom bearing race unless it is going to be replaced with a new bearing race. Do not reinstall a bearing that has been removed, as removal destroys the bearing.

1. Install the steering stem adjust nut (**Figure 21**) onto the steering stem to protect the threads during this procedure.

12

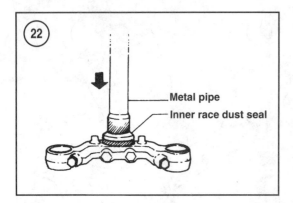

Metal pipe
Inner race dust seal

2. To remove the steering stem lower bearing assembly, carefully drive it up from the base of the steering stem with a drift and hammer; work around in a circle, driving it a little at a time. Remove the bearing assembly and the dust seal.

3. Remove the steering stem adjust nut.

4. Slide a new dust seal over the steering stem.

5. Slide the lower bearing assembly over the steering stem. Press the bearing onto the steering stem with a long piece of metal pipe that fits the inner race diameter (**Figure 22**). Make sure it is seated squarely and is all the way down.

FRONT FORK

The front suspension uses a spring-controlled, hydraulically-damped, telescopic fork.

The internal components of each fork assembly are unique. Do not intermix the components. To simplify fork service and to prevent the mixing of parts, the fork legs should be removed, serviced and installed individually.

Removal

1. Remove the front wheel as described in Chapter Eleven.

2. Remove the remaining front brake caliper as described in Chapter Fourteen.

3. Remove the front fender as described in Chapter Fifteen.

4. Loosen the upper fork tube pinch bolt (A, **Figure 23**).

5. If disassembling the fork leg, loosen (but do not remove) the fork bolt (B, **Figure 23**).

6. On GL1500C and GL1500CT models, perform the following:

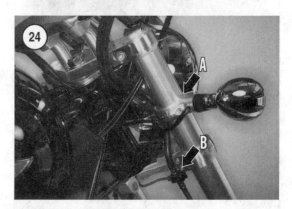

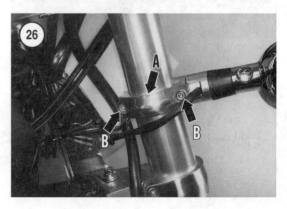

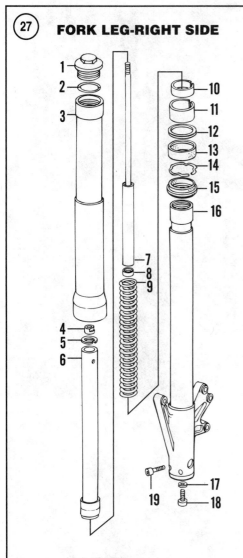

FORK LEG-RIGHT SIDE (27)

1. Fork cap
2. O-ring
3. Fork tube
4. Locknut
5. Spring seat
6. Spring collar
7. Fork damper
8. Oil lock piece
9. Fork spring
10. Slider bushing
11. Fork tube bushing
12. Backup ring
13. Oil seal
14. Stopper ring
15. Dust seal
16. Slider
17. Sealing washer
18. Allen bolt
19. Front axle clamp bolt

a. Measure the distance from the top surface of the lower fork bridge to the base of the front turn signal assembly clamp. Note this dimension for installation.

b. Remove the bolts (A, **Figure 24**) and clamp, then remove the front turn signal assembly. Reinstall the clamp and bolts onto the assembly to avoid misplacing these parts,

7. Loosen the lower fork tube pinch bolts (B, **Figure 24**).

8. Rotate the fork leg and slide it out of the fork bridge assembly.

Installation

1. Clean the upper and lower fork bridge of all dirt and other contamination.

2. Check the upper and lower fork tube pinch bolts for damage. Replace these bolts if any damage is observed.

3. Install the fork leg into the steering stem, aligning the top of the fork tube with the upper fork bridge.

4. Tighten the lower fork tube pinch bolts (B, **Figure 24**) to the torque specification in **Table 4**.

5. If loosened, tighten the fork bolt (B, **Figure 23**) to the torque specification in **Table 4**.

6. Tighten the upper fork pinch bolts (A, **Figure 23**) to the torque specification in **Table 4**.

7. On GL1500C and GL1500CT models, perform the following:

a. Install the front turn signal assembly onto the fork leg (**Figure 25**).

b. Install the clamp (A, **Figure 26**) and bolts (B, **Figure 26**) and tighten finger-tight.

c. Locate the front turn signal assembly so it is directed straight ahead and in the same position, as noted during removal.

8. Install the front wheel as described in this chapter.

9. Install the brake calipers as described in Chapter Fourteen.

10. Install the front fender as described in Chapter Fifteen.

Disassembly (Right Fork Leg)

Refer to **Figure 27** for this procedure.

1. Fabricate a fork holding fixture from a piece of heavy gauge metal. Drill the holes to match the

12

brake caliper mounting bolts holes. Install the fixture and mount it onto the base of the fork slider (A,
Figure 28).

2. Clamp the fork holding fixture in a vise (B, **Figure 28**) vertically.

3. Loosen and unscrew the fork cap (**Figure 29**)
from the fork tube.

4. Slide the fork tube down into the slider.

5. Hold onto the locknut with an open-end wrench
(A, **Figure 30**) and loosen and remove the fork cap
(B, **Figure 30**) from the fork damper.

6. Hold onto the spring collar and partially unscrew
the locknut (A, **Figure 31**) until the spring seat can
be slid out from under the locknut. Slide the spring
seat (B, **Figure 31**) out from under the locknut.

7. Slide the spring collar up and out of the fork
tube.

8. Remove the fork assembly from the vise.

9. Place the open end over a drain pan and drain the
fork oil. Slowly pump the fork slider and fork tube to
extract most of the fork oil.

10. Withdraw the fork spring from the fork assembly.

11. Reinstall the fork assembly in the vise and remove the Allen bolt and washer (**Figure 32**) from
the bottom of the slider.

12. Withdraw the fork damper and oil lock piece
from the fork assembly.

13. Carefully pry the dust seal (**Figure 33**) out of
the slider. Move the dust seal down the slider,

14. Remove the stopper ring, located above the oil
seal, from the slider.

15. There is an interference fit between the bushing
in the fork slider and the bushing on the fork tube. In
order to remove the fork tube from the slider, pull
hard on the fork tube using quick in and out strokes
(**Figure 34**). Doing this will withdraw the fork tube
bushing (A, **Figure 35**), backup ring (B) and oil seal
(C) from the slider.

16. Withdraw the fork tube from the slider.

17. Open the slider bushing slot (**Figure 36**) and
slide it off the fork tube.

18. Turn the fork tube upside down and slide off the
fork tube bushing, backup ring, oil seal, stopper ring
and dust seal (**Figure 37**) from the fork tube.

19. Inspect the components as described in this
chapter under *Inspection (Both Fork Legs)*.

Assembly (Right Leg Fork)

Refer to **Figure 27** for this procedure.

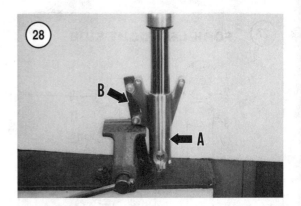

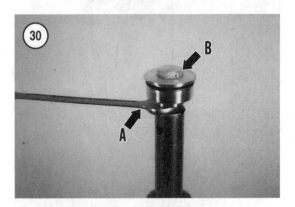

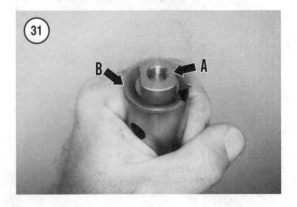

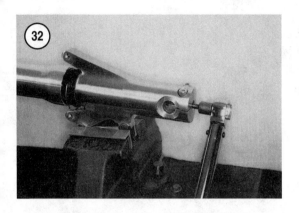

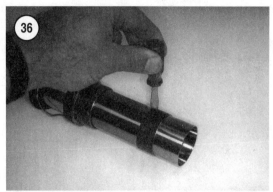

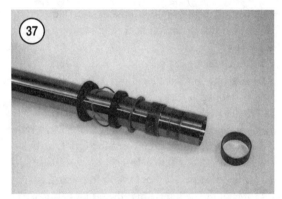

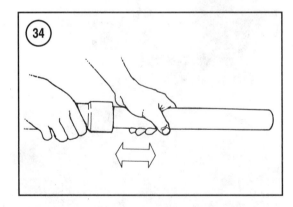

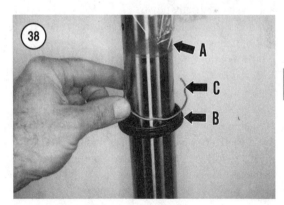

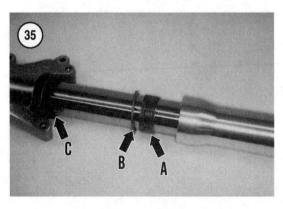

1. Coat all parts with fresh fork oil prior to installation.

2. Place a plastic bag or plastic wrap over the end of the fork slider (A, **Figure 38**). This will prevent damage to the seals when they slide over the open end of the fork slider. Apply fresh fork oil to the plastic surface.

3. Install the fork slider into a vise vertically.

4. Install the dust seal (B, **Figure 38**) and stopper ring (C, **Figure 38**) onto the fork slider.

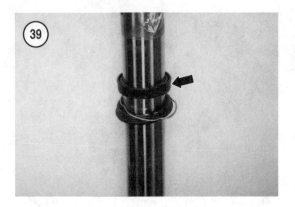

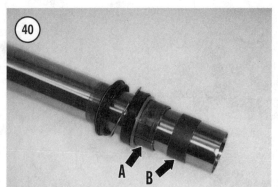

5. Position the oil seal with the marked side facing down and install the oil seal (**Figure 39**) onto the fork slider.

6. Remove the plastic from the fork slider.

7. Install the fork tube bushing (A, **Figure 40**) onto the fork slider.

8. To install the slider bushing, carefully spread the bushing open with a screwdriver, and slide it onto the fork tube, seating it between the fork tube bushing shoulders (B, **Figure 40**).

9. Apply fresh fork oil onto both bushings.

10. Install the fork tube into the slider (**Figure 41**) and push it partially down.

11. Install the oil lock piece (A, **Figure 42**) onto the end of the fork damper.

12. Install the fork damper (B, **Figure 42**) into the fork slider.

13. Apply a light coat of ThreeBond TB1432, or Loctite No. 242, to the Allen bolt threads prior to installation.

14. Install a new sealing washer and the Allen bolt into the fork slider and thread it into the fork damper.

NOTE
If the fork damper rotates while tightening the Allen bolt, temporarily install the fork spring, spring collar and fork cap. Tighten the fork cap securely. Remove the components temporarily installed.

15. Tighten the Allen bolt (**Figure 32**) to the torque specification in **Table 3**.

16. Drive the bushing (A, **Figure 43**) into the fork tube with a seal driver (B, **Figure 43**). Drive the bushing into place until it seats completely in the recess in the slider. Remove the installation tool.

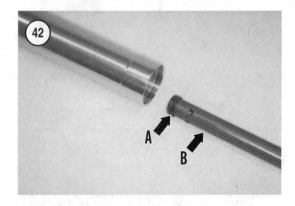

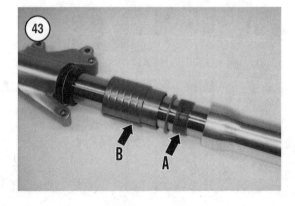

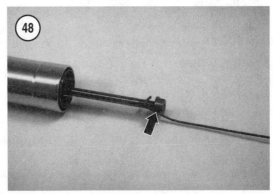

17. Use the same seal driver and drive the oil seal (**Figure 44**) into the slider until the groove in the slider can be seen above the top surface of the oil seal.

18. Install the stopper ring (**Figure 45**) into the slider groove. Make sure the clip seats in the groove completely.

19. Install the dust seal (**Figure 46**) and push it down until it seats completely (**Figure 33**).

20. Install the locknut (**Figure 47**) onto the damper rod and tighten securely.

21. Clamp the slider holding fixture in a vise (**Figure 28**) vertically.

22. To fill the fork oil and bleed the fork damper, perform the following:

a. Fill the fork with the type and quantity of fork oil specified in **Table 1**.

b. Bend the end of a metal coat hanger or stiff wire and insert it into the fork tube. Grab hold of the locknut (**Figure 48**) and pull the damper rod up.

c. Hold onto the damper rod and remove the coat hanger.

d. Slowly push the damper rod all the way down and then pull up to its limit (**Figure 49**). Repeat this 8-10 times. When the rod is first moved, it will move freely since there is no oil in the damper rod housing. As the oil fills the housing, the damper rod movement will become stiff.

23. Keep the fork assembly in the vertical position.

24. Check and adjust the fork oil level as follows:

a. Measure the fork oil level from the top of the fork (**Figure 50**). Use an oil level gauge, such as the one shown in **Figure 51**, to check and adjust the fork oil level. Otherwise, use a tape measure or ruler to set the oil level. Refer to **Table 1** for the correct oil level.

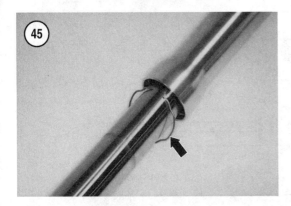

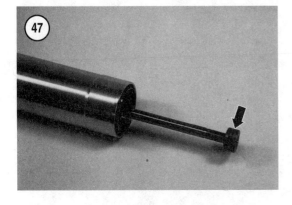

12

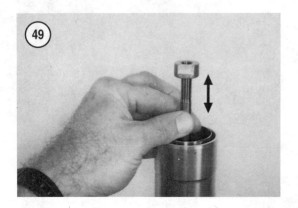

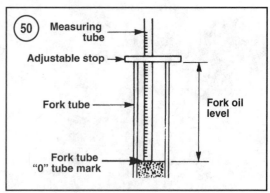

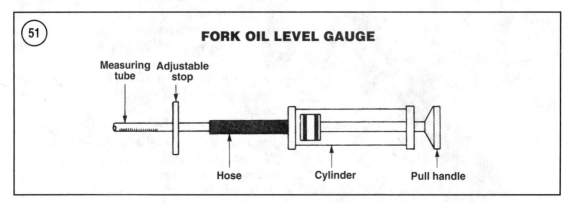

FORK OIL LEVEL GAUGE

b. If the oil level is too high, use the gauge or something similar to siphon some of the oil out of the fork tube. If the oil level is too low, pour some fork oil into the fork tube. Recheck the oil level.

25. Position the fork spring with the tapered end or close wound coils (**Figure 52**) going in last, then install the spring.

26. Position the locknut so that about half of the locknut threads are visible above the end of the damper rod.

27. Attach the same wire used in Step 22 onto the damper rod under the locknut (**Figure 48**) and secure it.

28. Correctly position the spring collar above the fork assembly and insert the wire up through the spring collar (**Figure 53**).

29. Hold onto the end of the wire and slide the spring collar down into the fork tube.

30. While holding up on the wire, press down on the spring collar and slide the spring seat under the locknut. Remove the piece of wire.

31. Tighten the locknut by hand until it bottoms on the damper rod (**Figure 54**).

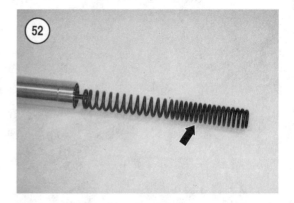

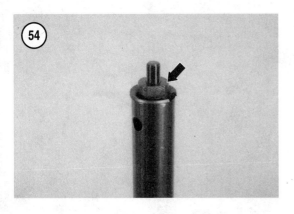

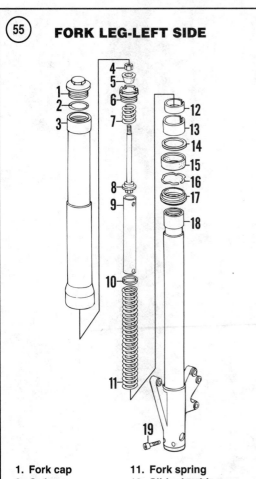

FORK LEG-LEFT SIDE

1. Fork cap
2. O-ring
3. Fork tube
4. Locknut
5. Stopper rubber
6. Inner fork bolt
7. Rebound spring
8. Rebound rod
9. Spring collar
10. Spring seat
11. Fork spring
12. Slider bushing
13. Fork tube bushing
14. Backup ring
15. Oil seal
16. Stopper ring
17. Dust seal
18. Slider
19. Front axle clamp bolt

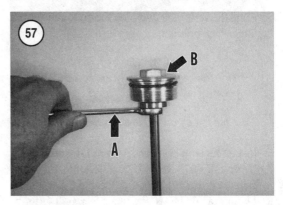

32. Install a new O-ring seal onto the fork cap and apply fork oil to the O-ring.

33. Install the fork cap onto the damper rod and thread it on until it stops.

34. Hold onto the locknut with an open-end wrench and tighten the fork cap to the torque specification in **Table 3**.

Disassembly (Left Leg Fork)

Refer to **Figure 55** for this procedure.

1. Fabricate a fork holding fixture from a piece of heavy gauge metal. Drill the holes to match the brake caliper mounting bolts holes. Install the fixture and mount it onto the base of the fork slider (A, **Figure 28**).

2. Clamp the slider holding fixture in a vise vertically (B, **Figure 28**).

3. Loosen and unscrew the fork cap (**Figure 56**) from the fork tube.

4. Place an open-end wrench on the rebound rod locknut (A, **Figure 57**) and unscrew the fork cap (B, **Figure 57**).

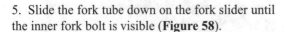

5. Slide the fork tube down on the fork slider until the inner fork bolt is visible (**Figure 58**).

WARNING
The inner fork bolt is under spring pressure. If the special Honda tool is not available, have the fork inner bolt removed by a Honda dealership.

6. Install the Honda special 44 mm locknut wrench tool (part No. 07VMA-MZ0010A) onto the inner fork bolt (**Figure 59**). Properly mesh the teeth of the tool with the notches in the inner fork bolt (**Figure 60**).

7. Slowly unscrew the bolt (A, **Figure 61**) and allow the fork spring to push the rebound assembly up (B, **Figure 61**) out of the fork assembly.

8. Remove the special tool from the inner fork bolt and remove the rebound rod assembly (**Figure 62**).

9. Remove the spring collar and the spring seat.

10. Remove the fork assembly from the vise.

11. Place the open end over a drain pan and drain the fork oil. Slowly pump the fork slider and fork tube to extract most of the fork oil.

12. Carefully pry the dust seal (**Figure 63**) out of the slider. Move the dust seal down the slider,

13. Remove the stopper ring, located above the oil seal, from the slider.

14. There is an interference fit between the bushing in the fork slider and the bushing on the fork tube. In order to remove the fork tube from the slider, pull hard on the fork tube using quick in and out strokes (**Figure 64**). Doing this will withdraw the fork tube bushing (A, **Figure 65**), backup ring (B) and oil seal (C) from the slider.

15. Withdraw the fork tube from the slider (D, **Figure 65**).

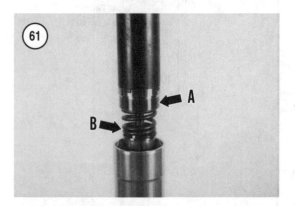

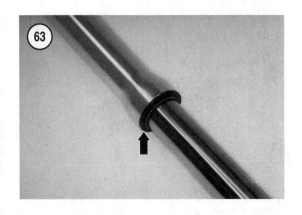

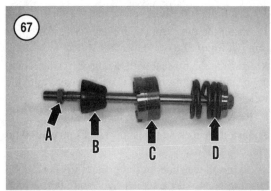

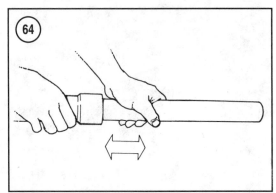

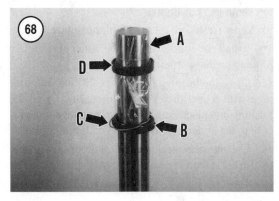

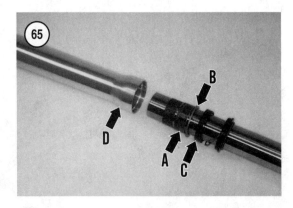

16. Open the slider bushing slot (**Figure 66**) and slide it off the fork tube.

17. Turn the fork tube upside down and slide off the fork tube bushing, backup ring, oil seal, stopper ring and dust seal (**Figure 65**) from the fork tube.

18. If necessary, disassemble the rebound rod assembly as follows:

a. Unscrew the locknut (A, **Figure 67**) from the rebound rod.

b. Slide off the stopper rubber (B), inner fork bolt (C) and rebound spring (D) from the rebound rod.

19. Inspect the components as described in this chapter under *Inspection (Both Fork Legs)*.

Assembly (Left Fork)

1. Coat all parts with fresh fork oil prior to installation.

2. Place a plastic bag or plastic wrap over the end of the fork slider (A, **Figure 68**). This will prevent damage to the seals when they slide over the open end of the fork slider. Apply fresh fork oil to the plastic surface.

3. Install the fork slider into a vise vertically.

4. Install the dust seal (B, **Figure 68**) and stopper ring (C, **Figure 68**) onto the fork slider.

5. Position the oil seal with the marked side facing down and install the oil seal (D, **Figure 68**) onto the fork slider.

6. Remove the plastic from the fork slider.

7. Install the fork tube bushing (A, **Figure 69**) onto the fork slider.

8. To install the slider bushing, carefully spread the bushing open with a screwdriver and slide it onto the fork tube, seating it between the fork tube bushing shoulders (B, **Figure 69**).

9. Apply fresh fork oil onto both bushings.

10. Install the fork tube into the slider (D, **Figure 65**) and push it partially down.

11. Drive the bushing (A, **Figure 70**) into the fork tube with a seal driver (B, **Figure 70**). Drive the bushing into place until it seats completely in the recess in the slider. Remove the installation tool.

12. Use the same seal driver and drive the oil seal (**Figure 71**) into the slider until the groove in the slider can be seen above the top surface of the oil seal.

13. Install the stopper ring into the slider groove. Make sure the clip seats in the groove completely.

14. Install the dust seal and push it down until it seats completely (**Figure 63**).

15. Fill the fork with type and quantity of fork oil specified in **Table 1**.

16. Keep the fork assembly in the vertical position.

17. Check and adjust the fork oil level as follows:

 a. Measure the fork oil level from the top of the fork (**Figure 50**). Use an oil level gauge, such as the one shown in **Figure 51**, to check and adjust the fork oil level. Otherwise, use a tape measure or ruler to set the oil level. Refer to **Table 1** for the correct oil level.

 b. If the oil level is too high, use the gauge or something similar to siphon some of the oil out of the fork tube. If the oil level is too low, pour some fork oil into the fork tube. Recheck the oil level.

18. Position the fork spring with the closely wound coils going in last, then install the spring (**Figure 72**).

19. Install the spring seat (**Figure 73**) and the spring collar (**Figure 74**) into the fork tube.

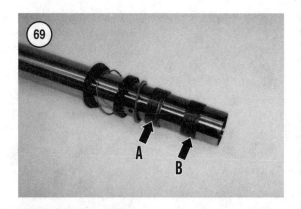

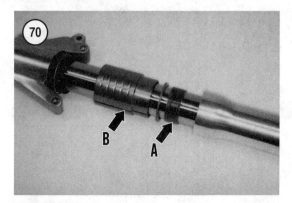

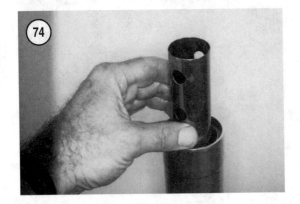

NOTE
If the rebound rod assembly was dis-assembled, screw the locknut down until it stops.

20. Install the rebound rod assembly (**Figure 75**) into the fork tube.

21. Install the same special tool used during disassembly onto the inner fork bolt (**Figure 59**). Properly mesh the teeth of the special tool with the notches in the inner fork bolt (A, **Figure 61**).

CAUTION
Do not cross-thread the inner fork bolt while starting it into the fork tube.

22. Push down on the special tool and thread the inner fork bolt into the fork tube (**Figure 59**). Tighten it to the torque specification in **Table 3**. Remove the special tool.

23. Push the rubber stopper down against the inner fork bolt.

24. Install a new O-ring seal (**Figure 76**) onto the fork cap and apply fork oil to the O-ring.

25. Install the fork cap onto the rebound rod and thread it on until it stops.

26. Hold onto the locknut with an open end wrench and tighten the fork cap (**Figure 77**) to the torque specification in **Table 3**.

27. Pull the fork tube up and install the fork cap into the fork tube. Tighten the fork cap to the torque specification in **Table 3**.

Inspection (Both Fork Legs)

1. Thoroughly clean all parts in solvent and dry them. Check the fork tube for signs of wear or scratches.

12

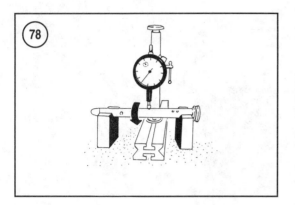

2. Check the damper rod for straightness with a dial indicator and V-blocks (**Figure 78**). Replace the rod if the runout is excessive (no runout specification available).

NOTE
Use the specification provided for fork tube runout as a guideline for dampner rod runout.

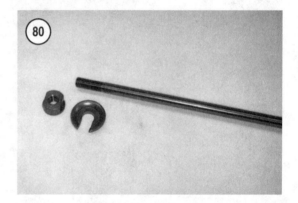

3. On the right fork leg assembly, inspect the following:
    a. Carefully check the spring collar and piston rings for wear or damage (**Figure 79**). Replace the piston ring, if necessary.
    b. Check the fork damper rod threads, the locknut threads and the spring seat (**Figure 80**) for damage.
    c. Check the threads in the base of the fork damper (A, **Figure 81**) for damage.
    d. Make sure the oil holes (B, **Figure 81**) are clear. Clean out with solvent if necessary and dry with compressed air.
    e. Move the rod up and down within the fork damper. It must move freely without binding.

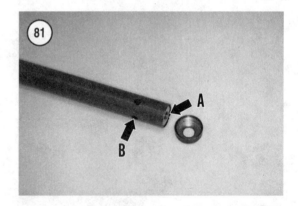

4. On the left fork leg assembly, inspect the following:
    a. Check the spring collar and spring seat for wear (**Figure 82**).
    b. Check all of the components of the rebound rod (**Figure 67**) for wear or damage.

5. Check the lower slider (A, **Figure 83**) for dents or exterior damage that may cause the upper fork tube to hang up during riding. Replace if necessary.

6. Check the upper fork tube (B, **Figure 83**) for straightness with a dial indicator and V-blocks. Replace the fork tube if the runout exceeds the wear limit in **Table 3**.

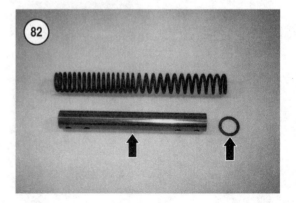

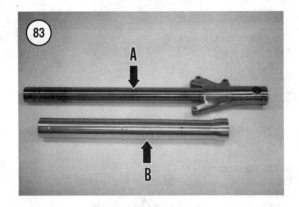

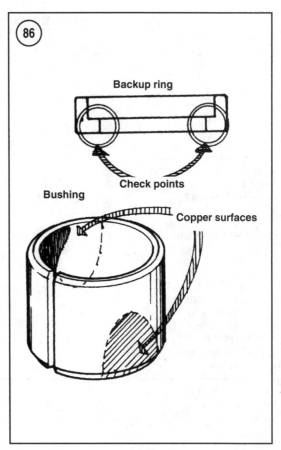

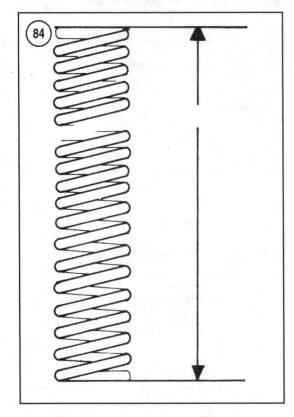

7. Check the lower slider for dents or exterior damage that may cause the upper fork tube to hang up during riding. Replace if necessary. Check the stopper ring groove in the slider for cracks or damage.

8. Measure the uncompressed length of the fork spring as shown in **Figure 84**. Replace the spring if it has sagged to the service limit dimensions in **Table 2**.

9. Inspect the slider and fork tube bushings (**Figure 85**). If either is scratched or scored, it must be replaced. If the Teflon coating is worn off so that the copper base material is showing on approximately 3/4 of the total surface, the bushing must be replaced. Also check for distortion on the check points of the backup ring; replace as necessary. Refer to **Figure 86**.

10. Inspect the backup ring for severe wear or damage.

11. Any parts that are worn or damaged should be replaced. Simply cleaning and reinstalling unserviceable components will not improve performance of the front suspension.

12

Table 1 FRONT SUSPENSION GENERAL SPECIFICATIONS

Front suspension	Telescopic fork (inverted)
Front fork travel	110 mm (4.3 in.)
Caster angle	
GL1500C, GL1500CT	32° 12 minutes
GL1500CF	32° 10 minutes
Trail	152 mm (6.0 in.)
Fork oil	
Type	Pro Honda Suspension Fluid SS-8
Quantity	
GL1500C, GL1500CT	
Right fork leg	667.5-672.5 cc
	(22.62-22.78 U.S. oz./23.51-23.69 Imp. oz.)
Left fork leg	741.5-746.5 cc
	(25.12-25.28 U.S. oz./26.11-26.29 Imp. oz.)
GL1500CF	
Right fork leg	666.5-671.5 cc
	(22.52-22.68 U.S. oz./23.41-23.59 Imp. oz.)
Left fork leg	731.5-736.5 cc
	(24.72-24.88 U.S. oz./25.71-25.89 Imp. oz.)
Fork oil level	
GL1500C, GL1500CT	
Right fork leg	135 mm (5.3 in.)
Left fork leg	142 mm (5.6 in.)
GL1500CF	
Right fork leg	136 mm (5.4 in.)
Left fork leg	148 mm (5.8 in.)

Table 2 FRONT SUSPENSION SERVICE SPECIFICATIONS

	Specification mm (in.)	Wear limit mm (in.)
Fork spring free length	344.2 (13.55)	337 (13.3)
Fork tube runout limit	–	0.20 (0.008)
Fork spring installation direction	Tapered end facing up	
Steering stem preload		
GL1500C and GL1500CT	0.8-1.2 kgf (1.8-2.6 lb.f)	
GL1500CF	0.5-1.0 kgf (1.1-2.2 lb.f)	

Table 3 FRONT SUSPENSION TORQUE SPECIFICATIONS

	N•m	in.-lb.	ft.-lb.
Handlebar			
Upper holder bolts	29	–	21
Lower holder nuts	64	–	47
Steering stem nut			
GL1500C, GL1500CT	103	–	76
GL1500CF	100	–	74

(continued)

Table 3 FRONT SUSPENSION TORQUE SPECIFICATIONS (continued)

	N•m	in.-lb.	ft.-lb.
Steering stem adjust nut			
GL1500C, GL1500CT	17	–	12
GL1500CF	13	115	–
Fork cap			
Bolt	34	–	25
Locknut	20	–	15
Left side fork inner bolt	98	–	72
Fork tube pinch bolts			
Upper	55	41	
Lower	25	18	
Damper rod Allen bolt*	20	15	

* Apply ThreeBond TB1342 or Loctite 242 (blue) to the fastener threads prior to installation.

12

CHAPTER THIRTEEN

REAR SUSPENSION

This chapter includes repair and replacement procedures for the rear suspension components.

Tire changing, tire repair and wheel balancing are covered in Chapter Eleven.

Table 1 and **Table 2** are located at the end of this chapter.

SHOCK ABSORBERS

Removal/Installation

Removal and installation of the rear shocks is easier if done separately. The remaining unit will support the rear of the motorcycle and maintain the correct relationship between the top and bottom shock mounts.

1. Park the motorcycle on level ground on the sidestand.
2. Remove the seat as described in Chapter Fifteen.
3. On models so equipped, remove the saddlebags as described in Chapter Fifteen.
4. Remove the exhaust system as described in Chapter Four.
5. On the left side, remove the upper bolt and washer and the lower special bolt (**Figure 1**) securing the shock absorber to the frame and final drive unit.
6. On the right side, remove the upper and lower shock absorber mounting bolts and washers (**Figure 2**).
7. Remove the shock absorber from the frame.
8. Install by reversing these removal steps. Tighten the bolts to the torque specifications in **Table 2**.

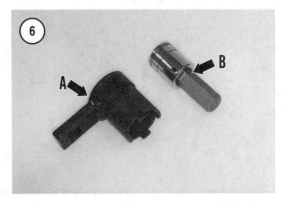

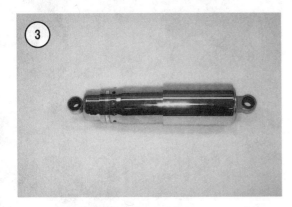

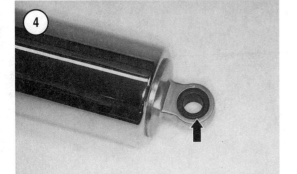

Inspection

The shock absorbers are not serviceable with the exception of replacing the upper and lower bushings.

1. Inspect the shock absorber for external damage and fluid leakage (**Figure 3**). Replace the shock absorber if leakage is noted.

2. Replace the bushings if the upper (**Figure 4**) and lower (**Figure 5**) bushings show wear or damage.

SWING ARM

The condition of the swing arm roller bearings can greatly affect handling performance; if worn parts are not replaced, they can produce erratic and dangerous handling. Common symptoms are wheel hop, pulling to one side during acceleration and pulling to the other side during braking.

A special Honda tool is required to loosen and tighten the left side pivot bolt locknut (Honda part No. 07908-4690003) (A, **Figure 6**). This tool is required for proper and safe installation of the swing arm. If this locknut is not tightened to the correct

13

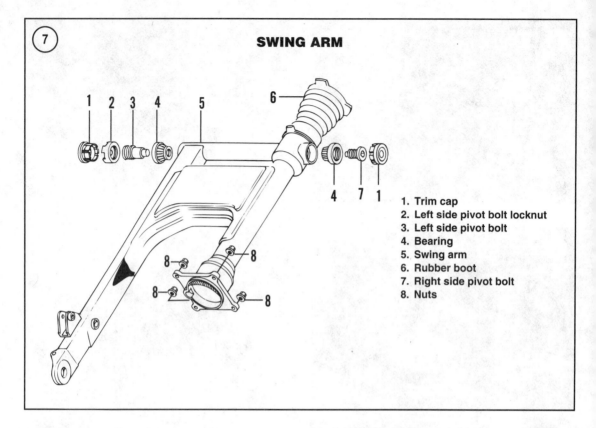

SWING ARM

1. Trim cap
2. Left side pivot bolt locknut
3. Left side pivot bolt
4. Bearing
5. Swing arm
6. Rubber boot
7. Right side pivot bolt
8. Nuts

torque, it may allow the left side pivot bolt to work loose. This could result in the swing arm working free from the left side of the frame, causing a serious accident. One additional tool is the 17 mm Allen hex socket (B, **Figure 6**).

Refer to **Figure 7** for these procedures.

Removal

1. Remove the exhaust system as described in Chapter Four.
2. Park the motorcycle on level ground and on a lift. Refer to *Motorcycle Lift* in Chapter One.
3. Remove the rear wheel as described in Chapter Eleven.
4. Remove the final drive unit and drive shaft as described in Chapter Eleven.
5. Remove the right- and left-side foot peg brackets as described in Chapter Fifteen.
6. Support the swing arm in its normal position and remove both shock absorbers as described in this chapter.
7. Remove the bolt and the rear brake master cylinder reservoir cover (A, **Figure 8**).

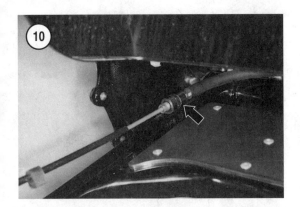

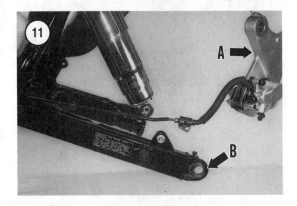

8. On the left side of the swing arm, perform the following:

    a. Remove the bolt securing the rear caliper brake hose to the end of the swing arm (**Figure 9**).

    b. Unhook the brake hose from the clamp on the swing arm (**Figure 10**).

    c. Tie the caliper and brake hose up to the frame with a bungee cord or piece of wire (A, **Figure 11**).

9. Remove the bolt and rear master cylinder chrome cover (B, **Figure 8**).

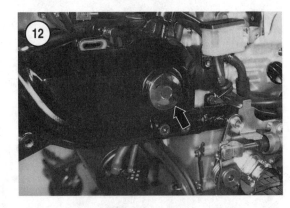

10. Grasp the rear end of the swing arm (B, **Figure 11**) and try to move it from side to side in a horizontal arc. There should be no noticeable side play. If play is evident and the pivot adjusting bolt is tightened correctly, the bearings may be worn or damaged.

11. Remove the trim cap (**Figure 12**) from the pivot bolt on both sides.

12. Loosen the left side locknut with the Honda locknut wrench (part No. 07908-4690003) (**Figure 13**). Remove the locknut (**Figure 14**).

13

CAUTION
Make sure the swing arm is supported prior to removing the pivot bolts. As soon as one of the pivot bolts is removed, the swing arm will be free and may fall out of the frame.

13. Remove the left and right pivot bolts with a 17 mm Allen hex socket (**Figure 15**).

14. Pull back on the swing arm and remove it from the frame. The drive shaft's universal joint will come out with the swing arm.

Bearing Inspection

NOTE
If the original bearings are going to be reused, they must be reinstalled in their original positions. Identify each bearing as it is removed so it can be installed in the same location.

1. Remove the left and right side bearings from the swing arm (**Figure 16**).

2. Pull the outer dust seal (**Figure 17**) off each bearing. Replace the dust seals if they are worn or damaged. Replace the oil seals if the motorcycle is a high-mileage vehicle.

3. Inspect the bearings for excessive wear or damage. Inspect the bearing races in the swing arm for scoring, wear or damage.

4. Each side of the swing arm is equipped with a grease retainer plate (**Figure 18**). Replace the grease retainer plate if it is loose or damaged.

5. Replace worn or damaged parts. If the bearings are damaged, replace the bearing, race and grease retainer plate as a set.

6. If necessary, replace the swing arm bearing assembly as described under *Bearing Replacement* in this chapter.

7. If the bearing assembly is acceptable, perform the following prior to swing arm assembly:

    a. Pack the outer dust seals with grease.

    b. Clean the bearings (**Figure 19**) with an aerosol type bearing degreaser and allow them to dry. Then pack each bearing thoroughly with grease. Make sure to work the grease between the bearing rollers and races thoroughly.

    c. Clean the bearing races in the swing arm with the bearing degreaser and wipe dry. Then apply grease to the face of each bearing.

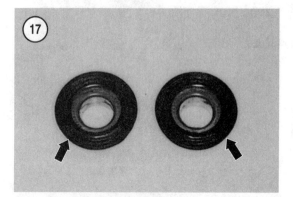

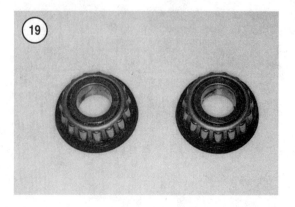

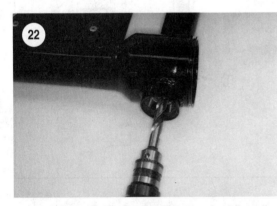

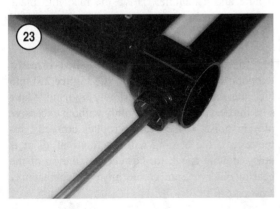

   d. Install an outer dust seal (**Figure 17**) onto each bearing.

   e. Install the bearings/dust seals (**Figure 20**) into the swing arm in their original locations.

8. Install the swing arm as described in this chapter.

Bearing Replacement

The swing arm is equipped with a roller bearing at each side. The inner race and roller bearing can be easily removed without force. The bearing outer race is pressed in place and must be removed with special tools. The outer race will be damaged during removal; do not remove it unless the bearing is going to be replaced.

Each side of the swing arm is equipped with a grease retainer plate (**Figure 18**).

The grease retainer plates are removed at the same time as the outer bearing race.

The special tools required to replace the swing arm bearing assembly are as follows:

   a. Bearing attachment (32 × 35 mm): Honda part No. 07746-0010100.

   b. Slide hammer shaft: commercially available from motorcycle and automotive parts houses.

   c. Driver handle: Honda part No. 07749-00100000.

   d. Bearing driver attachment (37 × 40 mm): Honda part No. 07746-0010200.

1. Remove the swing arm as described in this chapter.

2. Remove the dust seal and bearing assembly from each side of the swing arm (**Figure 16**).

3. Remove the rubber joint boot (A, **Figure 21**) and universal joint (B, **Figure 21**) from the right side of the swing arm.

4. Secure the swing arm in a vise with soft jaws.

5. Remove the left side bearing race and grease retainer plate (**Figure 18**) as follows:

   a. Drill a ½ inch hole in the right side grease retainer plate (**Figure 22**).

   b. Insert the slide hammer shaft partially through the drilled hole in the right side grease retainer plate (**Figure 23**).

   c. Working within the universal joint open area of the swing arm, install the 32 × 35 mm attachment onto the end of the slide hammer shaft and secure it with the nut (**Figure 24**). Tighten the nut securely.

13

d. Move the slide hammer shaft and attachment through the swing arm and against the left side grease retainer.

e. Tap on the end of the slide hammer shaft with a hammer and remove the bearing outer race and grease retainer plate from the left side. Discard both parts.

f. Pull the slide hammer shaft back toward the right side and remove the nut and the attachment. Withdraw the slide hammer shaft from the hole in the right side grease retainer plate.

6. Remove the right side bearing race and grease retainer plate (**Figure 18**) as follows:

a. Install the 32 × 35 mm attachment onto the end of the slide hammer shaft and secure it with the nut (**Figure 24**). Tighten the nut securely.

b. Insert the slide hammer shaft and attachment assembly in through the left side of the swing arm and against the right side grease retainer plate.

c. Tap on the end of the slide hammer shaft with a hammer and remove the bearing outer race and grease retainer plate from the right side. Discard both parts.

d. Withdraw the slide hammer shaft assembly from the left side.

7. Thoroughly clean out the inside of the swing arm with solvent and dry it with compressed air.

8. Apply a light coating of waterproof grease to all parts prior to installation.

NOTE
Either the right or left bearing grease retainer and bearing outer race can be installed first.

9. Install the grease retainer plate into the swing arm as shown in A, **Figure 25**.

WARNING
Never reinstall a bearing outer race that has been removed. During removal it becomes distorted and will no longer be aligned with the bearing. If reinstalled, it will damage the roller bearing assembly and create an unsafe riding condition.

10. To install the new roller bearing outer race, place the bearing driver outer over the bearing outer race and drive the race into place with the driver

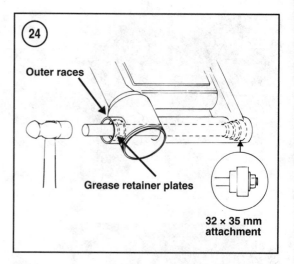

Outer races

Grease retainer plates

32 × 35 mm attachment

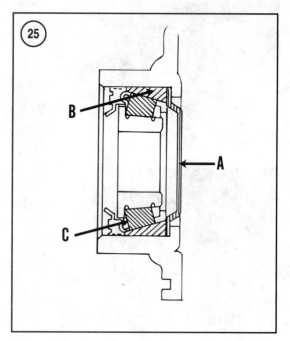

B

A

C

handle and a hammer. Drive the race into place slowly and squarely. Make sure it is properly seated (B, **Figure 25**).

11. To ensure the outer race was installed correctly, temporarily install the bearing (C, **Figure 25**) into the outer race and rotate it slowly by hand. Make sure the bearing rotates smoothly without excessive play or noise. If the bearing rotates correctly, remove it. If the bearing will not rotate at all or is noisy, double-check for correct installation of the bearing outer race and correct any problem that may exist.

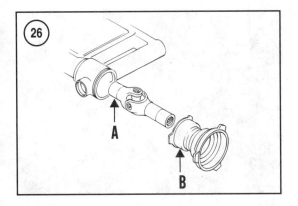

12. Repeat Steps 9-11 for the other grease retainer plate and the bearing outer race.

13. Install a new roller bearing and dust seal into each end of the swing arm.

14. Position the universal joint with the short end (A, **Figure 26**) going in first. Install the universal joint and the rubber joint boot (B, **Figure 26**) onto the right side of the swing arm.

15. Install the swing arm as described in this chapter.

Swing Arm Inspection

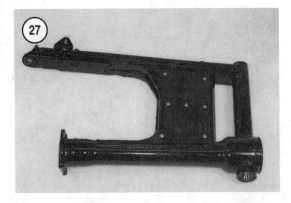

1. Clean the swing arm, pivot bolts and the locknut in solvent and thoroughly dry it with compressed air.

2. If the bearing inner races are not going to be replaced, apply engine oil to prevent rust.

3. Check the welded sections of the swing arm for cracks or fractures (**Figure 27**). If any are evident have the swing arm repaired or replace it.

4. Inspect the pivot bolts (**Figure 28**). Check the threads for wear or damage. Repair minimal thread damage with the correct metric die. Replace the pivot bolt(s) if thread damage is severe.

Installation

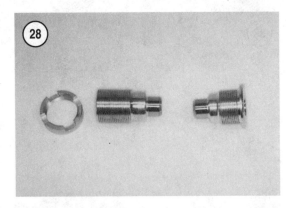

> *NOTE*
> *If the sidestand mounting bolts were removed, install them prior to installing the swing arm. These bolts are not accessible after the swing arm is installed.*

1. If removed, position the universal joint with the short end (A, **Figure 26**) going in first. Install the universal joint and the rubber joint boot (B, **Figure 26**) onto the right side of the swing arm.

2. Apply molybdenum disulfide grease to the splines on the output gear shaft (**Figure 29**).

3. If removed, install the bearing and dust seal assembly (**Figure 30**) onto each side of the swing arm pivot area.

4. Position the swing arm into the mounting area of the frame. Align the pivot bolt holes in the swing arm with the holes in the frame.

5. Apply a light coating of grease to the inner tip of both the right and left side pivot bolts.

6. Install the right side (**Figure 31**) and left side (**Figure 32**) pivot bolts, making sure the ends of

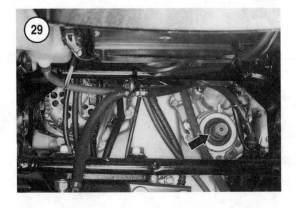

13

both pivot bolts are inside the inner bearing race. Tighten the bolts finger-tight at this time.

7. Lift the swing arm up and temporarily install the left side shock absorber. This will make it easier to align the universal joint with the output shaft.

8. Remove the driveshaft from the final drive unit. Wipe off all grease from the universal joint end splines. If the grease is left in place, the drive shaft may stick to the universal joint in Step 9 and pull the universal joint off the output shaft.

9. Insert the driveshaft into the swing arm (**Figure 33**) and mesh it with the universal joint splines.

10. Slowly rotate the drive shaft while pushing in on it until the universal joint splines are aligned with the output shaft splines. Push the universal joint all the way onto the output shaft until it bottoms. Hold onto the universal joint through the rubber boot and slowly pull the drive shaft out of the universal joint. Make sure the universal joint remains on the output shaft. Withdraw the driveshaft from the swing arm.

11. Pull the joint boot up and onto the output gear case (**Figure 34**). Make sure it is properly seated to keep out dirt and moisture.

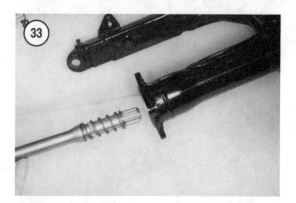

12. Install the drive shaft back into the final drive unit. Apply grease to the universal joint end splines of the driveshaft.

CAUTION
Prior to tightening the right side pivot bolt, make sure the left side pivot bolt is backed out and is not tight against the swing arm pivot area. If the left side pivot bolt is on tight, it will affect the tightening of the right side pivot bolt and lead to an incorrect tightening torque.

13. Make sure the swing arm is properly located in the frame and then tighten the right side pivot bolt (**Figure 35**) to the torque specifications in **Table 2**.

14. Tighten the left side pivot bolt (**Figure 36**) to the torque specification in **Table 2**.

15. Remove the left side shock absorber.

16. Move the swing arm up and down several times to make sure all components are properly seated.

17. Retighten the left side pivot bolt to the torque specification in **Table 2**.

18. On the left-hand side, perform the following:

    a. Install the pivot bolt locknut (**Figure 14**).

    b. Hold onto the left pivot bolt with a 17 mm Allen wrench (A, **Figure 37**) to make sure the pivot bolt does not move while tightening the locknut.

NOTE
*Position the torque wrench on the locknut wrench at a 90° angle, as shown in **Figure 38**. By doing this, the locknut can be tightened to the specified torque value without having to calculate the effect of the extension of the locknut wrench. If the torque wrench is positioned straight out from the locknut wrench, it will add a torque advantage and the torque value must be calculated as described in Chapter One.*

    c. Use the Honda swing arm pivot locknut wrench (part No. 07908-4690003) and a torque wrench (B, **Figure 37**) as follows. Tighten the locknut to the torque specification in **Table 2**.

19. Once again, move the swing arm up and down several times to make sure all components are properly seated.

20. Install the trim cap (**Figure 12**) over the pivot bolt on both sides.

21. Untie the caliper and brake hose from the frame (A, **Figure 11**) and carefully lower it.

22. On the left side of the swing arm, perform the following:

    a. Reposition the brake hose into the clamp on the swing arm (**Figure 10**)

    b. Move the brake hose into position on the swing arm and install the bolt (**Figure 9**). Tighten the bolt securely.

13

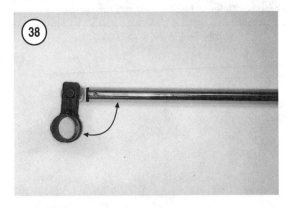

23. Install the rear master cylinder and reservoir chrome covers, then tighten the bolts securely.

24. Install both shock absorbers as described in this chapter.

25. Install the right and left side foot peg brackets as described in Chapter Fifteen.

26. Install the final drive unit and drive shaft as described in Chapter Eleven.

27. Install the rear wheel as described in Chapter Eleven.

28. Install the exhaust system as described in Chapter Four.

Table 1   REAR SUSPENSION GENERAL SPECIFICATIONS

Rear suspension	Swing arm/shock absorber
Rear suspension travel	120 mm (4.7 in.)
Shock absorber	Nitrogen gas filled damper

Table 2 REAR SUSPENSION TIGHTENING TORQUES

	N•m	ft.-lb.
Swing arm		
Left side pivot bolt		
GL1500C, GL1500CT	19	14
GL1500CF	22	16
Left side pivot locknut *		
GL1500C, GL1500CT	113	83
GL1500CF	98	72
Right side pivot bolt		
GL1500C, GL1500CT	103	76
GL1500CF	98	72
Left side shock absorber		
Upper bolt	26	19
Lower bolt	34	25
Right side shock absorber		
Upper bolt	26	19
Lower bolt	23	17
Damper holder plate screws	20	15

* A special tool is required to obtain an accurate torque reading. Refer to text for tool and procedure.

CHAPTER FOURTEEN

BRAKES

The brake system consists of dual discs on the front wheel and a single disc brake on the rear. This chapter describes repair and replacement procedures for all brake components.

Table 1 and **Table 2** are located at the end of the chapter.

DISC BRAKES

The front disc brakes are actuated by hydraulic fluid and controlled by a hand lever at the front master cylinder. The rear disc brake is actuated by hydraulic fluid and controlled by the foot pedal at the rear master cylinder. As the brake pads wear, the brake fluid level drops in the reservoir and automatically adjusts for wear.

When working on hydraulic brake systems, it is necessary that the work area and all tools be absolutely clean. Any tiny particles of debris in the caliper assembly or the master cylinder can damage the components. Also, sharp tools must not be used inside a caliper or on a piston. If there is any doubt about the ability to carry out any service on the brake system correctly and safely, refer the job to a Honda dealership or brake specialist.

> *WARNING*
> *Whenever working on the brake system, do **not** inhale brake dust. It may contain asbestos, which can cause lung injury and cancer. Wear a face mask that meets the Occupational Safety and Health Administration*

(OSHA) requirements for trapping asbestos particles, and wash both hands and forearms thoroughly after completing the work.

Consider the following when servicing the disc brakes:

1. Disc brake components rarely require disassembly, so do not disassemble them unless necessary.

2. Do not allow any brake fluid to contact any plastic parts or painted surfaces, as damage will result. If spilled, wash the area thoroughly with soap and water and rinse with clean water.

3. Always keep the reservoir covers installed to prevent dust and moisture from entering and contaminating the brake fluid.

> *NOTE*
> *When adding brake fluid to either brake master cylinder reservoir, poke a small hole into the seal of the brake fluid container next to the edge of the pour spout. This will help control the flow of brake fluid and will help eliminate fluid spillage, especially while adding fluid to the small reservoirs.*

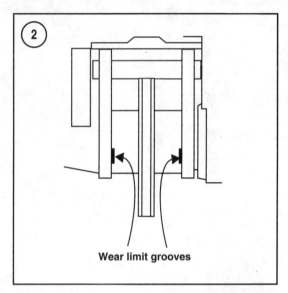

Wear limit grooves

4. When adding brake fluid, use only brake fluid that is clearly marked DOT 4 from a sealed container. Always use the same brand name; do not intermix fluids, as different brands may not be compatible. Brake fluid absorbs moisture, which greatly reduces its ability to perform correctly. Purchase brake fluid in small containers and discard any small leftover quantities. Do not store brake fluid with less than 1/4 of fluid remaining, as this small amount will absorb the moisture within the container.

> *CAUTION*
> *Do not intermix silicone-based (DOT5) brake fluid, as it will cause brake system failure.*

> *CAUTION*
> *Never reuse brake fluid; contaminated brake fluid can cause brake failure. Dispose of used brake fluid according to local or EPA toxic waste regulations.*

5. Use new brake fluid or isopropyl alcohol to clean and lubricate new parts for the brake system. Never clean any internal brake components with any petroleum-based solvents, as this will cause rubber parts to swell, permanently damaging them.

6. Whenever any part of the system is loosened, the brake system is considered to be open and must be bled to remove all air from the system. If the brake feels spongy, this usually means there is air in the system. Bleed the brake system as described under *Bleeding the System* in this chapter.

FRONT BRAKE PAD REPLACEMENT

There is no recommended mileage interval for replacing the brake pads. Pad wear depends greatly on riding habits and conditions. Periodically inspect the pads for wear and replace them when the wear limit grooves (**Figure 1** and **Figure 2**) reach the edge of the brake disc. To maintain an even brake pressure on the disc, always replace both pads in both calipers at the same time.

CAUTION
*Inspect the pads more often when the wear limit grooves (**Figure 2**) approach the disc. On some pads, the wear line is very close to the metal backing plate. If pad wear is uneven, the backing plate may come in contact with the disc and cause damage.*

1. Review the information listed under *Disc Brakes* in this chapter.

2. To prevent the accidental application of the front brake lever with the caliper assembly removed, place a spacer between the front brake lever and the handgrip. Hold the spacer in place with tape or a large rubber band.

3. When new pads are installed in the caliper, the master cylinder brake fluid level will rise as the caliper pistons are repositioned. Perform the following:

   a. Clean the top of the master cylinder of all debris. Remove the cover (**Figure 3**), set plate, diaphragm and float from the master cylinder.

   b. Use a syringe to draw some of the brake fluid from the reservoir to prevent any fluid overflow in the following step.

   c. Constantly check the reservoir to make sure brake fluid does not overflow. Remove brake fluid, if necessary, before it overflows.

NOTE
The pistons should move freely. If there is evidence of them sticking in the cylinder, the caliper should be removed and serviced as described in this chapter.

CAUTION
Do not allow the master cylinder reservoir to overflow when performing Step 4. Brake fluid will damage most surfaces it contacts.

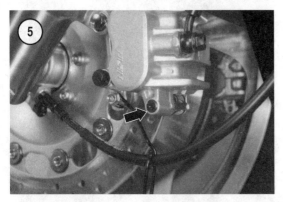

14

4. Hold the caliper body (from the outside) and push it toward the brake disc (**Figure 4**). This will push the pistons back into the caliper to make room for the new thicker brake pads.

5. Remove the pad pin plug (**Figure 5**), then loosen and remove the pad pin (**Figure 6**).

NOTE
If the brake pads are to be reused, handle them carefully to prevent oil and grease contamination.

6. Carefully slide both brake pads out from the caliper (**Figure 7**).

7. Account for the pad spring (**Figure 8**); it may or may not remain in the caliper.

8. Inspect the brake pads (**Figure 9**) for uneven wear, damage or contamination. Both brake pads should show approximately the same amount of wear. If the pads are wearing unevenly, the caliper is probably not sliding correctly on the support bracket. Replace both brake pads as a set.

9. Carefully remove any rust or corrosion from the disc.

10. If removed, install the pad spring (**Figure 10**) into the caliper prior to installing the brake pads (**Figure 8**).

11. Position the brake pads with the pad pin hole (**Figure 11**) at the bottom of the caliper and install both brake pads into the caliper (**Figure 12**). Index the upper end of the brake pad into the retainer in the caliper assembly. Refer to **Figure 13** and **Figure 14**.

12. Push both brake pads in against the pad spring and insert the pad pin (**Figure 15**) through the caliper and both brake pads. Tighten the pad pin (**Figure 6**) to the torque specification in **Table 2**.

13. Install the pad pin plug (**Figure 5**) and tighten it to the torque specification in **Table 2**.

14. Roll the motorcycle back and forth and activate the brake lever until it is firm and the pads are seated.

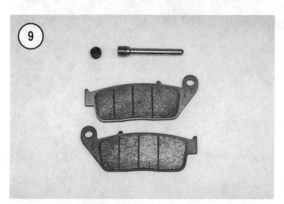

WARNING
Use DOT 4 brake fluid from a sealed
container. Other types may vaporize
and cause brake failure. Always use
the same brand name; do not intermix
silicone-based (DOT 5) brake fluid,

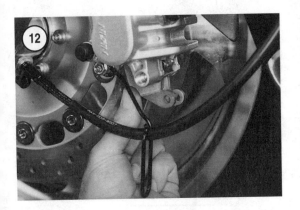

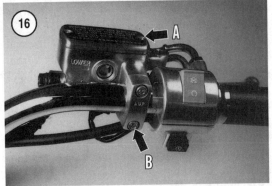

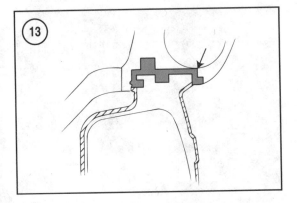

as it can cause brake component dam-age and lead to brake system failure.

15. Refill the master cylinder reservoir, if neces-sary, to maintain the correct fluid level. Install the float, diaphragm, set plate and cover. Install and tighten the cover screws securely.

WARNING
Do not ride the motorcycle until the brakes are operating correctly with full hydraulic advantage. If neces-sary, bleed the brake as described in this chapter.

16. Break the pads in gradually for the first 2-3 days of riding by using only light pressure as much as possible. Immediate hard application will glaze the new pads and greatly reduce their effectiveness.

FRONT MASTER CYLINDER

Removal/Installation

CAUTION
Cover all surrounding areas with a heavy cloth or plastic tarp to protect them from accidental brake fluid spills. Wash brake fluid off any sur-faces immediately, as it will destroy the finish. Use soapy water and rinse completely.

1. Remove the master cylinder cover (A, **Figure 16**), set plate, diaphragm and float.
2. Use a syringe to draw all of the brake fluid out of the master cylinder reservoir.
3. Disconnect the brake light switch wires (A, **Figure 17**).

14

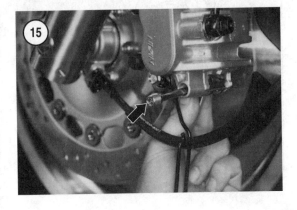

4. Remove the banjo bolt (B, **Figure 17**) securing the brake hose to the master cylinder.

5. Remove the brake hose and place the loose end into a reclosable plastic bag to prevent debris from entering. Tie the loose end of the hose to the handlebar.

6. Remove the clamping bolts and the holder (B, **Figure 16**) securing the master cylinder to the handlebar and remove the master cylinder.

7. Install by reversing these removal steps while noting the following:

   a. Position the master cylinder onto the handlebar.

   b. Position the clamp with the UP mark facing up. Align the master cylinder holder with the index mark on the handlebar (**Figure 18**). Tighten the upper bolt first, then the lower bolt to the torque specification in **Table 2**.

   c. Install the brake hose onto the master cylinder. Make sure to place a *new* sealing washer on each side of the fitting and install the banjo bolt (B, **Figure 17**). Position the projection on the hose fitting against the stopper on the master cylinder (**Figure 19**).

   d. Tighten the banjo bolt to the torque specification in **Table 2**.

   e. Bleed the brake as described under *Bleeding the System* in this chapter.

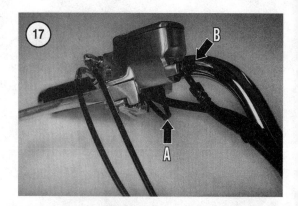

Disassembly

Refer to **Figure 20**.

1. Remove the master cylinder as described in this chapter.

2. Remove the screw securing the brake light switch (**Figure 21**) and remove it from the bottom of the master cylinder.

3. Remove the brake lever nut and pivot bolt (**Figure 22**) and remove the brake lever.

4. Remove the piston boot (**Figure 23**) from the area where the hand lever actuates the piston assembly.

5. If still in place, remove the screw securing the top cover and remove the cover, set plate, diaphragm and float.

6. Support the master cylinder securely (**Figure 24**) and compress the piston assembly with a wooden dowel. Then remove the circlip (**Figure 25**) from the piston bore and allow the piston assembly to extend out slowly.

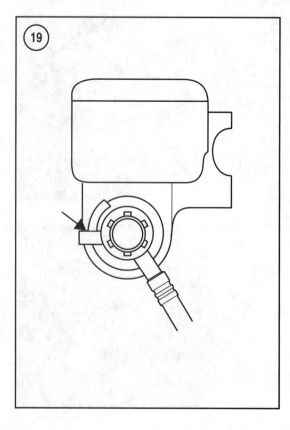

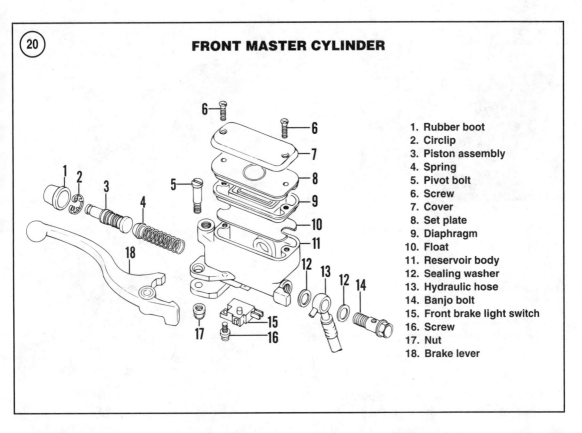

FRONT MASTER CYLINDER

1. Rubber boot
2. Circlip
3. Piston assembly
4. Spring
5. Pivot bolt
6. Screw
7. Cover
8. Set plate
9. Diaphragm
10. Float
11. Reservoir body
12. Sealing washer
13. Hydraulic hose
14. Banjo bolt
15. Front brake light switch
16. Screw
17. Nut
18. Brake lever

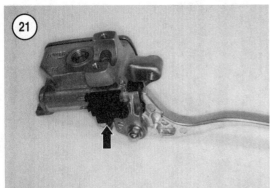

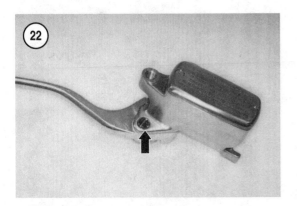

14

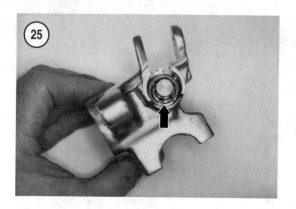

7. Remove the piston assembly from the master cylinder (**Figure 26**).

Inspection

1. Clean all parts in fresh DOT 4 brake fluid. Place the master cylinder components on a clean lint-free cloth after cleaning them.

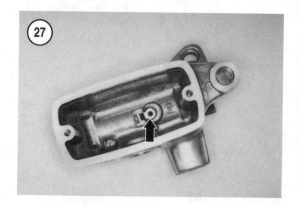

NOTE ·
*Do not lose the protector (**Figure 27**)*
in the master cylinder reservoir.

2. Check the piston assembly (**Figure 28**) for the following defects:
   a. Sagged or damaged spring (A).
   b. Primary (B) and secondary (C) cups that are damaged, swollen or show signs of deterioration. Do not attempt to remove the secondary cup (C) from the piston, as this will damage the cup.
   c. Damaged or scored piston. Also check the end of the piston (D) for wear or damage caused by the brake lever.
   d. Measure the piston outer diameter with a micrometer, as shown in **Figure 29**. Replace the piston if the diameter is less than the service limit in **Table 1**.
   e. The piston, piston cups and spring must be replaced as a set.

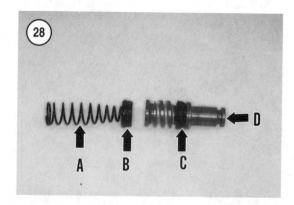

3. Check the master cylinder bore (**Figure 30**) for severe wear, cracks or scoring.

4. Measure the cylinder bore inner diameter with a bore gauge (**Figure 31**). Replace the master cylinder if the bore exceeds the service limit in **Table 1**.

5. Make sure the passages in the fluid reservoir are clear.

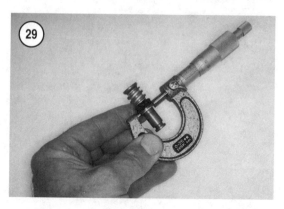

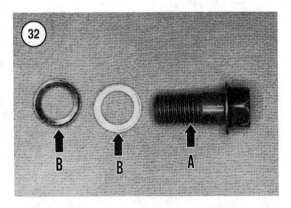

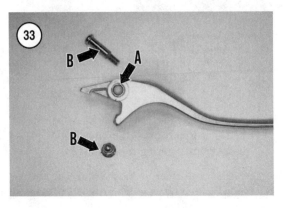

6. Check the master cylinder cover, set plate, diaphragm and float for damage.

7. Check the banjo bolt threads (A, **Figure 32**). If the threads are damaged or partially stripped, replace the master cylinder. Flush the banjo bolt with clean brake fluid.

8. Discard the sealing washers (B, **Figure 32**); always install new ones.

9. Check the brake lever pivot hole (A, **Figure 33**) for excessive wear or damage. Replace the lever if required.

10. Check the pivot bolt and nut (B, **Figure 33**) for wear and thread damage. Replace if necessary.

11. Replace all worn or damaged parts.

Assembly

Refer to **Figure 20** for this procedure.

1. Soak new cups in fresh DOT 4 brake fluid for at least 15 minutes to make them pliable. Coat the master cylinder bore with brake fluid.

2. The spring (A, **Figure 28**) has a small and large end. Install the small end of the spring toward the piston.

CAUTION
When installing the piston assembly, do not allow the cups to turn inside out; they will be damaged and allow brake fluid to leak within the cylinder bore.

3. Support the master cylinder so that the piston assembly faces up (**Figure 24**).

4. Install the piston assembly into the master cylinder in the order shown in **Figure 26**.

5. Compress the piston assembly and install the circlip (**Figure 25**) into the master cylinder bore groove. Release the piston and make sure the circlip is securely seated in the groove.

6. Install the piston boot so that it seats in the piston groove completely (**Figure 34**).

7. Install the brake lever as follows:

   a. Apply a light coating of silicone break grease to the brake lever pivot bolt, pivot bolt holes in the master cylinder and to the end of the piston.

   b. Install the brake lever (A, **Figure 35**) and secure it with the pivot bolt and nut (B, **Figure 35**). Tighten the nut securely, making sure the brake lever pivots smoothly with no sign of

14

binding and that it contacts the piston end correctly (**Figure 36**).

8. Install the switch (**Figure 21**) and secure it with the mounting screw.

9. Install the master cylinder as described in this chapter.

FRONT CALIPER

Removal

Refer to **Figure 37**.

It is not necessary to remove the front wheel to remove the caliper assemblies.

CAUTION
Cover the front fender with a heavy cloth or plastic tarp to protect it from accidental brake fluid spills. Wash brake fluid off any painted surfaces immediately, as it will destroy the finish. Use soapy water and rinse completely.

1A. If the caliper is *not* going to be disassembled for service, perform the following:

a. Place a container under the brake line at the caliper. Remove the banjo bolt and sealing washers (A, **Figure 38**) securing the brake line to the caliper assembly.

b. Remove the brake line and place the loose end into a reclosable plastic bag to prevent debris from entering. Tie the loose end of the hose to the front fork or handlebar.

c. Remove the caliper brake pads and pad spring as described in this chapter.

d. Remove the bolts (B, **Figure 38**) securing the caliper to the front fork. Remove the front caliper and place it in a reclosable plastic bag.

1B. If the caliper is going to be disassembled for service, perform the following:

NOTE
By performing substeps 2b and 2c, compressed air may not be necessary to removal the pistons during caliper disassembly.

a. Remove the brake pads as described in this chapter.

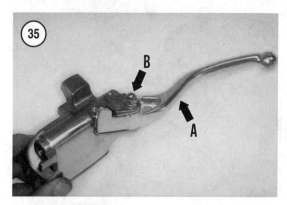

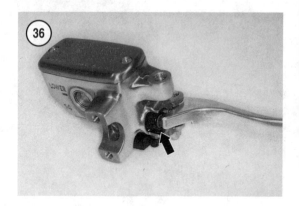

CAUTION
Do not allow the pistons to travel out far enough to contact the brake disc. If this occurs, the pistons may damage the disc during caliper removal.

b. Slowly apply the front brake lever to push the pistons partially out of the caliper assembly to ease removal during caliper service.

c. Place a container under the brake line at the caliper. Remove the banjo bolt and sealing

FRONT BRAKE CALIPER

1. Retainer
2. Pin boot
3. Piston
4. Dust seal
5. Piston seal
6. Caliper pin bolt
7. Caliper body
8. Bleed screw and cap
9. Pad pin
10. Pad pin cap
11. Outboard brake pad
12. Pad spring
13. Bracket pin boot
14. Inboard brake pad
15. Bracket pin bolt
16. Mounting bracket

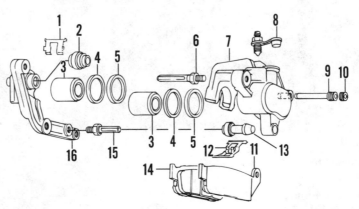

iper and take it to the workbench for disassembly and service.

2. If necessary, repeat for the other caliper assembly.

Installation

1. Carefully install the caliper assembly onto the disc.

2. Install *new* caliper mounting bolts (B, **Figure 38**) and tighten them to the torque specification in **Table 2**.

3. Install the brake hose onto the caliper with a *new* sealing washer on each side of the fitting. Install the banjo bolt and position the hose fitting against the stopper on the caliper (**Figure 39**). Tighten the banjo bolt to the torque specification in **Table 2**.

NOTE
The following illustrations show the caliper removed for clarity.

4. Install the brake pads and the pad spring (**Figure 40**) described in this chapter. Make sure the pads are seated correctly against the pad retainer (**Figure 41**).

5. If removed, repeat for the other caliper assembly.

6. Bleed the brake as described in this chapter.

7. With the front wheel off the ground, spin the front wheel and activate the brake lever until it is firm and pads are seated.

WARNING
Do not ride the motorcycle until the brakes are operating correctly with full hydraulic advantage.

washers (A, **Figure 38**) securing the brake line to the caliper assembly.

d. Remove the brake line and place the loose end into a reclosable plastic bag. Tie the loose end of the hose to the front fork or handlebar.

e. Remove the bolts (B, **Figure 38**) securing the caliper to the front fork. Remove the front cal-

14

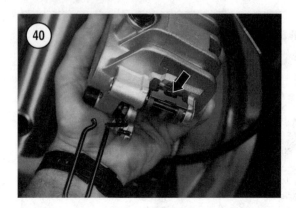

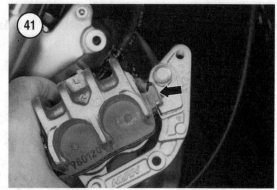

Disassembly

Refer to **Figure 37**.

1. Remove the brake caliper as described in this chapter.

2. Unscrew and remove the bleed screw and cap (**Figure 42**).

3. Remove the pad spring (**Figure 43**).

4. Pull the bracket (**Figure 44**) off of the caliper.

5. If the pistons were not partially removed during caliper removal, perform the following:

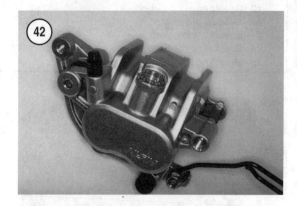

> *NOTE*
> *Compressed air is required for piston removal.*

> *WARNING*
> *Keep all fingers and hands out of the caliper bores when removing the pistons in the following steps. Wear shop gloves and apply compressed air gradually. Do **not** use high-pressure air or place the air hose nozzle directly against the hydraulic line fitting inlet in the caliper body. Hold the air nozzle away from the inlet, allowing some of the air to escape.*

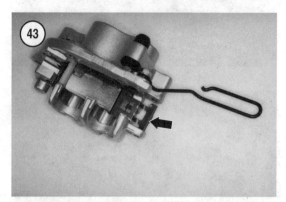

a. Pad the pistons with a piece of wood and shop cloth (A, **Figure 45**).

b. Perform this step close to a workbench top.

c. Apply the air pressure in short spurts to the hydraulic fluid passageway (B, **Figure 45**) and force out the pistons. Use a service station air hose if an air compressor is not available.

6. Remove the pistons from the caliper body (**Figure 46**).

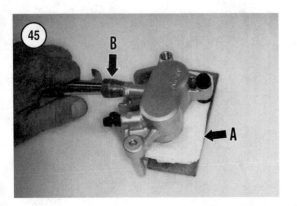

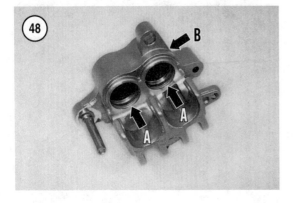

> *CAUTION*
> *In the following step, do not use a sharp tool to remove the dust seals from the caliper body. Do not damage the cylinder bore surfaces.*

7. Use a piece of plastic or wood and carefully push the dust and pistons seals (**Figure 47**) out of their grooves and discard all seals.

Inspection

> *CAUTION*
> *Never use petroleum-based solvents of any kind on the brake system's internal components. Any residual solvent remaining within the caliper component will cause the new seals to swell and distort.*

1. Clean the caliper parts (except brake pads) in isopropyl alcohol or fresh DOT 4 brake fluid. Wear eye protection and dry with compressed air. Then place the parts on a lint-free cloth while performing the following inspection procedure.

2. Make sure the fluid passageway in the base of the piston bore is clear.

3. Inspect the seal grooves (A, **Figure 48**) in both caliper bores for damage. If damaged, replace the caliper assembly.

4. Check the caliper bores for cracks, deep scoring or excessive wear. Measure the cylinder bores with a bore gauge (**Figure 49**). Replace the caliper housing if the bore is worn to the service limit in **Table 1**.

14

5. Inspect the banjo bolt threaded hole in the caliper body. If it is worn or damaged, attempt to repair it with a thread tap or replace the caliper assembly.

6. Inspect the bleed screw threaded hole in the caliper body. If worn or damaged, clean out with a thread tap or replace the caliper assembly

7. Inspect the bleed screw. Make sure it is clean. Apply compressed air to the opening and make sure it is clear. Install the bleed screw and tighten to the torque specification in **Table 2**.

8. Inspect the caliper body (B, **Figure 48**) for damage. Replace the caliper assembly if necessary.

9. Check the caliper pistons for scoring, excessive wear or rust. Then measure the piston outer diameter with a micrometer (**Figure 50**). Replace the piston if the outer diameter is less than the service limit in **Table 1**.

10. Check the caliper bracket (A, **Figure 51**) for cracks or other damage.

11. Check the rubber boots on the caliper housing and caliper bracket. Replace the boots if they are damaged or starting to deteriorate.

12. Check the pad retainer spring (B, **Figure 51**) on the caliper bracket for damage.

13. Replace all worn or damaged parts prior to assembly.

Assembly

1. Coat the new piston seals and dust seals with silicone grease (for brakes).

2. Coat the pistons and piston bores with clean DOT 4 brake fluid.

3. Carefully install the new piston seals (A, **Figure 47**) into the lower bore grooves. Make sure the seals are properly seated in their respective grooves.

4. Carefully install the new dust seals (B, **Figure 47**) into the upper bore grooves. Make sure the seals are properly seated in their respective grooves.

5. Position the pistons with the open end (**Figure 52**) facing out toward the brake pads. Install the pistons and push them in until they bottom (**Figure 53**).

6. Apply high-temperature silicone grease (for brakes) onto the caliper bracket pins and boots (**Figure 54**).

7. Install the retainer onto the bracket as shown in **Figure 55**.

8. Install the pad spring (**Figure 43**). Make sure it is seated correctly.

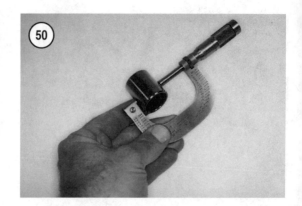

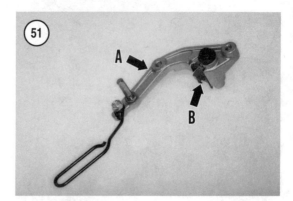

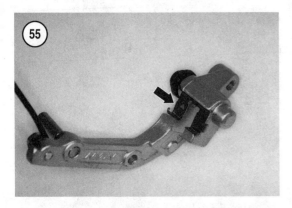

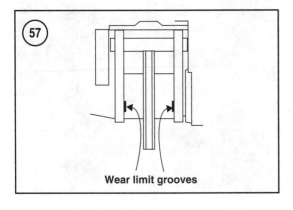

Wear limit grooves

REAR BRAKE PAD REPLACEMENT

There is no recommended mileage interval for replacing the brake pads. Pad wear depends greatly on riding habits and conditions. Periodically inspect the pads for wear and replace them when the wear limit grooves (**Figure 56** and **Figure 57**) reach the edge of the brake disc. To maintain an even brake pressure on the disc, always replace both pads in both calipers at the same time.

> *CAUTION*
> *Inspect the pads more often when the wear limit grooves (**Figure 57**) approach the disc. On some pads, the wear line is very close to the metal backing plate. If pad wear is uneven, the backing plate may come in contact with the disc and cause damage.*

1. Read the prior information listed under *Disc Brakes* in this chapter.

> *CAUTION*
> *If the rear brake pedal is inadvertently applied, the caliper pistons will be forced out of the cylinders in the caliper assemblies. If this occurs, the caliper assembly will have to be disassembled to reseat the pistons.*

2. To prevent the accidental application of the rear brake pedal with the caliper assembly removed, tie the rear brake pedal up to the front right side footpeg with a tie strap.

3. On models so equipped, remove the left side saddlebag as described in Chapter Fifteen.

4. When new pads are installed in the caliper, the master cylinder brake fluid level will rise as the caliper pistons are repositioned. Perform the following:

   a. Remove the bolt (A, **Figure 58**) securing the master cylinder cover (B, **Figure 58**) and remove the cover.

   b. Clean the top of the master cylinder of all debris. Remove the cover (**Figure 59**), set plate, diaphragm and float from the master cylinder.

   c. Use a syringe to draw out some of the brake fluid from the reservoir to prevent the fluid from overflowing in the following step.

   d. Constantly check the reservoir to make sure brake fluid does not overflow. Remove brake fluid, if necessary, before it overflows.

14

NOTE
The pistons should move freely. If there is evidence of them sticking in the cylinder, the caliper should be removed and serviced as described in this chapter.

CAUTION
Do not allow the master cylinder reservoir to overflow when performing Step 5. Brake fluid will damage most surfaces it contacts.

5. Hold the caliper body (from the outside) and push it toward the brake disc (**Figure 60**). This will push the pistons back into the caliper to make room for the new brake pads.

6. Remove the pad pin plug (**Figure 61**) and loosen and remove the pad pin (**Figure 62**).

7. Carefully slide the brake pads out from the caliper (A, **Figure 63**).

8. Clean the pad recess and the ends of the pistons with a soft brush. Do not use solvent, a wire brush or any hard tool that would damage the cylinders or pistons.

9. Carefully remove any rust or corrosion from the disc.

10. Account for the pad spring (**Figure 64**) which is now loose. It may or may not remain in the caliper.

11. Inspect the brake pads (**Figure 65**) for uneven wear, damage or contamination. Both brake pads should show approximately the same amount of wear. If the pads are wearing unevenly, the caliper is probably not sliding correctly on the support bracket. Replace both brake pads as a set.

12. If removed, install the pad spring (**Figure 64**) into the caliper prior to installing the brake pads.

13. Position the brake pads with the pad pin hole (B, **Figure 63**) at the bottom of the caliper and install both brake pads into the caliper (A, **Figure 63**).

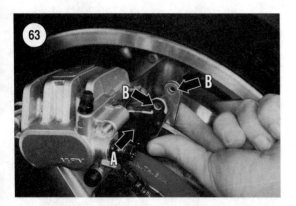

63

64

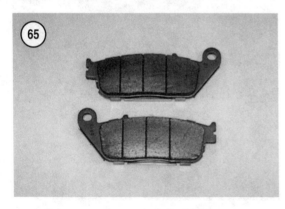

65

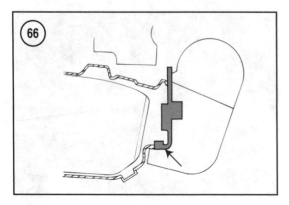

66

Index the forward end of the brake pad into the retainer in the caliper assembly (**Figure 66**).

14. Push both brake pads in against the pad spring and insert the pad pin through the caliper and both brake pads. Tighten the pad pin (**Figure 62**) to the torque specification in **Table 2**.

15. Install the pad pin plug (**Figure 61**) and tighten to the torque specification in **Table 2**.

16. Roll the motorcycle back and forth and apply the brake pedal until it is firm and the pads are seated.

> *WARNING*
> *Use DOT 4 brake fluid from a sealed container. Other types may vaporize and cause brake failure. Always use the same brand name; do not intermix silicone-based (DOT 5) brake fluid, as it can cause brake component damage leading to brake system failure.*

REAR MASTER CYLINDER AND RESERVOIR

Removal/Installation

1. Review the information listed under *Disc Brakes* in this chapter.

2. On models so equipped, remove the left side saddlebag as described in Chapter Fifteen.

3. Drain the fluid from the rear brake system as follows:

    a. Remove the bolt (A, **Figure 58**) securing the master cylinder reservoir cover (B, **Figure 58**) and remove the cover.

    b. Clean the top of the reservoir of all debris. Remove the cover (**Figure 59**), set plate, diaphragm and float from the reservoir.

    c. At the rear caliper, remove the bleed screw cover and loosen the bleed screw (**Figure 67**).

    d. Attach a bleed hose to the bleed screw and place the loose end into a container.

    e. Pump the brake pedal and force the brake fluid out of the rear brake system.

    f. Disconnect the bleed hose and tighten the bleed screw

> *WARNING*
> *Dispose of the old brake fluid according to local or EPA toxic waste regulations.*

Never reuse brake fluid, as contaminated brake fluid may cause brake failure.

14

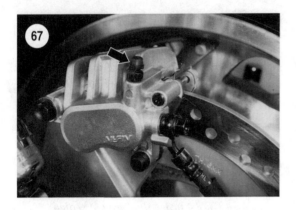

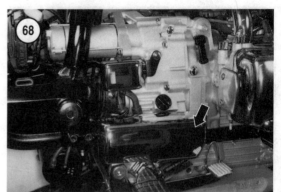

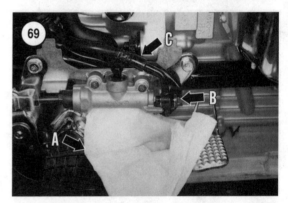

g. Temporarily install the float, diaphragm, set plate and cover onto the reservoir.

4. Remove the bolt and the rear master cylinder chrome cover (**Figure 68**).

5. Place a shop cloth under the master cylinder (A, **Figure 69**) to catch any residual brake fluid in the system.

6. Remove the banjo bolt and sealing washers (B, **Figure 69**) and disconnect the rear brake hose (C, **Figure 69**) from the front outlet of the master cylinder. Plug the hose to prevent residual brake fluid from spilling out and place it in a reclosable plastic bag.

7. Remove the snap ring (**Figure 70**) securing the reservoir hose to the master cylinder.

8. Remove the cotter pin securing the pivot pin to the master cylinder pushrod. Then remove the pivot pin and separate the brake rod clevis from the brake arm (**Figure 71**).

9. Disconnect the reservoir hose (A, **Figure 72**) from the master cylinder. Plug the hose to prevent residual brake fluid from spilling out.

10. Remove the two master cylinder mounting bolts (B, **Figure 72**) and remove the master cylinder from the frame. Drain all brake fluid remaining in the reservoir and discard it.

11. To remove the reservoir, remove the bolt (**Figure 73**) securing the reservoir to the frame.

12. Installation is the reverse of these steps, plus the following.

   a. If removed, install the rear master chrome cover mounting bracket (**Figure 74**) and align the bolt holes.

   b. Install the rear master cylinder mounting bolts (B, **Figure 72**) and tighten them to the torque specification in **Table 2**.

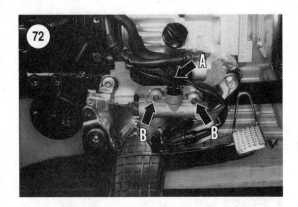

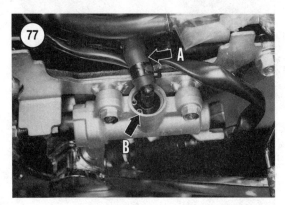

c. Install the rear brake hose onto the front fitting on the master cylinder with a *new* sealing washer on each side of the fitting. Install the banjo bolt and position the hose fitting against the stopper on the master cylinder (**Figure 75**). Tighten the banjo bolt to the torque specification in **Table 2**.

d. Install a new O-ring seal (**Figure 76**) into the master cylinder.

e. Install the reservoir hose (A, **Figure 77**) onto the master cylinder. Make sure the circlip seats correctly in the master cylinder groove (B, **Figure 77**).

f. Secure the brake rod clevis with a new cotter pin. Install the cotter pin through the clevis rod; bend the cotter pin arms over completely.

g. Bleed the rear brake as described in this chapter.

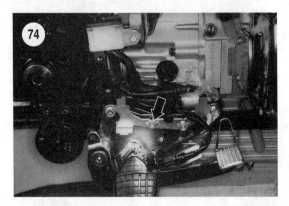

WARNING
Do not ride the motorcycle until the brakes are operating properly.

Disassembly

Refer to **Figure 78** for the following procedures.

14

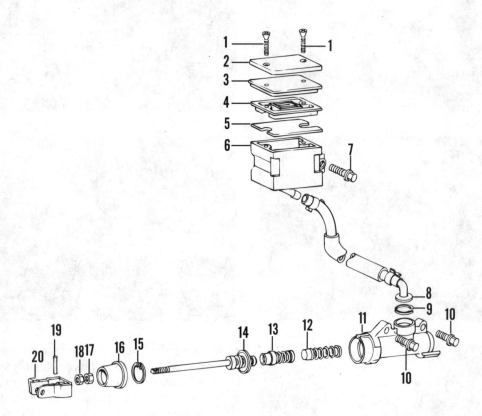

REAR MASTER CYLINDER AND REMOTE RESERVOIR

1. Screw
2. Cover
3. Set plate
4. Diaphragm
5. Float
6. Remote reservoir
7. Bolt
8. Reservoir hose
9. Circlip
10. Bolt
11. Master cylinder body
12. Spring
13. Piston
14. Pushrod
15. Circlip
16. Rubber boot
17. Adjust nut
18. Locknut
19. Pin
20. Clevis

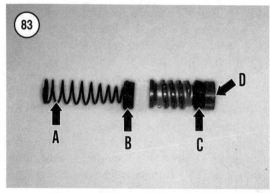

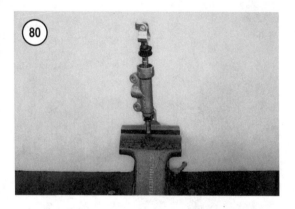

1. Pull the rubber boot (**Figure 79**) out of the master cylinder.

2. Support the master cylinder in a vise with soft jaws so that the pushrod faces up (**Figure 80**).

3. Compress the pushrod slightly and remove the circlip (**Figure 81**) from the master cylinder bore groove.

4. Remove the pushrod and piston assemblies (**Figure 82**).

Inspection

> *CAUTION*
> *Never use petroleum-based solvents of any kind on the brake system's internal components. Any residual solvent remaining within the components will cause the new seals to swell and distort.*

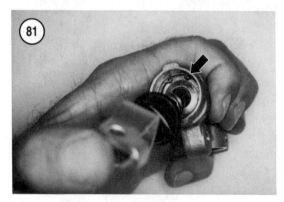

1. Clean the master cylinder parts in isopropyl alcohol or fresh DOT 4 brake fluid. Wear eye protection and dry with compressed air directing the air flow and residual fluid spray away. Then place the parts on a lint-free cloth while performing the following inspection procedure.

2. Check the piston assembly (**Figure 83**) for the following defects:

   a. Sagged or damaged spring (A).

   b. Primary (B) and secondary (C) cups that are damaged, swollen or show signs of deterioration. Do not attempt to remove the secondary cup (C) from the piston as this will damage the cup.

   c. Damaged or scored piston. Also check the end of the piston (D) for wear or damage caused by the pushrod.

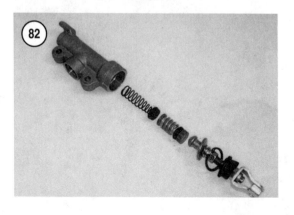

14

d. Measure the piston outer diameter with a micrometer as shown in **Figure 84**. Replace the piston if the diameter is less than the service limit in **Table 1**.

e. The piston, piston cups and spring must be replaced as a set.

3. Check the master cylinder bore (**Figure 85**) for excessive wear, cracks or scoring.

4. Measure the cylinder bore inner diameter with a bore gauge (**Figure 86**) and compare it to the specifications in **Table 1**. Replace the master cylinder if the bore diameter is worn to the service limit.

5. Make sure the fluid passages in the master cylinder are clear.

6. Check the master cylinder banjo bolt threads. If the threads are damaged or partially stripped, replace the master cylinder.

7. Flush the banjo bolt with clean brake fluid.

8. Replace the pushrod (A, **Figure 87**) if it is bent or if the adjuster threads are damaged.

9. Replace the pushrod boot (B, **Figure 87**) if it is deteriorated, torn or damaged.

10. Install a new O-ring seal (**Figure 88**) into the master cylinder body.

11. Flush the reservoir and the reservoir hose with clean DOT 4 brake fluid.

12. Replace all worn or damaged parts.

Assembly

Refer to **Figure 78** when performing this procedure.

1. If disassembled, assemble the pushrod assembly as shown in **Figure 87**.

2. Soak new cups in fresh DOT 4 brake fluid for at least 15 minutes to make them pliable. Coat the master cylinder bore with brake fluid.

3. When replacing the piston assembly, install the primary cup onto the small spring end as shown in B, **Figure 83**.

> *CAUTION*
> *When installing the piston assembly, do not allow the cups to turn inside out, as they will be damaged and allow brake fluid to leak within the cylinder bore.*

4. Apply a small amount of silicone brake grease onto the end of the piston (**Figure 89**) where it engages with the push rod.

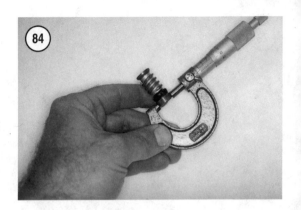

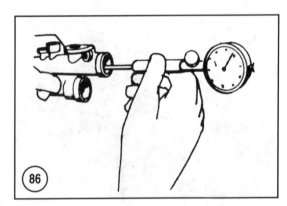

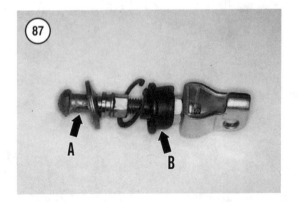

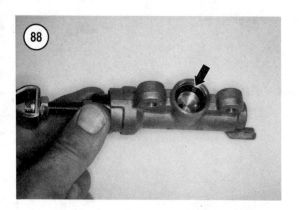

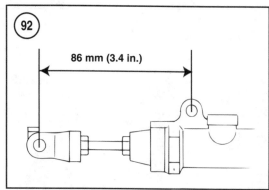

5. Install the piston assembly into the master cylinder in the order shown in **Figure 90**.

6. Support the master cylinder in a vise with soft jaws so that the piston assembly faces up (**Figure 80**).

7. Install the pushrod into the end of the piston, then compress the piston slightly.

8. Apply pressure to the pushrod so that its shoulder is below the circlip groove in the piston bore.

9. Install the circlip (**Figure 81**), making sure it seats in the groove completely. Push and release the pushrod a few times to check that the piston assembly is moving freely in the bore.

10. Seat the rubber boot into the piston bore (**Figure 91**).

11. Adjust the pushrod as follows:
    a. Set the brake rod clevis to the length shown in **Figure 92**.
    b. Operate the pushrod a few times and recheck the adjustment(s).

REAR CALIPER

14

Removal/Installation

Refer to **Figure 93**.

> *NOTE*
> *The manufacturer recommends the complete removal of the rear wheel. This is not necessary as described in this procedure. The rear wheel may be removed if so desired.*

> *CAUTION*
> *Do not spill any brake fluid on the painted portion of the rear wheel.*

REAR CALIPER

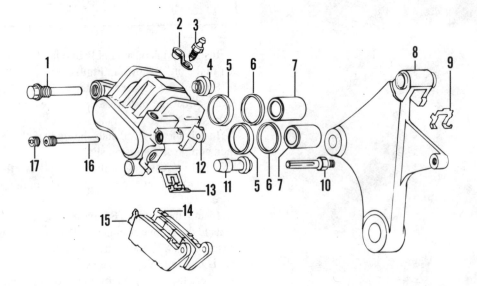

1. Bracket bolt
2. Cap
3. Bleed screw
4. Bracket bolt boot
5. Piston seal
6. Dust seal
7. Piston
8. Mounting bracket
9. Pad retainer
10. Caliper pin bolt
11. Bracket pin boot
12. Caliper body
13. Pad spring
14. Inboard brake pad
15. Outboard brake pad
16. Pad pin
17. Pad pin cap

Wash any spilled brake fluid immediately, as it will destroy the finish. Use soapy water and rinse completely.

1. On models so equipped, remove the left side saddlebag as described in Chapter Fifteen.

2. Remove the caliper brake pads and pad spring as described in this chapter.

3. If the caliper is *not* going to be disassembled for service, perform the following:

    a. Place a container under the brake line at the caliper. Remove the banjo bolt and sealing

washers (**Figure 94**) securing the brake line to the caliper assembly.

    b. Remove the brake line and place the loose end into a reclosable plastic bag to prevent the entry of debris. Tie the loose end of the hose to the frame.

4. If the caliper is going to be disassembled for service, perform the following:

NOTE

By performing sub steps 4a and 4b, compressed air may not be necessary for removal of the pistons during caliper disassembly.

CAUTION

Do not allow the pistons to travel out far enough to contact the brake disc. If this occurs, the pistons may scratch or gouge the disc during caliper removal.

    a. Slowly apply the rear brake pedal to push the pistons partially out of the caliper assembly for ease of removal during caliper service.

    b. Place a container under the brake line at the caliper. Remove the banjo bolt and sealing washers (**Figure 94**) securing the brake line to the caliper assembly.

    c. Remove the brake line and place the loose end into a reclosable plastic bag to prevent the entry of debris. Tie the loose end of the hose to the frame.

5. Shift the transmission into gear.

6. Support the motorcycle on a lift; see Chapter One.

7. Support the rear wheel with a jack (**Figure 95**) or on wooden blocks.

8. Remove the rear wheel axle nut (A, **Figure 96**) as described in Chapter Eleven.

9. Remove the rear caliper mounting bracket stopper bolt (B, **Figure 96**).

10. Push the rear axle out far enough to remove the caliper mounting bracket from between the wheel and swing arm (**Figure 97**).

11. Remove the rear caliper and mounting bracket.

12. Push the rear axle back into position and temporarily install the axle nut (A, **Figure 96**).

NOTE

If the caliper is not going to be serviced, place it in a reclosable plastic bag.

14

Installation

1. Remove the rear axle nut and push the rear axle out far enough to install the caliper mounting bracket in between the wheel and swing arm (**Figure 97**).

2. Place the rear caliper and mounting bracket into position and push the rear axle through the mounting bracket and swing arm.

3. Install the rear caliper mounting bracket stopper bolt (**Figure 98**) and tighten to the torque specification in **Table 2**.

4. Install the rear axle nut (A, **Figure 96**) as described in Chapter Eleven.

5. Install the brake hose with a *new* sealing washer on each side of the fitting, onto the caliper. Install the banjo bolt and position the hose fitting against the stopper on the caliper (**Figure 99**). Tighten the banjo bolt to the torque specification in **Table 2**.

6. Install the brake pads and the pad spring as described in this chapter.

7. Bleed the brake as described in this chapter.

8. Remove the jack or wooden blocks from under the rear wheel.

9. Remove the lift from under the motorcycle.

10. Roll the motorcycle back and forth and activate the brake pedal until the pedal is firm and the pads are seated within the caliper.

11. On models so equipped, install the left side saddlebag.

> *WARNING*
> *Do not ride the motorcycle until the brakes are operating correctly with full hydraulic advantage.*

Disassembly

Refer to **Figure 93** for this procedure.

1. Remove the brake caliper as described in this chapter.

2. Pull the bracket (**Figure 100**) off of the caliper.

3. Place a piece of wood and shop cloth over the end of the pistons and caliper body.

4. If the pistons were not partially removed during caliper removal, perform the following:

> *NOTE*
> *Compressed air is required for piston removal.*

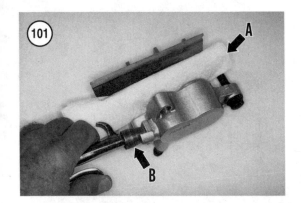

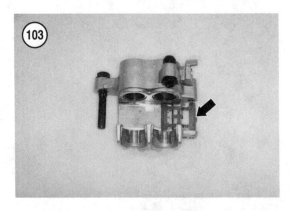

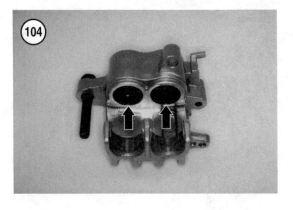

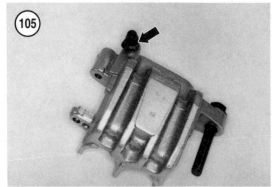

WARNING
*Keep all fingers and hands out of the caliper bores when removing the pistons in the following steps. Wear shop gloves and apply compressed air gradually. Do **not** use high-pressure air or place the air hose nozzle directly against the hydraulic line fitting inlet in the caliper body. Hold the air nozzle away from the inlet, allowing some of the air to escape.*

a. Pad the pistons with a piece of wood and shop cloth (A, **Figure 101**).

b. Apply the air pressure in short spurts to the hydraulic fluid passageway (B, **Figure 101**) and force out the pistons. Use a service station air hose if an air compressor is not available.

5. Remove the pistons from the caliper body (**Figure 102**).

6. Remove the pad spring (**Figure 103**) if it was not previously removed.

CAUTION
In the following step, do not use a sharp tool to remove the dust and piston seals from the caliper body. Do not damage the cylinder bore surfaces.

7. Carefully pry the dust and pistons seals (**Figure 104**) out of the caliper bore. Discard the seals. The seals must not be reused after removal, as they will not seal effectively.

8. Unscrew and remove the bleed screw and cap (**Figure 105**).

14

Inspection

CAUTION
Never use petroleum-based solvents
of any kind on the brake system's in-
ternal components. Any residual sol-
vent remaining within the caliper
component will cause the new seals to
swell and distort.

1. Clean the rear caliper parts in isopropyl alcohol or fresh DOT 4 brake fluid. Wear eye protection and dry with compressed air, directing the air flow and residual fluid spray away. Then place the parts on a lint-free cloth while performing the following inspection procedure.

2. Check the caliper bore for cracks, deep scoring or excessive wear. Measure the cylinder bores with a bore gauge (**Figure 106**). Replace the caliper housing if the bores are worn to the service limit in **Table 1**.

3. Check the caliper pistons (**Figure 102**) for scoring, excessive wear or rust. Then measure the piston diameter with a micrometer (**Figure 107**). Replace the piston if the outer diameter is less than the service limit in **Table 1**.

4. Check the rubber boots on the caliper housing and caliper mounting bracket. Replace the boots if they are hardened or damaged.

5. Check the pad spring for damage.

6. Check the pad retainer (**Figure 108**) on the caliper mounting bracket for damage.

7. Check the mounting bracket for cracks and damage (**Figure 109**).

8. Replace all worn or damaged parts prior to assembly.

Assembly

1. Coat the new piston and dust seals with silicone brake grease.

2. Coat the pistons and piston bores with clean DOT 4 brake fluid.

3. Carefully install the new piston seals (A, **Figure 110**) into the lower bore grooves. Make sure the seals are properly seated in their respective grooves.

4. Carefully install the new dust seals (B, **Figure 110**) into the upper bore grooves. Make sure the seals are properly seated in their respective grooves (**Figure 104**).

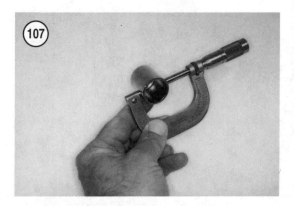
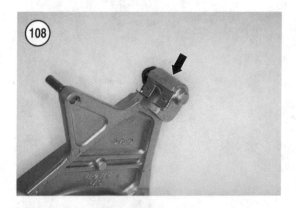

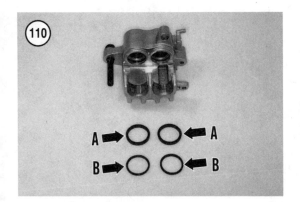

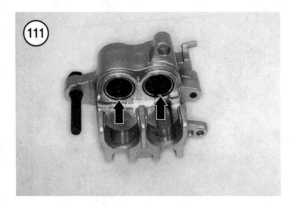

5. Position the pistons with the open end facing out toward the brake pads (**Figure 102**).

Install the pistons and push them in until they bottom (**Figure 111**).

6. Install the pad retainer onto the bracket as shown in **Figure 108**.

7. Apply silicone brake grease onto the caliper bracket pins and boots (**Figure 112**).

8. Install the caliper bracket onto the caliper housing (**Figure 113**).

9. Install the pad spring.

FRONT AND REAR BRAKE DISCS

Inspection

It is not necessary to remove the disc from the wheel to inspect it (**Figure 114**). Small radial marks on the disc are normal, but deep radial scratches—deep enough to snag a fingernail—reduce braking effectiveness and increase brake pad wear. If deep wear grooves exist, replace the disc.

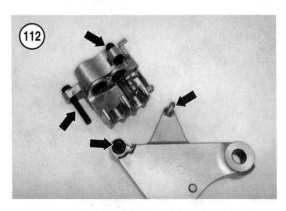

1. Remove the left side saddlebag on models so equipped, as described in Chapter Fifteen.

2. Measure the thickness of the disc at several locations around the disc with a micrometer (**Figure 115**) or vernier caliper. The disc must be replaced if the thickness in any area is less than specified in **Table 1**, or the minimum thickness marked on the disc as shown in **Figure 116**.

3. Make sure the disc bolts are tight before performing this check. Check the disc runout with a dial indicator as shown in **Figure 117**. Slowly rotate the wheel and observe the dial indicator. On all models, replace the disc if the runout equals the service limit in **Table 1**.

4. Clean the disc of any rust or corrosion and wipe clean with brake parts cleaner. Never use an

14

oil-based solvent that may leave an oil residue on the disc.

Removal/Installation

1. Remove the front or rear wheel as described in Chapter Eleven.

> *CAUTION*
> *Place a piece of wood or a vinyl tube in the calipers in place of the disc(s). This way, if the brakes are inadvertently applied, the pistons will not be forced out of the cylinders. If this occurs, the caliper will have to be disassembled to reseat the pistons and the system will have to be bled.*

> *CAUTION*
> *Do not set the wheel down on the disc surface, as it may get scratched or warped. Place the wheel on two blocks of wood or lean it up against a wall.*

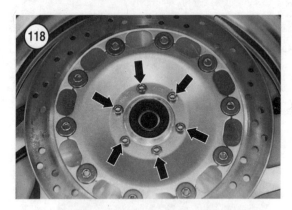

2. Remove the bolts securing the disc to the wheel and remove the disc. Refer to **Figure 118** for the front and **Figure 119** for the rear wheel.

3. Check the bolt threads and the wheel threads for damage. Clean threads with solvent or contact cleaner and blow dry. Replace damaged bolts.

4. Inspect the fasteners (**Figure 120**) securing the floating disc. If any are loose or damaged, the disc must be replaced.

5. Install by reversing these removal steps. Note the following.

6. On the front wheel, note that the brake discs have either an R (right side) or L (left side) stamped on them. Make sure to install the disc marked L on

the left side of the wheel and the disc marked R on the right side of the wheel.

7. On the rear wheel, the disc is marked REAR OUTSIDE (**Figure 121**). Make sure to install the disc with this marking facing out.

8. Tighten the disc mounting bolts to the torque specification in **Table 2**.

BRAKE HOSE REPLACEMENT

Front Brake Hoses

1. On GL1500CF models, remove the front fairing assembly as described in Chapter Fifteen.

2. Remove the master cylinder cover (A, **Figure 122**), then loosen the set plate, diaphragm and float. This will allow air to enter the reservoir and allow the brake fluid to drain out quickly in the next step.

3. Remove the banjo bolt and sealing washers (A, **Figure 123**) securing the brake hose to the left side caliper assembly.

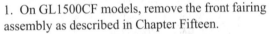

4. Remove the brake hose and place the end of the hose over a container and let the brake fluid drain out. Apply the front brake lever several times to force the fluid out of the brake hose. Dispose of this brake fluid properly; never reuse brake fluid.

5. Repeat Step 3 and Step 4 for the right side caliper assembly (A, **Figure 124**).

6. To remove the right side brake hose, perform the following:

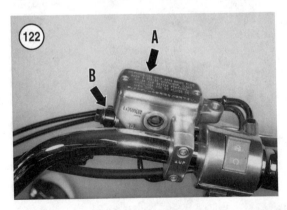

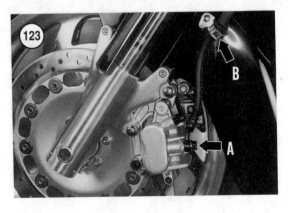

   a. If not already removed, remove the banjo bolt (A, **Figure 124**) securing the right side brake hose to the caliper assembly.

   b. Remove the banjo bolt (B, **Figure 122**) securing the right side brake hose to the master cylinder.

14

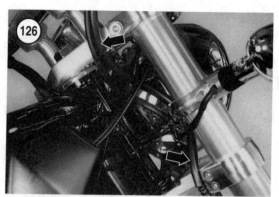

c. Unscrew the fitting (**Figure 125**) securing the crossover pipe to the right side brake hose.

d. Note the routing of the right side brake hose through the steering stem area and headlight case (**Figure 126**).

e. Disconnect the right side brake hose from the retainer on the front fender (B, **Figure 124**).

f. Carefully remove the right side brake hose from the frame. Immediately clean off any spilled brake fluid from all surfaces.

7. To remove the left side brake hose, perform the following:

a. If not already removed, remove the banjo bolt (A, **Figure 123**) securing the left side brake hose to the caliper assembly.

b. Unscrew the fitting (**Figure 127**) securing the crossover pipe to the left side brake hose.

c. Disconnect the left side brake hose from the retainer on the front fender (B, **Figure 123**).

d. Carefully remove the left side brake hose from the frame. Immediately clean off any spilled brake fluid from all surfaces.

8. To remove the crossover pipe, perform the following:

a. Unscrew the fitting (A, **Figure 128**) securing the crossover pipe to both the right and left side brake hoses.

b. Remove the mounting bolts (B, **Figure 128**) and remove the crossover pipe (C, **Figure 128**).

9. Install new hoses, crossover pipe, and new sealing washers in the reverse order of removal, noting the following:

a. Tighten the banjo bolts and fittings to the torque specification in **Table 2**.

b. Refill the master cylinder reservoir and bleed the front brake as described in this chapter.

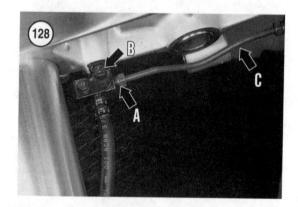

Rear Brake Hose

1. On models so equipped, remove the left side saddlebag as described in Chapter Fifteen.

2. Place a container under the brake line at the caliper. Loosen, but do not remove, the banjo bolt and sealing washers (**Figure 129**) securing the brake line to the caliper assembly.

3. Remove the rear wheel as described in Chapter Eleven.

4. Remove the bolt (A, **Figure 130**) securing the master cylinder reservoir cover (B, **Figure 130**) and remove the cover.

5. Clean the top of the reservoir. Remove the cover (**Figure 131**), then loosen the set plate, diaphragm and float. This will allow air to enter the reservoir and allow the brake fluid to drain out quickly in the next step.

6. Place a container under the brake line at the caliper. Remove the banjo bolt and sealing washers (A, **Figure 132**) securing the brake line to the caliper assembly.

7. Remove the bolt securing the rear caliper brake hose to the end of the swing arm (B, **Figure 132**).

8. Unhook the brake hose from the clamp on the swing arm (**Figure 133**).

9. Remove the bolt and chrome cover (**Figure 134**) from the rear master cylinder.

10. Remove the banjo bolt and sealing washers (A, **Figure 135**) to the rear master cylinder.

11. Remove the bolt securing the rear brake hose and clamp (B, **Figure 135**) to the frame.

12. Remove the bolt and move the rear master cylinder remote reservoir (C, **Figure 135**) and move it out of the way.

13. Note the routing of the rear brake hose assembly through the frame.

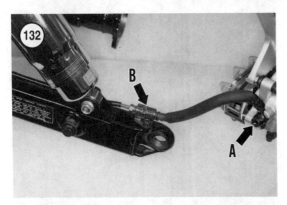

14

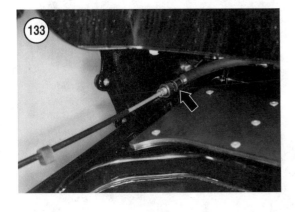

14. Carefully remove the rear brake hose assembly from the frame. Immediately clean off any spilled brake fluid from all surfaces.

15. Install a new hose assembly and new sealing washers in the reverse order of removal, noting the following:

    a. Tighten the banjo bolts to the torque specification in **Table 2**.

    b. Refill the master cylinder reservoir and bleed the rear brake as described in this chapter.

BLEEDING THE SYSTEM

Without a Brake Bleeder

1. On models so equipped, remove the left side saddlebag as described in Chapter Fifteen.

2. Remove the dust cap from the brake bleed valve.

3. Connect a length of clear tubing to the bleed valve on the caliper (**Figure 136**, typical).

4. Place the other end of the tube into a clean container. Fill the container with enough fresh brake fluid to keep the end submerged. The tube should be long enough so that a loop can be made higher than the bleed valve to prevent air from being drawn into the caliper during bleeding.

> *CAUTION*
> *Cover the top compartment, instrument cluster and front fairing with a heavy cloth or plastic tarp to protect it from accidentally spilled brake fluid. Wash brake fluid off of any surface immediately, as it will destroy the finish. Use soapy water and rinse completely.*

5A. On the front brake, clean the top of the master cylinder of all debris. Remove the screws securing the cover (**Figure 137**). Remove the set plate, diaphragm and float from the master cylinder reservoir.

5B. On the rear brake, perform the following:

    a. Remove the bolt (A, **Figure 130**) securing the master cylinder reservoir cover (B, **Figure 130**) and remove the cover.

    b. Clean the top of the reservoir of all debris. Remove the cover (**Figure 131**), set plate, diaphragm and float from the reservoir.

6. Fill the reservoir (**Figure 138**, typical). Insert the float, diaphragm, set plate and the cover loosely. Leave the cover in place during this procedure to

prevent brake fluid from spraying out of the reservoir.

> *WARNING*
> *Use brake fluid marked DOT 4 only. Others may vaporize and cause brake failure. Always use the same brand name; do not intermix, as many brands are not compatible. Do not intermix silicone-based (DOT 5) brake fluid, as it can cause brake component damage leading to brake system failure.*

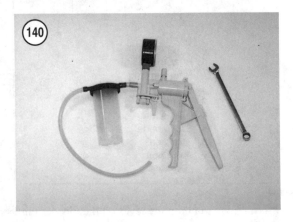

8. Continue to pump the lever (or pedal) and fill the reservoir until the fluid emerging from the hose is clean and free of bubbles.

NOTE
Do not allow the reservoir to empty during the bleeding operation or more air will enter the system. If this occurs, the procedure must be repeated.

9. Hold the lever in (or pedal down), tighten the bleed valve, remove the bleed tube and install the bleed valve dust cap.
10. If necessary, fill the reservoir to the upper level line.
11A. On the front master cylinder, install the float, diaphragm, set plate and cover (**Figure 137**). Install and tighten the cover screws securely.
11B. On the rear master cylinder, perform the following:
    a. Install the float, diaphragm, set plate and cover (**Figure 131**). Install and tighten the cover screws securely.
    b. Install the chrome cover (B, **Figure 130**) and bolt (A, **Figure 130**) and tighten securely.
12. Test the feel of the brake lever (or pedal). It should be firm and offer the same resistance each time it is operated. If it feels spongy, it is likely that there still is air in the system and it must be bled again. When all air has been bled from the system and the fluid level is correct in the reservoir, double-check for leaks and tighten all the fittings and connections.

WARNING
Before riding the motorcycle, make certain that the brakes are operating correctly by operating the lever or pedal several times.

Brake Bleeder Process

This procedure uses a brake bleeder (**Figure 140**) that is available from motorcycle or automotive supply stores or from mail order outlets.
1. On models so equipped, remove the left side saddlebag as described in Chapter Fifteen.
2. Remove the dust cap from the brake bleed valve.
3. Connect the brake bleeder and wrench to the bleed valve on the caliper (**Figure 141**, typical).

CAUTION
Cover the top compartment, instrument cluster and front fairing with a

14

7. Slowly apply the brake lever (or pedal) several times. Hold the lever (or pedal) in the applied position. Open the bleed valve about one-half turn (**Figure 139**). Allow the lever (or pedal) to travel to its limit. When this limit is reached, tighten the bleed screw. Occasionally tap the caliper assembly to assist in loosening any trapped air bubbles. As the fluid enters the system, the level will drop in the reservoir. Maintain the level at about 3/8 in. (9.5 mm) from the top of the reservoir to prevent air from being drawn into the system.

heavy cloth or plastic tarp to protect it from the accidental spilling of brake fluid. Wash brake fluid off of any surface immediately; it will destroy the finish. Use soapy water and rinse completely.

4A. On the front brake, clean the top of the master cylinder of all debris. Remove the screws securing the cover (**Figure 137**). Remove the set plate, diaphragm and float from the master cylinder reservoir.

4B. On the rear brake, perform the following:

   a. Remove the bolt (A, **Figure 130**) securing the master cylinder reservoir cover (B, **Figure 130**) and remove the cover.

   b. Clean the top of the reservoir of all debris. Remove the cover (**Figure 131**), set plate, diaphragm and float from the reservoir.

5. Fill the reservoir (**Figure 138**, typical). Insert the float, diaphragm, set plate and the cover loosely. Leave the cover in place during this procedure to prevent brake fluid from spraying out of the reservoir.

> *WARNING*
> *Use DOT 4 brake fluid only. Others may vaporize and cause brake failure. Always use the same brand name; do not intermix, as many brands are not compatible. Do not intermix silicone-based (DOT 5) brake fluid; it can cause brake component damage and lead to brake system failure.*

6. Open the bleed valve about one-half turn and pump the brake bleeder.

> *NOTE*
> *If air is entering the brake bleeder hose from around the bleed screw, remove the hose and apply several layers of Teflon tape to the bleed screw. This should make a good seal between the bleed screw and the brake bleeder hose.*

7. Occasionally tap the caliper assembly to assist in loosening any trapped air bubbles. As the fluid enters the system, the level will drop in the reservoir. Maintain the level at about 3/8 in. (9.5 mm) from the top of the reservoir to prevent air from being drawn into the system.

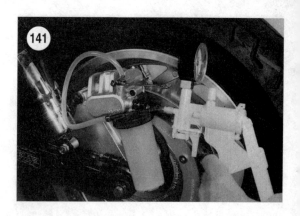

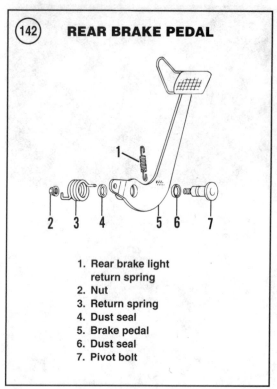

REAR BRAKE PEDAL

1. Rear brake light return spring
2. Nut
3. Return spring
4. Dust seal
5. Brake pedal
6. Dust seal
7. Pivot bolt

8. Continue to pump the lever on the bleeder until the fluid emerging from the hose is clean and free of bubbles. Tighten the bleed screw.

> *NOTE*
> *Do not allow the reservoir to empty during the bleeding operation, or more air will enter the system. If this occurs, the procedure must be repeated.*

9. When the brake fluid is free of air, retighten the bleed screw. Remove the brake bleeder tube and install the bleed screws dust cap.

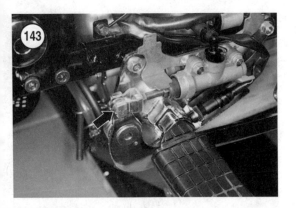

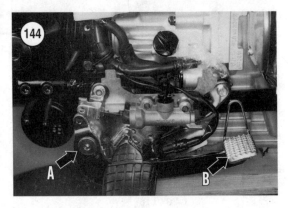

and the fluid level is correct in the reservoir, double-check for leaks and tighten all the fittings and connections.

> *WARNING*
> *Before riding the motorcycle, make certain that the brakes are operating correctly by operating the lever or pedal several times.*

REAR BRAKE PEDAL

Removal/Installation

Refer to **Figure 142**.

1. Remove the bolt (A, **Figure 130**) securing the master cylinder reservoir cover (B, **Figure 130**) and remove the cover.

2. Remove the cotter pin and pivot pin (**Figure 143**) from the rod eye on the end of the master cylinder pushrod.

3. Remove the nut securing the brake pedal mounting pivot bolt and remove the pivot bolt (A, **Figure 144**).

4. Partially remove the brake pedal (B, **Figure 144**) away from the footpeg holder bracket and disconnect the brake light switch return spring.

5. Remove the brake pedal and return spring.

6. Do not lose the dust seal on each side of the pivot bolt.

7. Install by reversing these removal steps while noting the following:

   a. Apply a light coat of multipurpose grease to all pivot areas before installing any components.

   b. Install the outer leg of the return spring into the hole in the brake pedal.

   c. Install the brake pedal and return spring onto the mounting bracket and hook the inner end of the spring onto the footpeg holder bracket.

   d. Tighten the pivot bolt and nut to the torque specification in **Table 2**.

10. If necessary, fill the reservoir to the upper level line.

11A. On the front master cylinder, install the float, diaphragm, set plate and cover (**Figure 137**). Install and tighten the cover screws securely.

11B. On the rear master cylinder, perform the following:

   a. Install the float, diaphragm, set plate and cover (**Figure 131**). Install and tighten the cover screws securely.

   b. Install the chrome cover (B, **Figure 130**) and bolt (A, **Figure 130**) and tighten it securely.

12. Test the feel of the brake lever (or pedal). It should be firm and offer the same resistance each time it is operated. If it feels spongy, it is likely that there still is air in the system and it must be bled again. When all air has been bled from the system

14

Table 1 and Table 2 are on the following pages.

Table 1 BRAKE SERVICE SPECIFICATIONS

	Specification mm (in.)	Wear limit mm (in.)
Brake pad thickness*		
Front master cylinder		
Cylinder bore inner diameter	14.000-14.043 (0.5512-0.5529)	14.055 (0.5533)
Piston outer diameter	13.957-13.984 (0.5495-0.5506)	13.945 (0.5490)
Front brake caliper		
Cylinder bore inner diameter	27.000-27.050 (1.0630-1.0650)	27.060 (1.065)
Piston outer diameter	26.935-26.968 (1.0604-1.0617)	26.927 (1.0601)
Rear master cylinder		
Cylinder bore inner diameter	14.000-14.043 (0.5512-0.5529)	14.055 (0.5533)
Piston outer diameter	13.957-13.984 (0.5495-0.5506)	13.945 (0.5490)
Brake rod clevis installed length	86 (3.4)	–
Rear brake caliper		
Cylinder bore inner diameter	27.000-27.050 (1.0630-1.0650)	27.060 (1.065)
Piston outer diameter	26.935-26.968 (1.0604-1.0617)	26.927 (1.0601)
Brake disc		
Runout		
Front and rear	–	0.3 (0.014)
Thickness		
Front	5.0 (0.20)	4.0 (0.16)
Rear	7.5 (0.30)	6.0 (0.24)

* Specification not provided by manufacturer. Replace brake pads when worn to the wear limit grooves.

Table 2 BRAKE TIGHTENING TORQUES

	N•m	in.-lb.	ft.-lb.
Brake disc bolts			
Front	20	–	15
Rear	42	–	31
Brake hose banjo bolts	34	–	25
Brake pedal pivot bolt	25	–	18
Caliper bleed screw	6	53	–
Front brake caliper			
Mounting bolt[1]	30	–	22
Pin bolt	23	–	17
Caliper bracket pin bolt	13	115	–
Front pad pin plugs	2.5	22	–
Front pad pins	18	–	13
Front master cylinder holder bolts	12	106	–
Front brake crossover pipe fittings	17	–	12
Rear caliper stopper pin bolt[1]	69	–	51
Rear caliper			
Pin bolt[2]	27	–	20
Pin retainer bolt	13	115	–
Caliper mounting bracket stopper bolt	69	–	51

(continued)

Table 2 BRAKE TIGHTENING TORQUES (continued)

	N•m	in.-lb.	ft.-lb.
Rear master cylinder			
Mounting bolts	12	106	–
Adjuster locknut	18	–	13
Reservoir bolts	12	106	–
Reservoir cover mounting bolt	10	88	–
Rear brake metal line joint	17	–	12

1. Replace with a new original equipment bolt
2. Apply ThreeBond TB1342 or Loctite 242 (blue) to the fastener threads prior to installation.

14

FRAME AND BODY

This chapter includes replacement procedures for components attached to the frame.

Frame and body torque specifications are in **Table 1** at the end of the chapter.

SEATS

Removal/Installation
(GL1500C and GL1500CT)

1. To remove the driver's seat, perform the following:

   a. Turn the ignition key clockwise in the seat lock (**Figure 1**) and unlock the rider's seat.

   b. Pull up on the front of the seat (**Figure 2**) and slide it forward to release the rear bracket from the frame stay. Remove the seat.

   c. Inspect the under side of the seat. Check the locking tabs (**Figure 3**) for damage. Replace the seat if the locking tabs are cracked or damaged. Do not try to repair the locking tabs, as this results in an unsafe riding condition.

   d. Install the seat and lock it into the rear bracket, then push the front down hard and lock it in place.

WARNING
After the seat is installed, pull up on it firmly and move it from side to side to make sure it is securely locked in

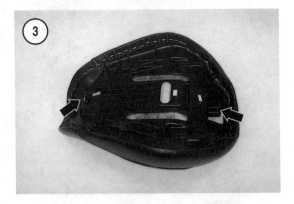

place. If it is not correctly locked in place it may move when riding the motorcycle. This could lead to the loss of control and possibly an accident.

2. To remove the passenger seat, perform the following:

   a. Remove the driver's seat as previously described.

   b. Remove the rear mounting hex bolt (**Figure 4**) and the front two Allen bolts (**Figure 5**). Remove the seat.

   c. Install the seat and the mounting bolts. Tighten the bolts securely.

   d. Install the driver's seat as previously described.

   e. Refer to the previous WARNING and make sure the seat is correctly locked in place.

Removal/Installation (GL1500CF)

Refer to **Figure 6**.

1. Remove the seat band cap nut and collar on each side and remove the seat band.

2. Turn the ignition key clockwise in the seat lock (**Figure 1**) and unlock the seat.

3. Pull up on the front of the seat and slide if forward to release the trunk stay and fender bracket. Remove the seat.

4. Inspect the underside of the seat. Check the locking tabs for damage. Replace the seat if the locking tabs are cracked or damaged. Do not try to repair the locking tabs, as this will result in an unsafe riding condition.

5. Insert the rear locking tab into the trunk stay, then insert the center locking tab into the fender bracket.

15

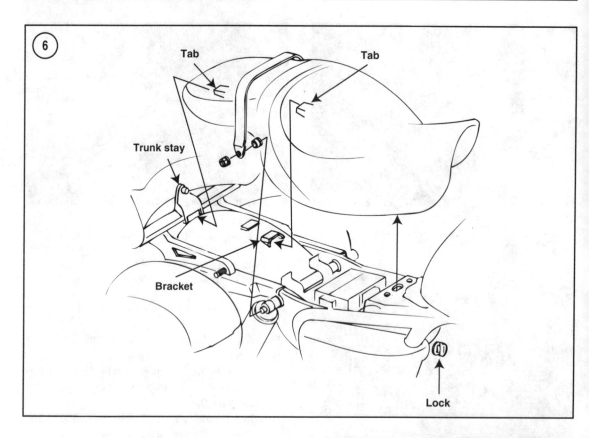

6. Push the front down hard and lock it in place. Make sure that the rear and center locking tabs are properly inserted into the trunk stay and fender bracket.

7. Install the seat band and the seat band cap nut and collar on each side. Tighten the cap nuts securely.

> *WARNING*
> *After the seat is installed, pull up on it firmly and move it from side to side to make sure it is securely locked in place. If it is not correctly locked in place, it may move when riding the motorcycle. This could lead to a loss of control and a possible accident.*

FRAME REAR SIDE COVERS

Removal/Installation

> *CAUTION*
> *The front locking tab is very easily broken, if not removed according to this procedure.*

1. Carefully release the rear portion of the side cover (A, **Figure 7**) from the frame boss.

2. Slowly pull out on the lower tab (B, **Figure 7**) and release the rear cover from the rubber grommet on the frame mount.

3. Gently pull out on the rear of the cover, then slowly pull back and release the front locking tab from the frame boss (C, **Figure 7**). Refer to the previous CAUTION.

4. Remove the side cover.

5. Make sure the rubber grommet is still in place on the frame lower mount.

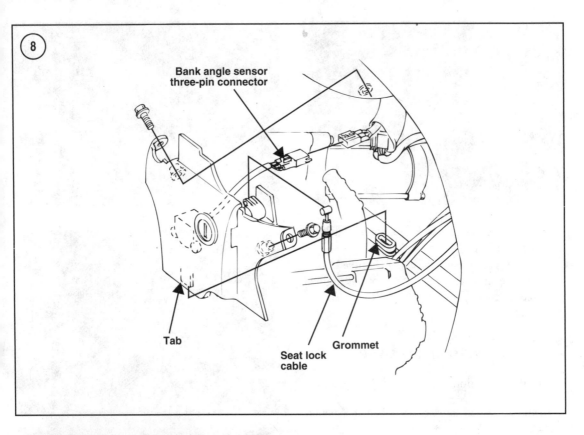

⑧

Bank angle sensor
three-pin connector

Tab

Seat lock
cable

Grommet

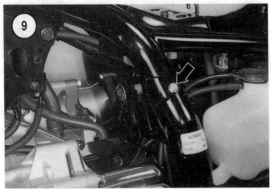

⑨

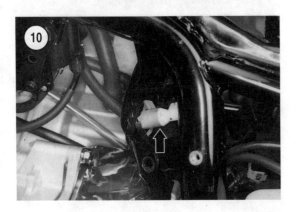

⑩

6. Carefully install the rear cover by reversing these removal steps.

CENTER COVER

Removal/Installation

Refer to **Figure 8**.

1. Remove the seat and frame rear side covers as described in this chapter.

2. Disconnect the bank angle sensor three-pin white electrical connector.

3. Remove the bolt and collar (**Figure 9**) on each side.

4. Carefully pull up on the center cover and release the tab from the rubber grommet on the frame mount. Pull the center cover away from the frame.

5. On the backside of the center cover, release the metal catch and loosen the latch assembly (**Figure 10**).

6. Disconnect the seat lock cable from the latch assembly.

7. Install by reversing these removal steps while noting the following:

15

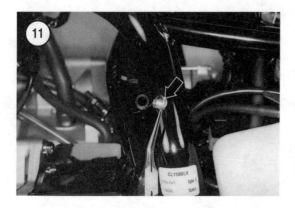

a. Reconnect the seat lock cable to the latch assembly.

b. Make sure to install the collar (**Figure 11**) under the mounting bolts. Do not overtighten the bolt as the surrounding plastic material may crack.

STEERING HEAD COVER

Removal/Installation

1. Remove the fuel tank as described in Chapter Eight.

2. Release the trim clip (A, **Figure 12**).

3. Release the cover boss (B, **Figure 12**) from the rubber grommet on the frame mount.

4. Remove the cover from the frame (C, **Figure 12**).

5. Make sure the rubber grommet (A, **Figure 13**) is still in place on the frame upper mount.

6. Install the cover onto the frame and press the upper tab (B, **Figure 13**) in to the rubber grommet

7. Align the trim clip hole with the one on the frame and install the trim clip (**Figure 14**). Push in on the center post on the trim clip to lock the trim clip in place.

8. On the left side, correctly position the clutch hose (**Figure 15**) in the cover notch. Do not pinch the hose.

RADIATOR COVER (GL1500CF)

Removal/Installation

Refer to **Figure 16** for this procedure.

1. Remove the three Allen bolts and collars securing the radiator cover to the frame.

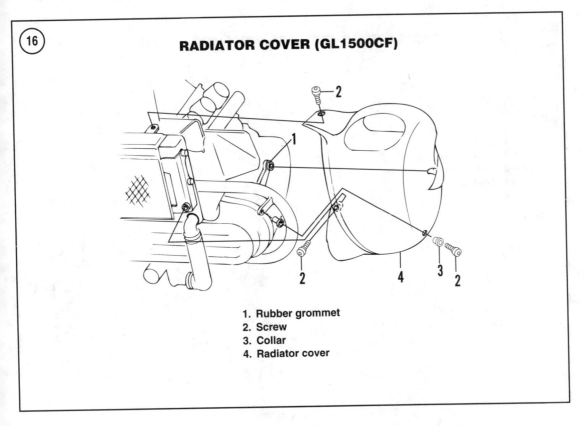

RADIATOR COVER (GL1500CF)

1. Rubber grommet
2. Screw
3. Collar
4. Radiator cover

2. Release the cover rear center boss from the rubber grommet on the frame mount.

3. Remove the radiator cover from the frame.

4. Make sure the rubber grommet is still in place on the frame rear center mount.

5. Be sure to install the collar under the mounting bolts. Do not overtighten the bolt, as the surrounding plastic material may crack.

6. Repeat for the other side if necessary.

Disassembly/Assembly

Refer to **Figure 17**.

1. Remove the radiator cover as previously described.

2. Remove the Allen bolts and screws securing the different panels together and separate the panels.

3. Assemble the panels and install the Allen bolts and screw. Do not overtighten the bolt and screws as the surrounding plastic material may crack.

WINDSHIELD (GL1500CT)

Windshield Replacement

Perform this procedure with the aid of an assistant.

Refer to **Figure 18**.

1. Remove the two lower bolts securing the windshield to the lower bracket.

2. Have an assistant hold onto the windshield and remove the two bolts, two collars and washers that secure the upper portion of the windshield to the upper brackets.

3. Remove the windshield.

4. If the windshield is being removed for service on another part of the motorcycle, wrap it in a blanket and store it out of the way to prevent it from being damaged.

5. Install by reversing these removal steps while noting the following:

   a. Be sure to install the collar and washer under the upper mounting bolts.

   b. Do not overtighten the bolt as the surrounding plastic material may crack.

15

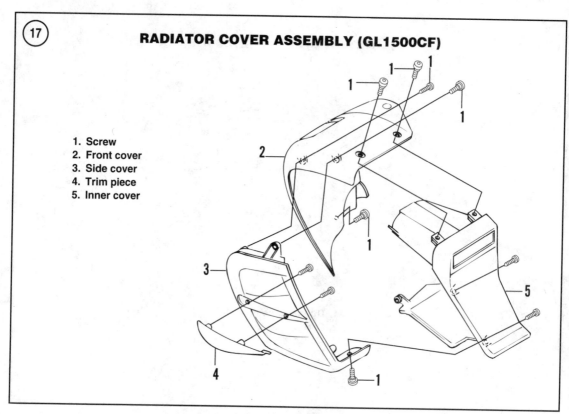

RADIATOR COVER ASSEMBLY (GL1500CF)

1. Screw
2. Front cover
3. Side cover
4. Trim piece
5. Inner cover

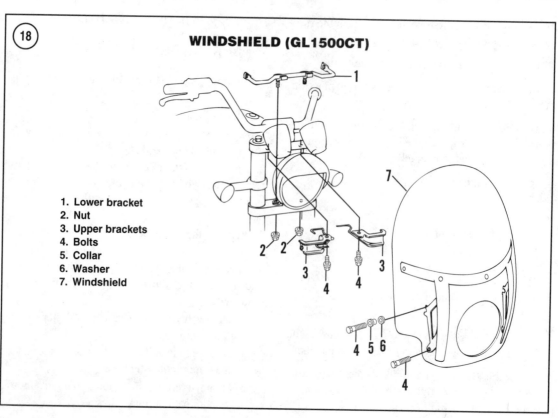

WINDSHIELD (GL1500CT)

1. Lower bracket
2. Nut
3. Upper brackets
4. Bolts
5. Collar
6. Washer
7. Windshield

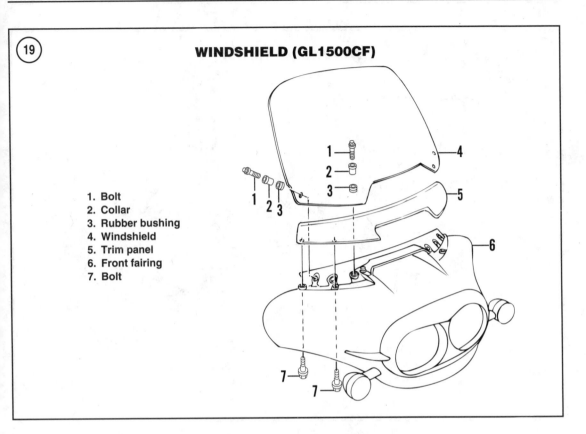

(19)

WINDSHIELD (GL1500CF)

1. Bolt
2. Collar
3. Rubber bushing
4. Windshield
5. Trim panel
6. Front fairing
7. Bolt

Mounting Brackets Removal/Installation

Refer to **Figure 18**.

1. Remove the windshield as previously described.

2. Remove the nuts securing the lower mounting bracket to the lower fork bridge and remove the bracket.

3. Remove the bolt securing the upper bracket to the upper fork bridge and remove the bracket. Repeat for the other side, if necessary.

4. Install by reversing these removal steps. Tighten the bolts and nuts securely.

WINDSHIELD (GL1500CF)

Replacement

Perform this procedure with the aid of an assistant. Refer to **Figure 19**.

1. Remove the right and left side front inner fairing as described in this chapter.

2. Working under the front fairing, remove the four bolts securing the trim panel and remove the trim panel.

3. Remove the two inner bolts and collars securing the windshield to the front fairing.

4. Have an assistant hold onto the windshield and remove the two outer bolts and collars securing the windshield to the front fairing.

5. Remove the windshield.

6. If the windshield is being removed for service on another part of the motorcycle, wrap it in a blanket and store it out of the way to prevent it from being damaged.

7. Install by reversing these removal steps while noting the following:

   a. Inspect the rubber bushing in each bolt attachment hole in the windshield. Replace as a set if they are starting to harden or deteriorate.

   b. Make sure to install the collar and washer under all four mounting bolts.

   c. Do not overtighten the bolt, as the surrounding plastic material may crack.

Windshield Cleaning (All Models)

Be careful cleaning the windshield; it can be easily scratched or damaged. Do not use a cleaner with

15

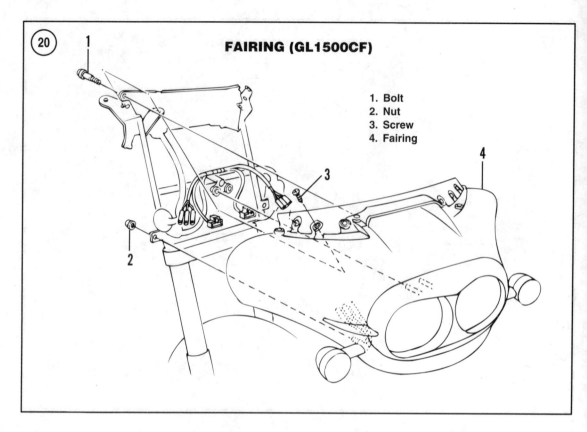

(20)

FAIRING (GL1500CF)

1. Bolt
2. Nut
3. Screw
4. Fairing

an abrasive or a combination cleaner and wax. Never use any type of cleaning solvent or petroleum product. These products will either scratch or totally destroy the surface of the windshield.

For normal cleaning, use a soft cloth or sponge and plenty of clean, cool water. Dry thoroughly with a soft cloth—do not press hard. If the windshield is very dirty, use a diluted mild detergent with a sponge and plenty of clean cool water. Be sure to rinse off all detergent residues. Any remaining detergent on the surface may cause surface cracking.

FAIRING (GL1500CF)

Removal/Installation

Perform this procedure with the aid of an assistant due to the size and weight of the fairing assembly.

Refer to **Figure 20**.

1. Remove the windshield as described in this chapter.

2. Disconnect the electrical connectors for the headlight assembly and both front turn signal assemblies.

3. Working under the front fairing, remove the two lower bolts securing the front fairing to the mounting bracket.

4. Have an assistant hold onto the front fairing and remove the four upper bolts securing the front fairing to the mounting bracket.

5. Remove the fairing.

6. If the fairing is being removed for service on another part of the motorcycle, wrap it in a blanket and store it out of the way to prevent it from being damaged.

7. Install by reversing these removal steps while noting the following:

   a. Do not overtighten the bolts as the surrounding plastic material may crack.

   b. Make sure the electrical connectors are tight and free of corrosion.

   c. Check and adjust the headlight as described in Chapter Eight.

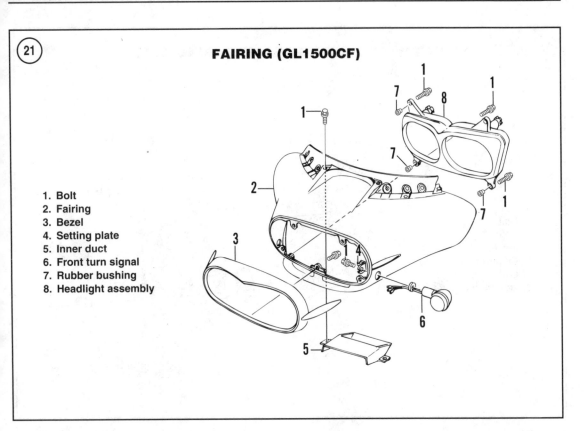

FAIRING (GL1500CF)

㉑

1. Bolt
2. Fairing
3. Bezel
4. Setting plate
5. Inner duct
6. Front turn signal
7. Rubber bushing
8. Headlight assembly

Disassembly/Assembly

Refer to **Figure 21**.

1. Remove the fairing as described in this chapter.

2. Remove the four screws and collars securing the headlight assembly to the front of the fairing panel. Remove the headlight assembly.

3. Remove the five screws securing the headlight bezel and remove the bezel.

4. Remove the bolts and setting plate securing the front turn signal assembly. Remove the turn signal assembly. Repeat for the other side if necessary.

5. Remove the two bolts securing the inner duct and remove the duct.

6. Install by reversing these removal steps. Do not overtighten the bolts and screws as the surrounding plastic material may crack.

Mounting Bracket Removal/Installation

Refer to **Figure 22**.

1. Remove the fairing as described in this chapter.

2. Disconnect the 20-pin white electrical connector from the combination meter.

3. Loosen, but do not remove, the upper mounting bolts securing the fairing and meter mounting bracket to the upper brackets.

4. Remove the bolts securing the fairing and meter mounting bracket to the lower bracket.

5. Pull the fairing and meter mounting bracket free from the upper brackets and remove the assembly.

6. If necessary, remove the bolts securing the upper brackets to the upper fork bridge and remove both upper brackets.

7. If necessary, remove the nuts securing the lower bracket to the lower fork bridge and remove the bracket.

8. Install by reversing these removal steps while noting the following:

   a. Tighten all bolts securely.

   b. Make sure the electrical connector is tight and free of corrosion.

Fairing Inner Panel Removal/Installation

Refer to **Figure 23**.

15

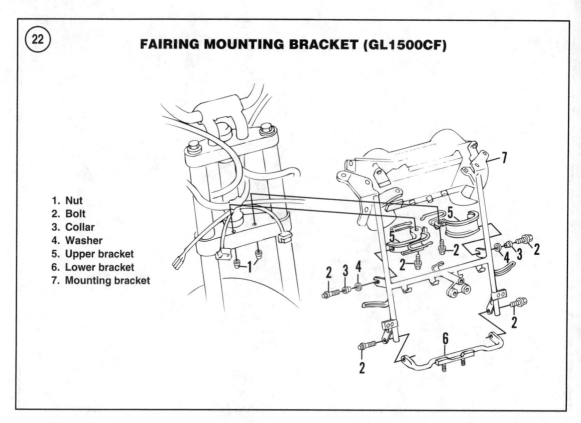

FAIRING MOUNTING BRACKET (GL1500CF)

1. Nut
2. Bolt
3. Collar
4. Washer
5. Upper bracket
6. Lower bracket
7. Mounting bracket

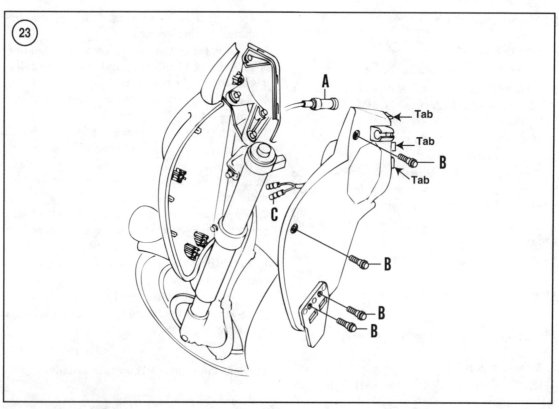

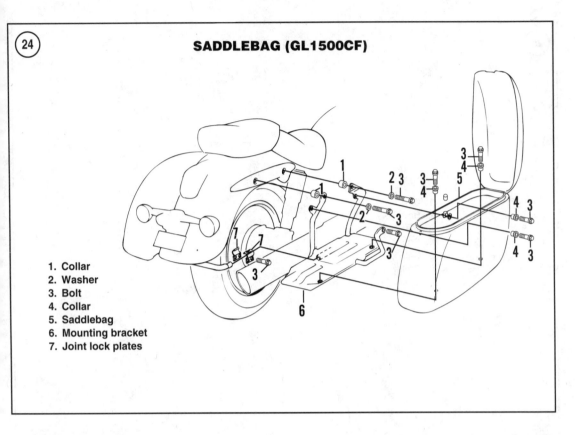

(24)

SADDLEBAG (GL1500CF)

1. Collar
2. Washer
3. Bolt
4. Collar
5. Saddlebag
6. Mounting bracket
7. Joint lock plates

1. On the left side only, disconnect the headset junction connector (A, **Figure 23**) from the holder.
2. Remove the four mounting bolts (B).
3. Carefully release the panel tabs from the front fairing.
4. Pull the panel part way from the front fairing and disconnect the speaker connectors (C).
5. Remove the panel.
6. If necessary, repeat for the other side.
7. Install by reversing these removal steps while noting the following:
   a. Do not overtighten the bolts and screws, as the surrounding plastic material may crack.
   b. Make sure all electrical connectors are tight and free of corrosion.

SADDLEBAG AND MOUNTING BRACKET (GL1500CF)

Refer to **Figure 24**.
1. Open the saddlebag lid.
2. Remove the two lower bolts and collars, then the two side bolts and collars and remove the saddlebag.

3. To remove the mounting bracket, perform the following:
   a. Remove the two bolts and remove the joint lock plates.
   b. Remove the three bolts and washers securing the mounting plate to the rear fender stay. Do not lose the collar spacers on the two top bolts.
4. Install by reversing these removal steps while noting the following:
   a. Do not overtighten the saddlebag mounting bolts as the surrounding plastic material may crack.
   b. Tighten all mounting bracket bolts securely. Be sure to install the collars on the two top bolts.

TRUNK (GL1500CF)

Trunk Removal/Installation

Refer to **Figure 25**.
1. Remove the seat and the right side rear frame cover as described in this chapter.

15

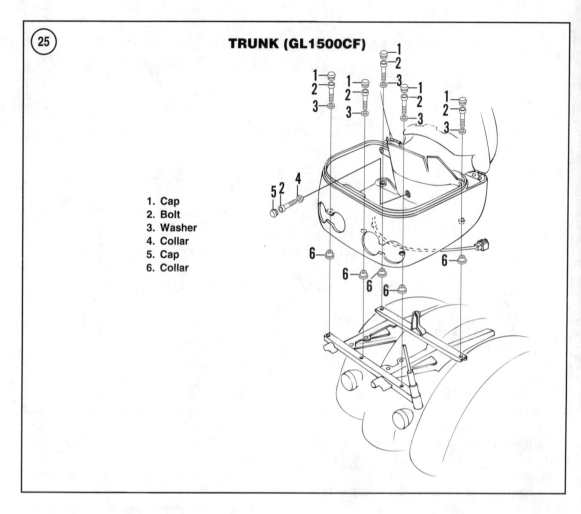

25

TRUNK (GL1500CF)

1. Cap
2. Bolt
3. Washer
4. Collar
5. Cap
6. Collar

2. Open the trunk lid.

3. Remove the screws, washers and rubber seats from inside the trunk.

4. Disconnect the three-pin electrical connector.

5. Within the trunk area, use a flat-blade screwdriver and pry loose the five trim caps over the mounting bolts.

6. Remove the front horizontal bolt and collar.

CAUTION
Due to the weight of the trunk lid in the open position, the trunk will tend to turn over toward the front of the motorcycle after the bolts are removed.

7. Hold onto the trunk and remove the five vertical bolts and washers securing the trunk to the trunk mounting bracket.

8. Remove the trunk and close the lid.

9. Install by reversing these removal steps while noting the following:

    a. Do not overtighten the trunk mounting bolts as the surrounding plastic material may crack.

    b. Install all trim caps over the mounting bolts.

Trunk Lid Removal/Installation

1. Open the trunk lid and support it in the open position.

2. Remove the screws securing the trunk lid supports from the trunk.

3. Remove the six screws securing the trunk lid hinges to the trunk and remove the trunk lid.

4. Install by reversing these removal steps. Do not overtighten the trunk lid mounting screws as the surrounding plastic material may crack.

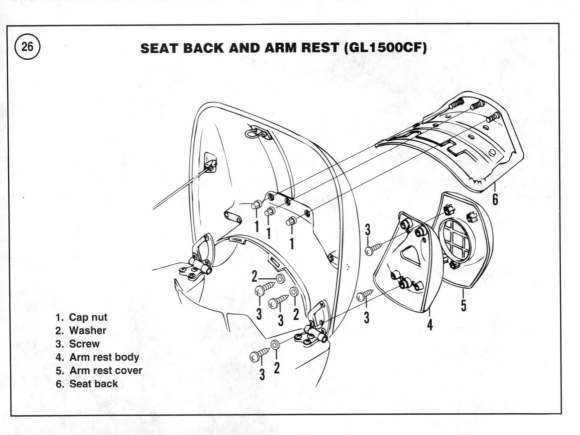

26 **SEAT BACK AND ARM REST (GL1500CF)**

1. Cap nut
2. Washer
3. Screw
4. Arm rest body
5. Arm rest cover
6. Seat back

27

SEAT BACK AND ARM REST

Removal/Installation

Refer to **Figure 26**.

1. Open the trunk lid.

2. Remove the three nuts securing the seat back to the trunk lid and remove the seat back.

3. Remove the three screws and washers securing the arm rest to the trunk and remove the arm rest.

4. If necessary, remove the four self-tapping screws securing the arm rest cover to the arm rest and remove the cover.

5. Install by reversing these removal steps. Do not overtighten the seat back and arm rest mounting screws, as the surrounding plastic material may crack.

FRONT FENDER

Removal/Installation

1. Remove the front wheel as described in Chapter Eleven.

2. Remove the brake hose guides (**Figure 27**) on each side of the fender.

3. Remove the two bolts (**Figure 28**) on each side securing the front fender to the fork legs.

4. Carefully remove the front fender out of the fork legs and remove it.

5. Install by reversing these removal steps. Tighten the bolts securely.

15

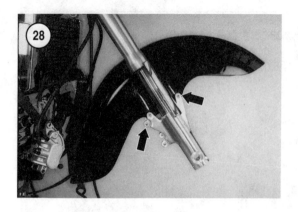

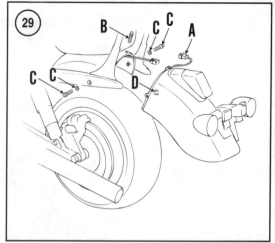

REAR FENDER

Removal/Installation

Refer to **Figure 29**.

1. Support the motorcycle on the sidestand.

2. On GL1500CF models, remove the seat as described in this chapter.

3. Working under the rear fender, disconnect the 6-pin or 4-pin electrical connector (A) for the taillight and license plate light assemblies.

4. Remove the following.

5A. On GL1500CT and GL1500CF models, perform the following:

   a. Open the saddlebag lids.

   b. Remove the two bolts and collars located on the inside surface of the saddlebag securing the saddlebag and the rear fender to the grab rail.

   c. Hold onto the rear fender and remove the 6 mm bolt (B) and remove the rear fender.

5B. On GL1500C models, perform the following:

   a. Remove the two bolts and collars (C) on the grab rail.

   b. Hold onto the rear fender and remove the 6 mm bolt (B) and remove the rear fender.

6. Install by reversing these removal steps while noting the following:

   a. Tighten the bolts to the torque specifications listed in **Table 1**.

   b. Make sure the electrical connector is tight and free of corrosion.

FOOTPEGS AND BRACKETS

Driver's Footpegs Removal/Installation

1. To remove the right side footpeg, perform the following:

   a. Remove the rear master cylinder (A, **Figure 30**) and rear brake pedal (B, **Figure 30**) as described in Chapter Fourteen.

   b. Remove the bolts (C, **Figure 30**) securing the footpeg assembly to the frame and remove it.

2. To remove the left side footpeg, remove the bolts (**Figure 31**) securing the footpeg assembly to the frame and remove it.

3. Install by reversing these removal steps. Tighten the bolts to the torque specifications listed in **Table 1**.

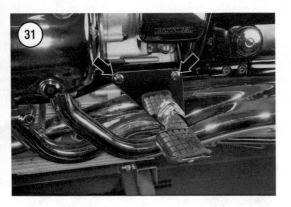

Passenger Footpegs Removal/Installation

1. Remove the exhaust system as described in Chapter Four.

2. Remove the bolts (**Figure 32**) securing the footpeg and bracket to the frame.

3. Remove the footpeg and bracket assembly.

4. Install the assembly and tighten the bolts to the torque specification listed in **Table 1**.

Table 1 FRAME AND BODY TIGHTENING TORQUES

	N•m	in-lb.	ft.-lb.
Sidestand			
Pivot bolt	10	88	–
Pivot bolt locknut	29	–	21
Driver footpeg bolt	26	–	19
Passenger footpeg			
Bracket bolt	39	–	29
Mounting bolt	39	–	29
Grab rail			
Front bolt (10 mm)*	39	–	29
Rear bolt (8 mm)*	26	–	19
Rear seat bolt			
(GL1500C, GL1500CT)	12	106	–
1. Apply oil to the threads and seating surfaces			

15

INDEX

16

16

WIRING
DIAGRAMS

1997-1999 GL1500C/CT INTERSTATE

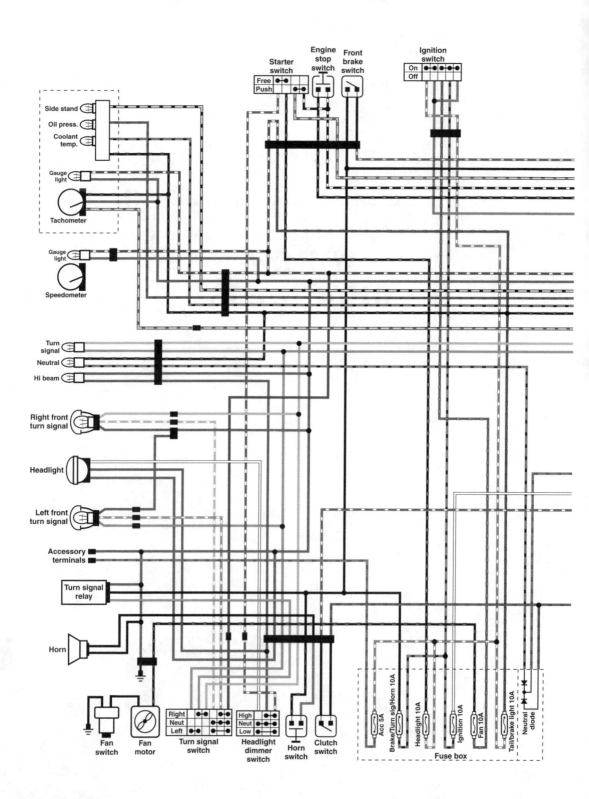

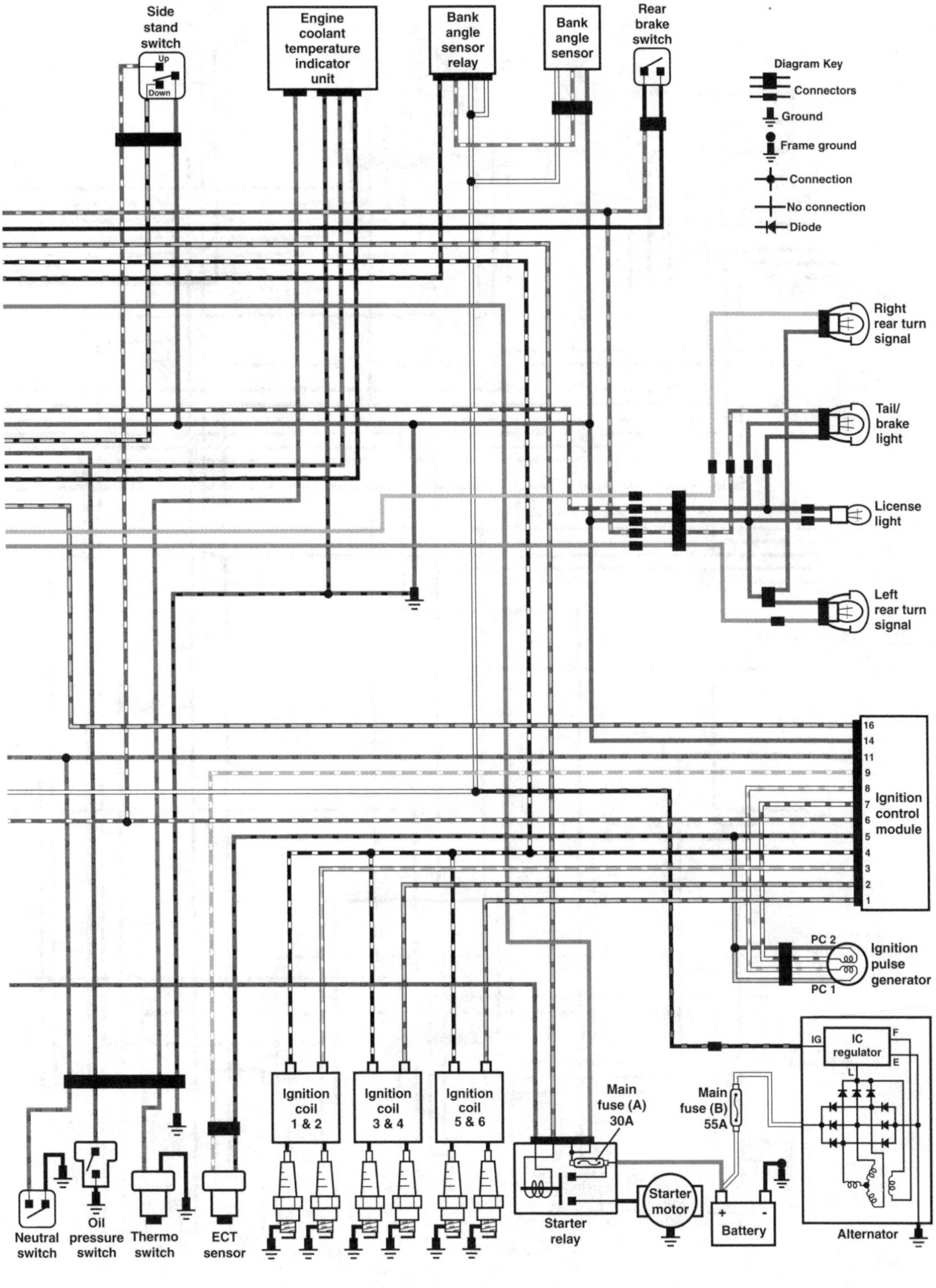

Side stand switch

Up

Down

Engine coolant temperature indicator unit

Bank angle sensor relay

Bank angle sensor

Rear brake switch

Diagram Key

Connectors

Ground

Frame ground

Connection

No connection

Diode

Right rear turn signal

Tail/ brake light

License light

Left rear turn signal

16
14
11
9
8
7
6
5
4
3
2
1

Ignition control module

PC 2

PC 1

Ignition pulse generator

IG   IC regulator   F

E

L

Neutral switch

Oil pressure switch

Thermo switch

ECT sensor

Ignition coil 1 & 2

Ignition coil 3 & 4

Ignition coil 5 & 6

Main fuse (A) 30A

Main fuse (B) 55A

Starter relay

Starter motor

Battery

Alternator

17

2000-ON GL1500C/CT INTERSTATE

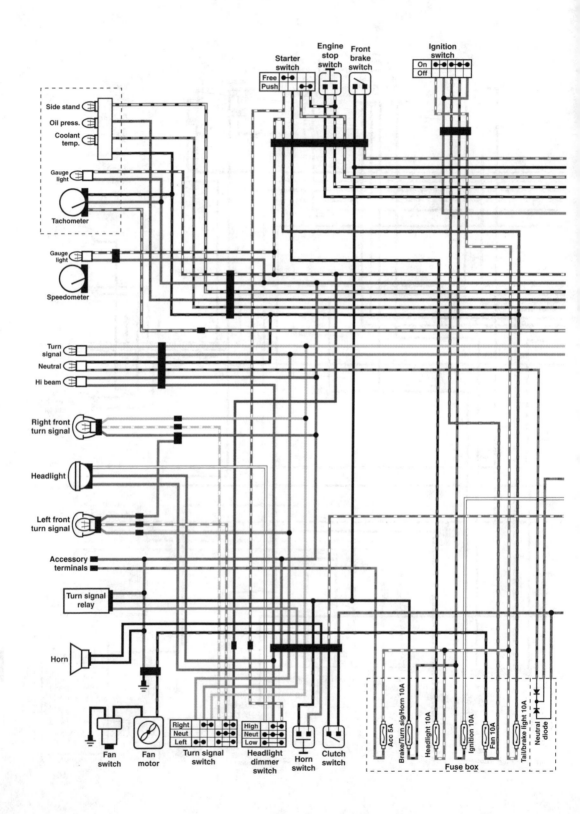

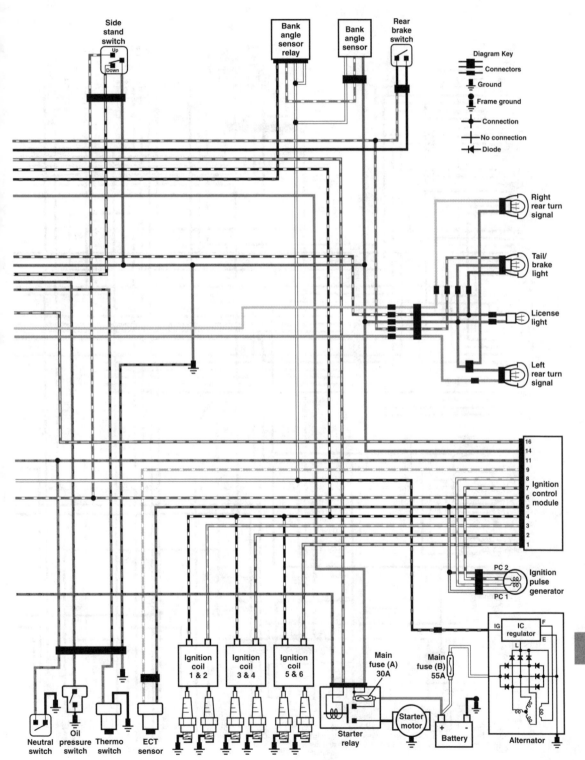

1999-2001 GL1500CF INTERSTATE

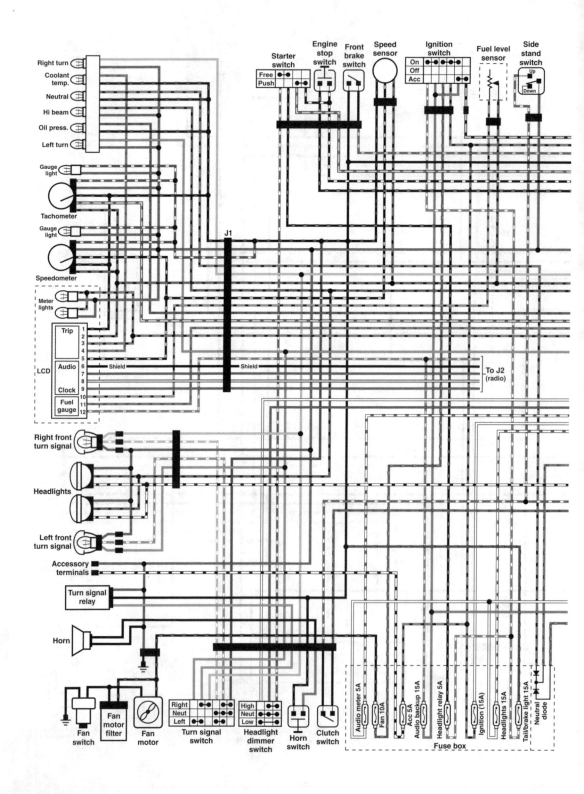

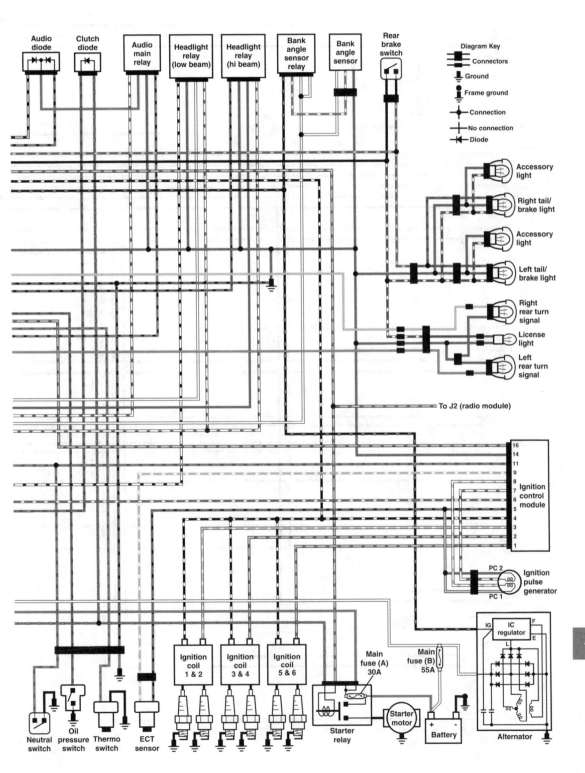

To J2 (radio module)

17

1999-2001 GL1500CF INTERSTATE RADIO

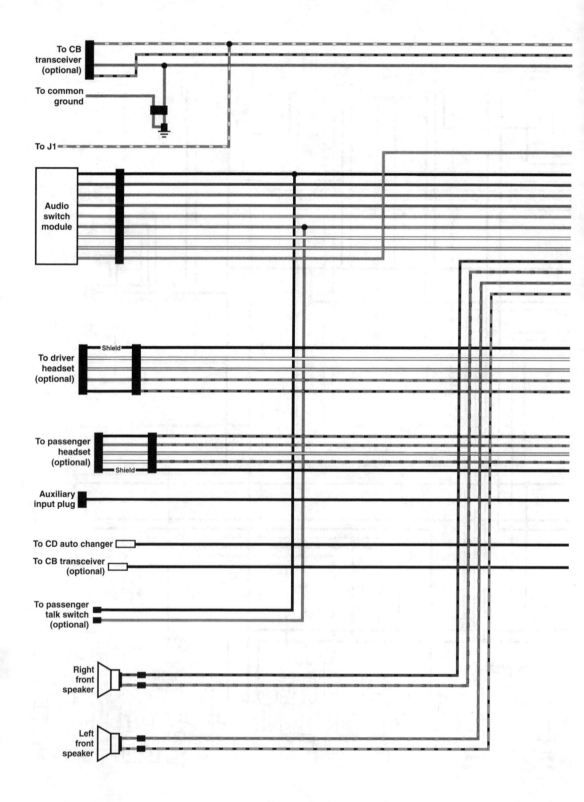

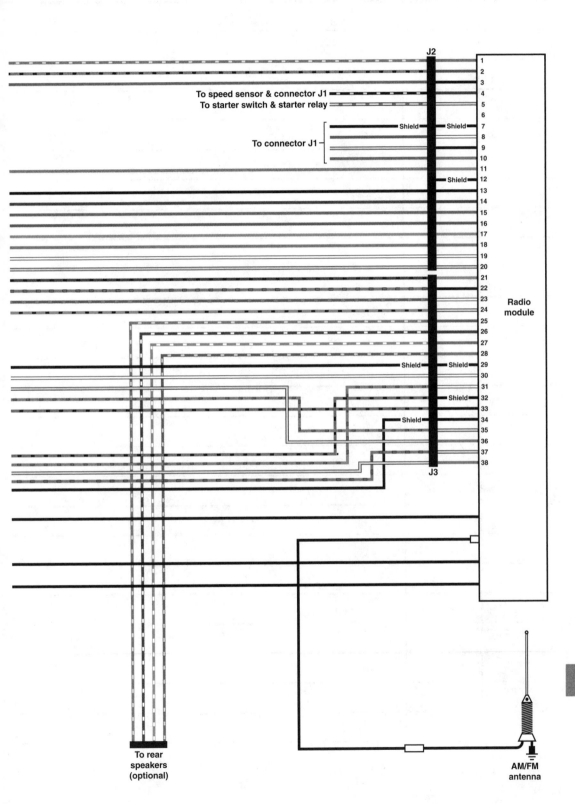

To speed sensor & connector J1

To starter switch & starter relay

To connector J1

Shield — Shield — 7

Shield — 12

Shield — Shield — 29

Shield — 32

Shield — 34

J2

J3

Radio module

To rear
speakers
(optional)

AM/FM
antenna

MAINTENANCE LOG

Date	Miles	Type of Service

Colour code.
G 159 P
G 159 W.